Business Policy and Strategic Management

(Text and Cases)

P. SUBBA RAO

Professor and Convener, Executive MBA Program
School of Business Administration
University of Papua New Guinea
Papua New Guinea (Australia)

Formerly: Professor and Dean
Faculty of Commerce and Management
Sri Krishnadevaraya University
Anantapur-515 003 (AP), India
E-mail: pulapas@rediffmail.com

Assisted by: Hima Bindu Chandra
President, Cybernit Software Solutions,USA

Himalaya Publishing House
ISO 9001:2015 CERTIFIED

First Edition : 1999
Edition : 2000, 2001, 2002, 2003, 2004
2005, 2006, 2007, 2008, 2009
Second Revised Edition : 2010
Edition : 2011, 2013, 2014, 2017, 2018
Edition : 2020, 2022
Edition : 2025

Published by : Mrs. Meena Pandey
for **HIMALAYA PUBLISHING HOUSE PVT. LTD.,**
"Ramdoot", Dr. Bhalerao Marg, Girgaon, Mumbai - 400 004.
Phone: 022-23860170, 23863863; **Fax:** 022-23877178
E-mail: himpub@bharatmail.co.in; **Website:** www.himpub.com

Branch Offices :

New Delhi : "Pooja Apartments", 4-B, Murari Lal Street, Ansari Road, Darya Ganj, New Delhi - 110 002. Phone: 011-23270392, 23278631; Fax: 011-23256286

Nagpur : Kundanlal Chandak Industrial Estate, Ghat Road, Nagpur - 440 018. Mobile: 09325409992, 09325908881

Bengaluru : Plot No. 91-33, 2nd Main Road, Seshadripuram, Behind Nataraja Theatre, Bengaluru - 560 020. Phone: 080-41138821; Mobile: 09379847017, 09379847005

Hyderabad : No. 3-4-184, Lingampally, Besides Raghavendra Swamy Matham, Kachiguda, Hyderabad - 500 027. Phone: 040-27560041, 27550139

Chennai : No. 34/44, Motilal Street, T. Nagar, Chennai - 600 017. Mobile: 09380460419

Pune : "Laksha" Apartment, First Floor, No. 527, Mehunpura, Shaniwarpeth (Near Prabhat Theatre), Pune - 411 030. Phone: 020-24496323, 24496333; Mobile: 09370579333

Cuttack : Plot No 5F-755/4, Sector-9, CDA Market Nagar, Cuttack - 753 014, Odisha. Mobile: 09338746007

Kolkata : 3, S.M. Bose Road, Near Gate No. 5, Agarpara Railway Station, North 24 Parganas, West Bengal - 700109. Mobile: 9674536325

DTP by : **Rajani Tambe**

Printed at : M/s. Giriraj Printers, Hyderabad. On behalf of HPH.

Dedicated

to

The Lotus Feet of

Sadguru Sainath Maharaj

PREFACE

Intensified competition among domestic private and public sector companies and multinational companies consequent upon globalisation along with strides in information technology brought paradigm shifts in strategic management of various companies. These shifts resulted in the emergence of new concepts like strategic intent, virtual organizations, strategic alliances, value chain analysis and the like.

The overwhelming response from the students, Lecturers, Professors and heads of various Business Schools of various universities in India, Papua New Guinea and other countries to my earlier edition of the book inspired me and my publishers to bring out this second and enlarged edition of the book on 'Business Policy and Strategic Management'.

The current edition is endowed with latest information and developments including value chain analysis, strategic intent, emergent strategies, internal and external environment analysis and the like in multiple modes like up-dated text, Boxes, Figures, Tables, Exhibits and Cases.

The current edition covers a number of latest developments, in addition to presenting the following new chapters:

- Global Strategic Management
- Functional Level Strategies
- Social Responsibilities and Ethics of Business
- Corporate Governance: A Strategy for Sustainable Development
- Corporate Strategic Failures

Many students particularly from Indian Universities, Business Schools and Management Institutes and the School of Business Administration, UPNG, Papua New Guinea and students from other universities across the developing countries provided on-line feedback for the earlier edition of the book. I, immensely thank them for their support and encouragement. Particularly, I would like to express my gratitude to Prof. Albert C. Mellam, Executive Dean and Prof. David Kavanamur, School of Business Administration, University of Papua New Guinea, Papua New Guinea and Prof M. Gangadhara Rao, my teacher and the Vice-Chancellor, GITAM University.

Mr. Niraj Pandey, Mrs. Ujjwale Pandey, Mr. Anuj Pandey, Mr. Vijay Pandey, Mrs. Poopathi and Mrs. Nimisha of Himalaya Publishing House have provided immense support in bringing out this revised edition. I thank all of them immensely.

My wife Mrs. Pulapa Rama Devi and my little friends Master Nitin Sai and Rohan Sai were put in inconvenience during the period of revising this book. I express my gratitude to them.

I request the students, teachers and other readers to write to me with their comments and suggestions via e-mail.

Port Moresby, Papua New Guinea

27th November 2009

Pulapa Subba Rao

pulapas@rediffmail.com

CONTENTS

1. THE STRATEGIC MANAGEMENT PROCESS **1 – 30**

(A) Why Strategy?
(B) What is Strategy?
(C) Why is Strategy More Complex?
(D) Strategic Management
(E) Strategic Management Process: Strategic Fit vs. Strategic Intent
Points to be Remembered – Key Words – Questions for Discussion – References

2. THE STRATEGIST AND STRATEGIC DECISION-MAKING **31 – 48**

(A) The Manager: Tasks and Roles
(B) The Strategist: Shareholders, Board of Directors and the CEO, Role of Executives in Strategic Management
(C) Strategic Decision-Making: Drivers of Success in, and Approaches to.
Points to be Remembered – Key Words – Questions for Discussion – References

3. ESTABLISHING CORPORATE DIRECTION **49 – 83**

(A) Introduction
(B) Vision
(C) Mission
(D) Business Definition
(E) Objectives
Points to be Remembered – Key Words – Questions for Discussion – References

4. EXTERNAL ENVIRONMENT SCANNING AND INDUSTRY ANALYSIS **84 – 128**

(A) Introduction
(B) International Environment
(C) Social and Cultural Environment
(D) Technological Environment
(E) Economic Environment
(F) Political Environment
(G) Natural Environment
(H) Industry Analysis
Points to be Remembered – Key Words – Questions for Discussion – References

5. INTERNAL ENVIRONMENT: CAPABILITIES AND COMPETENCIES **129 – 162**

(A) Resources and Capabilities
(B) Core Competencies
(C) Value Chain Analysis and Outsourcing
(D) Strengths and Weaknesses Analysis
(E) Competitive Strength Assessment
(F) Corporate Capability Factors
(G) Diagnosing Corporate Capabilities
Points to be Remembered – Key Words – Questions for Discussion – References

6. GLOBAL STRATEGIC MANAGEMENT 163 – 190

(A) Introduction
(B) Peculiarities of Global Strategic Management
(C) Value Creation
(D) Global Strategic Management Process
(E) Collaborative Strategies
Points to be Remembered – Key Words – Questions for Discussion – References

7. CORPORATE LEVEL STRATEGIC ALTERNATIVES 191 – 224

(A) Strategy Formulation: Situational Analysis
(B) Stability Strategies
(C) Growth Strategies
(D) Retrenchment Strategies
(E) Strategic Alliances
(F) Combination Strategy/Portfolio Restructuring
Points to be Remembered – Key Words – Questions for Discussion – References

8. BUSINESS UNIT LEVEL STRATEGIES 225 – 260

(A) Introduction
• Customer Needs
(B) Generic Strategies
• Low Cost Leadership, Differentiation, Focus
(C) Offensive Strategies and Competitive Advantage
(D) Defensive Strategies and Competitive Advantage
(E) Matching Strategy to Situation
(F) Thirteen Commandments for Formulating Successful Business Strategies
Points to be Remembered – Key Words – Questions for Discussion – References

9. FUNCTIONAL LEVEL STRATEGIES 261 – 293

(A) Functional Level Strategies: An Introduction
(B) Production/Operations Strategies
(C) Marketing Strategies
(D) Financial Strategies
(E) Human Resource Strategies
(F) Research and Development Strategies
(G) Information Strategies
(H) Integrated Functional Strategies
Points to be Remembered – Key Words – Questions for Discussion – References

10. STRATEGIC ANALYSIS AND CHOICE 294 – 327

(A) Introduction
(B) Criteria for Evaluating Strategic Alternatives
(C) The Input Stage
(D) The Matching Stage Corporate Portfolio Analysis
(E) Selection of the Matrix
(F) The Decision Stage
Points to be Remembered – Key Words – Questions for Discussion – References

11. STRUCTURAL IMPLEMENTATION **328 – 358**

(A) Analysing Strategic Change
(B) Managing Strategic Change
(C) Issues in Strategy Implementation
(D) Organisational Structure
(E) Approaches to Organisation Structure
(F) Matching Structure and Strategy
(G) Assessment of Organisational Structure
(H) Perspectives on the Methods of Organising
Points to be Remembered – Key Words – Questions for Discussion – References

12. BEHAVIOURAL IMPLEMENTATION **359 – 389**

(A) Positive Attitude and Mindset
(B) Leadership
(C) Corporate Culture
(D) Values
(E) Power
(F) Organisational Changes
(G) Organisational Development
Points to be Remembered – Key Words – Questions for Discussion – References

13. FUNCTIONAL IMPLEMENTATION: FUNCTIONAL ISSUES **390 – 427**

(A) Operational/Production Policies
(B) Marketing Policies
(C) Financial Policies
(D) Human Resource Policies
(E) Management Information System
Points to be Remembered – Key Words – Questions for Discussion – References

14. STRATEGIC EVALUATION AND CONTROL **428 – 453**

(A) Introduction
(B) Process of Strategic Control
(C) Reluctance to use Strategic Control
(D) Strategic Control and Environmental Factors
(E) Information for Strategic Control
(F) Implementing Strategic Control
(G) Successful Maintenance of Strategic Control
Points to be Remembered – Key Words – Questions for Discussion – References

15. STRATEGIC MANAGEMENT IN NON-PROFIT ORGANISATIONS **454 – 465**

(A) Introduction
(B) Categories of Non-Profit Organisations
(C) Mission, Objectives and Goals
(D) Strategy Formulation and Implementation
(E) Popular Strategies of Non-Profit Organisations
(F) Strategic Evaluation and Control
(G) Measures to Control the Constraints
Points to be Remembered – Key Words – Questions for Discussion – References

16. SOCIAL RESPONSIBILITIES AND ETHICS OF BUSINESS **466 – 488**

(A) Introduction
(B) Social Responsibilities of Business
(C) Business Ethics
(D) Value-Based Management
Points to be Remembered – Key Words – Questions for Discussion – References

17. CORPORATE GOVERNANCE: A STRATEGY FOR SUSTAINABLE DEVELOPMENT **489 – 500**

(A) Introduction
(B) Why Corporate Governance?
(C) Corporate Governance and Strategic Management
(D) Parties to the Corporate Governance
(E) Principles of Good Corporate Governance
(F) Mechanisms and Controls to ensure Good Corporate Governance
Points to be Remembered – Key Words – Questions for Discussion – References

18. CORPORATE STRATEGIC FAILURES **501 – 507**

(A) Introduction
(B) Enron Scandal
(C) Strategic Failure of Satyam Computer Services
(D) Failure of Dot.Coms
(E) Sony's Strategic Failures
(F) Conclusion
Points to be Remembered – Key Words – Questions for Discussion – References

GAME AND CASES **508 – 545**

(A) Game – Strategic Planning-Made Easy
(B) Method of Case Analysis
(C) Case Study-1: Bright Lightings Limited
(D) Case Study-2: Artos Industries Limited
(E) Case Study-3: Microsoft
(F) Case Study-4: Sony
(G) Case Study-5: Xerox Corporation

SUBJECT INDEX **546 – 550**

1 CHAPTER

THE STRATEGIC MANAGEMENT PROCESS

Chapter Outline

(A) Why Strategy?

(B) What is Strategy?

(C) Why is Strategy More Complex?

(D) Strategic Management

(E) Strategic Management Process: Strategic Fit vs. Strategic Intent

Points to be Remembered-Key Words-Questions for Discussion-References

Learning Objectives

After studying this chapter, you should be able to:

- Understand the concepts of strategy and strategic management
- Describe the process of strategic management
- Explain the nature of business policy and strategic management
- Study the key areas in developing a strategy
- Explain why crafting a strategy is complex?
- Describe the need for strategic management
- Explain the benefits and challenges of strategic management
- Describe the strategic management process

(A) WHY STRATEGY?

Different organisations having similar opportunities and resources perform differently due to their different strategies.

Different organisations having similar opportunities and resources perform differently. Consequently, some organisations succeed while others fail though both are in the same business. Similarly, organisations dealing with the same product and catering to the same group of customers perform quite differently. For example, Singapore Airlines has been growing at a faster rate than that of US Air. Dell computers has been doing well in highly competitive personal computers market, while Compaq and Apple have been struggling behind. Mittal Steel company has been growing by leaps and bounds and could bag 9 per cent of global steel market whereas the giants like Arcelor SA in the steel industry have been lagging behind. Why does Toyota dominate the automobile market?

Why do Coca-Cola and Pepsi-Cola attract the taste of all ages of soft drink customers worldwide?, though their products may adversely contribute to the obesity of some of their customers. (see Box 1.1). Why has Southwest Airlines been progressing dramatically while United Airlines filed for bankruptcy in 2002, US Airways filed bankruptcy in late 2005? How did Maruti Automobiles over take the former market leaders like Ambasador and Padmini? How did Virgin Blue overtake the traditional giants like Qantas and British Airways? How did most of the mobile phone companies like Airtel, Hutch and Vodafone overtake the leader Reliance? The answer for all these questions is the strategic management of the organisations. Thus, the strategies formulated and implemented by the managers of a company make or mar the growth rate, efficiency and the long run survival and development of the company.

The immediate questions that arise are: what is a strategy? What is strategic management process? How do managers craft strategies? In fact, managers of different organisations craft different strategies though they are endowed with similar opportunities and resources and challenged by more or less similar threats and weaknesses. Some strategies result in high efficiency, while some others lead to disaster. Why and how these drastic variations take place? An analysis management process would assist us to understand the abnormalities in the ultimate outcome.

Now, we shall study the meaning of a strategy.

BOX 1.1 OBESE PEOPLE HAVE 'SEVERE BRAIN DEGENERATION'

Obesity takes big toll on the brain

A new study finds obese people have 8 percent less brain tissue than normal-weight individuals. Their brains look 16 years older than the brains of lean individuals, researchers said today. Those classified as overweight have 4 percent less brain tissue and their brains appear to have aged prematurely by 8 years. The results, based on brain scans of 94 people in their 70s, represent "severe brain degeneration," said Paul Thompson, senior author of the study and a UCLA professor of neurology. "That's a big loss of tissue and it depletes your cognitive reserves, putting you at much greater risk of Alzheimer's and other diseases that attack the brain," said Thompson. "But you can greatly reduce your risk for Alzheimers, if you can eat healthily and keep your weight under control." The findings are detailed in the online edition of the journal, Human Brain Mapping. Obesity packs many negative health effects, including increased risk of heart

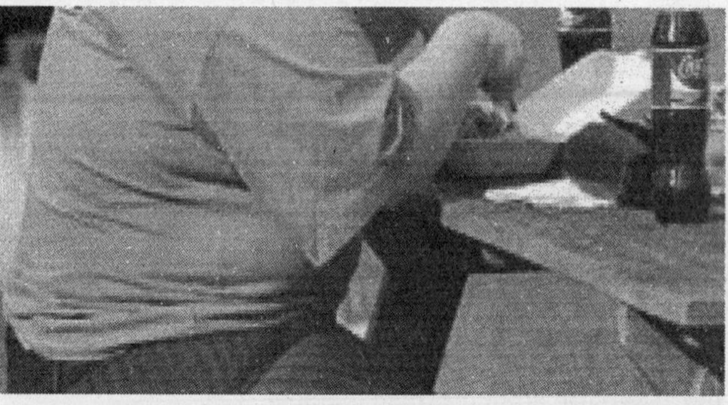

disease, Type 2 diabetes, hypertension and some cancers. It has also been shown to reduce sexual activity. More than 300 million worldwide are now classified as obese, according to the World Health Organization. Another billion are overweight. The main cause, experts say: bad diet, including an increased reliance on highly processed foods. Obese people had lost brain tissue in the frontal and temporal lobes, areas of the brain critical for planning and memory, and in the anterior cingulate gyrus (attention and executive functions), hippocampus (long-term memory) and basal ganglia (movement), the researchers said in a statement today. Overweight people showed brain loss in the basal ganglia, the corona radiata, white matter comprised of axons, and the parietal lobe (sensory lobe). "The brains of obese people looked 16 years older than the brains of those who were lean, and in overweight people looked 8 years older," Thompson said. Obesity is measured by body mass index (BMI), defined as the weight in kilograms divided by the square of the height in metres. A BMI over 25 is defined as overweight, and a BMI of over 30 as obese.

Source: http://news.yahoo.com/s/livescience/20090825/sc_livescience/obesepeoplehaveseverebraindegeneration (Accessed on 26/08/09).

(B) WHAT IS STRATEGY?

In simple terms, strategy is a planned or emergent course of action that is expected to contribute to the achievement of organisational goals. Strategy can also be an idea or a thought that is viewed to be productive to complete a course of action. A strategy is defined as, "a unified, comprehensive, and integrated plan that relates to the strategic advantages of the firm and to the challenges of the environment. It is designed to ensure that the basic objectives of the enterprise are achieved through proper execution by the organisation." Alfred D. Chandler defines strategy as, "the determination of the basic long-term goals and objectives of an enterprise and the adoption of the courses of action and the allocation of resources necessary for carrying out these goals." Strategy is defined by Arthur Sharplin as, "a plan or course of action which is of vital pervasive, or continuing importance to the organisation as a whole." James Brain Quinn defines the term strategy as, "the pattern of plan that integrates an organisation's major goals, policies and action sequences into a cohesive whole."

Strategy is a plan or course of action which is of vital pervasive, or continuing importance to the organisation as a whole.

Should Strategy be a Plan?

Analysis of definitions indicates that strategy is a long-run plan. Some authors view it as an integrated plan. Of late, it is viewed that strategy need not be a plan. Strategy sometimes emerges as a result of a situation or an incident as evident from some incidents that happened in various companies. One such incident happened in a biscuit manufacturing company.

One night at around 10 pm, the production manager of a biscuit company received a telephone call from his neighbours informing him that his wife was sick and they admitted her in a hospital in the town and asked him to rush to the hospital. The production manager narrated the problem to his deputy production manager and explained the conflicting situation of wife's health versus production responsibility and irresponsibility of the deputy production manager of drinking habit even while on duty. The deputy production manager volunteered to take charge of the production department and requested the production manager to go to the hospital and take care of his wife. Further he informed that he would not consume liquor and take care of production unit with full commitment on that night. The production manager was convinced of the commitment of the deputy production manager and left for the hospital.

The deputy production manager out of his joy of becoming the Acting Production Manager on that night consumed liquor twice the quantity that he normally consumes and went around the factory. He informed most of the employees that he was the Acting Manager of the Production Unit and asked every one to work seriously and efficiently and returned to his chambers. He was drowsy and slipped while coming back to his chambers. One of his hands fell on a part of a machine. He told to himself that people complicate the machine designs and removed that part and threw it on the floor. Later, he went to his chambers and slept.

One of the employees, next morning while going home after his night duty observed the part on the floor and placed it in its right position without complaining with a view to avoid any possible risk of being identified as the initial culprit.

The marketing manager after two weeks of time received a surprising feedback from the salespeople who visited the retailers that the company produced a new and delicious product and discontinued the same. The retailers requested the company to restore the production of that new product. The marketing manager was irritated for not being informed of the introduction of the new product and hence picked-up an argument with the production manager. But the production manager countered the argument and categorically informed that the company did not introduce any new product in recent times. However, after prolonged arguments, the marketing manager informed his counterpart that he would produce batch number and date of manufacturing of the new product and provided the same to the production manager after a few days by obtaining the same from one of the retailers.

Production manager after analyzing the information provided by the marketing manger found that the new product was produced on the night when he left the production unit for hospital. Then he called the Deputy Production Manager and asked him about the incident. After detailed discussions and analysis of his minute-to-minute activities, deputy production manager recollected the incident that he removed the divider which divides the wheat floor mix into two parts – where one side sugar is added and the another side salt is added. The supply chain where the sugar is added is connected to sweet biscuit production line and the supply chain where the salt is added is connected to salt biscuit production line. The removal of the divider by the deputy production manager led to the addition of both sugar and salt at the same place and resulted in the production of sweet-cum-salt biscuits. Thus, the company by an accident could produce a new product i.e., 'sweet-cum-salt biscuits'. And thereafter the company started commercial production of this new product that resulted in achieving the company's objectives and goals of enhancing market share and profit.

Strategies need not be planned and they can be emerged. As such, strategy is viewed as a planned or emergent course of action that is expected to contribute to the achievement of organisational goals.

Therefore, it is felt that strategies need not be planned and they can be emerged. As such, strategy is viewed as a planned or emergent course of action that is expected to contribute to the achievement of organisational goals.

Analysis of Definitions of Strategy

The analysis of various definitions of strategy presents the following points:

- Strategy is a central understanding of the strategic management process.
- Strategy is the determination of basic long-term goals and objectives of an organisation.
- It helps in determining the courses of action to attain the predetermined goals and objectives.
- It points to allocation of necessary resources for implementing the course of action.
- It develops the company from its present position to the desired future position.
- It is a set of decision-making rules having a common thread.

- The common thread pulls the policies, plans, goals, objectives of the different functional areas of business such as finance, marketing, production/operations and human resource together and interweaves them as a unified comprehensive and integrated plan, action and evaluation.
- It sets a clear direction.
- It is a course of unified actions either planned and/or emerged.
- Enterprise knows its strengths and weaknesses compared with those of its competitors.
- Enterprise devotes its hard-won resources to projects that employ its set of core competencies, the primary skills within the organisation.
- Identifies factors in the political and social environment that requires careful monitoring.
- Recognises which competitor's actions need critical attention.
- The competitive firm should have a rational, clear-headed notion, purged of wishful thinking of *(i)* its mission *(ii)* its external competitive environment (for analysing opportunities and threats) and *(iii)* its internal capabilities (including strengths and weaknesses). Now, we turn our discussion to the dimensions of the strategy, criteria for effective strategy, forms and kinds of strategies.

Criteria for Effective Strategy

Although each strategic situation is unique, there are some common criteria that tend to explain an effective strategy. Criteria for effective strategy include:

(i) Clear, decisive objectives: All efforts should be directed towards clearly understood, decisive and attainable overall goals. All goals need not be written down or be chronologically precise but they must be understood and be decisive.

Effective strategies are: Clear, concise, flexible, coordinated, surprise and secure

(ii) Maintaining the initiative: The strategy preserves freedom of action and enhances commitment. It sets the pace and determines the course of events rather than reacting to them.

(iii) Concentration: The strategy concentrates superior power at the place and time likely to be decisive. The strategy must define precisely what will make the enterprise superior in power, best in critical dimensions in relation to its competitors. A distinctive competency yields greater success with fewer resources.

(iv) Flexibility: The strategy must purposely have built in resources, buffers and dimensions for flexibility and maneuvers. Reserved capabilities, planned maneuverability and repositioning allows one to use minimum resource while keeping competitors at a relative disadvantage.

(v) Coordinated and committed leadership: The strategy should provide responsible, committed leadership for each of its major goals. Care should be taken in selecting the leaders in such a way that their own interests and values match with the requirements of their roles. Commitment and not mere acceptance is the basic requirement.

(vi) Surprise: The strategy should make use of speed, secrecy and intelligence to attack exposed or unprepared competitors at an unexpected time. Thus, surprise and correct time are very important.

(vii) Security: The organisation should secure or develop resources required, securely maintain all vital operating points for the enterprise, an effective intelligence system to prevent the effects of surprises by the competitors.

Forms and Kinds of Strategies

Strategy is a plan — a consciously intended course of action. Some of them may be unrealised or some other actions may emerge meanwhile. These two form a realised strategy as shown in Figure 1.1. Kinds of strategies are presented in Exhibit 1.1.

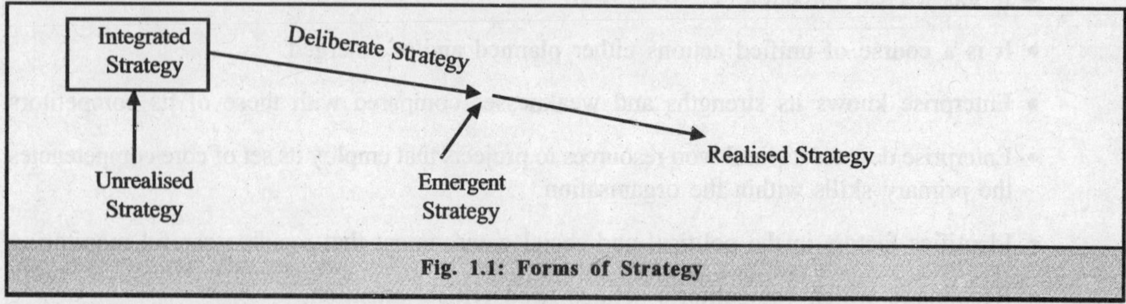

Fig. 1.1: Forms of Strategy

Exhibit 1.1: Various Kinds of Strategies, From Deliberate to Mostly Emergent

Planned Strategy: Precise intentions are formulated and articulated by a central leadership, and backed up by formal controls to ensure their surprise-free implementation in an environment that is benign, controllable, or predictable (to ensure no distortion of intentions); these strategies are highly deliberate.

Entrepreneurial Strategy: Intentions exist as the personal, unarticulated visions of a single leader, and so are adaptable to new opportunities; the organisation is under the personal control of the leader and located in a protected niche in its environment; these strategies are relatively deliberate but can emerge too.

Ideological Strategy: Intentions exist as the collective vision of all the members of the organisation, controlled through strong, shared norms; the organisation is often pro-active *vis-a-vis* its environment; these strategies are rather deliberate.

Umbrella Strategy: A leadership in partial control of organisational action defines strategic targets or boundaries within which others must act (for example, that all new products be high priced and at the technological cutting edge, although what these actual products are to be is left to emerge); as a result, strategies are partly deliberate (the boundaries) and partly emergent (the patterns within them); this strategy can also be called deliberately emergent, in that the leadership purposefully allows others the flexibility to maneuver and form patterns within the boundaries.

Process Strategy: The leadership controls the process aspects of strategy (who gets hired and so gets a chance to influence strategy, what structures they work within, etc.), leaving the actual content of strategy to others; strategies are again partly deliberate (concerning process) and partly emergent (concerning content), and deliberately emergent.

Disconnected Strategy: Members or subunits loosely coupled with the rest of the organisation produce patterns in the streams of their own actions in the absence of, or in direct contradiction to the central or common intentions of the organisation at large; the strategies can be deliberate for those who make them.

Consensus Strategy: Through mutual adjustment, various members converge on patterns that pervade the organisation in the absence of central or common intentions; these strategies are rather emergent in nature.

Imposed Strategy: The external environment dictates pattern in actions, either through direct imposition (say by an outside owner or by a strong customer) or through implicitly pre-empting or bounding organisational choice (as in a large airline that must fly jumbo jets to remain viable); these strategies are organisationally emergent, although they may be internalised and made deliberate.

Source: James Brain Quinn, Henry Mintzberg and Robert M. James (Eds.): "The Strategy Process", Prentice Hall, Englewood Cliffs, p. 16.

Need for Strategy

It is beyond doubt to state that every organisation necessarily formulate strategies. To state specifically, strategy is necessary in view of the following reasons:

(i) To have rules to guide the search for new opportunities both inside and outside the firm.

(ii) To take high quality project decisions.

(iii) To develop measures to judge whether a particular opportunity is a rare one or whether much better ones are likely to develop in the future.

(iv) To have an assurance that the firm's overall resource allocation pattern is efficient.

(v) To have and develop internal ability to anticipate change.

(vi) To save time, money and executive talent.

(vii) To identify, develop and exploit potential opportunities.

(viii) To utilise the delay principle, that is, delay the commitment until an opportunity is on hand.

Key Areas in Developing a Strategy

Managers have to consider the following key areas in developing a strategy:

(i) The type of goods and/or services that the firm will produce and will sell.

(ii) The mode of producing goods and rendering services.

(iii) Who are and will be the firm's customers.

(iv) The methods of financing the various operations of the firm.

(v) The amount of risk that the firm will take.

(vi) Methods of implementing the strategy.

(C) WHY IS STRATEGY MORE COMPLEX?

Globalisation along with strides in information technology brought paradigm shifts in the operations and modes of doing business in general and strategic management in particular.

Strategy crafting is complex due to global economic trends like boom and economic recession

The recent phase of globalisation after 1990 erased national political boundaries for the purpose of business. In addition, it set the phase for the emergence of global culture, global systems and practices, global products and services, standardisation of financial accounting principles and practices, logistics management systems like containerisation in case of sea transportation, establishment of manufacturing facilities throughout the world, preference for diversified human resources and sourcing the finance across the globe.

Significant shifts in globalization have been due to the establishment of World Trade Organisation, (WTO), creation of regional integrations like European Union and ASEAN, declining trade and investment barriers, growth in foreign direct investment, growth in multinational companies (MNCs), transformations of MNCs into transnational companies that consider the entire world as a single country for doing business and changes in mindset and attitude of customers.

Global Economic Trends

Globalisation along with its drivers like World Trade Organisation, declining trade and investment barriers, enlarging regional integrations brought unprecedented shifts in the growth rates of various economies. The significant trends include:

1. USA is no more the world's single largest market with the enlargement of European Union.
2. The enlarged European Union has emerged as a single largest world market with its more than 700 million potential customers.
3. European Union along with Western European countries have per capita income higher than that of USA.
4. China's economy is larger than that of Canada.
5. India has also been growing rapidly and now has emerged as the fourth largest economy in the world.
6. World's largest economies by 2050 would be USA, China, India, Japan UK, France, Germany and South Korea.
7. Russia and Italy are expected to decline by 2050.
8. Most of the MNCs headquarters in USA, and Europe are expected to earn more than 60% of their revenue from China and India by 2020. Therefore, MNCs have been crafting strategies to invest in the emerging markets like China and India, where the growth would be fast and sustainable in the future years. General Electric is now investing in China and India while FedEx is investing in India and Brazil.

Paradigm shifts that affect Strategic Management

The boundaries of industries have been changing due to the spectacular shifts in the nature of business strategies.

Change in Industry Boundaries: The shifts in globalisation and technology brought fundamental change in competition among the firms across the boundaries of industries and nations. In fact, the boundaries of industries have been changing due to the spectacular shifts in the nature of business strategies. For example, interactive computer networks and telecommunications have blurred the boundaries of the entertainment industry. Consequently, networks like ABC, NBC and Fox compete among themselves and also with AT&T, Sony and Microsoft. Similarly Coca-Cola and Pepsi Cola fight not only between themselves but also compete with Bisleri and a number of national/local mineral water producers. ICICI competes with commercial banks, development banks and also insurance companies.

Shifts in Mindset: The shift in mindset of the customer from the traditional low cost product to flexibility, speed, innovation, integration of a wide range of functions and/or services and information revolution brought a change in the mindset of the strategist. The change in the mindset of the strategist led to the shift in strategy crafting from the conventional competitive advantage based on low cost, large scale economics and huge advertising budget to the innovation, differentiation and enlarging the product functions and conveniences.

Change in National Boundaries: Globalisation wiped out the national political boundaries for the purpose of business. As such most of the businesses have been spreading their operations to various foreign countries. Consequently national companies started competing with MNCs not only at home but even in various other countries in addition to competing with other national companies. For example, Tata Steel competes with Mittal Steel at home and in foreign countries in addition to competing with Visakha Steels, and other companies in India. Crafting and implementing appropriate strategy that fits the turbulent environment is paramount. In addition, the corporate strategy needs to be coordinated and aligned with business unit's strategies in decentralised corporate structures in various countries and/or regions.

Hyper competition: The period post-1990s is marked by turbulent environment uncontrolled by any group of forces. "Assumptions of market stability are replaced by motions of inherent instability and change." Dynamics of strategic – maneuvering among the global and innovative combatants is caused by ever growing customer preferences, and partly due to the innovations of the competing firms. Hyper-competition is a condition of rapidly growing competition based on *(i)* price-quality positioning. *(ii)* innovative know-how *(iii)* establishing first-mover advantage and *(iv)* competition to protect their own brand and market and invade competitors' brands and markets. Thus, firms aggressively challenge the competitors' products and markets by enhancing their performance in order to improve their competitive position. As indicated earlier, the hyper-competition has been caused due to a number of interactive factors and the significant among them are globalisation and technology.(See Box 1.2).

Hyper-competition is a condition of rapidly growing competition based on *(i)* price-quality positioning. *(ii)* innovative know-how *(iii)* establishing first-mover advantage, and *(iv)* competition to protect their own brand and market and invade competitors' brands and markets.

BOX 1.2 ART OF HYPER-COMPETITION

Is the idea of sustained competitive advantage dead? Richard D'Aveni, professor of business strategy at the Amos Tuck School at Dartmouth College, believes it is. According to Mr. D'Aveni, business has entered a new era of hypercompetition, shifting dramatically from slow-moving stable oligopolies to an environment characterized by a quick-strike mentality on the part of companies aimed specifically at disrupting the competitive advantage of market leaders. Mr. D'Aveni says, he discovered in his consulting work that traditional strategic concepts were making companies weaker, not stronger. "The old structure was: define an industry, reduce the level of competition and then avoid competition where possible," he says. "But I found that successful companies were not doing any of these things. The best performers were disrupting markets, acting as if there were no boundaries to entry." In his book, "Hypercompetition: Managing the Dynamics of Strategic Maneuvering" (Free Press), Mr. D'Aveni argues, that competitive advantage is no longer sustainable over the long haul. Advantage, instead, is continually created, eroded, destroyed and recreated through strategic maneuvering. The old goal, Mr. D'Aveni says, was to increase profitability by legally restraining the level of competition in an industry. Companies avoided price wars, segmented the market to avoid head-to-head competition and tried to keep the number of competitors low by putting up entry barriers around their industries. Today, he points out, this strategy is "literally impossible." He says, four driving forces are contributing to the new era of hypercompetition: customer changes, including fragmenting tastes; rapid technological change; falling geographic and industry boundaries as markets globalize; and deep pockets among competitors due to the rise of giant global alliances in a raft of industries. "The way to go about winning today is to obsolete the current advantages of the leader," Mr. D'Aveni says. The Microsoft Corporation, for example, has long been considered invincible because it controls the operating system market for most of the world's personal computers. But suddenly, Mr. D'Aveni says, three efforts are under way simultaneously to make Microsoft's hegemony obsolete. For one, chip manufacturers are imbedding software directly into semiconductor chips, doing away with the need for separate operating software. For another, there is the move toward a low-priced, dumb terminal-like device that hooks directly into the Internet and takes advantage of software such as Sun Microsystems' Java. And last, there are the voice recognition systems, offered by the likes of the telecommunications companies, that will circumvent the need for current operating systems. "Everyone thought I.B.M. was invincible at one time, as well," Mr. D'Aveni notes. The Dartmouth professor foresees the untapped distribution capabilities of the Internet and the World Wide Web as the perfect vehicle for "disrupting the apple cart" of a variety of industries. "What will happen to publishing, for example," he asks, "when reporters or authors can transmit their work directly to the reader over the Internet? Why does Michael Crichton need a publisher when he can eliminate the middle man? No doubt the C.E.O.'s of the publishing houses are worried." Most difficult for market leaders is that tomorrow's competitors are not even on the radar screens of most companies, Mr. D'Aveni says. With weak entry barriers to most markets, he adds, the "unconventional player attacks suddenly from outside the industry with unexpected methods, often with devastating effect." Despite these new parameters, Mr. D'Aveni suggests that long-term dominance of an industry is still possible even though sustainable advantage has gone by the boards. It is possible to win in hypercompetition by mastering the art of dynamically repositioning oneself in four key arenas: price/quality, know-how/timing, stronghold creation/invasion and deep pockets.

http://www.strategy-business.com/press/16635507/14886 (Accessed on 31/08/09).

Enlarged opportunities: Globalisation enables the companies to source various inputs like material, finance, human resources, machinery and technology from different countries wherever the qualitative inputs at less cost and convenient terms and condition are available. For example, Dr. Reddy's Lab procure material from USA, human resources from India, machinery from Europe, produces in India and markets in Russia and African countries in addition to other developing countries. Wal-Mart has been contemplating procurement and production from many countries in the world to market in their 3,600 retail units. In fact, it treats operations in each country like a domestic company with local strategies with a global vision and mission.

Product Design, Quality and Service: Companies that go global design the products as per the preferences and conveniences of customers of foreign countries. In addition, they improve the quality of the product as well as the services due to the severe competition from the companies operating in the markets. For example, Toyota's product design, product quality and Jet Airlines – Boeing 777 has 132,500 major components and these components are produced in 545 different locations. A small optical company in the USA, *i.e.,* Swan Optical manufactures its eye wear in low cost factories in Hong Kong and China. Quality of service forced many automobile companies across the countries to improve their product and service including the Indian automobile companies.

Globalisation resulted in increase in, the efficiency of both MNCs as well as domestic companies producing quality product at less cost, supply of the product at the right time to the customer and provide better service as the customer buys the product from anyone who sells high quality product at less price with better service. In fact, customers today are secular and as such they are not loyal to any brand permanently.

Heavy Risks of Globalisation: Globalisation led to the closure of some of the domestic companies, particularly small companies in developing countries. In fact, thousands of small-scale companies were closed after globalisation due to their inability to compete with the MNCs. Further, even large-scale companies that had only a few products were forced to either expand or close down. Thus, globalisation complicates the process of strategic management due to the complex opportunities and threats created by the open of markets and severe competition.

Impact of Electronic Business (e-Business)

Neural networks combine computer software and chips that are capable of mimicking brain functions.

There have been dramatic developments in information technology during the last two decades. These developments enriches business communication, innovations in computer hardware and software, network of computers and network of production technology, machinery, product design, marketing systems, finance administration and human resource systems with computers. The next information technology breakthrough is the neural networks which will change the way the managers do their jobs. Neural networks combine computer software and chips that are capable of mimicking brain functions. For example, when a purchase order is issued to a vendor, he/she simultaneously enters the order in the online date base. The entire activities in the operation result in receiving goods, a person at the receiving end checks a computer terminal to ensure that the shipment received is proper condition the employee clicks the mouse to issue a cheque, otherwise, the employee is empowered to refuse the shipment. Further, information technology brought significant and dramatic changes through various techniques like:

- Business Process Re-engineering
- Enterprise Resource Planning and
- Supply Chain Management

Electronic business (e-business) consists of three areas, *viz., (a)* intranet within the organisation, *(b)* business-to-business (B2B) dealings and *(c)* business-to-customer (B2C) transactions.

Business-to-customer transactions include selling the goods and services through the internet to innumerable customers spread all over the world. Business houses establish virtual shops and offer goods and services to whoever visits their web sites. E-commerce is another aspect of e-business. Some other important aspects of e-business, which are successfully carried on through the internet are e-auctioning, e-banking, e-directories, e-engineering, e-travel services, e-operational resource management, e-supply and e-trading.

The emergence and growth of e-business has its impact on the way of doing business and thereby on the strategic management also as:

- **E-business provides with easy shopping:** Shopping on the internet provides with fascinating experience. A potential customer can turn to the web, browse different shops and place orders for a variety of goods and/or services without spending time and energy as it happens in traditional shopping.
- **E-business saves operating costs:** It saves operating cost by eliminating human intervention in order processing.(See Box 1.3).
- **E-business profoundly influencing the structure of business supply chains:** It changes the supply chains and their structure. For example, Chrysler Corporation by linking its supplies though a web-based network, reported savings of more than $3billion in cost of materials in 2007.
- **Higher degree of personalisation:** E-business allows higher degree of personalisation and customisation of products, services and relationships.
- **Round the clock facility:** E-business is around-the-clock advantage to the customer. E-business allows a fast and flexible execution and response to the market opportunities. The web enables a company to introduce a new product, get immediate customer reaction, refine and perfect the product without investment with greater assurance of success.

BOX 1.3 E-BUSINESS STRATEGIES

E-Business Strategies explores the use of advanced technologies that change the business dynamics of the physical aspect of real estate: the design, construction, and delivery of buildings.The global real estate, design, and construction industries are highly fragmented and notoriously inefficient. This course explores the ways in which firms can gain economies of scale, coordinate design and construction on a multi-firm basis, capture the benefit of new technologies, and change the competitive landscape. A similar metamorphosis has happened in adjacent service industries which use real estate, including finance, insurance, retail, investing, food services, and consulting; this course explores they how these disruptive business models will also change the cost and differentiation dynamics in this sector. **E-Business Strategies** is an interdisciplinary research course which highlights the application of leading edge technologies being developed at MIT, Harvard, and elsewhere. These include visualization, remote sensing, 3D solid modeling, knowledge management, and sophisticated supply chain and logistics optimization.

Source: http://web.mit.edu/1.464/www/ (Accessed on 31/08/09).

Organisational Adaptation and Learning Organisation

Organisations can and do adapt to changing environment factors by restructuring their activities and by imitating the successful organisations.

Significant environmental dynamism dominated by globalisation and information technology led to the organisational adaptation and further creation and/or emergence of learning organisations. Institution theory of organisations propose that organisations can and do adapt to changing environment factors by restructuring their activities and by imitating the successful organisations. In fact, strategic choice perspective proposes that organisations not only adapt to the changing environment, but have opportunity and power even to reshape their environments. Organisational learning theory proposes that organisation reactively adapt to the environmental changes and proactively improve organizational structure to fit the same to the possible future environmental shifts either caused or created by using the knowledge they learned from the environment. Thus, the organisations have become learning organisations.

Synergetic Outcome: Organisations are congregations of individual human resources. Organisations learn and acquire knowledge through individual employees. Organisational learning output is the synergetic outcome of individual learning of all employees. Organisations learn by creating conducive environment for knowledge creation and development through discussion, research, brain storming, etc. Organisations create conducive environment for their employees to analyse and foresee the environment and its influence on product design, demand, price and market share of the organisation.

Employees and Learning Organisations: Employees develop the knowledge for the organisation to prepare for the future by developing systems, structure and products. Flexibility allows the organisation to develop short-term thrusts within the long-term or a fixed period strategy, resulting in strategic flexibility. Strategic flexibility demands short-term flexibility due to environmental shifts in order to achieve the long-term strategic goal more efficiently and not be distracted by environmental turbulences.

Strategic Flexibility: Strategic flexibility takes place in learning organisation, where the knowledge is created, shared, acquired, transferred and used for understanding and foreseeing the future environment. Learning organisations, thus, prepare themselves for the future by changing the structure adequately before the environmental changes take place.

Knowledge is Competitive Advantage: Organisational learning has become imperative as organisational activities like product design, new product development, manufacturing, and supply chain have become competitive and intellectual. In addition, knowledge is accepted as competitive advantage. Procter and Gamble, Microsoft, and Reliance Industries encourage the employees to create and share information and knowledge and utilise the same for developing organisational competencies.

Learning Organisations and Competencies: Learning organisations develop competencies in problem solving logically, experimenting with new approaches, learning from past experiences, experiences of themselves and others and transferring the knowledge quickly and utilisation of such knowledge for their own and others experiences for efficient strategic implementation by arresting or mitigating the possible deviations.

Learning Organisations and Action Learning: Learning organisation adopt action-learning and action research techniques for knowledge creation. For example Motorola through its action-learning tool allows the marketing, manufacturing, finance and human resource personnel to meet and argue through brain storming sessions and agree on the new products, new markets, customer groups, customer needs and pricing before taking up commercial production. These sessions force the future possible issues and problems and provides for a successful strategy implementation.

(D) STRATEGIC MANAGEMENT

Introduction

One can generalise and say that the strategic management is the process of management of strategic decision-making, implementation and control. It is not a complete meaning of strategic management though as it fails to cover many important aspects of strategic management. One should know that the nature of strategic management is different from that of management. Managers in most cases deal with day to day issues and problems of operational control. These issues and problems include procuring raw materials, scheduling production process, inventory control, producing goods, procuring finances, investing, capital budgeting, working capital management, procuring human resources, settling their problems, selling the products, creating demand, advertising, sales promotion, marketing research and the like. All these tasks are important, but the managers perform these tasks based on general guidelines provided to them. Therefore, these tasks are vital for efficient implementation of strategy but it is not the entire scope of strategic management. Then, what is strategic management?

Definitions of Strategic Management

"Strategic management is concerned with deciding on strategy and planning how that strategy is to be put into effect." It can be thought of as having these elements within it, *viz.*, strategic analysis, strategic choice and strategic implementation as shown in Fig.1.2 Strategic analysis seeks to understand the strategic position of the firm. Strategic choice is to do with the formulation of possible course of action. Strategic implementation is concerned with planning how the choice of strategy can be implemented. According to Samuel C. Certo and J. Paul Peter, "Strategic management is a continuous, interative, cross-functional process aimed at keeping an organisation as a whole appropriately matched to its environment." A series of steps that a manager must take are identified by this definition. These steps include performing an environmental analysis, establishing organisational direction, formulating organisational strategy, implementing organisational strategy and exercising strategic control.

Strategic management is concerned with deciding on strategy and planning how that strategy is to be put into effect.

Schellenberger and Bosenan define the term strategic management as, "the continuous process

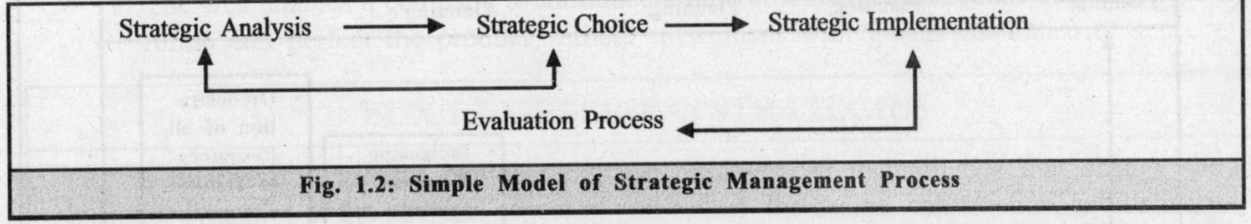

Fig. 1.2: Simple Model of Strategic Management Process

of effectively relating the organisation's objectives and resources to the opportunities in the environment." or, "strategic management is primarily concerned with relating the organisation to its environment, formulating strategies to adapt to the environment and assuring that implementation of strategies taken place."

Analysis of the Definitions of Strategic Management

The study of the above mentioned definitions of strategic management presents the following analysis:

(i) Strategic management is a continuous process but that does not mean that the organisation never finishes its strategic work. Managers will always be focusing or reflecting on some aspect of strategic management, though different aspects of strategic management require different emphasis and effort of varying intensity at different times.

(ii) Though the process of strategic management starts with the step of performing an environmental analysis, and moves on to strategic control, it comes back as environmental analysis. Thus, strategic management consists of a series of steps repeated cyclically.

(iii) Various activities of strategic management draw the inputs from various functional areas of management. Thus, strategic management process integrates human resources with marketing, production/operations and finance. All these functional areas of management, in a comprehensive effort, contribute simultaneously to create an effective plan or output. Thus, the cross-functional team members work together and the organisation will enjoy the benefits of synergy.

The members can visualise the overall position of where the firm is and what it needs to do in the future in order to achieve a sustainable competitive advantage. This process will encourage commitment of key executives to strategic plan.

(iv) Strategic management identifies its purpose as ensuring that an organisation as a whole appropriately matches its ever changing environment. Organisations must modify their strategies in accordance with the changes in its environment. For example, announcement of new economic policy by the Government of India in 1991 shook the environment and consequently most of the business firms modified their strategies. Similarly, the recent recession after 2008 also influenced business organizations to modify their strategies in the direction of reducing operations resulting in job cuts.

Historical Development of Strategic Management

Almost all the disciplines passed through different stages in their evolutionary process and reached their present stage. Strategic management is not an exception to this. Though the formulation of a strategy seems to be simple, it is very difficult to accomplish it. Many organisations develop their strategic management process over periods of several years, adjusting and tailoring them to meet specific needs of the organisation.

Different phases of development of strategic management are presented in Figure 1.3.

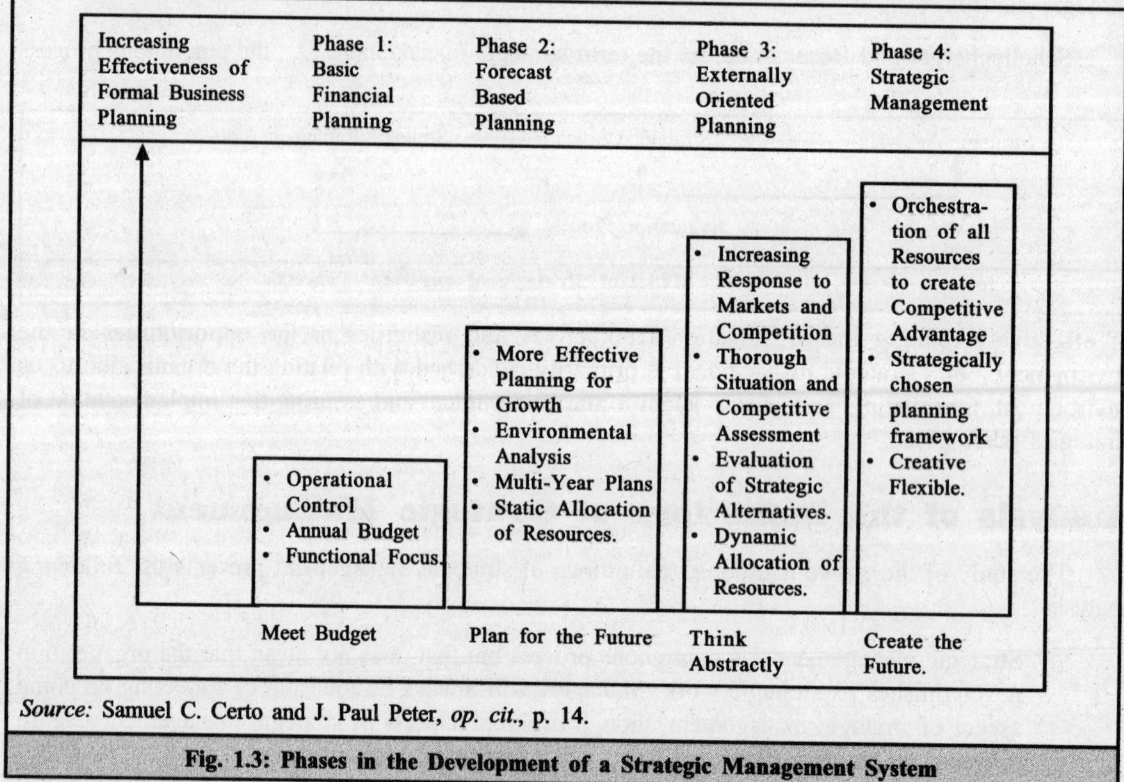

Source: Samuel C. Certo and J. Paul Peter, *op. cit.*, p. 14.

Fig. 1.3: Phases in the Development of a Strategic Management System

***Phase 1:* Basic Financial Planning:** The first phase of the strategic development is fairly a simple routine of basic financial planning. The main concern during this phase is simply meeting annual budget requirement, operational functions like production, marketing, finance and human resources and emphasising on the operational control.

***Phase 2:* Forecast-based Planning:** During this phase, the primary concern is mainly on effective plans, environmental scanning, plan for the future and allocation of resources.

***Phase 3:* Externally-oriented Planning:** There is a remarkable shift during this phase. The notable developments include: increasing response to markets and competition, complete situational analysis and assessment of competitive strength, evaluation of strategic alternatives and allocation of resources based on changing needs from time to time.

***Phase 4:* Strategic Management:** The focus shifts over time from meeting the budget to planning for the future, to thinking abstractly, to working to create desired future. To create future decision-makers, orchestrate and integrate all their organisation's resources to gain a competitive advantage. They build flexibility into the organisational planning process, and foster a supportive, participative climate within the organisation.

Thus, developing an effective and efficient strategic management process can be a long and difficult task. It requires sustained effort, enormous patience and sharp political skills. Strategic management requires efficient leadership.

Now, we shall discuss the need for strategic management.

Need for Strategic Management

Some managers argue that why should firms engage themselves in strategic management? They argue that firms can exist, develop and continue in business without strategic management. Some other managers argue that strategic management is essential in this competitive era. Exhibit 1.2 presents the reasons for and reactions to the value of strategic management. The following factors help us to know the need for strategic management.

Exhibit 1.2: Reasons for and Reactions to the Value of Strategic Management

Pros	*Cons*
1. Strategic management allows firms to anticipate changing conditions.	• Conditions change so fast, managers can't do any planning, especially long-term planning.
2. Strategic management provides clear objectives and direction for employees.	• Objectives must often be vague and general.
3. Research in strategic management is advancing so that the process can help managers.	• Managers pay little attention to research, and studies are not well done.
4. Business which perform strategic management are more effective.	• There are many reasons for success, and many firms are effective without formal planning.
5. Environment is not static. It is more dynamic and global environment also affects most of the firms. Strategic management helps in understanding environment and formulate strategy to suit to the environmental dynamism.	• Environmental dynamism can't be assessed.

Source: Adapted from Lawrence R. Jauch and William F. Glueck. "Business Policy and Strategic Management." McGraw Hill Book Company. New York. p. 18.

Strategic management is needed due to change process, to provide guidelines, field of study, better performance, systematic decisions, communication, allocation of resources and holistic approach.

1. Due to Change: Everything, except change is not permanent. It does mean that only change is permanent.Change makes planning difficult. But, firms may pro-act to the change rather than just react to it. Strategic management encourages the top executives to forecast change and provides direction and control. It will also allow the firm to take advantage of the opportunities provided by the changes in the environment and avoid the threats or reduce the risk as the future is anticipated. Thus, strategic management allows an enterprise to base its decisions on long-range forecasts.

2. To Provide Guidelines: Strategic management provides guidelines to the employer about the organisation's expectations from them. This would minimise conflict between job performance and job demands. Thus, it provides incentive for employer and helps the organisation in achieving its objectives.

3. Developed Field of Study by Research: Strategic management was just based on case studies or anecdotal evidence 30 years ago. But recently, there are methodological problem researches in this field of study. More systematic knowledge in this area is available at present. Therefore, today it is worthwhile to study strategic management.

4. Probability for Better Performance: There is no clear research evidence that strategic management leads to higher performance. But the majority of studies suggest that there is a relationship between better performance and formal planning. It is also stated that businesses which plan strategically have a higher probability of success than those which do not have.

5. Systematise Business Decisions: Strategic management provides data and information about different business transactions to managers and helps them to make decisions systematically.

6. Improves Communication: Strategic management provides effective communication of information from lower level managers to middle level managers and to top level managers.

7. Improves Coordination: Strategic management improves coordination not only among the functional areas of management, but also among individual projects.

8. Improves Allocation of Resources: Strategic planning helps in deciding upon most feasible and viable projects and thereby improves the allocation of resources to the viable projects.

9. Helps the Managers to have a Holistic Approach: Strategic management helps the managers to have complete understanding of the company and to have a holistic approach towards business problems and proportions.

Benefits of Strategic Management

Several corporations and institutions have been using strategic management. Organisations reap several benefits from effective strategic management. The benefits of strategic management include:

(i) Strategic management helps an organisation to be proactive rather than reactive in shaping its future.

(ii) It helps organisations not only to respond to its relevant environment, but also to initiate and influence its environment and thereby exert control over its destiny.

(iii) It helps organisations to make effective strategies through the use of a more systematic, logical and rational approach to strategic choice.

(iv) It helps the organisations to achieve understanding and commitment from all managers and employers. Managers and employers become creative and innovative when they understand and commit to the company's strategic management. This process results in employee empowerment. Empowerment is the act of strengthening an individual's sense of effectiveness.

(v) It encourages the organisations to decentralise the management process involving lower level managers and employees.

(vi) A significant number of research studies have suggested that a well-designed strategic management can boost profits.

(vii) A number of research studies have also indicated that systematic long-run planning resulted in high performance of the businesses.

(viii) It strengthens the employee commitment to and participation in formulating long-term goals.

(ix) Organisations foresee the environmental changes. Therefore they reduce the chance of being affected by the changes in the environment, market place and actions of competitors.

(x) It helps for increased employee productivity, reduced resistance to change, clear understanding of performance-reward relationship.

(xi) It enhances problem-prevention capabilities of organisations as it promotes interaction among managers at all levels.

(xii) It often brings order and discipline to a firm.

(xiii) It allows for identification, prioritisation and exploitation of opportunities.

(xiv) It provides an objective view of management problems.

(xv) It represents a framework for improved control of activities.

(xvi) It minimises the effects of adverse conditions and changes.

(xvii) It allows major decisions and supports established objectives.

(xviii) It allows fewer resources and less time to be devoted for correcting erroneous or *adhoc* decisions.

(xix) It helps to integrate the behaviour of individuals into a total effort.

(xx) It provides a basis for the clarification of individual responsibilities.

(xxi) It gives encouragement to forward thinking.

(xxii) It provides cooperative, integrated and enthusiastic approach to tackling problems and opportunities.

(xxiii) It encourages favourable attitude towards change.

(xxiv) It gives a degree of discipline and formality to the management of business.

(E) Strategic Management Process: Strategic Fit vs. Strategic Intent

As we have discussed earlier, strategic management is a process of series of steps. The basic steps in strategic management process are:

- Identify corporate vision, mission, objectives and goals.
- Analyse the corporate external environment to identify opportunities and threats.
- Scan the corporate internal environment to identify strengths and weaknesses of the company.
- Revise the corporate mission, if there is any drastic deviation in the external environment.

- Craft the strategic alternatives based mostly on the corporate opportunities and strengths. Also consider strategies for correcting company's weaknesses, when the opportunities are significant and distinct. Similarly consider crafting strategies by correcting the threats, as and when possible, and when the company has distinctive strengths or competencies.
- Select the best corporate strategy. Craft business unit level and functional level strategies based on corporate strategy.
- Implement the strategy.
- Evaluate and control the strategic implementation process in order to achieve the best performance. Fig. 1.4 presents the strategic management process.

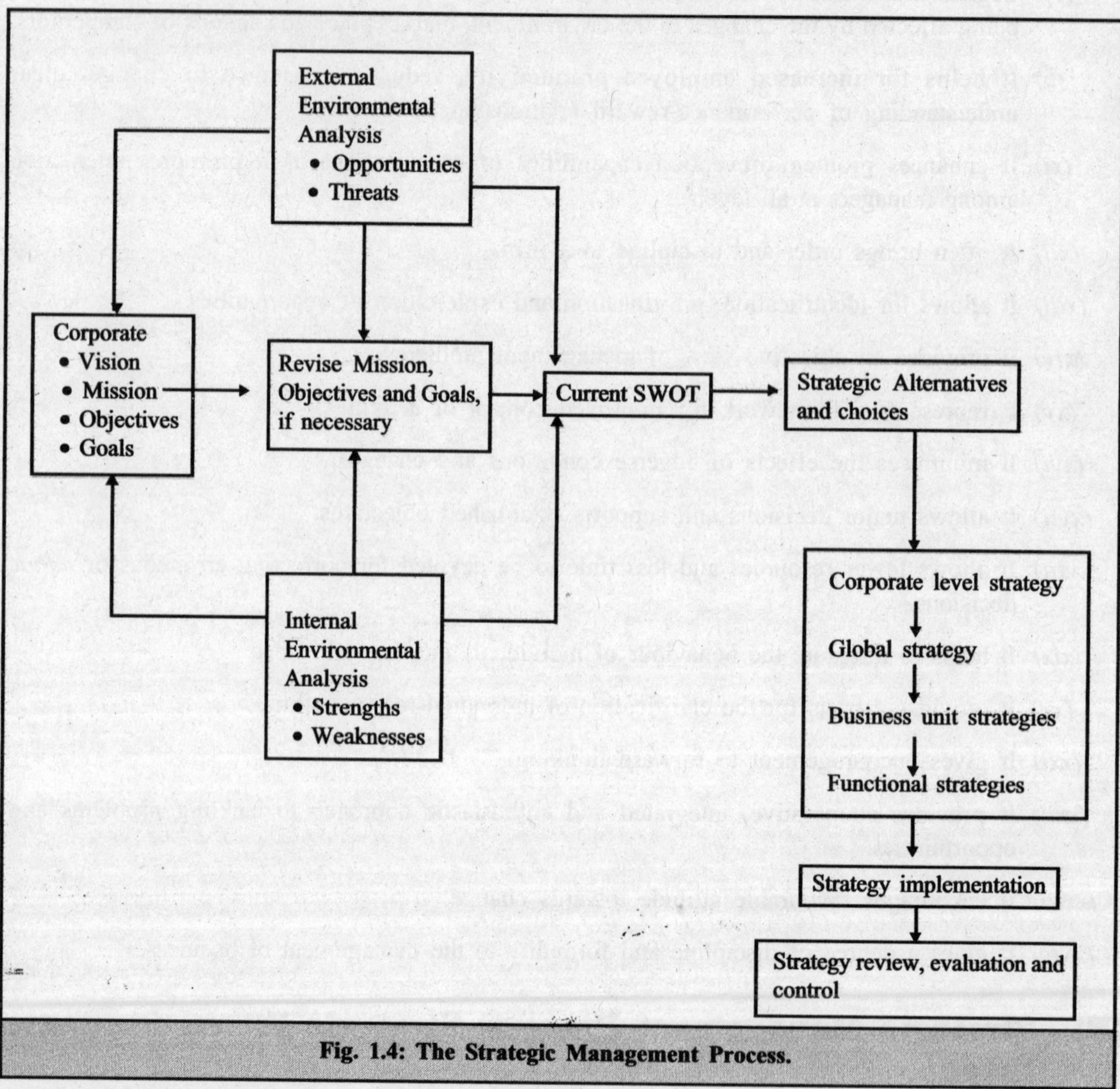

Fig. 1.4: The Strategic Management Process.

Vision and Mission Statements

There is a confusion in the usage of the terminology of vision and mission as some companies use them distinctively, while others use them interchangeably. Thus, some companies define vision and mission statements separately, while others define only mission statement. These two terms are used separately in this book.

Vision statements visualise the future of the company. An organisation's vision statement answers the question: "What do we want to become?" or "What can we become?" Normally, mission statements are defined based on vision statements. Vision statement of a life insurance company is “To take care, your life's primary goal”.

Mission statement defines the scope of business operations of a firm that distinguishes it from similar firms. The mission statement of **Ford Motor Company is:** “We are a global family with a proud heritage passionately committed to providing personal mobility for people around the world.” While the mission statement of **Microsoft** is: At Microsoft, we work to help people and businesses throughout the world realize their full potential. This is our mission. Everything we do reflects this mission and the values that make it possible”.

Strategic management process includes: formulation of vision, mission, objectives, goals, strategies based on SWOT analysis.

Organisation defines objectives based on its mission. Objectives specify the end towards which an activity is aimed at, long-range objectives specify the results that are desired in pursuing organisation's mission. For example, achieving high level of customer satisfaction is the long-run objective of ICICI Bank. The short-term objectives prefer targets normally of less than one-year's duration. Short-term objective of ICICI Bank is to make the transactions and procedures flexible for the convenience of the customer. Thus, objectives are open-ended statements.

Goals are defined based on the objectives. Goals are closed-ended statements. Goal in 2008 of ICICI Bank in relation to customer service is to complete each transaction of a customer in less than 10 minutes time.

External Environment Analysis (or Opportunities and Threats Analysis): Organisations analyse external environment in order to find the opportunities to achieve organisational goals as well as objectives. Similarly, external environmental analysis points out the possible threats to the achievement of organisational goals. External environment consists of social, technical, economic, political, legal, and government factors. These factors provide opportunities to certain business organisations, (see Box 1.4), while they pose threats to some other organisations. For example, economic liberalisation announced by the Government of India provided opportunities to various multinational companies to conduct business in India and to the Indian business houses like Reliance, Tata and Birla to expand and diversify their business activities.

External environmental analysis provides business opportunities and threats.

In fact, opportunity of one category of companies would be a threat to other category of companies. For example, globalisation and liberalisation has been the opportunity for MNCs and large scale domestic companies in India as well as abroad, but it had been a great threat for most of the small firms like A.P. Lightings Limited and non-dynamic public sector companies like Hindustan Machine Tools in India and Banking Corporation of PNG in Papua New Guinea.

BOX 1.4 DIPLOMATS PROVIDE OPPORTUNITY FOR WORLD'S MOST EXPENSIVE HOTELS

Starwood Hotels

The Royal Penthouse Suite at the President Wilson Hotel in Geneva commands $65,000 a night for its four-bedroom penthouse.

Amid the recession, rock stars, diplomats and other celebrities find solace from the doom and gloom by spending their time in sanctuary provided by the world's most luxurious and expensive hotels. While many of us are tightening our belts, shortening our summer holidays or even abandoning them, hoteliers to the rich and famous claim to have no trouble filling their most exclusive accommodations, and in the case of the most expensive suite in the world, managing to double its rate to $65,000 (€45,642) a night. In an annual survey by Financial News' sister publication Wealth Bulletin, the Royal Penthouse Suite at the President Wilson Hotel in Geneva, Switzerland, tops the list as the most expensive hotel room in 2009, commanding $65,000 for its four-bedroom penthouse — twice as much as patrons paid a year ago for its luxurious settings and views of Lake Geneva and Mont Blanc. The hotel's management puts the rise down to "buoyant demand" from government officials and U.N. diplomats. Last year's winner, the iconic Ty Warner Penthouse at the Four Seasons Hotel in New York, came second this time, at $35,000, $1,000 up from last year. New entries this year were the third-placed Presidential Suite at the Hotel Cala di Volpe in Sardinia, the Villa La Cupola Suite at the Westin Excelsior in Rome and the Presidential Suite at the Ritz-Carlton in Tokyo. Despite the past year's financial and economic turmoil, prices at the best hotel suites have risen by an average of 10% this year. Herbert Ypma, founder of the Hip Hotels brand, said: "The very high end hasn't suffered all that much. A lot of hotels used to having upmarket clientele are getting the benefit of them taking far more time off than usual — so they have more time to stay in hotels. Money was never the issue, time was."Hoteliers said that although the number of business travellers has fallen in the past year, government officials have taken their place in the best rooms and suites.President Barack Obama and his entourage took over the entire Ritz-Carlton Hotel in Moscow for three nights in June. The President Wilson Hotel said heads of state and other high-level government officials are fuelling demand for its hugely expensive Royal Penthouse Suite. Vivian Deuschl, spokeswoman for Ritz-Carlton Hotels, said demand is also coming from wealthy leisure travellers: "Last year they might have taken three or four cheaper holidays. This year they are taking one big vacation, but pulling out all the stops." The 10 most expensive hotel suites according to Wealth Bulletin's survey for 2009 are:

1. The Royal Penthouse Suite, President Wilson Hotel, Geneva — $65,000 per night: Complete with a cocktail lounge, the Royal Penthouse Suite at the President Wilson is so exclusive that bookings reportedly have to be made through the hotel's chairman. The suite occupies the entire top floor of the hotel. It is reached by a private elevator, has four bedrooms overlooking Lake Geneva and Mont Blanc and comes with six bathrooms. Equipped with bulletproof windows and doors, it is almost exclusively reserved for celebrities or state heads, ideal with the United Nations headquarters a five-minute drive away.

2. Ty Warner Penthouse, Four Seasons Hotel, New York — $35,000 per night: Business at the Ty Warner Penthouse at the Four Seasons Hotel in New York has remained as buoyant as when the suite opened in 2007, according to a spokeswoman. The nine-room suite has walls inlaid with thousands of pieces of mother-of-pearl. There is an indoor-outdoor Zen garden, a private spa room with a screen of living bamboo and a book-lined library, which has a grand piano at its centre.

3. The Presidential Suite, Hotel Cala di Volpe, Costa Smeralda, Sardinia — $34,000 per night: The Presidential Suite at Hotel Cala di Volpe near Porto Cervo, averages around $34,000 a night, although during the peak summer season will cost as much as $45,000. Located in the hotel tower, the multi-level Presidential Suite, sprawls across 2,500 sq ft and has three bedrooms, three bathrooms, a private gym, a steam room and a wine cellar. It is crowned by a rooftop terrace with an outdoor saltwater swimming pool.

4. Villa La Cupola Suite, Westin Excelsior, Rome — $31,000 per night: Villa La Cupola Suite in Rome's Westin Excelsior embodies all things Roman and excessive: a cupola, a Pompeii-style Jacuzzi, frescoes and stained glass windows detailing allegories of a mythological figure paired with a modern one, such as Atlas and Television, Hypnosis and Neurosis, Hermes and Marketing and Hermaphrodite and Fashion. Located on the fifth and sixth floors, the suite covers 6,099 sq ft and has an additional 1,808 sq ft of balconies and terraces overlooking Via Veneto.

5. The Presidential Suite, Ritz-Carlton Tokyo — $25,000 per night: The Presidential Suite, on the top floor of the city's tallest building, has spectacular views of Mount Fuji and

Roppongi Hills, as well as an expansive vista of Tokyo's impressive cityscape. It occupies 2,368 sq. ft., For refreshments, guests may enjoy the $18,000 Diamonds-Are-Forever Martini, which comes with a one-Karat Bulgari diamond at the bottom.

Ritz-Carlton

The Presidential Suite at Tokyo's Ritz-Carlton.

6. The Bridge Suite, The Atlantis, Bahamas — $22,000 per night: The 10-room Bridge Suite is actually a bridge spanning the two towers of the Atlantis Hotel. The 23rd-floor suite is decked with marble floors, a grand piano and a 22-carat gold chandelier. It was known in former times as "the Michael Jackson Suite" because of his regular stays. Prices have come down from $25,000 last year and fees are negotiable. Nevertheless, the suite is so exclusive the hotel does not even advertise it.

7. The Imperial Suite, Park Hyatt Vendôme, Paris — $20,000 per night: The Imperial Suite at the Park Hyatt in Paris provides guests with an "in-suite-spa" concept — with the bathroom/spa comprising a whirlpool bath, a steam shower room and a massage table. The 2,500 sq ft penthouse suite has a huge living room, a dining room, a kitchen and a work area.

Burj Al Arab

The Royal Suite at the Burj Al Arab in Dubai.

8. Royal Suite, Burj Al Arab, Dubai — $19,600 per night: Since it was built in the mid-1990s, the Burj Al Arab has become one of the world's most instantly recognizable hotels with its billowing sail-like structure stretching out on an artificial island into the Gulf of Arabia. The Royal Suite on the 25th floor has a marble-and-gold staircase, leopard print carpets, its own private lift and a rotating four-poster canopy bed.

9. Royal Armleder Suite, Le Richemond, Geneva — $18,900 per night: The Royal Armleder Suite at the Le Richemond Hotel is named after the wealthy family who used to own the famous hotel before Rocco Forte bought it in August 2004. The three-bedroom suite, which stretches over 2,500 sq ft on the seventh floor, has a 1,000 sq ft terrace with panoramic views of Lake Geneva, a real log fire and floor-to-ceiling bulletproof windows. Olga Polizzi, Rocco Forte's sister and well-known hotel interior designer, designed the suite.

10. The Ritz-Carlton Suite, The Ritz-Carlton, Moscow — $16,500 per night: To stay at the best suite in Moscow's Ritz-Carlton would cost around $16,000 a night — $500 less than last year. Furnished in Russian imperial style, the 2,370 sq. ft. suite has views of famous Moscow sites including the Kremlin and Red Square. The suite comes with the necessity for the security — conscious Russian billionaire — a panic room with its own energy and telecommunications facilities.

Source: http://finance.yahoo.com/real-estate/article/107608/diplomats-help-boost-rates-at-worlds-most-expensive-hotels.html(Accessed on 31/09/09).

Opportunities or threats depend upon perceptions as the same factor may be viewed as opportunity by one company while it may appear as threat to another. For example, more than one third of the low income group population in India was viewed as an opportunity by Coca-Cola to introduce Coca-Cola in a small bottle naming it "*Chota Cola*," *(Chota in Hindi language means small)* while its rival viewed the low income group as a loss of market. Environmental factors that may appear as threat at one point of time would turnout to be opportunities appearing at another point of time, once the company changes its strategy. For example the consumer goods giant Whirlpool introduced its washing machines in India in 1994. But it failed miserably because of the difference in women's clothing *viz.*, the *saree* which was much thinner in material than those dress material used in US was not suitable for its machines. However, instead of accepting defeat, Whirlpool adopted to this cultural difference by coming up with a suitable model.

The model not only succeeded but also became a market leader. A cultural threat turned into a huge opportunity once Whirlpool changed its strategy.

On-time sales of most of the products including grocery would be a threat to most of the traditional sellers. Similarly, information technology creates opportunities for the fast moving and changing firms and but poses threats to the firms doing business with out-dated technology.

Organisations analyse the external environmental factors and identify the opportunities and threats based on the company's current products, services systems and practices.

Internal Environment Analysis (or Strengths and Weaknesses): Internal environment consists of structures, resources, values, competencies, cultures, and systems of a company. Internal environmental analysis helps to identify company's strengths and weaknesses in relation to the market, customer needs and all other external environmental factors.

Internal environmental analysis provides business's strengths and weaknesses.

Internal environmental factors include organisation structure, finance, marketing, production/operations, human resources, information management and research and development capabilities of a company in terms of markets.

In fact, the same internal environmental factors seem to be strength in one kind of market and a weakness in other kind of markets. For example, the technology of Digicel, a mobile company is a strength of the company in smaller and relatively less developed and competitive markets like Papua New Guinea, Fiji and West Indies and is a weakness in highly competitive markets like USA, Europe and India. Therefore, companies have to assess their strengths based on the external environment under which they operate or propose to operate.

Companies identify their strengths and weaknesses in each of the functional area as well as overall organisational structure like producing high quality products, customised products and convenient products for the customers, efficient delivery of the products, efficient customer service, low cost and high productivity.

In addition, companies evaluate strengths and weakness against those of the competitors in order to find superiority or deficiency in each of the strengths and weaknesses. In addition, strengths and weaknesses are also identified against company's objectives and goals, in order to assess whether the company has capabilities to achieve its goals or not. For example, one of the objectives of Deccan Airlines is to provide passenger air travel at the lowest price compared to other domestic airlines in India. So Deccan Airlines evaluated its strengths in terms of low cost flights organisation structure that contribute to the low cost of operation per unit.

Thus, companies evaluate their strengths and weaknesses relative to the:

- external environmental factors
- markets in which currently operating and propose to operate

- objectives and goals of the companies and
- competitor's strengths and weaknesses.

Exhibit 1.3 presents some environmental factors to monitor strategic management process.

Exhibit 1.3: Some Environmental Factors to Monitor for Strategic Management Process

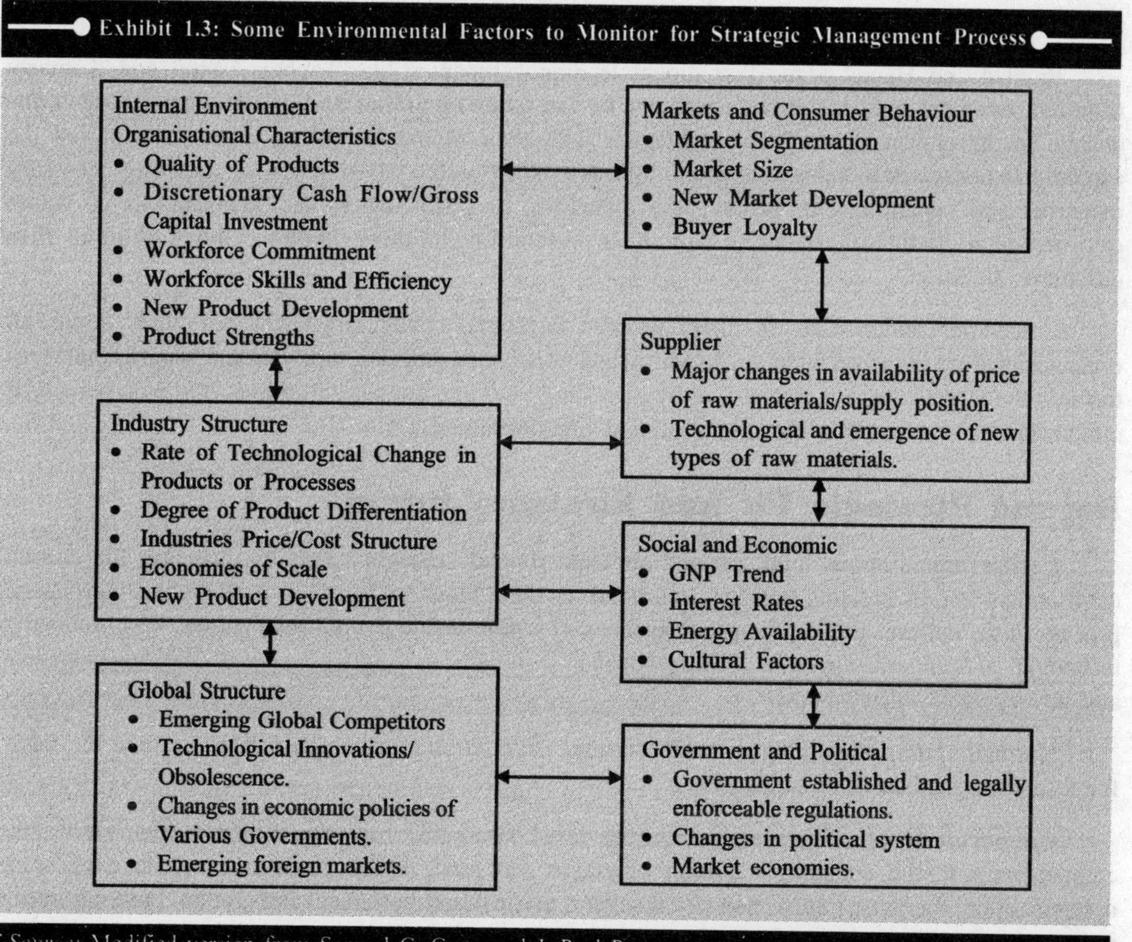

Source: Modified version from Samuel C. Certo and J. Paul Peter. *op.cit.*, p. 16.

SWOT Analysis and Strategy Formulation

The next logical step is to bring the alliance between opportunities and appropriate strengths, taking stock of weaknesses in relation to opportunities, study the possibility of correcting the weaknesses and study the threats, altering the strengths to convert the threats into opportunities. This process helps the organisation to make use of the opportunities to the full extent by aligning its strenghts to the opportunities. This alignment further enables the company to formulate appropriate corporate strategies. The companies also strive to modify its products and/or correct their weaknesses in order to fit them with the opportunities and then formulate strategies. The example of Coca-Cola's alternation in the bottle size and introduction of "Chota Cola" holds good in clarifying this concept. Thus, companies strive to bring the match among S-W-O-T in order.

Strategic Fit vs. Strategic Intent

Traditionally companies used to bring the fit between their current strengths and opportunities and formulate strategies in those areas where there is a fit between strengths and opportunities. C.K. Prahlad and Gary Hamel criticise the strategic fit model as it fixes the mindsets of the companies based on their current strengths and current environments and therefore fails to deals with the future environment and acquiring additional companies and resources.

Businesses, intent is preferring the situation of acquiring necessary resources and capabilities to achieve the objectives or goals under the circumstances of future environmental challenges and/or opportunities.

Prahlad and Hamel argue that global leading companies like Toyota, Canon and Komastu acquired resources and capabilities necessary for the future environmental opportunities ahead of the change in the environment. These companies with their global leadership objective acquired the capabilities necessary to achieve such an objective. They prefer this situation of acquiring necessary resources and capabilities to achieve the objectives or goals under the circumstances of future environmental challenges and/or opportunities. According to them, strategic intent is more than unfettered ambition.

Companies under strategic intent process formulate challenging/ambitious goals, focus all organisational resources on winning, acquiring additional competencies, motivate and inspire employees towards the targets, sustain enthusiasm by providing new operational definitions based on perceived circumstances and towards the organisational transformation.

Beyond Strategic Fit and Strategic Intent

Certain organisations think beyond strategic fit and strategic intent by changing the current environment and/or creating new environments to their favour. This is by influencing the change process of the culture, altering the political factors by influencing the political parties, by introducing technological changes, by initiating different economic initiatives like granting loans, deferring payments and advance/delayed payments.

Normally companies initially craft corporate level strategies, which further become the basis for formulating global level strategies.

Corporate-level strategies: Corporate level strategies link the opportunities, strengths/ competencies to the company's overall objective and goal. These strategies include expansion, diversification, mergers, joint ventures, takeovers, vertical and horizontal integration, entering into a new market and/or foreign country. Corporate level strategies affect the strategies and operations of all business units and functional level units.

Global strategies: Global strategies include a decision to enter foreign markets. This strategy includes which countries to enter and the mode of entry. Global strategy is based on the corporate strategy.

Fig. 1.5 presents strategic management process at different levels.

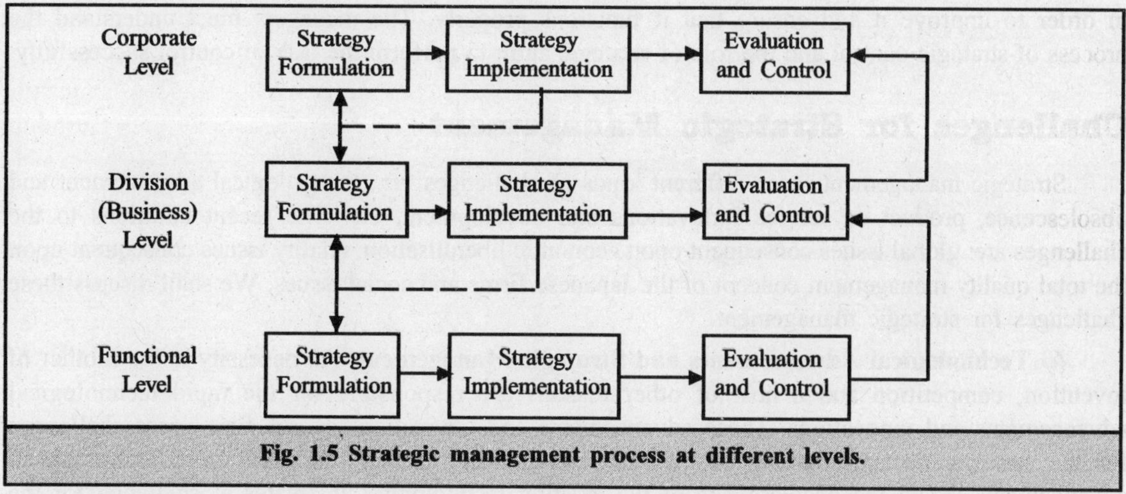

Fig. 1.5 Strategic management process at different levels.

Business level strategies: Business level strategies encompasses two or more functional units in crafting and implementing a strategy, for example, cost leadership strategy encompasses the integrated contribution of all functional areas. Other business level strategies include differentiation, niche market, total quality and fast delivery.

Functional level strategies: These strategies are more or less related to each function like production/operations, marketing, finance, human resource, information management and research and development. These are the ultimate strategies which are linked to corporate and business level Strategies. For example, managing cultural diversity is the human resource management strategy, while the merger is the corporate strategy.

Exhibit 1.4 presents the characteristics of strategies at different levels.

Exhibit 1.4: Characteristics of Strategies at Different Levels

	Organisational Level	*Strategic Business Unit Level*	*Functional Level*
Purpose	Implement Mission	Achieve organisation strategies	Support business unit and organisational strategies
Internal Activities	Control contribution of divisions, business units to mission	Coordinate with other units developing distinctive competence	Manage daily operating problems
Key Questions	What business are we in? What business should we be in?	Are changes threatening or creating opportunities for our products or markets?	Are we on schedule?
External Activities	Monitor general and specific environment.	Focus on an industry, product, market.	Anticipate changes required from new business units and organisational strategies
Time Frame	Long term (3 years plus)	Intermediate (1-3 years)	Daily (below one year)
Performance Measures	Vague, flexible	Measurable, moderately flexible	Detailed and specific

Source: Joe G. Thomas, "Strategic Management," Harper & Row, Publishers, New York, 1988, p. 46.

Strategic Evaluation and Control: The final step of strategic management process is strategic evaluation and control. It focuses on monitoring and evaluating the strategic management process in order to improve it and ensure that it functions properly. The managers must understand the process of strategic control and the role of strategic audit to perform the task of control successfully.

Challenges for Strategic Management

Challenges of strategic management include: Technological advancement, innovations, global issues, quality issues, economic boom and recession and social issues.

Strategic management faces different kinds of challenges *viz.,* technological advancement and obsolescence, product or service innovations and development, etc. The recent additions to the challenges are: global issues consequent upon economic liberalisation, quality issues consequent upon the total quality management concept of the Japanese firms and social issues. We shall discuss these challenges for strategic management.

***(i)* Technological Advancements and Strategic Management:** As necessity is the mother of invention, competition and a host of other reasons are responsible for the rapid technological advancements and innovations. These advancements and innovations of one firm poses challenges for the strategic decision-making of the competing firms. Further, the continuous technological advancements led to the obsolescence of the existing technologies. It creates a challenge for the strategic management of those firms using obsolete technologies. The strategic managers should be fully aware of technological advances and innovations while formulating strategies (See Box 1.5).

BOX 1.5 TECHNOLOGY AND IBM

- IT strategy: establishing the overall IT strategy for an enterprise – including the SOA Strategy, Application Support Strategies, Governance models and innovative technology strategies.
- Enterprise and Service Oriented Architecture: helping to establish/evaluate an overall enterprise architecture and/or SOA for the business.
- IT performance management: helping to improve IT processes to deliver higher quality at reduced costs.

Why IBM

Technology strategy consultants provide the intersection of business and technology, supporting our clients in enhancing competitiveness and creating new sources of economic value from technology. Our consultants work with CIOs and their peers in the boardroom, seeking to close the gap between business and information technology. The Global Business Services technology strategy practice is a recognized market leader in innovative technologies, service-oriented architecture (SOA), and IT strategy. Our consultants have demonstrated experience creating value for clients and serving as trusted business advisors. And we can bring value to your organization through the unmatched worldwide capabilities, relationships and research of IBM. With nearly 3,500 strategy professionals worldwide, the IBM strategy and change practice is part of IBM Global Business Services, one of the worlds leading management consulting practices. Working across all major sectors, IBM has inherent business expertise across more than a dozen industries. This includes communications, distribution, financial services, and the industrial and public sectors. Our consultants have demonstrated experience creating value for clients and serving as trusted business advisors to our clients worldwide.

Source: http://www-935.ibm.com/services/us/index.wss/offerfamily/gbs/a1029389 (Accessed on 31/08/09)

***(ii)* Product/Service Innovation and Development and Strategic Management:** Technological advancements and innovations together with changes in consumer tastes and preferences, needs and conveniences led to the continuous product/service development and innovation of new products.

The firms with new products/services widely accepted by the customers enjoy distinctive strategic advantage whereas other firms in the same industry suffer from strategic disadvantage. This leads to further competition and creates new challenges for strategic management. Strategic managers are expected to be aware of these developments and innovations in the industry while formulating their strategies.

***(iii)* Global Issues and Strategic Management:** With the announcement of economic liberalisation in India and consequently opening up of the economy to the rest of the world in 1991, business activities have tended to cross national boundaries more intensely and frequently. Due to the increase in scale and variety of operations of multinational and transnational corporations in the country, even firms with no international operations are experiencing the impact of globalisation on their markets and operations. Since this trend is expected to continue, almost all the organisations, irrespective of their size, nature of operations and markets will have to consider global issues in their strategic management process.

The strategic managers must be fully aware of critical international variables that might considerably affect their strategic operations, before they determine how their strategic management process can most effectively accommodate global environmental factors.

***(iv)* Quality Issues and Strategic Management:** The quality movement, spearheaded by W. Edwards Dening has had a significant impact on the method of strategic management process of organisations in the 1990s. Sea changes took place in the concept of quality. The concept of post-production quality control changed into Total Quality Management (TQM). It further changed to feed forward and zero-defect of the product. Further, quality today does mean an organisation — wide commitment to enhance the value of goods or services to the customer at each and every stage — from the stage of product design, raw material, every stage of production process, to the place of marketing (or selling) to post sale service. Japanese firms once produced cheap products, presently they are producing not only low cost but most qualitative products. In fact, today's customers feel happy to buy a Japanese-made product in view of its quality. Hence, Japanese firms enjoy strategic advantage position in this regard. (See Box 1.6).

BOX 1.6 QUALITY STRATEGY, STRATEGIC CONTROL SYSTEMS AND ORGANIZATIONAL PERFORMANCE

Despite calls for the development of systems to control the implementation and monitoring of strategic plans, prior studies suggest that few American or European firms employ formal strategic control systems. Using survey data from the automotive and computer industries in Canada, Germany, Japan, and the United States, we examine whether organizations following a quality-oriented strategy have adopted the strategic control practices discussed in the quality management literature. Our results indicate that organizations placing greater emphasis on quality in their strategic plan do tend to make greater use of quality-related strategic control practices. However, we find no evidence to support the claim that Japanese organizations link their control systems more closely to their competitive strategies than organizations in the other countries. Instead, Japanese manufacturers appear to make greater use of many of the strategic control practices regardless of their organization's strategic emphasis. The performance consequences of the strategic control practices vary somewhat by industry, suggesting that strategic control systems should be adapted to the organization's competitive environment. Finally, several strategic control practices are negatively associated with performance, consistent with claims that formal strategic control systems can actually hinder performance in some circumstances by focusing attention on formal and rigid action plans, targets, and information gathering when flexible and creative strategic responses may be more appropriate.

Source: http://knowledge.wharton.upenn.edu/paper.cfm?paperID=512(Accessed on 31/08/09)

Managers involved in the strategic management process at all levels are expected to understand the history of this movement and its day-to-day developments in order to appreciate the crucial role it plays in modern organisational strategy.

***(v)* Economic Boom and Recession:** Both economic booms as well as economic recession affect the strategic management process. Economic boom provides the opportunities for the increase in demand as well as business operations and economic recession in general create threats. Companies should foresee the trends that result in recession and formulate strategies accordingly. In fact most of the companies failed to foresee the economic recession of 2008 and beyond.

***(vi)* Social Issues and Strategic Management:** Since the organisation is part and parcel of the society, most of the organisations are of the view that, social responsibility is the managerial obligation to act, protect and promote both organisational interests and welfare of the society. Strategic management process of an organisation will be affected by recognising this obligation.

The strategic managers should have a clear idea about *(i)* the societal constituencies that the organisation will serve us the obligation, *(ii)* the areas of the business to be affected by this obligation, *(iii)* method of conducting social audit to facilitate the strategic management process, and *(iv)* the areas of strategic advantages that the organisation will be enjoying.

POINTS TO BE REMEMBERED

- Different organisations having similar opportunities and resources perform differently.
- Strategy is a unified, comprehensive and integrated plan/course of action that relates to the strategic advantages of the firm and the challenges of the environment.
- Strategy is necessary to have and develop internal ability.
- Globalisation and strides in information technology makes strategic management complex.
- Strategic management is concerned with deciding on strategy and planning how that strategy is to be put into effect.
- Strategic management passes through the stages of financial planning, external oriented planning and to strategic management.
- Strategic management is essential due to change and for better performance.

KEY WORDS

- Strategy
- Strategic Management
- Forecasting
- Electronic Business
- Challenges
- Opportunities
- Change
- Financial Planning
- External Planning
- Business Decisions
- Environment
- Advantages

QUESTIONS FOR DISCUSSION

(1) What is strategy? State a few definition of strategy.

(2) Should a strategy be a plan?

(3) What are the dimensions of strategy? Discuss different forms of strategy.

(4) Why do organisations need strategies?

(5) What are the key areas in developing strategies?

(6) State the historical developments of strategic management.

(7) Define the term strategic management.

(8) Discuss the need for and benefits of strategic management.

(9) What are the challenges to strategic management?

REFERENCES

1. James Brain Quinn, "*Strategies for Change*" in James Brain Quinn, Henry Mintzberg and Robert M. James (Ed). "The Strategy Process," Prentice-Hall, Englewood Cliffs, New Jersey, 1988, pp. 8-9.
2. Alfred D. Chandler, "*Strategy and Structure*," in the "History of American Enterprise," M.I.T. Press, Cambridge, 1962, p. 13.
3. Thomas L. Wheelen, J. David Hunger and Krish Rangarajan, "*Strategic Management and Business Policy*", Pearson, 2007, p.7.
4. James Brain Quinn, "*Strategies for Change*," Richard D. Irwin Inc., Homewood III, 1980, p. 7.
5. Delivering the Goods at FedEx, Business Week, June 2005, pp.60-62
6. Michael A Hitt, Robert E. Hoskisson and R. Duane Ireland, "*Management of Strategy*", Thomson, 2007, p.7.
7. R.M. Grant, "*Strategic Planning in a Turbulent Environment: Evidence from the oil majors*", Strategic Management Journal, 24: 491-517.
8. Thomas L. Wheeler, J. David Hunger and Krish Ramgarajan, '*Strategic Management and Business Policy*', Pearson, 2004, pp. 63-64.
9. R.A.D. Aveni, "*Coping with Hypercompetition: Utilising the New 7's Framework*", Academy of Management Executive, 9(3) 1995, p. 4b.
10. R.A.D. Aveni, "*Corporate Spheres of Influence*", MIT Sloan Management Review, 2004, 45(4), pp. 38- 46.
11. Wal-Mart at a Glance, 2005, www.walmart.com
12. Thomas L. Wheelen, J. David Hunger and Krish Rangarajan, "*Strategic Management and Business Policy*", Pearson, 2007, p.7.
13. A.Y. Lewin and H. W. Voloberda, "*Prolegomena on Coevolution: A Framework for Research on Strategy and New Organisational forms*", Organisational Science, October 1999, pp. 519-534.
14. D.A. Garvin, "*Building a learning or mitigating the possible deviations*", July-August 1993, p.80.
15. T.T. Bedwin, *et.al.*, "*The Evolution of Learning Strategies in Organisation*", Academy of Management Executive, November 1997, p. 47-58.
16. James A.F. Stoner, "*Management*," Prentice-Hall of India (P) Ltd., New Delhi, 1984, p. 87.
17. Quoted in Chandan J.S., "*Fundamentals of Modern Management*," Vikas Publishing House (P) Ltd., New Delhi, 1986, p. 1.
18. Harold Koontz and Cyril O'Donnel, "*Essentials of Management*," McGraw-Hill Book Company, New York, 1978, p. 4.
19. Robert T. Justis, Richard J. Judd and David B. Stephens, "*Strategic Management* and Policy," Prentice- Hall Inc. New Jersey, 1985, p. 3.
20. Azhar Kazmi, "*Business Policy*," Tata McGraw-Hill Publishing Company Ltd., New Delhi, 1992, p. 4.

21. R.A. Gordon and J.E. Howell, "*Higher Education for Business*," Columbia University Press, New York, 1959.

22. Samuel C. Certo and J. Paul Peter, "*The Strategic Management* Process," Richard D. Irwin Inc., Chicago, 1993, p. 5.

23. R.A. Gordon and J.E. Howell, *op.cit.*

24. Gerry Johnson and Keven Scholes, *op. cit.*, p. 10.

25. Mathew J. Kiernam, "*The New Strategic Architecture*," *The Executive,* February 1993, pp.7-21.

26. H. Igor Ansoff, "*Implementing Strategic Management*," Prentice-Hall, New Jersey, 1984.

27. Lawrence R. Jauch and William F. Glueck, "*Business Policy and Strategic Management*," McGraw-Hill Book Company, New York, 1988, p. 4.

28. *Ibid.*, p. 11.

29. Alfred D. Chandler, "*Strategy and Structure*," in the "History of American Enterprise," M.I.T. Press, Cambridge, 1962, p. 13.

30. Arthur Sharplin, "*Strategic Management*," McGraw-Hill Book Company, New York, 1985, p. 6.

31. James Brain Quinn, "*Strategies for Change*," Richard D. Irwin Inc., Homewood III, 1980, p. 7.

32. Samuel C. Certo and J. Paul Peter, *op.cit.*, p.6.

33. James Brain Quinn, "*Strategies for Change*" in James Brain Quinn, Henry Mintzberg and Robert M. James (Ed). "The Strategy Process," Prentice-Hall, Englewood Cliffs, New Jersey, 1988, pp. 8-9.

34. H. Igor Ansoff, "*Concept of Strategy*," in *Ibid.*, pp. 12-13.

35. R.N. Anthony and J. Dearden, "*Management Control Systems*," Irwin, 1976 Quoted in *Ibid,* p. 10.

36. C.K. Prahalad and G. Hamel, "*The Core Competence of The Corporation*," *Harvard Business Review*, May-June 1990, pp 79-91.

37. *Ibid.*

38. Samuel C. Certo and J. Paul Peter, *op.cit.*, p. 8.

✦ ✦ ✦

CHAPTER 2

THE STRATEGIST AND STRATEGIC DECISION-MAKING

Chapter Outline

(A) The Manager: Tasks and Roles

(B) The Strategist: Shareholders, Board of Directors and the CEO, Role of Executives in Strategic Management

(C) Strategic Decision-Making: Drivers of Success in, and Approaches to.

Learning Objectives

After studying this chapter, you should be able to:

- Know the tasks and roles of managers;
- Describe how the shareholders and Board of Directors can become strategists;
- Analyse the role of CEO as a strategist;
- Explain various executives as strategists;
- Discuss various types of decisions;
- Study the different approaches to strategic decision-making.

(A) THE TASKS OF A MANAGER

Mintzberg challenges the traditional view that managers plan, organise, direct and control. The point is that these words are too vague to understand the reality of managerial work.

Research studies stated that, "managers work at an unrelenting pace, and their activities are characterised by brevity, variety, and discontinuity and that they are strongly oriented to action and dislike reflective activities." In addition, managerial task, "involves performing a number of regular duties including ritual and ceremonial negotiations, and processing of soft information that links the organisation with its environment." Further it is stated that, "the manager's programmes — to schedule time, process information, make decisions and so on — remain locked deep inside their brains." Hence, management specialist has to concentrate his/her efforts on the specialised functions of the organisations, where he/she could more easily analyse the procedures and qualify the relevant information. This is due to the increasing pressure on his job from customers, subordinates with more democratic norms, demands from the government and increasing influences from outsiders.

Roles of a Manager

Managers perform different roles as shown in Figure 2.1. As can be seen from the figure, formal authority gives rise to three informational roles. The two sets of roles enable the manager to play the four decisional roles.

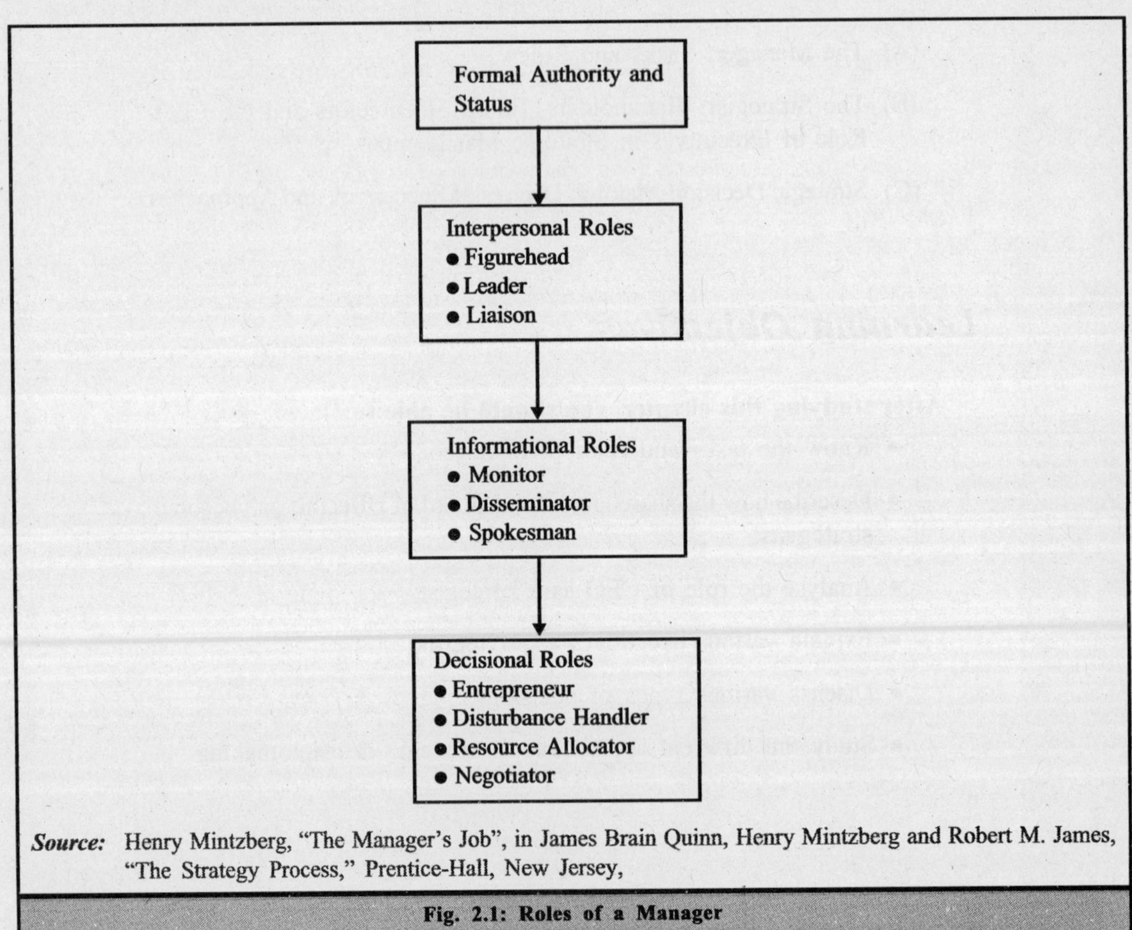

Source: Henry Mintzberg, "The Manager's Job", in James Brain Quinn, Henry Mintzberg and Robert M. James, "The Strategy Process," Prentice-Hall, New Jersey,

Fig. 2.1: Roles of a Manager

Interpersonal Role

The important interpersonal roles of strategists are:

Figurehead Role: Managers perform the duties of a ceremonial nature as head of the organisation or a strategic business unit or a department. Duties of interpersonal roles include routine, involving little serious communication and less important decisions. However, they are important for the smooth functioning of an organisation or a department.

Interpersonal roles of managers include: figurehead, leader and liaison.

Leader Role: The manager, as in charge of the organisation/department, coordinates the work of others and leads his/her subordinates. Formal authority provides greater potential power to exercise and get the things done.

Liaison Role: As the leader of the organisation or unit, the manager has to perform the functions of motivation, communication, encouraging team spirit and the like. Further, he/she has to coordinate the activities of all his/her subordinates, which involves the activity of liaison.

Informational Role

Manager emerges as the nerve centre of his/her organisation/department in view of his interpersonal links with his/her subordinates, peers, superiors and outsiders. Therefore, the manager has to play the information role effectively to let the information flow continuously from one corner to other corner.

The information roles of a manager include:

Monitor Role: As a result of the network of contacts, the manager gets the information by scanning his/her environment, subordinates, peers, and superiors. Managers, mostly collect information in verbal form often as gossip, hearsay, speculation and through grapevine channels.

Disseminator Role: Manager disseminates the information, he/she collects from different sources and through various means. He/she passes some of the privileged information directly to his/her subordinates, who otherwise have no access to it. The manager will play an important role in disseminating the information to his/her subordinates when they don't have contact with one another.

Informational roles of managers include: monitor, disseminator and spokesman.

Spokesman Role: Some insiders and/or outsiders control the unit/department or the organisation. The manager has to keep them informed about the developments in his/her unit. The manager has to keep his/her superior informed of every development in his/her unit, who in turn informs the insiders and outsiders. Directors and shareholders must be informed about the financial performance, customers must be informed about the new product developments, quality maintenance, government officials about implementation of law, etc.

Decisional Roles

Information is an important and basic input to decision-making. The managers play a crucial role in decision-making system of the unit. Only the manager can commit the department to new course of action and he has full and current information to take set of the decisions that determine the department's or organisational strategy. The decisional roles of the manager are:

Entrepreneurial Role: As an entrepreneur, the manager is a creator and innovator. He/she seeks to improve his/her department, adapt to the changing environmental factors. The manager would like to have new ideas, initiates new projects and initiates the developmental projects.

Decisional roles of managers include: Entrepreneurial, disturbance handler, resource allocatur and negotiator.

According to Peter F. Drucker, "the manager has the task of creating a true whole that is larger than the sum of its parts, a productive entity that turns out more than the sum of the resources put into it."

Disturbance Handler Role: Entrepreneurial role describes the manager as the voluntary initiator of change, the disturbance handler role presents the manager as involuntarily responding to pressures. Pressures of the situation are severe and highly demand the attention of the manager and as such the manager cannot ignore the situation. For example, workers strike, declining sales, bankruptcy of a major customer, etc., are some such situations.

The manager should have enough time in handling disturbances carefully, skilfully and effectively.

Resource Allocator Role: The most important resource that a manager allocates to his/her subordinates is his/her time. The manager should have an open-door policy and allow the subordinates to express their opinions and share their experiences. This process helps both the manager and his/her subordinates in making effective decisions. In addition, the manager should empower his/her subordinates by delegating his/her authority and power.

Negotiator Role: Managers spend considerable time in the task of negotiations. He/she negotiates with the subordinates for improved commitment and loyalty, with the peers for cooperation, coordination and integrations, with workers and their unions regarding conditions of employment, commitment, productivity, with the government about providing facilities for business expansion, etc.

These negotiations are integral part of the manager's job for only he/she has authority to commit organisational resources and is nerve centre of information.

Though the different roles of a manager are discussed separately for convenience, they are, in fact inseparable. The manager has to perform these roles simultaneously by integrating one with the another. Thus, the major role of the manager is integrating all the roles while playing managerial role or performing his tasks. In fact, the manager cannot play any one role while isolating the other roles. As a strategist, the manager has to integrate all the roles in decision-making while performing his/her tasks.

(B) THE STRATEGIST

It is a general view that the general manager in an organisation is the main executive in understanding the process of strategy formulation. But this is a very narrow view of defining a strategist. Anyone in the organisation who controls key or precedent setting actions can be called a strategist. It is also viewed that the strategist can be a collection of people. However, the senior general managers are key candidates for such a role as their perspective is broader than any of their subordinates. A ***strategist*** is a person who designs and plans action and policy to achieve a goal. (see Box 2.1).

BOX 2.1 DO YOU THINK YOU ARE A STRATEGIST?

It is a cliché that everyone thinks they're a strategist. The reason everyone thinks they're a strategist is because they don't know what a strategist does. **Get a reality check. Odds are you are not a strategist.** Strategy requires thinking conceptually and creating something from nothing. So, for the most part, if you need to see something in order to do strategy then you are not doing strategy, you're doing editing. Strategists usually favour thinking about the future instead of the present; strategists I admire are bored by what is and focus on what could be. Also, strategy means constantly making decisions based on incomplete information. It means taking intellectual leaps of faith that could derail many departments in an organization, and doing that with confidence.The best thing you can do for your career is to take a personality test to understand your strengths. If you are an INTJ you really are a strategist. If you are not an INTJ, the fewer letters you have that match that, the further away from strategist you are. So get some self-knowledge before you declare yourself a strategist. **If you're not a strategist, find work that plays to your strengths.** So look, most of you aren't strategists. But so what? It doesn't mean you're not brilliant. There are many ways to be brilliant. It is a misconception that the strategists do all the important work and everyone else does grunt work. There's plenty of important, interesting work that is detail-oriented and highly creative, such as building a space ship or doing cinematography. A lot of people think that if they are not creative or technical then they are strategists. This is not always true. A strategist thinks very big picture and also thinks ahead in time. People who are not artists or programmers and think in terms of the here and now are managers. If you do that with charisma, you're a leader. **If you are a strategist, then quit talking about it and do it.** Most people I have managed have told me, at one point or another, that their strength is strategy. For the most part, I hear this as "I don't know how to execute what you're asking me to execute." This is why the best way to understand how to do strategy is to execute on other peoples' strategies. You see first-hand what the common pitfalls of strategy are. Stop complaining that you are a frustrated strategist because today people at all levels in the organization are getting more opportunity to show their talent as strategists. This trend is partly a result of management theorists focusing on improving work for the lower ranks – not because improving entry-level work is ethical, but because the topic of how to be a better leader is exhausted, and academics need something fresh to write about, according to the Wall Street Journal. An example of this trend toward glorifying the low-ranking employee is the book Followership: How Followers are Creating Change and Changing Leaders, by Barbara Kellerman, professor at Harvard's Kennedy School of Government. Research like Kellerman's should drive home to you that if you're a strategist, you can do it from anywhere in the org. chart. So think of a great strategy in your entry-level job and then develop a strategy to convince people in the company to listen to you. That's a test of your strategic strength right there. And if you're not doing strategy in your current job, you might consider that you are like the guy who thinks he is a novelist but is not writing a novel: People do what their strengths are regardless of what their job description is. Real leaders will lead in any situation they find themselves. Real writers will always write, no matter what their day job is. And real strategists will always think in terms of the conceptual future, from any job they have.

Source: http://blog.penelopetrunk.com/2008/01/10/do-you-think-youre-a-strategist-youre-probably-wrong/

Normally the strategists include: shareholders, board of directors, chief executives officer, entrepreneurs, intrapreneurs, senior managers, middle level managers and lower level managers.

Shareholders and Strategic Management

The shareholders are the owners of the company.

The shareholders are the owners of the company. But it is not possible for them to manage the day to day operations of their company their company as they are: *(i)* mainly occupied in various activities, *(ii)* large in number, *(iii)* scattered throughout the length and breadth of the country and *(iv)* not expected to have managerial skills. Hence, they elect the directors to act as their representatives and manage the company. The role of the shareholders is limited to certain statutory requirements of the Companies Act, 1956. However, very crucial strategic decisions are to be taken by the shareholders in their meetings. The representative of the shareholders, *i.e.,* the board of directors share the responsibilities and activities of management with the executives at different levels.

The Board of Directors and Strategic Management

Board of directors represents the shareholders of the company.

Board of directors represents the shareholders of the company. Mostly, the directors are elected by the shareholders and they in turn elect the Managing Director. The ultimate authority of the Joint Stock Company lies with the board of directors. However, the authority of the board is subject to the limitations imposed by the Memorandum of Association, Articles of Association of the Company and the relevant provisions of the Companies Act, 1956.

Strategic Responsibilities of Board of Directors

Formulation of Mission, Objectives and Policies: Board of directors must take the long run view and have long run perspective for the company. The board formulates, reviews and reformulates the company's mission, objectives and policies which form the basis for strategy formulation and implementation.

Designing Organisational Structure: The board designs the structure of the organisation based on the objectives, policies, environmental factors, degree of competition, role of quality, expectations of employees, etc.

Selection of Top Executives: The board should assume the responsibility of screening and selecting the top executives who can formulate and implement the strategies. Senior/top executives are key personnel in the process of strategy implementation.

Financial Sanctions: The important financial decisions like sanctioning of finances to various projects, reserves, distribution of profit to shareholders and repayment of loans and advances, etc., are taken by the board. Further, the board reviews the financial performance of the company from time to time and reformulates the financial policies.

Link between the Company and External Environment: The board acts as a vital and continuous link between the company and external environment like government, other companies, social and economic institutions, etc.

Legal Functions: The board of directors also performs certain legal functions required as per the Companies Act, 1956 like criminal liabilities

Role of Board in Strategic Management

Board of directors of many companies, in recent times, have actively engaged themselves in strategy formulation. Added to this, with the appointment of outsiders as directors to the boards, more boards are involved with linking strategy with the consequent corporate action. These boards are supporting new strategies, mobilising resources, protecting the organisation from outside threats and linking the company with powerful outsiders.

Boards actively involve themselves in formulating vital strategies like mergers, acquisition, takeover, expansion, diversification, backward and forward linkages, etc., evaluation of corporate strategy and performance, advising, guiding and directing the chief executives in strategic management, feeding the data and information back and forward to the top level executives in strategy formulation and implementation.

The Chief Executive Officer and Strategic Management

The Chief Executive Officer (CEO) is designated as the Managing Director or President or General Manager or Chairman or Executive Director. The CEO is the person responsible for the functioning of the entire organisation. He cannot really delegate all his or her strategic responsibilities to anyone else, despite the fact that the board of directors and other officers can play a major role in this process.

Role of CEO in Strategic Management

CEO is the key strategist.

Among all the strategists, the Chief Executive Officer (CEO) is the key person in strategic management. He/she is the link between the board and top level executives of the organisation. Being the topmost general manager of the organisation, he/she integrates different functional areas of management and visualises the total organisation. He/she also foresees the external environmental factors and their impact on the business. He/she organises the whole data, ideas and information and conceptualises them.

The CEO looks forward based on his/her past experience and ability to understand the future changes. He/she evaluates the present mission, objectives, policies and strategies against the future probable changes and reformulates them, if necessary. Further, he/she formulates new objectives, policies and strategies as and when grand changes in the environment like economic liberalisations and technological advancements take place.

The CEO provides information and data to the board regarding strategy formulation. He provides the observations of strategy evaluation to the board and advises it either to continue the present strategy or to reformulate it or formulate a new strategy.

The CEO provides data regarding external environment to the senior managers, guides and helps them in formulating, implementing and evaluating and reformulating strategies as strategic business units are based on the corporate strategies.

Entrepreneurs and Strategic Management

"Entrepreneurs are individuals who start a business from scratch." Many entrepreneurs start a business like this. "The entrepreneur always searches for change, responds to it and exploits it as an opportunity." The qualities of an entrepreneur include:

Entrepreneurs are individuals who start a business from scratch.

(i) Zeal to do something new.

(ii) Enthusiasm, idealism, sense of purpose.

(iii) Independence of thought and action.

(iv) Having creative and innovative ideas.

(v) As initiators, they motivate others to follow or imitate them.

(vi) Proactive rather than reactive in actions.

The entrepreneur is the chief strategist in entrepreneurial firm. By virtue of his/her qualities discussed above, the entrepreneur formulates creative objectives and novel strategies and thereby exploits the market. As he/she is proactive in actions, he/she initiates the change and creates the opportunities for himself/herself and reaps the fruits. Then he/she acts as a guide and pathfinder to others. Thus, the entrepreneur, controls and moulds the external environmental factors to his/her favour through his/her innovative strategies.

The entrepreneur inspires his/her subordinates in strategy formulation, implementation and evaluation. He/she closely participates along with the subordinates in strategy reformulation. Strategic management is just like play to the entrepreneurs and he/she makes it a play for his/her subordinates also.

The entrepreneur will face problems if he/she expands the organisation into a larger one. He/she has to meet the challenges of competition, appointing competent managers who should be intelligent and smart enough to see the future beyond the entrepreneur's vision. It would be very difficult for the entrepreneurs to recruit the executives with these qualities. Hence, it would be prudent for the entrepreneurs, to consider this limitation while formulating expansion and diversification strategies.

Chief of the Family Operated Firm and Strategic Management

A family operated firm is a business whose major ownership, management and control is by a family and most of the key executives are family members. The chief of the family (or *karta* of the family) is the main strategist. The chief strategist of the family must consider the preferences of the family members who are active in the management of the firm and/or family. Normally, the family members render full support to the chief and do not interfere in normal activities of the business. Therefore, the family chief formulates the strategies like entrepreneurs. Women are also entering into family businesses, in recent times. The chief of the business takes the strategic decision by involving other members of the family in the process. In fact, he/she encourages and develops other members for strategic management.

A family operated firm is a business whose major ownership, management and control is by a family and most of the key executives are family members.

The family operating businesses will also have certain limitations in expanding the business into a large one, as in entrepreneur's business, though it may not be of the same magnitude. Hence, the chief of the family business should also consider the limitations while formulating expansion and diversification strategies.

Strategic Business Unit Level Strategists

The diversified businesses, multi-product, multi-service, multi-divisionalised firms are organised into Strategic Business Units (SBUs). The head of each SBU is its chief executive, if the company is structured based on the modern principles of organisation like, autonomy, freedom, responsibility and empowerment. Under such circumstances, corporate strategists encourage the SBU level chief executives in formulating their strategies.

SBU chief executives play a vital role in strategic management at their level as the chief executive at corporate level. The SBU level chief executive performs the roles similar to those of Managing Director and attempts to achieve the best results in his/her business units within the facilities and resources provided, autonomy and freedom sanctioned and under the overall guidelines of the corporate objectives and policies.

Intrapreneur is a creator within an organisation like SBU.

Intrapreneurship: With a view to avail the benefits of entrepreneurship, the corporate world started providing an entrepreneurial climate in their SBUs. In other words, the SBU chief executive is given freedom and autonomy to develop new ventures, to have a vision like an entrepreneur, etc. This concept is often described as "intrapreneurship."

With the increase in operations, production of new varieties of goods and/or rendering services, need for developing new ventures, the SBU manager is encouraged to start new ventures, or the SBU itself may be a new venture established within the present corporation. For example, Sparkle India Ltd., provided autonomy to its tungsten divisional head to formulate and implement his own strategies and play the role of an entrepreneur. The chief of this SBU empowered his employees and developed them into an autonomous team which could work without the chief.

SBU chief, under these circumstances plays the role of an entrepreneur and a strategist. SBU chiefs may have to be replaced when the entrepreneurial activities are completed as with independent entrepreneurs. This situation was more evident in Sparkle's India Ltd's tungsten wire division.

Corporate-Level Planners and Strategic Management

Corporate level planners are the supporting staff to the strategists. The large business firms provide the planning staff to their chief executives who are busy with their prime responsibilities. The planners are specialist staff with skills in strategic management techniques, process, analysis, etc. In addition, the planning staff are also trained in various strategic management techniques.

Senior Managers and Strategic Management

Senior managers include second line managers at the corporate office, divisional office, zonal office, SBUs functional heads, etc. These managers also play due role in strategic management process. Most companies form committees for strategy formulation, implementation and evaluation. The committees are constituted with the senior managers as members.

The senior managers perform various functions of strategic management like environmental scanning, finding out business opportunities, formulation of alternative strategies, performing SWOT analysis, examining the strategies, participating in the decision-making process along with other members of the committees.

Middle-Level Managers and Strategic Management

Middle level managers include immediate subordinates to the heads of various functional managers like production manager, marketing manager, finance manager and human resource manager. These managers mostly are executives and therefore, they mostly participate actively in implementation of functional strategies. However, they help the functional heads in formulating functional strategies like production strategy and marketing strategy. They collect the data and information, scan the relevant environment, identify the opportunities, develop the alternative strategies, perform SWOT analysis relating to functional strategies and participate in strategic decision-making process along with the functional head. These middle-level managers get the required on-the-job training to become functional strategists in the future. Thus, they perform the job of strategy implementation, learn the skill for the future strategist for the organisation and help the functional head in strategic management.

Lower-Level Executives and Strategic Management

Lower-level executives are the junior managers or managers at the bottom level of the managerial hierarchy. These managers normally take routine decisions which are just repetitive. As far as strategic decisions are concerned, lower-level executives mostly play the role of corporate planning staff. They collect data and information, classify them, tabulate them and present them to the middle-level executives. They also play their role in strategy implementation. They implement the orders of the middle-level executives and mostly perform the work at grass-root level to supervise the work performed by their subordinates. However, they can offer new ideas and suggestions to the top management regarding business opportunities. They also communicate the new concepts of strategic management to the middle-level management that they have learned in their business schools in the recent past.

Lower-level executives are the junior managers or managers at the bottom level of the managerial hierarchy.

This process allows the company to share the ideas of the young blood and the lower-level executives get the opportunity of learning practical issues of strategic management and equip themselves with talents necessary to formulate and implement strategies.

(C) STRATEGIC DECISION-MAKING

Introduction

Managers in the business world often fail to make a decision at the right time and allow the opportunities to be grabbed by the competitors and the problems remain or magnify and culminate into a crisis. Decisions should be taken at the right time and implemented after problems have been thoroughly analysed. Decision-making means to come to a conclusion and implement it. Decision-making is defined as "the selection based on some criteria of one behaviour alternative from two or more possible alternatives." The need for decision-making arises only when there are two or more alternative solutions for a problem.

Values and Alternatives: To select one solution from the available alternatives, each alternative should be evaluated in terms of probable outcomes in comparison with other alternative solutions. The comparison should be based on values in terms of financial, social, psychological, technological and political. These values are often conflicting with each other and make the decision-making process a critical one. Concentrating on the important facets of the problem will help in reducing the conflict. However, taking strategic decisions is much more complicated task.

Drivers of Success in Strategic Decision-Making

Sides and Associates has identified six drivers for success in strategic decision making. These six drivers as presented in Fig 2.2 are: strategic context, leadership, roles, process, tools and technology and management and controls. Strategic context deals with strategic priorities, consistent criteria, risk profile, stakeholders' priorities, and organiational goals.

The drivers of success in strategic decision-making are: strategic context, leadership, roles, process, tools and technology and management and controls. Strategic context deals with strategic priorities, consistent criteria, risk profile, stakeholders' priorities, and organiational goals.

Leadership includes senior executives' role in providing freedom to junior managers in decision making, input for decision-making and supplying adequate and right information at the right time. In addition, democratic and participative styles of leaders enhance decision-making culture in the company. Roles include collaborative, challenging and contributory roles of the individuals in committee and team/group decision-making. Process includes open versus closed communication as well as wider participation versus limited participation in decision-making. Strategy to be effective should be open communication and wider participation with the inbuilt devil advocacy in the process. Tools and technology includes cross-functional teams, quantitative techniques, modelling and institutional learning systems. Management and controls should include the measures that contribute to the enhancement of output as well as reducing the input requirement. These measures enhance the efficiency and profitability that contributes to the organisational goals.

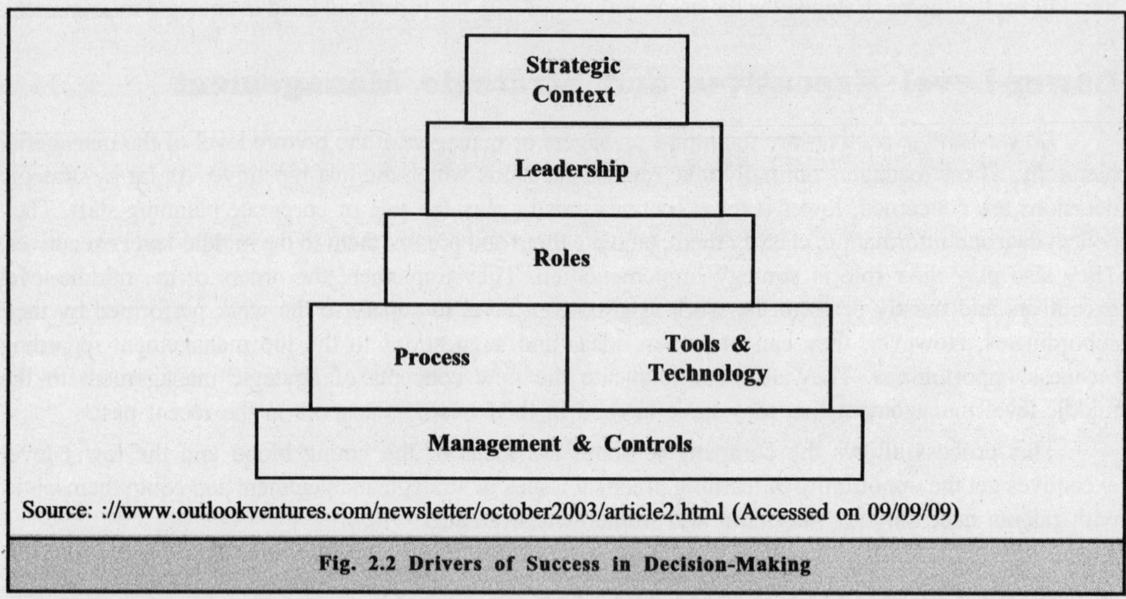

Source: ://www.outlookventures.com/newsletter/october2003/article2.html (Accessed on 09/09/09)

Fig. 2.2 Drivers of Success in Decision-Making

Types of Decision

Decisions are classified into routine and strategic or programmed and non-programmed decisions. Routine or programmed decisions are taken by an established or systematic procedure. The decision-maker, in general, knows the situation in routine or programmable decisions. Managerial decisions covered by policies, procedures and rules are taken by following established guidelines.

Strategic or non-programmed decisions have little or no precedent. They are relatively unstructured and generally require a more creative approach. The decision-maker must develop a procedure to be followed. Generally, it is difficult to make non-programmed decisions compared to programmed decisions.

Approaches to Strategic Decision-Making

Different theories have suggested different approaches of decision-making. These approaches are discussed hereunder:

(a) The Intuitive-Emotional Approach

Decision-maker under the intuitive-emotional approach takes decisions based on intuition which is characterised by the use of hunches, inner feelings or the 'gut-feeling' of the decision-maker.

Decision-maker takes decisions based on intuition which is characterised by the use of hunches, inner feelings or the 'gut-feeling' of the decision-maker. Decision-maker who makes decisions based on intuition, practices management exclusively as an art. This decision-maker prefers habit or experience, (see box 2.2) relative thinking, and instincts using the unconscious cognitive process. The decision-maker takes into account a number of alternatives into consideration, but simultaneously jumps one step in analysis and search for another and back again.

BOX 2.2 STRATEGIC DECISION-MAKING IN JAPANESE TRADING COMPANIES

The research task on strategic decisions-making in Japanese trading companies was conducted over a twelve-month period between 2000-2001, at five well-known Japanese kaisha headquartered in Tokyo. Results from the study indicate that the prominence of distinctive Japanese managerial practices such as nemawashi and settai in developing information sources. As well it was it was found that these practices strongly influence how information sources are accessed. Executive decision-makers from the Presidential level to Divisional Manager level who participated in this study were emphatic in the belief that strategic decision-making in most situations is reliant upon the network of information sources cultivated by dicision-makers as well as their skill in accessing the various sources and experiences.

http://jmo.e-contentmanagement.com/archives/vol/9/issue/1/article/403/strategic-decisionmaking-in-japanese-trading

(b) The Rational-Analytical Approach

In the rational-analytical approach, the decision-maker is intelligent and rational. The decision-maker makes the choice in full awareness of all available feasible alternatives to maximise advantages. The decision-maker considers all alternatives as well as consequences of all possible choices, orders these consequences in the light of a fixed scale of preferences, and chooses the alternative that procures the maximum gain.

In the rational-analytical approach, the decision-maker is intelligent and rational.

The rational approval to decision-making includes the following steps:

(i) Recognise the need for a decision;

(ii) Establish, rank and weight criteria;

(iii) Gather available information and data;

(iv) Identify possible alternatives;

(v) Evaluate each alternative with respect to all the criteria; and

(vi) Select the best alternative.

(c) A Satisfying Approach

There are limits to human rationality. Therefore, an individual must take decisions based on limited and incomplete knowledge. In view of this, the individual decision-maker cannot optimise but only satisfy.

Optimising means choosing the best possible alternative. Satisfy means choosing the first alternative that meets the decision-maker's minimum standard of satisfaction.

Satisfying approach to decision-making is presented in Figure 2.3. If the decision-maker is satisfied that an acceptable alternative has been found, it is selected otherwise, the decision-maker searches for an additional alternative.

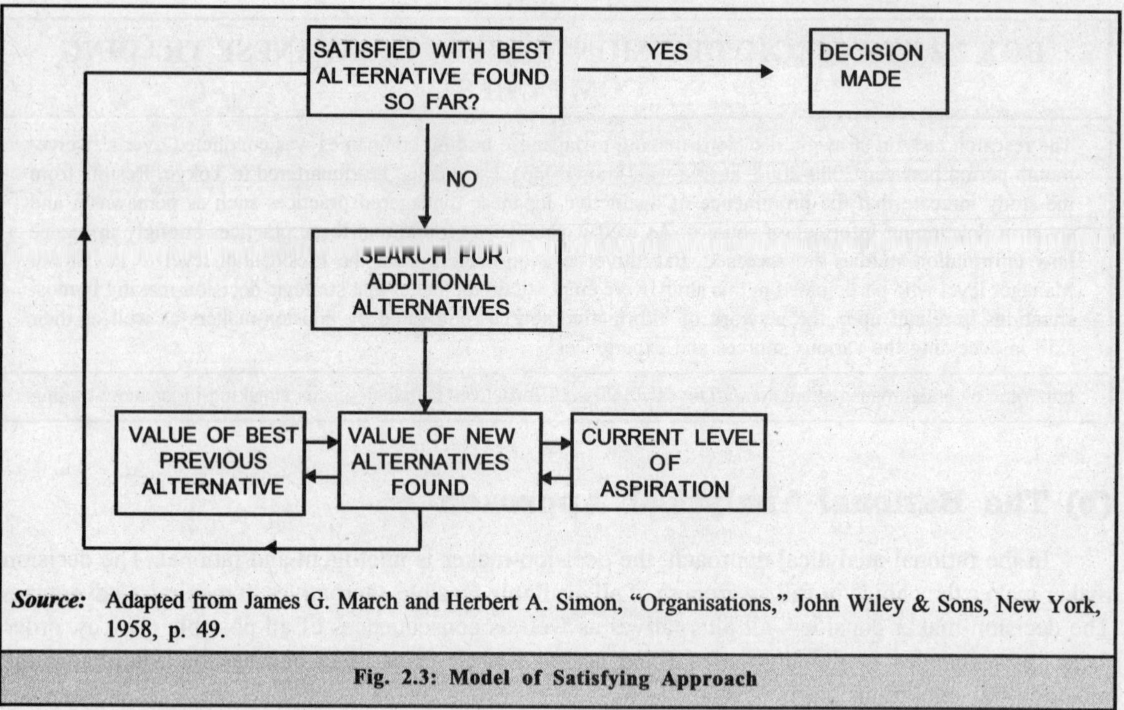

Source: Adapted from James G. March and Herbert A. Simon, "Organisations," John Wiley & Sons, New York, 1958, p. 49.

Fig. 2.3: Model of Satisfying Approach

BOX 2.3 STRATEGIC DECISION-MAKING TRAPS

"There are a series of traps that people fall into [in making decisions], that lead to incorrect judgements being reached, whatever the quality of the preceding analysis. The incidence of this is high. The cost, given that these are strategic decisions, is commensurately large..."Pragmatism leads to at least two biases that impact strategic decision-making. 1. Fact-based bias... we like to make decisions based on facts, [but]... To make strategic decisions, we need to be guided by a 'theory' that allows us to act before all the facts are in... a causal theory about the future - 'if we do this, then the following will happen' - lies at the heart of strategic decision-making. We cannot wait for all the facts. 2. 'Cut-through' bias... The second consequence of a pragmatic mindset is that it drives people to 'cut-through' and jump to a decision, by making a call. It is the other side of the fact-based bias. We wait for the facts, get impatient and cut-through... Unless it is done with great skill, it can lead to wrong decisions. "Following are the traps that people fall into. Trap one - over-simplification. Trap two - embedded assumptions... Many decisions are based on embedded assumptions that are not discussed, assumptions that often turn out to be wrong. Trap three - incomplete criteria... Many important decisions are made without an explicit, agreed set of criteria... Strategic decisions will have multiple options, to be tested against multiple criteria... Multiple weighings and multiple time periods. The human brain cannot reliably cope with such levels of complexity. In these circumstances, a formal, explicit process will yield a surer judgement... To avoid these traps, make the decision process visible. Work hard to consider the whole problem at the same time. This provides a great incentive to expedite the process. Identify important embedded assumptions. And spend real time talking through the decision criteria, weighings and scoring. This way, the decision process will do justice to the hard work done in fact gathering and analysis. Better decisions are the expected result."

http://bizzbangbuzz.blogspot.com/2008/02/strategic-decision-making-traps.html (Accessed on 09/09/09)

(d) Political-Behavioural Approach

Decision-Maker under political-behavioural approach considers all people and organisations in making decisions.

Normally, decisions made by organisations affect a variety of people and organisations. Hence, another view suggests that the corporations must consider all the people and organisations in making decisions. Corporations interact with a variety of stakeholders as the corporation and its stakeholders are mutually dependent on each other.

The employees exchange their human resources for fair salaries, benefits and harmonious industrial and human relations. Customers exchange their money for qualitative products and courteous services. Shareholders exchange their money for high rate of dividend and safety of their capital. Government provides security and protection and in turn expects payment of taxes regularly. Financial institutions exchange their finance for high rate of interest, security of principal amount and regular payment of interest. Suppliers of inputs expect fair terms of trade and continuous business. Competitors exchange information through chamber of commerce, trade and industry for mutual existence and development. The dealers expect continuous business. Thus, a stakeholder is an individual or organisation who can affect or is affected by the decision-making and achievement of organisational purpose and objective.

A Synthesis: The decision-maker being a human being possesses a rational and the emotional mind. Environment is a mixture of analysable and chaotic change and pressures. Therefore, decisions are made in a typically human way, using the rational, conscious analysis and intuitive, unconscious 'gut feeling' in light of political realities (see Box 2.4). Blending of these prescriptive and descriptive approaches helps to understand how decision-makers operate.

BOX 2.4 HOW COMPANIES MAKE GOOD DECISIONS: MCKINSEY GLOBAL SURVEY RESULTS

Do strong decision-making processes lead to good decisions? This McKinsey survey highlights several process steps that are strongly associated with good financial and operational outcomes. In the survey, we asked executives from around the world about a specific capital or human-resources decision their companies made in the course of normal business. We learned who was involved, what drove the decisions, how deep the analysis was, how unfettered the discussions, and how and where politics were involved. Respondents also described the financial and operational outcomes of the decisions. The results highlight the hard business benefits — such as increased profits and rapid implementation — of several decision-making disciplines. These disciplines include ensuring that people with the right skills and experience are included in decision-making, making decisions based on transparent criteria and a robust fact base, and ensuring that the person who will be responsible for implementing a decision is involved in making that decision. Finally, although corporate politics sometimes seems to undermine strong decision-making, some types of consensus-building and alliances apparently can help create good outcomes.

http://www.mckinseyquarterly.com/Strategy/Strategic_Thinking
How_companies_make_good_decisions_McKinsey_Global_Survey_Results_2282

Process of Strategic Decision-Making

Though, we have studied different approaches to strategic decision-making, the research suggests that the process of decision-making which actually takes place in organisations and give rise to strategic decisions possess the following five steps in the process: (Fig. 2.4) They are:

The steps in the process of strategic decision-making are: problem-awareness, problem diagnosis, development of alternative solutions, selection of the best solution and implementation of the best solution.

(i) Problem Awareness;

(ii) Problem Diagnosis;

(iii) The Development of alternative Solutions;

(iv) The Selection of a Solution; and

(v) Implementation of the Solution.

(i) Problem Awareness

Mostly individual employees identify the problems in various areas. Individuals when they get a 'gut feeling' that something is wrong, identify the problem. The awareness of a strategic problem mostly occurs to employees at grass-root level like sales people, machine operators, finance assistants, human resource assistants, etc. This awareness is likely to develop through a period of 'incubations' in which managers sense various stimuli that confirm and define a developing picture of a problem. Norburn and Grinyer call this stimuli as 'signals' or 'ear twitchers' and are of three types.

(a) Internal performance measurements like level of turnover or profit performance.

(b) Customer reaction particularly to the quality and price of the products and/or services.

(c) Changes in the environment, particularly in terms of competitive action, technological change and economic conditions.

These three factors together provide a picture of the deviation of an organisation's circumstances from the planned or expected one. This can be the deviation from a normal trading pattern.

The accumulation of stimuli will clearly indicate the existence of the problem in the organisation. This 'triggering point,' will soon be highlighted by the formal information system in the form of decline in sales, profit, and increase in the rejection level in the production department.

Successful business performance depends upon the ability of management in sensing its environment. Therefore, managers should respond when the problem is identified by the individual employees at the bottom level.

(ii) Problem Diagnosis

After the individual employees are aware of the problem and it is passed onto the managers, managers will gather the information and define the problem.

Information, may be gathered in the following ways:

(i) Information may be explored to determine the facts of the problem in detail. Such information may be gathered on a verbal and informal basis.

(ii) Rationalise the information and stimuli relevant to the problem so as to clarify the situation.

(iii) Act diplomatically to establish peer groups or political support for individual views of the problem.

Try to define the problem through debates and discussions and also get organisational view or consensus on the problem to be solved. The problem, then may take a clear shape by interweaving managerial experience of the executives and political process in the organisations. Some executives, may not accept to proceed ahead or define the problem and ask for additional information or the triggering of a different problem owing to different managerial experience and different views in right of social and political process. In such a situation, the process reverts back to the stage of triggering.

(iii) The Development of Solutions

After the problem is diagnosed clearly, the tendency of managers is that of searching for ready-made solutions. They do this process: *(i)* through memory search in which the managers seek for known, existing or attempted solutions, or *(ii)* passive search which entails waiting for possible solutions to be offered. If the managers fail in these two searches, they search for their own past experiences and other managers. If they fail to find a solution even through this method, they attempt to designing solutions.

They start designing or developing solutions through a vague idea, gradually improve it, refine it by recycling it through selection routes back into problem identification or through further searches. This process of developing solutions takes place through discussions, data analysis, debates, consultations and brain storming sessions and by sharing management wisdom and experience. Data warehouses provide required data and information for the development of solutions (see Box 2.5). This can take place both in the form of structured and unstructured team works. The solutions once developed are to be refined until they are developed to the stage of perfection within the available human and other resources of the organisation.

(iv) The Selection of a Solution

After the alternative solutions are developed, the solutions have to be formally evaluated based on their inherent strengths and weaknesses and also based on the environmental threats and opportunities for implementation. These solutions are to be ranked on the basis of their weights in terms of strengths and opportunities after eliminating the non-viable solutions in view of their weaknesses and environmental threats for implementation.

After the formal evaluation and ranking is completed, the managers tend to re-evaluate the solutions based on the managerial judgement followed by political bargaining as the formal evaluation is not the predominant criterion for assessing the feasibility in practice. Therefore the techniques for evaluation of solutions also include social and political process. Quinn suggests that successful managers actively adopt consultation/bargaining process in order to challenge prevailing strategic inclinations and generate information from other parts of the organisation. The solutions may also be referred to the senior level to seek authorisation.

David Hickson and his colleagues in their study identified three broad types of decision-making processes. They are:

(i) Sporadic processes characterised by many delays and impediments, many sources of influence and information on decision, and therefore, protracted personal interactions and informal negotiation. This type of process exists mostly in public sector organisations.

(ii) Fluid processes in which there are fewer delays and sources of influence, and more formal channels of communication which takes rather less time.

(iii) Constricted processes in which information sources are more readily available and decisions can be taken within groups or by individuals without extensive reference to others in the organisation. This might be the case in a business with a dominant chief executive or where there is an issue which relates primarily to one part of an organisation.

The managers should keep in mind the various processes discussed above while selecting the solution for implementation. If the managers fail to arrive at a consensus, the process may be recycled to search for new design.

BOX 2.5 DATA WAREHOUSES: IMPROVE STRATEGIC DECISION-MAKING WITH COHERENT VIEWS OF DATA

The ability to make quick, well-informed decisions is critical to competitiveness and growth for most companies. Read the white paper to see how data warehouse solutions can deliver business insight across virtually any business process or function. You will also learn how they're particularly valuable for understanding sales, profiling customers, and analyzing business costs. The ability to make quick, well-informed decisions is critical to competitiveness and growth for small and large companies alike. In recent years, most companies have seen the amount of customer and company data in legacy systems, desktops, servers and intranets increase dramatically. Yet a lack of integration between systems makes it nearly impossible for companies to use the valuable data within disparate systems to their advantage. In many cases, instead of relying on hard data based on historical trends to drive strategic direction, decision makers rely heavily on experience, limited — sometimes outdated — information and intuition. Siloed data also makes it more challenging to comply with changing regulations.Data warehouses — which can provide a manageable, cost-effective central repository of company-wide data — can help you take control of growing data volumes. And with the help of online analytical processing (OLAP) and data mining tools, data warehouses can help you drive a business strategy based on documented trends rather than best guesses.

http://www.webbuyersguide.com/resource/white-paper/14702/Data-Warehouses-Improve-Strategic-Decision-Making-with-Coherent-Views-of-Data (Accessed on 09.09.09)

(v) Implementation of the Decision

Implementation of the selected solution is a part of the decision-making process as the process may be required to be recycled due to impediments in the process of implementation. The managers should secure the support of the top management for allocation of resources, time, etc., regarding the implementation of the decision. A detailed programme of action specifying the minute details of action, people who will execute it, when it will be implemented, who will provide all necessary resources, how it will be implemented and who will co-ordinate the work, is needed. Employees concerned will be entrusted with the work and relevant information should be fed to them before hand. The managers should also ensure for getting feedback about the progress of implementation. If the decision cannot be implemented due to major hurdles in the implementation process, the process may be recycled for the possible modification.

Conclusion

Strategists have to take care as decision-making process some times involves irriational thinking of some managers.

Strategic decision-making, though plays a vital role in strategy crafting, there is every chance for the failure of strategic decision-making due to various reasons including the irrational thinking of the managers, unreliability of data and information, failure of the managers in evaluating the environment, lack of experience on the part of junior managers in decision evaluation and the political behaviour of the employees (see Box 2.6). Hence, management has to take all possible care in evaluating the situations as objectively and accurately as possible against the environment and organisational mission and goals.

BOX 2.6 FLAWS IN STRATEGIC DECISION-MAKING: MCKINSEY GLOBAL SURVEY RESULTS

Irrational thinking does not just affect individual economic decisions; it affects corporate strategic planning as well. These results highlight the practices of companies that have made successful strategic decisions — and also reveal what the same companies have gotten wrong. Since its inception nearly three decades ago, behavioral economics has upset the pristine premise of classical economic theory — the view that individuals will always behave rationally to achieve the best possible outcome. Today it's clear that the vagaries of individual and group psychology can cause irrational decision-making by both individuals and organizations, resulting in less than ideal outcomes. Even the best-designed strategic-planning processes do not always lead to optimal decisions. A recent survey by McKinsey attempts to assess the frequency and intensity of the most common managerial biases in companies. Specifically, we asked executives about a single recent strategic decision at their companies that had a clearly satisfactory or unsatisfactory outcome, focusing on the role that various biases may have played. It is evident from the results that satisfactory outcomes are associated with less bias, thanks to robust debate, an objective assessment of facts, and a realistic assessment of corporate capabilities. A few clear paths to making successful decisions also are apparent. But even when a decision had a satisfactory outcome, executives note several areas where their companies are not all that effective, such as aligning incentives with strategic objectives and forecasting competitors' reactions. Also notable is that companies that typically...

http://www.mckinseyquarterly.com/Strategy/Strategic_Thinking
Flaws_in_strategic_decision_making_McKinsey_Global_Survey_Results_2284?gp=1 (09/09/09)

POINTS TO BE REMEMBERED

- Managers work at an unrelenting pace and their activities are characterised by brevity, variety and discontinuity.
- Managers perform different roles, *viz.*, interpersonal, informational and decisional.
- Shareholders are the owners of the company and they participate in mission formulation and strategy formulation and revision.

- Board of directors represent shareholders and take significant part in strategic management.
- Various managers like senior managers, middle level, strategic business unit level managers take part in strategy formulation
- Strategic decision is developing and selecting the best among alternatives.

KEY WORDS

- Strategist
- Tasks
- Roles
- Shareholders
- Board of Directors
- Chief Executive Officer
- Entrepreneur
- SBU Level Strategist
- Senior Managers
- Strategic Decision-Making
- Intuitive-Emotional
- Rational-Analytical

QUESTIONS FOR DISCUSSION

(1) What are the tasks and roles of a strategist?

(2) Discuss how the shareholders and board of directors become strategists.

(3) Who are the middle level and senior level strategists?

(4) What is strategic decision-making ?

(5) What are the different approaches to strategic decision-making?

(6) Discuss the process of strategic decision-making.

REFERENCES

1. Henry Mintzberg, "The Manager's Job", in James Brain Quinn, Henry Mintzberg and Robert M. James (Eds), *op. cit.*, p. 23.
2. *Ibid.*, pp. 25-26.
3. *Ibid.*, pp. 27-29.
4. Peter F. Drucker, "*The Practice of Management*," 1954, pp. 341-342.
5. Henry Mintzberg, *op. cit.*, pp. 30-31.
6. Melvin J. Stanford, *op. cit.*, p. 27.
7. *Ibid.*
8. Gerard R. Roche, "Much Ado About Mentors", *Harvard Business Review*, January-February, 1979, pp.14-28.
9. Peter F. Drucker, "How the Effective Manager Does It", *Fortune*, February, 1967.
10. Bill Sloan, "Life at the Top", *Dallas*, September, 1979, pp. 15-19.
11. Harry Levinson, "Criteria for Choosing Chief Executives", *Harvard Business Review*, July-August 1980, pp. 114-118.
12. Lawrence R. Jauch and William F. Glueck, *op. cit.*, p. 52.

13. Peter F. Drucker, "*Innovation and Entrepreneurship*", William Heinemann, London, 1985, p.25.
14. Lawrence R. Jauch and William F. Glueck, *op. cit.*, p. 54.
15. Charles H. Kepner and Benjamin B. Tregoe, "*The Rational Manager*", McGraw-Hill, New York, 1965, p. 40.
16. George Prince, "*Putting the Other Half of the Brain to Work*", Training, November 1978, pp. 58-59.
17. Lawrence R. Jauch and William F. Glueck, *op.cit.*, p. 21.
18. Lawrence R. Jauch and William F. Glueck, *op.cit.*, p. 20.
19. Lawrence R. Jauch and William F. Glueck, *op.cit.*, pp. 22-23.
20. Gerry Johnson, "*Strategic Change and the Management Process*", Basil Blackwell, 1987.
21. M.A. Lyles, "*Formulation Strategic Problems: Empirical Analysis and Model Development*", Strategic Management Journal, Vol.2, 1981, pp. 61-75.
22. D. Norburn and P. Grinyer, "*Directors Without Direction*," General Management, Vol.1, No. 2, 1973-4.
23. J.B. Quinn, "Strategy for Change," Irwin, 1980 and D. Miller and P. Friesen, "*Archetypes of Strategy Formulation*", Management Science, Vol. 24, No. 9, 1978.
24. Gerry Johnson and Keven Scholes, *op.cit.*, pp. 31-37.
25. David Hickson *et.al.*, "*Top Decisions: Strategic Decision-Making in Organisation*", Basil Blackwell, 1986.
26. Frederick C. Miner, Jr., "*Group versus Individual Decision-Making: An Investigation of Performance Measures, Decision Strategies and Process Losses/Gains*", Organisational Behaviour and Human Performance, 33, February 1984, pp. 112-124.

✦ ✦ ✦

3

CHAPTER

ESTABLISHING CORPORATE DIRECTION

Chapter Outline

(A) Introduction

(B) Vision

(C) Mission

(D) Business Definition

(E) Objectives

Learning Objectives

After studying this chapter, you should be able to:

- Know the meaning and characteristics of vision;
- Discuss the meaning and key elements of a mission;
- Formulate a vision and mission for an organisation;
- Discuss the content of a mission statement;
- Know the meaning of business definition;
- Develop a skill of formulating objectives based on objectives;
- Understand the reasons for changing a mission and objectives;
- Process the formulation of objectives.

(A) INTRODUCTION

We have discussed in Chapter-1 that corporate direction involves 6 tasks, *viz.*,

- Vision
- Mission
- Business Definition
- Objectives
- Goals
- Strategy and Tactics

We discuss the terms briefly before we analyse them in detail.

Vision

Vision statement indicates what the company wants to create in the future. A clear vision is essential to develop an appropriate mission statement.

Mission

Corporate direction is determined by vision, mission, business definition, objectives, goals, strategies, and tactics.

Organisations normally perform some function which is valued by the society as they are part and parcel of the society. Some functions are valued more highly than others depending upon the requirements of the society. Of course, these priorities change over time. Thus, organisations perform various functions to meet the societal requirements for their long run survival and legitimate existence. Organisations are likely to be allowed to survive over the long term. (See Fig 3.1).

Organisations define the basic reason for their existence in terms of a mission statement,— its purpose, image and character. Thus, mission statement provides a link between the societal requirements and organisational business.

Business Definition

Part of the mission statement is the definition of the business. A good business definition will include a statement of products, markets and functions. It should meet a certain criteria: it should be as precise as possible and indicate major components of strategy (products, markets, human resources and finance). It should also indicate how the mission is to be accomplished.

Objectives

Objectives are the ends towards which activity is aimed. They also represent end towards which organising, staffing, leading and controlling are aimed. The strategic business units also formulate objectives and they are related to the objectives of the firm and contribute to the firm's objectives. The strategic managers should be aware of the objectives of the firm, strategic business units and departments while formulating the strategies.

Goals

Goal is precise and is expressed in clear and specific terms. The goal for the objective of increase in the rate of profitability may be stated as increase in the percentage of net profit of the company to the equity capital employed from 15% in 2009 to 18% in 2011.

Strategy

A strategy is a unified, comprehensive and integrated plan/action that relates to the strategic advantages of the firm to the challenges of the environment. It is designed to ensure that the basic objectives of the enterprise are achieved through proper execution by the organisation.

Strategy is discussed in detail in Chapter 1.

Tactics

To be effective, strategies must be put into practice. Detailed programmes on the basis of strategies are to be formulated to put the strategies into practice. These detailed programmes are known as tactics. Tactics are the action programmes through which strategies are executed. Strategies must be supported by effective tactics.

Organisational decision varies from a broad master strategy at one end and minute tactics at the other. The strategists should have a clear understanding about the differences between strategy and tactics. Exhibit 3.1 presents strategy versus tactics.

Exhibit 3.1: Strategy Vs Tactics

	Strategy	*Tactics*
1.	Level of Conduct: Strategy is developed at the top level of the management and relates exclusively to decisions in the province of these levels.	Tactics are employed at and relate to lower levels of management.
2.	Regularity: The formulation of strategy is both continuous and irregular. The process is continuous, but the timing of decision is irregular for it depends upon and is triggered by the appearance of opportunities, new ideas, management initiative, crises and other non-routine stimuli.	Tactics are determined, for many companies, on a periodic cycle with a fixed time schedule, such as the annual budget process.
3.	Subjective Value: Strategic decision-making is more heavily weighted with subjective values.	Tactical decision-making is less weighted with subjective values.
4.	Range of Alternatives: The total possible range of alternatives from which a management must choose is far greater in strategy.	The total possible range of alternatives from which a management must choose is less in tactics.
5.	Uncertainty: Uncertainty is usually much greater in both formulation and implementation of strategy. It is difficult to assess the risks in strategy.	It is usually less in tactics. Risks are more easily assessed in tactics.
6.	Nature of problems: Strategic problems are generally unstructured and tend to be one of a kind.	Tactical problems are more structural and often repetitive in nature.
7.	Information Needs: Strategy formulation requires large amounts of information desired from and relating to areas of knowledge outside the corporation. Most of the relevant data needed relate to the future are difficult to get with accuracy and are tailored to each problem.	Tactical informational needs rely more heavily on internally generated data. Particularly from accounting system, and involve a higher proportionate use of historical information.
8.	Time horizons: Strategies, especially when successful, are intended to, and last for long periods of time. However, sometimes, the time dimension is very short.	Tactics cover a shorter duration and are more uniform for all parts of an operating programme.
9.	Reference: Strategy is original in the sense that it is the source or origin for the development of tactics.	Tactics are formulated within and in pursuit of strategies.
10.	Detail: Strategies are usually broad and with few details.	Tactics have many details.
11.	Type of personnel involved in strategy formulation: The strategies are formed at the highest level.	Tactics are formulated by lower-level executives. It is easy to evaluate tactics. Tactical results are quickly evident and much more easily identified with specific actions.

12.	Ease of Evaluation: It is difficult to evaluate strategies. It takes a number of years to evaluate strategy.	Tactics are developed principally from functional point of view.
13.	Point of View: Strategies are formulated from a corporate point of view.	Tactics have very near term focus.
14.	Importance: Strategies are of highest importance to an organisation.	Tactics are relatively less important as a whole

Vision statements of various companies include:

Source: Modified version from: George A. Steiner, John B. Niner and Edmund R.C. "Management Policy and Strategy," Macmillan Publishing Company, New York, pp. 13-14.

(B) VISION

Vision: What do we want to create? Where we want to go?

Vision and mission statements are powerful shapers of effective corporate cultures, for many organisations. These statements present the values, philosophies and aspirations, that guide organisational action. In fact, they motivate and inspire the current and future employees of the organisation.

What is Organisational Vision?

An organisational vision is the answer to the question: 'What do we want to create?" Shared visions in organisations, "create a sense of commonality that permeates the organisation and gives coherence to diverse activities." The corporate vision has the potential power to focus the collective energy of insiders and to give outsiders a better idea of what an organisation really is. In fact vision is the first step of strategic management process in an organization (see Fig 3.1).

Characteristics of Vision

(i) **Vision is developed through sharing across an organisation:** Famous stories of successful visions involve visions that have been widely shared across entire organisations. Of course, an individual leader, often a founder has a powerful impact on the others.

Vision and mission statements are supposed to encompass the ethical, financial and operational guiding lights of the company. Vision is referred to as "sky books for the soul." The focus of vision is to reach out hungrily for the future and drag it into present. Vision is the soul searching activity, where the companies intend to answer the question like 'why are we here, where are we and where would we like to proceed in the future.

Reason for Being: The vision is compelling but not controlling force that protracts the future. To quote Kwan Jzu (3rd century BC): "when planning for a year, sow corn, when planning for a decade, plant trees, when planning for a life, train and educate people."

Companies work for mission after the vision statement is conceptualised and direction of the company is determined.

Picture of Preferred Future

Most of the major achievements of a number of companies are attributable with powerful dreams about the future, organisational values determine organisational culture. Johnson and Johnson Credo puts it as, "We believe our primary responsibility is to the doctors, nurse and patients, mothers and all others who use our products and services." The values of British Airways is putting people first," of Jet Airways is "the joy of flying," and the BPL is "believe in the best." Exhibit 3.2 presents vision statements of certain selected companies.

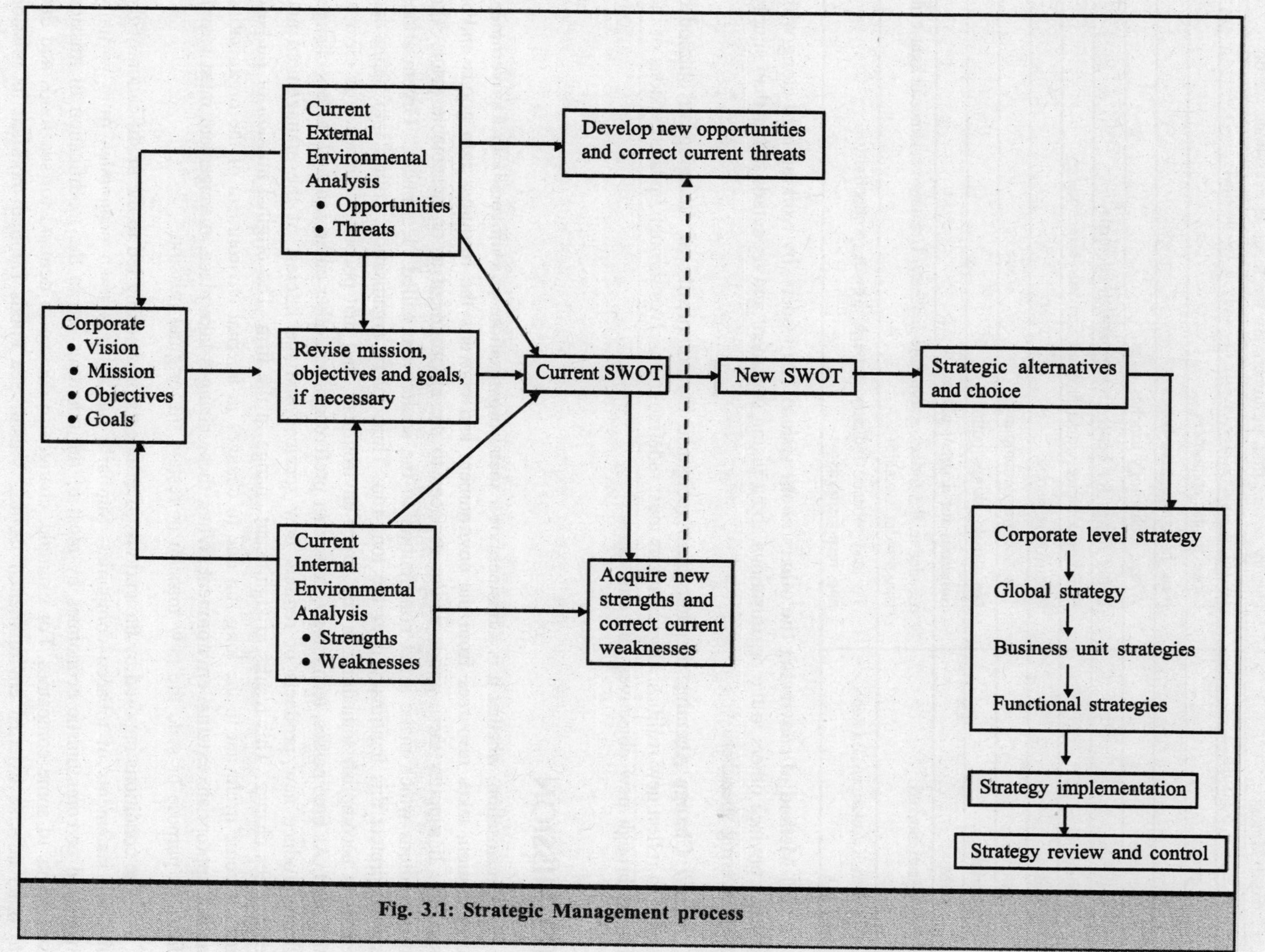

Fig. 3.1: Strategic Management process

Exhibit 3.2 Vision Statements of certain Selected Companies

Name of the Company	Vision Statement
Ford Motors	Quality covers first, customers are the focus of everything we do
Konsuke Matsoshita	To serve society and profits are only a by product
Wipro	Close to the customer
ITC	New horizons, new hopes
Siemens	Where technology touches lives
Du Pont	Better things for better living through chemistry
Hyundai	Building a better world through innovative technology
Nokia	Connecting people
Xerox	The document company
Philips	Let's make things better
IBM	Solutions for a small planet
Maruti Suzuki	Leader in the Indian automobile industry. Creating customer delight and shareholder's wealth
British American Tobacco	To lead tobacco industry through growth, productivity and responsibility

***(ii)* Method of convincing the others about vision:** The leaders, by working hard along with others, convince others in the organisations about vision statement and its details rather than simply by delivering speeches.

***(iii)* Change Agendas:** Leaders must recognise the complexity of changing an outmoded vision to reflect new realities. Organisations must redefine themselves through updated visions of the future through new objectives and strategies.

(C) MISSION

Organisation, whether it is a business or a social organisation, or a university or a government organisation, takes resources from the environment and converts the resources into goods and/or services. It supplies these goods and/or services to the environment at an acceptable price. The organisations which make a net contribution to the society are called "legitimate." Organisations should protect this legitimacy over the long-run. Thus, every organisation, comes into being and exists to accomplish something in the larger environment, and that purpose or mission is clear at that start. As time passes, technology, consumer preferences and other environmental factors change, firms produce new products or renders new services and the interest of the management and employees change. This results in significant change in the firm. The original mission or purpose may become irrelevant in the long run due to changes in internal environment of the organisation and/or appropriate external environment. When these changes take place, management must search for new purpose or state the new mission or restate the original mission.

Mission: Organisation, comes into being andexists to accomplish something in the larger environment.

The conditions imposed by the various governments on smoking led to the modification of the mission statements of tobacco companies. Similarly the shift to open economies from partially regulated or communistic economies by most of the countries led to the modification of mission statements of some companies. For example, changes in decline in demand for sea foods and due to other adverse external environmental factors, Vaisali Sea Foods Limited modified its mission statement from 'leader in the sea food industry' to 'serve the customer the best'. The company shifted its business emphasis to software industry by changing its mission statement.

What is Mission?

Mission is defined as, "an enduring statement of purpose that distinguishes one organisation from other similar organisations."

Mission: An enduring statement of purpose that distinguishes one organisation from other similar organizations.

Most of the organisations define the fundamental reason for their existence in terms of mission statement. Organisations do exist to satisfy a particular need of the society or to fulfill a particular deficiency in the society. Organisation, thus, finds a particular role for itself, to play in the society. By playing that particular role, the organisation meets the requirements of the society. The role that the organisation plays involves producing products and/or rendering services. For example, the society may have the need for having quick, reliable and cheap communication. Providing quick information would be the mission of that organisation. BSNL came into being to provide the facilities for providing fast, reliable and cheap mobile communication facilities. Thus, the mission of BSNL is to provide fast, cheap and reliable mobile communication facilities.

Similarly society has many needs like, cheap and fuel economy cars, acquiring knowledge, quick food, fast and comfortable travel, health care, entertainment, child care, and the like. Organisations do exist to produce the products and/or render services to satisfy these needs of the society. That particular role of the firm would be its mission.

Mission Statement: A mission statement is a declaration of an organisation's reason for being. When the mission of an organisation is carefully defined, it provides a statement to insiders and outsiders of what the corporation stands for — its purposes, image and character. The mission statement should be a long-term purpose of what the organisation is trying to become — the unique aim that differentiates it from similar organisations. The basic questions that must be answered are: What is our business? And what should it be? Mission statement provides direction and significance to all members of the organisation, regardless of their level.

The mission statement is where a company starts to show how this dream is going to become a reality. Companies identify major goals that must be accomplished. They indicate how they are going to operate to achieve the major goals. Mission statement is based on the organizational activities and background. Exhibit 3.3 presents mission description of activities, motto/slogan and mission statements of some selected companies.

Exhibit 3.3 Slogan/Motto, Activities and Mission Statements of Some Selected Companies

Name of the Company	Slogan/Motto	Description of Activities	Mission Statement
Ford Motor Company	Built for the road ahead	The instigator of the manufacturing revolution of mass production assembly lines, the Ford Motor Company is one of the largest manufacturers of transportation vehicles, particularly cars and trucks. The cars they manufactured include Ford, Lincoln, Mercury, Mazda, Volvo, Jaguar, Land Rover, and Aston Martin.	We are a global family with a proud heritage passionately committed to providing personal mobility for people around the world
American Standard Company	Raising the standard	The American Standard Company is into supplying air-conditioning systems, plumbing products, and automotive braking systems. Their products are well-known under the brands Trane(r) and American Standard(r) for their air conditioning systems, American Standard(r) and Ideal Standard(r) for their plumbing fixtures, and WABCO(r) for their electronic braking, stability, suspension and transmission control systems.	Be the best in the eyes of our customers, employees and shareholders.
The Walt Disney Company	"Global Entertainment Provider"	The Walt Disney Company operates a global entertainment portfolio of Media Networks, Parks and Resorts, Studio Entertainment, and Consumer Products. This wide array reaches out to the world through its television broadcasts, Internet businesses, theme parks, and the many ventures of The Walt Disney Company's subsidiaries.	The mission of The Walt Disney Company is to be one of the world's leading producers and providers of entertainment and information. Using our portfolio of brands to differentiate our content, services and consumer products, we seek to develop the most creative, innovative and profitable entertainment experiences and related products in the world.
NIKE Inc	Inspiration and innovation to every athlete"	Serving the sports and athletic industry, NIKE Inc. is known for manufacturing shoes, gear and apparel, particularly for athletes in a whole range of sports such as baseball, golf, tennis, football, etc. Its subsidiaries include Cole Haan, Bauer Nike Hockey, Hurley International, and Converse, with its brands being Air Jordan, Nike Golf, and Team Starter.	To bring inspiration and innovation to every athlete in the world.
Auto Owners Insurance	The "No Problem" People	Auto-Owners Insurance is one of the biggest insurance companies in the US that aspires to give only the best quality service. In addition to vehicle insurance, Auto-Owners also offers other products such as universal and whole life, homeowners, and long-term care insurance through its two subsidiaries, Home-Owners Insurance Company and Property-Owners Insurance Company.	Our goal is to provide the best claim service in the industry

Chevron	Human energy	Chevron is a global energy and oil company whose headquarters are in San Ramon, California. Aside from offering oil and natural gas, Chevron also develops hydrogen infrastructure, advanced battery systems, nano-materials and renewable energy applications.	At the heart of The Chevron Way is our Vision to be the global energy company most admired for its people, partnership and performance
Citigroup	Knowledge is your greatest asset	Citigroup is a financial institution divided into these major segments: Global Consumer, Corporate and Investment Banking, and Global Wealth Management. Citigroup Global Consumer business offers banking services such as bank accounts, deposits, loans, portfolio and investment management, insurance, etc. The Corporate and Investment Banking business involves banking transactions on an international level. Global Wealth Management involves having portfolio management and investment advisory services.	Our goal for Citigroup is to be the most respected global financial services company. Like any other public company, we're obligated to deliver profits and growth to our shareholders. Of equal importance is to deliver those profits and generate growth responsibly.
The Dow Chemical Company	Living, Improved Daily	The Dow Chemical Company is a chemical company whose specialty is into performance plastics, such as engineering plastics, polyurethanes, etc. Aside from this, Dow is also into performance chemicals, agricultural sciences, hydrocarbons and energy, etc.	To constantly improve what is essential to human progress by mastering science and technology
Graybar Electric Company	Works to your advantage	Graybar Electric Company is a company that acquires, stores, and distributes electrical, data, and communication components, such as wire, cable, and lighting products.	Graybar is the vital link in the supply chain, adding value with efficient and cost-effective service and solutions for our customers and our suppliers.
Harley-Davidson Inc.	Define your world in a whole new way.	Harley-Davidson, Inc., is the manufacturer of a line of motorcycles, with over 32 models of touring and custom Harleys. Aside from their line of motorcycles, Harley-Davidson also offers motorcycle accessories, motorcycle clothing apparel, and engines.	We fulfill dreams through the experience of motorcycling, by providing to motorcyclists and to the general public an expanding line of motorcycles and branded products and services in selected market segments
JPMorgan Chase	Strengthening communities	Operating in more than 50 countries all across the globe, JPMorgan Chase is a financial services institution whose expertise is in investment banking, financial transaction processing, asset and wealth management, and private equity.	The Corporate Governance & Nominating Committee exercises general oversight with respect to the governance of the Board of Directors.

Source: http://www.missionstatements.com/fortune_500_mission_statements.html (Accessed on 10/09/09)

Key Elements in Developing a Mission Statement

Mission statement is based on: *(i)* history of the organisation, *(ii)* organisation's distinctive competencies, and *(iii)* the organisation's environment.

Management must take into account three key elements in developing mission statements, *viz.*, *(i)* history of the organisation, *(ii)* organisation's distinctive competencies, and *(iii)* the organisation's environment.

***(i)* History of the Organisation:** Every organisation-manufacturing or service-oriented, profit or non-profit, large or small has a history of objectives, policies, accomplishments and mistakes. The critical characteristics and events of the past must be considered in formulating and developing a mission statement.

***(ii)* Distinctive Competencies of the Organisation:** Though an organisation can do many things, it should seek to do what it can do best. Distinctive competencies are the activities that an organisation does efficiently — so efficiently in fact, that an organisation with distinctive competency offers an advantage over similar organisations. Maruti Udyog Limited probably could enter the fertilizer business, but such a decision certainly would not take advantage of its major distinctive competencies. The organisation must have the competencies to capitalise the opportunities offered by the markets. An opportunity without the competence to exploit it is not really an opportunity, and in fact is an illusion for that organisation.

***(iii)* Organisation's Environment:** The management should identify the opportunities provided and threats or challenges posed by the environment before formulating a mission statement. Increase in the demand for civil construction industry during 1990s and before 207 provided an opportunity for steel industry, cement industry and electrical industry. Growth in software industry and photocopying reduced the demand for traditional publishing industry. For example, fast technological advancements in communication industry reduced the need for frequent travel and thus, may negatively affect the transport industry and hotel industry. Therefore, transport industry should consider the technological developments in communication industry, in developing its mission statement. (See Exhibit 3.4).

Exhibit 3.4: Mission Statement and Guiding Principles of Starbucks

- Mission statements: To be the premier purveyor of the finest coffee in the world while maintaining our uncompromising principles while we grow.
- Guiding principles to measure the appropriateness of decision.
- Provide a great work environment and treat each other with respect and dignity.
- Embrace diversity as an essential component in the way we do business.
- Apply the highest standards of excellence to the purchasing, roasting and fresh delivery to customers all of the time.
- Contribute positively to our communities and our environment.
- Recognise that profitability is essential to our future success.

Source: www.starbucks.com/aboutus/csr.asp

Elements of a Mission Statement

As explained earlier, the mission of an organisation is its uniqueness of purpose that distinguishes the organisation from other organisations. The mission statement indicates the nature and scope of business operations in terms of products and/or services, markets, customers and technology. The elements of the mission statement are:

(i) The mission statement should specify the products to be produced and/or services to be rendered, markets and/or customer groups to be served and the type of technology; (See Fig. 3.2).

(ii) The primary concern for survival and development through profitability;

(iii) The organisational philosophy in terms of basic beliefs, values, attitudes and aspirations; and

(iv) Management style to be practised.

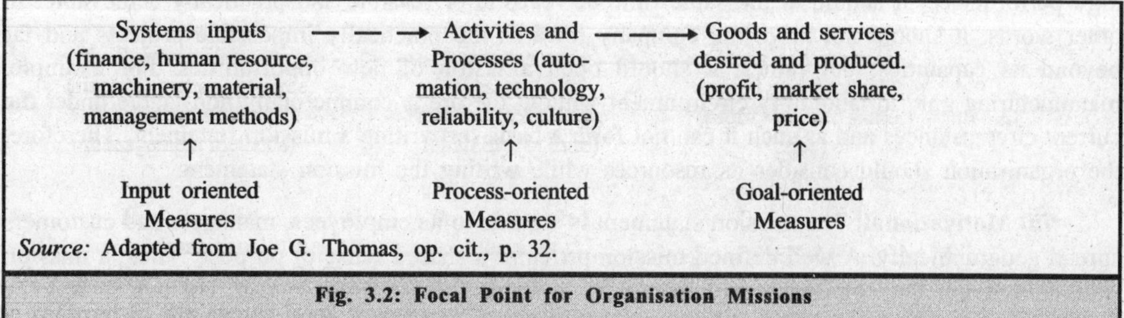

Source: Adapted from Joe G. Thomas, op. cit., p. 32.

Fig. 3.2: Focal Point for Organisation Missions

Characteristics of a Mission Statement

Developing an effective and useful mission statement is extremely difficult. Organisations spend a year or two in developing an effective and useful mission. When completed, it specifies the basic reason for the organisational existence, philosophy, identity, character and the image. It focuses on markets rather than products, it is also achievable, motivating and specific. It should also be clear, distinctive, indicate major components of strategy and how the policies are achieved. (See Exhibit 3.5).

***(i)* Market Rather Than Product Focus:** The customers are the key factors in determining an organisation's mission. Traditionally, many organisations defined their business by what they produced and in many cases named the organisation after their products (For example Andhra Pradesh Paper Mills Limited). Such organisations found that its mission is no longer relevant and its name may no longer describe what it does when their products and/or technologies become obsolete. Therefore, a more enduring way of defining the mission has become necessary. A key feature of mission statements has been an external rather than internal focus in recent years. Hence, it is viewed that, the mission statement should focus on the broad class of needs that the organisation is intending to satisfy (external focus) not on the physical product or service that the organisation is serving at present (internal focus). According to Peter F. Drucker,

Exhibit 3.5: Criteria for Good Mission Statements

- Precisely stated outcomes, given in measurable terms and with a specified completion data.
- Consistency with the environment in which the firm is operating or expects to operate.
- A description of how organisational activities will lead to the desired outcomes.
- Congruence with policies, procedures and plans as they apply to the organisation or business unit.
- An integration of major components of the organisation (scope of operations, resource allocation, competitive advantages and disadvantages).
- Attainability (realistic but challenging with existing or attainable resources)

Source: Joe G. Thomas, *op. cit.*, p. 32.

"A business is not defined by the company's name, statutes or articles of incorporation. It is defined by the want of the customer to be satisfied when he buys a product or service. To satisfy the customer is the mission and purpose of every business. The question "What is our business?" can therefore, be answered only by looking at the business from the outside, from the point of view of customer and market."

The view of Drucker is also applicable to non-profit and government organisations. Therefore, the organisations have to state the mission in terms of meeting the requirements of a particular group of customers and/or meeting a particular class of need.

Mission statement: Market focus, achievable, motivational, specific, clear, and distinctive.

***(ii)* Achievable:** Though the mission statements indicate that the organisations should achieve high performance, it should at the same time be realistic or feasible and practically achievable. In other words, it should not drive the company towards the practically impossible projects and far beyond its capacities, but rather, it should open a vision of new opportunities. For example, manufacturing gold in laboratory environment without the ore is commercially non-viable under the current circumstances and as such it can not form a basis for writing a mission statement. Therefore, the organisation should consider its resources while writing the mission statement.

***(iii)* Motivational:** The mission statement is a guide to its employees, managers and customers spread geographically. A well defined mission provides a shared sense of purpose. Thus, a mission should motivate the employees and managers to work for the organisation, customers and the society. It should also motivate the customer to feel pride for associating himself with that organisation. (See Box 3.1).

BOX 3.1 MISSION, VISION AND VALUES OF THE COCA COLA COMPANY

The world is changing all around us. To continue to thrive as a business over the next ten years and beyond, we must look ahead, understand the trends and forces that will shape our business in the future and move swiftly to prepare for what is to come. We must get ready for tomorrow today. That's what our 2020 Vision is all about. It creates a long-term destination for our business and provides us with a "Roadmap" for winning together with our bottler partners.

Our Mission

Our Roadmap starts with our mission, which is enduring. It declares our purpose as a company and serves as the standard against which we weigh our actions and decisions.

To refresh the world...

To inspire moments of optimism and happiness...

To create value and make a difference.

Our Vision

Our vision serves as the framework for our Roadmap and guides every aspect of our business by describing what we need to accomplish in order to continue achieving sustainable, quality growth.

People: Be a great place to work where people are inspired to be the best they can be.

Portfolio: Bring to the world a portfolio of quality beverage brands that anticipate and satisfy people's desires and needs.

Partners: Nurture a winning network of customers and suppliers, together we create mutual, enduring value.

Planet: Be a responsible citizen that makes a difference by helping build and support sustainable communities.

Profit: Maximize long-term return to shareowners while being mindful of our overall responsibilities.

Productivity: Be a highly effective, lean and fast-moving organization.

Our Winning Culture

Our Winning Culture defines the attitudes and behaviors that will be required of us to make our 2020 Vision a reality.

Live Our Values

Our values serve as a compass for our actions and describe how we behave in the world.

Leadership: The courage to shape a better future

Collaboration: Leverage collective genius

Integrity: Be real

Accountability: If it is to be, it is up to me

Passion: Committed in heart and mind

Diversity: As inclusive as our brands

Quality: What we do, we do well

Focus on the Market

Focus on needs of our consumers, customers and franchise partners

Get out into the market and listen, observe and learn

Possess a world view

Focus on execution in the marketplace every day

Be insatiably curious

Work Smart

Act with urgency

Remain responsive to change

Have the courage to change course when needed

Remain constructively discontent

Work efficiently

Act Like Owners

Be accountable for our actions and inactions

Steward system assets and focus on building value

Reward our people for taking risks and finding better ways to solve problems

Learn from our outcomes — what worked and what did not

http://www.thecoca-colacompany.com/ourcompany/mission_vision_values.html (Accessed on 05/09/09)

***(iv)* Specific:** The mission statement should be precise and specific and provide direction and guidelines for management's choices between alternative courses of action. Therefore, the mission statement, at the same time, should not be too narrow as it restricts the management's activities. If the mission is 'transporting the tourists,' it would be too narrow and if it is 'tourist business,' it would be too broad.

***(v)* Clear:** The mission statement should provide direction and guidance to the management and employees. Therefore, it should be stated in clear terms. Otherwise, it will result in confusion to all concerned. The mission of Nike Inc., is clear as it states "to Bring Inspiration and Innovation to every athlete in the world."

***(vi)* Distinctive:** As stated earlier, the mission statement of one organisation should be different from those of the similar organisations. In fact, different organisations serve the different markets or different groups of customers and use different technologies and produce different qualities of products (See Box 3.2).

BOX 3.2 YAHOO UPGRADED ITS MISSION STATEMENT — COMPARISON WITH THAT OF GOOGLE FOR DISTINCTIVENESS

Yahoo's mission question it is not as memorable as 'Don't be evil,' but Yahoo's new mission statement shows it's ready to leverage its unique strengths, says Fortune's Adam Lashinsky. And yet, now and again it's worth listening, either when a company changes its mission statement, or, worse, when one of the pooh-bahs can't necessarily articulate what the mission is. Take the case of Yahoo (Charts), the Internet's most successful punching bag. The only way to think of Yahoo as less than one of the great media companies of our day is in relation to Google (Charts), which is truly one of the great media companies of our day. Yahoo's strategy, execution and stock price have been stuck for months, a victim of its poorly played competition with Google. Part of Yahoo's problem has been that for all its lucrative online advertising businesses, it botched search, the best online business of them all for several years running. In an interview last summer with Yahoo CEO Terry Semel, I cited to him his arch-foe's disarmingly simple motto, "Don't be evil," and asked what Yahoo's motto is. After an uncomfortably long pause, Semel replied: "I don't know that we have a motto. Well, the mission of the company is, Deliver great value to our consumers and, basically, value them." Wrong. As it happened, Yahoo did have a mission statement, even if Semel, chief executive for five years, did not know it: "Our mission is to be the most essential global Internet service for consumers and businesses." That was broad stuff, and not bad as far as mission statements go. That Google had become far more essential for one of the most common Internet services consumers and business people seek - search - sort of derailed Yahoo's mission. Clearly it needed a new one.

Investors groan as Google grows

Now Yahoo has one. The company invited journalists to its Sunnyvale headquarters Tuesday for a presentation by three executives from its Santa Monica, Calif.-based media group. That is the outfit formerly run by ex-television executive Lloyd Braun and now run by Jeff Weiner, who has expanded his responsibilities from being Yahoo's top search executive. At the beginning of his presentation, Scott Moore, Yahoo's head of news and information, flashed a slide of Yahoo's mission statement, which, it turns out, was quietly rolled out internally around the time the company restructured its management late last year. The new line is equally broad. But it might fit a bit better than the old one. "Yahoo's mission," it reads, "is to connect people to their passions, their communities, and the world's knowledge. To ensure this, Yahoo offers a broad and deep array of products and services to create unique and differentiated user experiences and consumer insights by leveraging connections, data, and user participation."As with seemingly everything else, Yahoo's mission statement will suffer in comparison to Google's, which is to "organize the world's information and make it universally accessible and useful." What is good about Yahoo's new message is that it clarifies the differences between Google and Yahoo. The geeks in Mountain View may be organizing the world's information. The cool kids in Sunnyvale are connecting people to their passions. In other words, they are in the entertainment business, a time-tested and durable way of making money. The "deep array" of gizmos means Yahoo still tries basically anything that works online - as increasingly does Google as well. The line about leveraging connections, data and user participation, however, truly says something about how Yahoo sees itself. Its e-mail program is still the most popular online, it is increasingly willing to use its data as a come-on for advertisers, and by user participation, Yahoo is referring to its Yahoo Answers, Flickr and other social-networking services that give the 10-plus-year-old company some true hipness in a Web 2.0 world. Wall Street's hope for Yahoo is that if it can deliver with its new search-advertising platform, Panama, it can at least hold its own against Google and begin to leverage its unique strengths. If Yahoo's articulation of its own new mission statement is any indication, it might have half a chance.

Source: http://money.cnn.com/2007/02/01/technology/pluggedin_lashinsky_yahoo.fortune/ (Accessed on (05/09/09).

(vii) **Indicate Major Components of Strategy and Objectives:** The mission statement is broad in scope. It cannot be implemented without looking into the details. The objectives and strategies are formulated based on the mission. The mission statement without the objectives and strategies is incomplete. The organisation's mission statement, therefore, should indicate the objectives and strategies to be employed. (See Exhibit 3.3).

(viii) **Achievement of the Policies:** The strategies are also broad based although, not as broad as mission statements. Therefore, the mission statements of organisations should include major policies they plan to follow in the pursuit of their missions. These policies establish the ground rules for the organisation in its relationship with government, customers, suppliers, distributors, creditors, other similar organisations, technological parks, trade associations etc. (See Exhibit 3.3).

A Declaration of Attitude and Outlook

Mission statement should be broad in attitude and outlook in order to enable the generation of alternate objectives based on the changing environment and to allow the reconciliation of diverse needs of all stakeholders of the company. Mission statement should not be too lengthy, even though it should be broad in scope. Mission statement creates positive feelings and attitudes about an organisation. It should also inspire for positive action.

Customer Orientation

Mission statement indicates company's philosophy, purpose, markets, products, customers, aspiration, scope for creative growth, current and prospective activities, clarity for understanding, current and future aspiration of customers and the broader areas of the product utilities rather than the product. For example, AT&T's mission statement focuses on communication rather than telephones, Dr. Reddy's Lab's mission statement focuses an health rather than drugs and pharmaceutical products and Mobil's mission statement focuses on energy rather than oil and gas.

In fact, the changing customer needs determine the business. Today hotel customers need a variety of services in addition to core service like lodging, tour arrangements, etc.

Declaration of Social Policy

Mission statement indicates the company's desire to serve the society, accommodate the social imbalances social issues and desire to render responsibilities to various sectors of the society. The social policy also includes developing a product that combines both economic and social values, for example, Dr. Reddy's Lab produces medicines at low cost. Similarly, regional rural banks provide loans and advances at low interest rates, Maruti Udyog Limited produces low cost cars, Deccan Airlines in India, South West Airlines in USA provide air travel at less price. Thus, companies try to conduct business in a socially responsible way.

Functions of a Mission Statement

A mission statement:

(i) Should define what the organisation is and what the organisation aspires to be;

(ii) Should be limited enough to exclude some ventures and broad enough to allow for creative growth;

(iii) Should distinguish a given organisation from all others;

(iv) Should serve as a framework for evaluating both current and prospective activities; and

(v) Should be stated in terms sufficiently clear to be widely understood throughout the organisation.

Need For a Written Mission Statement:

King and Cleland recommend that organisations carefully develop a written mission statement for the following reasons:

1. To ensure unanimity of purpose within the organisation.
2. To provide a basis for motivating the use of organisational resources.
3. To develop a basis or standard for allocating organisational resources.
4. To establish a general tone or organisational climate, *e.g.,* to suggest a business like operation.
5. To serve as a focal point for those who can identify with the organisation's purpose and direction; and to deter those who cannot, from participating further in the organisation's activities.
6. To facilitate the translation of objectives and goals into a work structure involving the assignment of tasks of responsible elements within the organisation, and
7. To specify organisational purposes and the translation of these purposes into goals in such a way that cost, time and performance parameters can be assessed and controlled.

Contents of Mission Statements:

The type of information contained in a mission statement varies from company to company. But most mission statements address some common themes. These themes include:

Mission statement should include: Company's products, markets, technology, objectives, core values, self concept and public image.

Company Product or Service: This information identifies the goods and/or services produced by the organisation — what the company offers to its customers.

Markets: This information describes the markets and customers that the organisation intends to serve. Who these customers are and where they are located are common themes.

Technology: It includes topics such as the techniques and processes by which the company produces goods and/or renders services.

Organisational Objectives: As stated earlier, most mission statements refer to organisational objectives. These include, the general ways they propose for dealing with key stakeholders like shareholders, customers and employees.

Organisational Philosophy or Core Values: A statement of organisational philosophy commonly appears as part of the mission statement. An organisational philosophy statement reflect the basic beliefs and values that should guide organisation members in conducting organisational business.

Exhibit 3.6: Differences Between Image Positioning and Character Expression

Image Positioning	*Character Expression*
(i) To make company or product appealing.	• To build trust in business relationship.
(ii) Image leads, reality may follow.	• Reality leads.
(iii) Exaggerate trivial differences	• Dramatise significant differences.
(iv) Make claims, support with artificial evidence.	• Don't make claims, find ways to believably behave differently.
(v) Image positioning works even if it is at odds with reality.	• Consumers hunger for companies they trust. Images at odds with reality risk mistrust.
(vi) Communications are seen as messages to convey image.	• Communications are seen as behaviour to express character.
(vii) Depends on company-sponsored communications.	• Depends on news media and customer word-of-mouth.
(viii) Marketing seen as separate from delivery of goods and services.	• Marketing seen as integral to development and delivery of goods and services.

Source: Peter Laundry, "Learning from the Laramie Lawyer's Letter," "*Design Statements*," a Journal of the American Center for Design, Fall, 1992.

Organisational Self Concept: Mission statement necessarily contains the information on the self-concept of the organisation. Organisation self-concept is the company's own view or impression of itself. The company arrives at this self-concept by assessing its strengths and weaknesses, competition, and ability to survive in the market place.

Public Image: Mission statements normally contain some reference to the type of impression that the organisation wants to leave with its public. However, public forms the opinion of the company based on its activities and performances. It is viewed that traditional firms try to position an image and modern firms express their true characters. Exhibit 3.6 presents the differences between image positioning and character expression.

Inputs For The Company Mission

Strategic managers must recognise and acknowledge the legitimate claims of the stakeholders of the firm in defining and/or redefining company mission. These stakeholders can be divided into "insiders" and "outsiders." Insiders are individuals and groups including shareholders and employees of the firms. Outsiders are all other individuals and groups who are not insiders, but affected by the activities of the firm. Outsiders include: customers, suppliers of raw materials, government, employee unions, competitors, local committees, trade associations, general public and the like. These insiders and outsiders provide inputs for the formulation and reformulation of organisational mission as shown in Fig.3.3.

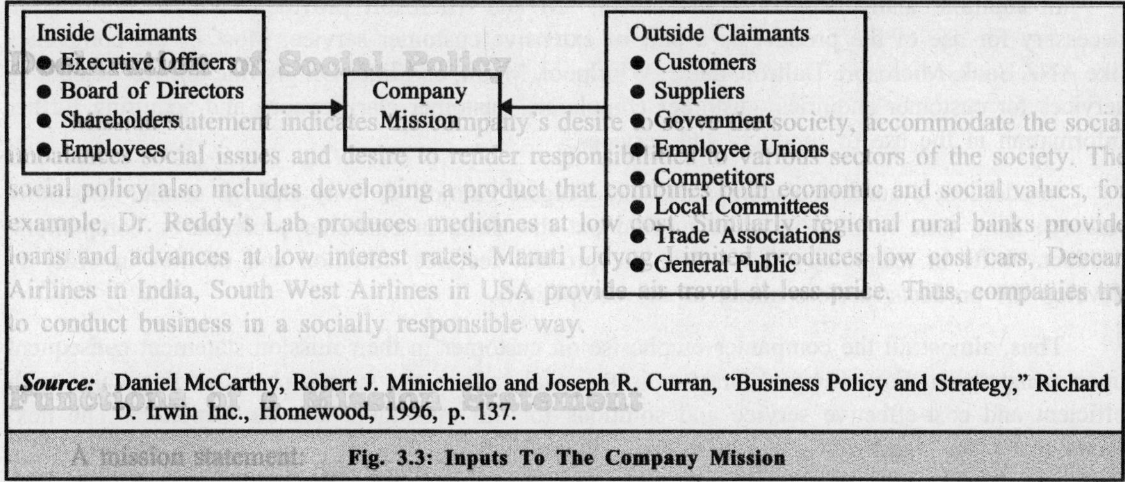

Source: Daniel McCarthy, Robert J. Minichiello and Joseph R. Curran, "Business Policy and Strategy," Richard D. Irwin Inc., Homewood, 1996, p. 137.

Fig. 3.3: Inputs To The Company Mission

When organisation attempts to define its mission so as to incorporate the interests of these various groups, the following steps must be taken:

(i) Identification of claimants;

(ii) Understanding claimant's specific demands *vis-a-vis* the company;

(iii) Reconciliation and prioritisation of the claims; and

(iv) Coordination of claims with other elements of the mission.

Broad Mission Statements

Studying the actual broad mission statements helps us to develop a skill for writing mission statements. It also helps us to evaluate mission statements. Exhibit 3.5 shows broad mission statements.

Recent Trends in Mission Components

Most of the companies of late are emphasising on the following four components in their mission statements:

- Customers and
- Quality
- Human Competency and
- Climate Change.

Companies change mission statements due to shift in emphasis on customers, quality, human resource and climate change

Customers: Globalisation and information technology strides provided greater opportunities to most of the multinational companies. These opportunities led to severe competition among MNCs and domestic companies. Consequently, companies started placing more emphasis on customer service as a strategy to attract and retain customers. "Customer is our king". "Customer is our top priority," and "Our business is centred around our customer" are the mottos that are claimed by most of the companies around the world.

Catterpillar, General Electric, Johnson & Johnson, Procter and Gamble, Colgate and Tata emphasise on customers by analysis of customer needs, design and redesign the products, add product function and modify the ingredients in addition to providing pre-sales and post-sales customer service. In fact, Xerox offers bonus to the employees for positive feedback and imposes penalties for the negative feedback from the customers.

In addition, many companies like Sears, 3M and Microsoft provide extensive information necessary for use of the product as a part of extensive customer service. Most of the companies like ANZ Bank, Microsoft, Daltron. datec, Whirlpool, Mobil, and Inter Oil provide toll-free telephone services for customer enquiries, customer complaints, customer clarifications and acquiring further information in the use of products and services.

In addition, a number of companies like Colgate Palmolive, Sony and LG conduct customer research from time to time in order to find out the shifts in customer preferences, competitors, product, shifts in technology that affect the product features, function and utilities in order to develop the products/services ahead of the competitors.

Thus, almost all the companies emphasise on customer in their mission statement consequent upon competition. For example, Graybar is the vital link in the supply chain, adding value with efficient and cost-effective service and solutions for our customers and our suppliers. The next factor that takes significant place in mission statement is 'quality'.

Quality: Quality is conformance of the product to the needs and expectations of customers. Quality is one of the most prime considerations for almost all the companies during the post-globalisation era as they 'produce what they can sell' rather than 'sell whatever they produce' as was in the past, for example, quality is the main concern for Ford as well as Toyota. Ford Motors focus on the rich income group while Toyota Motors focus on middle income group in those countries where it operates. Product quality, today, has become a universal theme in the global economy and continues to shape competitive dynamics in most of the companies. The third factor that takes significant place in mission statement is 'human competency'.

Human Competency: Human competency is the rare skills, talents and distinctive mind-set of the employees that contributes vitally for building distinctive competency to the company in crafting and achieving strategies based on strategic intent. For example, Virgin Blue could win over British Airways as well as Qantas in some routes mostly due to its distinctive human resources. In fact, Mr. Richard the CEO of Virgin group profoundly express that human resource is the top priority for the company as employees take care of customers, who in turn takes care of business, profits and shareholders. Even Deccan Airlines expressed the same opinion with regard to the role of human resources in strategy crafting and achievement. As such most of the companies realized the strategic role that the human resources play particularly after globalization.

Climate Change: Business organisations are now concerned more for the actions and a range of activities relating to combatting global warming, and to influencing political decisions on global-warming-related regulation, such as the Kyoto Protocol. Major multinationals have played and to some extent continue to play a significant role in the politics of global warming, especially in the United States, through lobbying of government and funding of global warming skeptics. Business also plays a key role in the mitigation of global warming, through decisions to invest in researching and implementing new energy technologies and energy efficiency measures. In fact the companies started incorporating their concern for climate change in their respective mission statements (See Box 3.3).

BOX 3.3 IMPACT OF CLIMATE CHANGE ON MISSION STATEMENT

Climate change is now a mainstream political issue. However, as yet there is no substantive framework for policy which offers coherence and consistency as to how national governments should cope with the long-term political challenges of climate change. In association with the Centre for the Study of Global Governance at the London School of Economics, this Policy Network project examines how best to develop this policy framework through a comparative political analysis of key western democracies. The project is led by Anthony Giddens, former director of the LSE, and Roger Liddle, vice-chair of Policy Network. Our objective is distinctive: to think about the challenges of climate change in a specifically political context. At present, public discussion of climate change tends to be partial and disparate. Loosely connected debates hinge on the evidence that climate change is occurring and estimates of its potential impact; the prospects for agreeing an international framework for an economic response to, for instance, carbon trading; futurology surrounding the potential for technological innovation that could solve the problem; and, scenario building that tends to emphasise the necessity for dramatic lifestyle changes. But the debate is often limited in scope and is too compartmentalised. To truly come to terms with the increasingly urgent need for mitigation and adaptation requires a broad policy perspective because the impact of climate change reverberates in every corner of the 21st century state. This project aims to offer an integrated platform from which to analyse and respond to the political challenges of climate change. Our primary focus is on public policy at the national level. Although an international agreement is a vital aspect of an effective global response to climate change, we cannot rely exclusively on international consensus as an impetus for action. No amount of discussion at an international level will be of any consequence if the countries mainly responsible for causing climate change do not make effective and radical responses to it. So, it is at the national level in the developed countries that real progress first has to be made. And it is through decisive national leadership at this level that a global solution can eventually be induced. Our "best practice" comparisons will concentrate on key western democracies, such as: the United Kingdom; Germany; Sweden; Spain; Poland; the United States at the federal level; and, Japan. We will also look at what role the European Union can play in encouraging national action and offering a framework for regional leadership combating the challenges of climate change. The aim of the project is to produce something of a complementary volume of study to that of the Stern Review in the form of two publications: an authoritative monograph written by Anthony Giddens; and a comparative collection of essays from national policymakers and senior academics synthesising the conclusions of the programme with a set of policy proposals for governments.

Framework

This volume of study will address the following political challenges posed and issues raised by climate change to western democracies:

- **The management of risk** – The prevailing scientific consensus on the effects of climate change is periodically questioned by those who want to scale-up and those who want to scale-down the present levels of urgency and severity in its assessment. How in these circumstances can democracies construct a prudent, long term and consistent policy agenda to manage these risks, whilst also building consensus around the agenda? To what extent is this agenda shared with the pursuit of energy security?
- **A return to planning?** – Effective national action on climate change requires a return in some form to long-term government planning. What new forms of interventionism would be most expedient, learning from the failures of the past? How can the climate change dimension be built into every relevant aspect of public policy? How can market-orientated approaches be balanced with state-centric ones in coping with vital issues of mitigation and adaptation, such as carbon pricing, the role of regulation, energy efficiency, transport and land use, the promotion of specific technological innovation by government, and lifestyle and behavioural changes?
- **Creating a political and public consensus for action** – How can the democratic penchant for partisanship and short-termism, within differing democratic cultures, be replaced by long-termism and a consensus-based policy agenda? How can an ambivalent public opinion, especially at times of economic uncertainty, be convinced of the merits of long-term action on climate change? What can governments do to induce sustained support for combating climate change?
- **The implications for social justice** – The social and economic costs of climate change will be large. How can you ensure that the impact of policies to address climate change are perceived as equitable by key groups in society and do not penalise those who are less fortunate? What are the prospects of ensuring that western democracies can be persuaded to carry the economic and political burden of climate change instead of countries in the developing world? Our goal is to consider the impact of these challenges and issues on western democracies in general and on specific nations in particular. In this process we will assess the national specificities of the politics of climate change: the successes, weaknesses and contradictions of existing policy; and, the links to national energy security agendas. This will allow for a wide-ranging "best practice" comparison.

Source: http://politicsofclimatechange.wordpress.com/the-politics-of-climate-change/ (Accessed on 06/09/09)

Product quality, today, has become a universal theme in the global economy and continues to shape competitive dynamics in most of the companies.

Redefining the Business/Mission Statement

Changes in external environmental factors like globalization, shift from regulated economies to market economies and development of information technology necessitated the companies to change their mission statements.

Some of the organisation are redefining their business definition and streamlining their growth direction. The examples include: merger of Brooke Bond with Lipton India, purchase of Glaxo Health food division by Heinz, HDFC took over Timesbank and Whirlpool took our Kelvinator. Some of the companies recently are redefining their mission statements. Changes in external environmental factors like globalization, shift from regulated economies to market economies and development of information technology necessitated the companies to change their mission statements. For example Vishal Food Products Limited shifted its business from exclusive food products to software business and as such it changed its mission statement from 'satisfying food needs of customers' to 'provide the best products and services to customers.' (See Box 3.4).

BOX 3.4 NATO LAUNCHES STUDY TO REDEFINE MISSION STATEMENT TO INCLUDE PIRACY, TERRORISM

BRUSSELS — NATO started a process Friday to update its outdated mission statement to focus on handling a resurgent Russia and threats such as piracy, terrorism and cyber attacks around the world. NATO's current mission statement, written in 1999, does not envision any missions outside its traditional theatre of operations in Europe and the North Atlantic." We will need a strategic concept that takes account of today's realities and tomorrow's challenges," NATO Secretary-General Anders Fogh Rasmussen told reporters before a meeting of the North Atlantic Council, the alliance's governing body. NATO's 28 member states hope that the new approach will help persuade an increasingly skeptical public in many European countries that the 60-year-old alliance remains relevant, two decades after the end of the Cold War."

The need for a new strategic concept is clear, the current one dates from 1999, before Sept. 11, before the conflict in Afghanistan, before cyber attacks, before piracy, and when NATO only had 16 members," Fogh Rasmussen said. "The world has changed, the threats have changed, and so has NATO." The task is made harder at a time of economic crisis and shrinking defense budgets, analysts say. Former U.S. Secretary of State Madeline Albright had been named to lead a panel that will craft NATO's mission statement. It met for the first time Friday with the North Atlantic Council and briefed its members on the concept. The draft will be submitted for consideration to the leaders of NATO's member nations at their summit in Lisbon, Portugal, next spring.

Albright said one of the Western alliance's principal challenges in the future would be its relations with a resurgent Russia. "It is important to know what the Russians have to say ... Russia can have a voice, but not a veto" over NATO operations, she said. Fogh Rasmussen, who took over as secretary-general in July, has said his top priorities would be guiding the war in Afghanistan to a successful conclusion, repairing ties with Russia that were further strained by last year's war with Georgia, and expanding NATO's partnership with moderate nations in North Africa and the Middle East.

Source: http://www.google.com/hostednews/canadianpress/article/ALeqM5g7pv02cVp1w_RhG5iBHiJJt41wsg (Accessed on 05/09/09).

Evaluation of Mission Statements

There is no one best mission statement for a particular organisation. Hence, good judgment is required in evaluating mission statements. Mission statements presented in Exhibit 3.6 are evaluated by David based on the ten criteria: customers, products or services, markets, technology, concern for survival, growth and profitability, philosophy, self-concept, concern for public image reconciliatory effectiveness and inspiring quality. These evaluations are presented in Table 3.1. A 'yes' in the table indicates that the given mission statement answers satisfactorily the question posed. A 'no' would mean a particular mission statement does not answer satisfactorily the question. This table indicates that the Mary Kay Cosmetics mission statement is the best example and the Nashua mission statement is the worst example. An effective mission statement addresses strategic concerns at the corporate, divisional and functional levels of an organisation.

(D) BUSINESS DEFINITION

Business definition is a part of mission statement. It is a description of the products, activities or functions and markets that the firm presently pursues. Products produced and/or services are the value created by the organisation for the customers. Markets are the classes of customers or geographic regions where the product and services are sold. Functions refer to the technologies or processes used to create and add value.

Meaning

A company's business is defined by what needs it is trying to satisfy, which customer groups it is targeting and the technologies it will use and the functions it will perform in serving the target market.

Three factors are to be taken into account while defining what business an organisation requires. They are:

1. Customer needs, or what is being satisfied.
2. Customer groups, or who is being satisfied.
3. The technologies used and functions performed-how customers' needs are satisfied.

Business definition deals with customer needs, customer functions and technologies.

Defining a business in terms of what to satisfy, who to satisfy and how the organisation will go about producing the satisfaction adds completeness to the definition. (Fig.3.4)

Table 3.1
An Evaluation Matrix of Example Mission Statements

Evaluative Criteria

Organisations	*Customers*	*Products or Services*	*Markets*	*Concern for Technology*	*Concern for Survival*
Avon Company	no	yes	yes	no	yes
Penn State Univ.	yes	yes	yes	yes	no
Univ. of Idaho	yes	yes	yes	no	no
Nashua Corporation	no	yes	yes	yes	no
Economics Lab	yes	yes	no	yes	yes
Harsco Corporation	yes	yes	yes	yes	no
General Tyre & Rubber	yes	yes	yes	yes	no
Mary Kay Cosmetics	yes	yes	yes	yes	yes

	Quality	*Concern for Self-Philosophy*	*Public Concept*	*Reconciliatory Image*	*Inspiring Effectiveness*
Avon Company	no	yes	yes	no	no
Penn State Univ.	yes	yes	yes	yes	yes
Univ. of Idaho	no	no	no	no	no
Nashua Corporation	no	yes	no	no	no
Economics Lab	yes	yes	yes	no	yes
Harsco Corporation	no	yes	no	no	yes
General Tyre & Rubber	no	yes	no	no	yes
Mary Kay Cosmetics	yes	yes	yes	yes	yes

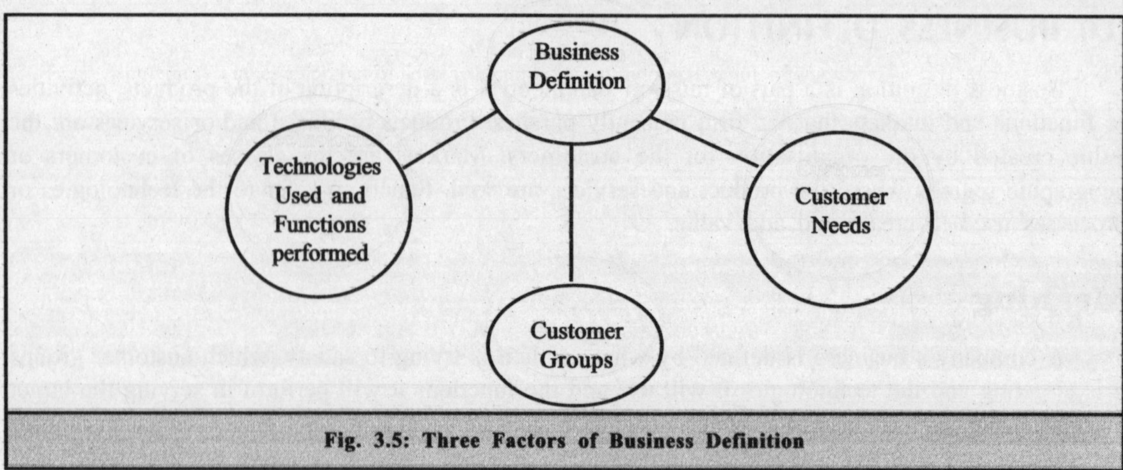

Fig. 3.5: Three Factors of Business Definition

An appropriate example of business definition that incorporates all three aspects is a paraphrase of Polaroid's business definition: "Performing and marketing instant photography to satisfy the needs of more affluent US and West European families for affection, friendship, fond memories and humour."

Broad or Narrow Business Definition?

Business definitions must be narrow enough to state exactly the business interest and also to have managerial values. Otherwise, managers cannot have clear direction or goal and do not know where to take the company. However, diversified companies should have broader business definitions than single-business enterprises. Exhibit 3.7 shows the dimensions of some broad definitions and some narrow definitions.

Exhibit 3.7: Dimensions of Some Broad Definitions and Some Narrow Definitions

Broad Definitions	*Narrow Definitions*
Beverages	Soft drinks
Footwear	Women's footwear
Furniture	Office furniture
Global Mail Delivery	Overnight Package Delivery
Travel and Tourism	Luxury buses in Goa

Criteria of an Effective Business Definition

An effective business definition should meet the following criteria:

(i) An effective business definition should include a statement of products, markets and functions;

(ii) The statement of the business definitions should be as precise as possible and indicate major components of strategy, *i.e.,* products, markets and functions. However, indication of how the mission is to be accomplished makes the statement further clear;

(iii) The statement should also indicate the kind of management desired and policies necessary to attain the mission; and

(iv) The statement should provide the necessary direction for the formulation of strategies.

(E) OBJECTIVES

The accomplishment of purpose or mission of an organisation requires the formulation of a number of objectives. Achievement of the organisational objectives, in turn, requires the formulation and fulfillment of departmental and unit goals. As presented in Figure 3.4, objectives can be structured as a hierarchy.

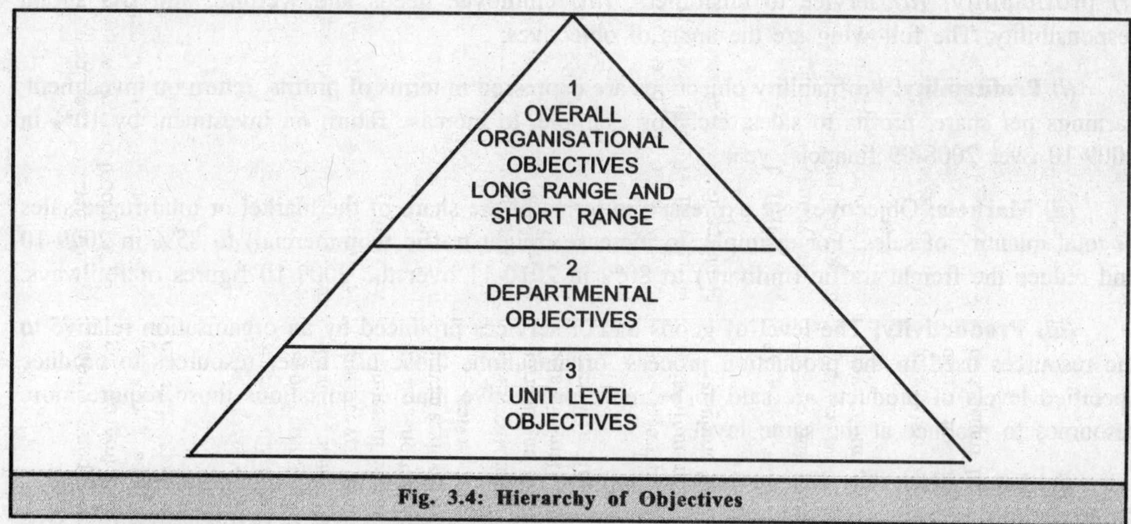

Fig. 3.4: Hierarchy of Objectives

Long-range objectives specify the results that are desired in pursuing the organisation's mission and normally extend beyond the current financial year of the organisation. Long-range objectives are notably speculative for distant years. Short-range objectives are performance targets, normally of less than one-year's duration, that are used by management to achieve the organisation's long-range objectives. The selection of short-range objectives is from an evaluation of priorities relating to long-range objectives. Departmental objectives, both long-range and short-range are formulated based on the respective long-range and short-range objectives of the organisation. Unit objectives are generally specific and are drawn from the departmental objectives.

Objectives Vs. Goals: The terms objectives and goals are differentiated by some managers based on generality and specificity of what an organisation seeks to achieve. For example, objective of an organisation is to improve its profitability whereas one of the goals of the organisation is to increase the net sales by 20% during 2010 over 2009. Thus, objectives are open-ended attributes and goals are close-ended attributes which are precise and expressed in specific terms. However, some managers use these two terms synonymously.

Objectives are based on mission statement and open-ended statements whereas goals are closed ended statements.

Formulating Objectives: The mission and directional course are converted into designated performance outcomes in the process of formulating objectives. Objectives represent a managerial commitment to achieve specified results in a specified period of time. They clearly spell out the quantity and quality of performance to be achieved, the time period, the process and the person who is responsible for the achievement of the objective.

An organisation's mission statement will be just a window-dressing, unless, it is translated into measurable and specific performance targets and managers are pressured to achieve these targets. Thus, objective formulation is a critical step in the strategic management process. It is viewed that, companies, whose managers formulate objectives for each key result area and then actively pursue actions to achieve their performance targets will out-perform the companies whose managers operate with hopes and mere good intentions.

Performance objectives must be stated in quantifiable or measurable terms. They must also contain a deadline for achievement.

Areas of Objectives

Objectives are set for all areas and departments of an organisation. Though the objectives can vary widely from one organisation to another organisation, they can be broadly divided into: *(i)* profitability, *(ii)* service to customers, *(iii)* employee needs and welfare, and *(iv)* social responsibility. The following are the areas of objectives:

***(i)* Profitability:** Profitability objectives are expressed in terms of profits, return on investment, earnings per share, profits to sales, etc. For example, to increase return on investment by 10% in 2009-10 over 2008-09 financial year.

***(ii)* Markets:** Objectives are expressed in terms of the share of the market or total rupee sales or total quantity of sales. For example, to increase freight traffic (commercial) to 85% in 2009-10 and reduce the freight traffic (military) to 80% in 2010-11 over the 2009-10 figures of Railways.

***(iii)* Productivity:** The level of goods and/or services produced by an organisation relative to the resources used in the production process, organisations those use fewer resources to produce specified levels of products are said to be more productive than organisations those require more resources to produce at the same level.

***(iv)* Innovation:** Any change made to improve methods of conducting organisational business. Organisational objectives should indicate innovations the organisation desires to implement.(See Box 3.5).

BOX 3.5 BAYER — EMPHASIS IN MISSION STATEMENT, INNOVATION AND OBJECTIVES

The corporate mission statement, featuring the slogan "Bayer: Science For A Better Life," summarizes the Group's goals, strategies and values. In the future, Bayer will focus on innovation and growth in the areas of health care, nutrition and high-tech materials.The mission statement underscores Bayer's willingness as an inventor company to help shape the future and our determination to come up with innovations that benefit humankind. Of special importance in this respect are new products emerging from Bayer's active substance research, the consumer health business, the growth markets of Asia and new areas such as biotechnology and nanotechnology, summarizes the Group's goals, strategies and values. In the future, Bayer will focus on innovation and growth in the areas of health care, nutrition and high-tech materials.

Source: http://www.bayer.com/en/mission-statement.aspx (Accessed on 05/09/09)

***(v)* Product:** These objectives are expressed in terms of sales and profitability by product line or product, target dates for development of new products and others.

***(vi)* Financial Resources:** These objectives are expressed in terms of the capital structure, new issues of common stock, cash flow, working capital, dividend payments and collection periods.

***(vii)* Physical Facilities:** These objectives are expressed in terms of machinery and equipment, fixed costs, units of production and other measures.

***(viii)* Organisation Structure and Activities:** These objectives are stated in terms of changes to be made in the policies of organisation structure or projects to be undertaken.

***(ix)* Manager Performance and Development:** These objectives are related to the quality and rate of development of managerial skills, knowledge and performance. Development of managerial performance is very important from the view point of the long-range success of the company and achievement of the other objectives of the company.

***(x)* Employee Performance and Attitude:** These objectives are related to the development of skills, knowledge and performance of non-managerial employees of the company. This area is also related to the development of favourable attitude of the employees towards the organisation. The significance of these considerations should be stressed through the formulation of organisational objectives.

***(xi)* Customer Service:** These objectives are related to the quality of the product, pre-sales and post-sales service, delivery times, promptly attending to the customer complaints, price, package and the like.

***(xii)* Social Responsibility:** These objectives are related to the obligation of business towards the society with a view to contribute to its welfare. Today, these objectives have become common to all the companies. For example to contribute to the medical facilities of the community where the company is located (See Box 3.6).

BOX 3.6 NIKE COMPANY: SOCIAL RESPONSIBILITY ISSUES

Nike has become one of those global companies targeted by a broad range of campaigning NGOs and journalists as a symbolic representation of the business in society. In Nike's case, the issues are those of human rights and conditions for workers in factories in developing countries. In the face of constant accusations, Nike has developed a considered response, supported by corporate website reporting. It now has a well developed focus for its corporate responsibility on improving conditions in contracted factories, aiming for carbon neutrality, and making sports available to young people across the world. The criticism continues, however.

Nike the company: Nike Inc produces footwear, clothing, equipment and accessory products for the sports and athletic market. It is the largest seller of such garments in the world. It sells to approximately 19,000 retail accounts in the US, and then in approximately 140 countries around the world. Just about all of its products are manufactured by independent contractors with footwear products in particular being manufactured in developing countries. The company manufactures in China, Taiwan, Korea, Mexico as well as in the US and in Italy. Who works in these factories?

The Global Alliance report on the factories in Indonesia gave the following workforce profile: 58% of them are young adults between 20 and 24 years old, and 83% are women. Nearly half of these workers have completed senior high school. Few have work-related skills when they arrive at the factory. 95% of the workers in the nine participating factories have received pay or wage increases in the last year, consistent with government minimum wage increases, and with small exceptions the bases wages in these factories are above the regions minimum wage – although critics would observe that doesn't add up to a great deal.

What are the issues?: Nike has around 700 contract factories, within which around 20% of the workers are creating Nike products. Conditions for these workers has been a source of heated debate, with allegations made by campaigns of poor conditions, with commonplace harassment and abuse. Nike has sought to respond to these allegations by putting into place a code of conduct for all of its suppliers, and working with the Global Alliance to review around 21 of these factories, and to pick up and respond to issues.

In Indonesia, the following was reported: 30.2% of the workers had personally experienced, and 56.8% had observed, verbal abuse. An average of 7.8% of workers reported receiving unwelcome sexual comments, and 3.3% reported being physically abused. In addition, sexual trade practices in recruitment and promotion were reported by at least two workers in each of two different factories, although a subsequent investigation was unable to confirm this. 73.4% of workers are satisfied with their relationship with direct line supervisors, 67.8% are satisfied with management.

Far and away, the main concerns expressed by workers relate to their physical working environment. A further report has been produced relating to a site in Mexico, which has experienced serious problems leading to labour disputes.In both cases, Nike responded to the audit reports with a detailed remediation plan.

What do the critics say?: Naomi Klein, in her widely read book "No Logo" deals quite extensively with Nike, accusing them of abandoning countries as they developed better pay and employment rights in favour of countries like China, where these are less of a cost. She points to a photo published in 1996 showing children in Pakistan stitching Nike footballs as an example of the use of child labour. Other critics have suggested that Nike should publicise all of its factories, and allow independent inspection to verify conditions there. Any auditing carried out by Nike should be made public. A lot of focus is given to wage rates paid by the company's suppliers. By and large, audits have found that wage rates are above the national legal minimum, but critics contend that this does not actually constitute a fair living wage. What does Nike say?

Nike accuses Naomi Klein of peddling inaccurate and old information. They point out that they have not abandoned countries as she claims, and remain in Taiwan and Korea despite the higher wages and labour rights. They admit that the 1996 photo documented what they describe as a "large mistake" when they began to order soccer balls for the first time from a supplier in Pakistan. They now operate stitching centres where the non-use of child labour can be verified.

Nike believe that the sharing with factory locations with independent third parties on a confidential basis enables them to monitor their supply chain properly. They state that disclosure of the factory names, plus details of audits of those factories, would be used by the NGOs simply to make further attacks rather than as part of a dialogue to help the company to address and resolve those problems which exist. As for wage rates, Nike feels that establishing what constitutes a "fair" wage is by no means as easy as its critics would have the public believe – and disparages the constant quoting of wage rates in US dollar equivalents, when these are meaningless given the different cost of living in the countries concerned. Nike are also visibly dismayed at how they have attained the status of lead focus in this area. They request that people look towards their competitors and see how many of them have taken the kind of measures the company has over the last few years.

Does anyone else support Nike?: The Global Alliance was quite complimentary. It said "Upon due consideration, members of the Operating Council unanimously expressed their judgment that upon learning of the alleged violations surfaced through the Global Alliance assessment process, that Nike had acted in good faith, and developed a serious and reasonable remediation plan."

http://www.mallenbaker.net/csr/CSRfiles/nike.html (Accessed on 05/09/09)

Characteristics of Effective Objectives

All organisations formulate objectives in one form or the other. The utility of objectives is determined by their level of effectiveness. The important guidelines for the formulation of effective objectives include:

Objectives should be specific, level of effort, change needed, measurable and consistent.

Specific Objectives: It becomes clear exactly what is to be achieved, when, how and by whom, when the objectives are formulated specifically. All organisational members know and understand what is expected of them, if the objectives are specific. Further they eliminate confusion. More specific objectives make it easier for management to develop realistic strategies. Thus, effective and specific objectives provide a foundation on which managers can construct appropriate organisational strategies.

Level of Effort: Objectives should be set realistically. Ground realities should be taken into consideration while deciding the efforts needed. Objectives should be set to that level, at which employers can extend themselves somewhat to achieve them. They should not be set at so high a level that employees become frustrated and stop trying to achieve them. Objectives that challenge employees' abilities are generally more interesting and more motivating than easily attained objectives. Therefore, managers should establish challengeable but reachable organisational objectives, and all employees should share this view.

Changing Objectives: Both internal environment and relevant external environment change continuously. These changes sometimes make the established objectives irrelevant. Therefore, the management should continuously assess and monitor the environmental changes and reformulate the objectives accordingly. In fact, managers must encourage all employees to identify changes and suggest required changes in the objectives.

Measurable Objectives: The objectives should be measurable in quantitative terms like 12% increase in profit per share over the last year's profit. A measurable objective is an objective stated in such a way that an attempt to attain it can be compared to the objective itself to determine whether it actually has been attained.

5. Consistent Long-run and Short-run Objectives: Organisational objectives that reflect a desirable mix of timeframes and that support one another should be established. Long-term objectives must be consistent with the organisational vision and mission, while short-run objectives must be consistent with long-run objectives. In short, short-run objectives should be derived from and lead to the attainment of long-run objectives. Figure 3.6 presents consistency of organisational objectives with mission.

Guidelines for Formulating Objectives

Managers should formulate the objectives with great care as they serve as basis for organisational activities. The following guidelines are taken into account while formulating the objectives:

Involve all those employees responsible for carrying it out: The management should identify and involve all those employees responsible for implementing the objectives. The people at the helm of affairs have better knowledge of the activities. They know best what can be achieved. Such people should be encouraged to participate in the process of objective formulation. Persons who are involved in the process of establishment of objectives have a strong commitment to achieve them. They gain a feeling of belongingness and importance. Top management should allow their subordinates to participate in the process, encourage them to express their views and ideas. These ideas should be discussed jointly and modified, if necessary before finalising the objectives. However, during periods of crisis, top management can formulate the objectives on its own and impose them on their subordinates, by explaining the reasons for such imposition. This practice makes the employees to commit themselves to achieve the objectives.

All objectives within an organisation should support the overall objectives: The organisational overall objectives should be the basis for the objectives of different departments like finance, human resources, marketing, production and research and development. In turn, the unit level objectives should be formulated based on the departmental objectives. In other words, objectives should be mutually consistent throughout the organisation.

Objectives should have some 'reach': Normally, most people put their effort to achieve the objectives when there is a reasonable challenge. People are motivated when a feeling of accomplishment can be given. Therefore, objectives formulated should provide some amount of challenge for accomplishing them.

Objectives should be realistic: Objective should provide not only challenging job but also be realistic from the view point of both internal and external environmental opportunities and threats or hindrances. It is also better to guard against trying to attain too much in a short period. In other words, objectives should not be over ambitious. A simply stated objective can be remembered.

Objectives should be contemporary as well as innovative: The manager should keep the objectives up-to-date. In other words, the manager should review the objectives periodically based on the changes in the organisational priorities and changes in external environment and make revisions, if necessary. In addition, the objectives should not be routine. The manager should invite the creative ideas from the employees and incorporate the innovative ideas in formulating the objectives. In fact, innovative objectives are highly essential for organisations in the market economies.

The number of objectives for each manager should not be too many: Too many factors cause confusion and neglect and too few permit waste and inefficiency. More number of objectives really diminishes the efficiency of major objectives and unduly emphasise minor objectives. Three or four objectives can be maximum for a manager at one point of time. If there are more objectives, they can be assigned to managers in a phased way.

Objectives should be ranked according to their relative priority: If the number of objectives are more than two, they should be ranked according to their relative priority. This practice gives clear guidelines to the manager and avoids confusion. Managers can attend to the first rank objective initially and after accomplishing it, they can attend to the second rank next and so on so forth. This practice helps the manager to allocate his resources and efforts accordingly and improves the managerial efficiency. The normal human tendency of working on easily achievable objectives and delaying the working on more difficult objectives can be minimised by this ranking method.

Objectives should be in balance within a given enterprise: The various objectives should not collectively point to an excess of any one condition. For example, the objective of customer service may be overstressed to the detriment of the objective of profit improvement. Similarly the objective of management development should be in balance with the growth and profit objective of the overall organisation.

Importance of Objectives

Why do organisations formulate objectives? And what is their importance? The following four factors explain the need for and importance of objectives.

Objectives help to define the organisation in its environment: The organisations justify their existence to their stakeholders in the environment like customers, government, creditors and society at large.

Objectives help in coordinating decisions and decision-makers: Stated objectives impose some constraints on the behaviour of employees and modify it towards the desirable direction. It coordinates decision-making process by different employees.

Objectives help in formulating strategies. Mission statements are translated into objectives and objectives are the basis for formulating strategies.

Objectives provide standards for assessing organisational performance: Objectives provide not only the direction to move to the organisation but also provides the ultimate goals and targets that the organisation is expected to achieve. These targets and goals become the standards to judge the organisational performance. Organisations without clear objectives will not have clear basis for evaluating their performance or success.

Objectives are more tangible targets than the mission statements: Mission statements are general as they are expected to be fulfilled in the long run. As such mission statements are not more tangible. Whereas, the objectives are the translated versions of the mission statement and as such they are more tangible. For example, the mission of Rayalaseema Passenger and Goods Transport is, "Providing transportation to the common man" and one of the objectives is fixing the lowest passenger tariff compared to rail transport and any other road transport.

Objectives help to reflect the changes in the environment: Objectives are revised to reflect the changes in the internal and external environment from time to time. Fig. 3.5 presents the changes in objectives.

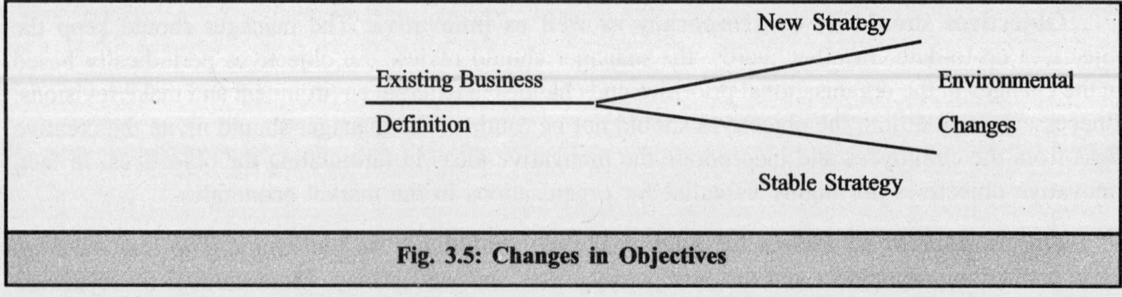

Fig. 3.5: Changes in Objectives

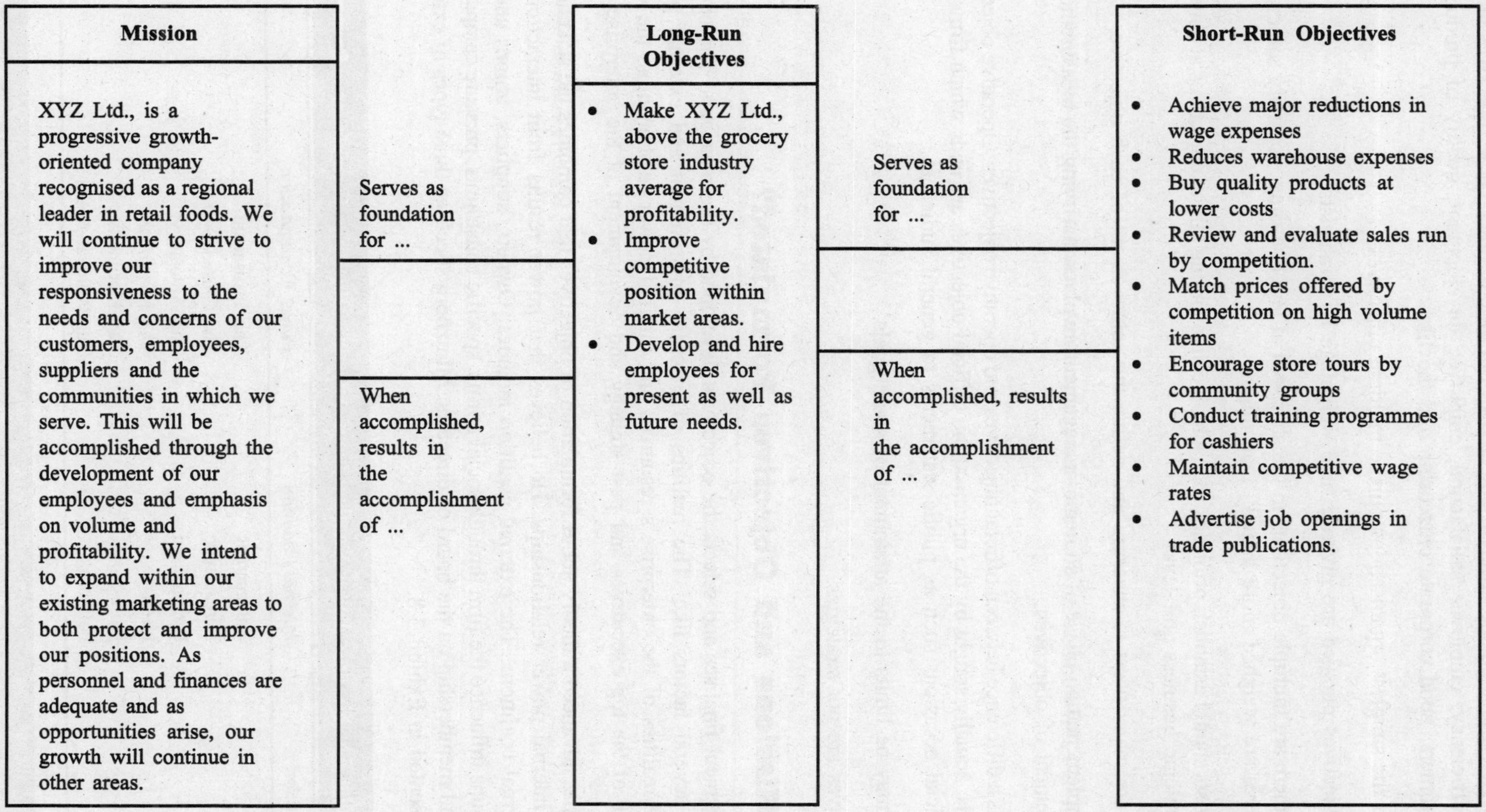

Mission

XYZ Ltd., is a progressive growth-oriented company recognised as a regional leader in retail foods. We will continue to strive to improve our responsiveness to the needs and concerns of our customers, employees, suppliers and the communities in which we serve. This will be accomplished through the development of our employees and emphasis on volume and profitability. We intend to expand within our existing marketing areas to both protect and improve our positions. As personnel and finances are adequate and as opportunities arise, our growth will continue in other areas.

Serves as foundation for ...

When accomplished, results in the accomplishment of ...

Long-Run Objectives

- Make XYZ Ltd., above the grocery store industry average for profitability.
- Improve competitive position within market areas.
- Develop and hire employees for present as well as future needs.

Serves as foundation for ...

When accomplished, results in the accomplishment of ...

Short-Run Objectives

- Achieve major reductions in wage expenses
- Reduces warehouse expenses
- Buy quality products at lower costs
- Review and evaluate sales run by competition.
- Match prices offered by competition on high volume items
- Encourage store tours by community groups
- Conduct training programmes for cashiers
- Maintain competitive wage rates
- Advertise job openings in trade publications.

Source: Adapted from Samuel C. Certo and J. Paul Peter, op. *cit., p.* 68.

Fig. 3.6: Consistency of Organisational Objectives with Mission - An Example.

Nature of Objectives

Different organisations pursue different objectives from time to time. These objectives include: Profit making, efficiency, employee satisfaction, employee development, quality of products or services for customers, good corporate citizenship and the like.

- All but the simplest organisations pursue multiple objectives.
- The objectives pursued are given a time weightage by strategists.
- Since there are multiple objectives in the short-run at any one time, normally some of the objectives are weighed more heavily than others.
- Strategists should establish priorities for each objective among all the objectives at corporate and strategic business unit level.
- There are many ways to measure and define the achievement of each objective.
- The implementation phase of strategic management involves clarifying the measurement of achievement of objectives.
- There is a difference between official objectives and operative objectives. Operative objectives are ends, actually sought by the organisation. Official objectives are ends which firms seek on official occasions such as public statements to general audiences.
- There may be limits to the attainment of some goals.
- Objectives are not strategies.

How are Missions and Objectives Formulated?

Top management finalises and selects the objectives developed by the managers. The choices are affected by several factors like: The realities of external environment and external power relationships, the realities of the enterprise's resources and internal power relationships, the value system and goals of the top executives and past strategy and development of the enterprise.

Mintzberg has advanced a theory about formulation of objectives that combines the stakeholder forces with the internal power relationships. He believes that power results from interactions of internal and external coalitions. The external coalition includes: Owners, suppliers, unions and the public. These groups influence the firm through social norms, specific constraints, pressure campaigns, direct controls and membership on the board of directors. Mintzberg specifies three types of external coalitions as presented in Exhibit 3.8.

Exhibit 3.8: Six Pure Power Configurations Affecting Objectives Formulation

External Coalition	*Internal Coalition*	*Power Configuration*
Dominated	Bureaucratic	The Instrument
Passive	Bureaucratic	The Closed System
Passive	Personalised	The Autocracy
Passive	Ideologic	The Missionary
Passive	Professional	The Meritocracy
Divided	Politicised	The Political Arena

Source: Henry Mintzberg, "*Power In and Around Organisations*," Prentice-Hall, Englewood Cliffs, N.J., p. 307.

The internal coalition includes top management, middle level managers, operators, analysts, and support staff. These groups influence the firm through the personnel control system, the bureaucratic control system, the political system, and the system of ideology.

Thus, the top manager sets the objectives subject to the environment. They are set by a complex interplay of past and present, internal and external role players.

The third factor affecting the formulation of mission and objectives is the value system of the top executives. These values will influence the perception of the advantages and disadvantages of strategic action and the choice of objectives. Exhibit 3.9 presents the extremes of six selected values.

Exhibit 3.9: Values Toward Various Groups in the Strategic Situation

1. Very Combative	Very Passive
2. Very Innovative	Non Innovative
3. Risk Oriented	Risk Aversive
4. Quality	Quantity
5. Autocratic	Participative
6. Personal Goals	Shareholder Goals.

The fourth factor affecting the formulation of mission and objectives is the awareness of management of the past development of the firm. Factors influencing the formulation of objectives and mission are shown in Figure 3.7.

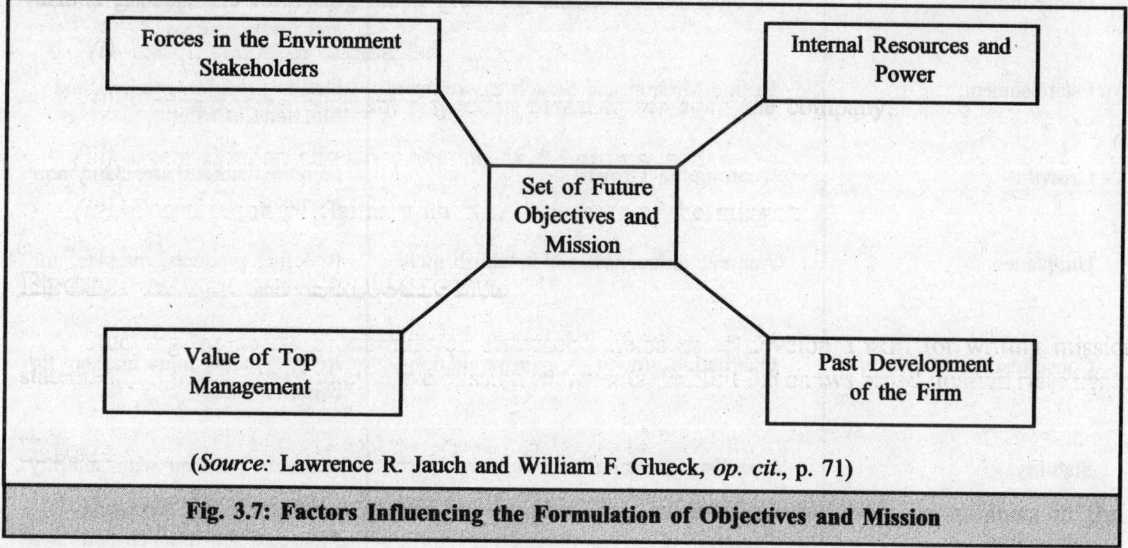

(*Source:* Lawrence R. Jauch and William F. Glueck, *op. cit.*, p. 71)

Fig. 3.7: Factors Influencing the Formulation of Objectives and Mission

Reasons for Change of Mission and Objectives

Generally organisations tend toward stability. Even then, their mission and objectives change over time. Objectives may change on the basis of gap between expected and desired states. These expected and desired states are influenced by some factors. These factors would lead to different perceptions regarding the gaps between goals and how the future goal states might be arrived at. The following are the reasons for change in mission and objectives.

1. *Change in Goal Orientation:* The goal orientations are altered by the aspiration levels of managers. The managers' aspiration levels change from time to time based on the past achievements of the organisation.

2. *Crisis Situations:* The crisis situations like economic liberalisations or any other change due to shift in government policy force the organisations to change their mission. Therefore, the organisations adapt their mission and objectives to the conditions of crisis situations.

3. *Changes in the Demands from Coalition Group:* The changes in the strengths and weaknesses of the members of coalition group and changes in the opportunities and threats of the external environment, the members change their interest. In addition, change in the government policies and international environment change the power configuration of the group. These changes make the enterprise shift from its state to new state of business. This brings the change in the mission and objectives of the enterprise.

4. *Changes in the Normal life-cycle of the Enterprise:* As the life-cycle of the human beings has different stages, the life cycle of the enterprise also has different stages. As the goals of human beings undergo changes from one stage to the another, the mission and objectives of an enterprise also undergo changes from one stage to the another of its life cycle due to changes in aspiration, needs etc. Exhibit 3.10 presents the change in organisational objectives and strategic focus at different stages.

Exhibit 3.10: Organisational Objectives and Strategic Focus at Different Stages of Organisational Life-Cycle

Stages of Organisational Life Cycle	*Organisational Objectives*	*Strategic Focus for an Organisation*
Incorporation:	Survival-create new entity	Identify an entrepreneurial idea and find resources
Establishment:	Define Mission and Search environment	Define products, markets and functions to offer
Growth:	Quantitative Growth	Increase market share; claim more territory
Uniqueness:	Achieve uniqueness and establish niche	Redefine products, markets, and functions.
Consolidation:	Qualitative growth — gain reputation	Reap rewards, mine markets for benefits
Stability:	Stabilise and contribute to society	Maintain position with stability
Reposition:	Survival	Procreate and retrench parts that are no longer healthy.

Source: Modified version from Lawrence R. Jauch and William F. Glueck. "Business Policy and Strategic Management." McGraw-Hill Book Company, New York. 1988. p. 72.

Process of Formulating Mission and Objectives

Having discussed various aspects of organisational direction in terms of mission and objectives, now we discuss the process of formulating organisational mission and objectives.

***Step 1:* Environmental Analysis:** The first step should reflect on the results of environmental analysis. Environmental analysis should provide managers with adequate information and data for reflection. The data and information from all the levels of environment — general, specific, operating and internal — should be collected. A cross-functional analysis of data and information and its results provide a basis for the establishment of organisational direction in terms of mission and objectives.

***Step 2:* Vision and Mission:** Environmental analysis serves as a foundation for the development and formulation of vision and mission. Managers should understand the information and data derived from the environment, its analysis and better equip themselves to have a visionary reflections. This reflection helps them to formulate and write the organisational vision. Organisational vision, in turn, becomes a solid foundation for establishing organisational mission. Managers should view the organisational mission by relating it to the societal needs. This stage helps the managers to write the mission statement.

Vision and mission statements reflect the organisation's relationship to its environment. This helps the organisation to increase its long-run profitability. It also helps the organisation to identify its core values and the direction to fulfill the vision.

***Step 3:* Organisational Objectives:** Organisational vision and mission serve as the basis for development of appropriate organisational objectives. Managers view that objectives should be consistent with the organisational vision and mission.

Organisations tend to evolve through stages in formulating the objectives more precisely.

(i) Formulation of general objectives, usually not in written form,

(ii) Formulation of general objectives, in written form,

(iii) Formulation of specific objectives, and

(iv) Ranking of specific objectives.

***Step 4:* Specific:** After the objectives are formulated by the top management of the organisation, they should be translated into specific targets (Exhibit 3.11) by the middle and lower level management. These specific targets help for the effective achievement of objectives at different levels.

Exhibit 3.11: Translation of Objectives into Specific Targets

Corporate Level Objectives	*Corporate and/or SBU Level Specific Targets*
(1) Improve Return on Capital	(1) Increase return on equity capital employed (after interest and taxes) from 15% to 18% in the next three years.
(2) Improve Overall Profit	(2) Increase overall profit margin from 5% to 8% in the next three years.
(3) Increase Shareholders' Return	(3) Increase earning per equity share from 10% to 15% in the next three years.
(4) Increase Sales	(4) *(a)* Increase sales in Andhra Pradesh in the next 3 years three times of the sales in 1997. *(b)* Penetrate into the market of Karnataka in 1998 and increase 5% of sales in Andhra Pradesh. *(c)* Start export to Eritrea in 1998 at least 10% of the company sales.
(5) Increase Manufacturing	(5) *(a)* Increase capital productivity by 10% in 1998. *(b)* Install new technology.
(6) Improve Industrial Relations	(6) *(a)* Settle 70% of the employee grievances in 1998 *(b)* Make the company strike-free by 1999.

POINTS TO BE REMEMBERED

- Vision: What do we want to create?
- Mission: An enduring statement of purpose that distinguishes one organisation from similar organisations.
- Key elements in mission are: environment, competencies.
- Mission statement should define the organisation.
- Mission is necessary to ensure unanimity of purpose within the company.
- Objectives are open-ended statements.

KEY WORDS

- Vision
- Mission
- Business Definition
- Contents
- Evaluation
- Inputs
- Function
- Broad
- Nature
- Guidelines
- Formulation
- Process

QUESTIONS FOR DISCUSSION

(1) What is a vision? Discuss its characteristics.

(2) What is a mission statement? What are the key elements in developing a mission statement?

(3) What are the contents of a mission statement?

(4) How do you evaluate mission statements?

(5) What is a business definition? Discuss broad and narrow business definitions.

(6) What are objectives? Discuss the characteristics of effective objectives.

(7) Discuss the importance of objectives.

(8) What are the reasons that result in changes in mission and objectives?

(9) Discuss the process of formulating mission and objectives.

REFERENCES

1. Peter Senge, "*The Fifth Discipline: The Art and Practice of Learning Organisation*," Doubleday, New York, 1990, p. 206.
2. *Ibid*., pp. 207-208.
3. Samuel C. Certo and J. Paul Peter, *op. cit.*, p. 56.
4. Lawrence R. Jauch and William F. Glueck, *op. cit.*, p. 58.

5. Peter Drucker, "*Management: Tasks, Responsibilities, Practices,*" Harper & Row, New York.
6. M.A. Hitt and R.D. Ireland, "*Corporate Distinctive Competence, Strategy and Performance,*" *Strategic Management Journal,* July-September, 1985, pp. 273-293.
7. C. Smart and I. Vertinsky, "Strategy and the Environment: A Study of Corporate Response to Crises," *Strategic Management Journal,* April-June 1984, pp. 199-214 and C. Stubbart, "Strategic Management in an Enacted World," *Academy of Management Review*, October, 1985, pp. 724-736.
8. P.K. Ghosh, "*Business Policy,*" Sultan Chand & Sons, New Delhi, 1993, p. 46.
9. *Ibid.*, p. 47.
10. Peter F. Drucker, "*Management,*" pp. 77-89.
11. *Ibid.*, p. 79.
12. Paul C. Nutt, "A Strategic Network for Non-Profit Organisations," *Strategic Management Journal,* January-March 1984, pp. 57-76.
13. James H. Donnelly Jr., James L. Gibson and John M. Ivancevich, "*Fundamentals of Management,*" Richard D. Irwin Inc., Homewood, 1992, pp.174-177.
14. Vern McGinnis, "The Mission Statement: A Key Step in Strategic Planning," *Business*, November-December 1981, p. 41.
15. W.R. King and D.I. Cleland, "*Strategic Planning and Policy,*" Van Nostrand Reinhold, New York, 1979, p. 124.
16. John A. Pearce II, "The Company Mission as a Strategic Tool," *Sloan Management Review,* Spring 1982, pp. 15-24.
17. Peter Laundry, "Learning From the Laramie Lawyer's Letter," *Design Statements*, Fall 1992, p. 5.
18. Daniel McCarthy, Robert J. Minichiello and Joseph R. Curran, "*Business Policy and Strategy,*" Richard D. Irwin Inc., Homewood, 1996, p. 136.
19. Fred R. David, *op. cit.*, p. 94.
20. Lawrence R. Jauch and William F. Glueck, *op. cit.*, pp. 59-60.
21. Arthur A. Thompson Jr. and A. J. Strickland III, *op. cit.*, p. 21.
22. Derek F. Abell, "*Defining the Business: The Strategic Point of Strategic Planning,*" Prentice Hall, Englewood Cliffs, 1980, p. 169.
23. Arthur A. Thompson and Jr. A.J. Strickland III, *op. cit.*, p. 22.
24. *Ibid.*, pp. 23-24.
25. *Ibid.*, p. 27.
26. *Ibid.*
26. Samuel C. Certo and J. Paul Peter, *op. cit.*, pp. 64-65.
27. Frederick Herzberg, "One More Time: How Do You Motivate Employees," *Harvard Business Review,* January-February 1968, pp. 53-62.
28. Samuel C. Certo and J. Paul Peter, *op. cit.*, pp. 65-67.
29. George R. Terry and Stephen G. Franklin, *op. cit.*, pp. 141-142.
30. Lawrence R. Jauch and William F. Glueck, *op. cit.*, p. 65.
31. *Ibid.*, pp. 62-64.
32. *Ibid.*, pp. 71-72.
33. Samuel C. Certo and J. Paul Peter, *op. cit.*, p. 67.
34. Lawrence R. Jauch and William F. Glueck, *op. cit.*, p. 75.
35. *Ibid.*
36. 1. J.W. Dean and D.E. Bowen. "Management Theory and Total Quality: Improving Research and Practice through theory Development", *Academy of Management Review*, 1994, 19p. 391-419.

✦ ✦ ✦

4

CHAPTER

EXTERNAL ENVIRONMENT SCANNING AND INDUSTRY ANALYSIS

Chapter Outline

(A) Introduction

(B) International Environment

(C) Social and Cultural Environment

(D) Technological Environment

(E) Economic Environment

(F) Political Environment

(G) Natural Environment

(H) Industry Analysis

Learning Objectives

After studying this chapter, you should be able to:

- Analyse the need for environment scanning for formulation of strategies;
- Study the social and cultural environment in order to find out the business appropriateness;
- Analyse the economic environment in order to find out the influence of income and expenditure pattern;
- Discuss the technological environment to find out the appropriateness of the technology;
- Explain the influence of the political environment on the business;
- Discuss the industry analysis in order to find out the growth of the industry.

(A) INTRODUCTION

William F. Glueck defined the term environmental analysis as, "the process by which strategists monitor the economic, governmental/legal, market/competitive, supplier/technological, geographic and social setting to determine opportunities and threats to their firms." "Environmental diagnosis consists of managerial decisions made by analysing the significance of data (opportunities and threats) of the environmental analysis."

BUSINESS ENVIRONMENTAL FACTORS

Business environmental factors are broadly divided into external environmental factors and internal environmental factors. External environmental factors that affect the business include Social and Cultural factors (S), Technological factors (T), Economic factors (E), Political/Governmental factors (P), International factors (I) and Natural factors (N) (STEPIN). Internal environmental factors influence/affect the business from within. They include: human resource management, trade unions, organisation structure, financial management, marketing management, production management, management/leadership styles, etc.

External environmental factors that affect the business include Social and Cultural factors (S), Technological factors (T), Economic factors (E), Political/ Governmental factors (P), International factors (I) and Natural factors (N) (STEPIN).

External environmental factors are further divided into micro external factors and macro external environmental factors. Micro external environmental factors include: competitors, customers, market intermediaries, suppliers of raw materials, bankers and other suppliers of finance, shareholders, and other stakeholders of the business firm.

External macro environmental factors include: social and cultural factors, technological factors, economic factors, political and governmental factors, international factors and natural factors. In recent times environmental protection has received greater attention in order to protect people, animals, plants and to maintain ecological balance. The analysis of internal environmental factors indicates the strengths and weaknesses of the business firm while the analysis of micro external and macro external environmental factors indicate the opportunities provided by the environment to the business. The strengths, weaknesses, opportunities and threats (SWOT) analysis helps to formulate strategies for the business firm. (See fig. 4.1).

Strategic Management and Environmental Analysis

Strategic management involves three levels of analysis, *viz.,* the organisation's macro environment/ general environment, the industry in which the organisation operates, and the organisation itself. We will discuss the first two levels in this chapter and the third level in the next chapter. Every company operates within a complex network of external environmental forces both international and national.

Need for Environmental Analysis and Diagnosis

External environmental analysis provides opportunities and threats, while internal environment provides for strengths and weaknesses.

Environmental analysis is the process by which strategists monitor the environmental factors to determine opportunities for and threats to their firms. Analysis also involves studying each factor minutely to find its nature, function and relationship. Strategic manager essentially searches for opportunities and threats, their sources and their impact on the business. Environmental diagnosis consists of managerial decisions made by assessing the significance of the data (opportunities and threats) of the environmental analysis. A strategist examines the relationship between the company's strategy and the environment. Then, he/she forecasts the future environment and compares the strategy with the future environment. If there are gaps, he/she reformulates the strategy after revising the business mission and objectives. Otherwise, he/she will continue with the present strategy as presented in fig. 4.2.

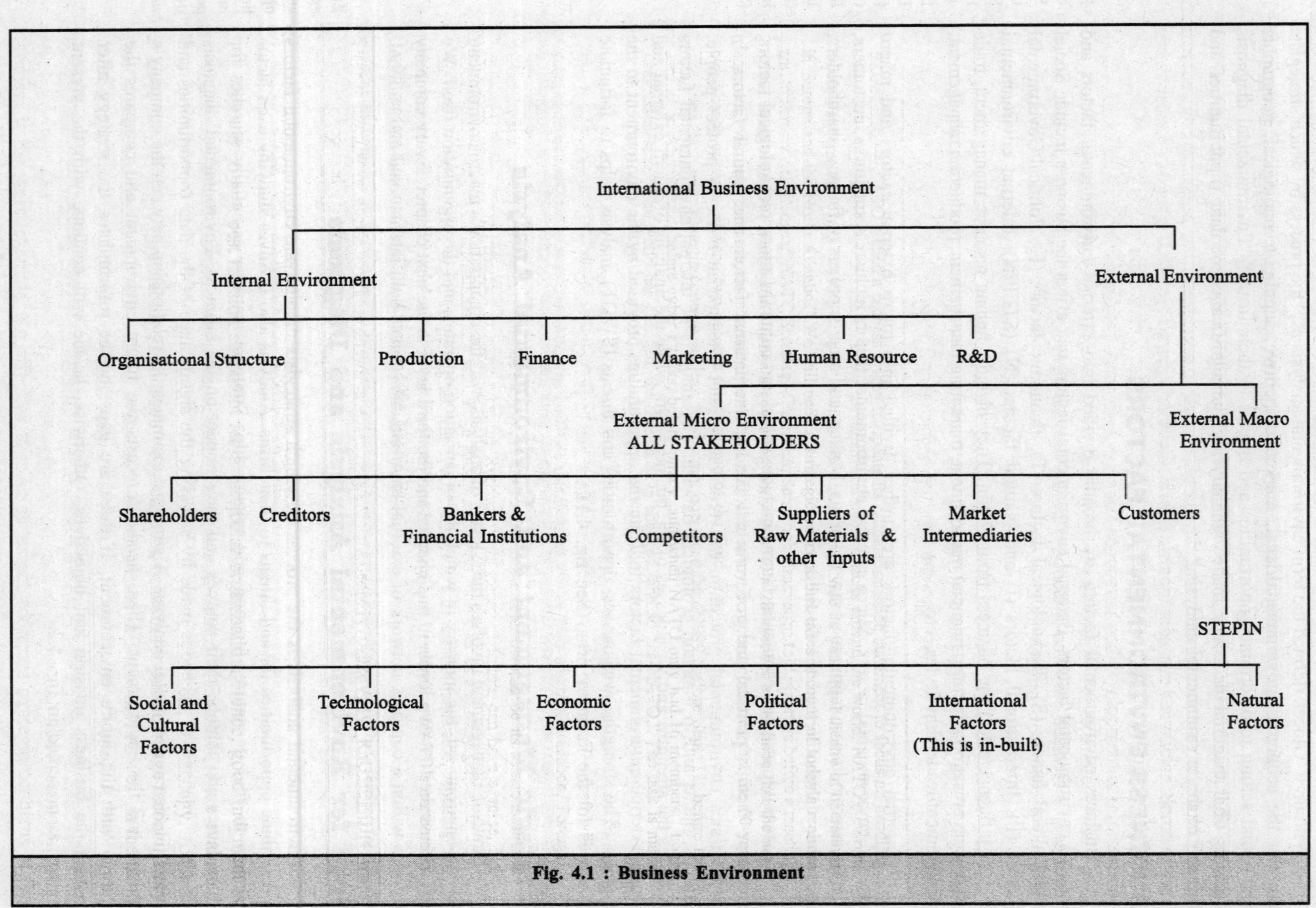

Fig. 4.1 : Business Environment

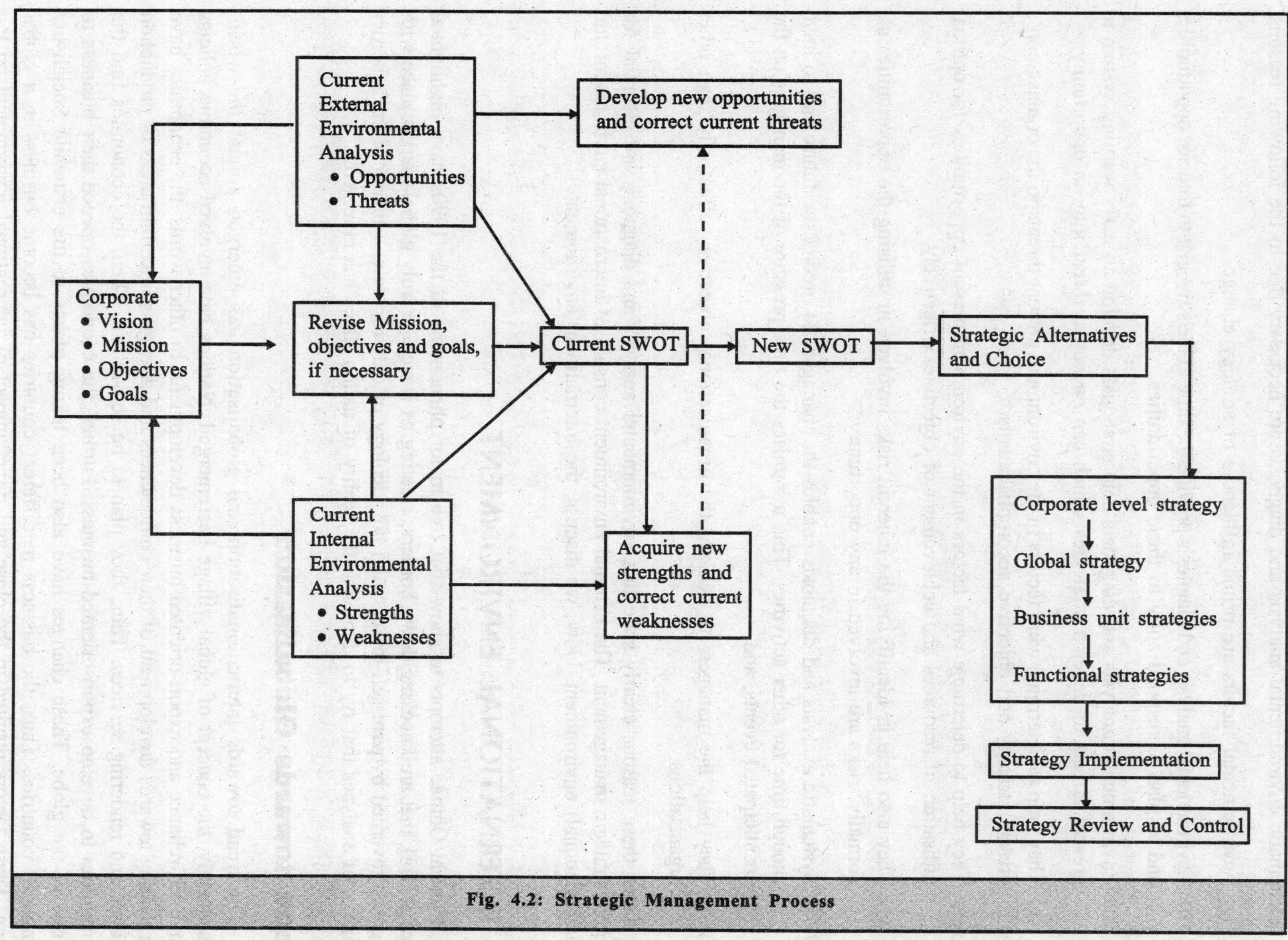

Fig. 4.2: Strategic Management Process

Systematic environmental analysis and diagnosis are necessary due to the following reasons:

(i) Environmental factors are prime influences of strategy change.

(ii) Environmental analysis and diagnosis provide the time to the strategist to forecast opportunities and to plan to respond aptly to these opportunities.

(iii) Environmental analysis and diagnosis help strategists develop an early warning system to prevent threats to develop strategies which can convert a threat into an opportunity.

(iv) They help to determine what factors in the environment present threats to the organisation's present strategy and objective accomplishments.

(v) They help to determine what factors in the environment present opportunities for optimal utilisation of resources and achievement of objectives effectively.

(vi) They also help in identifying the inherent risks involved in utilising the opportunities as, normally, risks are involved in any opportunity.

(vii) Systematic analysis and diagnosis enables the managers to predict the future and to have enough time for other activities. This minimises the time pressure of the managers on the unanticipated events, and

(viii) They help the managers to achieve the organisational objectives effectively than other organisations.

Thus, these reasons clearly state that environmental analysis and diagnosis are essential for effective strategic management. The external environment consists of international environment and general (national) environment. Now, we discuss, the international environment.

(B) INTERNATIONAL ENVIRONMENT

Kenichi Ohmae attempts to show that two major phenomena of the 1990s have highlighted forces at work that are knocking down borders, creating as it were, a truly global market place with its agents governed by pure self-interest and not ideology or culture. Now, a theory of cross-border affinities, of analyses that try to demolish the reality of nation-states has emerged.

Trend towards Globalisation

The trend towards internationalisation and globalisation has emerged around the world. Consequently, the concept of global village has emerged. Nations have evolved economic policies around self-reliance and export-oriented business development. In other words, the economies have been tending towards development of their competences and strengths in certain areas of production of goods and rendering services. Thus, they plan to be self-reliant. Then, the economies find the opportunities to develop export-oriented business. Further, the economies opened their business to the rest of the globe. These changes have also been taking places in the erstwhile Socialistic/ Communist countries. Thus, the business in different countries has become business in a global village. These factors resulted in the close and direct impact of international environment on the national business firms.

Nature of Globalisation: Globalisation refers to the process of integration of the world into one huge market. This type of unification calls for removal of all trade barriers among economies. At the organisational level, globalisation means: *(i)* the organisation commits itself heavily with several manufacturing locations around the world and offers products and/or services in several countries and *(ii)* ability to compete in domestic markets with foreign competitors.

A multinational company (MNC) or a transnational company (TNC) operates in more than one country, gains production, technology, marketing, financial, human resources and R&D advantages — in its costs and reputation over the domestic competitors.

Why do Companies go Global?

Companies go global due to the following reasons:

(i) Rapid shrinking of time and distance across the globe owing to the significant development of transportation and telecommunication facilities.

(ii) Inadequacy of and low purchasing ability in the domestic markets.

(iii) The short span of product life-cycle in the domestic market.

(iv) To have diversified portfolio of markets.

(v) To secure reliable and cheap inputs like raw material, finance and human resources.

(vi) Due to political stability in some countries and political disturbances in other countries.

(vii) To reduce high transportation costs.

(viii) To set up plants close to the raw material.

Companies go global due to: Rapid shrinking of time and distance across the globe owing to the significant development of transportation and telecommunication facilities; Inadequacy of and low purchasing ability in the domestic markets; The short span of product life-cycle in the domestic market.

Stages of Globalisation: There are four stages of globalisation as depicted in Exhibit 4.1. Companies at the first stage of globalisation have only passive dealings with foreign individuals and organisations. In the second stage, companies deal directly with their overseas interests. In the third stage, a company's international interests shape its overall make-up in an important way. In the final stage, the company sees its activities as essentially multinational as opposed to domestic.

Impact of International Environment on Domestic Business

Global environment consists of international political environment, policies of various governments, level of technology, social and cultural factors, level of economic development of different countries, level of industrial development, etc., has its impact on the business organisations of the domestic country. The impact is discussed hereunder.

(i) ***Configuring anywhere in the world:*** An MNC can choose the location of its plants or business units in different countries on the basis of availability of raw material, consumer markets, availability of cheap labour, etc. Thus, an MNC competes with the domestic company for inputs as well as selling the output.

(ii) ***Interlinked and interdependent economies:*** Economic policy of most of the nations is to develop the countries through inter-linkage and interdependence. Therefore, domestic industries also develop inter-linkage and interdependency with the foreign companies.

(iii) ***Minimisation of trade and tariff barriers:*** The recent trend towards globalisation in most of the nations in the world resulted in minimisation of trade and tariff barriers. Consequently, the protection provided to the home industry has been withdrawn. Therefore, the domestic industry is affected by the quality, price and convenience of the foreign products and services.

(iv) ***Effect on related industries and ancillary units:*** Globalisation may render many companies sick and defunct. This effect is more in case of ancillary industrial units and small scale industrial units compared to large scale industrial units. Globalisation of Indian economy in 1991 affected badly many ancillary industrial units.

(iv) ***Infrastructural resources and inputs at international prices:*** The prices of infrastructural resources like banking, transportation and telecommunications and inputs like raw materials and human resources adjust at international prices. In other words, prices of these factors, which were lower before globalisation would increase due to increase in demand for the same.

(vi) ***Increasing trend towards privatisation:*** Governments in many countries recently started withdrawing their capital from public sector industrial units and/or privatising these units after globalisation.

(vii) ***Entrepreneur and his unit have a central economic role:*** The trend of shifting the business from the bureaucrat to the entrepreneur has started consequent upon globalisation of business.

(viii) ***Mobility of skilled resources:*** The traditional factors of production *viz.*, land, labour, capital and organisation are no more immobile. Globalisation has resulted in the inflow of these factors into the potential developing countries.

(ix) ***Market side efficiency:*** Integration of global markets implies that costs, quality, processing time and terms of business become dominant competitive drivers.

(x) ***Formation of regional blocks:*** A final corollary to globalisation is the formation of trade blocks like North American Free Trade Area (USA, Canada and Mexico), European Economic Community and South Asian Preferential Trading Agreements. These regional blocks provide the opportunities to the business from within and creates threats to the business from other areas.

Now, we shall discuss the macro internal environmental factor. We start our discussion with social and cultural factors.

(C) SOCIAL AND CULTURAL ENVIRONMENT

Social and cultural factors in various countries of the globe affect business. These factors include attitude of the people to work, attitude to wealth, family, marriage, religion, education, ethics, human relations, social responsibilities, etc.

Cultural Attitude and Business

Dressing habits, living styles, eating habits and other consumption patterns, priority of needs are dictated/ influenced by culture of the land.

Dressing habits, living styles, eating habits and other consumption patterns, priority of needs are dictated/influenced by culture of the land. Some Chinese and most of the Indians do not consume beef. Thailand Chinese believe that consumption of beef is improper and Indian (particularly Hindus) believe that eating beef is a sin as they believe cow is sacred *(Kamadhenu)*. The eating habits vary widely. Chinese eat fish stomachs and bird's nest soup, Japanese eat uncooked sea food, Iraqis eat dried, salted locusts and snakes while drinking. The French eat snails, Americans and Europeans eat mostly non-vegetarian food. Indian eat mostly vegetarian food. It was surprising to the rest of the world to know that there were pure vegetarians in India. However, the foreign culture regarding food has been adapted very openly. *Indian food items like Chapati, Masala dosa and Hyderabadi biryani* have become popular in Europe and the USA whereas pizzas have become popular in India (see Box 4.1). In fact, the culture around the world has been evolving as global culture.

BOX 4.1: IN INDIA, PIZZAS ARE NOW THE FLAVOUR OF THE SEASON

Chicken tikka masala may be ruling the roost in Britain, but in curry country – India – pizzas are the flavour of the month. Take, for example, Neelam Mehta. Whenever she hears the question "What's for dinner, mum?" after she comes home from her Delhi office, her answer is often the same: "Pizza". "It's the easiest thing to do. Just pick-up the phone and order. I don't have to sweat it out in the kitchen at the end of the day," said Mehta, an Indian exporter with two teenage sons. Ever since India threw open its economic doors in the early 1990, a host of global pizza chains including Pizza Hut, run by Yum! Brands Inc., and Domino's Pizza have been fighting for a slice of the country's growing pizza market.

Source: Deccan Chronicle, July 22, 2003,

Similarly, dressing habits also vary from country to country based on their culture. We observe different dressing styles of the West, Middle East, India, Pacific, etc. Wearing '*saree*' by Indian women is influenced by the culture which in turn is influenced by the climate. However the *saree* culture in India is slowly decreasing with increase in women becoming more career oriented. Similarly, wearing 'burka/parda' by the women of the Middle East is another example of the influence of culture on the dressing habit.

Guidelines for the businessmen when they launch business in foreign countries: *(a)* resist the tendency to conduct business immediately on landing, and at all times, *(b)* offer favours as a business tool to generate allies, *(c)* contact, cultivate and conduct field work among at least one sample clientele to serve as an initial testing centre for the firm's product, *(d)* introduce the product line into the sample group by local firms of cause-related marketing and *(e)* extend product acceptance beyond the sample clientele into related market segments. Businessmen should follow these guidelines in order to prevent possible failures (See Box 4.2).

BOX 4.2: DISNEY IN FRANCE: CULTURAL ISSUES

Disney with its success in park business and entertaining children in USA entered Japan in 1983 and became successful there too so they decided to enter the French market too in 1986 owing to location advantage of Paris and availability of subsidies and incentives by French Government. However, Disney had problems negotiating with the French Government and faced unwillingness of French people to accept Disney. Despite these problems, Disney opened the park in 1992 summer. Soon after the opening, French farmers drove their tractors and blocked the entrance. Later, there were a number of operational disasters like Disney's policy of serving no alcohol, serving less quantity of breakfast, lunch timings, lack of teamwork for the employees of Disney of Paris. These problems resulted in a cumulative loss of $2 billion by the end of 1994.

Source: Adapted from Charles W.L. Hill, "International Business",: Tata McGraw-Hill, New Delhi, 2003, pp. 119-12.

Behavioural Factors Affecting Business

Cultural factors influence human behaviour. Cultural difference in various countries result in variation in human behaviour, consumer behaviour and behaviour of other stakeholders. Variation in behaviour can be ascertained through the social stratification of a country. Business should consider the behavioural patterns of social groups in hiring, marketing and in selecting suppliers of inputs and market intermediaries. Behavioural patterns can be studied based on ascribed group membership and acquired group memberships. Ascribed group membership is based on genders, age, family, caste, community, ethnic, racial and nation of origin. Acquired group membership is based on religion, political affiliation, professional and social associations. These memberships influence human behaviour of a society.

Behaviour based on Group Membership

Certain societies like USA reward people based on performance while other societies like Malaysia reward people based on ethnic group in addition to performance. Attitude towards female employment vary from country to country. Egalitarian societies do not discriminate employment of people based on sex whereas Arabian countries discourage females from seeking employment. Family membership is paramount rather than individual's achievements or traits – in certain societies like India, China and Southern Italy.

Impact of Culture on Consumer Behaviour

Culture influences the behaviour of the consumer though valid generalisations have not yet been developed. Montrose, Sommers and Jerome Kernan have made a beginning in this direction. They identify the value orientations that underline market behaviour as falling in six categories:

(1) Egalitarian or elitist; *(2)* prone to lay stress on accomplishment or on inherited attributes; *(3)* expected material or non-material rewards; *(4)* evaluating individuals or products in terms of objective norms or of subjective standards; *(5)* focused on the distinctiveness of the parts (intensiveness); and *(6)* oriented towards personal rather than toward group's gain. The U.S. consumer tends to have the attributes described by the first term in each pair. British attitudes tend to fall on the opposite side. A number of examples illustrate the significance of these differences.

"When performance orientation is coupled with a predisposition to be intensive - *i.e.*, to perceive many separate and distinct needs to be acted upon as well as a variety of ways in which these needs can be served — the probability of accepting new contingencies as real is greater than when an extensive value orientation prevails. Americans see more separate and distinct activities plus more separate and distinct products which can be used in their performance than do Canadians, Australians or Britons. Such a disposition supports their market for gadgets, the great array of household appliances accessories" (See Box 4.3).

BOX 4.3: CULTURE-BASED MARKET SEGMENTATION

A medium-sized Swedish engineering company manufactured fire-fighting equipment, but was incurring losses. In 1983 a new marketing director was appointed. After four years of work, turnover rose from £3 million to £10 billion and profitability was restored, mainly on the basis of a complete reappraisal of markets and marketing policy.

The marketing director found that the company had been dealing with about 100 country markets, but many produced orders only in small quantities, and these too intermittently. In total, the orders were a surprisingly small proportion of the turnover, but were just as costly and time-consuming to service as orders from the larger, steadier markets.

A careful process of selection showed that if the company concentrated more extensively on 50 markets, its chances of progress would improve, and of these 50, some 10 which looked the most promising were selected for constant and increasing attention; for example, visits were planned with increasing frequency. The company found that this core of key markets provided an almost ideal ratio, because only five or six countries accounted for 75 per cent of trade. A contraction of business in those few countries could prove very harmful. Recognising important national differences among the 10 key markets, with local issues and customer contracts, by reducing the total number of markets, but retaining those with significant trade, the company improved its profit performance.

Source: Edgar P. Hibbert, International Business, p.80.

Ageing Populations

Population ageing is constituted by a shift in the distribution of a country's population towards greater ages. An increase in the population's mean or median age, means a decline in the fraction of the population composed of children, or a rise in the fraction of elderly people.

Ageing population has seen an increase in many advanced countries as well as in some developing countries where advanced medical and health facilities are available. In addition, the baby-boom generation (people born in the 20-year period after World War II) in some countries like USA, UK and Australia continues to age. Added to this, the reduced birth rates in advanced countries and some developing countries like India and China has contributed to the ageing population.

An increase in the population's mean or median age, means a decline in the fraction of the population composed of children, or a rise in the fraction of elderly people.

Population ageing is a highly generalised process; it is most advanced in the most highly developed countries. Among the countries currently classified by the United Nations as more developed (with a population of 1.2 billion in 2005), the median age of the population rose from 29.0 years in 1950 to 37.3 in 2000 and it is estimated to rise to 45.5 by 2050. The corresponding figures for the world as a whole were 23.9 years for 1950, 26.8 for 2000 and 37.8 for 2050. Japan is one of fastest ageing countries in the world. There will be 9.3 people under the age of 20 for every person older than 65 by 2025. The ageing population would result in increased demand for medical care, pharmaceutical products and social security and decline in the demand for existing products like motor cycles, luxury cars and luxurious white goods.

Career Orientation of Women

Increase in career orientation of women particularly after globalisation has provided wider opportunities for fast foods and ready-made food industry, white goods, luxurious housing, automobile and the like. This trend is significant in India, China, Malaysia and Middle-East countries.

IN SUMMARY THE FOLLOWING FACTORS ARE TO BE SCANNED TO ASSESS THE SOCIAL AND CULTURAL ENVIRONMENT:

Demographic factors such as:

- population size and distribution
- age distribution
- education levels
- income levels
- ethnic origins
- religious affiliations
- gender distribution

Attitudes towards:

- materialism, capitalism, free enterprise
- individualism, role of family, role of government, collectivism
- role of church and religion
- consumerism
- environmentalism
- importance of work, pride of accomplishment

Cultural structures including:

- diet and nutrition
- housing conditions
- dressing habits
- work habits and work-culture
- punctuality

Source: Modified Version from: http://en.wikipedia.org/wiki/Environmental_scanning

(D) TECHNOLOGICAL ENVIRONMENT

Technological changes enabled business to take up the shape of transnational business through the concept of global business. International business, in fact, gained significance due to the amazing advancements in technology.

Technological environment has significant and direct influence on business in general and international business in particular. Technology is application of knowledge. J.K. Galbraith defines technology as "a systematic application of scientific or other organised knowledge to particular tasks." Technology advanced phenomenally during the past 50 years.

Technology changes are taking place at a faster rate. In fact, it brings changes in the society, economy and politics. Technology affects all walks of life, all countries and the entire globe. As stated by Alvin Toffler, "Technology feeds on itself. Technology makes more technology possible." Thus, technology is self-reinforcing. Technology brings the globe closer. Technology flows from the advanced countries to the developing world through the multinational corporations (MNCs), joint ventures, technological alliances, licensing and franchising.

Influence of Technology

Technology influences the way we live, we cook (electric rice cooker), we drink water (filtered and mineral water), communicate (telephone, fax, e-mail, videoconferencing, e-mail chatting, etc.), prepare for a class or a case, design or read a newspaper through the Internet, get marriage alliances (through the Internet), (computer aided), produce, sells (e-commerce), satellite networks electronic fund transfers, lasers, fibre optics, unmanned factories, miracle drugs, new diagnostic methods, new studies in technology like eye scanning for the password and using the remote for car will be changing our lives.

Technology and International Competition

Nations develop economically when they translate science into useful technology and in turn create wealth from innovations. Innovation is the useful adaptation of science or knowledge including invention of new products or processes. Invention is creation of entirely new things. A few companies or people invent but many companies adapt scientific knowledge to generate wealth by application and commercialisation.

Major inventions or discoveries do not remain private property for longer period. The inventions or innovation process and global competitiveness are two determinants of a nation's wealth. Japan concentrates on process innovation in automobiles, steel, telecommunication and microelectronics. Germany concentrates on innovations in chemicals, pharmaceuticals, automotive engineering, medical instruments and machine tools. Italy concentrates on innovations in textiles and leathers.

Scanning of Technological Environment

The level of technology is not the same in all the countries. Advanced countries enjoy the fruits of the latest technology while the developing nations face the consequences of obsolete or outdated technology. Therefore, MNCs have to understand technology, analyse it before entering the foreign markets. MNCs have to procure technological environmental information regarding:

- The level of technology of the industry in the home country.
- The level of technology of the industry in the proposed host country.
- Compatibility of the home country's technology with the host country's technology.

- If technology is not compatible, then select the appropriate technology for the host country, if possible. If not, select the host country's technology that suits the home country's technology.
- Study the compatibility of the technology to the culture of the host country including tastes and preferences of the host country's customers.
- Study the host country's Government policies regarding technology transfer.
- Study the modes of technology transfer like joint ventures, technological alliances, etc.
- Study the impact of technology on the environment of the home country including the laws pertaining to environmental pollution.

Technology and Globalisation

The Industrial Revolution resulted in large-scale production. The recent technological revolution took it further to the production of high quality products at lower costs. This forced the domestic companies to enter foreign countries in order to find markets for their products. Thus, technology is one of the important causes for globalisation.

Information Technology and Globalisation

As indicated earlier, information technology redefined the global business through developments like Internet, websites, e-mail, cyberspace, information super highways, Computer Aided Design (CAD), Computer Aided Production (CAP) and online transactions brought significant development in the global business. These facilities, according to M.J. Xavier, help the global companies in:

- Reducing the size of inventories
- Reducing delivery time
- Reducing unproductive waiting time
- Reducing the incidents of stock-outs and lost sales
- Responding to market changes at a faster rate
- Reducing rush orders
- Cutting down over production
- Reducing unnecessary movements of forwarding and back-tracking
- Reducing paper work and wasteful processes
- Planning production levels accurately
- Reducing/avoiding physical movement of employees, suppliers and customers.

MNCs have to understand and analyse more of economic environment of the foreign countries for strategy formulation.

Hence, we now discuss the economic environmental factors of the global countries.

IN SUMMARY THE FOLLOWING TECHNOLOGICAL FACTORS NEED TO BE ASSESSED:

- Efficiency of infrastructure, including: roads, ports, airports, rolling stock, hospitals, education, healthcare, communication, etc.
- Industrial productivity
- New manufacturing processes
- New products and services of competitors
- New products and services of supply chain partners
- Any new technology that could impact the company
- Cost and accessibility of electrical power

Source: Adapted from: http://en.wikipedia.org/wiki/Environmental_scanning

(E) ECONOMIC ENVIRONMENT

The economic environment of various countries directly influences international business. In fact, international economic environment and global business interact with each other. Global economy has undergone a sea change during the last 50 years. The change revolutionary has been after 1990. The results of these changes are emergence of global markets, establishment of World Trade Organisation, emergence of global business houses and global competitors rather than local competitors.

Economic Systems

There are three types of economic systems, *viz.*, Capitalism, Communism and mixed. Economic systems are based on resource allocation in the system.

Economic systems is an organisation of institutions established to satisfy human needs/wants. There are three types of economic systems, *viz.*, Capitalism, Communism and mixed. Economic systems are based on resource allocation in the system. They are market allocation in case of capitalistic, command/central allocation in case of communist and mixed allocations in case of the (Key questions to scan technological environment are given in Exhibit 4.1).

Exhibit 4.1: Key Questions of Technological Environment 

- What are the technologies within the corporation?
- Which technologies are utilised in the firm's business? Products? Components and Parts?
- How critical is each technology to each of these products and business?
- Which of these technologies are shared among different products and businesses?
- Which technologies are contained in purchased parts and materials?
- Which of these external technologies might become critical and why? Will they remain available outside the firm?
- What was the evolution of these technologies over time? In which companies were these technological changes initiated?
- What is the likely evolution of these technologies in the future?
- What have been the firm's investments in critical technologies over time?

- What were the investments and investment patterns of its leading technological competitors? Historical? Planned?
- What has been the investment in the product and in the process side of these technologies? For the firm and for its competitors? Design? Production? Implementation and service?
- What is the subjective ranking of different firms in each of these technologies?
- What are the firm's business and products?
- What is the cost and value-added structure of these parts, components, products, and businesses?
- What has been the historical, financial and strategic performance of the business, and what are the implications of these trends? In terms of cash generation and earnings characteristics? Investment requirements? Growth? Market position and market share?
- What are the applications of the firm's technologies?
- In which technologies applications does the firm currently participate and why? In which does the firm not participate and why?
- How attractive is each of these applications as an investment opportunity in terms of its market growth, its potential for profit improvement, and/or its potential for increasing technological leadership?
  - — Underlying growth characteristics?
  - — Evolution of customer needs and requirements?
  - — Current and emerging market segments; segment growth rates?
  - — Competitive positioning and likely strategies of key competitors?
- How critical are the firm's technologies to each of these applications?
- What other technologies are critical to the external applications?
- How do the technologies differ in each of these applications?
- What other technologies are critical to the external applications?
- What are the competing technologies in each application? What are the determinants of substitution dynamics?
- What is and will be the degree of technological change in each of these technologies?
- What are the applications that the firm should consider entering?
- What should be the priorities of technological resource investment?
- What technological resources are required for the firm to achieve its current business objectives?
- What should be the level and rate of corporate technology investments?
- Which technological investments should be curtailed or eliminated?
- What additional technologies will be required in order to achieve the current corporate business objectives?
- What are the implications of technologies and business portfolios for corporate strategy?

Source: Fred R. David, op. cit., pp. 115-117.

mixed economic system. In fact, there are no example of pure Capitalistic or Communist economics. All actual systems are mixed economic systems of varied degrees of market allocations and command allocations.

Capitalistic Economic System: Under this system, customer allocates resources. Customers' choice for product/services decide what will be produced by whom. This economic system provides for economic democracy, thus giving the customer, his choice for products/services.

Mixed Economic System: Under this economic system, major factors of production and distribution are owned, managed and controlled by the state. The purpose is to provide the benefits to the public sector, agrarian reforms, control over private wealth, regulation of private investment and national self-reliance.

The trend that is taking place in the globe today is the move towards privatisation, *i.e.,* move towards market allocation. U.K. France, Holland and India, *for example,* have reduced their command sector after 1990.

Communistic Economic System : In this economic system, private property and property rights to income are abolished. The State owns all the factors of production and distribution. It provides less scope for foreign investment and business (See Box 4.4).

BOX 4.4: COMMUNISM AND McDONALD'S

After a long negotiations between McDonald's and Soviet officials, the former entered Russian market in 1990. Moscow city council was a partner of McDonald's in the Russian Joint Venture. But McDonald's faced severe shortages in supply of building materials to build the restaurant as these requirements were not included in the central plan. The company was not provided with sufficient supply of wheat flour, sugar, mustard either due to non-inclusion in the central plan or due to inability of Soviet manufacturers to deviate from their standard output or due to the strict control that Soviet manufacturers should sell to the Soviet companies. Another problem was that certain products like iceberg lettuce, pickled cucumbers and the Russet Burbank potatoes used for McDonald's French fries were not produced or consumed in Russia. McDonald's educated Soviet farmers and cattle ranchers on how to grow and raise the products it needed.

McDonald's did not face any problem in respect to employees and customers and advertising. Russian television covered the event; it became almost impossible to accommodate the customers for the first time in January 1990 even though the Moscow's restaurant was biggest in the world. Customers favoured it though it was five times costlier than the normal local meal. Despite the crisis in 1998, McDonald's grew in Russia and had 73 stores by the end of 2001. McDonald's success in Russia enabled it to enter China and also become successful there.

Source: Adapted from John. D. Daniels, *et.al.*, '*International Business*', Pearson, Singapore, 2004, pp. 103-104.

Communism collapsed in the former USSR. Similarly, Communism collapsed in most of the African countries. This was mostly due to the changes towards privatisation. The degree of command allocation has been declining even in China. Cuba is an example of the last remaining predominantly Communist country. However, foreign, business faces a variety of problems in China (see Box 4.5).

BOX 4.5: PROBLEMS OF MICROSOFT IN CHINA

Microsoft entered China and planned to increased its sales to $100 million in 2000 from nil in 1994. Then Microsoft faced the problem of rampant piracy in China. It was estimated that about 90% of the software used in China was pirated. Even Government used pirated software. More so, China is an exporter of counterfeit software. China's judiciary also uses pirated software. Microsoft officials pressed Chinese officials to conduct raids but resulted in only collecting negligible penalties from those using pirated version even. It over backfired in some cases.

Microsoft then used the strategy of cutting the prices by 200 per cent and priced the software between US$ 100 to 200. But the pirated versions were sold at only US$ 5 to 20. So, Microsoft tried lobbying the US government to impress upon the Government of China to prohibit the use of pirated versions. At this time, China was trying to become a member of World Trade Organisation. Therefore, China accepted to protect the intellectual property rights of many US firms including Microsoft. US government signed for China's membership in World Trade Organisation in September 2000. US, however, lost its control over China in protecting intellectual property rights after signing for the China's membership in WTO.

Further, Chinese government declared that US could access the Chinese information system and network through Microsoft software. Chinese government encouraged the development of Chinese language version of the Linux operating system as an alternative to Chinese language version of Windows 2000.

Source: Adapted from Charles W.L.Hill, International Business. Tata McGraw Hill, 2003, pp.81-92

Countries classified by Income

The World Bank categorised economics into one of the following groups according to the per capita gross national income in 1999.

Low Income countries	US$ 755 or less
Lower Middle Income countries	US$ 756 to US$ 2,995
Upper Middle Income countries	US$ 2996 to US$ 9,265
Higher Income countries	US$ 9,266 or more

Macroeconomic Issues Affecting Business Decisions

Various macroeconomic issues like economic growth, inflation, balance of payments and transition to market economics affect business decisions.

(1) Economic Growth: The high economic growth rate of the countries lift the quality of life of their citizens in addition to providing an opportunity of expanding market share to international business firms. The stagnation or decline in economic growth of countries result in intense competition among the companies to retain their market share and/or to increase their market shares. The stagnation in global economy in 2001 and 2002 led to aggressive competition among the international business firms.

Managers of the multinational companies are interested in knowing the future economic growth rates of various countries in order to select the markets either to enter or concentrate or to commit more resources to the market. According to the Organisation of Economic Cooperation and Development (OECD), global economic recession in 2001 was highest in the last 20 years and European Union started recovering after this recession at a faster rate than that of Japan. However, China and India recorded continuous growth rates of around 7 per cent and 6 per cent respectively. Manager of multinational companies should know the growth rates of different countries on a continuous basis in order to avert the possible failures and enhance their market shares.

(2) Inflation: Inflation is another important factor that affects the market share of international business firms. Inflation affects rates, as the demand for money is high due to higher prices. Banks increase interest rates in order to attract deposits and governments raise interest rates with a view to combat inflation. Inflation also affects exchange rate of the domestic currency in terms of various foreign currencies. Inflation weakens the domestic currency and thereby makes exports dear and imports cheap.

Inflation forces people to spend their incomes immediately as happened in Brazil in the early 1990s when the inflation was rising at the rate of 1 per cent per day. High inflation affects exporting firms adversely and importing firms favourably. The rate of inflation has been declining since 1990. It came down from 4 per cent in early 1990s to 2.5 per cent in 2000 in advanced countries. International business managers have to continuously monitor inflation rates in order to manage cash flows in such a way that the adverse affects of inflation are kept at a minimum as managed by Pizza Hut in Brazil during 1990s.

(3) Balance of payments: Balance of payments position of a country is an outcome of international business and also affects the future of the international business. Export and import trade in goods and services affects current account position and flow of capital affects the capital account position. Excessive imports of goods, services and capital over exports result in negative balance of payments. Continuous negative balance of payments will lead to currency instability and control over imports and incentives to boost exports.

Excessive imports over exports also lead to external debt from foreign countries and international financial agencies. Heavily indebted countries in the world are Brazil ($238.0 billion), Mexico ($150.3 billion), China ($149.8 billion), Argentina ($146.2 billion) and Indonesia ($150.3 billion). Most of these countries have GDP higher than the external debt. Many African countries have external debt in excess of GDP. Many foreign investors pumped money into Argentina as the currency was pegged to U.S. dollar even when the economy was in recession in 1996. Argentina kept spending heavily and this resulted in Argentina's default to the tune of US $155 billion in external debt – the largest default by any country in history.

Managers of multinational companies should monitor the balance payments positions of the countries where they operate in order to take preventive measures rather than becoming a part of the debt trap or its adverse effects as happened in the Asian crisis.

(4) Economic Transition: Many former Communist/command economies and mixed economies are undergoing transition to market economies due to the failure of central planning and public sector to generate economic development. The collapse of the former USSR and the breaking of Berlin wall and foreign exchange crisis in India in 1991 and opening up of China towards extensive international trade paved the way for increased globalisation of business. This process enhanced the interest of the multinational companies in carrying out business in many parts of the world and conversion of many national companies in various countries into multinational companies.

Economic Transition includes:

- Liberalising economic activities, prices and market operations along with reallocating resources to their most efficient use.
- Dispensing with licensing system and regulated markets.
- Developing indirect, market-oriented instruments for macro-economic stabilisation.
- Achieving effective enterprise management and economic efficiency usually through privatisation.
- Imposing hard budget constraints which provide incentive to improve efficiency.
- Creation and establishment of institutional legal framework to secure property rights, the rule of law and transparent market entry regulations.

As indicated earlier, many countries initiated transformation from different economic systems like Communism/Socialism and mixed economies to market economies and they are in different stages of the transformation process. Most of these countries came across with various disabling factors such as:

- Opposition to liberalisation, privatisation and globalisation due to the vested interests of various groups and political parties.
- Ineffective enforcement of laws, rules and regulations due to the underground and virtual economy.
- Prevalence of corruption and illegal activities.
- Freezing of market transformation resulted in financial instability, low growth or reverse growth of the economy.

Many countries that faced these problems during the initial stages of transformation eventually overcame these problems. And some of the countries are in the process of overcoming these problems. Countries those overcame these problems experience the following environment or situation factors in the transformation process.

- Spread of benefits of market economy.
- Strong fiscal position in terms of increase in government income.
- Increase in confidence in banks and other financial institutions.
- Growth in industrialisation, employment and output.
- Increase in credibility and financial position of the government.
- Improvement in government's financial ability to finance and administer social safety net.
- Early recovery and adjustment to the market economic situations.
- Steady progress towards open and liberal markets.
- Development of market-friendly environment.
- Growth in foreign and domestic investment, further industrialisation, increase in employment, output, living standards and quality of life of the people.

Opportunity to MNCs

The process of liberalisation and transition provided significant opportunities to the multinational corporations to enter most of the countries of the world either by locating their manufacturing facilities or extending their markets or both. Privatisation helps multinational companies to acquire the pubic sector companies in the liberalised economies. Thus, MNCs are the immediate and greatest beneficiaries of liberalisation, privatisation and globalisation of world economies.

Transition Process

Transition processes vary from country to country. Russia changed both economic and political systems simultaneously. As such, the country faced severe consequences during its early stage of the process.

Transition processes vary from country to country. Russia changed both economic and political systems simultaneously. As such, the country faced severe consequences during its early stage of the process. Now, the country is comparatively comfortable in the transition process as the administrative constraints disappeared. In contrast, China opted for only economic transformation by strongly holding its political system of totalitarianism. China's economic growth rate is higher than that of other countries. India is the largest democracy in the world and it opted for economic transformation from mixed economy to market economy. India's economic growth rate is also significant compared to that of many countries in the world, though; it is a little bit less than that of China.

Economic vs Social Issues in Transition

Though the transition has set trends for economic growth of at least some countries and the economic future of other countries seems to be bright, the contribution of transition to the social issues, widening gap between rich and poor, poverty, child care, medical facilities and HIV/AIDS would be the future challenges to the world.

These problems would be paramount in lower-income countries in general and lower-income African countries in particular unless certain measures are taken immediately; it would affect the cause of humanity unable to reap the economic benefits of transition to market economy.

Indian Economic Environment

There are three distinct economic philosophies, *viz.,* Capitalism, Socialism and Communism. Economic environment refers to all those economic factors which have a bearing on the functioning of a business. Economic environment and business are mutually interdependent. In fact, the dependence of the business on the economic environment is more. The important economic factors that constitute the economic environment are:

(a) Growth strategy

(b) Economic system

(c) Economic planning

(d) Industry

(e) Agriculture

(f) Infrastructure

(g) Financial and fiscal sectors

(h) Removal of regional imbalances

(i) Price and distribution controls

(j) Economic reforms

(k) Population

(l) Per capita and national income.

India is one of the major economies in the world. India has developed her economy in different areas. The important facets of Indian economic environment (Fig. 4.3) are discussed hereunder:

(a) **Industrial Policy:** Industrial policy is the most important document which indicates the relationship between the government and business. The Industrial Policy Resolution previously laid emphasis on industrial development through the development of public sector. Industrial policy, 1991 was a major departure from the earlier policies. The significant objectives of this policy were: Self reliance, to build on the many-sided gains already made, removing regulatory system and other weaknesses, link the Indian economy to the global markets so that we acquire the ability to pay for imports, and to make us less dependent on aid, increasing competitiveness of industries for the benefit of the common man and ensuring running of public sector undertakings on business lines and to reduce their losses.

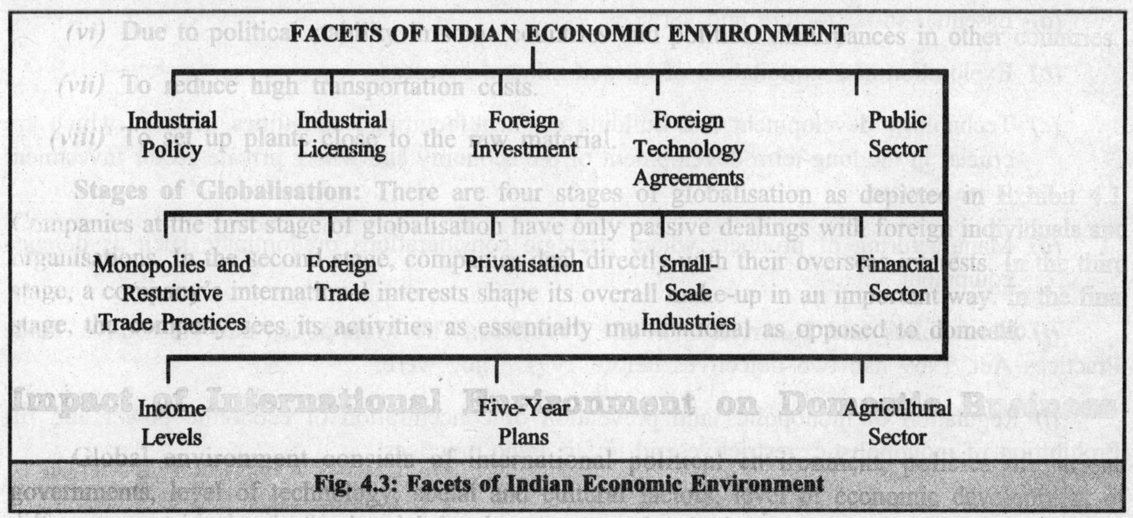

Fig. 4.3: Facets of Indian Economic Environment

(b) **Industrial Licensing:** Abolition of industrial licensing for many projects except those specified (13 in number), irrespective of levels of investment is worthwhile. These specified industries will continue to be subject to compulsory licensing for reasons related to security, strategic concerns, social reasons, problems related to safety, overriding environmental issues, manufacturing of products of hazardous nature and articles of elitist consumption.

(c) **Foreign Investment:** It has been decided to provide approval for direct foreign investment upto 51 per cent foreign equity in high priority industries requiring large investments and advanced technology. There shall be no hurdles in this process. This group of industries is generally known as the "Appendix-I Industries" and are areas in which FEMA companies have already been allowed to invest on a discretionary basis.

(d) **Foreign Technology Agreements:** Government of India now, provides automatic approval for technology agreements related to high priority industries within specified parameters, in order to inject the desired level of technological dynamism in Indian industry. Other industries can also avail similar facilities, if the agreements do not require free foreign exchange. Indian entrepreneurs can negotiate the terms of technology transfer. The hiring of foreign technicians and foreign testing of indigenously developed technologies do not, now, require prior clearance.

(e) **Public Sector:** The objective of the government before opening the Indian economy to the rest of the globe had been to establish socialistic pattern of society. This objective made the

government to give top priority for public sector to develop industrial sector in the country. Public sector played a dominant role by establishing industries in the areas of public utilities, infrastructure, development banks, capital goods industries, core and key industries and industries requiring huge capital resources.

In fact the government nationalised commercial banks, insurance industry and coal mines to achieve its objectives. Public sector was made responsible to achieve the objectives of the government like creation of employment opportunities, balanced regional development, providing infrastructural facilities and acting as a model employer. Public sector has played a crucial role in the country in the direction of these objectives. But, the public sector, in view of its conflicting dual roles of profit making and service rendering, could not do justice to any of these two objectives. Serious problems observed were: insufficient growth of productivity, poor project management, overmanning, absence of continuous technological up-gradation, inadequate attention to R&D and human resource development. These factors led to the disinvestment and privatisation of public sector in addition to liberalisation of the economy.

The most likely areas for public sector, in the future will be as follows:

(a) Essential infrastructure and services.

(b) Exploration and exploitation of oil and mineral resources.

(c) Technology development and building of manufacturing capabilities in areas which are crucial in the long-term development of the economy and where private sector investment is inadequate.

(d) Manufacturing of products where strategic considerations predominate such as defence equipment.

***(f)* Monopolies and Restrictive Trade Practices:** The Monopolies and Restrictive Trade Practices Act, 1969 had two objectives before 1991. They were:

(i) Regulation of monopolies and prevention of concentration of economic power and *(ii)* Prohibition of monopolistic, restrictive and unfair trade practices.

The economic liberalisation of 1991, aimed at achieving high productivity, competitive advantage to the domestic industry in the international market and economies of scale led to the amendment of the Act in 1991. The objectives of the amended Act are:

(i) Controlling monopolistic trade practices, and

(ii) Regulating restrictive and unfair trade practices.

***(g)* Foreign Trade:** It was widely recognised during the 1990s that the internationalisation of business, export-oriented industrial growth and self-reliance in the development of competencies were the highly essential factors for rapid economic development of the developing countries. Some countries believe in import substitution whilst majority of the countries believe in mutual dependence of the world nations for production and consumption. India recognised the significance of export and import trade for its development. This was quite evident in the new economic policy of 1991.

***(h)* Privatisation:** The word privatisation has been receiving much attention in business and government all over the world. Privatisation techniques have already been tried in countries like Great Britain, China, U.S.A., Turkey, Brazil, Eritrea, Mexico and Japan. The process of privatisation has already been started in India through disinvestment of government's shareholdings in public sector. The process of privatisation should be accelerated for effective functioning of public sector and rapid industrial growth. In fact, Government of India recognised the need for privatisation for rapid and efficient industrial growth.

(i) **Small Scale Industries:** It was argued that 'small is beautiful.' It was further believed that small is efficient, innovative and productive. Further, government viewed that small scale sector solves the problems of the country like unemployment, and regional imbalance. Consequently, the government provided huge financial and non-financial facilities to this sector. But the government realised that this sector failed to a greater extent in playing its role and is a misfit in the market economies. Exhibit 4.2 shows the SWOT analysis of this sector. It is clear from this exhibit that the protection and assistance of the government to this sector is reduced at least in the magnitude, if not in direction.

(j) **Financial Sector:** The financial sector consists of commercial banks, development banks, mutual funds, unorganised financial sector institutions, custodial service institutions, stock exchanges, underwriting and capital issue houses. The economic liberalisation brought significant changes in financial sector. The important ones among them are:

— Permission for Non-Resident Indians (NRIs) to enter the Indian stock market;

— Establishment of the Securities and Exchange Board of India;

— Setting up of the Investment Information and Credit Rating Agency of India (IICRA) and

— Establishment of Credit Rating Information Services of India Ltd. (CRISIL).

Exhibit 4.2: Small Sector: The SWOT Analysis

Strengths	◆ Flexibility in production volumes and design changes
	◆ Faster decision-making
	◆ Lower labour costs
	◆ Lower overheads
Weaknesses	◆ Often lack of management, marketing or financial skills
	◆ Technological obsolescence
	◆ Poor financing
	◆ Lack of marketing strength
Opportunities	◆ Large companies are outsourcing more to reduce their own costs
	◆ Promising export markets
	◆ Higher investment limits mean companies can expand and modernise
	◆ Big companies can take a larger equity stake in small ones
Threats	◆ With concessions disappearing, inefficient units will die
	◆ With de-reservation, competition will come from large companies
	◆ With import liberalisation, competition will come from MNCs and cheap inputs
	◆ Smaller, less aggressive companies will suffer.

(*Source:* Business India, June 15, 1995) quoted in K. Aswathappa, *op. cit.*, p. 357.

(k) **Infrastructure:** The infrastructural facilities improved significantly in India. But, India ranks very poorly in global competitiveness. This is a not welcome sign to invite foreign investment in a big way.

(l) **Income Levels:** The high growth rate of income indicates the level of economic development of the country. National income in India increased from Rs. 1,10,685 crores in 1980-81 to Rs. 2,00,265 crores in 1993-94. The per capita income increased from Rs. 1,630 in 1980-81 to Rs. 2,255 in 1993-94. The slow growth of per capita income compared to that of national income is due to higher growth rate of population.

(m) **Five-Year Plans:** Five-year plans were introduced from 1951-52 with a view to develop the economy on planned lines. The targets regarding national income were achieved during the First,

Sixth and Seventh Five-Year Plans. Agricultural sector, industrial sector and service sectors were developed during the different five year plans.

***(n)* Agricultural Sector:** Agricultural sector is a major component of our economic environment. The agricultural sector has been developed by means of green revolution and white revolution. Agricultural productivity ranks second in rice and wheat in the world. India achieved self sufficiency in agricultural output. This development paved the way for the development of agro-based industries.

***(o)* Consumers:** Inflation and economic flux causes sweeping changes in consumer buying patterns. As consumers perceive that more money is buying them less, many people are adopting the much publicised "buy now, save later' motto at the expense of future security.

Economic factors have a direct impact on the potential attractiveness of various company strategies. The various important economic variables that often represent opportunities and threats for companies include: monetary policy of the Reserve Bank of India, share prices, interest rates, tax rates and policies, employment trends, price variations, etc. They are presented in Exhibit 4.3.

Exhibit 4.3: Key Economic Variables that often Represent Opportunities and Threats for Companies

— Shift to a service economy in India
— Level of development of commercial banks
— Level of growth of development banks
— Level of availability of credit
— Saving philosophy and trends
— Level of disposable income
— Propensity of people to spend
— Interest rates
— Inflation rates
— Economies of scale
— Money market rates
— Government budgets
— Gross National Product trends
— Consumption patterns
— Unemployment trends
— Worker Productivity Levels
— Value of Rupee in terms of other currencies
— Stock market trends
— Foreign countries' economic conditions
— Import/Export factors
— Demand shifts for different categories of goods and services
— Income differences by region and consumer groups
— Price fluctuations
— Monetary policies
— Fiscal policies and tax policies and rates
— Industrial and licensing policies
— Agricultural policies
— Labour policies
— Policies of various trading blocks like SAARC, EEC, NAFTA
— Policies towards joint ventures

Source: Modified version Fred R. David, *op. cit.* p. 106.

IN SUMMARY THE FOLLOWING ECONOMIC FACTORS NEED TO BE SCANNED:

- GDP per capita
- Economic growth
- Unemployment rate
- Inflation rate
- Consumer and investor confidence
- Inventory levels
- Currency exchange rates
- Merchandise trade balance
- Financial and political health of trading partners
- Balance of payments
- Future trends

http://en.wikipedia.org/wiki/Environmental_scanning

(F) POLITICAL ENVIRONMENT

Political Ideologies

Political ideology is the body of complex ideas, theories and objectives that constitute a socio-political programme. Most of the countries at present are political by pluralistic as different people have various ideologies. Political ideologies of the people in the same country vary widely due to the variations in culture, ethnic groups, tribal groups, community groups, religious groups and the economic groups. These variations influence the people to form different political parties. Managers in multi-political party environment find it difficult to articulate the company's interest and formulae, its mission in order to balance them with the ideology of the political parties.

Democracy

The ideology of pure democracy aims that all citizens should be equal politically and legally, should enjoy freedom and participate in the political process. Pure democracy is not practically implemented and as such countries practice different forms of representative democracy, where citizens elect representatives to make decision on their behalf. Characteristics of contemporary and representative democracy include:

- Freedom of opinion, expression, press and freedom to organise.
- Freedom of electing the representative by voting.
- Limited terms for elected officials.
- An independent and fair judicial system with higher regard for individual rights and property.
- A non-political bureaucracy and defence infrastructure.
- An accessibility to the decision-making process.

Totalitarianism

Totalitarianism is extreme to democracy and is of two types *viz.*, theocratic and secular.

Totalitarianism is extreme to democracy and is of two types *viz.*, theocratic and secular. Religious leaders also assume the roles of political leaders and rule the country in theocratic totalitarianism, as is the case in Iran. One or a group of leaders or a single political party without aligning with any religion assume the power and rule the country with military force under secular totalitarianism as in case of Cambodia, Afghanistan before Taliban rule and Iraq under Saddam Hussein rule. Totalitarianism is also categorised as fascism, authoritarianism and communism. Fascism and authoritarianism are non-existent at present. Communism is also viewed as secular totalitarianism where political and economic systems virtually go together. Many former communist countries like Russia, Sweden and Estonia moved towards different degrees of capitalism and democracy. However, China, Vietnam and North Korea continue to be communist countries.

However, political and economic uncertainty prevails in those countries that shift from communism to capitalism and democracy due to their transition. These uncertainties cause problems to international business firms.

Political environmental factors also influence the operations of international business firms enormously. The influence of the political system of a country influences the business from multiple angles, *viz.*, deciding, promoting, fostering, encouraging, sheltering, directing and controlling the business activities. The success and growth of international business depend upon stable, dynamic, honest, people participative, secured political system in a country.

Countries with stable political system enjoyed the successful business operations. The USA is the best example for political stability and dynamism. Hence, business people prefer to locate their business operations in the USA. According to John Kenneth Galbraith, no country with a stable and honest Government has not had a reasonably satisfactory state of economic progress. The Government, in addition to being stable should also be efficient. Tanzania had a stable government during 1965 and 1985 with Nyerere as the head of the Government. He resigned in 1985 leaving a near-ruined country behind him. Zaire had similar experience with Mobutu and Zambia with Kenneth Kaunda.

John Kenneth Galbraith argues that, in all the advanced countries, "the early emphasis was not on capital investment but on political and then on cultural development. In USA, West Europe and more recently in Japan, a secure political context was stressed in both thought and action on economic development; it was considered the first requisite for economic progress."

In addition to the stable and dynamic governments, the political environment includes the policies and characteristics of political parties, the nature of the constitution and government system.

Some countries do not differ from other countries regarding the philosophies of the political parties, some other countries differ radically. Some countries are highly bureaucratic in decision making regarding foreign investment, technology imports, etc., while some other countries have simple and quick decision-making mechanisms with their democratic approach.

The characteristics of bureaucratic and communistic countries include:

- Limitations, controls and curbs on private enterprises.
- Rule of the trade is state trading and counter trading.
- Many restrictions on imports and foreign capital both inflow and outflow.
- Restrictions on international/multinational corporations.

The trend has changed even in communistic countries. They have been progressively shifting towards liberalisation, privatisation and globalisation (LPG). As many as 8,500 public sector enterprises were brought under the umbrella of private sector in over 80 countries up to 1991. The erstwhile communist countries including the former USSR countries and the China are in the direction from Marx to the Market.

The political philosophy of the developing countries shifted from self-sufficient to self-reliant. As such they compete among themselves to woo foreign capital, technology and managerial expertise.

The political philosophy of most of the governments seem to be broadly one of convergence. However, they differ widely in imposing restrictions and regulations, scope, trade policies, procedures, taxes, custom duties, incentive systems, etc.

Political Relations and International Business

Political friendship/friendly diplomatic relations result in the growth of bilateral or multilateral trade. *For example,* the friendly diplomatic relations between India and the former USSR helped not only the Indian companies but also the MNCs operating in India to have close business linkages with the former USSR. Similarly, the friendly diplomatic relation between Pakistan and the USA helped Pakistan companies to have close business linkages with the USA.

Political friendship/ friendly diplomatic relations result in the growth of bilateral or multilateral trade.

Hostilities between countries also affect the international business among the companies of these countries. Arab countries did not prefer to carry on business with the business firms of Israel. These countries preferred business relations with those countries which boycott Israel. Hence, countervailing laws were adopted in USA to prevent the US companies from complying with this boycott.

In USA, the firms follow the policy of 'maintenance of arm's length' with the competing firms. But in other countries, particularly in Europe and India, they come to an agreement among themselves regarding price, product design, division of markets, etc. This difference is mostly due to the fact that, the US market is large enough to accommodate any number of firms to operate independent of competing firms. But the size of the European countries is very small and the firms cannot enjoy large scale economies. Therefore, European firms divide the market among themselves either in terms of products, geographical areas or customers in order to have large scale economies.

Level of Economic Development and Political Stability: South Africa and Italy are economically developed countries. South Africa has been facing internal and external problems and Italy has been facing labour problems and internal dissension. Vietnam is politically stable but economically developing country. This is due to varied regional, ethnic, language, religious issues problems.

Political Risks: International business firms face political risks as and when there are changes in government policies and/or changes in political parties in power. Risks are based on the host government's actions like confiscation, expropriation, nationalisation, domestication and creeping expropriation.

- **Confiscation:** The process of nationalisation of a property without compensation is called confiscation. Chinese government's seizure of US property in 1949 when Chinese Communist party took power is an example of confiscation.
- **Expropriation:** Expropriation is the process of nationalisation of a property with compensation. Indian Government nationalised commercial banks with compensation in July 1969.
- **Nationalisation:** Nationalisation is the process of shifting the ownership of private property from private individuals or institution to the Government. Burma nationalised entire foreign trade. Poland and Czech Communists nationalised 100 per cent of their economy.

- **Domestication:** In domestication, foreign business firms relinquish control and ownership in favour of domestic investors either partly or fully. For example, Indian Leaf Tobacco Development Company Ltd., in India, Pepsi, General Motors and Barclays Bank in South Africa.
- **General Instability Risk:** These risks are due to social, political, religious unrest in the host country like the recent coup in Fiji and problems due to Muslim rebels in Philippines.
- **Operation Risk:** These risks are due to the imposition of controls on the foreign business operation (like production levels, marketing, finance and human resource) by the host government.

Indicators of Political Instability

Political instability can be viewed from the social unrest, attitudes of nationals and policies of host governments.

- **Corruption:** Corruption and bribery become acute and prevalent not only among bureaucrats but also among politicians during the early stages of political instability.
- **Social Unrest:** Social unrest is caused by clashes between or among community groups, religious groups and ethnic groups. For example, Christian-Muslim conflict in Lebanon, Hindu-Muslim conflict in India, White-Black conflict in the USA, the civil war between Serbs and Croats in 1991 in Yugoslavia, ethnic conflict between Christian in Armenia and Muslims in neighbouring Azerbaijan, etc.
- **Attitudes of Nationals:** The negative attitude of nationals towards foreign business and foreigners is a greater risk. These negative attitudes include exploitation, colonialism, repatriation, non-employment to foreigners, etc.
- **Policies of the Host Government:** Host Government's policies affect the operation of international business firms directly and internally or externally. For example, Janata Government in India asked Coca-Cola to leave the country in 1977 due to the policy of discouraging multinationals. The dispute between Chile and Argentina made Argentina to restrict exports (including the foreign companies operating in the country like General Motors, Peugeot and Renault) to Chile. The Enron Corporation's experience is another example.

Strategies to Minimise Political Risks

Minimise political risks by contributing to the change of the attitudes of the people and government of the host country like stimulation of the host country's economy, employment of nationals, sharing ownership, being civic minded, political neutrality, behind-the-scenes lobby, observation of political mood and reduction of exposure.

Political risks cannot be completely eliminated. However, they can be minimised by contributing to the change of the attitudes of the people and government of the host country like stimulation of the host country's economy, employment of nationals, sharing ownership, being civic minded, political neutrality, behind-the-scenes lobby, observation of political mood and reduction of exposure.

Stimulation of the Local Economy: The foreign company can stimulate the economic development of the host country by investing in their priority areas/portfolios. Further, the foreign company may encourage the local companies by purchasing the raw materials and other inputs from the latter, assist the local companies in technological aspects, using the local companies as ancillary units, etc. *For example,* IBM is the foreign company allowed to sell switchboards in France.

Similarly, the foreign company can stimulate the host economy by being export oriented. *For example,* AT&T entered France with an agreement with Generale de Electricity of France to produce digital switches and export to the USA.

Employment of Nationals: Most foreign companies feel that the people of developing countries are lazy, unintelligent, unmotivated, and less educated. As such foreign companies hire the people from advanced countries and do not employ the local people.

Multinational companies can minimise political risks by employing, developing and promoting the local people.

Sharing ownership: If the multinational company owns the entire capital by itself, it magnifies political risks. Hence, it is suggested that the foreign companies should allow the domestic investors to invest and share the ownership by converting the company into a public limited company. In fact, some countries have imposed a condition that the foreign companies can enter the domestic country only with the participation of local investors. Eritrea is an example in this case. Ownership can be shared through joint ventures. Ford chose to merge its automobile operations in South Africa with Anglo American by reducing its share to a minority position of 40 per cent.

Being Civic Minded: US based MNCs sometimes encounter the 'Ugly American' label abroad. The MNCs in addition to doing business in foreign countries, should be good corporate citizens there. MNCs may help the foreign countries in different ways like constructing schools, hospitals, roads, water reservoirs, etc. Du Pont supplied 1.4 million water jug filters to eight African countries. H. J. Heinz spent US$ 94,000 to fund infant nutrition studies in China. IBM donated computer equipment and expertise worth $ 60,000 to Costa Rica.

Political Neutrality: It is criticised that the MNCs actively involve themselves in political affairs of developing countries. It is suggested that the MNCs should not involve in political affairs or disputes among the local groups of the host countries from the point of view of long-run interests. Brazilian companies *for example,* do not get involved in the political activities of Central American countries.

Behind-the-Scene Lobby: Firms attempt to influence political decisions to help out the host countries. Mobil corporation issued newspaper advertisements urging US to sell missiles to Saudi Arabia. Pizza Hut came to China's rescue when the US mushroom industry asked for a quota against imports from China.

IN SUMMARY THE FOLLOWING POLITICAL FACTORS NEED TO BE SCANNED:

- Political climate - amount of government activity
- Political stability and risk
- Government debt
- Budget deficit or surplus
- Corporate and personal tax rates
- Payroll taxes
- Import tariffs and quotas
- Export restrictions
- Restrictions on international financial flows

Source: Adapted from: http://en.wikipedia.org/wiki/Environmental_scanning

Legal Environment

Laws of the land directly affect the international business wherever they operate. Therefore, international business managers should be aware of the legal systems and laws that are in-force in various foreign countries in addition to their home country as well as host country. Different forms of laws like common laws, civil laws, contract laws and theoretical laws and the degree of

Laws of the land directly affect the international business wherever they operate.

independence of the judiciary system vary from country to country. However, the countries in transition from Communism to market economy, mixed economic to market-economy and different types of totalitarianism to democracy and capitalism may not have perfect business laws. Therefore, international business managers should perform their activities cautiously.

Protection of Intellectual property

The output of intellectual activity like an invention, a screenplay, computer software, chemical formula for a new drug and the like are intellectual properties of those involved. Patents, copyrights and trademarks establish ownership rights over intellectual property rights. Patent provides exclusive rights to the inventor of a new product or process for a particular period to produce and market the product/process. Copyrights provide exclusive rights to the authors, publishers, composers and the like to publish and market their works. Trademarks are designs, icons, names used by the producers and marketers to differentiate their products/services from those of others. These trademarks are officially registered and become exclusive rights of the manufacture's who register them. Protecting intellectual property rights across the globe is a problem due to the volume of the task, cultural differences across the globe and limitations of various governments in enforcing the laws. World Trade Organisation is enforcing the intellectual property regulations. Governments in various member countries of the World Trade Organisation have been either formulating new laws or amending the existing laws in order to protect the intellectual property rights.

Product Safety and Product Liability

Products must adhere to certain safety standards as prescribed by product safety laws. Firms and its executives hold responsibility under product liability when injury, death or damage is caused by usage or consumption of product. These laws and standards are more comprehensive in USA compared to other countries. Differences in coverage of these laws among the countries result in variation in competitive advantage as well as non-uniformity of ethical standards to and among countries. Thus, the countries with less comprehensive product safety and product liability laws provide an opportunity to the business to reduce its cost and possess more competitive advantage than their counterparts in those countries, where the laws are more comprehensive.

Labour Laws: Labour legislations are enacted in various countries, mostly based on the resolutions of the International Labour Organisation. These legislations prescribe the minimum wages, trade union activities, employee–employer relations, collective negotiations, recruitment and employment practices, stipulations regarding working conditions, employee benefits, regulations and modalities of prevention and settlement of industrial disputes. However, MNCs force most of the governments to play an indifferent role with respect to implementation of labour laws. MNCs enter those countries where the cost of human resource is less in order to acquire competitive advantage through low labour costs (See Box 4.6). However, these practices sometimes result in exploitation of labour in developing countries.

BOX 4.6: NIKE IN VIETNAM: FAILURE OF IMPLEMENTATION OF LABOUR LAWS

Nike subcontracted its manufacturing operations in Vietnam. The operation employed 25,000 employees and most of them were young women. Their wages were as low as $40 a month and the working conditions in the factories were quite inferior. Nike's practices were widely criticised by media. Consequently Nike hired Andrew Young – former US Ambassador to UN to enquire into the working conditions of employees and present a report. Mr. Young did not conduct detailed study but reported that Nike was doing a good job in treating the workers. Mr. Young was criticised widely for his improper reporting. Then Nike joined a taskforce including industry leaders, human rights groups and labour leaders that resulted in reaching an accord for payment of local minimum wages in foreign factories and establishment of Fair Labour Association – an independent association to monitor the wages and working conditions. Later, Nike announced a number of initiatives and incentives to employees working with its subcontractors. It was widely criticised that the Fair Labour Association was not an independent body and the labour practices in Nike were unfair even during 2001.

Source: Adapted "Right Group says Nike isn't fulfilling Promises". – Wall Street Journal, May 16, 2001 and Charles W.L. Hill, Tata McGraw, New Delhi, 2004, pp.131-134.

IN SUMMARY THE FOLLOWING LEGAL FACTORS NEED TO BE SCANNED:

- Minimum wage laws
- Environmental protection laws
- Worker safety laws
- Labour laws
- Copyright and patent laws
- Anti-monopoly laws
- Sunday closing laws
- Municipal licences
- Laws that favour business investment

Source: Adapted from http://en.wikipedia.org/wiki/Environmental_scanning

(G) NATURAL ENVIRONMENT

Natural environment consists of ecological factors and climatic conditions that affect business. Topography of the region, rivers, climatic conditions, humidity, wheather conditions, etc., influence the business directly and indirectly. For example the output and quality of products in cotton textile industry are affected by the humidity in the weather. Similarly availability of water influences the soft drinks industry as well as brewery and mineral water industry.

In addition to affecting location strategies, the natural factors affect cost strategies, investment strategies, green-marketing strategies and quality strategies of different industries. Maintenance of pollution free environment, companies need to invest heavily on erecting additional machinery and equipment. Similarly certain climatic conditions favour the maintenance of high quality of output while other climatic conditions disfavour the quality of the product. Further the hilly geographical territories create problems for construction and maintenance of infrastructural facilities like roads, railway lines and telecommunication facilities. Therefore, companies have to scan natural environment to find out opportunities provided by and the threats posed by natural environment and to craft appropriate strategies.

Climate change is widely regarded as one of the most serious challenges the world faces with consequences that go far beyond its effects on the environment. Climate change has reached a tipping point in global awareness. Therefore, the companies need to maintain appropriate measures with regard to the challenges of climate change and its aftermath affects.

(H) THE INDUSTRY ENVIRONMENT

Industry is a group of firms producing (or rendering) the same or similar products (or services) which depend on others for inputs. The strategies of the firm will be affected by the attractiveness of the industry in which it chooses to do business and its relative competitive position within that industry. The important factors of this environment include:

Market, customer, demographic factors, geographic factors and competition.

The Market Environment

The market environment consists of all factors and groups having impact on the demand for the firm's products and/or services, competitors, etc. The factors influencing the firm's market environment include:

— Product design, configuration, demand, packing, uses, lifecycle, etc.

— Place of the market, special features of the market, etc.

— Place also includes customer related factors like customer taste, preference, needs, perceptions, values, bargaining abilities, satisfaction, dealers, distributors, wholesalers, retailers, etc.

— Price of the product, payment terms and conditions, special offers, discount, competitor's price, price of the substitute and complementary products etc.

— Promotional factors like expenditure and effectiveness of advertising, personal selling and sales promotion of the firm and competing firms.

Customer

The significant factor of the marketing environment is the customer. The strategists are mostly concerned with the customers of the firm and their needs and desires. In fact, the customer has become king to the strategists in the country with the liberalisation of the economy in 1991. The strategists are interested in not only the present customers but also the potential and future customers.

According to Lawrence R. Jauch and William F. Glueck, strategists include three factors as part of their industry analysis of customer sector, *viz.*, buyer identification, demographic factors and geographic locations of markets.

Buyer Identification: Markets normally indicate three distinct classes of customers. Different factors affect each class of customers in making their purchase decision as presented in Fig. 4.4. Strategists identify the nature of these customers and their utilities in order to avoid threats of loss of customers and to find or create opportunities for themselves to find new customers or to sell more to existing ones.

Demographic Factors

The demographic factors that influence the industry analysis include:

(i) Changes in population size and structure;

(ii) Age shifts in the population; and

(iii) income distribution and changes of the population.

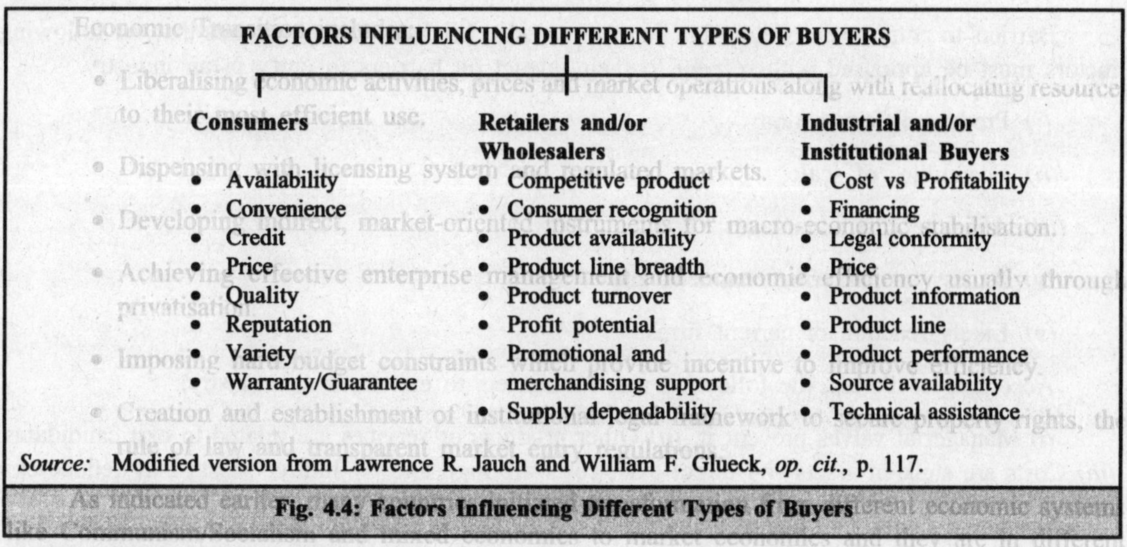

Source: Modified version from Lawrence R. Jauch and William F. Glueck, *op. cit.*, p. 117.

Fig. 4.4: Factors Influencing Different Types of Buyers

Geographic Factors

The strategists should also analyse the geographic environment to know the opportunities and threats as part of analysing customer sector. The strategist should think of extending the market to new locations.

Supplier: Suppliers provide material, capital and the likes to a firm. The strategist should analyse the supplier changes in the environment like price of the material, continuous supply of material, providing material on credit, etc. Michael Porter summarised this environment as follows:

(i) The power of the supplier to raise prices. The farther away the supplier is, the greater is his power.

(ii) The power of the supplier to raise the prices is less, if the buying firm is monopolist or oligopolist.

(iii) The power of the supplier to raise prices is greatest when the buyer is not an important customer or when the supplier can have forward linkage.

The power of the buyer can also affect the cost of suppliers. The power of the buyer can be maximum when *(i)* the buyer's firm is concentrated *(ii)* the buyer represents a significant portion of the supplier's business and *(iii)* if the buyer can virtually integrate backward.

Alternatively, the buyer's power would be minimum when *(i)* the buyer's firm is competitive *(ii)* the cost of switching to a substitute is high, *(iii)* the supplier's product is especially a vital part of the production process and *(iv)* the supplier can virtually integrate forward.

In addition to analysing the bargaining power of supplier and buyer, the strategist must analyse the environment to examine: *(i)* availability and cost of raw materials and sub-assemblies, *(ii)* availability and cost of energy, *(iii)* availability and cost of financial resources and *(iv)* availability and cost of labour.

Competitors

The strategist analyses the demand for and supply of the product that the firm produces. Further, he examines the level and nature of competition the firm faces and will face. Factors to be examined regarding competition are: *(i)* entry and exit of major competitors, *(ii)* substitutes and complements for current products and services and *(iii)* major strategic changes by current competitors (See Exhibit 4.2).

Barriers to entry or exit determine the entry or exit. Michael Porter contends that the following factors must be appraised with respect to their impact on barriers to entry in an industry.

(i) Product differentiation;

(ii) Economies of scale;

(iii) Absolute cost advantages;

(iv) Access to marketing channels; and

(v) Likely reaction of current firms.

According to Porter, the following are the barriers to exit from an industry:

(i) Managerial valves prevent it, *(ii)* Other products or services are related to exit candidates, *(iii)* Costs are sunk in assets *(iv)* direct exist costs are high and *(v)* Indirect costs may reduce exit behaviour. Exhibit 4.4 presents key questions about competitors.

Exhibit 4.4: Key Questions about Competitors

1. What are our major competitors' strengths?
2. What are our major competitors' weaknesses?
3. What are our major competitors' goals, objectives and strategies?
4. How are our major competitors most likely to respond to current economic, social, cultural, demographic, geographic, political, governmental, technological and competitive trends affecting the industry?
5. How vulnerable are our major competitors to our alternative company strategies?
6. How vulnerable are our alternative strategies to successful counter attack by our major competitors?
7. How are our products or services positioned relative to our major competitors?
8. To what extent are new firms entering and old firms leaving the industry?
9. What key factors have resulted in the present competitive position in the industry?
10. How have the sales and profit rankings of major competitors in the industry changed over recent years? Why have these rankings changed that way?
11. What is the nature of supplier and distributor relationship in this industry?
12. To what extent could substitute products or services be a threat to competitors in this industry?

Source: Fred R. David, p. 119.

The Concept of Driving Forces

Industry conditions change because important forces driving industry participants (competitors, customers, suppliers) alter their actions, the driving forces in an industry are the major underlying causes of changing industry and competitive conditions.

Industry conditions change because important forces driving industry participants (competitors, customers, suppliers) alter their actions, the driving forces in an industry are the major underlying causes of changing industry and competitive conditions. Several different factors can affect an industry powerfully enough to act as driving forces. The important among them are:

- Changes in the long-term industry growth rate;
- Changes in who buys the product and how they use it;
- Product innovation;
- Technological change;
- Marketing innovation;
- Entry or exit of major firms;
- Diffusion of technical know-how;
- Increasing globalisation of the industry;

- Changes in cost and efficiency;
- Emerging buyer preferences for a differentiated instead of a commodity product;
- Regulatory influences and government policy changes;
- Changing societal concerns, attitudes, life-style; and
- Reduction in uncertainty and business risk.

Competitor Analysis

Studying the actions and behaviour of close competitors is essential. Unless a company knows what competitors are doing, it ends up "flying blind" into battle. Therefore, successful strategists take great pains in scouting competitors — understanding their strategies, watching their strategies, watching their actions, sizing up their strengths and weaknesses and trying to anticipate what moves they will make next. This activity includes the following actions:

1. Identifying competitor's strategies: Strategists can get a quick profile of key competitors by studying where they are in industry, their strategic objectives and their basic competitive approaches (see Exhibit 4.4)
2. Evaluating who the industry's major players are going to be.
3. Predicting competitor's next moves.
4. Pinpointing the key factors for competitive success: Key success factors spell the difference between profit and loss and ultimately between competitive success and failure. A key success factor can be a skill or talent, a competitive capability or a condition a company must achieve, it can relate to technology, manufacturing, distribution, marketing or organisational resources. (See Exhibit 4.5).
5. Drawing conclusions about overall industry attractiveness. Whether an industry is relatively attractive or unattractive depends on several situational considerations.

Exhibit 4.5: Types of Key Success Factors

Technology-Related KSFs

- Scientific research expertise (important in such fields as pharmaceuticals, medicine, space exploration, other "high-tech" industries)
- Production process innovation capability
- Product innovation capability
- Expertise in a given technology

Manufacturing-Related KSFs

- Low-cost production efficiency (achieve scale economies, capture experience curve effects)
- Quality of manufacture (fewer defects, less need for repairs)
- High utilisation of fixed assets (important in capital intensive/high fixed-cost industries)
- Low-cost plant locations
- Access to adequate supplies of skilled labour
- High labour productivity (important for items with high labour content)
- Low-cost product design and engineering (reduces manufacturing costs)
- Flexibility to manufacture a range of models and sizes/take care of custom orders

Distribution-Related KSFs

- A strong network of wholesale distributors/dealers
- Gaining ample space on retailer shelves
- Having company-owned retail outlets
- Low distribution costs
- Fast delivery

Marketing-Related KSFs

- A well-trained, effective sales force
- Available, dependable service and technical assistance
- Accurate filling of buyer orders (few back orders or mistakes)
- Breadth of product line and product selection
- Merchandising skills
- Attractive styling/packing
- Customer guarantees and warranties (important in mail-order retailing, big ticket purchases, new product introductions)

Skills-Related KSFs

- Superior talent (important in professional services)
- Quality control know-how
- Design expertise (important in fashion and apparel industries)
- Expertise in a particular technology
- Ability to come up with clever, catchy ads
- Ability to get newly developed products out of the R&D phase and into the market very quickly

Organisational Capability

- Superior information systems (important in airline travel, car rental, credit card, and lodging industries)
- Ability to respond quickly to shifting market conditions (streamlined decision-making, short lead times to bring new products to market)
- More experience and managerial know-how

Other Types of KSFs

- Favourable image/reputation with buyers
- Overall low cost (not just in manufacturing)
- Convenient locations (important in many retailing businesses)
- Pleasant, courteous employees
- Access to financial capital (important in newly emerging industries with high degrees of business risk and in capital-intensive industries)
- Patent protection

Source: Arthur A. Thompson. Jr. and A.J. Strickland III. *op. cit.*, p. 82.

Michael Porter's Approach to Industry Analysis

According to Michael Porter, the business while analysing the environment should be concerned more with the intensity of competition is determined by various potential entrants, suppliers, industry competitors, rivalry among existing firms, buyers, substitutes, etc. (See Fig 4.5).

The collective and interactive, "strength of these forces determine the ultimate profit potential in the industry, where profit potential is measured in terms of long run return on invested capital."

Strategists can identify opportunities and threats in each of these competitive forces and rate their strength as high or medium or low force. No force is regarded as an opportunity. However, the business firms in the long run can change the threats into either opportunities or neutral forces through their strategies. But they have to craft their strategies in the short run within the limitation of these forces.

For example, a soft drink company in India could currently rate as follows:

Force	*Rate*	*Comments*
Rivalry	High	Coca-Cola and Pepsi cola.
Threat of potential entrants	Low	Industry reached maturity stage, sales growth is slow
Threat of substitutes	Low	Other soft drinks do not provide flavour close to Coca-Cola or Pepsi Cola
Bargaining power of the buyers	Low	Large number of buyers with negligible share in the total sales
Bargaining power of the suppliers	Medium	Coca-Cola and Pepsi Cola make large quantities of buying of sugar, water and carbon dioxide.
Development seconds market	Medium	Development of second market for books like www.amazon.com and cars
Threat of other stakeholders	Medium	Agitation against Coca-Cola and Pepsi Cola environmental concern, ingredients of the products are on 'high.'

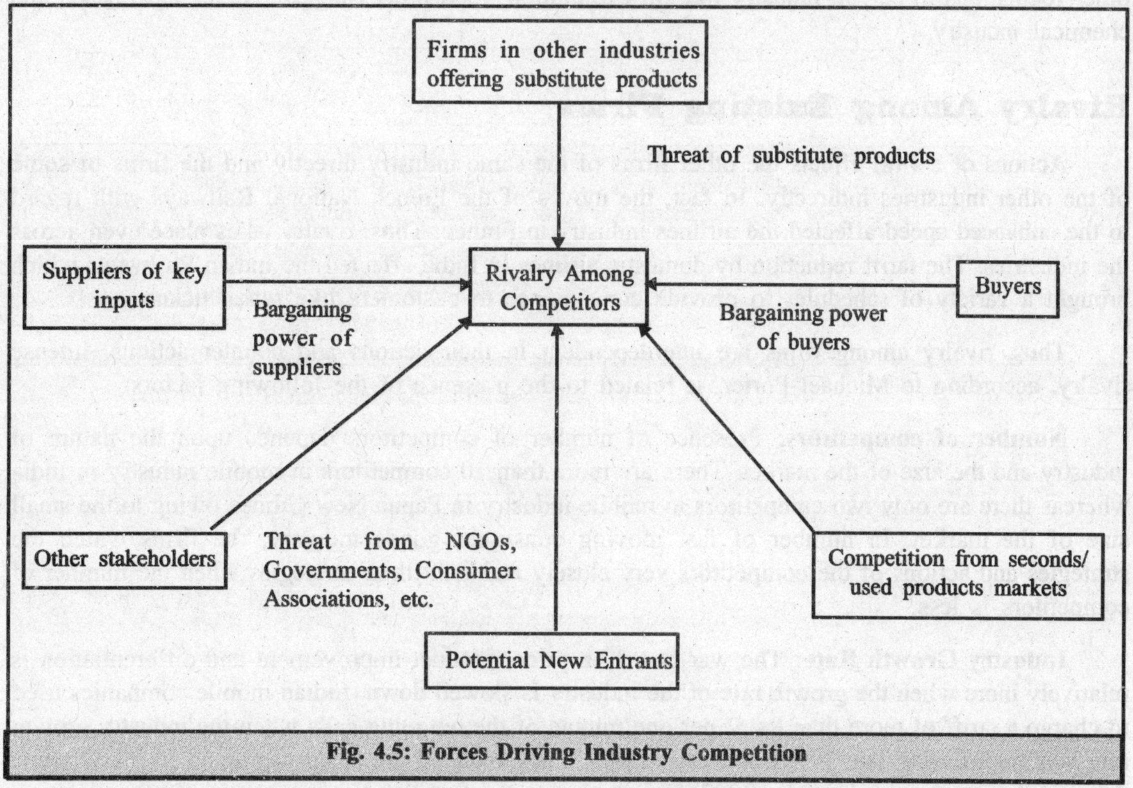

Fig. 4.5: Forces Driving Industry Competition

The soft drink industry is currently at high level of competitive intensity based on the above factors. In other words, the industry growth rate is low and the profit margins are narrowed down.

Now, we shall discuss each of these competitive focuses in detail:

Potential/threat of new entrants: Normally new entrants pose a threat to the existing firms as they enter the industry with new and creative management practices, new and improved product features, low price, latest technology, and write new promises to the customers. For example, Reliance mobiles entered mobile industry in India with latest technology, reduced price, wide area network and enhanced bandwidth. Similarly, Degicel entered mobile market in Papua New Guinea with wide area network, reduced price and latest technology.

However, the existing firms and/or the industry can create entry barriers: They include: Large scale operations sales and low prices provided, an advantage to Reliance mobile phones to prevent the entry of rivals in Indian mobile industry whereas the exorbitant tariff fixed by 'Be' mobile created an 'invitation to enter' the mobile market to Digicel mobiles in Papua New Guinea.

Product Differentiation: Product differentiation created by Coca-Cola like Sprite, Fanta, Diet coke, etc., created entry barriers to other companies and tough competition to Pepsi Cola.

Capital Requirement: The need for inventing large capital creates entry barrier for new entrants. For example, steel industry, airways and shipping companies need huge capital and therefore less number of new firms enter these industries.

Switching Costs: Entry barriers are created when the cost of switching to other businesses or systems is too high.

Accession to Distribution Channels: The existing firms can create a block to the access of the distribution channels by employing role distribution dealers.

Government Regulations: Government imposes entry barriers by imposing licensing and other regulations in certain industry like oil exploration, food processing, air travel, agro-based and chemical industry.

Rivalry Among Existing Firms

Actions of a firm affects the other firms of the same industry directly and the firms of some of the other industries indirectly. In fact, the moves of the French National Railways with regard to the enhanced speed affected the airlines industry in France. Thus, rivalry takes place even across the industries. The tariff reduction by domestic airlines in India affected the Indian Railways, which brought a variety of schedules to provide convenience to customers like *tatkal* tickets.

Thus, rivalry among firms are interdependent in their actions and counter actions. Intense rivalry, according to Michael Porter, is related to the presence of the following factors:

Number of competitors: Presence of number of competitors depends upon the nature of industry and the size of the market. There are more than 10 competitors in mobile industry in India whereas there are only two competitors in mobile industry in Papua New Guinea owing to the small size of the market. In number of fast moving consumer goods industry, the firms watch the strategies and actions of the competitors very closely and craft their strategies when the number of competitors is less.

Industry Growth Rate: The war based on price, product improvement and differentiation is relatively more when the growth rate of the industry is slowed down. Indian mobile companies used to charge a tariff of more than Rs. 2 per one minute of the outgoing calls when the industry growth rate was high during late 1990s and early 2000. They reduced the same to around Rs. 0.50 when the growth rate slowed down by 2007. This is due to the fact that the firms compete for the same market whose growth is slowed down.

Product/Service characteristics: The factors like availability and location proximity play vital role in the competition when the product/service characteristics are the same or do not matter much when compared to other factors like time and location proximity. For example, customers weigh the time and location proximity in buying food for immediate consumption and also when the product characteristics are the same.

Bargaining Power of Buyer

Current and potential bargaining power of the buyers determines the competitive strength of the firms for example, airlines, bargaining power in buying petrol is relatively high compared to that of a truck owner. Bargaining power of the buyer is relatively more in the following situations:

- Purchases form a larger share of the sales of company. For example, the quantity of books purchased by distance education department/centres of universities is larger, than publishing the total sales by a company. Similarly, the share of purloin of computers by colleges and universities is larger to the total purchases by a computer company.
- Ability of the buyer to implement backward integration strategy for example, the ability of Airlines Company or Indian Railways to have its own catering and the ability to start their own colleges and universities to educate the prospective employees like Kirlosker.
- Availability of alternative suppliers: Liberalisation of economies resulted in the alternative supply of products and services. For example, Air India was the major supplier of international air travel before 2000. Now, there are a wide range of alternatives.
- High share of the value of purchase: The buyer prefers to reduce the cost of buying when the share of value of purchase is relatively high. This is true in case of purchase of barley by a brewery.

Low Margins of the Buyer in sales

Market intermediaries when they are forced to maintain low margin bargain for low price. This is more applicable in case of fast moving consumer goods.

Bargaining Powers of Suppliers

Bargaining power of the supplier influences prices. Bargaining power of the suppliers of pharmaceuticals is more in Papua New Guinea and is one of the reasons for high cost of medical facilities in Papua New Guinea. Similarly, the bargaining power of OPEC is significant in supplying oil which resulted in increase in airfares in 2008.

The suppliers enjoy higher level of bargaining power under the following circumstances:

- When the suppliers in the industry is dominated by a few firms.
- When the supply of the product/service is less than the demand for it.
- When the product has distinctive attributes and difficult to switch over.
- When easy substitutes are not available like rail travel in India and air travel in Papua New Guinea.
- When suppliers can have forward linkage and direct dealing with customers like airline business.

Development of Second Market

Development of second/used products market poses a wide threat in some industries particularly in publishing and automobile industry. For example www.amazon.com facilitates second market for a wide range of used books posing a threat to the publishing industry. Similarly, a number of companies started the business in procuring such and supplying used cars to various foreign countries. Such trends pose competition to the firm in the publishing industry as well as automobile industry.

Relative Power of Other Stakeholders

Other stakeholders include political parties and non-government organisations. This is an additional factor for the Porter's model. For example; the products of Coca-Cola and Pepsi Cola have been challenged by the Bhartiya Janata Party activists on the ground that natural fruits, tender coconut and juices are far better than the cola product, in terms of health issues and price. These activities posed challenges to Coca-Cola and Pepsi Cola.

Some of the Papua New Guineans favour 'Be' mobile, a public sector unit, causing competition to Digicel mobile company in the country. Agitations by the consumer associations and voluntary organisations force governments to plan to enact special legislations and impose regulations to protect the consumer and the environment. These regulations enhance the cost of assets and production. The enhanced costs intensify the competition.

For example, water, air and sound pollution control measures imposed by the Government of India enhanced the cost of production of chemical industry.

Industry Boundaries

An industry is a group of firms that produce the same or similar products or render the same or similar services.

An industry is a group of firms that produce the same or similar products or render the same or similar services. Similar products indicate that they serve the same purpose for example, orange juice, grape juice, apple juice and mango juice serve the same purpose. So, firms producing different kinds of juices belong to the juices manufacturing industry. Different kinds of passenger cars like economy cars, luxury cars and cars-cum-truck serve similar purpose of conveyance. These firms belong to the automobile industry along with other automobile manufacturing firms. Sometimes, would be quite unclear to classify the industries for example, Coca-Cola producers beverages as well as mineral water which can include mineral water under beverages. The answer is partly 'Yes' as both these products satisfy the need of thirsty and partly 'No' as the beverages satisfy the need for excitement, unlike water.

Similarly some firms producing bicycles for riding also produce toy bicycles. How do we classify such companies? Such examples create a confusion over industry boundaries. These confusions complicate the task of crafting strategy as each operational area override other area of operations of the firm.

Industry definition is necessary:

(i) to determine the area in which the firm is competing.

(ii) to focus the attention of the strategies on the firm's competitors.

(iii) to identify the environment and common opportunities and threats.

(iv) to evaluate the strategies, goals and objectives of the firm.

Though industry definition is necessary, the following problems are involved in the process.

Growing competition forces companies to spread their operations to other industry. For example universities spread thir activities into publishing industry, hotel and transport industry.

Industry evolutions create industries within industries like telephone industry, mobile industry, e-mail and Internet within telecommunication industry.

Globalisation led to the creation of global industry.

Yet how to draw Boundaries

Despite these problems, executives have to design boundaries in order to focus on strategic management. The executives, therefore, should examine the following issues:

- Identify the goals of each portfolio of the company.
- Focus on the critical success factors of each portfolio of the business.
- Scan the firm's strengths to compete in other areas of the industry and if not, acquire such strengths.
- Future opportunities and threats that force the firm to enter areas of other industries.
- Acquisition of new strengths and reduction of future threats of entering new industries.
- Reduction of conflict, overlap and gap areas of strategies that result owing the expanding industry boundaries.

Environmental Scanning

The process of environment scanning has been far from being systematic except with regard to information relating to current developments. Environmental scanning requires information inputs which can be devised from different strategies like:

- Verbal information from audio-visual media, suppliers, sales people, etc.,
- Written and documenting information from newspaper, journal and reports,
- Information from management information system
- Industrial spying
- Forecasting reports.

1. Key Sources of Information for Environmental Scanning:

Once strategists have selected key environmental variables, the next step is to select key sources of environmental information for scanning. The sources of information include:

(i) The economic and business daily newspapers like The Economic Times, Business Standard, Business Line and Financial Express.

(ii) Journals and periodicals like Business India, Business World, Business Today, Update, Fortune India, Main Stream, Long Range Planning Journal, Economist, IMF World Economic Outlook, Harvard Business Review, Foreign Trade, Finance and Development, Environmental Trends & Scenarios, etc.

(iii) Institutional publications like Mumbai Stock Exchange Directory, the Centre for Monitoring Indian Economy, Kothari Industrial Directory of India, Publications of Market Research, Agencies like Operations Research Group, the National Council for Applied Economic Research, etc., annual reports of various companies, publications of professional organisations like Federation of Indian Chamber of Commerce and Industry.

(iv) Government publications like Economic Survey, Guidelines to India Bulletins, ICICI Portfolio Studies, Business Intelligence and Data, The State of Nation Report, Quarterly Survey of Industries, Indian Trade Journal, Yojana, etc.

(iv) Other publications include: United Nations Publications, World Economic Survey, International Financial Statistics, Economic Survey of Asia and the Far East, Commodity Trade Statistics, Year Book of International Trade Statistics, etc.

2. Approaches to Environmental Scanning:

The experiences of various pioneering companies reflect the emergence of four basic principles regarding effective implementation of environmental scanning function.

1. Environmental analysis must be linked, conceptually and practically to current planning and operations.
2. Environmental analysis serves a number of separate purposes, different analytic structures and systems may be required in order to achieve those different purposes.
3. Systems for environmental analysis must fit the culture and decision-making styles of the organisation and areas they serve.
4. Continuing support in spite of internal changes is required to sustain environmental analysis in an organisation over time.

3. Factors Affecting the Environmental Scanning:

Several factors affect the environmental scanning. These factors are classified as *(i)* Strategist related factors, *(ii)* Organisation related factors and *(iii)* Environment related factors.

(i) Strategist related factors include: age, family background, educational background, experience, socio-cultural background, motivational level, perception and cognitive styles, ability to face challenges, ability to cope up with stress, ability to motivate and lead people, ability to adopt to different cultures and problem situations, ability to form and lead team work, ability to forecast, judgement, analytical and interpretation skills etc.

(ii) Organisation related factors include the nature of the business, product or services and markets, age, size and complexity of the organisation, organisation structure and its nature etc.

(iii) Environmental factors include: complexity, volatility or turbulence, hostility and diversity of the environment.

The strategist may face the problem of comprehending massive information and a number of environmental factors. Hence, the strategist should select priority based environmental factors to forecast the future or scanning the environment.

4. Scanning Systems:

There are three types of scanning systems. They are:

(i) **Irregular Scanning Systems:** These consist of *ad hoc* studies in response to environmental crises.

(ii) **Regular Scanning Systems:** These consist of regular reviews of the environment or selected strategic environmental components. These reviews include annual planning exercises.

(iii) **Continuous Scanning Systems:** This is an ongoing activity. Established boundary, scanning offices often coordinate this activity. This is more future oriented system. Exhibit 4.6 compares these three scanning systems along several dimensions.

Techniques of Environmental Scanning:

1. *Expert opinion:* Knowledgeable people are selected and asked to assign importance and probability ratings to various possible future developments. The most refined version, the Delphi method, puts experts through several rounds of event assessment, where they keep refining their assumptions and judgements.

2. *Trend extrapolation:* Researchers fit curves (linear, quadriatic, or S-shaped growth curves) through past time series to serve as a basis for extrapolation. This method can be very unreliable if new developments alter the expected direction of movement.

3. *Trend correlation:* Researchers correlate various time series in the hope of identifying leading and lagging relationships that can support forecasts.

4. *Dynamic modelling:* Researchers build sets of equations to try to describe the underlying system. The coefficients in the equations are fitted through statistical means. Econometric models of more than 300 equations, for example, are used to forecast changes in the U.S. economy.

Exhibit 4.6: Comparison of Scanning Models

Irregular Model	*Regular Model*	*Continuous Model*
Media for Scanning Activity		
Ad hoc studies	Periodically updated studies	Structured data collection and processing systems
Scope of Scanning		
Specific events	Selected events	Broad range of environmental systems
Motivation for Activity		
Crisis initiated	Decision and issue oriented	Planning process oriented
Temporal Nature of Activity		
Reactive	Pro-active	Pro-active
Time Frame for Data		
Retrospective	Primarily current and retrospective	Prospective
Time Frame for Decision Impact		
Current and near future	Near-term	Long-term
Organisational makeup		
Various staff agencies	Various staff agencies	Environmental scanning unit.

Source: Liam Fahey and William R. King. "Environmental Scanning for Corporate Planning." *Business Horizons*. August. 1977. p. 63.

5. *Cross-impact analysis:* Researchers identify a set of key trends (those high in importance and/or probability) and ask, "If event A occurs, what will be the impact on all other trends?" The results are then used to build sets of "domino chains," with one event triggering others.

6. *Multiple scenarios:* Researchers build pictures of alternative futures, each internally consistent and with a certain probability of happening. The major purpose of the scenarios is to stimulate contingency planning.

7. *Demand/hazard forecasting:* Researchers identify major events that would greatly affect the firm. Each event is rated for its convergence with several major trends taking place in society and for its appeal to each major public group in the society. A higher convergence and appeal increases the probability that the event will occur. The highest-scoring events are then researched further.

5. Environmental Threat and Opportunity Profile: ETOP

Analysis of environmental information, data and factors, and determining opportunities and threats require a systematic technique. Lawrence R. Jauch and William F. Glueck suggest the technique of Environmental Threat and Opportunity Profile (ETOP). This technique conveniently summarises the diagnoses of all the various factors of the environment which is important to the strategic gaps facing the firm. The ETOP presents the impact of each environmental factor like economic, political and social on the organisation. Exhibit 4.7 presents an environmental threat and opportunity profile (ETOP) of a bank.

Exhibit 4.7: Environmental Threat and Opportunity Profile of a Bank

Environmental Factors		
Environmental Factors	+	Continued emphasis on infrastructural facilities including telecommunications
	+	Increase in educational levels and income levels
	+	Increase in business activity.
	–	Establishment of financing companies
Technological	+	Increased computerisation
	–	Shortage of computer operators and engineers.
Government	–	Economic liberalisation allowed private banks to operate and compete with the existing banks
Customer	–	Shift from the present banks to the newly established banks with modern facilities.
Supplier	–	Source of technology will become scarce
Competitor	+	Less competition from the existing banks
	o+	No competition from cooperative banks.
	–	Strength of the foreign banks in terms of technology, people and funds.

Note: '+' Indicates opportunity '–' Indicates Threat; 'o' indicates neutral impact.

POINTS TO BE REMEMBERED

- Strategic management involves three levels, *viz.*, the organisation's macro environment or general environment, the industry in which the organisation operates and the organization itself.
- Environmental factors are prime influences on strategy change.
- The trend towards globalisation has emerged around the world.
- Social and cultural factors influence business.
- Technological changes enabled business to take up the shape of transnational business through the concept of global business.
- Economic system is an organisation of institutions established to satisfy human needs/ wants.
- Political ideology is the body of ideas. Theories and objectives constitute a socio-political programme.
- Industry is a group of firms producing the same or similar products vets.

KEY WORDS

- Social Factors
- Cultural Factors
- Technological Factors
- Economic Factors
- Political Factors
- Global Factors
- Industry Analysis
- Competitor Analysis
- Multinational Companies
- Transnational Company
- Cultural Attitude
- Information Technology
- Economic Systems
- Balance of Payments
- Industrial Policy
- Small-scale Industry

QUESTIONS FOR DISCUSSION

(1) Why do you scan the business environment?

(2) What is economic environment? How do you use economic factors in determining opportunities and threats?

(3) What are the global factors that affect the business?

(4) Why do companies go global?

(5) What are the social and cultural factors that affect the business?

(6) What are the technological factors? How do they influence business?

(7) What are the political ideologies? How do political factors influence business?

(8) What is industry analysis? Discuss the demographic factors that influence the business.

(9) What is competitor analysis?

(10) How do you identify opportunities and threats of a business?

REFERENCES

1. William F. Glueck, *Business Policy and Strategic Management*, McGraw-Hill, 1980, p. 88.
2. Ibid., p. 88.
3. Lawrence R. Jauch and William F. Glueck, *op. cit.*, p. 86.
4. *Ibid.*, pp.
5. Kenichi Ohmae, "*The End of the Nation State: The Rise of Regional Economies.*"
6. Arun Kumar Jain, "*Managing Global Competition*," Competence Publishing House, Dehradun, 1994, p. 30.
7. *Ibid.*, p. 31.
8. Philip Kotler, "*Principles of Marketing*", Prentice-Hall of India, p. 576.
9. K. Aswathappa, "*Essentials of Business Environment*", Himalaya Publishing House, Mumbai, 1996, pp. 34-35.
10. Arun Kumar Jain, *op. cit.*, pp. 33-37.
11. K. Aswathappa, *op. cit.*, p. 47.

12. Jeffrey A. Fadiman, "Should Smaller Firms Use Third World Methods to Enter Third World Markets": The Project Heads as Point Man Overseas, *Journal of Business and Industrial Marketing*, 4 (winter/Spring 1989), pp. 17-28.
13. John D. Daniels, Lee H. Radebough and Daniel P. Sullivan, "*International Business*", Pearson Education, Singapore, 2004, p. 54.
14. Montose, Sommers and Jerson Kernan, "Why products flourish here": Fizzle There! *Columbia Journal of world business*, March-April 1967, p. 90
15. Quoted in David H. Holt and Karen W. Wigginton, "*International Management*", Thomson, 2002, p. 51.
16. Warren J. Keegan, op. cit., p. 80.
17. Quoted in John D. Daniels, *et. al.*, op.cit., p.124.
18. Olech Havrylyshyn and Thomas Wolf, "Determinants of Growth in Transition Economies", *Finance & Development*", June 1999, p. 12.
19. Robert Wesson, "*Modern Government-Democracy and Authoritarianism*", Prentice Hall, New Jersey, 1985, pp. 41-42.
20. John D. Daniels, *et.al.*, op.cit., p. 88.
21. Ibid., p.11.
22. Sak Onkvisit and John J. Shaw, "*International Marketing*", Prentice-Hall, New Delhi, 1999, pp. 135-58.
23. Charles W.l. Hill, *op.cit.*, p.50.
24. Lawrence R. Jauch and William F. Glueck, *op.cit.*, p. 117.
25. *Ibid.*, pp.117-118.
26. *Ibid.*, p. 120.
27. Azhar Kazmi, *op. cit.*, p. 115.
28. Samuel C. Certo and J. Paul Peter, *op. cit.* pp. 44-45.
29. James R. Bright and Milton E.F. Schoeman, "*A Guide to Practical Technological Forecasting*", Prentice-Hall, Englewood Cliffs, New Jersey, 1973. Quoted in Samuel C. Certo and J. Paul Peter, *op. cit.* p.48.
30. Lawrence R. Jauch and William F. Glueck, *op. cit.*, p. 138.
31. Michal E. Porter, "*Competitive Strategy*", Free Press, New York, 1980, p. 3.
32. John A. Pearce and Richard B. Robinson, "*Strategic Management,*" Tata Mc Graw-Hill Publishing Co. Ltd., New Delhi, 2005, pp. 99-99.

✦ ✦ ✦

5

CHAPTER

INTERNAL ENVIRONMENT: CAPABILITIES AND COMPETENCIES

Chapter Outline

(A) Resources and Capabilities
(B) Core Competencies
(C) Value Chain Analysis and Outsourcing
(D) Strengths and Weaknesses Analysis
(E) Competitive Strength Assessment
(F) Corporate Capability Factors
(G) Diagnosing Corporate Capabilities

Learning Objectives

After studying this chapter, you should be able to:

- Analyse organisational analysis and capabilities;
- Discuss the core competencies of the company;
- Analyse organisational strengths and weaknesses;
- Study the organisational capabilities;
- Identify the opportunities and threats;
- Assess organisation's competitive strengths;
- Discuss various corporate capability factors in each of the functional areas;
- Diagnose the corporate capability factors.

(A) RESOURCES AND CAPABILITIES

Organisations formulate strategies based on corporate strengths and weaknesses. Corporate strengths and weaknesses are determined based on organisational resources, capabilities and competencies.

Resources

Resources are all kinds of inputs like material, components, human resource, finance, etc.

Resources are all kinds of inputs like material, components, parts, machinery, equipment, capital, human resources including talented employees, competent technical personnel and efficient managers. Though the resources are more essential to an organisation, they alone do not yield a competitive advantage. However, competitive advantage of a firm is created through unique blending, bundling and building of all kinds of resources. For example, Dell computers interlinked technology and human resources to build an efficient business model. This model helped Dell to sell computers directly to customers by eliminating market intermediaries like dealers and retailers, which in turn, created a distinctive competitive advantage for the Dell Computer Corporation.

Organisational resources are tangible and intangible resources. Tangible resources can be seen and quantified like buildings, machinery, equipment and vehicles. Intangible resources are those rooted deeply in the organisation's history and that have accumulated over time. Examples of intangible resources are employee's knowledge, trust, ideas, scientific capabilities, capacity to innovate and managerial competence, reputation with customers like brand name and perception of product quality, durability and reliability and reputation with suppliers for efficient, effective, supportive and mutually beneficial interactions and relationships.

Why resources are valuable?

Organisational resources determine strengths and weaknesses. Managers can structure the composition of resources in order to maximise strengths and minimise weaknesses. The following factors help to determine what constitutes a valuable asset, capacity or competence.

1. **Competitive superiority:** Organisations with different resources have different degrees of competitive abilities. For example, the company with latest technology possesses competitive superiority over other companies. Similarly, companies with best talented and competent human resources enjoy the competitive superiority over other companies in terms of most efficient ideas, customer service, low cost and best quality. Similarly, patents determine the competitive advantage. For example, Coca-Cola's cola formula brought competitive superiority to the company.

2. **Resource scarcity:** When a particular resource contributing significantly to the value of the product/service is in short supply, such a resource determines the distinctive capability of a firm. Thus, the firms possessing such a scare resource possess distinctive capability over other firms.

3. **Inimitability:** If a particular resource possessed by a firm can't be imitated/copied easily by the competitors, such a resource provides distinctive capability to the firms in the long-run. In contrast the firms possess distinctive advantage only in the short-run, when the resource can be copied/imitated easily. For example, Wendy's idea of providing 'drive through' facility in its hamburger business provided a distinctive capability to the firm in short-run as this idea was copied and practiced easily by other fast-food restaurants. Thus, competitors copy/imitate the distinctive competency of the firm at least in the short-run. Therefore, firms should develop unique resources based on the following characteristics in order to sustain the distinctive capability.

• **Physically Unique Resources:** Physically unique resources are virtually impossible to copy/imitate. Design of the Maruti cars, Cola formula of Coca-Cola, beer ingredients, structure of ice beer of S.P. Brewery Limited, aroma of Bru Coffee are proved to be unique resources as their competitors could not copy them.

• **Path-dependent Resources:** Path-dependent resources are created by the firm over a period of time through their continuous effort. Therefore, it would be difficult for the competitors to acquire/imitate/copy of such resources. For example, Coca-Cola developed the present coke formula over a period of time. Similarly, LG developed a distinctive variety of refrigerator that can store special Korean pickle for over a year. Farex baby foods, Dr. Reddy Lab's low cost pharmaceutical products and Toyota automobiles are examples of the distinctive resources developed by the companies that can't be copied by the competitors.

• **Casual Ambiguity:** Certain firms create and/or develop competitive advantage that can't be known exactly by others and therefore can't be understood and imitated by the competitors. Casual ambiguous resources arise from subtle combinations of tangible and intangible assets, social and cultural factors, processes and organisational attributes the company possesses. For example, employee freedom and risk-taking culture of a biscuit company enabled an employee to play with the production process and machinery and develop sweet-cum-salt biscuits. Similarly, South-West Airlines developed a number of new methods and approaches by casual ambiguity consequent upon the breaking culture adapted by the company.

• **Economic Deterrence:** Economic deterrence occurs when the requirement of capital for establishing manufacturing facilities is quite large and the size of the market is small only to accommodate a single player. Hence, competitors may not enter the market. For example, Air Niugini has no competitor due to the large size of capital requirement to establish an airline company and small size of airways market in Papua New Guinea. Similarly, Pepsi-Cola Limited withdrew from the Papua New Guinea market due to the small size of the market and low rate of return on capital employed.

4. **Appropriate the Profits:** Different parties like owners/shareholders, human resources, input suppliers, output dealers contribute their resources to the success of the business and thereby to profits. Thus, the contributors of these resources are expected to share the profits created by the resource providers.

5. **Durability:** Durability deals with the extent of the time span that the value of resources remain. Value of some resources increase over time while the value of some other resources depreciates over the period. For example, the value of land appreciates over the period due to scarcity of land while the value of technology depreciates over the period due to the invention of new technology and displacement of old technology by the latest technology. The value of brands of most of the varieties of wine appreciates while the value of computer technologies, mobile telephone technologies and technologies of electronic products depreciates.

6. **Substitutability:** Easy developmental of substitute products depreciates the value of the resource of the product and *vice versa*. For example, development of mobile phones depreciated the value of 'pagers' and 'land phones'. Similarly, development of computers depreciated the value of manual and electronic type writers. Development of photocopying machines depreciated to value of carbon paper technology. Limited scope for development of alternatives for land enhanced the value of land.

Resource-Based View and Organisational Analysis

Companies must evaluate their resources in order to estimate their future competitive advantage. Organisations should analyse various resources to gauge the value of each resource to the firm as well as to its competitive advantage. The following guidelines are helpful to analyse an organisation's resources.

- Disaggregate Resources: Organisations should disaggregate their resources into minute aspects and scan each aspect of resources in order to assess organisation's capabilities.
- Utilise a Functional Perspective: After breaking the resources into minute areas, attribute each minute area to a concerned functional perspective.
- Look at Organisational Processes: After minute resource analysis, combine the analysis in order to present an unified view of the total organisation.

Resources and Competitive Advantage

Competitive advantage of a firm as well as its sustainability depends upon the firm's resources. Grant proposes a five-step resource-based approach to internal analysis.

Competitive advantage of a firm as well as its sustainability depends upon the firm's resources.

- Analyse the firm's resources in terms of strengths and weaknesses.
- Combine the firm's strengths into specific capabilities. Identify the capabilities that can help the firm significantly in achieving its mission. These corporate capabilities are viewed as distinctive capabilities, when the firm alone possesses these capabilities.
- Appraise the corporate capabilities in terms of their potential contribution to profit earning capacity of the firm as well as their sustainable contribution.
- Select the strategy that best exploits the firm's resources and capabilities relative to external environment.
- Identify resource gaps and bridge them for upgrading weaknesses.

Sustainability of Resource Advantage

As discussed earlier, resource advantage is not for ever. Some resource advantages sustain for a long period while some other resource advantages stay for a short period. Sustainability of resource advantage is determined by two characteristics, *viz.,* durability and inimitability.

Inimitability: Inimitability, as discussed earlier, is the rate at which a firm's resources are copied/duplicated by the competitors. Competitor's abilities to imitate include copying the product design by reverse engineering, copying the marketing strategies, scout the talent employees, suppliers of inputs and market intermediaries of the competitor and copying the production processes.

Imitation of a company's capabilities is dependent on three factors, *viz.,* transparency, transferability and replicability.

Transparency: Transparency is the degree of openness of a company's abilities, competencies and talent's that indicates the vulnerability for copying. For example, the formula of Coca-Cola's cola is not at all transparent and as such the competitors could not copy.

Transferability: Transferability is the degree and speed at which the competitors can acquire the capabilities of a firm. Product design, technology as well as production process of biscuits can be easily imitated. As such, most of the biscuit companies are more vulnerable for copying.

Replicability: Replicability is the competitor's ability to use copied resources for the success of the firm. Many movie making companies copy the theme of already released movies of the competitors.

Now, we shall discuss another factor of resource, capabilities and core competencies, i.e., capabilities.

Capabilities: Capabilities are the firm's capacity to deploy resources that have been purposely integrated to achieve a desired state.

Capabilities

Capabilities are the organisation's capacity to deploy resources that have been purposely integrated to achieve desired end state. Capabilities are the outcomes of interactions among tangible and intangible resources. For example, IBM's capabilities are the interaction of its tangible resources like its employees, knowledge and ideas with regard to product development and the market strategies employed over the period.

Capabilities are the organisation's capacity to deploy resources that have been purposely integrated to achieve desired end state.

Capabilities enable firms to create and exploit opportunities and develop sustained advantages. Dr. Reddy's Lab's capabilities enabled the company to create marketing opportunities in most of the developing countries particularly in Africa in addition to India. Capabilities are based on developing, carrying and exchanging information and knowledge through the firm's human capital. For example, Yahoo and Google's employees developed a number of products through exchange of information, knowledge, talent and expertise. Ranbaxy, Microsoft and Infosys believe in their intellectual capacity of their employees.

Intellectual capabilities: In fact, it is felt that a company builds capabilities not based on technology, and other physical assets but from the knowledge, skills, talents, intellectual capital and commitment of its human resources. Therefore, companies should concentrate on providing congenial work environment, so that individual employee's intellectual capital would be synergized into organisation's knowledge, skill and commitment that forms the company's intellectual capability.

Organisations in order to enhance their intellectual capability have been shifting into learning organisations by enabling their existing employees to learn continuously, developing alliances with the people of consultant organisations, and employing more competent people. In addition, organisations employ 'Chief Learning Officers' and 'Chief Knowledge Officers', who in turn convert the individual knowledge and talents into organisation knowledge and skill.

Thus, a company's human capital — individual and synergized — in the form of knowledge, skills, talent and commitment form the capabilities and a key source of its competitive advantage during this current century. Human knowledge takes the shape of the innovations, creations, new ideas, effective strategies, new product/services and enhanced functions/uses of the existing product or service.

Organisations, in addition to human capabilities, build capabilities in other areas like manufacturing, marketing and research and development. Manufacturing capabilities include designing a new product, effective production process that reduces manufacturing cycle time and minimises cost of production. For example, Mazda developed an innovative production process that reduced the assembly time. Other manufacturing capabilities include sophistication of production technology, and designing quality. Marketing capabilities include effective use of logistics management techniques, building up of brands and developing customer relationships. For example, Reliance Fresh and More Super Markets build the capabilities around using effective logistics management techniques, whereas McDonald's and Singapore Airlines build capabilities around customer relationship management and Gillette builds effective brand images. Research and development capabilities include exceptional focus on innovation as developed by Sony, exceptional technological capability by Corning and development of deep knowledge in the development of alternative materials as is the case with Kodak.

The Body Shop developed the capabilities in motivating, empowering and retaining employees while Hewlett-Packard build the capabilities around effective execution of managerial tasks. Organisations strive to convert capabilities into core competencies.

(B) CORE COMPETENCIES

Core competencies are a company's resources and capabilities that enable the firm to build competitive advantage over the competitors.

Core competencies are a company's resources and capabilities that enable the firm to build competitive advantage over the competitors. Companies build competitive advantage by procuring and multiplying resources, create abilities over them, and developing synergy of resources and capabilities. Core competencies enable the companies to formulate strategies and draw strategic actions by converting competencies into business activities. Thus, the companies achieve their goals of earning an expected profit, improve market share and satisfy their employees by using their core competencies.

For example, Vodafone India utilised its technical manpower and financial resources to build towers in Indian villages. This competency enabled the company to increase its share in the rural market and thereby its total market in India by 2% between 2005 and 2009. Similarly, Digicel (PNG) Ltd., also built towers in rural areas of Papua New Guinea in addition to urban centres by utilising its Financial, technical and resources. This capability enabled the company to acquire core competency over Be-Mobile Ltd., which was enjoying monopoly in mobile phone service in Papua New Guinea until 2007.

Thus, core competencies are those capabilities and resources that enable the company to perform and act to achieve its goals by adding or creating unique value to its goods and/or services better compared to its competitors in the long term. Therefore, all the resources and capabilities of a company need not result in competencies. It does mean that the resources and capabilities could be utilised in building a competitive advantage. These resources have competitive value and potential to serve as competitive advantage. Thus, some resources would represent a liability as the company may be weak over competitors in that resource area. Similarly, the firm may fail to utilise such resource during a particular time to build its competencies. For example, Deccan Airlines could not use its capabilities of seating capacity as its competitors like King Fisher due to its inabilities in maintaining punctuality during 2006.

When companies fail to convert certain resources into competencies, due to competition and external environmental threats, companies should find other markets or portfolios of business where such resources become capabilities. For example, Toyota introduced its outdated model and technology of home country in India and other developing countries.

How Many Core Competencies?

The mind boggling question at this juncture is how many core competencies are required for a company? It is obvious that a company can't have core competencies in all areas. McKinsey & Company identifies that their clients craft their strategies around them four core competencies. Core competencies of some selected companies are provided in the Exhibit 5.1.

Exhibit 5.1: Core Competencies of Some Selected Companies

Company	*Core Competencies*
McDonald	Real estate, restaurant operations, marketing and global infrastructure
Ford	Design, branding, sales, service operations
Honeywell	Technology, customer service
Brady Corporation	Safety, graphics, special products
Vodafone	Extensive coverage, technology, low cost
Dr. Reddy's Lab	Low cost, quality, wide range of product

Building Core Competencies

As indicated earlier, all capabilities need not be core competencies. Two tools help us to know whether a particular capability is a core competency or not. The first one consists of four specific criteria and the second one is value chain analysis.

Four criteria for determining core capabilities include:

- Valuable capabilities
- Rare capabilities
- Costly-to-imitate capabilities
- Non-substitutable capabilities

Valuable capabilities: Valuable capabilities create and add value by exploiting opportunities provided by external environment to the company. Digicel (PNG) Ltd.'s appropriate technical and financial capabilities enabled it to exploit the opportunities provided by the Papua New Guinea's environment like high cost of mobile services as well as instrument costs.

Similarly, non-availability of required quantity of petrol and other Petroleum products in Indian market were exploited by the technical, financial and skilled human resources of Reliance Petrochemicals Ltd. The vast experience of expertise of Wal-Mart in Retail Super-Market malls enabled it to exploit the retail market business in India.

The following exhibit presents the valuable capabilities of various companies and the opportunities that were exploited by them.

Exhibit 5.2 : Value capabilities and the opportunities exploited

Company	*Value capabilities*	*Opportunities exploited*
Sony Corporation	Expertise in designing, producing and selling	Portable disc players, easy to hold 8-mm video cameras market
Wal-Mart	Distribution capabilities	Market for low price for branded products. In fact, other retailers were charging high prices in USA.
J. Boag & Son Brewery	Brewing and marketing premium beer	Non-availability of premium beer
Vodafone (India)	Technical and financial capabilities	Entered rural mobile phone market in India by constructing towers in rural India.
Digicel (PNG) Ltd.	Technical and financial capabilities of medium level suitable for small markets.	High priced mobile services in a small market of Papua New Guinea.
Tata	Expertise in Automobiles	Small car market for low income group of India (Nano brand cars)
Dr. Reddy's Lab	Capabilities in bulk drugs, expertise in producing low cost pharmaceuticals	Exploited low-income customer markets in India and other Third World countries.

Rare: Rare capabilities are those that are possessed by the competitors rarely. In fact, many companies possess valuable capabilities, but not rare. Even having an innovative idea is also a rare capability. Companies with rare capabilities exploit external opportunities to a significant extent, compared to their competitors. The following capabilities possessed by the companies are viewed as rare capabilities.

Exhibit 5.3

Company	*Rare capabilities*	*Opportunities Exploited*
Coca-Cola	Idea of introduction of small size bottle of coke for low-income group	Successfully entered and exploited lower income group market
Coca-Cola	Product formula	Market leader
L & G	Idea and development of special refrigerator for storing traditional Korean food	Turned around the sick company
Dell	Business model of selling the product directly to customers	Successfully exploited the market.
Computershare Ltd.	Idea of development of share registry software	Became global share registry.
Eureka Vacuum Cleaners	Special sales approach based on problems of Indian housewives product formula	Grabbed the household market for vaccum cleaners.

Costly to Imitate Capabilities: Costly to imitate capabilities are those capabilities that pose complexity and thereby heavy cost to competitors to imitate. These capabilities include unique organisational culture, brand name, interpersonal relations, trust, network with customers, suppliers, creditors, etc.

The following exhibit presents the capabilities that are costly to imitate of some selected companies.

Exhibit 5.4

Company/Product	*Costly/Capabilities*
McKinsey	Organisational culture
Tata Group	Historical reasons
Colgate Palmolive	Product brand
Airtel	Clarity of voice
McDonald	Taste of the food
Starbuck	Coffee flavour
3 Roses Tea	Aroma

Other reasons for the costly capabilities to imitate include:

- Casual ambiguity in linking a company's capabilities, competencies and competitive advantage.
- Social complexity: Social complexity involves complex social relations among managers, suppliers, creditors, market intermediaries and government officials.

Companies that developed social complexity as a competitive advantage include Tata group, Reliance Industries, Hewlett-Packard, Sony, Walt Disney company, Merck, Harvey Norman, General Electric and Toyota.

Non-substitutable: Non-substitutable capabilities are those that do not have strategic equivalents. Non-substitutable capabilities include company's specific capacities like trust, relationships, product attributes, knowledge and expertise. Coca-Cola's formula can be regarded as non-substitutable capability.

The following table presents the possible outcomes from combinations of criteria for sustainable competitive advantage.

Table: Possible outcomes from the combinations of criteria for Sustainable Competitive Advantage

Value	*Rare*	*Costly*	*Non-substitutable*	*Competitive Consequences*	*Performance* Implications
No	No	No	No	Competitive Disadvantage	Below-average Returns
Yes	No	No	Yes/No	Competitive Parity	Average Returns
Yes	Yes	No	Yes/No	Temporary Competitive Advantage	About-average to Average Returns
Yes	Yes	Yes	Yes	Sustainable Competitive Advantage	Above-average Returns

Source: Adapted from Dallas Hanson, *et. al.*, p. 104.

(C) VALUE CHAIN ANALYSIS AND OUTSOURCING

Value is the amount buyers desire to pay for what a firm provides to them in the form of a product/service/product-cum-service. Creating value for buyers that exceeds the cost of manufacturing, marketing and other operations is one of the basic goals of any business unit's generic strategy. Business activities that transform inputs into desired output that customers value reflect the value chain. Value chain analysis examines and enhances the efforts of the business operations that contribute to the value to the customers. Value chain analysis views the business as a process of activities from the stage of raw material/inputs to the final stage of delivering the product including after sales service to the customer. Value chain analysis examines the areas of advantages of low cost and disadvantages of high costs. It further tries to further reduce the cost in the low cost areas and attempts to turn the high costs into low costs in order to reduce overall costs of all operations. Value Chain analysis, in addition to attempting to reduce the cost, also attempts to enhance the value to the customer. It enhances the value by contributing to the quality, convenience and comfort to the customer. Michael E. Porter contributed to identifying building blocks, assessing the value addition from each of the activities and linking their organisation's competitive advantage. The value chain display consists of total value of activities and margin. Value activities are of two types, *viz.*, primary activities and support activities (See Fig. 5.1)

Value chain analysis examines the areas of advantages of low cost and disadvantages of high costs.

Primary Activities: Primary activities are those business activities that relate and contribute directly to the manufacture, marketing of the product and creating and adding value in the chain of operations. Thus, primary activities form the sequence or chain through which raw materials/inputs are transformed into final product/service that the customers use including the post-sales service. Primary activities, thus, include:

- Inbound Logistics: These are the activities concerned with receiving, storing and issuing all kinds of raw materials and spare parts to the manufacturing/service centers. Materials handling, inventory management, stock control, storage, transportation are some of the functions involved in this activity.
- Operations: Production/operations activities aim at transforming inputs into products. These activities include machining, assembling, testing, packaging and delivering.
- Outbound Logistics: These activities include collection of finished goods, handling them, storing them, transporting them to marketing intermediaries and customers.
- Marketing and Sales: These activities include promotional programmes like advertising, personal selling and sales promotion, sales administration, product delivery and the like.
- Service: Service activities include pre-sales service to create demand and sales and post-sales service to enhance the value of product or service.

How do primary activities add to the value?

Primary activities add to the value of the product by reducing the cost as well as by improving the quality and convenience. Now, we shall discuss these aspects.

Inbound Logistics: Inbound logistics include quality verification of raw material at the source, transportation in good condition and efficiently, storage and warehousing economically and efficiently controlled. These activities ensure the quality of raw material that can contribute to the quality of the final product. In addition to performing these activities on time, ensure the timely distribution of the product to market intermediaries and the customer. Further efficient handling of these activities, better negotiations and maintenance of sound relationship with the supplier reduce the cost of inbound logistics. Inbound logistics contribute significantly to enhancement of value as raw materials account for more than 50% of product cost in majority of products.

Infrastructure and facilities for inbound logistics require heavy capital investment contributing significantly to the cost of final products. Therefore, firms employ modern techniques to reduce the investment requirement. For example, General Electric uses highly automated sorting and inventory systems that allow the material to move quickly from stores to the factory. This technique reduces the storage cost as well as inventory cost significantly. Some firms outsource these activities, and thus reduces the requirement of heavy investments.

Inbound activities play a vital role even in service industries like banking, insurance companies, hospitals, educational institutions, telecommunication services and transportation services. Procurement of medical equipment, pharmaceuticals and stationery influences the quality and cost of the services in hospitals. Similarly, efficient handling of inputs play vital role in determining quality, cost, convenience and customer satisfaction in hotel industry as well as in educational institutions.

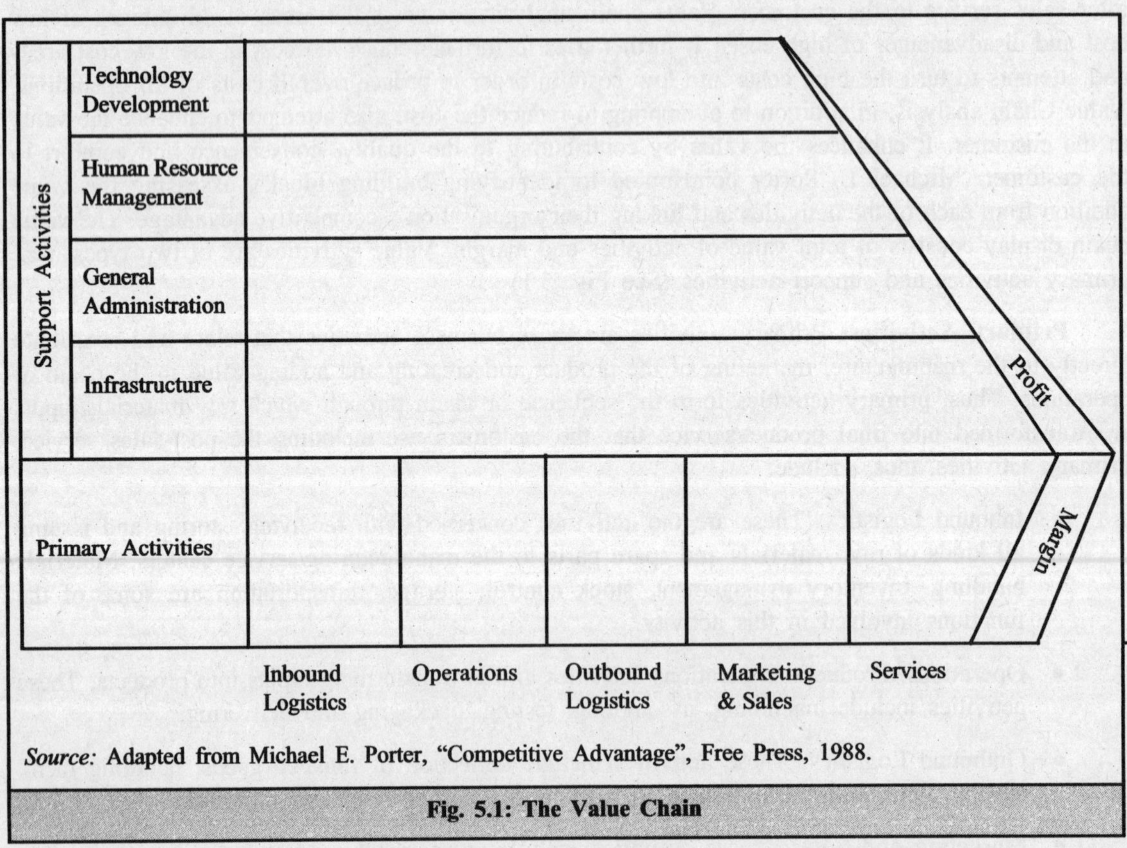

Source: Adapted from Michael E. Porter, "Competitive Advantage", Free Press, 1988.

Fig. 5.1: The Value Chain

Operations: Operations/production deal with the conversion process that transforms the inputs into output. Value is added or created when the input is converted into output. Operations aim at creation and innovation which in turn enhances the value of the product. Further the objectives of zero defect products ensure quality and dependability of the product.

Product design directly contributes to the value as customers that would pay higher price for the product designed in accordance with their unexhibited/unexpressed needs as well as conveniences. Appropriate type of process contributes to the cost reduction, speed of production and improved quality. Similarly, selection and practice of other production activities, appropriate technology, facilities like capacity, aggregate planning and scheduling of operations, efficient management of inventory and planning and control of quality contribute to the value.

Outbound Logistics: Outbound logistics begin after the completion of the production process and end with the distribution of the product either to the market intermediaries in case of indirect marketing and to the customer in case of direct marketing. Thus, the activities of outbound logistics include storage/warehousing, transportation, handling of products, negotiation with market intermediaries and inventory management. Efficient performance of these activities enables the firm to deliver on the products in taste to the customer, reduce delivery time and storage. Thereby, it reduces the cost of inventory.

Strides in information technology resulted in Internet-based marketing, helps the marketing intermediaries like wholesalers and retailers to maintain lowest level or close to zero level inventory. Some of the companies producing fast moving consumer goods track the inventory, orders, transportation, storage and the like. Dr. Reddy's Lab tracks the transportation, storage and inventory. P&G reduced the transportation time and the complexities in tracking the products by using Internet–based on-line inventory management. Efficient and fast outbound logistics of P&G enabled it to track the fast moving products, sharing the information with super markets about the customer tastes and demands and thereby develop new ideas for future product development. Thus, efficient and Internet-based online outbound logistic activities reduce cost, increases innovation and delivers the products intact.

Marketing and Sales: Marketing and sales activities include product development and mix, pricing, place of markets including channels of distribution like wholesalers, retailers, sales force and network marketing and promotional mix including advertising, personal selling and sales promotion. Companies select different marketing strategies like leader or follower strategies, total market or niche or focus strategies, single product line or multiple product line strategy, direct marketing or indirect marketing strategies and specified place marketing or online marketing. Companies select the strategies in order to reduce the marketing costs and enhance the convenience and comfort to the customers. Some of the hotels in India in order to enhance the convenience to the customer introduced phone ordering and home delivery. Even super markets follow this strategy. Most of the airlines including Singapore Airlines, Indian Airlines and Air Nuigini introduced online ticket booking in order to reduce the marketing cost and thereby ticket price and enhance customer convenience. Even Indian Railways and many road transport companies introduced online ticket booking. Firms also advertise online using Internet that reduces cost and reaches customers fast.

In fact, some companies design excellent marketing strategies that enable the customer to be willing to pay the price that is quite higher than the product cost, thus, enhancing the value. For example, Coca-Cola, Pepsi-Cola and other cola drinks as well as mineral water companies price their products significantly higher than the cost of the production of their respective products. They could do so mostly due to their marketing and sales efforts.

Service: Pre-sales and post-sales services are quite essential for consumer durable, convenience and luxury goods. Customers would be willing to pay more when the service and thereby the continuous and perfect functioning of the product is guaranteed and/or ensured. For example, automobiles, refrigerators, TVs, educational instruments like computers, overhead projectors/multimedia projectors and photocopying machines need after sales services. Excellent after sales service ensures continuous and perfect functioning of the product and thus, enhances customer's value.

In addition, the service reduces the replacement cost of the product as well as working cost. For example, the excellent service facilities provided by Maruti Udyog Limited throughout the country enhanced the running life and reduced running cost of its cars.

Support Activities: Other activities of the business are support activities which provide support to the primary activities of the business, and hence, they are referred to as support activities. Support activities help the company enhance the customer value and reduce the cost by bringing coordination among primary activities and providing necessary inputs for the primary activities. Support activities include:

- Technology development
- Human resource management
- General administration
- Infrastructure

Technology Development: Technology is improved continuously both in production and in other operations. It is developed through innovation and continuous up-gradation. Technology revolution including the revolution in the information technology brought paradigm shifts in the production process, product functions and utilities, speed of manufacturing, quality of products in terms of zero-defect production, fast delivery of the products and information processing. Technology development enables the companies to add multiple functions to the product. For example, mobile phone today carries the functions of a clock, alarm, calculator, tape recorder, camera and video camera. Similarly, multiple functions are added to computers. Thus, technology development enhances the customer value by adding a variety of functions to the existing product. In addition, it reduces the cost of the product in terms of the utility of all functions put together. Technology development supports the primary activities. Inbound logistics are helped by transportation technology, materials handling technology, and storage technologies. For example, containerisation made the sea transportation become more convenient. Jet planes help fast movement and air conditioning of containers helps in the export of even perishable products to foreign countries.

Production and operations are directly helped by the technology development. Automation of production process, coding of stores activities and movement of the raw materials enable the production process to be economical, fast and of high quality. Designing and production of customized products, computer-aided design and computer-aided production became possible due to technology development. Technology enables outbound logistics for efficient and fast delivery in addition to intact delivery to the customer. As indicated in case of inbound logistics, containerisation, increase in speed of transport vehicles and other technologies relating to storage enhanced the efficiency of outbound logistics.

Product development, advertising, sales promotion and service activities are performed most efficiently due to technological development. Thus, developments in technology support the outbound logistics and service activities.

Human Resource Management: Human resource plays a dominant role in the successful and profitable performance of a firm. In fact, human resource makes or mars the performance of a company. The motivated, committed and efficient human resources significantly support primary activities. Skilled and trained human resources provide necessary support for all primary activities. In fact, all primary activities are performed by human resources.

Human resource is also referred to as human capital and asset. It determines the competitive advantage and distinctive competency of a firm. Efficient human resource management in terms of selection of right people, development, motivation, employee empowerment and the like provide required human effort for successful operation of all primary activities. Efficient human resource contributes towards increase in productivity which in turn reduces cost of production. In addition, efficient human resources contribute to the quality, customer convenience and comfort and thereby enhance value and profit margin of the company.

General Administration: General administration includes organisational structure, management style, leadership style, policies and procedures. General administrative policies and practice can be enabling or disabling. Enabling policies and practices include: flat and horizontal structure, employees empowerment, decentralisation, empowerment of employees in decision-making, strategy formulation and implementation, employee motivation, leading the employees progressively and development of commitment. These enabling policies of general administration support the primary activities, which in turn contribute to the reduction of cost and enhancement of value and profit margin.

Infrastructure: Infrastructural activities include accounting, finance, information system, pay roll, legal affairs, public relations and corporate governance. Expenditure on these activities is called overhead expenses as this expenditure can not be isolated. Infrastructure activities contribute to the value addition by supporting and enabling the primary activities. In addition, the efficient functioning of infrastructure activities contributes to the cost reduction, and thereby increase profit margin.

Outsourcing

Outsourcing is the long-term contracting out of mostly non-core business processes to an outside provider to help achieve increased value for the business. Availability of highly qualified skill pool and faster adaptation of well-defined business processes lead to higher productivity gains without compromising on quality. Outsourcing creates and adds value to the business by

- enabling the executives to concentrate on strategic areas,
- improving processes and saving money, and
- increasing business capabilities.

Outsourcing has been increasing in order to meet the growing international demand for lucrative and customer-interaction centres. Many organisations worldwide are outsourcing these services to locations like India, China, South Korea and Malaysia.

Outsourcing has been increasing in order to meet the growing international demand for lucrative and customer-interaction centres.

Many companies acquire the capabilities by outsourcing some of the business operations. Ford Motor Company could acquire the capabilities of reducing the cost of key parts by outsourcing. Nissan Motor Company outsourced the maintenance of its North American Computer Systems to IBM in order to reduce its costs. Dell Computers concentrates on creating value through its distribution channels by outsourcing most of its manufacturing and customer service activities. Nike and Reebok concentrates on their core competencies of designing and marketing by outsourcing production activities. In fact, small firms were developed in Vietnam and other countries due to the outsourcing of production activities by Nike and Reebok. These companies could further enhance their core capabilities and competencies by outsourcing the business processes in which they lack core competencies.

Organisational Analysis

Organisational appraisal is the process of monitoring an organisation's internal environment to identify strengths and weaknesses that may influence the firm's ability to achieve goals. The internal environment of an organisation includes forces that operate inside the organisation with specific implications for managing organisational performance. Internal environmental factors which come from within collectively define both trouble spots that need strengthening and the core competencies that the firm can build. An organisation can better analyse how much activity might add value or contribute significantly to shape an effective strategy by systematically examining its internal environment. Michael Porter has proposed a method for such an evaluation. This method is called value chain analysis. Value chain analysis can identify internal core competencies. Internal core competencies can be identified by analysing functional areas of business. The purpose of analysing an organisation's internal environment is to identify and evaluate organisational strengths and weaknesses.

(D) STRENGTHS AND WEAKNESSES ANALYSIS

Organisational analysis requires data and information about the internal environment. SWOT analysis refines this information by applying a general framework for understanding and managing the environment under which a company operates. (The acronym SWOT stands for strengths, weaknesses, opportunities and threats). A SWOT analysis consists of evaluating a company's internal strengths and weaknesses and its external opportunities and threats. SWOT analysis underscores the basic point that strategy must produce a good fit between a firm's internal capability (its strengths and weaknesses) and its external situation (its opportunities and threats).

1. Identifying Strengths and Weaknesses

A strength is a strong point for the company, *i.e.,* something a company is good at doing or a characteristic that gives it an important capability.

A strength is a strong point for the company, *i.e.,* something a company is good at doing or a characteristic that gives it an important capability. A strength can be a skill, a competence, a valuable organisational resource or competitive capability or achievement that gives the company an advantage. A weakness is something the company does not have or does poorly (in comparison to competitors or standards) or a condition that puts it at a disadvantageous positions. A weakness may or may not make an organisation competitively vulnerable, depending on how much it matters in the competition battle.

SWOT analysis of a company is presented in Exhibit 5.5. The lists of strengths and weaknesses have to be evaluated after they have been identified. Important and crucial strengths are to be identified. These factors count more in determining performance, in competing efficiently and in formulating powerful strategy. Similarly some weaknesses can be fatal whereas others can be easily remedied. Such weaknesses should also be spotted out. Strengths are like strategic assets and weaknesses are like competitive liabilities. Unlike in financial balance sheet, the strengths/assets should be more than the weaknesses/liabilities in the strategic balance sheet.

A company's strengths are more significant. They can be used as cornerstones of the strategy. They are the basis for building competitive advantages. If a company does not have strengths to build competitive advantages, the management has to develop competencies quickly. These competencies can be the basis for building competitive advantages.

Successful strategists seek to exploit what a company does best — its expertise, strengths, core competencies and strongest competitive capabilities. At the same time, the successful strategists seek to correct the competitive weaknesses. Otherwise, these weaknesses hurt the company's performance, and disqualify it from pursuing an attractive opportunity. In essence, an organisation's strategy should be well-fitted to company's strengths, weaknesses and competitive capabilities. Thus, the company should build its strategy around the strengths and avoid the area of weaknesses.

2. Distinctive/Core Competencies

The company should consolidate its production, technological, marketing, finance and human resource know-how into competencies to enhance its competitiveness. A distinctive or core competence is something a company does especially well in comparison to its competitors. The distinctive competence is the unique capability it gives an organisation in capitalising upon a particular opportunity; the competitive edge it may give a firm in the market place and the potential for building a distinctive competence and making it the cornerstone of strategy. Thus, a distinctive competence is, "any advantage a company has over its competitors because it can do something which they cannot or it can do something better than they can."

Distinctive or core competencies empower a company to build competitive advantage. Core competencies include excellent quality maintenance, lowest production cost, latest technology utilisation, ability to provide required service, ability to develop new products, high creditworthiness, etc.

Distinctive or core competencies empower a company to build competitive advantage. Core competencies include excellent quality maintenance, lowest production cost, latest technology utilisation, ability to provide required service, ability to develop new products, high creditworthiness, etc. The benefits of core competences in formulating strategies include: (a) the company gets an added capability in going after a particular market opportunity, (b) the company gets the competitive edge it can yield in the market place, and (c) its potential for being cornerstone of strategy.

3. Identifying Opportunities and Threats

Opportunities and threats of a company can also be seen in Exhibit 5.5. There are differences between the industry's opportunities and a firm's opportunities except in one firm industry. Some firms are in better position than other firms in the same industry, in utilising the opportunities. This situation is based on the firm's strengths and weaknesses. The industry opportunities most relevant to a specific firm are those that offer significant avenues for growth and those where a firm has the most potential for competitive advantages. Certain external environmental factors pose threats to a firm. These threats include: adoption of latest technology by the competitors, inflow of high quality and improved products from foreign markets, entry of multinational and transnational corporations, change in the customer's preferences, change in governmental policies, failure of the markets, etc.

Strategy must be formulated to *(i)* pursue opportunities suited to the firm's strengths or competencies, and *(ii)* provide a defense against threats posed by the environment. The SWOT analysis should appraise a firm's strengths, weaknesses, opportunities and threats and draw conclusions about the firm's attractiveness. Exhibit 5.6 presents strategy-making questions.

Exhibit 5.5: SWOT Analysis — What to Look for in Sizing up a Company's Strengths, Weaknesses, Opportunities, and Threats

Potential Internal Strengths

- Core competencies in key areas
- Adequate financial resources
- Well thought of by buyers
- An acknowledged market leader
- Well-conceived functional area strategies
- Access to economies of scale
- Insulated (at least somewhat) from strong competitive pressures
- Proprietary technology
- Cost advantages
- Better advertising campaigns
- Product innovation skills
- Proven management
- Ahead on experience curve
- Better manufacturing capability
- Superior technological skills
- Others

Potential Internal Weaknesses

- No clear strategic direction
- Obsolete facilities
- Super profitability because?
- Lack of managerial depth and talent
- Missing some key skills or competences
- Poor track record in implementing strategy
- Plagued with internal operating problems
- Falling behind in R&D
- Too narrow a product line
- Weak market image
- Weak distribution network
- Below-average marketing skills
- Unable to finance needed changes in strategy
- Higher overall unit costs relative to key competitors
- Others

Potential External Opportunities

- Serve additional customer groups
- Enter new markets or segments
- Expand product line to meet broader range of customer needs
- Diversify into related products
- Vertical integration (forward or backward)
- Falling trade barriers in attractive foreign markets
- Complacency among rival firms
- Faster market growth
- Others

Potential External Threats

- Entry of lower-cost foreign competitors
- Rising sales of substitute products
- Slower market growth
- Adverse shifts in foreign exchange rates and trade policies of foreign governments
- Costly regulatory requirements
- Vulnerability to recession and business cycle
- Growing bargaining power of customers or suppliers
- Changing buyer needs and tastes
- Adverse demographic changes
- Others

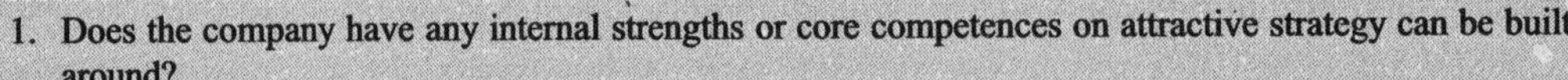

Exhibit 5.6: Strategy-Making Questions

1. Does the company have any internal strengths or core competences on attractive strategy can be built around?
2. Do the company's weaknesses make it competitively vulnerable and/or do they disqualify the firm from pursuing certain opportunities? Which weaknesses does strategy need to correct?
3. Which opportunities does the company have the skills and resources to pursue with a real chance of success? (Remember: opportunity without the means to capture it is an illusion).
4. What threats should managers be worried about most, and what strategic moves should they consider in crafting a good defense?

Source: Adapted from Arthur A. Thompson Jr., and A.J. Strickland III, *op. cit.*, p. 90.

4. Strategic Cost Analysis

One of the critical strengths of a company is its cost position relative to competitors. Cost comparison is critical particularly for those companies producing consumer goods. Therefore, assessing whether a company's costs are competitive with those of its close rivals is a necessary and crucial part of a company's internal environmental analysis. Cost differences among rivals can stem from many factors like prices of raw materials, salary levels and cost of transportation. The lower a company's costs are below those of rivals, the company has an advantage over its competitors. Otherwise, it becomes competitively vulnerable to the company. Strategic cost analysis involves comparing a company's cost position relative to key competitors, activity by activity from raw materials purchase to the price paid by ultimate customers.

(E) COMPETITIVE STRENGTH ASSESSMENT

Systematic assessment of whether a company's competitive position is strong or weak relative to close rivals is an essential step in company's situational analysis. Particular elements to single out for evaluation are: (1) how strongly the firm holds its present competitive position, (2) whether the firm's position can be expected to improve or deteriorate if the present strategy is continued, (3) how the firm ranks relative to key rivals on each important measure of competitive strength and industry key success factor, (4) whether the firm has a net competitive advantage or disadvantage, and (5) the firm's ability to defend its position in light of industry's driving forces, competitive pressure, and the anticipated moves of rivals."

Exhibit 5.7 lists some indicators of strengths and weaknesses in a competitive position showing whether a firm's competitive position is improving or slipping. Competitive strengths and competitive advantages empower a company to improve its long term market position.

Exhibit 5.7: The Signs of Strength and Weakness in a Company's Competitive Position

Signs of Competitive Strength	Signs of Competitive Weakness
• Important core competencies	• Confronted with competitive disadvantages
• Strong market share (or a leading market share)	• Losing ground to rival firms
• A pace-setting or distinctive strategy	• Below-average growth in revenues
• Growing customer base and customer loyalty	• Short on financial resources
• Above-average market visibility	• A slipping reputation with customers
• In a favourably situated strategic group	• Trailing in product development
• Concentrating on fastest-growing market segments	• In a strategic group destined to lose ground
• Strongly differentiated products	• Weak in areas where there is the most market potential
• Cost advantages	• A higher-cost producer
• Above-average profit margins	• Too small to be a major factor in the marketplace
• Above-average technological and innovational capability	• Not in good position to deal with emerging threats
	• Weak product quality
• A creative, entrepreneurially alert management	• Lacking skills and capabilities in key areas
• In position to capitalise on opportunities	

Source: Arthur A. Thompson Jr. and A.J. Strickland III, *op. cit.*, p. 96.

1. Scanning, Forecasting and Other Data Sources for SWOT:

Organisations require cross-functional cooperation to collect data about present and future environments. SWOT analysis becomes a team effort performed by functional specialists from finance, human resources, marketing, production etc. Information gathered from key employees can also help managers to better understand the internal environment of the organisation.

Organisations require cross-functional cooperation to collect data about present and future environments.

Scanning systems can take many different forms. They are:

(i) *Irregular Scanning Systems:* These consists largely of *ad hoc* studies, often in response to environmental crisis.

(ii) *Regular Scanning Systems:* These systems revolve around regular reviews of the environment or selected strategic environmental components.

(iii) *Continuous Scanning Systems:* These systems continuously monitor components of the organisational environment.

Internal environmental forecasting is a critical step in SWOT analysis. It is the process of identifying strategic issues that will affect an organisation's environment at some future time.

Strategic Issues Need To Be Addressed

Effective strategy-making requires a thorough understanding of the strategic issues a company faces. This step puts the company's overall situation into perspective and identifies the situation where management needs to focus its strategic attention.

Strategists should consider the following issues:

1. Whether the present strategy is adequate in light of driving forces at work in the industry.
2. How closely the present strategy matches the industry's future key success factors.
3. How good a defense the present strategy offers against the five competitive forces — future ones, not necessarily past or present ones.
4. In what ways the present strategy may not adequately protect the company against external threats and internal weaknesses.
5. Where and how the company may be vulnerable to competitive attack from one or more rivals.
6. Whether the company has competitive advantage or must work to offset competitive disadvantage.
7. Where the strong spots and weak spots are in the present strategy.
8. Whether additional actions are needed to improve the company's cost position, capitalise on emerging opportunities and strengthen the company's competitive position.

These considerations should indicate whether the company can continue the same basic strategy with minor adjustment or whether it should undertake a major overhaul.

(F) CORPORATE CAPABILITY FACTORS

Corporate capability is the inherent capacity or potential of a company to use its strengths and overcome its weaknesses.

Corporate capability is the inherent capacity or potential of a company to use its strengths and overcome its weaknesses with a view to avail the opportunities provided and face the threats posed by its external environment. Corporate capability factors are also called strategic factors, strategic advantage factors, corporate competence factors, etc. The areas of company capability factors include: general management, marketing, finance, human resource and research development.

Now, we discuss the corporate capability factors in general management and functional management areas, *viz.*, marketing management, financial management, production/operations management, human resource management and research and development.

1. Corporate Capability Factors in General Management

Management is the art of getting things done by the people. It is concerned with the accomplishment of organisational objectives by utilising physical, financial and human resources. Managers perform five basic functions, *viz.*, planning, organising, directing, staffing and controlling. (see Exhibit 5.8).

Planning: Planning is deciding in advance what do to, how to do it, when to do it and who is to do it. Planning bridges the gap from where we are, to where we want to go. Planning minimises the risk and maximises the advantages of opportunities. The purpose of every plan and all supporting plans is to facilitate accomplishment of organisational purpose and objectives. Planning is the cornerstone of effective strategy formulation. Planning is also essential for successful strategy implementation and strategy evaluation. In fact effective planning determines organising, staffing, motivation, leading and controlling. (See Fig. 5.2).

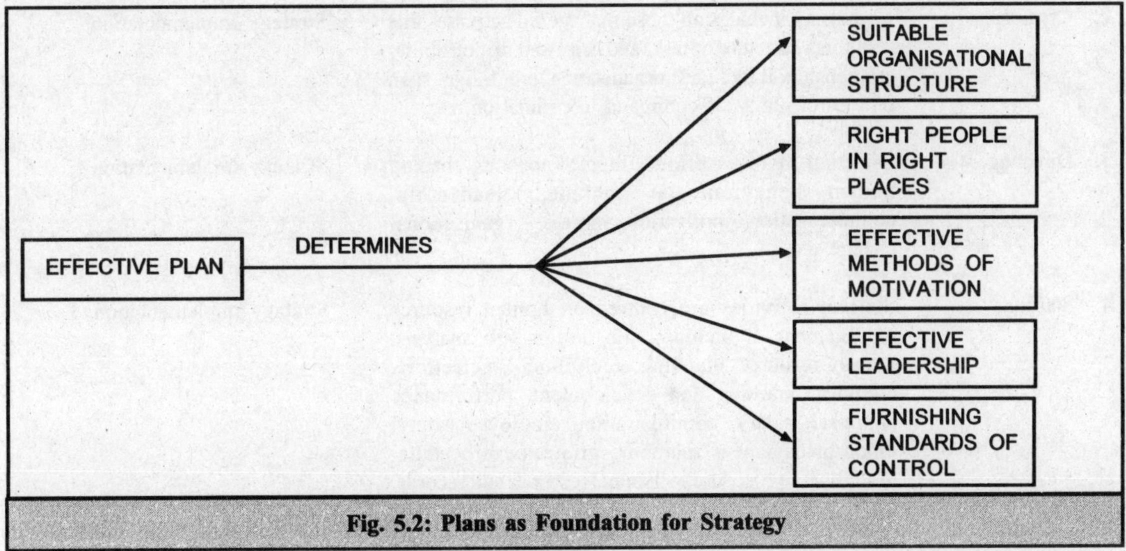

Fig. 5.2: Plans as Foundation for Strategy

Planning logically precedes the execution of all other managerial functions as managerial operations in organising, staffing, leading and controlling are designed to support the accomplishment of enterprise objectives. First, the top management must formulate an enterprise's mission, objectives, strategies before divisional and functional managers can effectively set goals. Therefore, planning to be effective, must begin at the top of an organisation and filter down. The three levels of planning analogous to the three levels of strategic management, are, corporate, strategic business unit and functional. Enterprises that use formal planning approaches are generally more profitable than those that do not.

The reasons for positive impact of planning on organisational and individual performances are:

(i) Planning allows an organisation to identify and take advantage of environmental opportunities, it permits an organisation to minimise the impact of environmental threats, as well. It also determines the likelihood that future trends and events could be harmful or beneficial to an enterprise.

(ii) An enterprise can develop synergy through planning. Synergy exists when members of a team pool together their knowledge and skills. In synergy, the sum of the efforts of all the members of a team is more than the total of all the individual efforts. It can be called the 1 + 1 = 3 effect. All members can work together towards the achievement of desired goals. Synergy can result in powerful competitive advantages.

(iii) Planning enables an enterprise to adapt to changing environments, and shape its own destiny. The strategy management is a formal planning process that allows an organisation to pursue proactive rather than reactive strategies. Thus, the efficient enterprises strive to control and mould their future, rather than merely reacting to external forces and events as they occur.

Exhibit 5.8: The Basic Functions of Management

Function	Description	Most Important at the Stage of Strategic Management Process
1. Planning:	Planning consists of all those managerial activities related to preparing for the future. It includes: forecasting, formulating objectives, policies and goals.	Strategy Formulation
2. Organising:	Organising includes all those managerial activities that result in a structure of task, authority and responsibility relationship. It includes: organisation, job design, span of control, unity of command, coordination, etc.	Strategy Implementation
3. Directing:	Directing involves efforts directed towards shaping human behaviour. It includes: leadership, communication, motivation, morale, organisational change, etc.	Strategy Implementation
4. Staffing:	Staffing activities are centred on human resource management. It includes: job design, job analysis, human resource planning, recruitment, selection., employee training and development, performance appraisal, salary, administration, employee safety, union-management relations, grievance procedure, disciplinary procedure, personnel research and records.	Strategy Implementation
5. Controlling:	Controlling refers to all those managerial activities directed towards assuring that actual results are consistent with planned targets. Key areas are: quality control, financial control, sales control, inventory control, expense control, etc.	Strategy Evaluation

Source: Fred R. David., *op. cit.*, p. 150.

Organising

An organisation is a means to an end. It is essential to carry out the pre-determined course of action. An organisation is a "structure and process by which cooperative group of human beings allocate its task among its members, identifies relationships and integrates its activities towards common objectives." Complex relationships exist between the specialised departments and the general departments as many top managers are seeking the advice from the specialist managers. Thus, organisation establishes relationships among the employees so that they can collectively contribute to the attainment of company goals.

An organisation structure facilitates the contribution of individuals to the attainment of company objectives. It does so by people with minimum unsought consequences or costs. A well organised firm can formulate, implement and evaluate strategies effectively than a disorganised firm. The organisation function includes: combining the tasks into positions, positions into jobs, combining jobs to form departments, and bringing relationships among departments.

Jobs are analysed on the basis of tasks, positions, duties and responsibilities. Jobs are combined into departments based on enterprise function, territory, product, customers, process or equipment, etc. One of the increasingly used forms of organisation is referred to as matrix or project organisation. The essence of matrix organisation normally is the combination of functional and product forms of departmentation in the same organisation structure. As companies and customers have become increasingly interested in end results, there has been pressure to establish responsibility in someone to ensure results.

Organisations can also be structured on the basis of line and staff. Line and staff are viewed as relationships but not as departments. The relationship existing between two managers due to delegation of authority and responsibility and giving or receiving instructions or orders is called line relationship. The relationship between two managers is said to be a staff relation, when it is created due to giving and taking advice, guidance, information, help or assistance, counselling and the like, in the process of attaining organisational goals.

Staffing

The process of staffing is also called personnel management. Personnel management is planning, organising, directing and controlling and procurement, development, compensation, integration and maintenance of people for the purpose of contributing to the individual, organisational and social goals. It is also called human resource management. Human resource managers assist line managers in performing staffing activities like job analysis, human resource planning, recruitment, testing, interviewing, selecting, inducting, placing, appraising performance, training, developing, career planning and rewarding, disciplining, transferring, promoting, demoting, retrenching and dismissing employees.

The human resource management function is not only a significant task but also a complicated one. Hence, all organisations including the small organisations need to employ a special manager for this function. The increasing globalisation of business activity, expansion and diversification of the organisations both product/service-wise and geography-wise resulted in complexity of the task. These factors make the personnel manager to concentrate on managing cultural diversities, quality of work life and the like. The managers sometimes find it difficult to implement the strategies like joint ventures, mergers, etc., in view of the changing trends in human resource management. The strategists, particularly the chief executive officers are becoming increasingly aware of the vitality of human resources in strategic management.

Directing

The next logical function after completing planning, organising and staffing is the achievement of organisational objectives. The basic function of management is motivating, commanding, leading and activating people. The willing and effective cooperation of employees for the attainment of organisational objectives is possible under proper direction. Tapping the maximum potentialities of the people is possible through motivation and command. Coordination deals with the task of blending efforts in order to ensure successful attainment of an objective.

Controlling

The controlling function of management includes all those activities undertaken to ensure that actual performances confirm to planned performances. The controlling activities include:

(i) Establish performance standards,

(ii) Measure actual performance,

(ii) Compare actual performance to planned performance standards,

(iv) Take corrective actions.

The controlling function is particularly significant for efficient strategic evaluation. Exhibit 5.9 depicts check list of corporate capabilities in general management.

This list can be helpful in determining specific strengths and weaknesses in management. Positive answers to these questions indicate capabilities or strengths of the management in that area concerned. Negative answer to any of these questions indicates the weakness of the management in that area.

Exhibit 5.9: Corporate Capabilities in General Management: Checklist

Planning

1. Does the organisation have clearly stated goals and objectives?
2. Does the organisation have an overall strategy for competing in its basic industry?
3. Does the organisation monitor and anticipate competitor's actions and reactions in the marketplace?
4. Does the organisation monitor and anticipate the needs of key customers, suppliers, distributors, creditors, shareholders and employees?
5. Does the organisation have an effective budgeting process?
6. Does the organisation use a strategic management approach to corporate decision-making?
7. Does the organisation have a written mission statement?
8. Does the organisation have contingency plans?
9. Does the organisation have synergy?
10. Does the organisation allocate resources based on stated goals?
11. Does the organisation have objectives, strategies, goals, and policies that are mutually consistent, supportive, and clearly communicated?

Organising

1. Does the enterprise have a clear organisational structure as evidenced by a formal organisational chart?
2. Does the organisational chart reflect the most desirable structure for the firm?
3. Does the organisational chart exhibit acceptable spans of control?
4. Are similar activities appropriately grouped together in the organisational chart?
5. Are staff functions, such as personnel, shown appropriately in the organisational chart?
6. Is the unity of command principle adhered to in the organisational chart?
7. Do the organisation's managers delegate authority well?
8. Does the organisation have and use written job descriptions?
9. Does the organisation have and use written job specifications?
10. Are the organisation's jobs meaningful, rewarding and challenging?

Directing

1. Is employee morale high?
2. Is managerial morale high?
3. Is job satisfaction high?
4. Is a participative management style used?
5. Is creativity encouraged?
6. Are absenteeism rates in the organisation low?
7. Are turnover rates in the organisation low?
8. Have the managers identified the number and composition of informal groups in the organisation?
9. Are the norms of informal groups in the organisation favourable to management?
10. Does a good system for two-way communication exist in the organisation?
11. Are managers in the organisation good leaders?
12. Does the organisation have a good system of rewards and sanctions?
13. Does the organisation and its employees adapt well to changes?

14. Are employees able to satisfy individual needs through the organisation?
15. Are department policies reasonable and supportive of stated goals?

Staffing

1. Does the organisation have a personnel manager or human resource department?
2. Does the organisation hire employees only after careful recruiting, interviewing, testing and selecting?
3. Does the organisation provide employee training and management-development programmes?
4. Does the organisation provide reasonable employee benefits?
5. Does the organisation have an effective performance evaluation system?
6. Does the organisation have a good wage and salary administration system?
7. Does the organisation have stated grievance procedures?
8. Does the organisation have stated disciplinary policies?
9. Does the organisation have a career planning system for its employees?
10. Does mutual trust and respect exist between line managers and personnel managers in the organisation?
11. Are working conditions in the organisation clean and safe?
12. Does the organisation have equal employment opportunities?
13. Does the organisation have an affirmative action programme?
14. Does the organisation promote employees from within?
15. Does the organisation provide employee counseling?
16. Are union-management relations good in the organisation?
17. Does the organisation have a code of ethics?

Controlling

1. Does the organisation have an effective financial control system?
2. Does it have an effective sales control system?
3. Does it have an effective inventory control system?
4. Does it have an effective expense control system?
5. Does it have an effective production control system?
6. Does it have an effective management control system?
7. Does it have an effective quality control system?
8. Does it have computer-assisted control system?
9. Have the productivity standards been established in all departments of the organisation?
10. Does the organisation regularly monitor favourable and unfavourable variances in the control process?
11. Are corrective actions taken promptly to improve unfavourable variances?
12. Are rewards and sanctions in the organisation supportive of established control systems?
13. Is unethical behaviour effectively controlled in the organisation?
14. Are the organisation's control systems prompt, accurate and thorough?

Source: Adapted from Fred R. David, *op. cit.*, pp. 157-159.

2. Corporate Capability Factors in Functional Areas of Management

Competitive advantage refers to all aspects of an organisation that allow it to compete more effectively than its rivals. Functional competence refers to the strengths of the organisation in the functional areas of management, *viz.*, marketing, finance, production/operations, human resources and research and development.

Competitive advantage refers to all aspects of an organisation that allow it to compete more effectively than its rivals.

3. Marketing Management

Marketing has been defined as the human activity directed for satisfying needs and wants through exchange processes. Joel Evans and Barry Berman suggest that there are nine basic functions of marketing. They are: (1) Customer Analysis, (2) Buying, (3) Selling, (4) Product and Service Planning, (5) Price Planning, (6) Distribution, (7) Marketing Research, (8) Opportunity Analysis, and (9) Social Responsibility.

1. Customer Analysis: Examination and evaluation of customer needs, desires and wants is called customer analysis. Customer analysis involves administering customer surveys, analysing consumer information, evaluating market positioning strategies, developing customer profiles and determining optimal market segmentation strategies. Customer analysis information can be essential in developing an effective mission statement.

2. Buying: Buying means obtaining the goods and services needed to produce and sell a product. The function of buying includes evaluating alternative suppliers, selecting the best suppliers, arranging acceptable terms with suppliers and procurement.

3. Selling: Selling includes marketing activities like advertising, sales promotions, publicity, personal selling, sales forces management, customer relations and dealer relations.

4. Product and Service Planning: This function includes new product design and development, testing market, product and brand positioning, warranties, packaging, product options, product features, product style, product quality, scrapping old products and customer service.

5. Price Planning: Factors affecting pricing decisions include customers, government, channel members and competitors. Major pricing policies are penetration pricing and skim-the-cream pricing.

6. Distribution: This function includes warehousing, physical distribution channels, distribution coverage, retail site locations, sales territories, inventory levels and location, transportation carriers, wholesaling and retailing.

7. Marketing Research: Marketing research is systematic gathering, recording and analysing data about problems relating to the marketing of goods and services.

8. Opportunity Analysis: Opportunity analysis is an appraisal of the costs, benefits and risks associated with marketing related and/or strategic decisions.

9. Social Responsibility: Social responsibility includes organisation's obligation to offer products and services that are safe, ethical and reasonably priced.

Companies can identify marketing strengths and weaknesses by undertaking a comprehensive marketing audit. Exhibit 5.10 presents corporate capabilities checklist in marketing management.

Exhibit 5.10: Corporate Capabilities in Marketing — Checklist

A Marketing Systems Audit

1. Is the marketing intelligence system producing accurate, sufficient, and timely information about marketplace developments with respect to customers, prospects, distributors and dealers, competitors, suppliers, and various publics?
2. Are company decision-makers asking for enough marketing research, and are they using the results?
3. Is the company employing the best methods for market and sales forecasting?
4. Is the marketing planning system well conceived and effective?
5. Is sales forecasting and market potential measurement soundly carried out?
6. Are sales quotas set on a proper basis?
7. Are the control procedures adequate to ensure that the annual goals are being achieved?
8. Does management periodically analyse the profitability of products, markets, territories, and channels of distribution?

9. Are marketing costs periodically examined?
10. Is the company well organised to gather, generate, and screen new-product ideas?
11. Does the company do adequate concept research and business analysis before investing in new ideas?
12. Does the company carry out adequate product and market testing before launching new products?

A Marketing Productivity Audit

1. What is the profitability of the company's different products, markets, territories, and channels of distribution?
2. Should the company enter, expand, contract, or withdraw from any business segments and what would be the short- and long-run profit consequences?
3. Do any marketing activities seem to have excessive costs? Can cost-reducing steps be taken?

Source: Philip Kotler, Marketing Management: Analysis, Planning and Control, Prentice Hall Inc., Englewood Cliffs, New Jersey, 1984, pp. 767-70.

4. Financial Management

The best measure of a company's competitive position and overall attractiveness to investors is the company's financial position. Determining an organisation's financial strengths and weaknesses is essential in formulating strategies. Basic decision areas of finance are: the investment decision, the financing decision, and the dividend decision.

1. The Investment Decision: The investment decision (also called capital budgeting) is concerned with allocation and reallocation of capital to projects, products, assets and divisions of an organisation.

2. Financing Decision: The financing decision is concerned with determining the best financing mix or capital structure for the organisation.

3. Dividend Decision: Dividend decisions involve such issues as the percentage of earnings paid to the shareholders, the stability of dividend paid over the period to the shareholders, and the repurchase or issuance of stock.

Exhibit 5.11 shows useful financial checklist of corporate capabilities. The positive answers to the questions in the checklist are the financial strengths and the negative answers are the financial weaknesses of the company.

Exhibit 5.11: A Financial Checklist of Corporate Capabilities

Liquidity:

1. Have the firm's liquidity ratios been increasing over time?
2. Are the firm's liquidity ratios above industry averages?

Leverages:

1. Have the firm's leverage ratios been increasing over time?
2. Are the firm's leverage below industry averages?

Activity:

1. Have the firm's activity ratios been moving favourably over time?
2. Do the firm's activity ratios compare favourably with industry's average?

Profitability:

1. Have the firm's profitability ratios been increasing over time?
2. Are the firm's profitability ratios above industry's average?

Growth:

1. Have the firm's growth ratios been increasing over time?
2. Are the firm's growth ratios above industry's averages?

Source: Fred R. David, *op. cit.*, p. 177.

5. Production/Operations Management

The next element in evaluating the strategy of an organisation is its production or operations management. Operations management has been defined as managing the resources required to produce the products or render services provided by an organisation. One of the goals of a firm is to develop a distinctive competence which separates it from its competitors. Production decisions/strategies reflect decisions of quality, product design and configuration, cost, customer service, production efficiency, and response time. A firm, through operating strategies in these areas, may be able to develop its own reputation, differentiating it from its competitors.

Roger Schroeder suggests that production/operations management consists of five decision areas, *viz.*, process, capacity, inventory, human resource and quality. Corporate capabilities checklist in production or operations management is shown in Exhibit 5.12. The "yes" answer to some questions shows the strengths of an organisation in those areas and the "no" answer presents the weaknesses of an organisation in those areas concerned.

Exhibit 5.12: Corporate Capabilities in Production/Operations Management 

Process

1. Are the facilities located effectively?
2. Are the facilities designed effectively?
3. Should the organisation be integrated backward or forward to a greater extent?
4. Are transportation costs for receiving and shipping excessive?
5. Is the process technology that is being used appropriate?
6. Is an effective and efficient flow or sequence of operations being used to convert inputs into outputs?
    - Line flow — characterised by a linear sequence of operations used to make the product or service; extremely efficient but also extremely inflexible. Examples are cafeterias and automobile assembly lines.
    - Intermittent flow — characterised by production in batches at intermittent intervals; equipment and labour are organised into work centres by similar types of skill or equipment. Examples are the flow operations used by fast-food restaurants and hospitals.
    - Project flow — characterised by a sequence of operations used to produce a unique product; no real product flow; used when there is a great need for creativity and uniqueness. Examples are developing a new product or building a ship.
7. Is the product or service being made to order, made to stock, or both? Is this activity most effective and efficient?
    - Made to order — processing activities are keyed to individual customer orders; process consists of customer placing an order, firm responding with a price and delivery date, and customer accepting or rejecting the offer. Delivery time and control of order flow are critical. Examples are a restaurant operation and painting a portrait.
    - Made to stock — process consists of producing a standardised product line; inventories are maintained to meet, say, a 95 percent service level of orders. Forecasting, inventory management, and capacity planning are critical. Examples are a furniture plant and oil refinery.

Capacity

1. Is overall demand for the product or service regularly and effectively forecasted?
2. Are the appropriate economies of scale achieved?
3. Are the factories, warehouses, and stores located effectively?
4. Are there appropriate number of factories, warehouses, and stores?
5. Are the factories, warehouses, and stores of an appropriate size?
6. Have aggregate planning costs been determined and minimised?
    - Hiring and firing costs
    - Overtime and under-time costs

- Inventory-carrying costs
- Subcontracting costs
- Part-time labour costs
- Cost of stock-out or back order

7. Are loading, scheduling, and dispatching activities performed effectively?
8. Have strategies been developed for dealing with non-uniform demand?
9. Does the firm have an effective and efficient production control system?

Inventory

1. Have the costs of producing or buying needed inventories been examined?
2. Have inventory carrying costs been determined?
3. Have inventory ordering costs been determined?
4. Have purchasing, receiving and shipping costs been determined?
5. Have stock-out costs been determined?
6. Have service level versus inventory level considerations been examined?
7. Have appropriate production lot sizes been determined?
8. Does the firm have an effective inventory control system?
   - Single-bin system
   - Two-bin system
   - Card-file system
   - Computerised system
   - Economic Order Quantity (EOQ) system
   - Materials Requirements Planning (MRP) system
   - Order-point systems

Work Force

1. Have time and motion studies been completed on all operations-related jobs?
2. Have production jobs been designed effectively and efficiently?
3. Are production management employees competent, efficient, and motivated?
4. Are production standards clear, reasonable and effective?
5. Have the productivity rewards and sanctions been established?
6. Have reasonable and effective operations policies been established?
7. Are absenteeism and turnover rates low among production employees?
8. Is employee morale high among production employees?
9. Are the firm's operations managers effective leaders?

Quality

1. Does the organisation have an effective and efficient quality control system?
2. Have the following quality control costs been determined and evaluated?
   - Prevention costs, such as the cost of training and development programmes, and marketing studies to determine customers' quality needs and desires?
   - Appraisal costs, such as the cost of determining the quality of incoming raw materials, sampling procedures, finished goods inspections and tests, and operating laboratories?
   - Internal failure costs, such as the cost of scrap material, downtime, retesting, and inspections?
   - External failure costs, such as the cost of refunds, repairing products, replacing products and setting customer complaints?

Source: Fred R. David, *op. cit.*, pp. 182-184.

6. Human Resource Management

Human resource plays not only significant but a crucial role in building and developing an organisation. It is said that the difference between two organisations in terms of competencies is due to differences in the capabilities of their human resources. But management of human resources is more complicated than management of any other resources.

Human resource management consists of five important strategic decision areas, *viz.*, employment, human resource development, compensation, human relations and industrial relations.

A survey of CEOs spotlighted productivity improvement, employee communications and management succession planning as areas of strategies for human resource management. Exhibit 5.13 depicts corporate capabilities checklist in human resource management.

Exhibit 5.13: Corporate Capabilities in Human Resource Management

Human Resources Management (HRM)

(a) What are the corporation's current HRM objectives, strategies, policies, and programmes?
- *(i)* Are they clearly stated or merely implied from performance and/or budgets?
- *(ii)* Are they consistent with the corporation's mission, objectives, strategies, policies, and with internal and external environments?

(b) How well is the corporation's HRM performing in terms of improving the fit between the individual employee and the job? Consider turnover, grievances, strikes, layoffs, quality of work life.
- *(i)* What trends emerge from this analysis?
- *(ii)* What impact have these trends had on past performance and how will they probably affect future performance?
- *(iii)* Does this analysis support the corporation's past and pending strategic decisions?

(c) How does this corporation's HRM performance compare with that of similar corporations?

(d) Are HRM managers using appropriate concepts and techniques to evaluate and improve corporate performance? Consider job analysis programme, performance appraisal system, up-to-date job descriptions, training and development programmes, attitude surveys, job design programmes, quality of relationship with unions.

(e) What is the role of the HRM manager in the strategic management process?

Source: Thomas L. Wheeler and J. David Hunger, *op. cit.*, p. 43.

7. Research and Development

Research and development is concerned with the creation of knowledge, the design of goods and services and the operation of production process. Survival and development of most of the competitive firms depend upon the successful research and development activities. Research and development strategies should address: (1) the focus of R&D activities (pure or applied research), (2) the relationship of R&D activities to other functional areas (e.g., marketing, human resource, etc.), (3) the aggressiveness of the firm's R&D posture, (4) the time horizon for results expected from the R&D department, (5) new product development, and (6) pilot plans or prototype testing. Four approaches to determine R&D budget allocations have been used. They are: (1) financing as many project proposals as possible, (2) using a percentage-of-sales method, (3) budgeting for R&D about what competitors spend, and (4) deciding how many successful new products are needed and working backwards to estimate the required R&D investment. Exhibit 5.14 presents corporate capabilities in research and development. Like the previous checklists, "no" answers to the key questions indicate potential weaknesses and "yes" answers suggest areas of strengths.

Exhibit 5.14: Corporate Capabilities Checklist in Research and Development

1. Has the organisation examined the research and development practices in its basic industry?
2. Does the organisation have the personnel needed to conduct successful research and development?
3. Does the organisation have the facilities and equipment needed to conduct successful research and development?
4. Does the organisation have the information flows and resources needed to conduct successful research and development?
5. Has the organisation investigated the relative benefits of focusing R&D efforts on existing versus new products?
6. Has the organisation examined the trade-offs between developing new and improved products on the one hand, and developing new and improved production processes on the other?
7. Has the organisation established a research and development department?
8. Does the organisation allocate sufficient human capital resources to conduct successful research and development?
9. Does the organisation capitalise on available sources of new product ideas?
10. Is the organisation prepared to take the risk of instituting long periods of research without discovering ideas that have commercial value?
11. Is the organisation prepared to take the risk of financing long periods of product development and testing without eventual successful marketing of the product?
12. Does the organisation have, or can it obtain, needed capital to exploit discoveries if and when they are made?
13. Has the organisation examined the potential benefits of using outside agencies or individuals to conduct basic and applied research for the firm?
14. Has the organisation established clear research and development goals and policies?
15. Does the organisation understand the research and development strategies of is major competitors?
16. Has the organisation considered joint ventures in research and development?
17. Is the organisation knowledge about domestic and foreign licenses, royalty fees, patents, trademarks, and other regulatory concerns applicable to research and development activities in its basic industry?
18. Does the organisation have an overall research and development strategy?

Source: Fred R. David, *op. cit.*, p. 187-188.

(G) DIAGNOSING CORPORATE CAPABILITIES

There are two important methods of analysing and diagnosing corporate capabilities. They are: (1) Functional-Area Profile and Resource Deployment Matrix and (2) Strategic Advantage Profile.

1. Functional-Area Profile and Resources Deployment Matrix

This method requires the preparation of a matrix of functional areas with characteristics common to each other. This approach allows the firm to analyse the strategic deployment of funds and its strengths and weaknesses over time as compared with those of competitors. Each area must be considered with respect to what its policies and approaches were, are and will be. The analysis can be done on a piecemeal basis, with each area independently of others. However, the strengths and weaknesses must be compared in relation to one another. Weaknesses must be compared with strengths as weaknesses may prevent the company from taking advantage of an opportunity. Similarly, strengths and weaknesses may be compared to the external environmental factors. Most of the strategists are concerned with how their firms are placed strategically in relation to the competitors. It is also important to compare strengths and weaknesses relative to their overall significance to the strategy of the firm.

2. Strategic Advantage Profile

Strategic advantage profile provides, "a picture of the more critical areas which can have a relationship with the strategic posture of the firm in the future.

Once the corporate capability profile (CCP) is prepared and the key areas for diagnosis have been analysed, it is useful to prepare a strategic advantage profile (SAP). Strategic advantage profile provides, "a picture of the more critical areas which can have a relationship with the strategic posture of the firm in the future. Exhibit 5.15 presents an example of a SAP for a hypothetical firm. This exhibit indicates that, this firm has weaknesses in competition, mobilising finances by issuing equity capital, quality control, personnel managers and middle and junior managers with outdated management styles. These disadvantages preclude certain strategies such as competition based on quality, introduction of product changes, expansion of production and marketing. This company can go for the stability strategy. However, it requires the analysis of external environmental opportunities and threats to draw the conclusions on strategies.

Exhibit 5.15: Strategic Advantage Profile

Internal Area	*Competitive Strength (+) or Weakness (–)*
1. Marketing	+ Excellent pre-sales and post-sales service
	+ Complete understanding of consumer preference changes to sales representatives.
	– Close competition.
	+ Selling at consumer's door step.
2. Finance	+ High Rate of Profit
	+ Credit worthiness is favourable for raising loans
	– Low Rate of Dividend, Unfavourable Stock Market Conditions
3. Production/Operations:	+ Excellent Technology
	+ Excellent sources of raw materials
	– Poor Quality Control
4. Human Resources	+ Capable employees
	– Managers with personnel but not human resource management skills
	+ Favourable compensation package
5. Research and Development	0 Picking up now.
6. General Management	+ Top Management with Progressive Ideas
	– Middle and Junior Management with outdated management styles.

Note: + Indicates Strength; 0 indicates neutral; – indicates weakness.

3. Company Situation Analysis

There are five steps to conduct company situation analysis. They are:

(1) Evaluating how well the current strategy is working.

(2) Doing a SWOT analysis.

(3) Identifying the corporate capability factors.

(4) Evaluating the company's cost position relative to competitors.

(5) Assessing the company's competitive position and competitive strength.

(6) Determining the strategic issues and problems the company needs to address.

Exhibit 5.16 provides a format for company situation analysis. The concepts and techniques discussed in this chapter are the basis for preparing the company situation analysis.

Exhibit 5.16: Company Situation Analysis

1. STRATEGIC PERFORMANCE INDICATORS

Performance Indicator	**20...**	**20...**	**20...**	**20...**	**20...**
Market share	....	....	....	....	....
Sales growth	....	....	....	....	....
Net profit margin	....	....	....	....	....
Return on equity investment	....	....	....	....	....
Others	....	....	....	....	....

2. INTERNAL STRENGTHS

INTERNAL WEAKNESSES

EXTERNAL OPPORTUNITIES

EXTERNAL THREATS

3. COMPETITIVE STRENGTH ASSESSMENT

Rating scale: 1 = Very weak; 10 = Very strong.

Key Success Factor/ Firm		**Firm**	**Firm**	**Firm**	**Firm**	
Competitive Variable	**Weight**	**A**	**B**	**C**	**D**	**E**
Quality/product performance	....	....	....	....	....	....
Reputation/image	....	....	....	....	....	....
Raw material access/cost	....	....	....	....	....	....
Technological skills	....	....	....	....	....	....
Manufacturing capability	....	....	....	....	....	....
Marketing/distribution	....	....	....	....	....	....
Financial strength	....	....	....	....	....	....
Relative cost position	....	....	....	....	....	....
Others	....	....	....	....	....	....
Overall strength rating	....	....	....	....	....	....

4. Conclusions Concerning Competitive Position
(Improving/slipping? Competitive advantages/disadvantages?)

5. Major Strategic Issues/Problems the Company must Address

Source: Arthur A. Thompson Jr. and A.J. Strickland III. *op. cit.*: p.100.

POINTS TO BE REMEMBERED

- A strength is a strong point for the company.
- The distinctive competence is the unique capability it gives an organisation.
- Systematic assessment of whether a company's competitive position is strong or weak relative to close rivals is called competitive strength assessment.
- Corporate capability is the inherent capacity or potential of a company.
- Corporate capability in general management includes organisational structure, hierarchies and synergy.

- Resources are all kinds of inputs like material, components, parts, machinery, human resources, etc.
- Variable capabilities create and add value by exploiting opportunities provided by and threats posed by the external environment.
- Value is the amount buyers desire to pay for what a firm provides to them in the form of a products/service/product-cum-service.
- Core competencies are a company's resources and capabilities.

KEY WORDS

- Strength
- Weakness
- Distinctive Competence
- Core Competence
- Value Chain Analysis
- Threats
- Opportunities
- Unique Resources
- Cost Analysis
- Transferability
- Replicability
- Rare capabilities
- Intellectual Capabilities
- Primary Activities
- Outsourcing

QUESTIONS FOR DISCUSSION

1. What are organisational resources and capabilities? Why are organisational resources valuable?
2. Discuss resource-based view of organisational analysis.
3. What are organisational capabilities? How do you identify then?
4. What are core competencies? How many core competencies are required for a company?
5. How do you build core competencies?
6. What is value chain analysis? How do primary activities add value?
7. How do you identify organisational strengths?
8. How do you identify organisational weaknesses?
9. How do you assess competitive strengths of an organisation?
10. How do you identify corporate capability factors of different functional areas?

REFERENCES

1. Yeoh and Roth, "*An Empirical Analysis*", p. 638 in McGrath, Macmillan and Venkataraman, "*Defining and Developing Competencies*", p. 652.
2. D. L. Deeds, D. Decarolis and J. Coombs, "Dynamic Capabilities and New Product Development in High Technology Ventures", *Journal of Business Venturing*, No. 15, 1994, pp. 211-29.
3. R. Hall, "The Strategic Analysis of Intangible Resources", *Strategic Management Journal*, no. 13, 1992, pp. 136-139.

4. John A. Pearce and Richard B. Robinson, "*Strategic Management*". Tata McGraw-Hill Publishing Company Limited, New Delhi, 2007, p. 153.
5. R.M. Grant, "The Resource-Based Theory of Competitive Advantage: Implications for Strategy Formulation," *California Managers Review*, Spring 1991, pp. 114.
6. Thomas L. Wheelen, J. David Hunger and Krish Rangarajan, "*Strategic Management and Business Policy*", Pearson, 2006, p. 77.
7. Dallas Hanson *et. al.*, "*Strategic Management*", Thomson Learning, Victoria, 2002, p. 94.
8. Hilt, Nixon, Clifford and Coyne, "*The Development*", p. 3.
9. B. Mc Evily and A. Zaheer, "Building Ties: A Source of Firm's Heterogeneity in Competitive Capabilities", *Strategic Management Journal*, 20, pp. 1133.
10. M.T. Hansen, N. Nhoria and T. Tierney, "What is Your Strategy for Managing Knowledge?", *Harvard Business Review*, 77(2), pp. 106-16.
11. Leonard Barton, Bower, Clark and Wheelwright, "How to Integrate Work and Deepen Expertise", *Harvard Business Review*, 72 (5), p.123.
12. Brush and Artz, "Towards a Contingent Resource-Based Theory", *Strategic Management Journal*, 15, pp. 271-90.
13. C. Ames, "Sales Soft? Profits Flat? It's time to Rethink Your Business", *Fortune 25*, June, pp. 142-146.
14. Dallas Hanson *et. al.*, "*Strategic Management*", Thomson Learning, 2002, p. 99.
15. *Ibid.*, p. 100.
16. L.B.Ward "Dell Sales Overtake company", *Dalls Morning News*, 24 January 2000. pp.1-2.
17. Computershare 2001, Computershare Limited, Home Page, 19 February 2001, Quoted in Dalls Hanson, *op. cit.*, p. 101.
18. Reed and De Fillippi, "*Casual Ambiguity*".
19. C. Eliezer, "Gudinski is back for a second Act", *Business Review Weekly*, 12 November 1999, pp. 161-165.
20. Robert A. Pitts and David Lei, "*Strategic Management*", Thomson, 2006, p. 92.
21. Robert A. Pitts and David Lei, *op.Lit.*, p. 95.
22. Burt "*Ford expects to Farm Out*", p. 1.
23. P. Landers, "Nissan Retains IBM to Manage its Computers", *Wall Street Journal*, 29 October 1999, p. A15.
24. Samuel C. Certo and J. Paul Peter, *op. cit.*, pp. 36-37.
25. Michael Porter, "*Competitive Advantage*", Free Press, New York, 1985.
26. Samuel C. Certo and J. Paul Peter, *op. cit.*, p. 39.
27. Arthur A. Thompson Jr., and A.J. Strickland III, *op. cit.*, p. 87.
28. *Ibid.*, pp. 87-88.
29. C.K. Prahld and Gary Hamel, "The Core Competence of the Corporation", *Harvard Business Review,* 90:3, May-June 1990, pp. 79-93.
30. Arthur A. Thompson Jr., and A.J. Strickland III, (1984), p. 67.
31. Arthur Sharplin, "*Strategic Management*", McGraw-Hill, New York, 1985, pp. 93-94.
32. *Ibid.*, p. 90.
33. *Ibid.*, p. 95.
34. Samuel C. Certo and J. Paul Peter, *op. cit.*, p. 46.
35. *Ibid.*
36. Arthur A. Thompson Jr., and A.J. Strickland III, *op. cit.*, p. 98.
37. Fred R. David, "*Fundamentals of Strategic Management*," Merrill Publishing Company, London, 1986, p. 151.
38. Z. Malik and Karger, "Does L.R. Planning Improve Company Performance", *Management Review,* September 1975, pp. 27-31.
39. Fred. R. David, *op. cit.*, pp. 151-152.
40. Philip Kotler, "*Marketing Management*", Prentice-Hall, Englewood Cliffs, New Jersey, 1984, p. 4.
41. J. Evans and B. Berman, "*Marketing*", Macmillan, New York, 1982, p. 17.
42. Fred R. David, *op. cit.*, pp. 160-167.

43. James Van Horne, "*Financial Management and Policy*", Prentice-Hall, Englewood Cliffs, New Jersey, 1974, p. 10.

44. R. Chase and N.J. Aquilano, "*Production and Operations Management*", Richard D. Irwin, Homewood, 1985, p. 5.

45. R.J. Schonberger, "*Operations Management*", Business Publications Inc., Plano, 1985, p. 34.

46. P. Subba Rao, "*Essentials of Human Resource Management and Industrial Relations*", Himalaya Publishing House, Mumbai, 1996.

47. Joe G. Thomas, *op. cit.*, p. 165.

48. Fred R. David, *op. cit.*, p. 185.

49. Lawrence R. Jauch and William F. Glueck, *op. cit.*, p. 170.

6

CHAPTER

GLOBAL STRATEGIC MANAGEMENT

Chapter Outline

(A) Introduction
(B) Peculiarities of Global Strategic Management
(C) Value Creation
(D) Global Strategic Management Process
(E) Collaborative Strategies

Learning Objectives

After studying this chapter, you should be able to:

- Analyse the meaning of strategy and strategic management process;
- Discuss the role of value creation in global strategic management;
- Analyse the global company and international environment in order to find out SWOT;
- Formulate the strategies and implement the best strategy;
- Know the peculiarities of global strategic management;
- Analyse global collaborative strategies.

(A) INTRODUCTION

The first chapter has provided us an insight into what is international business and nature, (of international business) basis (for international business), benefits (of international business) and the problems of international business. We have learnt the environmental scanning of international business, trading blocks and the World Trade Organisation, which would help us to understand the strengths (S) and weakness (W) of an international firm and the opportunities (O) provided and threats (T) posed by the international business environment. This background helps us to study the present chapter on 'Global Strategic Management'.

Now, we shall proceed to the policy and strategy of international business. Some of you might have studied a course on 'Business Policy and Strategic Management.' Those who studied this course can understand the fundamental nature of policy and strategy in guiding the direction of the business.

Now, we discuss briefly what is vision, mission and strategy for the benefit of those who have not yet studied a course on 'Business Policy and Strategic Management.'

Vision: What do we want to create?

Vision: An organisational vision is the answer to the question: "What do we want to create?" Shared visions in the organisations create a sense of commonality that permeates the organisation and gives coherence to diverse activities." The corporate vision has the potential power to focus on the collective energy of insiders and to give outsiders, a better idea of what an organisation really is.

Mission: An enduring statement of purpose that distinguishes one organisation from other similar organisations.

Mission: An organisation takes inputs from the environment, converts the inputs into output and supplies the same to the society. These contributions to the society are legitimate. The organisation should protect this legitimacy in the long run. Thus, every organisation comes into being and exists to accomplish something in the larger environment, and that purpose or mission is clear at the start. *For example*, the purpose of AT&T to provide telephone services, LG to produce and supply televisions, refrigerators, etc., Delta Airlines reduced to provide air transport, etc.

Mission is defined as, "an enduring statement of purpose that distinguishes one organisation from other similar organisations." Organisations define the fundamental reason for their existence in terms of a mission statement. Organisations exist to satisfy a particular need of the society or to fulfil a particular deficiency of the global society.

Policy: Policies are general statements or understandings which guide channel thinking and action in strategic decision-making.

Strategy : A unified, comprehensive and integrated plan that relates to the strategic advantages of the firm to the challenges of the environment.

Strategy: Strategy is an unified, comprehensive and integrated plan that relates to the strategic advantages of the firm to the challenges of the environment. It is designed to ensure that the basic objectives of the enterprise are achieved through proper execution by the organisation.

Strategic Management: Strategic management is concerned with deciding on the strategy and planning how that strategy is put into effect. According to Samuel C. Certo and J. Paul Peter, "Strategic management is a continuous, iterative cross functional process aimed at keeping an organisation as a whole appropriately matched to its environment."

Strategic management of a global company is distinct from that of a domestic company due to its peculiarities. Having discussed the concepts of strategy and strategic management, now we shall analyse the peculiarities of global strategic management.

(B) PECULIARITIES OF GLOBAL STRATEGIC MANAGEMENT

Strategic management of the global companies has peculiar features compared to those of a national company. Those include:

- International strategic management is concerned with the flow of goods and services across the countries. It deals with the opportunities, threats, challenges and risks in various markets in the world.
- Strategies of the global corporations are formulated by analysing the global environment. In some cases, strategies are formulated for the cluster of markets or countries.
- Global Strategic Management is an integrated strategic management of a global company. *For example,* the strategic management of Procter and Gamble formulates strategies for its operations in India, the UK, the USA, etc., and integrates all these strategies in order to make a global strategy.
- Global strategic management is concerned with the impact of the present decision on the future. The management has to assess the impact of the strategic decisions on the future product path, future markets, etc.
- Global strategic management is mostly action oriented. All the managers are the active players in this process.
- Global strategic management is a continuous and dynamic management. The changing business environment across the globe influences and interacts with the global corporation. *For example,* Microsoft continuously monitors its relevant environment as they deal in a highly ever changing environment.

Global strategic management is a continuous and dynamic management.

The global corporations review both long range plans and short range plans. However, the time span for the global strategic management is mostly long range.

- The global strategic management process scans the environment of all the countries. It also studies the interaction among the environments of various countries.
- The global strategic management process studies the strategies and reaction of their global competitors and the competitors in various countries.
- The global corporations operate in their home country as well as in various foreign countries. Hence, the global strategic management process integrates the domestic operations and the operations in the foreign countries.
- The global Corporation's portfolios include business in various countries and different products and/or services. Therefore, the global strategic management determines the priorities among the international portfolios.
- The global strategic management designs the organisational structure based on the divisionalised geographical structure.
- The global strategic management mostly depends upon the cultural differences among the countries, differences in the laws of the land, policies of the government, political environments in various countries, etc.
- The global strategic management is more critical on the control front mainly due to unique factors influencing the international business.

Having discussed the peculiarities of global strategic management, we now discuss the process of global strategic management.

(C) VALUE CREATION

A firm's objective of long run profitability can be efficiently achieved when the customers place more value on the products or services. This situation enables the firm to charge a higher price compared to that of the competitors and also the cost of output. A customer would prefer to pay the price to the extent that would equate his/her expected value from the product/service or consumer surplus. However, the firms charge the price that would be less than that of the consumer surplus, due to the competitive situation. Therefore, the price charged by the firms is normally less than that of the value placed by majority of the customers on the product. The difference between the value of the product to the customers and the cost of producing that product is referred to as the 'value creation'.

A firm can increase its profits by creating a high value to the product and/or reducing the cost of production. The companies should try to enlarge the gap between the value and cost of production compared to that of the competitors. They can achieve this through low cost strategy and differentiation strategy, as low cost strategy helps for producing at low cost and differentiation strategy helps for enhancing the value for the product.

Firms can enjoy low cost leadership by availing location economies, low transportation costs, the economies of experience, curve effects and economies of scale. Location economies can be derived by locating the firm in those countries where comparative cost advantages in manufacturing automobiles and electronics, exist. *For example,* Japan has comparative cost advantages in producing computer software, pharmaceuticals, biotechnology products, etc., and India and China have comparative cost advantages in labour intensive products.

Strategic Choices

International business firms can use four basic strategies, *viz.*, international strategy, multidomestic strategy, global strategy and transnational strategy.

International strategy: The international business firms adopted this strategy in order to transfer the valuable skills and products developed in the home country to the foreign markets where such skills and products area not available. This strategy produces results when *(i)* the company has core competencies which the foreign competitors do not possess, *(ii)* the firm faces weak pressure for local responsiveness and cost reductions. *For example*, Trukai Rice and steamships (both are Australian companies) transfer the skills and products from Australia to Papua New Guinea. McDonald, Southern Cross University also adopted the international strategy.

Multidomestic strategy: The international business firms adapting this strategy customise products and marketing strategies to the host country requirements and environment. The international business firms establish their production, marketing, finance and R&D facilities in various host countries. *For example*, UniLever established Hindustan Lever Limited in India. Similar examples include Nestle, Procter and Gamble and Colgate Palmolive.

Global strategy: The international business firms adapting this strategy concentrate on profit earning though cost minimisation. Therefore, these firms produce standard products, by locating the manufacturing and other facilities in certain locations where the cost of production/ operations is the lowest. They select other cost reduction strategies in order to achieve low cost leadership in the industry. The firms like Intel and Texas Instruments adopted this strategy.

Transnational strategy: According to Christopher Bartlett and Sumantra Ghoshal, international business firms should pursue low cost leadership-cum-local responsive or customisation strategy due to the intensive global competition. Firms can achieve this strategy by exploiting experience based economies and location based economies. Firms should transfer experience based core competencies and also customise their operations/product to the local requirements. They also emphasise that the transfer of experience based economies and skills should flow not only from home firm to foreign subsidiary, but also from foreign subsidiary to home company and from one foreign subsidiary to another foreign subsidiary. They referred this learning process as 'global learning'. This process of simultaneous value creation is called 'transnational strategy'. The firms adopting this strategy simultaneously reduce cost and increase value creation and addition. *For example,* Caterpillar learned greater cost economies when it faced severe competition from Komastu and Hitachi during 1980s.

Strategic Alliance: Strategic alliance is an agreement between two or more competitive international business firms in order to serve a global market. Strategy alliance normally takes place among the companies carrying out a similar line of business.

(D) GLOBAL STRATEGIC MANAGEMENT PROCESS

The strategist understands the vision, mission, objectives and goals of an organisation before starting the strategic management process. The international strategic management process starts with the organisational analysis of the international company in order to know its strengths and weaknesses. The next step is the analysis of the international environmental factors in order to know the opportunities provided by the environment and the threats posed by the environment.

The goals of the international company alongwith the SWOT analysis lead to the formulation of alternative strategies. The strategist analyses the alternatives and selects the best strategy. Then, the strategist implements the best strategy. Further, this process requires evaluation of the strategy implementation process in order to see that the strategy is implemented as planned.

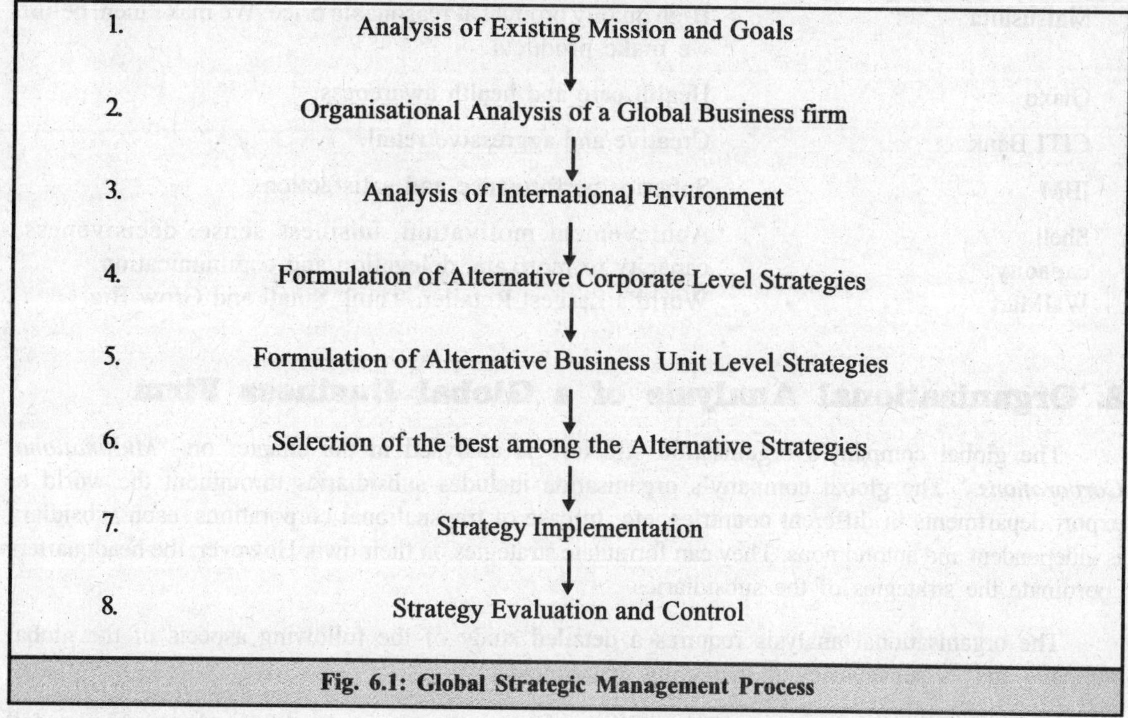

Fig. 6.1: Global Strategic Management Process

GLOBAL STRATEGIC MANAGEMENT PROCESS

1. Analysis of Existing Mission and Goals

Most of the companies initially start as domestic firms and transform into an international company at a later stage. Further, it goes on adding new products to its portfolio and/or adding new countries to the existing portfolio.

The global companies normally modify the mission statement as most of the companies initially start as domestic firm and transform into an international company at the later stage.

The company finds that the existing mission statement would be redundant when it significantly adds the product and/or country portfolios to the existing portfolio. Then, the global company prefers to reformulate the existing mission statement.

For example, Dr. Reddy's Labs original mission statement was, *"To become market leader in the Indian Pharma industry"*. The company after 1991, found that this mission statement was redundant as it expanded its activities to many developing countries. Then, it modified its mission statement as:

"To achieve global leadership in protecting the health of masses."

Thus, the global company has to modify the mission statement, if necessary. The global company also changes its goals depending upon the changes in the environment. The next step in this direction is the organisational analysis of a global firm.

Vision and Philosophies of Major MNCs

MNC		Vision/Philosophy.
AT&T	:	Develop telecommunication system that enables any person in the world to speak to anyone at a cheap price, fast and clearly.
GM	:	Attracting and developing people.
GE	:	Mergers, acquisition and strategic alliances.
Matsushita	:	High quality product at reasonable price. We make men, before we make products.
Glaxo	:	Health care and health awareness.
CITI Bank	:	Creative and aggressive retail.
IBM	:	Superior performance and satisfaction.
Shell capacity	:	Achievement motivation, business sense, decisiveness, capacity to motivate, delegation and communication.
WalMart	:	World's Largest Retailer. Think Small and Grow Big.

2. Organisational Analysis of a Global Business Firm

The global company's organisation structure is analysed in the chapter on *"Multinational Corporations."* The global company's organisation includes subsidiaries throughout the world or export departments in different countries, etc. In case of transnational corporations, each subsidiary is independent and autonomous. They can formulate strategies on their own. However, the headquarters coordinate the strategies of the subsidiaries.

The organisational analysis requires a detailed study of the following aspects of the global company and its subsidiaries or marketing departments:

- **Organisation Structure:** The analysis of an organisation structure includes: Flat or tall organisation, team structure or individual based structure, geographical or strategic business unit structure, etc. This analysis requires identification of strengths and weaknesses of the company with regard to the structure. The flat and team structures are regarded as strengths for a global company. In addition, the autonomous team structures are regarded as the greatest strengths of a global company. In contrast, the tall structures and mechanical structures are regarded as weaknesses for a global company. The next important factor is marketing.

- **Marketing:** The marketing analysis includes the analysis of 4 Ps, *viz.*, product, price, promotion and place. The global company analyses each of these factors in detail and identifies its strengths and weaknesses in each of the aspects of all the 4 Ps. *For example,* product design suitable to the culture of the host country is a strength and a higher price in the developing countries is a weakness.

Exhibit 6.1: Organisational Analysis and Its Contribution to Strategic Management

Marketing	*Production/Operations*	*Finance*	*Human Resources*
Market:	**Scope of Operations:**	**Sources of Funds:**	Manpower Planning
Geographic scope and	Extent of Vertical	Use of debt	Recruiting
target segments	Integration	**Development of Funds:**	Employment
Unserved potential	Owned/Contracted	Dividend payment	Development
Product:	**Functions performed:**	percentage	Retaining compensation
Physical or Tangible	Sourcing	Additions to fixed assets	Job security
Supplementary Service/	Number, size, location of	and working capital	Culture
benefits.	plants	Liquidity position	Quality of work life
Technological level	Logistical spread	Capital structure	
Extent of Product Line	Value added product line	Earnings per share pattern:	
Focus of Development	**Types of Operations:**	Smoothed or varying	
Price:	Process type	Growth	
Relative Price Level and	Flexibility/specialised	Internal Acquisition Stock	
Range	Break-even volume	Cash	
Use of Price Level and	Operations Leverage/		
Changes	Contribution Margin		
Promotion:	Focus of Plants		
Use and Role of Sales	Capital/Labour Intensity		
Force	**Development:**		
Use of Untapped	Process/Product		
Culture	Technology Risk Level		
Choice and use of	Engineering Content		
Media	**Operations Control:**		
Push or Pull Emphasis	Plants focus		
Place (Distribution):	Stability of Line		
Number of Channels	Size and Role of		
Channel Role	Inventory control		
Services Rendered	Operations/Scheduling		
Margins Allowed	Quality		
	Cost Reduction		
	Practices		
	Labour		
Product Development	Skill Level		
	Supervision needed		
	Union status		
	Cost Position		
	Experience level		

Source: Kenneth J. Hatten, Mary Louise Hatten, *'Strategic Management,'* Prentice Hall Inc., New Jersey, 1987, p. 17.

The next factor is production.

- **Production:** The strategist of the global company analyses each of the areas of production. These areas include: Sourcing of materials, location of plants, logistics spread, plant layouts, sourcing the human resources, quality considerations, cost considerations, inventory levels, inventory management, etc. The strategist has to analyse each factor and identity the strengths or weaknesses of each of the minute factors.

The next organisational factor is finance.

- **Finance:** The strategist, on the similar lines of the production has to identify the strengths and weakness for each of the finance factors. The important finance factors include sources of finance, capital structure, earning per share and the like. *For example*, sourcing the finance from International Finance Corporation (IFC) is a strength as IFC provides loans at the lowest rate for a quite long period.

The next internal factor is human resources.

- **Human Resources:** The strategist of a global company analyses each of the human resource management areas and identifies its strengths and weaknesses. The human resource management factors include: sourcing of manpower, the skill of employees, cultural compatibility of the employees with the cultures of various countries, cost of employees, etc. *For example,* sourcing employees from India is a strength for the global business, from the point of view of cost and cultural compatibility. *Exhibit 6.1* presents organisational analysis and its contribution to strategic management.

Exhibit 6.1 summarises the organisational analysis of a global company and its contributions to identify the strengths and weaknesses. *For example,* Toyota is strong in organisational culture, L&T is strong in technology and P&G is strong in product innovation and development.

After identifying the strengths and weaknesses of the global company, the strategist has to analyse the international environment in order to find out the opportunities provided and the threats posed by the international environment.

Now, we shall study the international environment. International environment is explained in the chapter on *"International Business Environment."* We now identify the opportunities provided and the threats posed by the environment to the global business.

3. Analysis of International Environment

Strategic management of a global organisation requires an understanding and analysis of international business environment in order to assess opportunities and threats. The strategist formulates alternative strategies to exploit the opportunities provided by the environment by using company strengths. Most of the MNCs have the strength of technology and the environment of developing countries provides the opportunity of high quality and low priced products. Therefore, MNCs exploit the opportunities by formulating the strategy of entering the developing countries.

Global business environment factors include:

- Political-legal Factors
- Economic Factors
- Technological Factors
- Social Factors

For example, Sony formulated the strategy of low priced televisions to enter the expanding Indian middle class. Similarly, Cavan Case designed a product of *"Fair Ever"* by using saffron as an input to exploit the opportunity afforded by Indian ladies.

Global business environment factors include:

(a) Political-legal Factors

(b) Economic Factors

(c) Technological Factors

(d) Social Factors.

Now, we shall discuss these factors in order to assess opportunities and threats.

(a) **Political-Legal Factors:** All countries have their own political systems and legal framework that affect business. These laws relate to hiring and firing of native employees and exporting of certain percentage of products in order to earn foreign exchange. These laws may provide an opportunity or pose a threat to the businesses going abroad. Major world political and legal trends also influence the businesses going across the national boundaries. During 1980s, and 1990s, many governments in the world tended towards markete conomies and privatised the public sector and reduced the government control over business. Hence, the world political and legal environment provided opportunities for business to grow internationally.

(b) **Economic Factors:** Growing economic activities, increasing gross national product and per capita income are indicators of opportunities for business. Contraction in economic activities and reduction in incomes are indicators for threats for business. The challenging international economic variables for strategists are interest rates, inflation rates and foreign exchange rates. High inflation rates and devaluation of currencies pose threats to international business.

(c) **Technological Factors:** Technology plays a major role in global business. Technology is one of the main bases for joint ventures particularly in the developing world. Manufacturing companies in technologically advanced countries locate their production plants in the developing countries where cheap labour and raw materials are available. Developing countries generally welcome such companies. The benefits to the developing countries from such companies include: influx of financial resources, employment opportunities for native people, creation of an opportunity to the domestic manufacturers to acquire new technologies, opportunity for workforce to acquire new skills through training, increase in revenue to the government and the like. As such, most of the newly industrialising nations like India, Singapore, South Korea, Brazil and Spain invite foreign companies. The benefits to technologically advanced firms going to the newly industrialising nations include low cost of production, business growth, exports to the third nations, increase in profits and corporate leadership.

However, some developing countries expect from the technologically advanced foreign companies assistance to local entrepreneurs, establishment of research and development facilities, and the introduction of products relevant to the home country. These relationships provide on-the-job training to local employees but the overall long term contribution to the host countries is questionable in the minds of some leaders of the developing countries. This type of problems with multinational companies are common in developing countries due to varying interests of host countries and MNCs. Therefore, the host country and the MNCs should have a clear understanding and agreement about the interests of each other. In fact, in an economic and technological sense, both parties need each other and both will benefit from a sound relationship.

The important technological issue in the global business from the point of view of the developing nations is appropriate technology. Labour saving devices (like robots) that are economically justifiable in highly advanced countries where labour is costly, may be more costly than labour intensive types of production in less developed countries where unemployment level is high and wage rate is low. Therefore, the developing world needs labour intensive technology to solve the problem of unemployment. Therefore, MNCs should think about the technology appropriate for the conditions of the host country. Sometimes, technology is developed just accidently. *(See Box 6.1).*

BOX 6.1: TECHNOLOGY DEVELOPMENT GUIDED BY DREAM

Sidetrack

While developing his famous sewing machine, Issac Singer, at one point was faced with a problem that seemed insurmountable: how to get the thread to run through the needle smoothly and continuously without breaking or getting stuck.

One night he had a dream. He dreamt that he was being chased by tribals carrying large spears. As they drew closer he noticed that every spear had a hole just below the point of the blade. He awoke with a start.

The next morning he made a needle with its eye near the point instead of at the top. That solved his problem. The thread could now run consistently through the needle. His invention was complete and the Singer Sewing Machine soon became the premier sewing machine in the world.

Source: *The Hindu,* Dated: February 3, 2001.

(d) **Social Factors:** Every country has its own distinctive culture, *i.e.,* generally accepted values, traditions, and patterns of behaviour. Different social and cultural factors of different countries will affect MNCs. Some cultures accept bribery and payoffs as a fact of life, whereas others punish them severely. In Nigeria, the accepted 'dash' (money under the table) ranges from 15% of a multi-billion dollar contract to a few naira to get a hotel operator to place a phone call. In some countries, the amounts paid to the minor officials to expedite the executions of their duties is called "lubrication" or "grease the palms." MNCs must carefully monitor each country's norms to ensure their actions are in line with the local practice. Managers of MNCs must be aware of the wide variance in working practices around the world and should be totally familiar with those in the country where they are stationed. It is common in Europe for the employers to pay the amount according to the number of family members of employees or because of unpleasant working conditions. Fiji Island miners receive a daily half hour "Sex break," to fulfil marital obligations. People in Eritrea need two hours lunch break as all the family members have a long lunch together.

Difference in language and social norms will affect the marketing mix for a particular country. Product presentation, packaging, distribution channels, pricing and advertising must be attuned to each culture. In Japan, perfume is hardly used. Even if a product is desired by the public, literal translation of product names and slogans can ruin sales. *For example*, Pepsi Cola's "Come alive" jingle was translated into German as "Come alive out of the grave." An advertisement for ink by the Parker Pen Company, when translated into Spanish gave the false impression that the product helped prevent pregnancy.

Religious beliefs may also make a significant impact on a country's business practices. *For example*, banks in Pakistan stopped paying interest to depositors in 1985 to conform with Islamic law. In Japan, each time Mazda manufactures a new car model, a Shinto Priest clad in traditional white robe, sandals, and black lacquered head gear conducts 'honourable purification,' rites on the new product with the top management in attendance. In some countries, it is customary to take a nap after lunch. In some countries, religious requirements call for taking several breaks during the workday to pray. In India, "Vastu" and "auspicious time" are widely followed to begin transactions including business.

Cross-cultural differences in norms and values require modifications in managerial behaviours. Social norms that are not well understood by outsiders often constrain business transactions. Japanese business executives expect their clients or suppliers to interact socially with them after working hours. In fact, these social settings are requirements for serious business relationships.

Scanning Environment: Companies intending to go globally have to analyse the internal environment also in order to assess their strengths and weaknesses. Campo-Flores suggests that a corporation's chances for success are enhanced if it has or can develop the following capabilities:

(i) *Technological lead:* An innovative approach or a new product or a new process gives one a short term monopoly position.

(ii) *A strong trade name:* Snob appeal of a well-known product can permit a higher profit margin to cover the initial entry costs.

(iii) *Advantages of scale:* A large corporation has the advantage of low unit costs and a financial base strong enough to weather setbacks.

(iv) *A scanning capability:* An ability to search successfully and efficiently for opportunities will take on greater importance in international dealings.

(v) *An outstanding product or service:* A solid product or service is more likely to have a staying power in international competition.

(vi) *An outstanding international executive:* The presence of an executive who understands international situations and is able to develop a core of local executives who can work well with the home office is likely to result in the building of a strong and long lasting international organisation.

Analysis of internal and external environment indicates international SWOT analysis. Now, we study the international SWOT analysis.

International SWOT Analysis

The company, should evaluate its strengths, weaknesses and opportunities and threats of international environment before making a final decision about going global. The company can use the following questions in evaluating its strengths and weaknesses.

Global Company evaluates its
- Strengths,
- Weaknesses
- Opportunities
- Threats

(i) Do the companies' have a strong market position in the respective countries in which they operate?

(ii) Do the companies' quality of the products/services compare favourably with those of their respective world competitors?

(iii) Do the companies' have technological advantage in the world regions where they will operate their major businesses?

(iv) Do the companies' have a strong brand reputation in the countries in which they sell their products or services?

(v) Do the companies' managers and employees have more talent than those of their world competitors?

(vi) Do the companies' financial profile compare favourably with that of the industries?

(vii) Are the companies' consistently more profitable than their world rivals?

(viii) Are the companies' product and process research and development efforts likely to produce better results than their competitors?

(ix) Are the companies, various world operations subject to unionisation?

The following questions will help the companies to evaluate the opportunities and threats of the external environment:

(i) What threats and opportunities do political and legal factors present?

(ii) What threats and opportunities do the economic factors present?

(iii) What threats and opportunities do technological factors present?

(iv) What threats and opportunities do social factors present?

(v) What is the size of the industry?

(vi) What are the growth rate and growth potential of the industry?

(vii) Is the industry cyclical? If so, can the cyclicality be smoothened out across different world markets?

(viii) Is the industry subject to fluctuations in demand because of seasonal factors? If so, can these seasonal factors be smoothened out across different world markets?

(ix) How intense is world competition in the industry?

(x) What is the median industry probability? What is its potential probability?

(xi) Is the industry susceptible to unionisation?

(xii) What is the rate of innovation in the industry?

After studying the SWOT analysis, the strategist has to formulate alternative strategies, keeping in mind the SWOT analysis. *(See Box 6.2).*

BOX 6.2: TOYOTA VS GENERAL MOTORS: EVALUATING SWOT CAREFULLY

During the first three months of 2007, Toyota sold more cars and trucks worldwide than General Motors for the first time ever, as the Japanese company moved closer to becoming the world's largest automaker in terms of annual global sales. For most of the twentieth century, GM was synonymous with the power and innovation of US industry. Today, the Detroit based auto manufacturer — which has been steadily losing market share for three decades and posted more than $12 billion in losses over the last two years — is retrenching its operations, shedding tens of thousands of jobs and shuttering its factories. Toyota's first quarter sales rose 9.2 per cent to a record 2.35 million vehicles. GM reported that it sold 2.26 million vehicles in the January-to-March period. Fifty years after Toyota entered the all important US market, the company controlled 15.6 per cent of the share, up from 9.3 in 2000, while GM's share fell to 23.1 per cent in 2006 — its lowest percentage since the 1920s — down from 28.1 per cent just seven years ago.

Globally, GM outsold Toyota 9.1 million to 8.8 million in 2006. But the Japanese auto company's sales rose 8 per cent last year, and it expects to sell 9.34 million vehicles in 2007, in large measure due to growing demand in the North American market. Toyota has six assembly plants in North America with a total production capacity of 1.8 million vehicles a year, and it expects the output to rise to 2.2 million by 2010 as two more new plants come on line. Meanwhile, GM is cutting the North American production by 1 million units.

The *Wall Street Journal* noted that Toyota executives were "becoming more cautious about the prospects for future growth" and that its big Tundra pickup truck had gotten off to a slow start despite large discounts because of the highly competitive nature of the small truck market. "The company has announced plans to build a US plant in Mississippi capable of producing 150,000 vehicles, initially Toyota Highlander sport-utility vehicles, starting in 2010. At one point, however, Toyota had been considering a plant that would open a year earlier and build one-third more vehicles."

4. Formulation of Alternative Corporate Level Strategies

Formulation of corporate level alternative strategies of a global business are different from those of domestic company. The global company first decides the country to enter and then formulates the corporate level strategies. *(See Box 6.3).*

BOX 6.3: SPOTLIGHT ON STRATEGY: THE SONY MAVICA

The *Wall Street Journal* reported on the success of Sony's Mavica product in the market for digital cameras. Despite higher price and less functionality, the Sony Mavica is the market leader in its category and is an excellent example of successful high-tech strategies in action.

Consider the following examples:

Example One

WSJ Article Excerpt: "No one had foreseen the Sony Mavica taking off as it did...because we were all concentrating on the resolution" says Gary Rado, executive vice president of the U.S. unit of Japan's Casio [a Sony competitor].

Critical Issue: Customers view products very differently than the people who supply them. In technology based companies, the tendency is to try to sell products on the basis of price, special features and technical specifications.

Strategy Employed: Rather than competing on technical specifications, Sony focussed on the "intangible" factors that are especially attractive to most customers.

Example Two

WSJ Article Excerpt: The Mavica stores its pictures on a standard floppy disk. Among Mavica's digital competitors, there are at least five non-interchangeable storage systems.

Critical Issue: Mainstream customers are most concerned about the company they are buying from, the quality of the product they are buying, **industry standards**, and the infrastructure of supporting products and system interfaces.

Strategy Employed: Sony took advantage of the industry's lack of standards (which are very important to non-technical buyers) and designed the Mavica to work with a standard storage device, the floppy disk.

Example Three

WSJ Article Excerpt: "So many products out there, so much clutter," says Ed Pullen, a senior industry analyst at a research firm ZD a StoreBoard in La Jolla, Calif.

Critical Issue: Lack of differentiation is the leading cause of failure among high-tech products. To gain a strong product position, a company must differentiate its product from all other products in the market. Differentiation is possible on the basis of many different factors: quality/reliability, ease of use, functions/features, applications, benefits, price/performance, or cost of use, to name just a few.

Strategy Employed: Sony has clearly captured the ease-of-use position in the market for digital cameras. This makes the Mavica significantly different than other products on the market, which leads to public endorsements from industry analysts. "A child could figure it out," says Ron.

Source: Adapted from http://www.hightechstrategies.com

The strategies which can be formulated are broadly classified as corporate level strategies and business unit level strategies.

Corporate Level Strategies: Corporate level strategies in general are of four categories, *viz.*,

(i) Stability Strategies: Maintenance of *status quo* and sustainable growth strategies.

(ii) Growth Strategies: These strategies include internal growth, concentration strategies, mergers, takeover/acquisition, horizontal integration, conglomerate diversification, vertical integration and joint ventures.

(iii) Retrenchment Strategies: These strategies include: turnaround, captive company, transformation, divestment and liquidation. *(See Exhibit 6.2)*

Exhibit 6.2: Alternative Generic Strategies Defined and Exemplified

Strategy	*Definition*	*Example*
Forward Integration	Gaining ownership or increased control over distributors or retailers	Coca-Cola Company purchased its largest franchised bottler, JTL, for $ 1.4 billion.
Backward Integration	Seeking ownership or increased control of a firm's suppliers	Apple Computer Company created a new company-owned software subsidiary called Claris Corp.
Horizontal Integration	Seeking ownership or increased control over competitors	Delta bought Western AirLines; Maytag bought Magic Chef.
Market Penetration	Seeking increased market share for present products or services in present markets through greater marketing efforts	Lance developed a salesforce of 2,300 persons in thirty-five states; Lance's strategy includes no advertising expenditures.
Market Development	Introducing present products or services into new geographic areas	Kindercare plans to open one hundred new day care units in 1988.
Product Development	Seeking increased sales by improving and modifying present products or services	Apollo Computer introduced a $ 57,900 high performance workstation for engineers. Union Pacific, a big Western railroad, bought Overnite Transportation, a big Eastern trucker.
Concentric Diversification	Adding new, but related products or services	Ford Motor Co. bought PMI Mortgage Insurance Co., the nation's fourth largest mortgage insurance company.
Conglomerate Diversification	Adding new, unrelated products or services	Pepsi Co bought the Kentucky Fried Chicken Company.
Horizontal Diversification	Adding new, unrelated products or services for present customers.	
Joint Venture	Two or more sponsoring firms forming a separate organisation for co-operative purposes	Dupont and Xerox created a new company called DX Imaging to develop and manufacture copying equipment based on a new type of liquid toner technology.
Retrenchment	Regrouping through cost and asset reduction to reverse declining sales and profits	Firestone closed plants in Illinois, Oklahoma, and lowa, due to shrinking demand for farm and off-highway tyres.
Divesture	Selling a division or part of an organisation	Bank America sold the Charles Schwab division for $230 million.
Liquidation	Selling all of a company's assets, in parts, for their tangible worth	GenCorp liquidated the RKO General Broadcasting Group.
Combination	Pursuing two or more strategies simultaneously	Ralston Purina sold its Purina animal feed business to British Petroleum and at the same time bought Union Carbide's battery division.

Source : Fred R. David, *"Concepts of Strategic Management"*, Merrill Publishing Company, Toronto, p. 66.

(iv) *Combination Strategies:* These strategies include all possible combinations of the strategies. *(See Box 6.4).*

The companies, before deciding which markets to go, should know the risks involved in a nation's market. There are many risks involved in going internationally including shifting borders, unstable governments, foreign exchange problems, corruption and technological pirating.

BOX 6.4 : NOKIA NEWBORNS UNCOVERED: COMBINED STRATEGY

Taking place at Bangkok, Thailand, Showcase Nokia 2007, held simultaneously with 3GSM World Congress for Asia Pacific, saw top decision makers of Nokia share and discuss important strategies and product developments with journalists from the region. Of the points presented, the most significant point was that Asia Pacific will continue to remain as the biggest market segment for Nokia and that the current figure of three billion mobile subscriber base worldwide will be breached. "Nokia expects that in 2007, the 3 billion mobile subscriber mark will be crossed, with the Asia Pacific region contributing significantly to this growth. Although Nokia is known to most as one of the largest manufacturers of mobile phones, nearly all the topics covered had little or nothing to do with handsets *per se*, revolving mainly around major areas of business mobility, mobile Internet and mobile computing. On the business mobility front, Nokia reinforced the company's commitment to dissolve barriers impeding the adoption of business mobility solutions. For this, Nokia announced a hardware/software combination of a trio of new E-series handsets namely the E61i, E65 and E90 Communicator, and Intellisync Mobile Suite 8.0 mobileware. The Nokia Intellisync Mobile Suite in particular is a comprehensive software platform designed to equip both companies and individual users with a single graphical based point of management for e-mails, files and applications, database, documents, and also Nokia devices.

The prevalence of the Internet has really allowed Nokia and other manufacturers to take product design to the next level and there's little to argue that it has single handedly raised consumer expectation and satisfaction from one of the most cherished portable devices around. With consumers just beginning to embrace mobile Internet, Nokia is meeting this growing market by introducing more handsets with Internet capabilities. These include the new Nokia 3110 classic, 6110 Navigator, N77, 6088, 1325 and 1265. Though all phones support basic web browsing, the actual Internet experience actually varies, with the N77 being the most engaging of these newborns as it has a large 2.4-inch screen and also lets you enjoy TV programming on the go via DVB-H technology. The N-series will continue to remain as the flagship series of Nokia, especially now that Nokia has cooperated with YouTube to bring YouTube videos into all N-series handsets, new and old. Already destined to become a common feature in mobile phones, GPS is expected to break new grounds by bringing location based services to your palm. In this regard, Nokia has announced long term plans to become a significant player of mobile phoncs cmbedded with GPS modules by providing consumers with a range of additional benefits, including access to the latest updated maps and points of interest. Granted the company has acquired gate 5, a leading supplier of mapping, routing and navigation software and services, there is no doubt that location based experiences will increasingly be at the core of the Nokia portfolio of mobile phones, be it for the enterprise sector or consumer space.

Source: Adapted from http://www.hardwarezone.com

Deciding which Markets to Enter

Some companies operate in a number of countries, while some companies operate in a fewer countries with a deeper commitment. Ayal and Zif have suggested that a company should enter fewer markets when:

(i) Market entry and market control costs are high,

(ii) Product and communication adaption costs are high,

(iii) Population and income size and growth are high in the initial countries chosen, and

(iv) Dominant foreign firms can establish high barriers to entry

The firms can choose to enter the markets with high market attractiveness, high competitive advantage and low risk. Fig. 6.2 shows bases for evaluating which markets to enter.

Market Attractiveness

Competitive Advantage		High (H)	Medium (M)	Low (L)	Risk
	H	China	India		
	M				L
	L	Germany			
Competitive Advantage	H				Risk
	M			Romania	H
	L				

Source: Modified version from Philip Kotler, *op. cit.*, p. 409.

Fig. 6.2: Evaluating which Markets to enter

Corporate Level Strategies of a Global Business

After deciding the country to enter, the company has to decide the best mode of entry. There are nine common modes of entry, *viz.*,

(i) Indirect Exporting *(ii)* Direct Exporting *(iii)* Licensing
(iv) Joint Ventures *(v)* Direct Investment *(vi)* Acquisitions
(vii) Production Sharing *(viii)* Management Contracts *(ix)* Turnkey Operations

Indirect Exporting : Exporting through independent intermediaries to various countries.

(i) **Indirect Exporting:** Indirect exporting means exporting through independent intermediaries to various countries. There are four types of intermediaries, *viz.*,

(a) Domestic based exporter: Domestic based exporter buys the products from the manufacturer and he in turn exports them to various countries.

(b) Domestic based export agent: Domestic based export agent negotiates with the domestic producers and foreign purchasers for exports. He co-ordinates the domestic producers and foreign purchasers. He collects commission for his services.

(c) Co-operative organisation: A number of producers producing the same or similar products form into a co-operative organisation. This cooperative organisation will carry on exporting activities on behalf of the member producers. This type of arrangement is used by the producers of agricultural products.

(d) Export management company: This company manages the exports by charging a fee.

Indirect exports cost less to the producers and the producers can concentrate on the manufacturing as the export arrangements are taken care by the intermediaries.

(ii) **Direct Exports:** Companies depend on indirect marketing during the early stage of their exports. Eventually, they may decide to export directly in order to get more benefits and economies of scale. The investment and risk will be greater compared to the indirect exports. Therefore, companies develop a relationship with all stockholders of the foreign market, even before they enter the foreign market.

The methods of direct exports are as follows:

(a) *Domestic Based Export Department or Division:* A separate export department or an export division within the marketing department may be created by the company to look after the exports. This department/division will perform all the functions and complete the procedures relating to exports.

(b) *Overseas Sales Branch or Subsidiary:* The company may establish overseas sales branch(es) in one or more foreign countries. These sales branches perform the functions of export marketing and also fulfil the procedural formalities. These branches also make the host countries to feel the presence of the company. These branches perform customer service in addition to performing other marketing functions in the host country.

(c) *Travelling Export Sales Representatives:* The company can send the sales representatives to various foreign countries to explore business and also to execute the business.

(d) *Foreign Based Distributors or Agents:* The company appoints foreign based distributors or agents to deal with the exports and sell the company's products. These distributors or agents may be given exclusive rights to represent the company and its products. Alternatively, they may be given limited rights as well as responsibilities.

Companies have to participate in international exhibitions and trade fairs and exhibit their products.

(e) *E-Business:* The domestic company can sell directly to the various foreign customers through electronic business by making portals or websites on the internet. Most of the companies have their own websites which are also linked to various search engines of other popular websites like *www.yahoo.com, www.rediff.com, etc.* The companies should make their websites worldwide and worldly-wise. *(See Box 6.5).*

(iii) **Licensing:** Under this approach, the licensor licenses a foreign company to use its production process, trade mark, patent, trade secret or other item value for a fee or royalty. The manufacturer enters a foreign market with a little risk. The foreign company gains the advantages of production expertise or technology or a well-known product without having to start from scratch. Coca-Cola enters different foreign markets by licensing bottlers around the globe. It supplies them syrup, trains the personnel of the foreign companies in producing and selling the product.

Licensing: Under this approach, the licensor licenses a foreign company to use its production process, trade mark, patent, trade secret or other item value for a fee or royalty.

There are different forms of licensing arrangement. One form of licensing is management contract. Under this arrangement, a company sells a management contract to the owners of a foreign hotel, airport, hospital or other organisation to manage these businesses for a fee. The firm provides management expertise.

The second form of licensing is contract manufacturing. Under this method, the firm engages local manufacturers to produce the product. The third form of licensing is franchising. The franchiser offers a franchisee a complete brand concept and operating system. The franchisee pays certain fees to the franchiser.

(iv) **Joint Ventures:** The Foreign investors and the local manufacturer join together to form a joint venture. The joint venture involves technological transfer, market sharing and investment sharing. The foreign investor and local producer share ownership and control. Joint venture is an appropriate strategy for technological, economic and political reasons. Some governments need a domestic manufacturer's participation in ownership and control in allowing the foreign firm to enter the domestic market. The two firms substitute their resources, skills and expertise in forming a joint venture. Some joint ventures are successful and run for many years. But, some foreign investors after gaining the knowledge of

Joint Ventures: Foreign investors and local manufacturer join together to form a joint venture.

marketing conditions, consumer behaviour and culture of the people may divorce the local investor and start its independent company. Similarly, the local investor after getting the technology transferred may divorce the foreign company and have his complete ownership and control. The other problems of joint ventures include: cultural variations of the two companies, variations in the policies of reinvestment of profits, competition between the two firms for critical managerial positions and the like. Further, joint ownership may hamper a multinational company from carrying out specific manufacturing and marketing policies on a worldwide basis.*(See Box.6.5)*.

BOX 6.5: VODAFONE, ESSAR SORT OUT DIFFERENCES OVER INDIAN JV

Vodafone Group and India's Essar Group have reached an agreement on running Hutchison Essar, the Indian mobile phone operator in which Vodafone plans to acquire a controlling interest.

Under the agreement, Vodafone will have operational control of the joint venture, while Essar, which holds 33 per cent of the equity, will have rights consistent with its shareholding, including proportionate board representation, Vodafone said.

Hutchison Telecommunications International Ltd. (HTIL), announced in February that it had entered into an agreement to sell its 67 per cent direct and indirect equity and loan interests in Hutchison Essar to a subsidiary of Vodafone for a total cash consideration of $11.1 billion.

Under the agreement announced, Hutchison Essar will be renamed Vodafone Essar, and in due course the business will market its products and services under the Vodafone brand, Vodafone said. The services are currently being marketed under the Hutch brand.

Ravi Ruia, vice chairman of the Essar Group, will become chairman of Vodafone Essar, and Arun Sarin, CEO of Vodafone, will become the joint venture's vice chairman.

The appointment of Ruia as chairman appears to be a concession to the demand of the Essar Group that they run the Indian company jointly with Vodafone. Essar said it would cede operational control to Vodafone, but wanted to be consulted on strategic decisions relating to the joint venture.

Essar will also have certain liquidity rights. Between the third and fourth anniversaries of completion of the transaction, and subject to regulatory requirements, it will have an option to sell its 33 per cent shareholding in Vodafone Essar to Vodafone for $5 billion, or an option to sell between $1 billion and $5 billion worth of Vodafone Essar shares to Vodafone at an independently appraised fair market trading value, Vodafone said.

Vodafone needs Essar as a partner because of the Indian government restrictions limiting foreign equity holdings in Indian companies to 74 per cent.

Source: Adapted from http://www.infoworld.com

Direct investment is the ultimate way of going internationally.

(v) **Direct Investment:** Direct investment is the ultimate way of going internationally. The direct investment includes involvement of a company in ownership and control of foreign based assembly or manufacturing or service facilities. The foreign company *(i)* can buy part of the local manufacturing facilities, or *(ii)* can buy full interest in the local company, or *(iii)* can build its own facilities on its own. The company after producing in a foreign country can meet the customer needs in that country and export to other countries. This strategy helps the company to widen the market and get distinct advantages.

The Advantages of Direct Investment include:

(a) Getting raw material, labour and other inputs at cheaper prices.

(b) Getting foreign government incentives like cheap finance, tax concessions, subsidies and the like.

(c) Savings in cost of transportation of products to other countries.

(d) Creating jobs in the host country and build up a positive image in the host country.

(e) Building-up of closer relationships with host country's government, customers and market intermediaries makes its products more acceptable in the local market.

(f) Acquiring full control on its investment and market and develop manufacturing and marketing policies to serve the long-term needs and international objectives.

Disadvantages: In spite of these advantages, direct investment suffers from the risks and disadvantages. The disadvantages include:

(i) The company exposes its large investments to political risks, and commercial risks like blocked or devalued currencies, worsening markets or expropriation.

(ii) The laws of foreign government require the company to employ people without required skills, payment of higher salaries and payment of higher rates of taxes.

(iii) The host country may impose discriminative conditions on the foreign companies.

(iv) The political instability in host country also affect the foreign company's business.

(vi) **Acquisitions:** A foreign company rather than starting the business from scratch, acquires an already established company in the host country. The foreign company can buy the established company in its entirety rather than on piecemeal basis. Synergistic benefits can be enjoyed by the foreign company if it acquires a firm strong complementary product lines and efficient distribution network. If information about the potential companies in the host country is not available, it would be difficult for the foreign company to acquire. The government's restrictions on the ownership and control is a limiting factor for acquisition. *For example,* the Government of Eritrea imposes a restriction that foreigners cannot have 100 per cent ownership. Instead, they should have a joint ownership with Eritrean investors. *(See Box 6.6).*

BOX 6.6: TATA BUYS CORUS GROUP: LARGEST ACQUISITION BY AN INDIAN COMPANY

The most dramatic change in the Indian business in the past decade has been the surge in ambition. Take Ratan Tata, the Mumbai based tycoon who won the race to buy Britain's Corus Group, beating his Brazilian rival Benjamin Steinbruch in a closely contested auction.

At £6.2 billion, or $12 billion, Tata Steel's offer may be a pygmy by U.S. standards of deal making.It is, however, the largest ever attempted by an Indian company and, when completed, may just make the league table of Top 30 all cash transactions globally. Ratan Tata calls it "a moment of great fulfilment."

Several analysts are suggesting that Tata has gone overboard in trying to best Steinbruch's Companhia Siderurgica Nacional, or CSN. Tata Steel raised its offer to 608 pence a share, from 455 pence initially. CSN bid 603 pence. The leveraged deal, they say, may have put the 100 years old Indian company's finances at risk. Tata Steel shares fell by almost 11 per cent in Mumbai after this.

If Tata Steel were to create, from scratch, 19 million tons of steelmaking capacity comparable in quality to what Corus possesses, it would end up investing 70 per cent to 85 per cent more than it is paying now. Or at least that's what Tata's own calculations show.

Besides, setting up a new factory, a three to five year project if everything goes well, has a great execution risk.

Even in a developing country such as India — which you would assume would welcome the jobs associated with a new steel plant — it isn't easy to make such investments. Invariably, the iron ore exists in places where the poorest of the poor live. And they are nervous about displacement.

Acquiring Corus will also give Tata access to the European customers of steel, especially in the automobile and aerospace industries.

Corus will benefit from access to Indian iron-ore reserves as well as a virgin market for steel. India's per capita steel consumption is still about 35 kilograms, or 77 pounds, a year, or about one-tenth of a developed country levels.

The Tata-Corus combination will be the world's fifth biggest steel producer.

(vii) **Production Sharing:** The term production sharing combines the higher labour skills and technology available in the developed countries with the lower cost labour available in the developing countries.

(viii) **Management Contracts:** Large MNCs may have a large amount of management talent at its disposal. Management contracts offer a means through which an MNC may use part profits and personnel to assist a firm in a host country for a specified fee and period of time. MNCs earn some income from their investment and continue the operations until the local management is trained and developed. These arrangements help the developing economies that have the capital but do not have skilled manpower, and managerial skills necessary.

Turnkey operations are typically contracts for the construction of operating facilities in exchange for a fee.

(ix) **Turnkey Operations:** Turnkey operations are typically contracts for the construction of operating facilities in exchange for a fee. The facilities are transferred to the host country or the firm when they are complete. Normally, the customer is a government department or agency. The foreign company supplies some of its own equipment for the project.

These strategies are explained in detail in the chapter on *"Modes of Entering Global Markets"*.

The strategist of a global firm has to formulate business unit level strategies for the global firm.

5. Formulation of Alternative Business Unit Level Strategies

The global companies formulate business unit level strategies based on the corporate level strategies, organisational strengths and environmental opportunities. The important strategies at this level include:

(a) Low cost leadership strategy

(b) Focus or Niche strategy

(c) Differentiation strategies.

(a) **Low Cost Leadership Strategy:** The global companies plan to reduce the cost of production, cost of marketing, etc., by locating the firms close to the raw materials or close to the markets, adopting latest technology, etc. The strategy of low cost leadership provides the global company two options, *viz.*, fix the price at a lower level compared to that of the competitors or to increase the profit margin or both.

(b) **Focus or Niche Strategy:** Transnational companies formulate specific strategies for specific markets whereas international and multinational corporations apply the same strategy in a number of countries. The transnational companies are expected to think globally and act locally. Thus, they become global companies. The niche strategy refers to focussing on a small market. Transnational companies adopt the focus strategy for each local market in order to compete with the domestic companies.

(c) **Differentiation Strategy:** Transnational companies mostly adopt the differentiation strategy. They differentiate the product policies, price policies, service policies from country to country and from one customer group to other customer group, etc. This strategy helps them to compete with the local companies and also create a positive impression among the customers of various countries.

In addition to these strategies, the business unit level strategies of global business include other strategies.

(d) **Offensive Strategies:**

- Attacking competitor's strengths
- Attacking competitor's weaknesses
- Simultaneous attacks on many fronts
- End-run offensives
- Guerrilla offensive strategies
- Pre-emptive strategies

(e) **Defensive Strategies:**

Defensive strategies include:

- Protecting company's competitive position, and
- First mover advantage.

The important business unit level strategy is international product portfolio.

International Product Portfolio

Strategic planning seeks to match markets with products and other corporate resources with a view to strengthen and analyse strategies. Strategists should take into consideration, the country, attractiveness and product strength. However, MNCs plan around either product or market, but not both.

Strategic planning seeks to match markets with products and other corporate resources with a view to strengthen and analyse strategies.

Harrell and Kiffer propose portfolio analysis that can be applied to international markets. *Figure 6.3* shows matrix for plotting products. Country attractiveness is shown on the vertical line and the competitive strength of a particular product is shown on the horizontal line. Market size, market growth rate, government regulations and economic and political factors determine the country's attractiveness. Market share, product fit, contribution margin and market support determine the competitive strength. Companies with high product competitive strength and high country attractiveness can invest for growth. Contrary to this situation, the companies with low product competitive strengths and low country attractiveness can choose a strategy of harvest or divest. Those falling in the upper right box can choose for divestment or joint venture. Those falling in the centre and lower left boxes are probably good candidates for 'milking.' They can produce strong cash flows in the short run.

Country Attractiveness / Competitive Strengths	High		Low
High	Invest/ Grow		Dominate/ Divest Joint Venture
		Selectivity Strategies	
Low			Harvest/ Divest Combine/ License

Source: G.D. Harrell & R.O. Kiefer, *"Multinational Strategic Market Portfolios"*, MSU Business Topics, Winter 1981, p. 7.

Fig. 6.3: Matrix for Plotting Products

6. Selection of the Best among the Alternative Strategies

The global company after formulating the alternative strategies has to select the best among the alternative strategies. The strategists analyse the alternative strategies, rank them and select the best among them. The techniques of strategic analysis include:

- **Boston Consultancy Group Matrix:** According to this matrix, the strategy with high industry growth rate and high relative market share *(called stars)* is the best strategy.
- **General-Electric Nine-cell Matrix:** According to this matrix, the strategy with long term industry attractiveness and high business strength is the best strategy.
- **Directional Policy Matrix:** According to this matrix, the strategy with high business sector prospects and high competitive abilities of the company is the best strategy.

Thus, the strategist selects the strategy with highest industry attractiveness (having highest opportunities) (O) and highest strengths (S).

The next logical step in the strategic management process is strategy implementation.

7. Strategy Implementation

After selecting the best strategy, the global company implements it in order to achieve its goals. The factors of strategy implementation include:

The factors of strategy implementation include:
- Partner selection
- Organisational structure
- Behavioural implementation
- Marketing implementation
- Financial implementation
- Production implementation
- Human resource implementation.

(a) Partner selection
(b) Organisational structure
(c) Behavioural implementation
(d) Marketing implementation
(e) Financial implementation
(f) Production implementation
(g) Human Resource implementation.

(a) **Partner Selection:** Selection of a sound and competent partner is a must for successful implementation and running of a joint venture or licensing. The Policies of both the countries and complexities of the host country market can be balanced by selecting a right partner. This is the key to the success of the strategy. Lasserre proposes a model describing the many variables to be considered by both sides when assessing a partnership. *Fig. 6.4* presents assessing partners to implement the joint venture and licensing strategies. Both the parties need to assess the strategic fit of each company's project strategy and fit of each company's respective resources. This process requires one to two years, prior contacts between the two parties.

(b) **Organisational Structure:** MNCs tend to go through three common evolutionary stages in structuring their operations and programmes. During the initial entry, an MNC offers products in the foreign market through licensing or an export department as discussed earlier. In the second stage, the MNC establishes a local operating division in the host country. The MNC develops its market and it reaches the maturity stage. The MNC during this stage consolidates operations under a regional management organisation. Attention is given to a wider range of investment opportunities like joint ventures and mergers.

As *(i)* the profit contribution from the foreign operations increases, *(ii)* the organisation gains experience, *(iii)* the need for international specialists arises, *(iv)* the level of complexity increases, and *(v)* internal conflicts arise, and pressure is mounted to exercise more control over the operations of the foreign subsidiaries. These conditions generally result in the establishment of an international division.

The international division is responsible for imports, exports, licensing, contracts, direct sole ownership and joint ownership. This structure will result in more efficient coordination, more effective fending off of threats and better capitalising on opportunities through more timely decisions.

If the international division depends on the domestic divisions, for its resources, it may not get the resources on priority basis. This will affect the efficiency of foreign division. As the international division continues to increase in size, the strategist develops another structure, *i.e.,* global organisation structure. *Exhibit 6.3* summarises some of the structural arrangements possible in each stage of MNC development. The global structure-functional design is based on the geographical and functional structure.

Exhibit 6.3 : International Activity and Structure

Stage	*Activities*	*Organisation Responsible for International Activities*	*Executive In Charge*
ONE	Exports directly and indirectly, but trade is minor.	Export department.	Export manager, reporting to domestic marketing executive.
	Exports become more important.	Export division.	Division manager.
TWO	Company undertakes licensing and invests in production overseas.	International division.	Director of international operations, usually vice-president.
	International investments increase.	Sometimes international headquarters of a company as wholly owned as subsidiary [of domestic parent company].	President, who is the vice-president in the parent company.
THREE	International investments substantial and widespread; diversified international business activities.	Global organisational structure by geographic areas, product lines, functions, or some combination. Also worldwide staff support.	No single executive in charge of international business.

Source: Adapted from W.A. Dymsza. *Multinational Business Strategy* (New York: McGraw-Hill Book Company. 1972). p. 22.

(c) **Behavioural Implementation:** The major part of the strategy implementation in a global business is behavioural implementation. The cultural environment varies widely from country to country. When the global company decides to enter a foreign country, it has to train the existing employees in the culture of the foreign country. In addition, MNCs should train the expatriates in the culture of the parent country.

In addition, the employees of the MNCs should also be trained in the values, norms and beliefs of the country which it planned to enter. The employees should be trained in cross-cultural management, if the strategy selected is joint ventures.

Thus, appropriate behavioural training should be imparted to the employees depending upon the strategy.

(d) **Marketing Implementation:** The strategist has to design the product, price, promotion and other marketing strategies in order to achieve corporate level strategies and goals. *(See Box 6.7).*

BOX 6.7: NOKIA'S ONE GLOBAL BRANDING STRATEGY

One global strategy for Nokia, "1,001 reasons" for mankind: But is the message the right one to achieve a global identity for the Nokia brand?

NOKIA CORP., the world's largest cellphone maker, is going global with its advertising, a first for the company, as it tries to create a stronger, more unified identity in the increasingly tough cellphone branding war.

The corporate campaign, which carries the slogan "1,001 reasons to have a Nokia imaging phone," is rolling out across Europe, Africa and Asia, showing up in television, print and online ads. Nokia also plans to bring it to the U.S., tentatively in several months. It aims to send one message in all countries where Nokia is sold, a strategy that departs from past approaches that used different images and messages in different countries.

For Nokia, Grey Worldwide agency SEK & Grey created the ads for Europe, the Middle East and Africa. Another agency, Bates Advertising in Singapore, part of WPP Group, is handling the Asia Pacific region. The two worked together to come up with one campaign. Instead of expressing one best difference in their products over those of the competitors, Nokia decided that an additional thousand reasons are better than one great one. Not only that, but as Pekka Rantala, senior vice president of marketing for Nokia's multimedia business teases, Nokia does not tell you what the reasons are, just that there are 1,001 of them. Mr. Rantala envisions future ads for Nokia identifying at least some of these 1,001 reasons.

For Nokia, a global company based in Finland, staying with this strategy will create future ads lost in the white noise of global culture, falling short of developing human connections so necessary for market traction, in any language.

(e) **Financial Implementation:** The global company plans for sourcing the finance depending upon the strategy. If the strategy is low cost leadership, then the global company plans to get finance from International Finance Corporation. If the strategy is to enter foreign countries through joint ventures, it gets the finance from the host country. Similarly, the global company takes the capital budgeting decisions, depending upon the strategy. Thus, the financial plans are implemented depending upon the strategy.

(f) **Production Implementation:** Production implementation is very closely related to the strategy. If the strategy is low cost leadership, then the production facilities are located close to the raw material or customers. Manufacturing facilities are located in a number of countries due to the possibility of production through online.

(g) **Human Resource Implementation:** The global company recruits the people, trains and develops them based on the strategy. If the culture of the country plays a vital role in strategy implementation, the global company mostly appoints the people from the host country. If the skill and talent of the human resources play a dominant role in the strategy implementation, it employs the human resources from the entire world. Similarly, the company develops the employees in behavioural aspects, if the culture plays vital role in strategy implementation.

Activities of Strategy Evaluation & Control Include:
- Establish the standards of strategic management process
- Measure the performance of the process at every stage
- Compare the performance with the standards
- Observe the deviations
- Take corrective steps

Thus, the global company implements the strategy. The next logical step in the strategic management process is strategic evaluation and control.

8. Strategy Evaluation and Control

The strategic management process may not be implemented as planned due to changes in environmental factors, incompatibility of strategies to the conditions of the host country, etc. Therefore, the global company has to evaluate the process and control it. The activities in this regard include:

- Establish the standards of strategic management process
- Measure the performance of the process at every stage
- Compare the performance with the standards
- Observe the deviations
- Take corrective steps

The specific areas of strategic evaluation and control include:

(i) Financial measures

(ii) MNC – host country relationships

(iii) Contributory relationships

(iv) Reinforcing relationships

(v) Frustrating relationships, and

(vi) Undermining relationships.

(i) **Financial Measures:** The international performance in the area of finance can be evaluated through return on investment, budget analysis and historical comparisons. Multiple performance indicators should be used in view of the differences among countries which magnify the usual problems of comparability.

(ii) **MNC-Host Country Relationships:** The host countries, particularly, the third world nations expect benefits from MNCs. These benefits include: technology transfer, creation of employment opportunities, tax revenues, build up domestic businesses through joint ventures and creating a competitive business environment. But the host countries find themselves in a double bind regarding the repatriation of profits. If, the MNCs export their 100% profits, it affects the host countries, balance of payments. The Developing countries did not receive much benefits from the technology transfer from MNCs. Given the pros and cons of MNCs' presence, Fayerweather proposes four basic relations, *viz.*, contributory relationship, reinforcing relationship, frustrating relationship and undermining relationship.

(iii) **Contributory Relationship:** If an MNC contributes directly to the achievement of goals, in a host nation without any negative effect, such a relationship is called contributory relationship. In this relationship, the MNC and the local partner of the host country help each other.

(iv) **Reinforcing Relationship:** The actions of an MNC reinforce the achievement of the goals of the host nation, but tend to have some negative side effects.

(v) **Frustrating Relationship:** Actions of an MNC challenge the goals of the nation or impede its immediate functioning in ways to which the nation cannot respond effectively so that its government is frustrated.

(vi) **Undermining Relationship:** The effect of an MNC is to reduce the basic logic (in terms of norms, values, and philosophy) of a nation, so that its functioning is weakened or undetermined. Poor countries have often been swindled out of a decent return for their produce in the name of market mechanism, deprived of their economic independence, reduced by imported life styles, foreign value system, irrelevant research designs — all in the name of freedom of choice.

(E) COLLABORATIVE STRATEGIES

International business firms either perform their business operations on their own or collaborate with other companies. In fact, companies, in some situations, collaborate with their competitors also. Their collaboration choices are influenced by several factors including physical, economical, scale of operations, make or buy or make and buy decisions, societal factors, competitive environment and their objectives and strategies.

Motives for Collaborative Strategies

Some of the motives for collaborative strategies are common for both domestic business and international business. These include spread and reduced costs, specialise in core competencies, avoid or counter competition, secure vertical or horizontal integration, learn from other companies and sharing of capacities.

Spread and reduced costs: It is economical to buy the products from other specialist companies when the quantity required is small and uneconomical to produce. Companies with less capacities can outsource the capacities from the companies with larger capacities. This arrangement helps both the companies to reduce and spread the costs and also reduce the start up and waiting time. This facility also reduces the level of investment of small companies.

Specialise in Core Competencies: Companies have certain core competencies and as such they perform the activities concerning core competencies most efficiently compared to other activities. Therefore, companies prefer to depend on other companies for other operations through licensing. *For example*, Coca-Cola licensed their logos to other companies to put them on clothing.

Avoid or Counter Competition: Some markets are not large enough to accommodate competitors. For example, Papua New Guinea's market is not so large as to accommodate both Coca-Cola and Pepsi-Cola. Therefore, Pepsi-Cola withdrew from the market. Nearly 30 communication companies have formed New World, a broad band fibre optic network, in order to connect the USA with Latin America and Caribbean.

Vertical and Horizontal Integration: Vertical and horizontal linkages or integrations allow the companies to concentrate on the core competencies, operate on small scale and emphasise as a portion of the supply chain.

Learn from Other Companies: Collaborative strategies in the form of joint ventures enable the companies to learn about their partner's technology, production process, methods and systems and markets. Governments of China, Malaysia and Papua New Guinea allow foreign companies.

Sharing Capacities: Companies can jointly share their production, service, marketing, human resource and other capacities in order to operate on an optimum scale.

Motives for Collaborative Arrangements: Motives for collaborative arrangements for international business include: gain location — specific assets, overcome governmental constraints, diversify geographically and reduce exposure in risky environments.

Gain Location — Specific Assets: It would be difficult for MNCs to conduct business in some countries, on their own due to country specific environmental factors like political, cultural, economic and competitive. Therefore, MNCs seek collaboration with the domestic companies that have strengths in managing the local business. Wal-Mart initially entered Japan on its own and failed to conduct business successfully. Then it opted for strategic alliance with 'Seiyu' — a Japanese company which is familiar with local consumer tastes and rules of establishing retail stores.

Overcome Governmental Constraints: Many countries like Malaysia, Papua New Guinea, Eritrea and Mexico impose limits on foreign ownership. Some countries like China and India impose restrictive conditions on exclusive foreign ownership. The USA and Mexico prohibit exclusive foreign companies to carry out certain business operations. Further, it would be difficult for foreign companies to protect their intellectual property rights like patents and copyrights in certain foreign markets like China. MNCs adapt collaborative strategies with the local companies to enter foreign markets by solving these problems.

Diversify Geographically: The foreign companies adapt collaborative strategies to enter various foreign markets due to diversities of cultures, geographical conditions, etc.

Minimise Exposure in Risky Environments: Political, economic and security factors create risky business environments in different countries. It would be difficult for MNCs to understand and face these risky environments. Therefore, they enter such foreign markets through strategic alliances with local companies which have knowledge and skills of facing such risky environments.

Types of Collaborative Strategies: Collaborative strategies include franchising, licensing, joint ventures, outsourcing which are management contracts and turn-key projects, etc. These strategies are discussed in detail in Chapter 4 on 'Modes of Entering International Business'.

POINTS TO BE REMEMBERED

- The corporate vision has the potential power to focus the collective energy of insiders and to give outsiders a better idea of what an organisation really is.
- Strategy is a competitive, unified and integrated plan. Companies formulate grand strategies and generic strategies.
- Strategies of a global company are different from a domestic company.
- Environmental insensitive products do not require significant adaptation to the environmental factors and *vice versa* is true in case of environmentally sensitive products.
- The different stages of a transnational corporation include: domestic company, international company, multinational company, global company and transnational company. The strategies differ from one stage to another stage.

KEY WORDS

- Vision
- Strategy
- Business Unit Level Strategies
- Defensive Strategies
- Environmental
- Direct Exports
- Strategic Analysis
- Strategic Control
- Mission
- Grand Strategies
- Offensive Strategies
- Licensing
- Scanning
- Turnkey Operations
- Strategy Implementation

QUESTIONS FOR DISCUSSION

1. What is strategic management? Explain the process of strategy formulation.
2. What are the peculiarities of global strategic management?
3. Explain the strategies to be adopted by a global company in case of environmentally sensitive products.
4. Discuss the strategies to be employed by a global company.
5. What is international SWOT analysis? How is it used in formulating global strategies?

REFERENCES

1. Peter Senge, *"The Fifth Discipline: The Art and Practice of Learning Organisation"*, New York, 1990, p. 206.
2. *Ibid.*, pp. 207-208.
3. Samuel C. Cento and J. Paul Peter, *op.cit.*, p. 56.
4. Gerry Johnson and Keven Seholes, *op.cit.*, p. 10.
5. Samuel C. Cento and J. Paul Peter, *op.cit.*, p. 10.
6. Bartlett and Ghoshal *"Managing Across Borders"*, Quoted in Charles W.L. Hill , *op.cit.*, pp. 424-425.
7. Peter Lorange, John Ross and Peggy Simicic Bronn, *"Building Successful Strategic Alliances"*. Long Range Planning, December 1992, pp. 10-17.
8. J.D. Daniels, E.W. Ogram and L.H. Radebaugh, *"International Business: Environment and Operations,"* Addison-Wesley, Reading 1982, p. 640.
9. D. Ricks and J.S. Arpan, *"International Business Blunders"*, Ohio: Grid Inc., Columbus, 1974.
10. Warren J. Keegan, *"Global Marketing Management"*, Prentice-Hall of India, New Delhi, 1995, p. 32.
11. *Ibid.*
12. *Ibid.*, p. 34.
13. John Fayer Weather, *"International Business Management: A Conceptual Framework"*, McGraw-Hill, New York, 1969.
14. Warren J. Keegan, *op.cit.*, p. 39.
15. *Ibid.*, p. 41.
16. S. Chang, "The Gods and the U.A.W. Are Smiling: Mazda's New Boss Plans to Make Cars and Jobs for Yanks," *People*, February 18, 1985, pp. 90-91.
17. P. Wright, "Doing Business in Islamic Markets," *Harvard Business Review*, Vol. 59, No. 1, January-February 1981, pp. 34-40.
18. Chang and Campo-Flores, pp. 602-604, Quoted in Thomas L. Wheelen and J. David Hunger, *op. cit.*, p. 272.
19. Wright, Pringle and Kroll, *op. cit.*, pp. 233-234.
20. Thomas L. Wheelen and J. David Hunger, *op.cit.*, p.285.
21. M. Ul Haq, *"The Poverty Curtain: Choice of the Third World"*, Columbia University Press, 1976.
22. Rabock and Simmonds, *"International Business and MNCs"*, p.419.
23. *Ibid.*
24. Dymsza, *"Multinational Business Strategy"*, pp.23-26.
25. Fayer Weather, *op.cit.*, p.124.
26. John Wilman, "*Coca-Cola Aims to Put Fizz into Fashion*", Financial Times, January 2, 1999, p.1.
27. New World Ready to Build Caribbean Fiber System, Fiber-Optics New 20, No. 26, June 2000, p.1.
28. Yumiko Ono and Ann Zimmerman, "Wal-Mart Enters Japan with Seiyu Stake" Wall Street Journal, March 15, 2002, B5.
29. G.D. Harrell and R.D. Keifer, *op.cit.*, p.5.

✦ ✦ ✦

7 CHAPTER

CORPORATE LEVEL STRATEGIC ALTERNATIVES

Chapter Outline

(A) Strategy Formulation: Situational Analysis
(B) Stability Strategies
(C) Growth Strategies
(D) Retrenchment Strategies
(E) Strategic Alliances
(F) Combination Strategy/Portfolio Restructuring

Learning Objectives

After studying this chapter, you should be able to:

- Undertake strength, weakness, opportunity and threat (SWOT) analysis;
- Discuss various stability strategies;
- Analyse various growth strategies like mergers, takeovers, horizontal integration, vertical integration and joint ventures;
- Explain retrenchment strategies like turnaround strategies, captive company strategy, divestment strategy and liquidation strategy;
- Craft combination strategy and portfolio restructuring;
- Discuss various forms of strategic alliances.

(A) STRATEGY FORMULATION: SITUATIONAL ANALYSIS

Strategy formulation is often referred to as strategic planning or long range planning. This process is primarily analytical and not action oriented. The strategy formulation process is concerned with developing a corporation's mission, objectives, strategy and policy. This process involves scanning external and internal environmental factors, analysis of the strategic factors and generation and evaluation and selection of the best alternative strategy appropriate to the analysis.

Evaluation of Current Results

Henry Mintzberg, after much research found that strategy formulation is typically not a regular, continuous process. "It is small, often an irregular, discontinuous process, proceeding in fits and starts. There are periods of stability in strategy development, but also there are periods of flux, of grouping, of piecemeal change and of global change."

Performance results are generally periodic measurements of developments that occur during a given time period like return on investment, profits after taxes, earnings per share and market share. The current performance results are compared with the current objectives and with that of the previous year's performance results. If the results are equal to or greater than the current objectives and past year's results, the company will mostly continue with the current strategy otherwise, the strategy formulation process begins in earnest.

The strategic managers must evaluate the mission, objectives and policies, management styles and skills.

The strategic managers must evaluate the mission, objectives and policies. In fact, the strategic managers are evaluated in terms of management style, values and skills by the top management. Henry Mintzberg has pointed out that a corporation's objectives and strategies are strongly affected by the top management's view of the world. This view determines the mode to be used in strategy formulation. These modes include: entrepreneurial mode, adaptive mode and planning mode as presented in Exhibit 7.1.

Entrepreneurial Mode: Strategy is formulated by one powerful individual. The focus is on opportunities rather than on problems. Strategy is guided by the founder's own vision of direction.

Adaptive Mode: This strategy formulation mode is characterised by reactive solutions to the existing problems rather than a proactive search for new opportunities.

Planning Mode: Analysts assume main responsibility for strategy formulation. Strategic planning includes both the proactive search for new opportunities and the reactive solution of existing problems.

SWOT Analysis

SWOT analysis helps the organisation, to emphasise on its strengths and moderate the impact of its weaknesses, uncover its strengths that have not yet been fully utilised and correct or make up for the weaknesses.

Underlying any successful selection of strategies is an analysis of the firm's internal strengths and weaknesses and the opportunities provided and the threats that are posed by the external environment. As explained earlier, the process of examining the firm and its environment is known as SWOT (strengths, weaknesses, opportunities and threats) analysis. The management should identify and analyse various factors (see Exhibit 7.2) to identify the strengths, weaknesses, opportunities and threats. This analysis will help the company to position itself to take the advantage of the opportunities provided by the environment and to minimise the threats posed by the environment. This analysis will also help the organisation, to emphasise on its strengths and moderate the impact of its weaknesses. Further, the organisation can uncover its strengths that have not yet been fully utilised and correct or make up for the weaknesses. Matching environmental information with the knowledge of the organisation's capabilities enables management to formulate efficient and realistic strategies for attaining organisational goals.

Corporate Profiles

SWOT analysis helps the management in determining in which business or businesses the company should be operating. The three types of corporate profiles are: *(i)* the firm can compete in one business or industry, *(ii)* the firm can compete in several related businesses or industries, *(iii)* the firm can compete in several unrelated businesses or industries. The firm benefits from the specialised knowledge, by competing in only one industry. But, operating primarily in one industry, increases a firm's vulnerability to business cycles. Firms competing in related businesses and/or markets/countries transfer the improvements in production or efficiencies in operation of one business to other businesses or markets or countries.

However, these firms also face the problems of shrinkage in consumer demand or price competition. These problems can be overcome by operating in unrelated businesses. But, the firms operating in unrelated businesses face the problems in managing diverse and unrelated businesses efficiently. SWOT analysis helps in determining which of these strategies is most appropriate for a particular firm. The strategist must analyse the firm's critical weaknesses or valuable strengths based on internal environmental analysis in the context of abundant opportunities provided or critical threats posed by the external environment. (See Fig.7.1)

Exhibit 7.1: Characteristics and Conditions of Three Modes

Characteristics	*Entrepreneurial Mode*	*Adaptive Mode*	*Planning Mode*
Motive for Decisions	Proactive	Reactive	Proactive & Reactive
Goals of Organisation	Growth	Indeterminate	Efficiency & Growth
Evaluation of Proposals	Judgmental	Judgmental	Analytical
Choice made by	Entrepreneur	Bargaining	Management
Decision Horizon	Long term	Short term	Long term
Preferred Environment	Uncertainty	Certainty	Risk
Decision Linkages	Loosely coupled	Disjointed	Integrated
Flexibility of Mode	Flexible	Adaptive	Constrained
Size of Moves	Bold Decisions	Incremental Steps	Global Strategies
Vision of Direction	General	None	Specific
Condition for Use			
Source of Power	Entrepreneur	Divided	Management
Objectives of Organisation	Operational	Non-operational	Operational
Organisational Environment	Yielding	Complex, dynamic	Predictable, Stable
Status of Organisation	Young, small, or strong leadership	Established	Large

Source: H. Mintzberg, "Strategy Making in Three Modes," *California Management Review*, Vol. XVI, No. 2, p.49, in Thomas L. Wheeler and J. David Hunger, *op. cit., p. 147.*

Exhibit 7.2: Framework for SWOT Analysis

Sources of Possible Environmental Opportunities and Threats:

Economic Forces Political-Legal Forces Social Forces Technological Forces

Industry Forces

Possible Organisational Strengths and Weaknesses

Advertising	Distribution	Leadership	Product/Service Quality
Brand names	Economies of Scales	Location	Promotion
Channel Management	Environmental Scanning	Management	Public relations
Company Reputation	Financial Resources	Manufacturing and operations	Purchasing
Computer Information System	Forecasting	Market Share	Quality control
Control Systems	Government Lobbying	Organisational Structure	Research & Development
Costs	Human Resources	Physical facilities/ equipment	Selling
Customer Loyalty	Inventory Management	Product/Service Differentiation	Technology.
Decision-Making	Labour Relations		

Source: Peter Wright, Charles D. Pringle and Mark J. Kroll, *op. cit.*, p. 70.

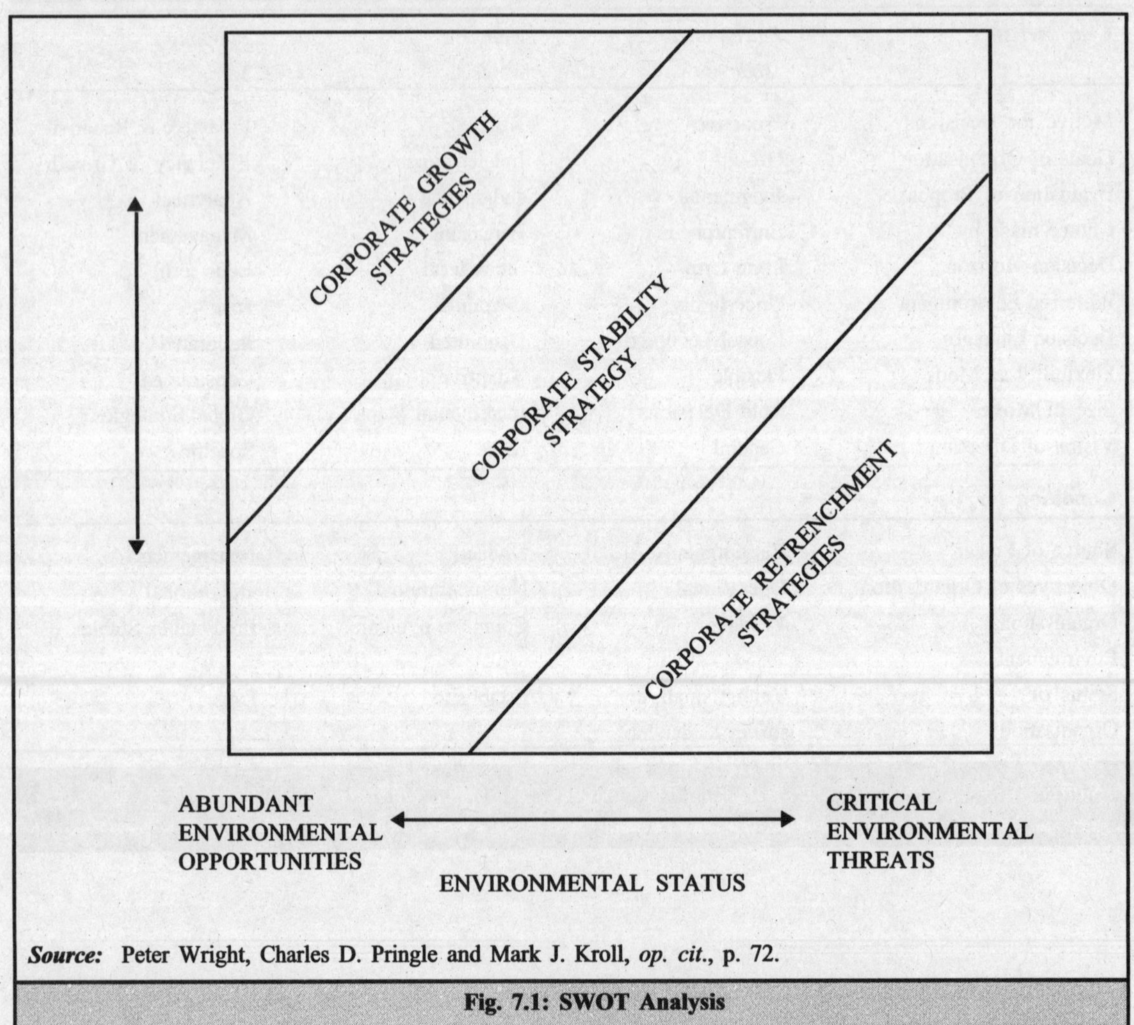

Source: Peter Wright, Charles D. Pringle and Mark J. Kroll, *op. cit.*, p. 72.

Fig. 7.1: SWOT Analysis

Strategic Alternatives

Strategic alternatives revolve around the question of whether to continue or change the business enterprise which is currently in or improve the efficiency and effectiveness with which the firm achieves its corporate objectives in its chosen business sector.

After analysing the environment and assessing the internal environment, the next step in the strategic planning process is to develop strategic alternatives to help the organisation in achieving its objectives. Different kinds of strategic alternatives are presented in Fig. 7.2. "Strategic alternatives revolve around the question of whether to continue or change the business enterprise which is currently in or improve the efficiency and effectiveness with which the firm achieves its corporate objectives in its chosen business sector." Glueck and Jauch identify four grand strategies, *viz.*, stability, expansion, retrenchment and combination of these three strategies. Now, we discuss these strategies.

KINDS OF GRAND STRATEGIES

Stability Strategies	Growth Strategies	Retrenchment Strategies	Combination Strategies
• Maintenance of Status Quo • Sustainable Growth	• Internal Growth • Concentration Strategies • Mergers • Takeover/ Acquisition • Horizontal Integration • Conglomerate Diversification • Vertical Integration • Joint Ventures	• Turnaround • Captive Company • Transformation • Divestment • Liquidation	Portfolio Restructuring

Fig. 7.2: Different Kinds of Grand Strategy Alternatives

(B) STABILITY STRATEGIES

Some firms adopt stability strategy instead of using growth strategies. Firms attempt to maintain their size, level of production and sales, serving almost the same customer groups, performing the same customer functions, produce with the same technologies and operate the current lines of business. These firms do not attempt to grow either through increased sales or through the development of new products or markets. Companies belonging to mid-day industries like cement, chemicals, plastics, banking, fertilizers and iron and steel adopt stability strategies.

Companies experiencing volatilities diversify to the stable portfolio businesses.

Stability through Diversification: Companies belong to sunrise and sun-setting industries like pharmaceutical, software, bio-technology, paper and textile mostly experience output, sales and profit swings either due to a declining demand or due to environmental uncertainties. Such companies diversify into those areas where they can experience stability in output, sales and profits. For example, DOW Chemical, Dupont, BASF and ICI diversified into plastics, fertilizers and synthetic fibers which are stable in business operations. Bayer AG purchased Roche Holding which is a consumer drug company to balance the portfolios in terms of output, sales and profits. Similarly, Bayer started the portfolios like pesticides, seeds, health care and advanced plastics. Similarly, Tata Iron and Steel Company diversified into automobiles, software, food, etc., and Reliance entered into petroleum, communication and retail business in order to enjoy the stability of earnings from different businesses.

Stability through Minor Functional Strategies: Some companies belonging to sun-setting/ non-growth industries like hotel, automobile and publishing adopt minor functional strategies like service strategies, modernisation and customisation strategies in order to have stability in sales revenue and profits. For example, most of the hotels adopted the strategy of home delivery, publishing companies adopted the strategy of publishing the books based on the requirements of a specific customer group and textile companies modernised the factories in order to have stability of sales and profits.

This strategy can be of five types, *viz.*, maintenance of *status quo* and sustainable growth.

- Maintenance of *Status-Quo*
- Sustainable Growth
- Pause/Proceed with Caution Strategy
- No Change Strategy
- Profit Strategy

Maintenance of *Status Quo*

Stability strategies include: maintenance of status-quo, sustainable growth, pause/proceed with caution strategy, no change strategy, and profit strategy.

The firms adopting this strategy maintain the same level of operations. Small business firms desire satisfactory level of operations rather than growth.

Sustainable Growth: Slow growth is more desired rather than maintenance of *status quo*. In fact, it is very difficult to maintain *status quo*. Therefore, a sustainable growth strategy is more optimistic than the zero growth.

Pause/Proceed With Caution Strategy

The companies test the environment and particularly the market conditions, whenever they introduce a new product or service. At that time, they observe the reactions of the market and proceed in accordance with the positive reactions of the market. They pause the business operations including production and marketing, if the market reactions are negative. Thus, the companies follow pause and proceed strategies until the environment reaches the stability stage. Once the environment is stable, the company would follow stability strategy. Companies, thus, follow *ad hoc* strategies until the environment is under volatile conditions. Dell Computers experienced abnormal growth in demand in early 1990s and it could not manage the increased demand. Then, the company followed this strategy until it could meet the increased demand.

No Change Strategy

Companies continue the same strategy until the internal environment and external environment remain more or less constant. Even though, there would be minor changes in the environment like enhancement of opportunities or threats, there would be offset by the entry of new firms into the industry or exit of existing firms from the industry. In other words, when the opportunities increase in the form of increase in demand, new firms enter the industry. In case of increase in threats in the form of decline in demand, the existing firms exit from the industry.

Profit Strategy

Profit strategy aims at maintaining the same level of profit (earned during favourable economic conditions) even during uncertain and unfavourable economic conditions, through window dressing. Thus, the companies support themselves artificially through any one or combination of the following tactics:

- boosting up of sales revenue by presenting gross sales,
- reducing operating expenditure,

- presenting the income earned through sale of assets as operating income,
- reducing the depreciation amount by using different methods of calculation of depreciation, and
- presenting the bad debts as debtors.

Companies should use this strategy cautiously and rarely or otherwise they experience the situation experienced by Satyam Computers during late 2008.

Reasons for Adopting Stability Strategies: Firms adopt the stability strategies due to the following reasons:

(i) Managers of small businesses desire a satisfactory level of profits rather than increased profits.

(ii) Maintenance of *status quo* involves less risk than a more growth strategy.

(iii) Change of any form may disrupt the current working relationships and the consequences may be detrimental to the organisation.

(iv) Change may upset the smooth operations and result in poor performance especially, if the firm considers itself successful with the present level of operations.

(v) Changing operations to pursue a more aggressive growth strategy usually requires an increased investment and managerial support. Firms, which cannot provide resources, may continue with the stability strategy.

(vi) Some executives maintain with the stability strategy due to inertia for change.

(vii) In some cases, firms are forced to adopt stability strategy, if they operate in a low growth or no growth industry.

(viii) Sometimes, firms may find that the cost of growth is more than the benefits of the same.

(ix) Firms that dominate their industry through their superior size and competitive advantage may pursue stability to reduce their chances of being prosecuted for engaging in monopolistic practices, and

(x) Smaller firms that concentrate on specialised products or services may choose stability because of their concern that growth will result in reduced quality and customer service.

Despite these reasons for adopting stability strategy, there is a danger of pursuing the stability strategy. The danger is that the environment may change and cause the firm or its product line to become obsolete. Hence, firms plan for adopting growth strategies.

(C) GROWTH STRATEGIES

Organisations may select a growth strategy to increase their profits, sales and/or market share. They also pursue a growth strategy to reduce the cost of production per unit. Growth strategies involve a significant increase in performance objectives. These strategies are adopted when firms remarkably broaden the scope of their customer groups, customer functions and alternative technologies either singly or in combination with each other. The different types of growth strategies are discussed hereunder:

Growth strategies include: internal growth and concentration strategies.

1. Internal Growth Strategy

Internal growth is achieved through increasing the firm's production capacity, employees and sales. Some firms prefer this strategy to the strategy of external growth as internal growth preserves their efficiency, quality and image unlike in external growth.

2. Concentration Strategies

Firms pursue concentration strategies to grow while remaining relatively simple. The total efforts of the firm are concentrated on a limited combination of customer groups, customer functions, alternate technologies and products.

Eureka Vacuum Cleaners added new functions to the vacuum cleaners like cleaning beds, cleaning domestic drainage in addition to cleaning the floor by adding a few more equipment to the original products, in order to serve the domestic customers in multiple activities. Similarly, Nokia added camera, audio and video camera, and internet facility to their mobile phones in order to meet the diversified needs of the same customer groups.

Advantages: Lauenstein and Skinner argue that most of the effective organisations focus on a narrow set of objectives. A firm can gain a competitive advantage by concentrating on a specific technology, product or market. Firms pursuing this strategy are frequently able to identify new developments and trends within the industry and respond to them. Exhibit 7.3 presents strategic alternatives available to the firms pursuing concentration strategies. However, firms change their strategies from concentration strategies despite the advantages.

Exhibit 7.3: Strategic Alternatives Available to the Firms Pursuing Concentration Strategies

Focus on Customer:

- Increase usage by present customers:
  - Increase purchase size or frequency
  - Improve product location
  - Expand product line (sizes, options, styles)
  - Expand shelf space
- Attract Competitors' Customers:
  - Increase promotional efforts
  - Initiate price cuts
- Attract Nonusers of the product:
  - Advertise new uses
  - Offer special prices and promotions
  - Increase product availability (new geographic uses)

Focus on Product:

- Differentiate product from its competitors
- Increase Rate of Product Obsolescence
  - Change styles
  - Change options
  - Change colours
- Develop new uses for the product
- Improve product servicing

Focus on Technology:

- Develop new equipment to improve efficiency
- Develop new products
- Find uses for by-products
- Improve quality

Source: Joe G. Thomas, *op. cit.*, p. 203.

Problems: There are certain potential problems of concentration strategies. They are:

(i) One of the greatest problems is the risk associated with putting "all the corporate eggs in one basket."

(ii) The introduction of substitute products may also be very detrimental to a firm following a concentration strategy. The substitute products can make a firm's product obsolete particularly when the firm concentrates on only one product or product line.

(iii) A company pursuing concentration strategy may also be affected by the disruption in the supply of essential and crucial raw material.

(iv) Sometimes, the market segment becomes unattractive owing to limited growth opportunities, and availability of substitute products or absence of essential resources. In such a case, a firm pursuing a concentration strategy may become locked into one area of business and become unable to move into another line of business.

Exhibit 7.4 presents the reasons for change of a firm from concentration strategies.

Exhibit 7.4: Reasons for Change of a Firm From Concentration Strategies

1. *Temptations of diversification* — Spreading risks by operating in multiple areas decreases the threat of any one area causing the firm to fail. However, diversification spreads resources over several areas, similarly decreasing the probability that the firm can be a strong force in any area.
2. *Need to meet short term goals* — When the firm is not strong in an area, managers tend to experience pressures to do what is necessary to meet the plan (budget or quota) in the short run rather than focusing on a long range success. Many times short term sales and profits can be increased by moving into new businesses.
3. *Underestimation of present opportunities* — Spreading resources too thin may cause an organization to overlook opportunities in its existing field. Similarly, resources may limit a firm's ability to capitalize on opportunities that do develop.
4. *Impatience to grow* — Small firms often feel they are too small to be important in their field. Growth becomes a primary objective. Once they have moved into other fields to increase sales and profits, however, diversified firms discover that they lack the management and financial resources needed to operate the diverse organization.
5. *Overconfidence* — A company doing well may conclude it has superior ability and can be successful in almost any business. Management often forgets the years of experience it took to earn the success being achieved. Such firms lack this experience in the new business.
6. *Misjudging success requirements* — Problems of the new business are often more complex and resistant to solution than expected. Connections between the new and old businesses are often superficial and only marginally related to the problems of the new venture.
7. *Pressure to use idle capacity* — Firms with excess resources, especially manufacturing facilities, feel compelled to put unused resources to work immediately. Rather than wait for growth to utilize the capacity, firms often rush into the first available alternative to begin using idle resources.
8. *Siren song of integration* — Forward or backward integration creates opportunities to control resources or markets and to "absorb the profits of the middleman." Many times, the acquiring firm lacks the expertise of the middleman. Furthermore, the acquiring organization rarely is able to operate the supplier/market at its most efficient capacity, thus, incurring diseconomies of scale.
9. *Dangers of pride* — Even after entering a new field that turns sour, managers are often reluctant to admit to making a mistake. Commitment to this strategy escalates. Resources are devoted to supporting the struggling venture to save the managers, pride, rather than allocating those resources to more profitable, growing projects.

Source: M. Lauenstein and W. Skinner, "Formulating a Strategy of Superior Resources," *Journal of Business Strategy*, pp. 4-10 in Joe G. Thomas, *op. cit.*, pp. 202-203.

(3) Merger Strategy

A merger is a combination of two or more businesses in which one acquires the assets and liabilities of the other in exchange for stock or cash or both. Companies are dissolved and assets and liabilities are combined and new stock is issued.

Many firms prefer to grow through mergers. Combination of two or more firms is known as a merger. When the firms of similar objectives and similar strategies combine into one firm, such combinations are called mergers. "A merger is a combination of two or more businesses in which one acquires the assets and liabilities of the other in exchange for stock or cash or both. Companies are dissolved and assets and liabilities are combined and new stock is issued." Mergers can take place within one nation or across nations.

Types of Mergers: Mergers can be classified into the following types:

(i) *Horizontal Mergers:* Horizontal mergers are combinations of firms engaged in the same business. Merger of Tata Steel with Natsteel of Singapore and Videocon with Thomson, SA, an electronics company of France are examples of horizontal merger.

(ii) *Vertical Mergers:* Vertical mergers are combination of different firms engaged in activities complementary to each other like supply of raw materials, production of goods and marketing. For example, combination of firm engaged in mining of iron ore, and iron and steel company. Merger of A. P. Lightings with Philips is an example for vertical integration.

(iii) *Concentric Mergers:* Concentric mergers are combination of firms related to each other in terms of customer groups or customer functions or alternative technologies. For example, combination of firms producing televisions, washing machines, and kitchen appliances.

(iv) *Conglomerate Mergers:* Conglomerate mergers are the combination of firms unrelated to each other in terms of customer groups, customer functions and alternative technologies. For example: combination of a publishing company and an automobile company.

Reasons/Motives for Merger

Two or more firms have to act for merger. One of them is the buyer and the other one is the seller. Both these firms have motives for combination. Availability of readymade or built-in manufacturing facilities, well known brands or brand loyalty, captive market share, loyal customers, advanced technology, efficient distribution channels, financial soundness, etc., are attractive factors resulting in the merger. Exhibit 7.5 presents the buyer's motives and seller's motives for merging.

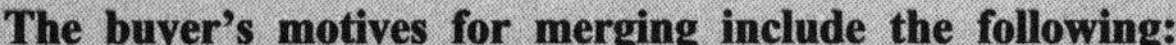

Exhibit 7.5: The Buyer's and Seller's Motives for Merging

The buyer's motives for merging include the following:

- To increase the value of the firm's stock. Mergers often lead to increases in the stock price and/or price-earnings ratio.
- To increase the growth rate of the firm.
- To make a good investment. A firm may make a better use of funds by purchasing instead of plowing the same funds into internal expansion.
- To improve the stability of the firm's earnings and sales. This is done by acquiring firms whose earnings and sales complement the firm's peaks and valleys.
- To balance or fill out the product line.
- To diversify the product line when the current products have reached their peak in the life cycle.
- To reduce competition by purchasing a competitor (possible violation of the Sherman Act).
- To acquire a needed resource quickly – for example, high quality technology or highly innovative management.
- For tax reasons. It may be desirable to purchase a firm with prior tax losses which will offset the current or future earnings.
- To increase efficiency and profitability, especially if there is synergy between the two companies. (Synergy is discussed later in the chapter.)

The seller's motives for merging include the following:

- To increase the value of the owner's stock and investment in the firm.
- To increase the firm's growth rate by receiving more resources from the acquiring company.
- To acquire the resources to stabilise operations and make them more efficient.
- For tax reasons. If the firm is owned by a family or an individual, a merger makes it easier to deal with estate tax problems.
- To help diversify the owning family's holdings beyond the present firm.
- To deal with top management problems such as management succession for an entrepreneur or dissension among top managers.

Source: Lawrence R. Jauch and William F. Glueck, *op. cit.*, p. 229.

Critical Issues in Merger: There are four critical areas of merger. They are: strategic issues, financial issues, managerial issues and legal issues.

***(i)* Strategic Issues:** These issues relate to commonality of strategic interests for mergers between the firms. Strengths of one firm may be the weaknesses of the other firm and *vice versa.* Both the firms get the advantage of the strengths of each other after the merger. Further, the impact of synergy would help both the organisations after merger to achieve the objective efficiently.

***(ii)* Financial Issues:** These issues include *(a)* valuation of seller firm, *(b)* Sources of financing for merger, etc. Value of the selling firm may be assessed based on the assets, market standing, earning potential, share prices, etc. Source of financing would be based on shares through exchange of debt and equity. However, other sources of financing are used rarely.

***(iii)* Managerial Issues:** Managerial issues are critical in mergers. There would be significant changes in the top management level and chief executive of the firm after merger. Further, professional management may not be given due consideration after merger. Even the staff members at middle and lower levels may also be changed after merger. To make the merger a smooth one, there should be an understanding between the buyer and seller about the top level management, staff at all levels and professional management. Further, steps should also be taken to train the employees of both the firms about the organisational culture of each other.

***(iv)* Legal Issues:** Legal issues in mergers are concerned with the provisions of the various laws relating to mergers. These provisions of the laws include: Chapter V of the Companies Act, 1956, the MRTP Act and Section 72A (I) of the Income Tax Act.

Advantages and Disadvantages of Mergers

Mergers as a growth strategy are popular in many countries. There are certain advantages of mergers for both the buying and selling firms. These advantages include:

(i) The firm after the merger will enjoy the economies of large scale operations.

(ii) The firm after the merger can utilise the funds to the maximum extent and get the benefit of profit growth.

(iii) The firm will be in a position to diversify the activities, increase the level of operations and level of profits.

(iv) The more effective and efficient utilisation of resources will result in higher productivity.

(v) Revival of sick units and avoidance of mortality of loss making organisation can be possible through merger.

(vi) Entrepreneurs often find it easy to buy an existing firm with established markets rather than establishing a new company.

(vii) The merger provides the buying company an easy entry into the market along with the customers' loyalty.

(viii) The merger also helps the buying company in having easy access to the sources of raw material, finance and human resources.

(ix) The problems of procuring skilled employees and developing them can be solved through mergers.

(v) The organisational life cycle can be expanded for a longer period through mergers.

Despite these advantages, mergers and acquisitions are not always successful due to their disadvantages.

Disadvantages

(i) The psychological problems of the top management of the merging firms after merger may result in disbanding of merger.

(ii) Negative attitude of the senior partner towards the junior firm may result in the failure of the merger.

(iii) The executives of the acquired firm may get low status, low level authority and power.

(iv) Research studies find that the performance and profitability of the combined firms tend to decline compared with that of the merging firms, before merger.

(v) The mergers will lead to concentration of economic power, monopolistic conditions and thereby political power, higher prices, restricted supply, black marketing, etc.

Reasons for failure of mergers are presented in Exhibit 7.6.

Exhibit 7.6: Reasons for Failure of Mergers

Business Week reviewed a sample of firms completing mergers and identified seven reasons for the failure of mergers.

1. Paying too much for the acquired firm.
2. Assuming that a growing market or product will continue its recent outstanding performance.
3. Leaping into a merger without carefully studying its consequences.
4. Diversifying into areas in which the firm had too limited knowledge.
5. Buying too large a firm and thus, incurring an excessively large debt.
6. Trying to merge disparate corporate cultures.
7. Counting on key personnel staying after the merger.

Source: "Do Mergers Really Work," *Business Week*, June 3, 1985, pp. 88-91.

Guidelines for Effective Mergers

In view of the failure of some of the mergers due to the disadvantages discussed above, the firms should follow the guidelines for the success of the mergers. The guidelines for effective mergers are:

(i) Mergers must be carefully planned.

(ii) Human considerations should also be given sufficient care as that of financial resources.

(iii) The valuation of a merger candidate is an important process.

(iv) Legal factors must be carefully assessed.

(v) Mergers which create synergy are likely to be more successful.

(vi) The benefits of merger, the positions and the authority in the combined firm should be distributed to the people of both the firms with due considerations.

(vii) A separate plan and a detailed programme should be prepared.

(viii) Authority and responsibilities should be clearly written for executing the programme of merger.

(ix) The activities of merger should be controlled through the technique of feed-forward and management information system.

(4) Takeovers or Acquisitions Strategy

Sometimes firms want to grow through the strategy of takeover or acquisition. Takeover (or acquisition) is defined as, "the attempt (often sprung as a surprise) of one firm to acquire ownership or control over another firm against the wishes of the latter's management (and purchase some of its stakeholders)." But, in practice, takeovers can be hostile (against the wishes of the acquired firm) or friendly (through mutual consent of buyer and seller like in merger). Takeover strategy is currently the most popular strategy in India, particularly after the economic liberationisation.

Takeover is the attempt (often sprung as a surprise) of one firm to acquire ownership or control over another firm against the wishes of the latter's management (and purchase some of its stakeholders).

Exhibit 7.7 presents the examples of acquisitions.

Exhibit 7.7

Acquirer	*Acquiree*	*Industry*
Tata Steel, India	Corus Group, UK	Steel
Hindalco, India	Novelis, Canada	Steel
Videocon, India	Daewoo Electronics, Korea	Electronics
Dr. Reddy's Lab, India	Beta Pharma, Germany	Pharmaceutical
SuzCon Energy, India	Hansen Group, Belgium	Energy
HPCL, India	Kenya Petroleum Ltd., Kenya	Oil and Gas
Ranbaxy Labs, India	Terapia SA, Romania	Pharmaceutical
VSNL, India	Teleglobe, Canada	Telecom

Advantages of Takeovers

(i) Takeovers ensure management accountability.

(ii) Takeovers provide easy growth opportunities.

(iii) They create mobility of resources from one activity to another activity.

(iv) They avoid gestation periods and problems involved in new projects.

(v) They provide the chance of survival to the sick units and provide alternatives to the disinvestment strategy.

However, the strategy of takeovers, suffers from disadvantages.

Disadvantages

The disadvantages of takeovers are:

(i) Professionalisation of the management may be replaced by money power.

(ii) Takeovers do not create any real assets to the society.

(iii) They result in monopoly and concentration of economic power.

(iv) They are detrimental to the society.

(v) Interests of the minority shareholders are not protected.

These disadvantages sometimes result in the failure of some takeovers.

Guidelines for Effective Takeovers

Prasanna Chandra recommends a six step procedure for effective takeovers. This procedure includes:

(a) Spell out the objectives.

(b) Indicate how the objectives would be achieved.

(c) Assess managerial quality.

(d) Check the compatibility of business styles.

(e) Anticipate and solve problems early.

(f) Treat people with dignity and concern.

Guidelines for effective takeover offered by an executive are presented as follows:

(i) Specify clearly the acquisition objectives, especially the earning objectives.

(ii) Workout and specify the gains of shareholders of both the firms.

(iii) Be sure that the management of the acquired company is or can be made competent.

(iv) Note the existence of important dovetailing resources but do not expect perfect compatibility.

(v) Initiate the process of merger with active involvement of the chief executive.

(vi) Clearly define the business that the company is in.

(vii) Identify and check on the strengths, weaknesses and key performance factors for both the firms.

(viii) Anticipate problems and discuss them early with the other firm so as to create a climate of trust.

(ix) Be sure that the takeover does not pose a threat to the present management team.

(x) People should be of prime consideration in planning for takeover and structuring the organisation.

(5) Horizontal Integration

Many companies expand by creating other firms in their same line of business. For example, Tata group established Tata Financial Services, Tata Capital and Tata Investment Corporation in the same line of business.

The reasons for engaging in this process of horizontal integration are:

(a) to increase the market share, *(b)* to reduce the cost of operations per unit of business through the large scale economies, *(c)* to get greater leverage to deal with the customers and

suppliers, *(d)* to promote the products and services more efficiently to a larger audience, *(e)* to have greater access to the channels of distribution, *(f)* to enjoy increased operational flexibility, *(g)* finally, to take the advantage of the benefits of synergy. When the combination of two or more business units (existing and created) results in greater effectiveness and efficiency than the total yielded by those businesses, when they were operated separately, then synergy has been attained.

(6) Conglomerate Diversification

Horizontal integration strategy aims at related diversification. In other words, diversification occurs, when the existing firm creates another business unit in the same industry. But, firms may also expand through unrelated or conglomerate diversification. In other words, firms create new business units that are unrelated to its original business. For example, Gujarat Gas Ltd., created another business unit, *i.e.,* Gujarat Finance Company Ltd.

Under conglomerate diversification firms enter new and unrelated portfolios of business.

Other examples of Conglomerate diversification include establishment of unrelated businesses by Tata group like Tata Steel, Tata Consultancy Services, Tanishq Jewellery, Tata Tele Services and Tata Tea. Similarly, Aditya Birla group established unrelated businesses like Ultra Tech Cement, Indian Aluminium, Bihar Caustic and Chemicals, Idea Cellular, Birla Sun Life Insurance and PSI Data Systems.

Benefits: The benefits of conglomerate diversification are:

(a) Reduction of risks. This benefit is particularly important for businesses that operate in industries subject to rapid technological change, *(b)* economies of large scale operations, *(c)* financial stability, *(d)* increase in profits, and *(e)* attain managerial competence.

Reasons for Adopting Conglomerate Strategy

The firms adopt conglomerate strategy in order to:

(a) achieve growth rate higher than what can be realised through expansion,

(b) make effective use of financial resources with retained profits exceeding immediate investment needs,

(c) avail the potential opportunities of profitable investments,

(d) achieve distinctive competitive advantage and broader stability,

(e) improve the price-earnings ratio and bring about a higher market price of shares.

(7) Vertical Integration

Another growth strategy is vertical integration, in which new products and/or services, which are complementary to the existing product and/or service lines, are added. Vertical integration is characterised by the extension of the company's business definition in three possible directions from the existing business, *viz., (i)* backward integration, *(ii)* forward integration, and *(iii)* both backward and forward integrations. Backward vertical integration occurs when the firms acquire or create the company that supply the firm, the raw materials or components and other inputs. Forward vertical integration occurs when the firms acquire or create the company that purchases its products and/ or services. Indian Railways established their own production units like Chittaranjan Locomotive Works, Diesel Locomotive Works, Integral Coach Factory, Rail Wheel Factory and Rail Coach Factory. These business units help Indian Railways to produce the coaches and engines necessary for them. Thus, these business units are the examples of backward linkage strategy. Indian Railways also established Catering and Tourism Corporation, which is an example for the forward linkage. Fig. 7.3 shows both backward and forward linkages.

***Vertical integration can be (i)* backward integration, *(ii)* forward integration, and *(iii)* both backward and forward integrations.**

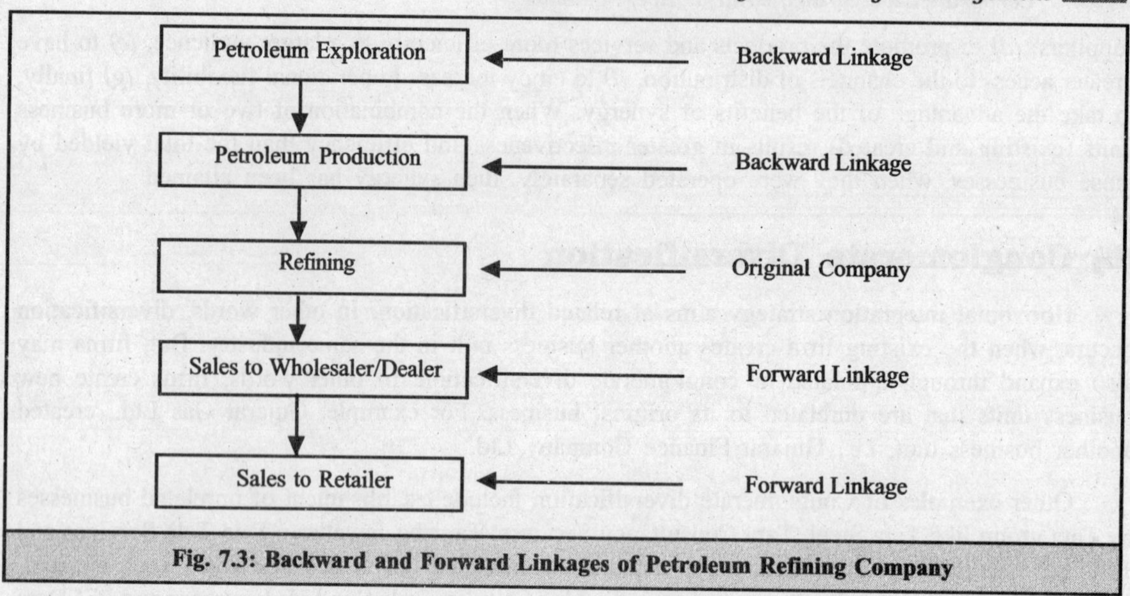

Fig. 7.3: Backward and Forward Linkages of Petroleum Refining Company

Advantages of Backward Integration Strategy

Backward integration strategy is adopted by many firms in view of its advantages. They include:

(i) Firms adopting this strategy can have a regular and uninterrupted supply of raw materials, components and other inputs.

(ii) Quality control of the raw material, components and parts can be ensured easily.

(iii) Firms can earn higher rate of return on investment in view of better use of overhead facilities and spread of overhead costs.

(iv) Firm can increase its power of negotiation with other suppliers in view of access to information on costs.

(v) Indirect taxes payable on purchase of inputs can be minimised, and

(vi) Firm can enjoy the economies of large scale operations.

Disadvantages: Though this strategy is advantageous to the companies, some companies find that this strategy is not desirable in view of the certain disadvantages associated with it. They are:

(i) Technological upgradation in one of the firms makes backward integration technically not feasible.

(ii) Technological upgradation in one of the firms, necessarily forces the management to upgrade the technology of the remaining firms. This process demands for heavy financial investment.

(iii) Adverse economic conditions in the main firm also affect the firm supplying raw materials, components, etc.

(iv) Transfer pricing may be a problem, if the supplying firm doesn't have freedom.

Forward Integration: Many firms start their operation in a limited fashion, and later expand them vertically, when they accumulate enough financial resources. The firms develop forward integration due to the advantages.

Advantages: Advantages of forward integration are:

(i) Firms can acquire greater control over sales, prices and level of output.

(ii) Firms can improve their competitive position.

(iii) Firms can reduce their overall costs.

(iv) This strategy enables the firms to improve the scope of quantity control at different stages.

(v) Firms can develop their own network for consumer feedback.

(vi) Firms can have their own facilities for providing pre-sales and post-sales service.

Disadvantages: Despite the advantages, sometimes the firms avoid this strategy in view of its disadvantages. They are:

(i) Since the firm produces the final products with its own components, and sells the final products as well as components, the firm may involve in a conflicting situation of competing with its own customers.

(ii) Sometimes it is difficult to cope up with the changes in technology,

(iii) The firm may face financial problems as this strategy demands for large scale operations.

In brief, there are many reasons for pursuing a diversification strategy and many different means to achieve that diversification. Exhibit 7.8 presents an overview of the various types of diversification alternatives available to a firm.

(8) Joint Ventures

Joint ventures are partnerships in which two or more firms carry out a specific project or corporate in a selected area of business. Joint ventures can be temporary, disbanding after the project is finished, or long term. The ownership of the firms remains unchanged. "Even a successful joint venture may not last forever. Nor does the collapse of a joint venture always imply failure. Actually, corporate partnerships are formed for specific and time bound objectives which, once achieved, leave little reason for the alliance to be continued. Joint ventures that last longer do so because their objectives have been redesigned."

Joint ventures are partnerships in which two or more firms carry out a specific project or corporate in a selected area of business.

When Do Joint Ventures Form?

Joint ventures form:

1. When an activity is uneconomical for an organisation to do alone.
2. When the risk of business has to be shared, and therefore, is reduced for the participating firms.
3. When the distinctive competence of two or more organisations can be pooled together.
4. When setting up of an organisation requires surmounting hurdles such as import quotas, tariffs, nationalistic political interest and cultural roadblocks.

Characteristics of Joint Ventures

The characteristics of joint ventures are:

(i) Every joint venture has a scheduled life-cycle, which will end sooner or later.

(ii) Every joint venture has to be dissolved when it has outlived its life-cycle.

(iii) Changes in the environment force the joint ventures to be redesigned regularly.

(iv) Joint ventures between Indian companies and transnationals also follow life-cycle.

(v) Transnationals seek to absorb their partner's competencies.

Exhibit 7.8: An Overview of the Various Types of Diversification Alternatives Available to a Firm

	Concentric Diversification (Related)		*Conglomerate Diversification (Unrelated)*	
	Internal	External	Internal	External
Horizontal Integration	Develop new products for current markets.	Buy a firm with products similar to existing products.	Develop totally new and unrelated products.	Merge with a firm having a distinct product line.
Vertical Integration	Move into new markets with current products.	Buy a firm with distribution channels in a new market.	Diversify into new markets with new products.	Acquire a firm that allows entry into a new market segment.
Backward:	Develop a production facility for raw materials used in current products.	Purchase facilities to produce component parts for existing products.	Develop capabilities to produce raw materials unrelated to existing products.	Acquire a producer of component parts not needed in current production processes.
Forward:	Develop retail outlets for existing products.	Acquire a retail outlet to sell existing products.	Open retail outlets that do not handle current product line.	Purchase a retail outlet that will not handle existing products.

Source: Joe G. Thomas, *op. cit.*, p. 214.

Types of Joint Ventures

1. Formation of a joint venture between two firms of the same industry of the same country.
2. Formation of a joint venture between two firms of different industries but of the same country.
3. Formation of a joint venture between two firms of two countries locating the business in the domestic country.
4. Formation of a joint venture between two firms of two countries locating the business in the foreign country.
5. Formation of a joint venture between two firms of two countries and locating the business in the third country.

Reasons for the Formation of Joint Ventures

Joint ventures are undertaken for a variety of reasons like, political, economic and technological.

1. In some countries, foreign firms are allowed to operate only if they enter into a joint venture with a local partner.
2. Size of the project may be so large and one company cannot accomplish it. Then, one firm enters into a joint venture with another firm to accomplish the project.
3. Some projects require multidimensional technology that no one firm possesses. Therefore, firms with different, but compatible technologies may join together.
4. One firm with technological competence and another firm with managerial competence join together.
5. A foreign firm with technological competence joins with a domestic firm with marketing competence.

Strategic Issues Involved in Joint Ventures

The strategic issues in the formation of joint ventures are:

1. Sharing the strengths of each other and eliminating the weaknesses of both the firms by acquiring the other's strengths. For example, the domestic firm acquires technology from a foreign company and the foreign firm acquires the knowledge of the domestic markets channels, culture, etc., after formation of a joint venture and working jointly for the objective.
2. Eliminating or reducing competition by forming a joint venture by the competing firms.
3. Increasing market share more than the sum of the market share of individual firms by forming a joint venture.
4. To acquire the strengths of the other firm in diversified industrial areas including technology, marketing, and management.
5. Unfavourable business conditions (or threats) in the existing industry may force the firm to join with the other firms of another industry.
6. Favourable business conditions (opportunities) in other industries may encourage the firm to form a joint venture with the firm of that industry.

Advantages of Joint Ventures: The advantages of joint ventures include:

(i) Firms undertake joint ventures to spread development costs.

(ii) Joint ventures allow the firms with expertise in different fields to combine their knowledge and resources.

(iii) Joint ventures are useful as a form of 'trial marriage' to see if firms can work together before undertaking a merger.

(iv) Joint ventures are more useful in entering international markets. After simple exporting activities, joint ventures are usually the next step for firms entering the foreign markets.

(v) Joint ventures provide quick access to channels of distribution, thus, reducing the marketing cost.

(vi) Partner in the domestic country (host country) assists in interpreting local customs and culture and translating the technical language.

(vii) Joint ventures reduce the investment in the host country and minimise the risk of nationalisation of business.

(viii) Joint ventures provide a means of achieving the legally required joint ownership.

(ix) Joint ventures minimise the commercial/business risk to both the partners.

(x) Joint ventures provide the facility of foreign technology to the host partner.

(xi) Joint ventures provide the chance to combine the strengths of two partners and utilise the opportunities provided by the environment. Thus, the joint ventures make the impossible things possible.

Disadvantages: Despite a number of advantages of joint ventures, some problems crop up due to joint ventures. They are:

(i) Problems of equity participation by the foreign and home partners

(ii) Foreign exchange regulations imposed by both the governments

(iii) Absence of proper coordination between/among partners

(iv) Differences of culture and customs of both the partners

(v) Division of profits with other firms

(vi) Loss of control of the other firm; and

(vii) Possible conflict and blaming each other at the time of failure

Exhibit 7.8 presents the situations when a company needs to consider diversifications

(D) RETRENCHMENT STRATEGIES

Retrenchment strategies include: Turnaround strategies, captive company strategy, divestment strategy, transformation strategy and liquidation strategy.

The third major class of strategic alternatives available to a firm is retrenchment strategies. Growth strategies and stability strategies are generally adopted by firms that are in satisfactory competitive positions. But, when a firm's position is disappointing or, at the extreme, when its survival is at stake, then retrenchment strategies may be appropriate. Retrenchment strategies include: Turnaround strategies, captive company strategy, divestment strategy, transformation strategy and liquidation strategy.

Reasons for Adopting Retrenchment Strategies: As stated earlier, the firm's poor performance is the major reason for adopting retrenchment strategies. To be specific, the reasons include:

1. Prevalence of poor economic conditions.
2. Competitive pressures may also cause firms to curtail their operations.
3. Operating and production inefficiencies may also cause firms to pursue retrenchment strategies.
4. Inability of the firm to implement latest technology caused by technological revolution.
5. The company is not doing well or perceives itself as doing poorly.
6. The company has not met its objectives and there is pressure from shareholders, customers or others to improve performance.
7. The external environment poses threats and internal strengths are insufficient to face the threats.
8. Better opportunities in the environment are perceived in other area of business/other markets where a firm's strengths can be utilised.

(1) Turnaround Strategy

Improving internal efficiency can be done by adopting turnaround strategy. The aim of turnaround strategy is to transform the organisation into a learner and more effective business. Turnaround means reversing the negative trend.

The aim of turnaround strategy is to transform the organisation into a learner and more effective business.

Indicators of Adopting Turnaround Strategy: Adoption of turnaround strategy is necessary during the adverse conditions of the firm. Specifically the indicators include:

1. Incurring losses continuously.
2. Declining demand for product and/or services.
3. Increasing cash outflows and/or declining cash inflows.
4. Declining sales and declining market share.
5. Declining production and/or productivity.
6. Increasing debt and debt service.
7. Continuous problems of working capital.
8. High rate of employee turnover and employee job dissatisfaction.
9. Significant decrease in the market price of the share. Turnaround strategy should aim at setting a reverse trend to this declining or negative situation.

Approaches of Turnaround Strategy

Approaches of turnaround strategy should concentrate on diagnosing the problem accurately and adopting a right approach. The approaches of the strategy include: *(i)* surgical, and *(ii)* Human resource development.

Surgical approach: The surgical approach is mostly mechanic and requires a tough attitude of the top executive. The executive issues direction for change, fires employees, closes down divisions/plants, drops the product lines, replaces the machinery, issues production, controls the marketing and finance and fixes the accountability for results. This approach continues until the firm is turned around. Later the chief executive relaxes the tough environment and controls.

Human Resource Development (HRD) Approach: Human resource development approach involves:

(1) The chief executive conducts a series of meetings, encourages the managers to be open, understand each other, understand the problems and diagnose the root cause for poor performance of the firm.

(2) He encourages the employees to suggest methods of turning around, policies, gives a detailed programme through a thorough participation, and is actively involved in discussions in the form of brain-storming sessions.

(3) He encourages employees to decide the technique, acquire skills and knowledge, modify their behaviour, etc.

(4) He encourages the managers and employees to implement the solutions offered by them in a highly co-ordinated, and a committed team spirit.

(5) This team spirit is continued at least until the firm is turnaround.

This approach, though difficult, gives effective results.

Who will Manage the Process?: Basically, either the present executive and his team or a new executive will manage the process.

(i) The present chief executive along with his team will manage the turnaround process. The chief executive will be helped by the outside consultants continuously.

(ii) Since the present team is responsible for the poor performance of the business, they will withdraw on their own from the different positions. Then, the shareholders will appoint a new team to manage the turnaround process.

(iii) If the present chief executive and his team does not withdraw from the position, the shareholders will replace the existing team particularly, the chief executive. The shareholders appoint a new chief executive and the team. This new team and chief executive will manage the process.

Activities of Turnaround Process

The management should carefully undertake different activities of the turnaround process. They include:

1. Diagnosing the problem accurately.
2. Analysing the products, its quality, design, configuration, uses, suitability to the changing customer tastes, preferences and needs, etc., against the competitors' products and substitute products.
3. Analysing the production process, technology, competition, competitors' strategies, market segment positioning, etc.
4. Analysing the financial position, cost of capital, cost control, etc.
5. Feedforward of information to various decision areas and control areas.
6. Take up activities systematically, feedback and control the deviations immediately through action research.

The elements in a turnaround strategy are presented in Exhibit 7.9.

(2) Captive Company Strategy

A captive company strategy is another form of retrenchment strategy. This strategy is pursued when a firm sells the majority of its products to one customer (wholesaler/dealer) who in turn performs some of the functions normally done by an independent firm. Companies may undertake a captive strategy as one means of reducing labour costs and reducing the size of employees.

Under captive strategy firm sells majority of its products to one customer or outsources its production activities.

The customer, in this strategy, provides the product design to the captive manufacturer, who in turn, produces according to this design and supplies the products to the customer. The firm need not involve the cost of product design and marketing. The firm can also minimise the risks of marketing.

A captive strategy may also be effective for a new company. The firms with marketing problems and the small companies who cannot launch the full range of marketing activities on their own may adopt a captive strategy. However, the companies may go for their own marketing strategy after they develop their own business. The major limitation of this strategy is that the company is limited by the activities of its captor.

Exhibit 7.9: Matching Corporate Strategic Alternatives to Fit an Undiversified Firm's Situation

Market Growth Rate	COMPETITIVE POSITION: WEAK	COMPETITIVE POSITION: STRONG
	Strategy Options	**Strategy Options**
Rapid	*(In probable order of attractiveness)* • Reformulate single business concentration strategy. (To achieve turnaround) • Acquire another firm in the same business (to strengthen competitive position). • Vertical integration (forward or backward if it strengthens the competitive position) • Diversification • Be acquired by/sell out to a stronger rival • Abandonment (a last resort in the event all else fails).	*(In probable order of attractiveness)* • Continue single business concentration — International expansion (if market opportunities exist). • Vertical integration (if it strengthens the firm's competitive position) • Related Diversification (to transfer skills and expertise built up in the company's core business to adjacent businesses)
Slow	**Strategy Options**	**Strategy Options**
	(in probable order of attractiveness) • Reformulate single business concentration strategy (to achieve turnaround). • Merger with a rival Firm (to strengthen competitive position). • Vertical Integration (only if it strengthens the competitive position substantially) • Diversification • Harvest/Divest • Liquidation (a last resort in the event all else fails).	*(in probable order of attractiveness)* • International expansion (if market opportunities exist) • Related Diversification • Unrelated Diversification • Joint venture into new areas • Vertical integration (if it strengthens competitive position) • Continue single business Concentration (achieve growth by taking market share from weaker rivals.)

Source: Arthur A. Thompson Jr. and A.J. Strickland III. *op. cit.*, p. 165.

(3) Transformation Strategy

Under transformation strategy, firms make a major change in its outlook and operations.

Another retrenchment strategy is the transformation strategy. A transformation occurs when a firm makes a major change in its outlook and operations, usually including moving from one kind of business to another. Changes in strategy are quite substantial. These strategies are difficult to implement because they require a great deal of flexibility on the part of the entire organisation.

Companies may undertake this strategy when:

1. Returns on current operations are lower than desired.
2. Opportunities in other areas are especially attractive.
3. Investments needed in the current operations exceed when the firm is willing or able to spend.
4. A strong, flexible management team exists.
5. The firm has a strong financial base to support its transformation.

Under the divestment strategy company sells or 'spins off' one of its business units under the divestment strategy.

(4) Divestment Strategy

Divestment is another form of retrenchment strategy. The company sells or 'spins off' one of its business units under the divestment strategy. Divestment strategy is usually adopted when the company is performing poorly or when it no longer fits the company's strategic profile.

Causes for Adopting Divestment Strategy

1. Divestment strategy is frequently used when the firm wants to increase the efficiency of a strategic business unit or a major operating division or a product line which has failed to achieve the desired results.
2. Firms may also adopt this strategy when their market share is negligible to be competitive or when the market size is too small to earn the desired profit.
3. The availability of better alternatives may also cause the firms to divest. The limited resources often force the firms to divest the resources from a less profitable business to a more profitable business.
4. The need for increased investment at later stages in providing safety facilities and infrastructure facilities causes the firms without additional funds, to divest.
5. Firms sometimes also divest parts of businesses they have acquired, as the unit may not fit in the original business of the firm.
6. A continuous increase in the cash outflows more than that of cash inflows from a particular unit forces the firm to divest that unit.
7. The firm's inability to meet the competition, causes the firm to divest.
8. The technological change and inability of the firm to invest additional financial resources forces the firm to divest.
9. Divestment of a part of the business is necessary to allow the remaining business to survive.
10. Divestment of unprofitable wings is necessary as part of the merger agreement.
11. Divestment, sometimes, is necessary to abide by the provisions of the law.

Approaches of Divestment

There are three approaches of divestment. The firm may select one approach depending upon the need for adopting this strategy.

1. Firms may pursue a divestment strategy by spinning off a part of the business as an independent entity both financially and managerially.
2. Firms may also divest by selling a business unit to another firm. Mergers are the result of one firm selling a part of its operations to another firm.
3. Another form of divestment is simply closing down a portion of the firm's operations.

Cautions in Adopting Divestment Strategy

1. Generally, the firms delay in making a decision to divest as it reflects the failure of the firms. The delay in adopting this strategy results in the financial loss of the financial sound units also. Therefore, the firms should take the decision of divesting a loss making unit at the right time.
2. The buying firm normally undervalues the assets of the divesting firm or part of the firm. Hence, the firm should find the right time, when it can get a better value of the divesting portion. Adopting divestment strategy, always is not due to business failure. It may be due to shifting from a less profit making business to a more profit making business. The delay in adopting divestment strategy may result in liquidating a portion of the business or a business unit.

(5) Liquidation Strategy

The liquidation strategy is generally considered as the most extreme retrenchment strategy. This strategy involves closing down a business organisation and selling its assets. This is the last alternative strategy as its consequences are severe. The consequences include: loss of jobs of all employees and termination of the opportunities of the firm. Adoption of this strategy implies the total failure of the firm.

Liquidation strategy involves closing down a business organisation and selling its assets.

Reasons for Adopting Liquidation Strategy

1. Partnership firms and small business organisations liquidate when one or more partners/ shareholders want to withdraw from the business.
2. When the sole trader wants to withdraw or retire or take-up another job, he has to liquidate the business, unless one of his family members runs the firm.
3. Liquidation is necessary, when one of the partners has to withdraw and all other partners express their inability to buy the withdrawing partner's share.
4. Liquidation may also occur when a firm is worth more as closed down than surviving. In other words, the value of assets of the firm are more worthwhile than the rate of return earned by the firm.
5. Sometimes, owners may receive a "Godfather offer," for their business. The owners may receive a highly attractive offer and they feel that liquidating the business is more worthwhile. Then, the owners will adopt the liquidation strategy.

BOX 7.1 IT'S TOO LATE TO SAVE SEARS

The long awaited turnaround story at Sears may never happen. Why? Because reclusive hedge fund impresario and Sears Holding Corp., Chairman Edward Lampert doesn't know how to run a retail business, says Jeff Matthews of hedge fund RAM Partners. After Sears posted a surprise quarterly loss, a Barron's report on August 24, stated the stock could fall another 50%. Lampert shot back with a letter claiming the article was "inaccurate" and "biased." Matthews says facts are facts: Shopping at Sears remains a lacklustre experience, five years after Lampert bought the company and merged it with Kmart. "They've totally lost touch with the American consumer," says Matthews, who has no position in Sears stock.

- **Lack of investment in stores.** "The stores are terrible; they don't look any better than they did five years ago. In fact, they look worse." Matthews notes Wal-Mart spends tens of billions a year on stores, while Sears is spending about $200 million. That's no way to compete.
- **No retail expert at the helm.** For more than 18 months, Sears has had an "interim" CEO, Matthews notes. Until they hire someone more permanent with retail know-how they're doomed, he says. "I kept waiting for five years: when is he going to hire the guy? Never happened."

Source: http://finance.yahoo.com/tech-ticker/article/320517/It%27s-Too-Late-to-Save-Sears-Matthews-Says?tickers=shld,azo,wmt,cost,dia,spy,XRT (Accessed on 12/09/09)

Consequences of Liquidation

Normally, large scale organisations do not adopt this strategy in view of the consequences of the liquidation strategy. The consequences include:

Liquidation strategy involves closing down a business organisation and selling its assets.

1. There would be a closure or elimination of an agency performing economic functions in the set-up of economic institutions of the country. Therefore, the Government does not encourage the liquidation of business, unless it is warranted.
2. All the jobs of employees will also be liquidated consequent upon the adoption of this strategy. Hence, the employees and trade unions do not welcome this strategy.
3. Different types of stakeholders of the business like creditors, dealers, financial companies, banks, customers and suppliers will have to suffer as the obligations of the firm towards them will be fully or partially unmet. Hence, these stakeholders prefer not to adopt this strategy, unless, it is a must.
4. The shareholders of the firm will forego their share capital either in full or in part. They mostly prefer running of the business than its closure.
5. Further, it would be difficult to find a buyer as it involves larger amount of finance.

In view of these consequences, the firms should adopt this strategy very carefully and in a planned way. This process would enable the company to get maximum proceeds by selling the assets and meet the obligations of the various stakeholders.

Strategic alliances are teaming and allying with other companies either of the same industry or another industry, with a view to help to perform all kinds of business/service activities necessary for a customer in the supply chain.

(E) STRATEGIC ALLIANCES

Strategic alliances are long term relationships between the companies designed to achieve an objective faster and more effectively than if either of the firms does so on its own. Strategic alliances are like teams that contribute to synergy. Strategic alliances are teaming and allying with other companies either of the same industry or another industry, with a view to help to perform all kinds of business/service activities necessary for a customer in the supply chain. For example, alliances among an automobile company, finance company, spare parts producing company and a service company enable them to meet a unified facility for buying and maintaining a car by a customer. Thus, alliance bridges gaps in providing a whole facility. Similarly, the alliance among road transport, Civil Aviation Authority, immigration authority and an airline company and security company enables them to provide a total facility of air travel to a foreign country.

Strategic alliances enable for entering new markets, learning new technologies, developing new products, providing product/service extensions and providing a total package of product and/or service. Strategic alliances produce both the advantages as well as risks to all partners as well as final beneficiary. Alliance relationships sometime result in turbulent environment, hence, the partners have to coordinate the activities carefully and collaborate with each other efficiently.

Characteristics of Strategic Alliances: Characteristics of strategic alliances include:

- Firms of an alliance remain independent, but join together to collaborate like a single firm, to provide the total but part by part, in the supply chain.
- Firms of an alliance coordinate with each other in addition to performing efficiently.
- Firms link with each other on a long term basis.
- Strategies are crafted in a unified manner with a win-win attitude.
- Partners share strengths, thus eliminating the weaknesses. In other words, the strengths of one partner wipes out the weaknesses of other partner. Thus, the relationship is reciprocal.
- Alliances are for mutual benefit by pooling technology, resources, investments and bearing risks mutually and jointly.
- All firms of an alliance perform part by part, but provide all the parts of supply chain in a coordinated manner.

Objectives of Strategic Alliances

- Different partners of an alliance possess strengths as well as core competencies in various areas. In fact, the area of strength of one partner would be the area of weakness of another partner. In other words, one partner is strong in production and weak in marketing and *vice versa* would be true in case of another partner. The alliance between these two partners would ultimately bring strengths both in production and marketing. Thus, an alliance brings benefits to the alliance firms that would not be possible individually either through internal development or external acquisition.

Thus, the major objective of an alliance is to get the maximum benefit through collaboration which would be impossible either through internal growth or external growth.

- The second objective of a strategic alliance is to encourage the partners to develop new technologies, new markets, attract new group of customers and develop new products/ services rather than doing by oneself all activities in the supply chain.
- The third objective of an alliance is to learn from the alliance partners how to expand and diversify into new areas in the future. Thus, alliances enable the firm to have a transnational step before actually entering into new areas.
- The fourth objective is to create and develop new resources and thereby, new core competencies. These new core competencies enable the firms to minimise or avert possible future risks. Thus, alliances reduce potential risks when a firm pursues new strategies.

- The fifth objective of alliances is to reduce the cost of establishment and operations. Firms can reduce the cost of implementing a strategy by partnering with an experienced firm in the core area of operation. For example, Air India formed an alliance with Singapore Airlines in Singapore-San Francisco route, wherein Singapore Airlines has the experience and knowledge in operations and Air India has competence in marketing in India.
- The sixth objective is to minimise or avoid risks. Firms invariably have to bear heavy risks if they develop the entire supply chain. In contrast, they share the risks by forming into alliances. The sharing of risks would reduce the burden and the risk element of the alliance firms. Sometimes, risks can also be averted, if the partner firms have expertise in the market concerned. For example, Air Nuigini averts the risks of the Australian market through the alliance with Qantas.

Areas of Strategic Alliances

Firms form strategic alliances in the following areas:

- **New Market Entry:** Companies form strategic alliances, when they enter new markets. The firms intend to enter new markets and enter into alliance with those companies which are already in the market. For example, a new pesticides company forms alliance with the existing fertilizer company. Alliance between Coca-cola and Nestle benefitted both the companies in marketing each other's products.
- **Supply Chain Integration:** Strategic alliances are formed among the companies engaged in various operations of the supply chain. For example, the alliance among Goodman Fielder-wheat flour manufacturing company, Paradise Biscuits-biscuit manufacturing company and Food World — a retailer.
- **Design an Integrated Product-cum-Service:** Firms of different industries form alliance in order to develop an integrated product-cum-service. For example, Indian Railways along with A.P. Tourism Corporation provide an integrated service. Similarly, Apollo Hospitals and A.P. Tourism Corporation provide 'medical tourism' service.
- **Shaping Industry Evolution:** Different firms of the same industry align themselves to develop a new product. For example, Toshiba and Samsung formed an alliance to develop advanced memory chips and Intel and Hewlett-Packard joined to develop 64-bit Itanium microprocessor. Biogen and Glaxo SmithKine formed an alliance to develop tissue regeneration. Millennium Pharmaceuticals and American Home Products formed an alliance to develop genetic mapping technology. Creative BioMolecules and Biogen formed an alliance to develop kidney treatments.

Similarly, Apple iPod development, production and marketing were done by the alliance among Apple iPod, a consultant and HP. Sony teamed up with once-rival Samsung Electronics to develop the flat screen television. DaimlerChrysler joined with General Motors in USA to produce transmission and fuel cells. Ford joined with Toyota and Toshiba to produce hybrid motors.

- **Mutual Learning and Applying Technology, Methods and Systems:** Partners of strategic alliance learn technology, methods and systems from each other who has expertise and is familiar with such areas. This process helps the partners to acquire others' capabilities. For example, A.P. Lightings which was a partner and an alliance acquired the marketing methods and systems from its partner, i.e., Philips.

Forms of Strategic Alliance

Strategic alliance can take several forms. The significant among them are:

- Licensing
- Franchising
- Co-marketing
- Cross-marketing
- Co-production
- Outsourcing
- Knowledge Sharing
- Joint Ventures
- Equity Participation

Forms of strategic alliance include: Licensing, franchising, co-marketing,cross-marketing,co-production, outsourcing, knowledge sharing, joint ventures, equity participation.

Licensing: Manufacturers leases the right to use its intellectual property, i.e., technology, work methods, patents, copyrights, etc., to another partner of the alliance. For example, Coca-Cola company of USA and Coca-Cola Amatil (PNG) Limited in Papua New Guinea.

Franchising: Franchising is a form of licensing. Under franchising, the franchisee — a partner of the alliance operates the business under the name of another company called franchisor. Under franchising, the franchisee pays a fee to the franchisor and the franchisor in turn provides various facilities to the franchisee like trade marks, operating systems, product reputations and continuous support systems like advertising, employee training, and quality assurance programmes.

Co-marketing: The partners of a strategic alliance market the products jointly. For example, Air Nuigini and Qantas perform marketing on Port Moresby-Brisbane route.

Cross-marketing: Under cross-marketing arrangements, each partner helps another partner in marketing its products. For example, McDonald's helps to sell Walt Disney company's toys with happy meals. Soap manufacturers market the shampoos and toothpaste companies market tooth brushes.

Co-production: Partners of the alliance produce jointly by using the manufacturing facilities of either of them. This arrangement is mostly used when the production capacities of one of the partner are underutilized while another partner's demand is more than its capacity. Alternatively, this strategy is adopted when the size of the market is small for two or more than two produce to manufacture. For example, private electricity generating companies used to generate power for A.P. State Electricity Board. IBM used to get its production from Motorola and Toshiba.

Outsourcing: Outsourcing is the long term contracting out of non-core business processes to an outside provider to help achieve increased shareholder value. Availability of highly qualified skill pool and faster adaptation of well defined business processes leads to higher productivity gains without compromising on quality. One partner of the strategic alliance outsources the non-core business processes from another partner of the alliance in order to enable its executives to concentrate on core business processes to improve the efficiency of the process and to increase organisational capabilities. Bata outsourced its manufacturing operations to small scale industries in Kanpur and Kharagpur. Nike outsourced its production activities to small scale industries in Vietnam. Many US and European software companies, insurance companies, banks and hospitals outsourced their back-end office operations to companies in India due to the availability of high quality human resources at lowest cost.

Knowledge Sharing: Companies form alliances in order to share and then create new knowledge and thus create value to the activity. Companies from different industries are forming alliances by forming into a larger knowledge-creating web. For example, companies like Nokia, Motorola, Vodafone, Deutsche Telecom, Microsoft and other companies formed alliance in order to develop the industry's next generation of wireless telephone and data communication system.

Joint Ventures: Two or more firms form alliance to create a new business entity that is legally separate and distinct from its parents. Joint ventures are established as corporations owned by the funding partners in the predetermined proportions. The American Motor Corporation entered into a joint venture with Beijing Automotive Works called Beijing Jeep to enter the Chinese market by producing jeeps and other vehicles. Joint ventures involve shared ownership. Joint ventures provide required strengths in terms of required capital, latest technology, required human talent, etc. and enable the companies to share the risks in the markets.

Equity Participation: Strategic alliances also take through equity participation. For example, Xerox of the USA and Fuji of Japan form alliance together through equity participation, in order to explore new markets in Europe and Pacific Rim. Having studied different types of strategic alliances, now we shall study the advantages of strategic alliances.

Advantages of Strategic Alliances

- **Win-win outcomes:** Alliances and collaborative arrangements normally result in win-win outcomes to the parties.
- Alliances help in racing against rivals for **market leadership**.
- Alliances help in acquiring **new competencies**, improve supply chain efficiently and gain economies of scale.
- Alliances help in entering critical markets and building a **potent market presence**.
- Alliances help in gaining **knowledge about unfamiliar markets** and cultures through alliances with local markets.
- Alliances help in acquiring **skills and competencies** that are concentrated in certain geographical locations like software design in USA, and back-end facilities in India.
- Alliances help in acquiring **new technologies, new expertise and competencies** faster than that would be possible through internal efforts. Strategic alliances produce not only advantages, but also result in certain risks, costs and losses.

Now, we shall study the disadvantages.

Disadvantages of Strategic Alliances

Firms acquire competencies and knowledge from each other in an alliance. But, sometimes, the collaborators may turn to be a competitor after acquiring the competencies from the partner of the alliance. The alliance may turn into a most undesirable competition under such situations. The other risks and costs of alliance include:

Increase in Incompatibility of Partners: Incompatibility between partners of the alliance takes place when the partners fail to honour commitments of each other. Similarly, when the goal of the alliance is accomplished, the continuation of alliance would be at risk. Similarly, partners may not require the continuation of alliance, once they acquire the strengths from other partners. For example, Hewlett-Packard and Dell Computers formed an alliance to sell HP-branded printers. But, Dell started producing and selling printers under its own brand in 2002.

Risk of Knowledge/Skill Drain: Firms of the alliance acquire the knowledge and skill from the partners and use such skills for the development of their business. For example, Sony acquired the knowledge and skills of distinctive consumer electronics and skill from Apple, while building the laptop computers for Apple. Sony used this knowledge to enter the personal computer industry.

Risk of Dependence: Alliances sometimes can often become dependent excessively on their partner. This in turn, result in loss of skills in that area of operation in the country, in addition to extension of dependency for other lines of products. For example, the US automobile industry was extensively dependent on the Japanese automobile industry for the production of small cars. This dependency resulted in the development of skills and expertise of the Japanese while the skills of the employees of US automobile industry became redundant. The US outsourced the production of VCR and DVD to the Far Eastern Companies and development software and back-end operations to companies in India. These situations contributed to the economic downturn and consequently led to the increase in unemployment in USA.

Cost of Coordination: The success of strategic alliance mostly depends on an effective coordination of operation of the partners. In fact, the partners have to coordinate all the activities meticulously. Hence, coordination becomes a costly affair. In addition, the different cultures of the partners complicates the process of coordination. Management styles, methods, approaches and practices vary from one partner to the another partner of the alliance. Similarly, the production technologies, production systems and practices also vary from one partner to the another. These varying systems and practices result in complication of coordination and thereby, enhances the cost of coordination.

Cost of Learning: Partners should learn from each other with regard to management styles, culture, operations and production. Most of the companies feel that they know everything and as such they fail to learn. Daewoo has a similar experience with Caterpillar and Samsung with US forklift maker Clark Equipment.

Cost of Inflexibility: A strategic alliance forms after a thorough analysis of the environment and capabilities of the partners as well as competitors. But, the environmental factors as well as the capabilities of the partners may vary owing to various reasons. The partners are expected to be flexible and adaptable to the environmental shifts. Firms fail to be flexible and adaptable contributing to the failure of the alliance. IBM and Apple — the partners of an alliance of development of a new operating system and multimedia technologies failed to understand the changed competitive environment of Microsoft. Consequently, the alliance failed to produce the results.

Cooperation and Competition: The firms of an alliance start with an intention of co-operation. But, when the firms acquire the competencies of the other partner, they may tend to break the alliance and compete with the partner. Thus, today's collaborator may turn into tomorrow's competitor. For example, Atlantic Coast decided to compete directly with its partner in alliance.

Shifting Loyalties of Staff: The executives and employers of the partner companies drawn for the alliance operations, may shift their loyalties from their parent companies to the alliance firm as they work closely with the alliance firm.

(F) COMBINATION STRATEGY (OR) PORTFOLIO RESTRUCTURING

Combination strategy combines stability, growth and retrenchment strategies.

This strategy is the combination of stability, growth and retrenchment strategies. Combination strategies may involve implementation of two or more strategies. In some cases, particularly during the periods of rapid environmental change, adoption of combination strategy would be necessary. Firms may liquidate one unit, develop another unit and allow the third unit to survive simultaneously to improve the efficiency of the business and maximise the profitability. Once the company's profitability is satisfactory, it may adopt a growth strategy. This strategy is common for large scale organisations with multiple units, diversified products and national or global markets. The combination of survival, growth and retrenchment strategies may be either simultaneous or sequential. This strategy is also called portfolio restructuring strategy as it is the mix and percentage make up of the different types of businesses in the portfolio. It involves both divestment and acquisition/takeover.

1. An Integrative Model of Strategic Alternatives:

We have discussed the organisational appraisal that enables us to identify the organisation's strengths and weaknesses and environmental analysis that helps to find the opportunities provided by and threats posed by the external environment. Fig. 7.4 provides an integrative model for recognising strategic alternatives that would be appropriate for a firm that evaluates itself as proposed by Joe G. Thomas.

As can be seen from this exhibit, the firms whose strengths, match with the environmental opportunities are the ideal firms. These ideal firms can adopt the strategies like concentration, vertical integration and horizontal integration.

Firms, whose strengths do not match with the opportunities provided by the environment but face with the environmental threats are the threatened firms. In other words, these firms are internally strong but externally are faced with threats from external environment. These firms may adopt the strategies like limited growth, concentric diversification, conglomerate diversification, transformation and joint venture.

Firm's Internal Analysis	FIRM'S ENVIRONMENTAL SITUATION: Opportunities are Provided	FIRM'S ENVIRONMENTAL SITUATION: Threats are Posed
Strong	**Ideal Firm:** • Concentration • Vertical Integration • Horizontal Integration	**Threatened Firm:** • Limited Growth • Concentric Diversification • Conglomerate Diversification • Transformation • Joint Ventures
Weak	**Opportune Firm:** • Turnaround • Concentration • Captive Company • Limited Growth • Mergers • Joint Ventures • Divestment • Liquidation	**Troubled Firm:** • Turnaround • Divestment • Liquidation

Source: Modified version from Joe G. Thompson, *op. cit.*, p. 227.

Fig. 7.4: An Integrative Model of Strategic Alternatives

The internally weak firms provided by environmental opportunities are opportune firms. These firms can adopt the strategies like turnaround, concentration, captive firm, limited growth, mergers, joint ventures, divestment and liquidation.

The internally weak firms posed which are threats by the environment are troubled firms. These firms can adopt the strategies of turnaround, divestment and liquidation. Leveraged buyouts have allowed firms to divest unprofitable segments of a business by selling them to entrepreneurs who often are able to return the segment to profitability.

POINTS TO BE REMEMBERED

- Strategy formulation is often referred to as Strategic Planning.
- Successful Strategy Selection is an analysis of the firm's internal strengths and weaknesses and the opportunities provided and threats posed by external environment.
- SWOT analysis management determines in which businesses the company should be operating.
- Corporate level strategies include stability strategies, growth strategies, retrenchment strategies and combination strategies.
- Stability strategies include maintenance of *status quo* and sustainable growth.
- Growth strategies include internal growth, concentration strategies, mergers, takeovers/ acquisitions, horizontal integration, conglomerate diversification, virtual integration and joint ventures.
- Retrenchment strategies include turnaround, captive company, transformation and liquidation.

KEY WORDS

- Stability strategies
- Sustainable growth
- Internal growth
- Concentration strategies
- Mergers
- Takeover
- Acquisition
- Horizontal integration
- Conglomerate diversification
- Vertical integration
- Joint ventures
- Turnaround
- Captive company
- Divestment
- Liquidation
- Portfolio restructuring

QUESTIONS FOR DISCUSSION

(1) What is SWOT analysis? How do you use SWOT analysis in crafting strategies?

(2) What are the Stability Strategies? Discuss their advantages and disadvantages.

(3) What are Growth Strategies? Discuss their pros and cons.

(4) What are Joint Ventures? Explain the circumstances under which the joint ventures are appropriate.

(5) What is a Merger? Explain the circumstances under which the mergers are appropriate.

(6) What is Acquisition? Explain the circumstances under which the acquisitions are appropriate.

(7) What are Retrenchment Strategies? Discuss each of them.

(8) What is Turnaround? Explain the circumstances under which the turnaround is appropriate.

(9) Discuss Combination Strategies in detail.

REFERENCES

1. Henry Mintzberg, "Planning on the Left side and Managing on the Right," *Harvard Business Review,* July-August, 1976, p. 56.
2. Thomas L. Wheelen and J. David Hunger, "*Strategic Management and Business Policy,*" Addison-Wesley Publishing Company, Reading, 1986, p. 146.
3. Henry Mintzberg, "Strategy Making in Three Modes," *California Management Review,* Winter 1973, pp. 44-53.
4. Thomas L. Wheelen and J. David Hunger, *op. cit.*, pp. 146-147.
5. Peter Wright, Charles D. Pringle and Mark J. Kroll, "*Strategic Management*", Allyn and Bacon, Boston, 1992, p. 70.
6. W.F. Glueck and L.R. Jauch, "*Business Policy and Strategic Management*", McGraw-Hill, 1984, New York, p. 209.
7. *Ibid.*, p. 241.
8. Joe G. Thomas, *op. cit.*, pp. 197-198.
9. Peter Wright, Charles D. Pringle and Mark J. Kroll, *op. cit.*, p. 76.
10. Joe G. Thomas, *op. cit.*, pp. 203-204.
11. Lawrence R. Jauch and William F. Glueck, *op. cit.*, p. 229.
12. Harry Levinson, "A Psychologist Diagnoses Merger Failure", *Harvard Business Review*, March-April, 1970.
13. Thomas Hogarty, "The Profitability of Corporate Mergers", *Journal of Business,* Vol. 4, No. 3, 1970, pp. 317-327.
14. Lawrence R. Jauch and William F. Glueck, *op. cit* p. 231.
15. Arthur A. Thompson Jr., and A.J. Strickland III, *op. cit.*, p. 90.
16. Prasanna Chandra, "*Financial Management: Theory and Practice*", Tata McGraw-Hill, New Delhi, 1987, pp. 660-661.
17. Willard Rockwell Jr. "How to Acquire a Company", *Harvard Business Review,* Vol. 46, No. 5, October 1968, in P.K. Ghosh, *op. cit.*, p. 218.
18. Peter Wright, Charles D. Pringle and Mark J. Kroll, *op. cit.*, p. 73.
19. H. Igor Ansoff, "*Corporate Strategy*", McGraw-Hill, New York, 1965, p. 127.
20. P.K. Ghosh, *op. cit.*, p. 185.
21. Peter Wright, Charles D. Pringle and Mark J. Kroll, *op. cit.*, p. 76.
22. Sundeep Khanna, "Paradigm Shifts in Partnership", *Business Today* 7-21, October 1996, p. 81.
23. Thompson and Strickland, *op. cit.*, pp. 92-93.
24. Sundeep Khanna, *op. cit.*, p. 80.
25. S. Jain, "*International Marketing and Management*", Mass: Kent; Boston, 1984.
26. Peter Wright, Charles D. Pringle and Mark J. Kroll, op. cit., p. 77.
27. Glueck and Jauch, *op. cit.*, p. 219.
28. P.N. Khandwalla, "Two Routes to Turnaround", *Business World,* 12-25, April, 1989, pp. 17-19.
29. G.A. Mirchandani, "Turning a Business Around", *Business India,* March 7-20, 1988, p. 110-11 in Azhar Kazmi, *op. cit.*, p. 168.
30. "Despite Ford Venture, Mexico Faces Struggle to be Competitive", *Wall Street Journal,* January 11, 1984, p. 1. In Joe G. Thomas, *op. cit.*, p. 218.
31. Joe G. Thomas, *op. cit.*, pp. 220-221.
32. Peter Wright, Charles D. Pringle and Mark J. Kroll, *op. cit.*, p. 78.
33. Joe G. Thomas, *op. cit.*, pp. 219-220.
34. *Ibid.*, pp. 221.
35. *Ibid.*, pp. 226.
36. Arthur A. Thompson and A.J. Strickland, *op. cit.*, p. 180.
37. "Steel Entrepreneurs Seek Profits in Plant that Big Firms Discarded as Uneconomical", *Wall Street Journal,* May 15, 1984, p. 33. in Joe G. Thomas, *op. cit.*, p. 228.

✦ ✦ ✦

8 CHAPTER BUSINESS UNIT LEVEL STRATEGIES

Chapter Outline

(A) Introduction
- Customer Needs

(B) Generic Strategies
- Low Cost Leadership, Differentiation, Focus

(C) Offensive Strategies and Competitive Advantage

(D) Defensive Strategies and Competitive Advantage

(E) Matching Strategy to Situation

(F) Thirteen Commandments for Formulating Successful Business Strategies

Learning Objectives

After studying this chapter, you should be able to:

- **Discuss customer needs from multiple perspectives.**
- **Analyse the value creation and value chain analysis from the perspective of low cost and product differentiation.**
- **Study low cost strategies and ways to achieve low cost.**
- **Explain the differentiation strategy and approaches to achieve differentiation strategy.**
- **Study focus or niche strategy and approaches to achieve differentiation strategy.**
- **Study various offensive strategies in order to achieve a competitive advantage.**
- **Analyse various defensive strategies and to achieve a competitive advantage.**
- **Discuss the ways and means to match a strategy to the situation.**

(A) INTRODUCTION

Strategy is an integrated, comprehensive and unified plan/course of action. Business unit level strategy is a co-ordinated, integrated and a comprehensive action or plan. The purpose of business unit level strategy is to provide a value to customers by gaining a competitive advantage through exploiting the core competencies in specific individual product/service markets. Business unit level strategies are designed based on the firm's belief about where and how it has an advantage over its competitors.

Customers: Customers are the basis for crafting a business unit level strategy, because the customer's needs and expectations determine the product/service configuration. Product configuration determines the competencies that a firm should possess to deliver the product expected by the customers, including the place, price and time of delivery. A firm to implement its business unit level strategies successfully should possess these competencies.

Possess competencies to serve customers: Firms possessing these competencies deliver a superior value to the customers in order to achieve its goals. Firms adopt corporate level strategies in order to acquire competencies necessary to implement business unit level strategies. For example, i2 technologies acquired Smart Technologies in order to possess the competencies to provide internet-based customer relationships. Similarly, General Motors crafted a strategy to use i2's software in order to possess the competencies to foster training hubs on internet. Thus, firms acquire competencies to serve the customers based on its business unit level strategy.

Firms select a group of customers based on their missions through market segmentation.

Decide customer needs: Firms select a group of customers based on their missions through market segmentation. Markets are segmented based on a variety of factors. Factors for consumer market segmentation include: demographic (age, income, sex, etc.), and socio-economic (social class/community, stage in the family lifecycle, etc.), geographic (region, nationality, culture, etc.), psychological (personality traits, leadership/followership styles, etc.) and consumption (frequent, occasional and rare users) and perceptual factors. Factors for industrial markets include: end-use segments, product segments, geographic segments, common buying factors segments and customersize segments. Firms normally concentrate on major customer groups while crafting business unit level strategies. The teenage population in most of the countries is a major segment as it has special needs and is earning money to satisfy them. Firms should identify their targeted customer group, who in turn, provide an opportunity to achieve their goals through implementation of a business unit level strategy.

Use competencies to satisfy customer needs: Now, firms use the competencies they acquired to satisfy the selected needs of the customers. Firms craft strategies to match their competencies with the targeted customer needs. Hewlett-Packard uses its engineering core competencies to manufacture products that are renowned for quality as expected by its customer group. Hewlett-Packard targets customers who do not want to face troubles while using the systems. Hewlett-Packard prices its product as the percentage of client's transactions revenue.

Thus, firms craft business unit level strategies to achieve their missions and goals.

Types of Business Unit Level Strategies

Business unit level strategies include: cost leadership, differentiation and focused

A firm's position in the industry relative to its competitors determines the business unit level strategies that the firm can craft. The firms enjoying a significant market share and which are in the growth stage can be as better off as compared to their competitors. Michael E. Porter suggested three generic business-unit level strategies, *viz.*, cost leadership, differentiation and focused. Focused strategy in turn can be focused cost leadership and focused differentiation strategy as presented in figure 8.1.

Competitive Scope	Competitive Advantage: Cost	Competitive Advantage: Uniqueness
Broad Target	Cost Leadership	Differentiation
Narrow Target	Focused cost leadership	Focussed Differentiation

Source: Michael E. Porter, "Competitive Advantage", *Free Press*, New York, 1985, p.12

Fig. 8.1: Four Generic Strategies

A firm should have an edge over the competitors in getting customers and defending against competitive forces to have a competitive advantage. The sources of competitive advantage include: Producing top quality products/rendering superior quality services, offering the best quality customer service, producing at minimum cost compared to that of the competitors, selecting a more convenient geographical location, superior product design compared to the competitors' brands, producing a more reliable and longer lasting product, having the most committed human resources and offering the customer more value for money (combination of configuration, quality, service, right time, place and price). A company must provide what the customer will perceive as 'the best value' — either cheap and the good or the best product that is worth paying. Companies, to be successful, should invest aggressively in creating a sustainable competitive advantage for, it is the single most dependable contributor to above average profitability. A company, should develop alternative strategies at the business unit level, after developing corporate level strategies. (See Fig. 8.2).

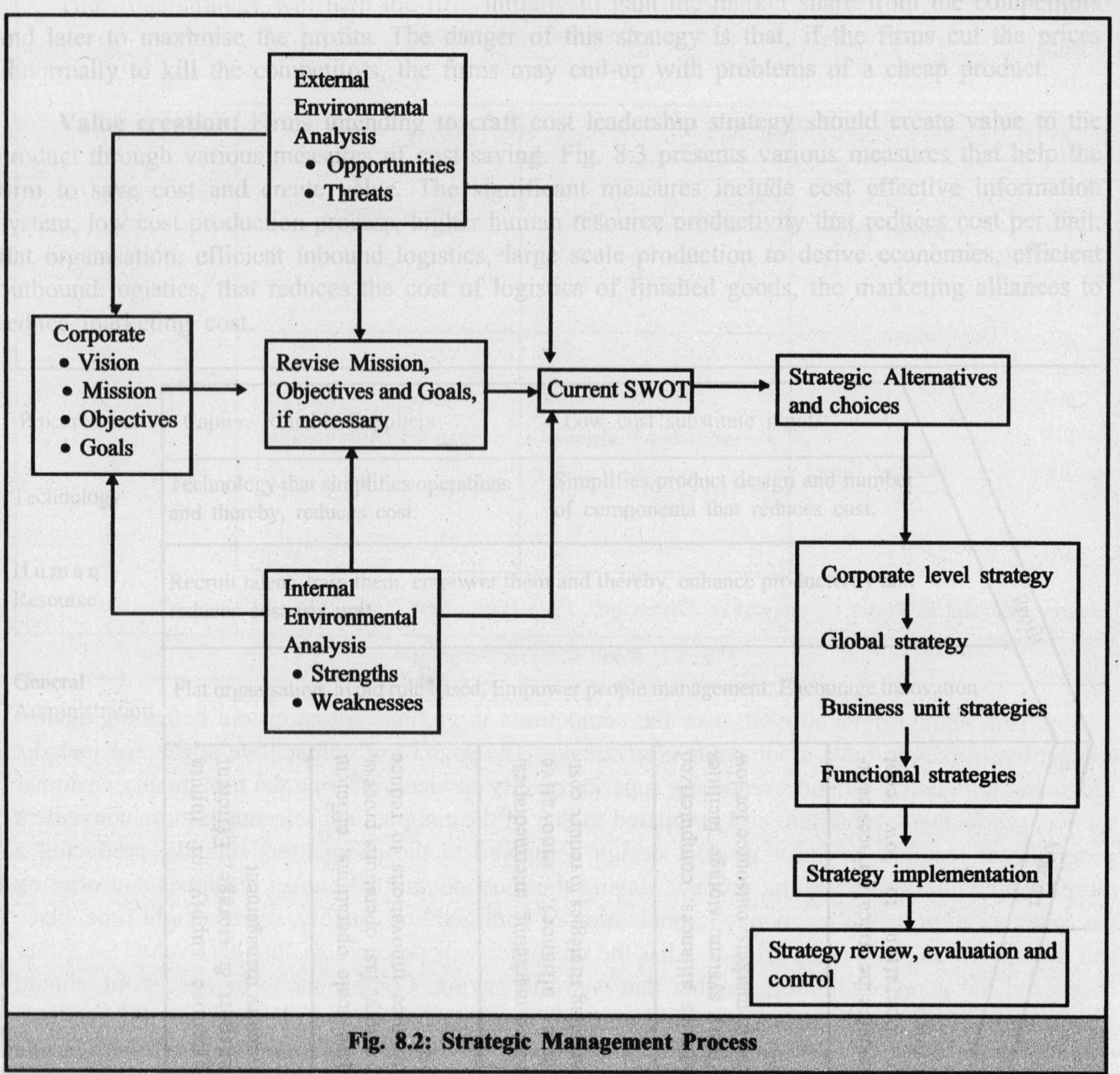

Fig. 8.2: Strategic Management Process

(B) GENERIC STRATEGIES*

Competitive strategy includes all the moves and approaches a firm has taken and is taking *(i)* to attract buyers, *(ii)* to withstand competitive pressures and *(iii)* to improve its market position. A firm's strategy can be mostly offensive or mostly defensive depending upon the market conditions. There would be countless strategies that the firms adopt in different situations. But, all these strategies can be broadly divided into the following three categories:

1. Striving to be the overall low cost producer in the industry (a low-cost leadership strategy).
2. Seeking to differentiate one's product offering from the rival's products (a differentiation strategy).
3. Focusing on a narrow portion of the market rather than the whole market (a focus or niche strategy).

Exhibit 8.1 depicts the distinctive features of these three generic competitive strategic approaches.

* The treatment in this section draws heavily from Thompson and Strickland, *op. cit.*, pp. 102-122.

Exhibit 8.1: Distinctive Features of the Generic Competitive Strategies

Type of Feature	*Low-Cost Leadership*	*Differential*	*Focus*
Strategic target	• A broad cross-section of the market.	• A broad cross-section of the market.	• A narrow market niche where the buyer, needs and preferences are distinctively different from the rest of the market.
Basis of competitive advantage	• Lower costs than competitors.	• An ability to offer buyers something different from competitors.	• Lower cost in serving the niche or an ability to offer niche buyers something customised to their requirements and tastes.
Product line	• A good basic product with few frills (acceptable quality and limited selection).	• Many product variations, wide selection, strong emphasis on the chosen differentiating features.	• Customised to fit the specialized needs of the target segment.
Production emphasis	• A continuous search for cost reduction without sacrificing acceptable quality and essential features.	• Invent ways to create value for buyers.	• Tailor-made for the niche.
Marketing emphasis	• Try to make a virtue out of product features that lead to low cost.	• Build in whatever features buyers are willing to pay for. • Charge a premium price to cover the extra costs of differentiating features.	• Communicate the focusser's unique ability to satisfy the buyer's specialized requirements.
Sustaining the strategy	• Economical prices/good value. • All elements of strategy aim at contributing to a sustainable cost advantage — the key is to manage costs down, year after year, in every area of the business.	• Communicate the points of difference in credible ways. • Stress constant improvement and use innovation to stay ahead of imitative competitors. • Concentrate on a few key differentiating features; use them to create a reputation and brand image.	• Remain totally dedicated to serving the niche better than other competitors; don't blunt the firm's image and efforts by entering other segments and adding other product categories to widen market appeal.

Source: Arthur A. Thompson and A.J. Strickland, *op. cit.*, p. 104.

1. A Low-cost Leadership Strategy

The low-cost leader's basis for, competitive advantage is lower overall costs than the competitors. The low cost strategy is a powerful approach in markets where most of the customers are price sensitive. The purposes of striving to be a low-cost producer are:

The low cost strategy is a powerful approach in markets where most of the customers are price sensitive.

(i) to fix the price for the products at the lower level compared to that of the competitors,

(ii) to gain the maximum market share from the competitors, or

(iii) to earn a high profit margin and thus, maximise the profits.

Thus, this strategy will help the firm initially to gain the market share from the competitors and later to maximise the profits. The danger of this strategy is that, if the firms cut the prices abnormally to kill the competitors, the firms may end-up with problems of a cheap product.

Value creation: Firms intending to craft cost leadership strategy should create value to the product through various measures of cost saving. Fig. 8.3 presents various measures that help the firm to save cost and create value. The significant measures include cost effective information system, low cost production process, higher human resource productivity that reduces cost per unit, flat organisation, efficient inbound logistics, large scale production to derive economies, efficient outbound logistics, that reduces the cost of logistics of finished goods, the marketing alliances to reduce marketing cost.

Support activities					
Procurement	Captive Reliable Suppliers		Low cost substitute inputs		
Technology	Technology that simplifies operations and thereby, reduces cost.		Simplifies product design and number of components that reduces cost.		
Human Resource	Recruit talent, train them, empower them and thereby, enhance productivity and reduces cost per unit.				
General Administration	Flat organisation, avoid rule based, Empower people management. Encourage innovation				
	Systemise supply of inputs transport & storage, Efficient inventory management	Large scale operations, efficient inventory, fast operations process, introduce innovations to reduce cost.	Reduce marketing intermediaries, create alliances, innovative marketing strategies to reduce cost.	Logistics alliances, computerized delivery system, storage facilities close to markets, outsource for low cost.	Outsource the critical services/back-end operation to low cost providers.
	Inbound Logistics	Operations	Marketing & Sales	Outbound Logistics	Service

Profit

Margin

Fig. 8.3: Value Creating Activities to Reduce Cost

Ways to Achieve Cost Advantage

The firm should see that their costs in all areas of production are lower than that of the competitors. There are two ways to accomplish this goal. They are:

(a) out-managing rivals on efficiency and cost control and/or

(b) finding creative ways to cut cost producing activities out of the activity cost chain.

These two approaches can be used independently or simultaneously. Firms to get a low cost advantage should pursue cost savings exhaustively throughout the activity cost chain. All areas without exception should be taken care of.

Organisational culture of such firms should be symbolically reinforced by Spartan facilities, salaries and benefits to executives and employees are based on demand and supply factors, exhaustive search for low cost materials, find the ways and means to control budget expenditure, minimisation of wastage, recycling of wastage and empowerment of employees to minimise cost.

Necessary Conditions for Success of Low-cost Strategy

The following conditions should also be present in order to enable a firm to achieve low-cost leadership strategy. The significant among them are:

Low-cost Plus Conveniences

Low-cost strategy helps to compete with the current competitors and allows creating entry barriers to the prospective competitors. But, sometimes it would be difficult to compete with the major competitors exclusively based on low cost. Companies, under such circumstances should provide additional conveniences to the customers. For example, Disco SA, could not compete with the retail giants like Wal-Mart and Carrefour of France in South American countries exclusively based on low-cost strategy. Then it provided additional conveniences like home delivery, online ordering and childcare facilities to compete in the market in addition to low cost. Tiger Airways provide low-cost plus time convenience to its customers.

Low cost to be successful should be associated with additional product functions as well as conveniences.

Loyalty and relationship with suppliers: Prices of inputs significantly influence the margin maintained by a firm as well as in maintaining the low cost. But, suppliers, sometimes tend to increase the price. Bargaining power of the firm with suppliers would influence the latter to maintain a low price. However, small firms can't have better bargaining power to influence the suppliers. Under such situations, the loyalty and good relationship with the supplier help the firm in getting the inputs at a less and competitive price.

Cost leaders should be satisfied with average returns: Cost leaders continuously strive for reduction of cost. At the same time potential new entrants as well as existing competitors observe the cost leader's strategies. Therefore the cost leader should be satisfied with average profits by charging low prices rather than enjoying higher profit margins. The option of enjoying higher profit margins, would provide a chance to the new entrants to enter the market with a low price than that of the cost leader. For example, Telikom (PNG)'s strategy of higher prices and profit for mobile phone services before 2007 attracted Digicel to enter Papua New Guinea's mobile market and grow as the market leader in mobile market of Papua New Guinea. However, Acer Computer Corporation of Taiwan followed the low profit margin strategy and fixed the price at a low level. The Corporation could follow the low price strategy due to its core competency in building cutting edge on personal computers faster and cheaper than those of the competitors.

Thus, the cost leaders can strive in the market and enjoy market leadership by creating an entry barrier to the potential new entrants until they are satisfied with average returns.

Development of product and material substitutes: The low cost leaders, in order to maintain the market leadership should invest on research and development in order to develop the substitute products as well as substitute material. A.P. Paper Mills, in order to maintain a low cost of production developed a substitute material for bamboo. CDs and DVDs emerged as substitutes for audio and video tapes. When the demand for bicycles was on a declining trend, Hero Cycles established a joint venture with Honda in order to produce motor bicycles.

Steps to Minimise Cost

1. Firms intending to be a low cost producer should appraise each cost creating activity and should identify the factors driving the cost of the activity.
2. Firms have to identify the controllable and uncontrollable costs, immediate and postponable costs, present and future costs, etc.
3. Firms have to use their knowledge about the controllable costs, postponeable costs, to manage and control these costs, month after month or year after year.

4. Wherever and whenever, it is possible, firms have to eliminate the whole activity from the activity cost-chain.
5. Firms have to control costs to keep the products affordable.
6. Firms have to reengineer processes to improve time utilisation and minimisation of wastage.
7. Firms have to forge relationships with vendors to minimise costs.
8. Firms have to build global capacities, if the domestic market is large enough.
9. Firms have to steer clear of diversification even, if synergies are available.
10. Firms have to focus on the chosen segments without straying into new ones.

Advantages of Being a Low-cost Producer

The low cost producing firms get some attractive defenses against five competitive forces:

1. Strong position to compete with the rival competitors. The low-cost firm is in a strong position to compete with rival competitors, offensively based on price, to defend against price war conditions, to use the appeal of a lower price, to win sales from rival competitors and earn high profits in price competitive markets.
2. The low-cost firm has a partial profit margin protection from powerful customers.
3. The low-cost firm is more insulated than competitors from powerful suppliers.
4. The low-cost firm can prevent the entrance of potential competitors into the market through price-cuts.
5. The low-cost firm is better positioned than high-cost rivals against the substitute products.

Conditions for the Effectiveness of Low-cost Strategy

The low-cost leadership strategy is particularly effective when:

1. Price competition among rival sellers is a dominant competitive force.
2. The industry's product is essentially standardised.
3. There are few ways to achieve product differentiation that have value to buyers.
4. Most buyers use the product in the same ways.
5. Buyers shop for the best price without incurring much cost and inconvenience.
6. Buyers are large and have a significant power to bargain down prices.

The Risks of a Low-cost Producer Strategy

The low-cost leadership strategy has its disadvantages. They are:

1. Technological advancements adopted by the rivals may result in cost reduction for rivals multiplying the advantage. Past investments and hard won gains of the low-cost producer will be lost.
2. Rival firms may initiate the low-cost methods adopted by the low-cost producer, thus, making any advantage short lived.
3. It would be very hard to the low-cost producer, to introduce changes in product design, production process, etc., in order to incorporate the buyers' preferences.

4. The declining buyer is sensitive to price due to increase in buyer's income which leaves the low-cost producer behind.

Thus, heavy investments in cost reduction activities can lock a firm into both its present technology and its present strategy, leaving it vulnerable to technological advancements and changing buyers' preferences and tastes other than a lower price. This situation is more significant in times of increase in the buyers' income brackets consequent upon the country's economic development.

2. Differentiation Strategies

Generally, customers' needs, tastes and preferences vary from one customer to the another customer. These differences in customers' tastes, preferences and needs can be satisfied by producing the product with different attributes. This situation results in adoption of a differentiation strategy by the producer to satisfy the diversified needs of the customer by a standardised product. The producer to make this strategy successful should study the different needs, tastes and preferences of various classes of customers. Further, he should study the buying and consumption behaviour of different classes of customers. The producer, then should incorporate the features into the product offering based on the study. This will make the product much suitable to the different customers compared to the competitors' offerings. Consequently, most of the customers will prefer this product to the rivals/competitors.

Differentiation strategy is used by the producer to satisfy the diversified needs of the customer by a standardised product.

Competitive advantage results when more customers become strongly attached to the attributes of a differentiator's product offering.

Value Creation for Differentiation Strategy

Firms intending to pursue differentiation strategy should create value for product differentiation through various measures. Fig. 8.4 presents various measures that contribute to product differentiation. The significant measures include: technology development that contribute to product variations, capabilities of human resources to invent new products, flat organisation structures that provide freedom to employees to think and develop different products, procure quality inputs and the like.

Firms intending to pursue differentiation strategy should create value for product differentiation through various measures.

Conditions for Successful Differentiation Strategy

Crafting and implementing differentiation strategy successfully depends upon the following conditions:

Crafting and implementing differentiation strategy successfully depends upon customer loyalty for differentiation, customer willingness to pay premium price, bargaining power of suppliers, new potential entrants and substitute products.

Customer Loyalty for Differentiation

Normally, customers prepare to buy the products at the lowest price. However, customers prefer to pay a high price when the product design configuration and the services associated with the product are of their choice. Thus, the customers would be loyal to the brand whose product features match with their preferences. As the customers, loyalty to a brand increases, customer's sensitivity to the price increases is reduced. "This relationship between brand loyalty and price sensitivity insulates a firm from competitive rivalry." For example, Gujarat Gas Company provides all associated and necessary services to its customers including on-the-spot repair services in addition to supplying gas. Hence, customers prefer to buy from Gujarat Gas Company rather than from its competitors, though the price is higher than that of the competitors.

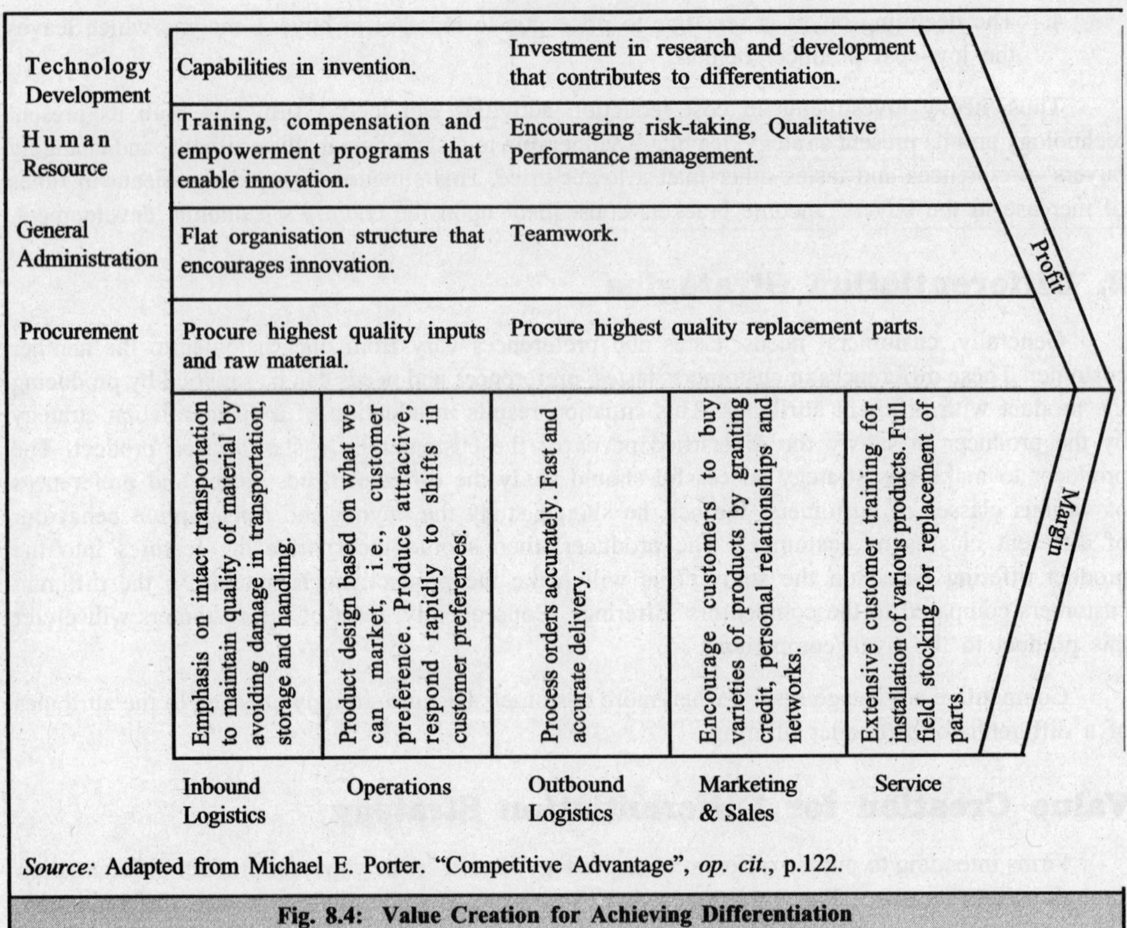

Source: Adapted from Michael E. Porter. "Competitive Advantage", *op. cit.*, p.122.

Fig. 8.4: Value Creation for Achieving Differentiation

Customers' Willingness to Pay Premium Price

Some customers belonging to upper income group pay the premium price for the differentiated products based on quality, convenience and prestige. Business class air passengers and full economy class passengers are the best examples as they are willing to pay a premium price compared to special fares class passengers who will not enjoy any conveniences for altering the dates of journey. Similarly, Indian Railways, differentiate services like A.C. two tier, A.C. three tier, *tatkal* class (tatkal refers to *ad-hoc* arrangement for journey without required prior plan), sleeper class and ordinary class as the upper income group passengers are willing to pay as high as 20 times to that of the ordinary class fares.

Bargaining power of suppliers: Firms relying on differentiation strategy need high quality of inputs for producing high qualitative differentiated products. The suppliers of inputs expect a higher price as the firm charges a premium price. For example, farmers supplying vegetables to the super markets expect a higher price for their produce than that in unorganised markets due to two reasons, *viz.*,(i) They supply high quality produce to super markets and (ii) super markets charge higher price than that of unorganised markets.

Potential Entrants: The risk of potential entrants would normally be comparatively less as it needs heavy investments and also it would be rather difficult to produce differentiated and high quality products in the short run.

Substitute products: Firms producing high quality differentiated products bear the risks of substitute products. Therefore, firms have to continuously improve the products through further differentiation. Titan continuously upgrades the models of its watches in order to minimise the risk of substitute products.

Advantages of Efficient Differentiation

The efficient differentiation brings the following advantages to the differentiator:

(a) The product commands a premium price for the producer.

(b) More number of units is sold as additional customers are won over by the differentiating features.

(c) The product gains greater customer loyalty to its brand.

(d) Differentiation enhances the profitability when the cost of differentiation is less than the extra price of the product.

Disadvantages of Differentiation

Though, differentiation brings some advantages, some times, its results in loss to the producer. They are:

(a) Differentiation is unsuccessful when the customers do not value the additional features significant enough to buy the product in profitable quantities.

(b) Differentiation results in a loss when the cost of differentiation is more than the extra price of the product.

Approaches to Differentiation

Differentiation may take several forms. Important among them are:

(i) A different taste

(ii) Special features

(iii) Superior service

(iv) Spare parts availability

(v) Overall value to the customer

(vi) Engineering design and performance

(vii) Product reliability

(viii) Quality manufacturer

(ix) Technological leadership

(x) A full range of services

(xi) Complete line of products

(xii) Top-of-the-line image and reputation.

Achieving Differentiation: Anything a company can do to create customer value represents a potential basis for differentiation. A company should build the value creating attributes into the product at an acceptable cost after finding suitable sources of buyer values. The producer should make sure that the incorporated attributes should *(i)* raise the product's performance, or *(ii)* make the product more economical to use, or *(iii)* enhance customer satisfaction in tangible or intangible ways. Differentiation possibilities can grow out of activities performed anywhere in the activity cost chain.

Need for Differentiation: Producers would like to differentiate their products/services as it works as an attractive strategy due to the following reasons:

(i) Differentiation provides some buffer against the rival's strategies, as customers become loyal to the brand or model they like most and often like to pay a higher price.

(ii) Differentiation erects entry barriers in the form of customer loyalty and uniqueness that the newcomers find hard to overcome.

(iii) Differentiation mitigates the bargaining power of major customers as the competitors' products are less attractive to them.

(iv) Differentiation helps a company fend off threats from substitutes.

(v) Efficient differentiation creates lines of defence for dealing with competitive forces as it provides, a price advantage and thereby a higher profit margin.

Situations Suitable for Differentiation Strategy

Differentiation strategy works better under the following situations:

(i) Where there are many ways to differentiate the product/service and most of the customers feel these differences as valuable.

(ii) Where the customers' tastes, preferences, needs and uses of the item are diverse.

(iii) Where a few competitors follow differentiation strategy.

(iv) Where the differentiation strategies are least subject to quick or inexpensive imitation by the competitors. In other words, it should be difficult to the competitors to copy quickly and profitably.

(v) Where the differentiation is based on, *(a)* technical superiority, *(b)* quality, *(c)* more customer supportive services and *(d)* more value for the money.

Real Value, Perceived Value and Signals of Value

Michael E. Porter explains that customers pay for only those product features which they perceive. Therefore, the price premium of the differentiated product should be based on the value actually delivered to the customer and more particularly the value the customer perceives. Buyers, without an experience in using the product and enough judgmental skills may perceive the value based on the signals like seller's word-of-mouth reputation, attractive packaging, extensive advertisements and personal selling, sellers' facilities, list of customers, firm's market share, etc. These signals of value may be significant when *(a)* the nature of differentiation is subjective or hard to qualify, *(b)* customers purchase the product for the first time, *(c)* customers infrequently repurchase the product, and *(d)* customers are not sophisticated.

Limitations of a Differentiation Strategy

There is no guarantee that the differentiation will always result in an efficient competitive advantage. This is due to the limitations of the differentiation strategy. These limitations include:

(i) Buyers may perceive a little value in uniqueness of the product.

(ii) A significantly low cost strategy may defeat a differentiation strategy.

(iii) Trying to differentiate on the basis of something that does not lower a customer's cost or enhance a customers' well-being (as perceived by the customer).

(iv) Over differentiating results in high cost and high price compared to that of the competitors, or product quality or service levels exceed the customer's needs.

(v) Trying to charge too high a price premium (the higher the premium, the more number of customers can be lured away by lower priced competitors).

(vi) Ignoring the need to signal value and depending only on tangible product attributes to achieve differentiation.

(vii) Not understanding or identifying what customers consider as value.

Differentiation-cum-Low-Cost Strategy

Combining differentiation strategy and low-cost strategy results in giving customers more value for the money with an emphasis on more than minimally acceptable quality, service, features and performance. The purpose is to meeting or exceeding customer's expectations on different product attributes like quality, service, design, performance, features and price. Thus, the producer creates a superior value for the product. In essence, such a hybrid strategy helps a company to combine the competitive advantage appeals of both low-cost and differentiation.

Combining differentiation strategy and low-cost strategy results in giving customers more value for the money with an emphasis on more than minimally acceptable quality, service, features and performance.

3. Focus and Specialisation Strategies

Focussing begins by choosing a market niche where customers have distinctive preferences or requirements. Thompson and Strickland define the term 'niche' as, "geographic uniqueness, by specialised requirements in using the product or by special product attributes that appeal only to niche members." A strategist's basis for competitive advantage is either lower costs than the competitors, in serving the market niche or an ability to offer niche members something different from that of competitors. If the buyer's needs can be satisfied through a low cost based product compared to the rest of the market, the producer can adopt a focus strategy based on low-cost. Alternatively, if there is a customer segment that demands unique product attributes, then the producer can adopt a focus strategy based on differentiation.

Situations Where the Focus Strategy is Efficient: A focus strategy will be efficient in the following situations:

(i) The market segment is large enough to be profitable.

(ii) The market segment has a good growth potential.

(iii) The market segment is not significant to the success of major competitors.

(iv) The focusing producer has the skills and resources to serve the segment efficiently.

(v) The focusing producer can defend himself against the challengers based on the customer goodwill he has built up and his superior ability to serve customers in the segments.

(vi) When it is costly or difficult for the competitors to meet the specialised needs to the niche.

(vii) When no other competitor is attempting to specialise in the same target segment.

(viii) When a company does not have enough resources to pursue a wider part of the total market.

(ix) When the industry has many different segments and allows a focuser to select an attractive segment based on his strengths and capabilities.

Advantages of Focus Strategy: The advantages of a focus strategy are as follows:

(i) Specialised skills of a producer adopting the focus strategy in serving the target market niche provide a basis for defending against five competitive forces.

(ii) The focused company's competence in serving the market niche creates entry barriers for new firms. Therefore, it is harder for firms outside the niche to enter.

(iii) This strategy also presents a hurdle to the producers of substitute products to enter the niche market.

(iv) The powerful customers' bargaining power is also lowered as the competitor's ability to serve their needs is less as compared to the focused firm.

(v) The niche strategy combined with low-cost and differentiation strategies will enable the producer to enhance the market share and profitability (See Fig. 8.5).

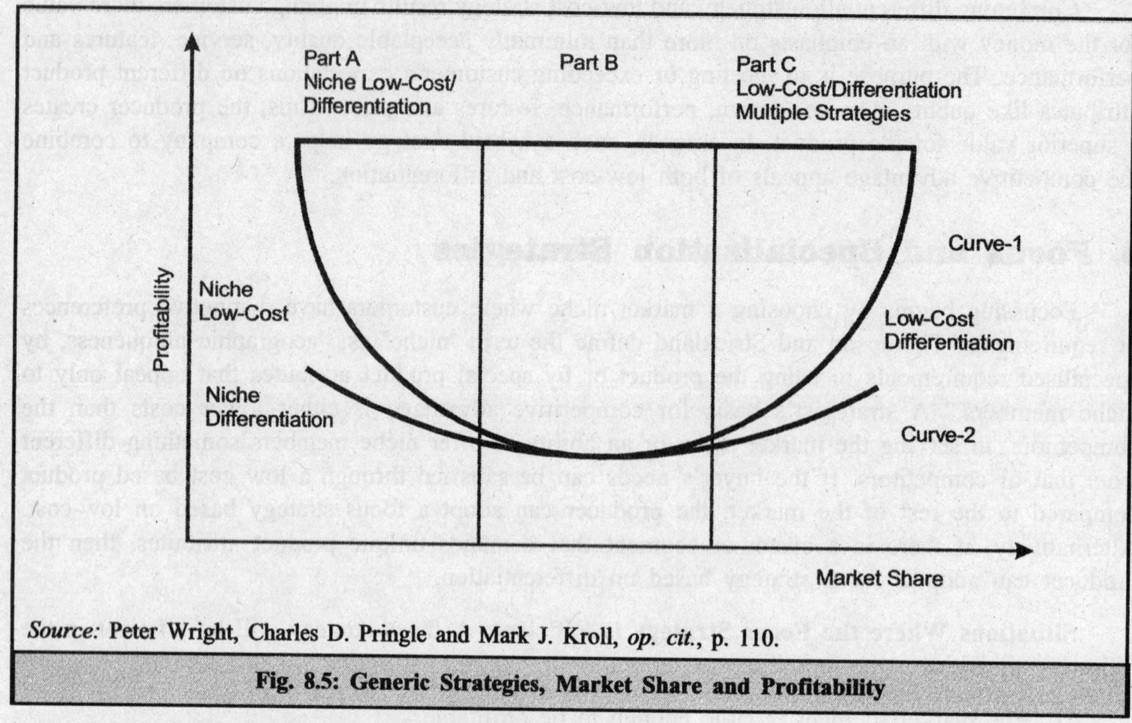

Source: Peter Wright, Charles D. Pringle and Mark J. Kroll, *op. cit.*, p. 110.

Fig. 8.5: Generic Strategies, Market Share and Profitability

Limitations of a Focus Strategy

(i) Competitors may find ways and means to match the focused firm in serving the niche.

(ii) The niche customers' taste, preferences and needs may shift towards the product attributes desired by the whole market.

(iii) The high rate of profitability of the focused firm may attract the competitors to share the profits. The summary of the generic strategies is presented in Exhibit 8.2.

Exhibit 8.2: Summary of Generic Business Unit Strategies and Their Ramifications

Generic Business Unit Strategy	*Emphasis of Business Unit*	*Market Coverage*	*Characteristics of Products and Services*	*Market Demand*	*Pricing*
Niche Low-cost	Lower Overall costs	Niche	No frills	Elastic	Depending on industry forces, low to average.
Niche Differentiation	Specialised quality	Niche	Highly differentiated	Inelastic	High
Niche Low-cost/ Differentiation	Specialised quality and low costs	Niche	Highly differentiated	Inelastic	High
Low-cost	Lower overall costs	Industrywide	No frills	Elastic	Depending on industry forces, low to average
Differentiation	Quality	Industrywide	Differentiated	Relatively inelastic	Depending on industry forces, average to high
Low-cost Differentiation	Quality and Low cost	Industry-wide	Differentiated	Relatively inelastic forces	Depending on industry average to high
Multiple Strategies	Mixed	Mixed	Mixed	Mixed	Mixed

Source: Peter Wright, Charles D. Pringle and Mark J. Kroll, *op. cit.*, p. 109.

Focused Cost Leadership

Focused strategy enables the firm to concentrate on a particular customer group and the cost leadership strategy enables the firm to produce the product/sell the product at the lowest price in the industry. Focused costs leadership strategy in its turn enables the firm to sell the product to the targeted group of customers at the lowest price. Coca-cola introduced 'chota cola' (Chota in Hindi language means small) for low income group at the lowest price in India. Similarly, Ikea-furniture Company provides low cost furniture to the young people. 'Nano' car of Tata focuses on rural customers and aims at selling the car at the lowest price.

Focused Differentiation Strategy: Firms adopting this strategy differentiates products for different markets/customer groups. Maruti Udyog Limited provides different models of cars for different groups of customers. Corporate Intermediate colleges in Andhra Pradesh, India provide different levels of education along with varied services and facilities to different student groups based on their merit scores. Colleges differentiate the students into groups based on their initial examination scores and then provide different levels of education to prepare them for engineering and medical admissions in universities and colleges of different rankings.

Focused cost leadership strategy enables the firm to sell the product to the targeted group of customers at the lowest price.

(C) OFFENSIVE STRATEGIES AND COMPETITIVE ADVANTAGES

An offensive strategy, if successful, can open up a competitive advantage over the competitors. Fig. 8.6 shows the building and eroding of competitive advantage. Strategic moves are successful in producing a competitive advantage during the build up period. The build up period can be short in service industries and it can be longer in capital intensive and technologically sophisticated industries. It would be better for the firm, if an offensive move builds up a competitive advantage quickly. Otherwise the competitors may understand and respond to it.

There is a benefit period, after a successful competitive offensive. The firm can enjoy the fruits of competitive advantage. If the competitors take longer time to launch the counter offensives, the firm can enjoy the benefits for a longer period. The *vice versa* is true if the competitors react quickly. The firm earns above average profits during the benefit period. The best strategic offensives give a major competitive advantage and long benefit periods.

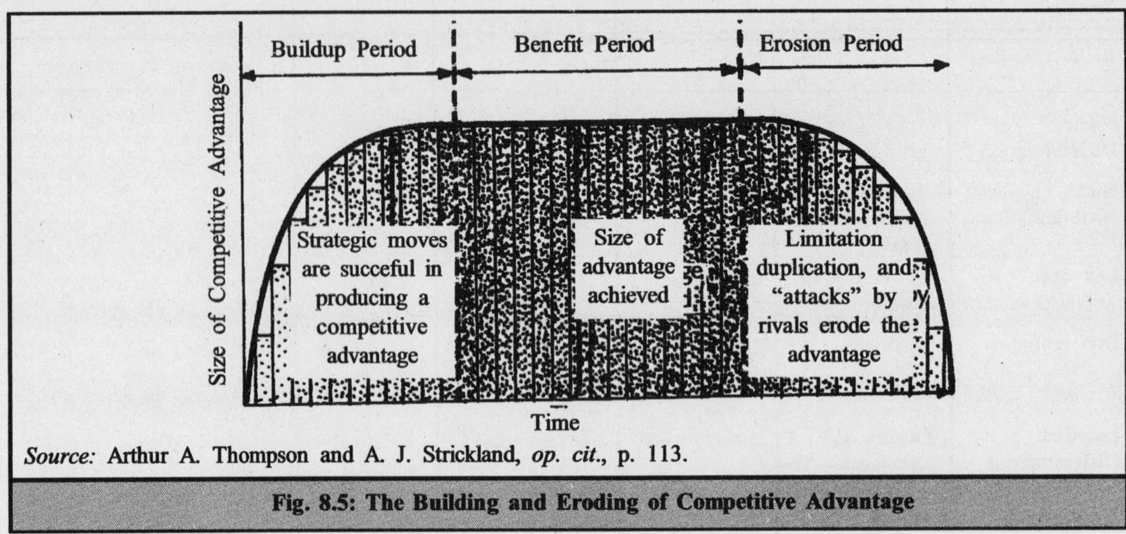

Source: Arthur A. Thompson and A. J. Strickland, *op. cit.*, p. 113.

Fig. 8.5: The Building and Eroding of Competitive Advantage

The erosion period begins as and when the competitors react with counter offensives. A company, therefore, must devise a second strategic offensive to sustain its initial advantage during the benefit period itself. A firm must plan in advance of competitors and initiate creative strategic offensive before the competitors.

There are six basic ways to mount strategic offensives. They are:

(a) Attacks on competitor's strengths

(b) Attacks on competitor's weaknesses

(c) Simultaneous attack on many fronts

(d) End-run offensives

(e) Guerrilla offensives

(f) Pre-emptive strikes

Attacking Competitors' Strengths

Firms attack the competitor's strengths by going head-to-head against the rivals due to the following reasons:

(i) To gain a market share by overpowering weaker competitors and challenging them where they are strongest.

(ii) To whittle away at a strong competitors' competitive advantage. Success is measured by how much the competitive gap is narrowed.

The effectiveness of strength-against-strength offensive challenge depends on the amount of surplus of benefit of the strategy over its costs. The initiator, to be successful, should need the competitive strength and resources.

Types of Attacks: The types of attacks on competitor's strengths involve:

(a) Price cutting

(b) Comparison advertisements

(c) New features that appeal to competitor's customers

(d) New plant capacity in a competitor's backyard

(e) New models that match those of the competitor's

(f) A good product with a lower price

(g) Get cost advantage and then only attack through lower price

(h) Focus on the competitor's geographic area.

Therefore, challenging larger, entrenched competitors with aggressive price cutting is foolhardy unless the aggressor has either a cost advantage or a greater financial strength.

Attacking Competitor's Weaknesses

Firms, in this offensive approach, focus their competitive attention directly on the competitor's weaknesses. The weaknesses that can be challenged successfully are presented in Exhibit 8.3.

Exhibit 8.3: Weaknesses of Rivals that can be Challenged Successfully

- Attack geographic regions where a rival has a weak market share or is exerting less competitive effort.
- Attack buyer segments that a rival is neglecting or is weakly equipped to serve.
- Attack rivals that lag on quality, features, or product performance; in such cases, a challenger with a better product can often convince the most performance-conscious customers of lagging rivals to switch to its brand.
- Attack rivals that have done a poor job of servicing customers; in such cases, a service-oriented challenger can win a rival's disenchanted customers.
- Attack rivals with weak advertising and brand recognition; a challenger with strong marketing skills and a good image can often move in on lesser known rivals.
- Attack market leaders that have gaps in their product line; challengers can exploit opportunities to develop these gaps into strong, new market segments.
- Attack market leaders who are ignoring certain buyer needs by introducing product versions that satisfy these needs.

Source: Arthur A. Thompson and A.J. Strickland, *op. cit.*, pp. 114-115.

Challenging competitors where they are most vulnerable is more likely to succeed than challenging them where they are strongest, particularly, if the challenger has advantages in the areas where the competitors are weak.

3. Simultaneous Attacks on Many Fronts

A grand offensive involving several major initiatives may be sometimes launched by the aggressors. The purposes of aggressors in adopting a grand offensive are to throw a rival off balance, scatter its attention, and force it into channeling resources to protect all its sides simultaneously. The types of attacks include: change the product attributes including configuration, features, flavour, creation of new market segments, price cuts, new services, new channels of distribution, changes in promotional activities, etc.

4. End-Run Offensives

End-run offensives dodge head-to-head confrontations, instead of concentrating on innovative product attributes, technological advances and early entry into less contested geographic markets. In other words, end-run offenders avoid aggressive price cuttings, escalated advertising or any other costly efforts to out throw the competitors.

5. Guerrilla Offensives

A guerrilla offensive uses the hit-and-run principle, selectively attacking where and when an underdog can temporarily exploit the situation to its own advantage. There are several ways to adopt a guerrilla offensive.

Ways of Adopting Guerrilla Offensive

(i) Attack a narrow well-defined segment that is weakly defended by the competitors.

(ii) Attack areas where competitors are overextended and have spread their resources more thinly. These areas include: *(a)* going after their customers in less populated geographic areas, *(b)* enhancing delivery schedules at times when competitors' deliveries are running behind, *(c)* adding to quality when the competitors produce less quality products, *(d)* increasing technical services when customers are confused by the number of competitors' models and features.

(iii) Make small, scattered, random raids on leaders with tactics like *(a)* occasional lowballing on price in order to win a big order or steal a key order, *(b)* increase promotional activities, *(c)* increase legal actions charging anti-trust violations, patent infringement and unfair trade practices.

Suitability of Guerrilla Offensives

Guerrilla offensives are well-suited under the following areas:

(i) Small challengers who have neither the resources nor the market visibility to mount a fullfledged attack.

(ii) When the competitors are big enough, resourceful, have wide and a large market and are very hard to be attacked.

(iii) When the cost of full-fledged attack is more than that of its benefits.

6. Pre-emptive Strategies

Pre-emptive strategies involve moving first to secure an advantageous position which the competitors are foreclosed or discouraged from duplicating. The efficient pre-emptive strategy will not totally block competitors from following or copying. But, this strategy gives an important position to the firm. Further, this strategy keeps the competitors in a disadvantaged position which can't be easily circumvented.

Methods of Employing Pre-emptive Moves: The methods of employing pre-emptive moves to win a prime strategic position are:

(i) Expand production capacity ahead of the market in hope of discouraging the competitors from following it.

(ii) Secure the best source of raw material and/or the most reliable, high quality suppliers through long term contracts or backward vertical integration.

(iii) Secure the best geographical locations.

(iv) Obtain the business of prestigious customers.

(v) Built a psychological image in the minds of customers that is unique and hard to copy and that establishes a compelling appeal.

(vi) Secure exclusive or dominant access to the best distributors in an area.

Competitive Advantage Potentials

Competitive advantage potentials offer the strongest basis for a strategic offensive. These competitive advantage potentials include:

(i) Developing a lower-cost product design.

(ii) Making changes in production operations that lower costs and/or enhance differentiation.

(iii) Developing product features that deliver superior performance or lower user costs.

(iv) Giving customers more responsive post-sale service and support.

(v) Escalating the marketing effort in an under-marketed industry.

(vi) Pioneering a new distribution channel.

(vii) Eliminating wholesalers/distributors/dealers and selling directly by to the ultimate consumer/ users.

A strategic offensive must be tied to

(a) Competitive strengths or key skills like cost reduction capabilities, customer service skills, technical expertise, etc.

(b) Strong functional competence. This includes engineering and product design, manufacturing expertise, advertising and promotion, marketing know-how, etc.

(D) DEFENSIVE STRATEGIES AND COMPETITIVE ADVANTAGES

All firms are subject to attacks from competitors in a competitive environment. These attacks cause risks to the firms being attacked. The defensive strategy aims at lowering the risk of being attacked, weakens the impact of any attack that occurs and influences the challengers to aim their efforts at other competitors. Thus, the foremost purpose of defensive strategy is to protect the competitive advantage and fortify the firm's competitive position.

1. Methods of Protecting the Competitive Position:

There are several methods of protecting the firm's position. The first approach involves trying to block the challengers' avenue for mounting an offensive. The options of this approach are presented in Exhibit 8.4. The second approach to a defensive strategy entails signalling strong retaliation if a challenger attacks. These retaliatory counter measures include:

(i) Publicly announcing management's commitment to maintain the firm's present market share.

(ii) Publicly announcing plans to construct adequate production capacity to meet increasing demand in future, and sometimes building ahead of demand.

(iii) Giving out advance information about a new product, technological breakthrough or the planned introduction of important new brands or models viewing that challengers will delay their own moves until they see if the signalled actions are true.

(iv) Publicly committing the firm to a policy of matching the prices or terms offered by competitors.

(v) Maintaining a war chest of cash and marketable securities.

(vi) Making an occasional strong counter-response to the moves of weak competitors to enhance the firm's image as a tough defender.

2. First-Mover Advantages and Disadvantages

Because of first-mover advantages and disadvantages, when to make a move is often as crucial as what move to make. In other words, when to make a strategic move is often as crucial as what move to make.

Advantages of First-Mover are

(i) Pioneering helps to build the firm's image and reputation with buyers.

(ii) Early commitments to the suppliers of all types of inputs, new technologies, distribution channels and cost advantage.

(iii) First-time customers remain strongly loyal to pioneering firms in making frequent purchases.

(iv) Moving first constitutes a pre-emptive strike, making imitation extra hard or unlikely.

Exhibit 8.4: Options to Block Challengers' Avenues for Mounting an Offensive

- Broadening the firm's product line to close off vacant niches and gaps to would be challengers.
- Introducing models or brands that match the characteristics which the challengers' models already have or might have.
- Keeping prices low on models that most closely match the competitors' offerings.
- Signing exclusive agreements with dealers and distributors to keep the competitors from using the same ones.
- Granting dealers and distributors sizeable volume discounts to discourage them from experimenting with other suppliers.
- Offering free or low-cost training to buyers' personnel in the use of the firm's product.
- Making it harder for competitors to get buyers to try their brands by (1) giving special price discounts to buyers who are considering trial use of rival brands, (2) resorting to high levels of couponing and sample giveaways to buyers most prone to experiment, and (3) making early announcements about impending new products or price changes so that the buyers postpone switching.
- Raising the amount of financing provided to dealers and/or buyers.
- Reducing delivery times for spare parts.
- Increasing warranty coverage.
- Patenting alternative technologies.
- Protecting proprietary know-how in products, production technologies, and other parts of the activity-cost chain.
- Signing exclusive contracts with the best suppliers to block access to the aggressive rivals.
- Purchasing natural resource reserves ahead of present needs to keep them from the competitors.
- Avoiding suppliers that also serve competitors.
- Challenging rivals' products or practices in regulatory proceedings.

Source: Porter, *Competitive Advantage*, pp. 489-494 Quoted in Thompson and Strickland, *op. cit.*, pp. 118-119.

First-Mover Disadvantages include

(i) Pioneering leadership is much more costly and only a negligible experience curve effects accrue to the leader.

(ii) Technological change is so rapid that early investments are soon obsolete.

(iii) It is easy for the latecomers to crack the market because customer loyalty to pioneering firms is weak.

(iv) Skills and technical know-how developed by the market leaders can be easily copied or even surpassed by late movers.

Appropriate timing, therefore, is an important ingredient in deciding whether to be aggressive or cautious.

(E) MATCHING STRATEGY TO SITUATION*

An industry's environment and a company's situation determine the type of strategy that suits the company's business. According to Thompson and Strickland there are eight kinds of industry's environment and company situations. They are:

(i) Competing in a young, emerging industry.

(ii) Competing during the transition to industry maturity.

(iii) Competing in mature or declining industries.

(iv) Competing in fragmented industries.

(v) Competing in international markets.

(vi) Strategies for industry leaders.

(vii) Strategies for runner-up firms.

(viii) Strategies for weak and crisis-ridden firms.

1. Strategies for Competing in Emerging Industries

An industry, which is in the early formative stage is called an emerging industry. Most of the firms, in an emerging industry are in start-up mode, adding people, acquiring or constructing facilities, gearing up production, trying to broaden distribution and gaining customer acceptance. These firms face problems regarding product design, technology and marketing. Emerging industries pose unique challenges to the strategy makers. These challenges are depicted in Exhibit 8.5. The two critical strategic issues confronting firms in an emerging industry are: *(i)* how to finance the start-up phase, and *(ii)* what market segments and competitive advantage to go after to secure a leading industry position. Either low-cost or differentiation competitive strategies are appropriate.

* The treatment in this section draws information heavily from Thompson and Strickland, "Strategic Management."

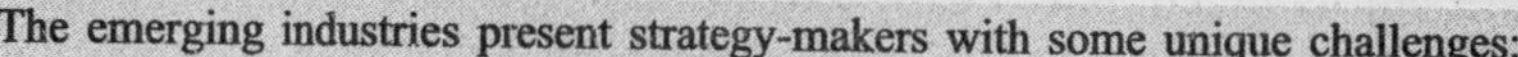

Exhibit 8.5: Strategies for Competing in Emerging Industries

The emerging industries present strategy-makers with some unique challenges:

- Because the market is new and unproven, there are many uncertainties about how it will function, how fast it will grow, and how big it will get; the little historical data available is virtually useless in projecting future trends.
- Much of the technological know-how tends to be proprietary and closely guarded, having been developed in-house by pioneering firms; patent protection is sought for competitive advantage.
- Often, there is no consensus on which production technologies will be most efficient and which product attributes the buyers will prefer. The result is industry-wide absence of product and technological standardisation, wide differences in product quality and performance, and a situation where each firm has to pioneer its own approach to technology, product design, marketing, and distribution.
- Entry barriers tend to be relatively low; additional start-up companies and large outsiders will enter if it becomes more evident that the industry's future is promising.
- Experience curve effects often permit significant cost reductions as volume builds.
- Firms have little hard information about competitors, how fast products are gaining buyer acceptance, and users' experiences with the product; there are no trade associations gathering and distributing information.
- Since all buyers are first-time users, the marketing task is to induce initial purchase and overcome customer concerns about product features, performance reliability, and conflicting claims of rival firms.
- Many buyers expect first-generation products to be rapidly improved, so they wait to buy until technology and product design mature.
- Firms may have trouble securing ample supplies of raw materials and components (until suppliers gear up to meet the industry's needs).
- Many companies find themselves short of funds to support the needed R&D and to get through several lean years until the product catches on.

Source: Michael E. Porter, "*Competitive Advantage*," Free Press, New York, 1980, pp. 216-223. Quoted in Arthur and Strickland, *op. cit.*, p. 126.

Focusing strategies may be viable when finances are limited. One of the most challenging business strategy problems is dealing with all the risks and opportunities of an emerging industry. Companies need to observe some guidelines to be successful in an emerging industry. Exhibit 8.6 presents these guidelines.

Exhibit 8.6: Guidelines for Companies to be Successful in Emerging Industries

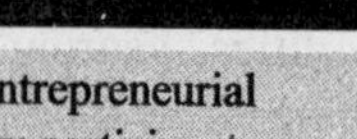

1. Try to win the early race for industry leadership by employing a bold and a creative entrepreneurial strategy. Because an emerging industry has no established rules of the game and industry participants often try a variety of strategic approaches, a pioneering firm with a powerful strategy can shape the rules and become the industry leader.
2. Push hard to perfect the technology, improve product quality and develop attractive performance features.
3. Try to capture any first-mover advantages associated with more models, better styling, early commitments to technologies and raw materials suppliers, experience curve effects and new distribution channels.
4. Search out new customer groups, new geographical areas to enter, and new user applications. Make it easier and cheaper for the first time buyers to try the industry's new product.
5. Gradually shift the advertising emphasis from building product awareness to increasing frequency of use and creating a brand loyalty.
6. Move quickly when technological uncertainty clears and a "dominant" technology emerges; try to pioneer the "dominant design" (but be cautious when technology is evolving so rapidly that early investments are likely to become obsolete).
7. Use price cuts to attract price-sensitive buyers into the market.

8. Expect large, established firms looking for growth opportunities to enter the industry as their perceived risk of investing in the industry lessens. Try to prepare for the entry of powerful competitors by forecasting *(a)* who will enter (based on present and future entry barriers) and *(b)* the types of strategies they will employ.

Source: Phillip Kotler, "*Marketing Management*," Prentice-Hall, Englewood Cliffs, N.J., 1984, p. 336 and Porter, "*Competitive Advantage*," Quoted in Thompson and Strickland, *op. cit.*, p. 127.

Strategies for Competing During the Transition to Industry Maturity: Rapid industry growth may be for some period. As the growth rates slack off, the transition usually produces fundamental changes in the industry's competitive environment. Slower rates of market growth cause competitive pressures to intensify, often producing a shakeout of weaker competitors and reduces profit margins throughout the industry. The fundamental changes in the industry's competitive environment produced by the transition are presented in Exhibit 8.7.

Firms can make several strategic moves to strengthen their competitive moves, when market growth slows and competitive pressure builds up. These strategic moves include:

(i) *Pruning the Product Line:* Too many product versions prevent the firms from achieving the economies of long product runs. The prices of slow-selling products may not cover their costs. Strategies to match company strengths include: *(a)* pruning product lines, *(b)* concentrating sales efforts on items whose margins are highest, *(c)* reduce the costs where the firm has a competitive advantage.

Exhibit 8.7: Fundamental Changes in industry's Competitive Environment Produced by the Transition

1. *Slowing growth in buyer's demand generates more head-to-head competition for market share.* Firms that want to continue on a rapid growth track start looking for ways to take customers from the competitors. Outbreaks of price-cutting, increased advertising, and other aggressive tactics are common.
2. *Buyers become more sophisticated, often driving a harder bargain on repeat purchases.* Since buyers have an experience with the product and are familiar with the competing brands, they are better able to evaluate different brands, and will negotiate with sellers to get a better deal.
3. *Competition often produces a greater emphasis on cost and service.* As all sellers begin to offer the product attributes that buyers prefer, buyer choices increasingly depend on which seller offers the best combination of price and service.
4. *Firms have a "topping out" problem in adding production capacity.* Slower rates of industry growth mean showdowns in capacity expansion. Each firm has to monitor the rivals' expansion plans and time its won carefully to minimise their oversupply conditions in the industry. Adding too much capacity too soon can adversely affect the company profits well into the future.
5. *Product innovation and new end-use applications are harder to come by.* Producers find it increasingly difficult to develop new product features, find further uses for the product, and sustain buyer excitement.
6. *International competition increases.* Growth-minded domestic firms start to seek out sales opportunities in foreign markets. Some companies, looking for ways to cut costs, relocate plants to countries with lower wage rates. Greater product standardization and diffusion of technological know-how reduce entry barriers and make it possible for enterprising foreign companies to become serious market contenders in more countries. Industry leadership passes to companies with the biggest global market share and strong competitive positions in most of the world's major geographic markets.
7. *Industry profitability falls temporarily or permanently.* Slower growth, increased competition, more sophisticated buyers, and occasional periods of overcapacity put pressure on industry profit margins. Weaker, less efficient firms are usually the hardest hit.
8. *The resulting competitive shakeout induces a number of mergers and acquisitions among former competitors, drives some firms out of the industry,* and, in general produces industry consolidation. Inefficient firms and firms with weak competitive strategies can survive in a rapid growth industry. But the much stiffer competition in the industry, maturity stage exposes competitive weakness and results in a survival-of-the fittest market contest.

Source: Porter, "*Competitive Advantage*," pp. 238-240. Quoted in Thompson and Strickland, pp. 128-129.

(ii) *More Emphasis on Process Innovation:* The purposes of re-investing the production can involve mechanising high-cost activities, revamping production lines to improve labour efficiency and increased use of advanced technology. Japanese firms have successfully used production process innovation to become lower-cost producers of higher-quality products.

(iii) *A Stronger Focus on Cost Reduction:* A tough price competition forces the firms to reduce unit costs. The effort to reduce costs include: bargain with the suppliers of inputs to reduce the prices, switch to lower priced components, development of more economical product designs, cut unnecessary tasks out of activity-cost chain, increasing production and distribution efficiency and trim administrative overhead.

(iv) *Increasing Sales to Present Customers:* Attracting customers from competitors may not be appealing an increasing sales to the existing customers in a mature market. Strategies to increase sales to the existing customers include: broadening the lines offered to include complementary products and ancillary services, finding more ways for customers to use the product and performing more functions for the buyers.

(v) *Purchasing Rival Firms at Bargain Prices:* Sometimes distressed rivals can be acquired cheaply. An acquired firm's customer base can provide expanded market coverage. The most desirable acquisitions are those that will significantly enhance the acquiring firm's competitive strength.

(vi) *Expanding Internationally:* A firm may seek to enter foreign markets where attractive growth potential still exists as its domestic market matures. Foreign expansion is particularly attractive when the outdated equipment is usable for export production or in plants of third world countries. Such opportunities arise when: *(a)* foreign buyers have less sophisticated needs, *(b)* end-use applications are much simpler, *(c)* foreign competitors are smaller, less formidable and do not adopt latest technology, and *(d)* when a domestic firm's skill and reputation are readily transferable to foreign markets.

(vii) *Strategic Pitfalls:* The strategic pitfalls include: *(a)* The firm may steer a middle course between low cost, differentiation and focusing. This compromise will make the firm to end up with a fuzzy strategy, *(b)* sacrificing long-term competitive position for short-term profit, *(c)* waiting too long to respond to price cutting, *(d)* getting caught with too much capacity as growth slows, *(e)* overspending on marketing efforts to boost the sales growth, and *(f)* failing to pursue cost reduction soon enough and aggressively enough.

Strategies for Firms in Mature or Declining Industries

Many firms operate in industries where demand is growing slower than the economy average — or even declining. Strong competitors can achieve good performance even in a stagnant market environment while weak companies adopt the strategies like, cash-flow maximisation, selling-out, and closing down.

Businesses competing in slow growth or declining industries have to accept the difficult realities. Strong competitors may be able to take sales from weaker competitors. The exit of weaker firms help the stronger firms to increase their market share. The strategies to be adopted by the firms to succeed in stagnant industries are presented in Exhibit 8.8.

Dangers in the stagnating market are:

(a) Getting trapped in a profitless war of attrition;

(b) Diverting too much cash out of a business too quickly; and

(c) Being overly optimistic about the industry's future and waiting complacently for things to get better.

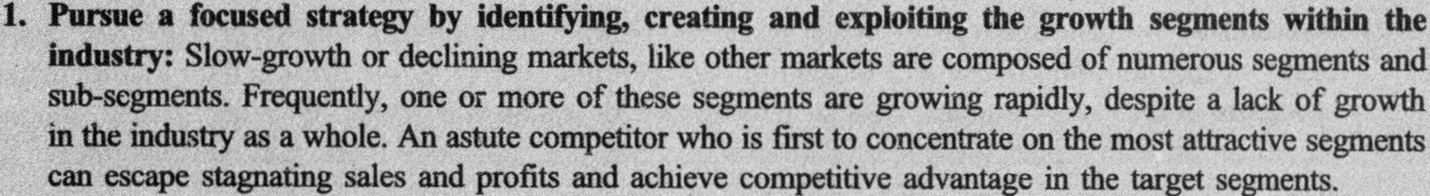

Exhibit 8.8: Strategies for Firms in Stagnant Industries

1. **Pursue a focused strategy by identifying, creating and exploiting the growth segments within the industry:** Slow-growth or declining markets, like other markets are composed of numerous segments and sub-segments. Frequently, one or more of these segments are growing rapidly, despite a lack of growth in the industry as a whole. An astute competitor who is first to concentrate on the most attractive segments can escape stagnating sales and profits and achieve competitive advantage in the target segments.
2. **Stress differentiation based on quality improvement and product innovation:** Either enhanced quality or innovation can rejuvenate the demand by creating important new growth segments or inducing buyers to trade up. Successful product innovation opens up an avenue for competing besides meeting or beating rivals' prices. Differentiation based on innovation has the additional advantage of being difficult and expensive for rivals to imitate.
3. **Work diligently and persistently to drive costs down:** When increases in sales cannot be counted on to generate increased earnings, firms can improve profit margins and return on investment by continuously reducing the operating costs and increasing efficiency. They can achieve a lower-cost position by: (1) improving the manufacturing process via automation and increased specialization, (2) consolidating underutilized production facilities, (3) adding more distribution channels to ensure the unit volume needed for low-cost production, (4) closing low-volume, high-cost distribution outlets, and (5) revamping the activity cost chain to eliminate some cost producing tasks.

Source: R.G. Hamermesh and S.B. Silk, "How to Compete in Stagnant Industries," *Harvard Business Review*, Vol. 57, No. 5, Sep-Oct. 1979, p. 161. Quoted in Thompson and Strickland, *op. cit.*, pp. 130-131.

3. Strategies for Competing in Fragmented Industries

A number of industries are populated with thousands of small firms without a substantial market share. The outstanding feature of a fragmented industry is the absence of market leaders with king-sized market shares. Some industries are fragmented due to the following reasons:

- Low entry barriers allow small firms to enter quickly and cheaply.
- Absence of large scale economies permits small companies to compete with large scale firms on equal cost footing.
- Demand for product is in small qualities.
- Market is local.
- Market accommodates a large number of small firms as the market is large and diverse (health care, energy).
- High transportation cost limits the area of operation and market.
- Local regulatory requirements make each geographic area unique.

Firms in fragmented industries generally are in a weak bargaining position with buyers and suppliers. Suitable competitive strategy options of a fragmented industry are presented in Exhibit 8.9.

Exhibit 8.9: Suitable Competitive Strategy Options for Fragmented Industry

- **Constructing and operating "formula" facilities** — This is an attractive approach to achieving low cost when firms must operate facilities at multiple locations. Such firms design a standard facility, construct outlets in favourable locations at a minimum cost, and then operate them in a super efficient manner. McDonald's and 7-Eleven have pursued this strategy to perfection, earning excellent profits in their respective industries.
- **Becoming a low-cost operator** — When the price competition is intense and profit margins are under constant pressure, firms can pursue no-frills operations featuring low overhead, use of high-productivity/ low-cost labour, tight budget control, and total operating efficiency. Successful low-cost producers can play the price-cutting game and still earn profits above the industry average.

- **Increasing customer value through integration** — Backward or forward integration may contain opportunities to lower costs or enhance the value given to customers (like cutting to size, assembling components before shipment to customers, or providing technical advice).
- **Specializing by product type** — When products come in many models and styles, a focused strategy based on specialization in one area of the line can be very effective. Some firms in the furniture industry specialize in only one furniture types such as brass beds, rattan and wicker, lawn and garden, and early American. In auto repair, firms specialize in transmission repair; body work; and mufflers, brakes, and shocks.
- **Specializing by customer type** — A firm can cope with the intense competition of a fragmented industry by catering to those customers (1) who have the least bargaining leverage (because they are small in size or purchase small amounts), (2) who are the least price sensitive, (3) who are interested in additional services, unique product attributes, or other "extras," (4) who place custom orders, or (5) who have special needs or tastes.
- **Focusing on a limited geographic area** — Even though a firm in a fragmented industry is blocked from winning a big industry-wide market share, it can still gain significant internal operating economies by blanketing a local/regional geographic area. Concentrating facilities and marketing activities on a limited territory can produce greater sales force efficiency, speed delivery and customer services, and permit saturation advertising — while avoiding the diseconomies of trying to employ the strategy on a national scale. Convenience food stores, banks, and department store retailers have been successful in operating multiple locations within a limited geographic area.

In fragmented industries, firms have a wide degree of strategic freedom — many different strategic approaches can exist side by side.

Source: Thompson and Strickland, *op. cit.*, pp. 133-134.

4. Strategies for Competing in International Markets

Firms 'go international' for three basic reasons. They are: *(i)* desire to seek out new markets, *(ii)* a competitive need to achieve lower costs, *(iii)* a desire to access natural resource deposits in other countries. International strategy has to be situation driven and requires a careful analysis of the industry's international aspects. Special care should be taken regarding, how national markets differ in customer needs, habits, tastes, preferences, distribution channels, long-run growth potential, driving forces, and competitive pressures.

Situational considerations: In addition to the above differences there are four situational considerations that are unique to international operations. They are:

(i) Production Cost Variations: The cost of production of different products and services vary from country to country due to variations in wage/salary levels, human resource productivity, inflation rates, energy costs, tax rates, cost of raw material, cost of services and the like. The low cost countries become major production centres and the products produced in these countries are exported to the markets in other countries. Companies with facilities in these countries have a competitive cost advantage over those that do not have. India is an example for low production cost for many products including computer software.

The concept of manufacturing share (different from brand share or market share) is another important production cost consideration in the international competition. Manufacturing share is important as it is a better indicator than market share. Worldwide a low-cost producer is a powerful advantage.

(ii) Fluctuating Exchange Rates: The fluctuations in exchange rates complicates the issues of locational cost advantages.

(iii) Host Government Trade Policies: The host government's policies relating to import tariffs, quotas, and local content requirements on goods produced within the country, etc., affect the strategies. In addition, the regulations regarding technical standards, product certification, prior approval of capital investment, withdrawal of funds from the country and requirement of ownership share by local investors complicate the foreign companies. Local companies may be encouraged to compete with the foreign companies by providing finance at a low interest rate, subsidies on raw materials, etc.

Multi-country vs. Global Competition: Multi-country competition takes place country-by-country. In multi-country competition, rival firms vie for national market leadership. In global competition, prices and competitive, conditions across country markets are strongly linked. Leading competitors compete head-to-head in many different countries. In a globally competitive industry, rival firms vie for worldwide leadership. A global competitor's strength is directly proportional to its portfolio of country based competitive advantages. Differences between multi-country and global strategies are presented in Exhibit 8.10.

Exhibit 8.10: Differences between Multi-country and Global Strategies

	Multi-country Strategy	*Global Strategy*
Strategic arena	Selected target countries and trading areas.	Most countries which constitute critical markets for the product (at least North America, the European Community, and the Pacific Rim [Australia, Japan, South Korea, and Southeast Asia]).
Business strategy	Custom strategies to fit the circumstances of each host country situation; little or no strategy coordination across countries adapted to local needs.	Same basic strategy worldwide; minor country-by-country variations where essential.
Product-line strategy		Mostly standardized products sold worldwide.
Production strategy	Plants scattered across many host countries.	Plants located on the basis of maximum competitive advantage (in low-cost countries, close to major markets, geographically scattered to minimize shipping costs, or use of a few world-scale plants to maximize economies of scale — as most appropriate).
Source of supply for raw materials and components	Suppliers in host country preferred (local facilities meeting local buyer needs; some local sourcing may be required by the host government).	Attractive suppliers from anywhere in the world.
Marketing and distribution	Adapted to practices and culture of each host country.	Much more worldwide coordination; minor adoption to host country situations if required.
Company organisation	From subsidiary companies to handle operations in each host country; each subsidiary operates more or less autonomously to fit the host country conditions.	All major strategic decisions are closely coordinated at global headquarters; a global organisational structure is used to unity the operations in each country.

Source: Thompson and Strickland, *op. cit.*, p. 139.

Thus, a company's strategic approach is shaped by these situational considerations along with the cultural and political differences among the various countries.

Types of International Strategies: There are six types of international strategies for companies going internationally. They are:

(i) License foreign firms to use the company's technology or produce and distribute the company's products. (The firm gets the royalty income).

(ii) Maintain a national (one-country) production base and export goods to foreign markets, using either company owned or foreign controlled forward distribution channels.

(iii) Follow a multi-country strategy: In this, company's international strategy is crafted country by-country to be responsive to the customer needs and conditions in each country.

(iv) Follow a global low cost strategy: The Company produces at the lowest cost and supplies to most of the buyers or all strategically important markets in the world.

(v) Follow a global differentiation strategy: The firm, adopting this strategy, differentiates its product on the same attributes in all countries to create a consistent image and a consistent competitive theme.

(vi) Follow a global focus strategy: The Company, by adopting this strategy, aims at serving the same identifiable niche in each of many strategically important country markets.

Global Strategy and Competitive Advantage

The company can gain a competitive advantage with a global strategy approach in two ways. They are: *(i)* acquiring global competitor's ability to locate its activities among nations in a manner that lowers costs or achieves greater product differentiation, and *(ii)* acquiring the global competitor's ability to coordinate its activities in ways that a domestic-only competitor cannot.

Locating Activities: With a global strategy, a firm can pursue sustainable competitive advantage by locating activities in the most advantageous countries and coordinating strategic actions worldwide.

Co-ordinating Activities and Strategic Moves: By aligning and coordinating company activities in different countries, a firm can build a sustainable competitive advantage in several ways like, *(i)* shifting production from one country to another to take advantage of exchange rate fluctuations, of changing wage rates, energy costs, etc. *(ii)* enhancing its brand reputation, and *(iii)* challenging rivals.

Strategic Alliances: Strategic alliances are cooperative agreements between firms that go beyond normal company-to-company but do not pursue merger or full partnership. The forms of alliance are: joint research efforts, technology sharing, joint use of production facilities, marketing one another's products, producing or assembling jointly, etc.

Strategic alliances are a means for companies in globally competitive industries to strengthen their competitive positions while still preserving their independence. These are more effective in combating disadvantage than in gaining a competitive advantage.

Strategic Intent: Competitors in international markets adopt different strategies. They also have different strategic objectives or intent. There are four types of competitors, *viz.,* firms with global dominance strategic intent, firms with a defending domestic dominance intent, firms with host-country responsiveness intent and firms with domestic only strategic intent.

Profit Sanctuaries and Critical Markets: Profit sanctuaries are country markets where a company has a strong or protected market position and derives substantial profits. In other words, a nation becomes a company's profit sanctuary when a company, because of its strong competitive position or protective governmental trade policies, derives a substantial portion of its total profits from the sale in that nation.

To defend against the global competitors, firms have to compete in all critical markets. Critical markets are markets in countries, *(i)* that are the profit sanctuaries of key competitors, *(ii)* that have big sales volume, *(iii)* that contain prestigious customers whose business is strategically important to have, *(iv)* that offer exceptionally good profit margins due to weak competitive pressures.

The Competitive Power of Cross-Subsidisation: Cross-subsidisation involves using profits earned in one or more country markets to support a competitive offensive against the key rivals or to gain an increased penetration of a critical market.

5. Strategies for Industry Leaders

The competitive positions of industry leaders generally range from stronger than average to powerful. Leaders enjoy a well-known reputation. The strongly entrenched leaders have proven strategies (low cost leadership or differentiation). The strategic concerns of industry leaders are: *(a)* sustaining a leadership position, *(b)* becoming the dominant leader, and *(c)* large market share.

The competitive positions of industry leaders generally range from stronger than average topowerful. Leaders enjoy a well-known reputation. The strongly entrenched leaders have proven strategies (low cost leadership or differentiation).

Three contrasting postures are open to an industry leader and dominant firms.

1. Stay-on-the-Offensive Strategy: This strategy is based on the principle that the best defense is a good offence. Offensive minded leaders try to be "first-movers" to build a sustainable competitive advantage and a solid reputation as the leader. Staying on offensive requires continuous, innovation, development of new products, better performance features, quality enhancements, improved customer service, reducing cost of production, discovering new uses of the products, attracting new users, etc. A leader's growth rate should be more than or at least equal to that of the industry. Otherwise, he will lose ground to the competitors.

2. Fortify and Defend Strategy: This strategy is to make it very difficult for new firms to enter and for challengers to gain ground. Specific defensive actions are:

(a) Attending to increase competitive ante for challengers and new entrants by spending more on promotional programmes, customer service and research and development.

(b) Introducing more of the company's own brands.

(c) Making it very difficult to the customers to switch to rival products.

(d) Broadening the product line to close off possible vacant niches for competitors to slip into.

(e) Keeping prices reasonable and attractive quality, design, etc.

(f) Building new capacity ahead of the market demand to block the market expansion potential of competitors.

(g) Investing more to remain cost competitive and technologically progressive.

(h) Patenting alternative technologies.

(i) Signing exclusive contracts with the best suppliers of inputs and dealers or distributors.

3. Follow-the-Leader Strategy: The objective of this strategy is to enforce an unwritten tradition that smaller firms follow the industry leader in adjusting prices up or down. The leader uses its competitive muscle to thwart and discourage the would be challengers. The small rivals are signalled by the leader about the consequences of any move to cut into the leader's business. The leader's retaliation strategies include: quickly cut the prices, large scale promotional programmes, offering better deals to the major customers, pursue the distributors not to carry the rival's products, demarketing the rival's products through the salesmen, scouting the best executives of rivals, etc.

6. Strategies for Runner-Up Firms

Runner-up firms acquire weaker market positions than the industry leaders. Some runner-ups play the role of market challengers. They adopt offensive strategies to gain a market share. Others behave content followers. A challenger firm interested in improving its market standing should adopt a strategy aimed at building a competitive advantage of its own. "Rarely can a runner-up improve its market position by imitating the leading firm. A cardinal rule in offensive strategy is to avoid attacking a leader head-on with an imitative strategy, regardless of the resources and staying power an underdog may have."

Runner-up companies have more strategic flexibility and can consider any of the following six approaches.

1. Vacant Niche Strategy: This strategy involves concentrating on consumer or end-use applications that the major firms have neglected. An ideal vacant niche is sufficient in size and scope to be profitable, has some growth potential, is well-suited to a firm's own capabilities and skills and is outside the interest of the leading firms.

2. Specialist Strategy: A specialist firm concentrates on: a single product, a particular end-use, a special customer group or a particular geographical area. The purpose is to build a competitive advantage through product uniqueness, expertise in special purpose products or specialised customer service.

3. "Ours-is-Better-Than-Their Strategy": This strategy uses a combination of focus differentiation strategy keyed to product quality. Sales and marketing efforts focus on quality and conscious and performance oriented buyers. Fine craftsmanship, prestige quality, frequent innovations, and close contact with customers are the approaches of this strategy.

4. Content Follow Strategy: Follower firms refrain from initiating trend-setting strategic moves and from aggressive attempts to steal the customers away from the leaders. They prefer approaches that will not provoke competitive retaliation. They follow focus and differentiation strategies that keep them out of the leader's strategies.

5. Growth via Acquisition Strategy: Strengthening a company's position to have a larger market share is possible through a merger with or acquiring weaker rivals.

6. Distinctive Image Strategy: Some runner-up companies use a variety of strategic approaches by standing out from competitors. These approaches include: creating a reputation for the lowest prices, providing prestige quality at a reasonable price, providing superior customer service, designing unique product attributes, emerging as a new product introducers and devising creative advertising.

Obstacles to Small Firms

Small firms have to overcome the following obstacles:

(i) Less economies of scale in production, distribution and sales promotion.
(ii) Difficulty in gaining customer recognition.
(iii) An inability to afford mass media advertising on a large scale.
(iv) Difficulty in funding capital requirements.

Runner-up firms do not face these problems, and they can hold the strategies against big business houses.

Strategies to Overcome these Obstacles: The problems of small firms can be surmounted and a profitable competitive position can be established by:

(i) Focusing on a new market segment where the company's strengths can yield a competitive edge.

(ii) Developing technical expertise that will be highly valued by customers.

(iii) Aggressively pursuing the development of new products for customers in the target market segments.

(iv) Using innovative, "dare-to-be different," "beat-the-odds" entrepreneurial approaches to out manage stodgy, slow-to-change market leaders.

Runner-up firms, by making a leapfrog technological breakthrough, can gain a market share. This is possible, if the leaders become complacent.

7. Strategies for Weak Businesses

A firm in a declining competitive position (or also-ran position) has four basic strategic options:

(i) *Modest Strategic Offensive:* If it has the financial resources, it can adopt a modest strategic offensive focused to low cost of production or new differentiation.

(ii) *Aggressive Defense:* It can adopt an aggressive defense, using variations in the present strategy and fighting hard to keep sales, market share, profitability and competitive position at current levels.

(iii) *Immediate Abandonment:* It can opt for an immediate abandonment and get out of the business either by selling out to another firm or by closing down the operations.

(iv) *Harvest Strategy:* It can adopt a harvest strategy keeping reinvestment to a bare minimum and maximising short term cash flows in preparation for an orderly exit. This strategy is a middle course between preserving the status quo and exiting as soon as possible. This is an endgame strategy.

Harvesting Strategies Include

(i) Cut operating budgets to rock-bottom and pursue stringent internal cost control.

(ii) Capital investment in the new equipment is minimal or zero depending upon the current conditions of the fixed assets.

(iii) Cut promotional expenses gradually.

(iv) Reduce quality in not so visible ways.

(v) Curtail non-essential customer services.

(vi) Reduce equipment maintenance.

Conditions for Harvesting

(i) When the industry's long term prospects are unattractive.

(ii) When building up the business would be too costly or not profitable enough.

(iii) When the firm's market share is becoming increasingly costly to maintain or defend.

(iv) When reduced levels of competitive effort will not trigger an immediate fall off in sales.

(v) When the enterprise can redeploy the freed resources in higher opportunity areas.

(vi) When the business is not a major component in a diversified corporation's portfolio of existing businesses.

(vii) When the business does not contribute other desired features like sales, stability, prestige, or a well-rounded product line to a company's overall business portfolio.

Crisis Turnaround: Turnaround strategies include: *(i)* revise the existing strategy, *(ii)* launch efforts to boost revenues, *(iii)* pursue cost reduction, *(iv)* sell off assets to raise cash to save the remaining part of the business, and *(v)* use a combination of these efforts. Turnaround situations and strategies are discussed in Chapter 7.

(F) THIRTEEN COMMANDMENTS FOR FORMULATING SUCCESSFUL BUSINESS STRATEGIES

Business experiences over the several years prove that disastrous courses of action can be avoided by following certain principles of employing strategies. The lessons from the past experiences can be summarised into 13 commandments. These commandments help the strategists in formulating effective strategic plans. Exhibit 8.11 presents these 13 commandments for formulating effective strategies. Exhibit 8.12 presents a summary checklist of the most important situational considerations and strategic options.

Exhibit 8.11: Thirteen Commandments for Formulating Effective Strategies

1. *Always put top priority on formulating and executing moves that enhance the company's competitive position for the long term and that serve to establish it as an industry leader.* In competitive markets, a strongly entrenched leadership position pays off year after year, but the glory of meeting one year's financial targets quickly passes. Shareholders are never well-served by managers who let short term financial considerations override strategic initiatives that will bolster the company's long term competitive position and strength.
2. *Understand that a clear, consistent competitive strategy, when well-crafted and well-executed, builds reputation and recognisable industry position; a strategy aimed solely at capturing momentary market opportunities yields fleeting benefits.* The pursuit of short-run financial opportunities without long term strategic guidance tends to produce the worst kind of profits; one shot rewards that are unrepeatable. Over the long haul, a company that has a well conceived competitive strategy aimed at securing a strong market position will outperform and defeat a rival whose strategic decisions are driven by short-term financial expectations. In an ongoing enterprise, the game of competition ought to be played for the long term, not the short-term.
3. *Try not to get "stuck back in the pack" with no coherent long term strategy or distinctive competitive position, an "average" image, and little prospect of climbing into the ranks of the industry leaders.*
4. *Invest in creating a sustainable competitive advantage* — it is the single most dependable contributor to above average profitability.
5. *Play aggressive offence to build a competitive advantage and aggressive defence to protect it.*
6. *Avoid strategies capable of succeeding only in the best of circumstances* -- competitors will react with counter-measures and market conditions are not always favourable.
7. *Be cautious in pursuing a rigidly prescribed, inflexible strategy* — changing market conditions may render it quickly obsolete. Any strategy, to perform satisfactorily, must be adaptable to fresh market circumstances. Strategic themes involving "top" quality or "lowest" cost should be interpreted as relative to competitors and/or customer needs rather than based on arbitrary management standards.
8. *Don't underestimate the reactions and the commitment of rivals* — especially when they are pushed into a corner and their well-being is threatened.
9. *Be wary of attacking strong, resourceful rivals without a solid competitive advantage and ample financial strength.*
10. *Consider that attacking competitive weakness is usually more profitable than prices attacking competitive strength.*
11. *Take care not to cut without an established cost advantage* — only a low-cost producer can win at price-cutting over the long term.
12. *Be aware that aggressive moves to wrest market share away from rivals often provoke aggressive retaliation in the form of marketing "arms race" and/or price wars — to the detriment of everyone's profits.* Aggressive moves to capture a bigger market share invite cutthroat competition particularly when the market is plagued with high inventories and excess production capacity.
13. *Employ bold strategic moves in pursuing differentiation strategies to open up meaningful gaps in quality, service, or performance features.* Tiny differences between the rivals' competitive strategies and product offerings may not be visible or important to buyers.

Source: Thompson and Strickland, *op. cit.*, pp. 155-157.

Exhibit 8.12: Matching Strategy to Situation
(A checklist of optional strategies and generic situations)

Industry Environments	*Company Positions/ Situations*	*Situational Consideration*	*Market Share and Investment Options*	*Strategy Options*
• Young, emerging industry • Rapid growth • Consolidating to a smaller group of competitors • Mature/slow growth • Ageing/declining • Fragmented • International/ global • Commodity product orientation • High technology/ rapid changes	• Dominant leader – Global – National – Regional – Local • Leader • Aggressive challenger • Content follower • Weak/distressed candidate for turn-around or exit. • "Struck in the middle"/no clear strategy or market image	• External – Driving forces – Competitive pressures – Anticipated moves of key rivals – Key success factors – Industry attractiveness • Internal – Current company performance – Strengths and weaknesses – Opportunities and threats – Cost position – Competitive strength – Strategic issues and problems	• Growth and build a bigger market share by growing faster than industry as a whole – Invest heavily to capture growth potential • Partly and defend – Protect market share; grow at least as fast as the whole industry – Invest enough resources to maintain competitive strength and market position • Retrench and retreat – Surrender weakly held positions when forced to, but fight hard to defend core markets/ customer base – Maximise short term cash flow – Minimise reinvestment of capital in the business • Overhaul and reposition – Try to turn around • Abandon/liquidate – Sell out – Close down	• Competitive approach – Overall low-cost leadership – Differentiation – Focus/ specialisation • Offensive initiatives – Attack – End run – Guerrilla warfare – Preemptive strikes • Defensive initiatives – Fortify/protect – Retaliatory – Harvest • International initiatives – Licensing – Export – Multi-country – Global – Forward – Backward

Source: Thompson and Strickland, *op. cit.*, p. 158.

POINTS TO BE REMEMBERED

- Customers are the basis for crafting a business unit level strategy.
- Firm's select a group of customers based on its mission.
- Firms position in the industry relative to its competitors' determines the business unit level strategies that the firms can craft.
- Firms intending to craft a cost leadership strategy should create value to the product through various measures of cost saving.
- Low-cost strategy helps to compete with the current competitors and allows to create entry barriers to the prospective competitors.
- Firms intending to pursue differentiation strategy should create value for product differentiation.
- Relationship between brand loyalty and price sensitivity insulates a firm from competitive rivalry.
- Lower-cost leader's basis for competitive advantage is lower overall costs than that of the competitors'.

KEY WORDS

- Low-cost strategy
- Focus strategy
- Value chain analysis
- Differentiation approaches
- First-mover advantages
- Emerging industry
- Declining industries
- Harvesting
- Differentiation strategy
- Value creation
- Low-cost leader
- Low-cost approaches
- Follower
- Fragmented industries
- Industry leaders
- Weak firms

QUESTIONS FOR DISCUSSION

1. How do companies craft strategic business unit level strategies based on customer needs?
2. What is low-cost strategy? How does value chain analysis help to achieve a low-cost strategy?
3. Discuss different approaches to a low-cost strategy.
4. What are the advantages and risks of low-cost strategy?
5. What is differentiation strategy? Discuss its approaches.
6. Discuss the advantages and risks of differentiation strategy.
7. What are the offensive strategies? How do the offensive strategies help to achieve a competitive advantage?

8. What are the defensive strategies? How do these strategies help to achieve a competitive advantage?
9. What are the thirteen commandments for formulating successful business strategies?

REFERENCES

1. Arthur A. Thompson Jr., and A.J. Strickland III, *op. cit.*, p. 102.
2. Michael E. Porter, "*Competitive Strategy: Techniques for Analyzing Industries and Competitors*," Free Press, New York, 1980.
3. Arthur A. Thompson Jr., and A.J. Strickland III, *op. cit.*, pp. 105-106.
4. "Competing on Costs," *Business Today*, July 7-21, 1997, p. 70.
5. Arthur A. Thompson Jr., and A.J. Strickland III, *op. cit.*, pp. 106-107.
6. *Ibid.*, p. 107.
7. *Ibid.*
8. *Ibid.*, p. 108.
9. Michael E. Porter, *op. cit.*, pp. 138-142.
10. *Ibid.*, pp. 160-162.
11. Arthur A. Thompson Jr., and A.J. Strickland III, *op. cit.*, p.111.
12. Ian C. Macmillan, "*How Long Can You Sustain a Competitive Advantage*" in Lian Fahey, "*The Strategy Planing Management Reader*," Prentice Hall, Englewood Cliffs, New Jersey, 1989, pp. 23-24.
13. Ian C. Macmillan, "*Controlling Competitive Dynamics by Taking Strategic Initiative*," The Academy of Management Executive, Vol. 2, No. 2, May 1988, p. 111.
14. Phillip Kotler and Ravi Singh, "*Marketing Warfare in the 1980s*." The Journal of Business Strategy, Vol. 1, No. 3, Winter 1981, pp. 30-41, Phillip Kotler, "*Marketing Management*," Prentice Hall, Englewood Cliffs, New Jersey, 1984, pp. 401-406.
15. Phillip Kotler, "*Marketing Management*," p. 402.
16. William E. Rothschild, "*Surprise and Competitive Advantage*," Journal of Business Strategy, Vol. 4, No. 3, Winter 1984, pp. 10-18.
17. Michael E. Porter, "*Competitive Strategy*," pp. 241-246. Quoted in *Ibid.*, p. 129.
18. Macmillan, "*How Business Strategies Can Use Guerrilla Warefare Tactics*," Journal of Business Statistics, Vol. 1, No. 2, Fall 1980, pp. 63-65. Kathryn R. Harrigan, "*Strategic Flexibility*," Lexington Books, Lexington, 1985, pp. 30-45 and Liam Fahey, "*Guerrilla Strategy: The Hit and Run Attack*," In Fahey, "*The Strategic Planning Management Reader*," pp. 194-197 Quoted in Thompson and Strickland, *op. cit.*, pp. 115-116.
19. *Ibid.*, pp. 116-117.
20. Ian C. Macmillan, "*Pre-emptive Strategies*," *Journal of Business Strategy*, pp. 16-26. Quoted in Thompson and Strickland, *op. cit.*, 116-117.
21. Michael E. Porter, "*Competitive Advantage*," *op. cit.*, pp. 520-522.
22. Macmillan, "*Controlling Competitive Dynamics*," pp. 112-116.
23. Michael E. Porter, "*Competitive Advantage*," pp. 495-497 Quoted in Thompson and Strickland, *op. cit.*, pp. 119-120.
24. *Ibid.*, pp. 232-233.
25. Peter Wright, Charles D. Pringle and Mark J. Kroll, *op. cit.*, pp. 124-126.
26. Boston Consulting Group, "*Perspectives on Experience*," The BCG, 1976. G. Hall and S. Howell, "The Experience Curve from An Economist's Perspective," *Strategic Management Journal*, 6, 1985, pp. 197-212.
27. T. Peters and N. Austin, "*A Passion for Excellence*," Random House, New York, 1985, p. 53.
28. R.D. Buzzell and B.T. Gale, "*The PIMS Principles*," Free Press, New York, 1987.
29. Peter Wright, Charles D. Pringle and Mark J. Kroll, *op. cit.*, p. 130.
30. *Ibid.*, p. 131.
31. *Ibid.*
32. *Ibid.*, p. 135-136.
33. C.F. Gibson and R.L. Nolan, "*Managing the Four Stages of EDP Growth,*" in L.M. Salerno, ed., "*Catching up with the Computer Revolution*," Wiley, New York, 1983, pp. 25-43.

34. Peter Wright, Charles D. Pringle and Mark J. Kroll, *op. cit.*, p.138.
35. *Ibid.*, p. 140.
36. C.W.L. Hart, "*The Power of Unconditional Service Guarantees,*" The McKinsey Quarterly, Summer 1989, pp. 75-76.
37. Arthru A. Thompson and A.J. Strickland, *op. cit.*, p. 125.
38. Charles W. Hofer and Dan Schendel, "*Strategy Formulation: Analytical Concepts,*" West Publishing, St. Paul, Minn, 1978, pp. 164-165.
39. Arthur A. Thompson and A.J. Strickland, *op. cit.*, p. 128.
40. Michael E. Porter, "*Competitive Strategy,*" pp. 241-246. Quoted in *Ibid.*, p. 129.
41. Michael E. Porter, "*The Competitive Advantage of Nations,*" Free Press, New York, 1990, pp. 53-61.
42. Arthur A. Thompson and A.J. Strickland, *op. cit.*, pp. 134-136.
43. Michael E. Porter, *op. cit.*, p. 65.
44. Prahalad and Doz, "*The Multinational Mission,*" p. 52.
45. *Ibid.*, p. 61.
46. Philip Kotler, "*Marketing Management," Porter, "Competitive Advantage,*" and Ian C. Mac Millan, "*Seizing Competitive Initiative,*" *The Journal of Business Strategy,* Vol. 2, No. 4, Spring 1982, pp. 43-57.
47. Arthur A. Thompson and A.J. Strickland, *op. cit.*, p. 147.
48. Michael E. Porter, "*Competitive Advantage,*" p. 514.
49. Philip Kotler, "*Marketing Management,*" pp. 397-412, R.G. Hamermesh, M.J. Anderson Jr., and J.E. Harris, "*Strategies for Low Market Share Businesses,*" *Harvard Business Review,* Vol. 56, No. 3, May-June 1978, pp. 95-102 and Porter, "*Competitive Advantage,*" Chapter 15. Quoted in Thompson and Strickland, pp. 151-152.
50. Hamermesh, Anderson and Harris, "*Strategies for Low Market Share Business,*" p. 102.
51. Phillip Kotler, "*Harvesting Strategies for Weak Products,*" Business Horizons, Vol. 21, No. 5, August 1978, pp. 17-18.
52. V.P. Rindova and C.J. Fombrun, "Constructing Competitive Advantage: The Role of Firm-Constituent Interactions." *Strategic Management Journal*, Vol. 20. pp. 691-710.
53. Michael E. Porter, "What is Strategy?", Harvard Business Review, 1998, 74 (6), pp. 61-78.
54. A. Goldstein," GM to use i2 Software: Stocks Soar", Dallas Morning News, 20 January 1999.
55. S.C. Jain, "*Marketing Planning and Strategy,*" South-western College Publishing, 2000, p. 120.
56. Hewlett-Packard, 1999, www.hp.com
57. P. Burrows, "The Hottest Property in the Valley", *Business Week*, 30 August 1999, pp. 69-77.
58. Michael E. Porter, "Competitive Strategy", *The Free Press*, New York, 1985, p.2.
59. Acer Computer Corporation, 2000. www.acer.com.
60. Dallas Hanson *et. al.*, *Strategic Management*", Thomson, Australia, 2002, p. 139.

✦ ✦ ✦

9

CHAPTER

FUNCTIONAL LEVEL STRATEGIES

Chapter Outline

(A) Functional Level Strategies: An Introduction

(B) Production/Operations Strategies

(C) Marketing Strategies

(D) Financial Strategies

(E) Human Resource Strategies

(F) Research and Development Strategies

(G) Information Strategies

(H) Integrated Functional Strategies

Learning Objectives

After studying this chapter, you should be able to:

- Discuss production/operation strategies at a functional level;
- Explain the research and development strategies;
- Analyze the strategies in marketing, human resource and information areas;
- Integrate the functional strategies to achieve superior efficiency;
- Substantiate how the functional strategies result in superior quality, superior customer service and superior guarantee.

(A) FUNCTIONAL LEVEL STRATEGIES — AN INTRODUCTION

All organisations, irrespective of their size, nature and scope of business must perform the functions like production/operations, finance, marketing, human resource and research and development. Careful planning, execution and co-ordination of these functions are highly essential for efficient strategic planning, implementation and control. The strategic managers at the functional level should understand the interrelationship of these functions in formulation of the strategies. The activities of all the functional areas are interwoven in attaining their purposes as well as the purpose of the total firm as shown in Fig. 9.1. In fact, these functional areas of a firm are like different organs of a human body. Therefore, it is needless to say that the organisational strategies are implemented at the functional levels.

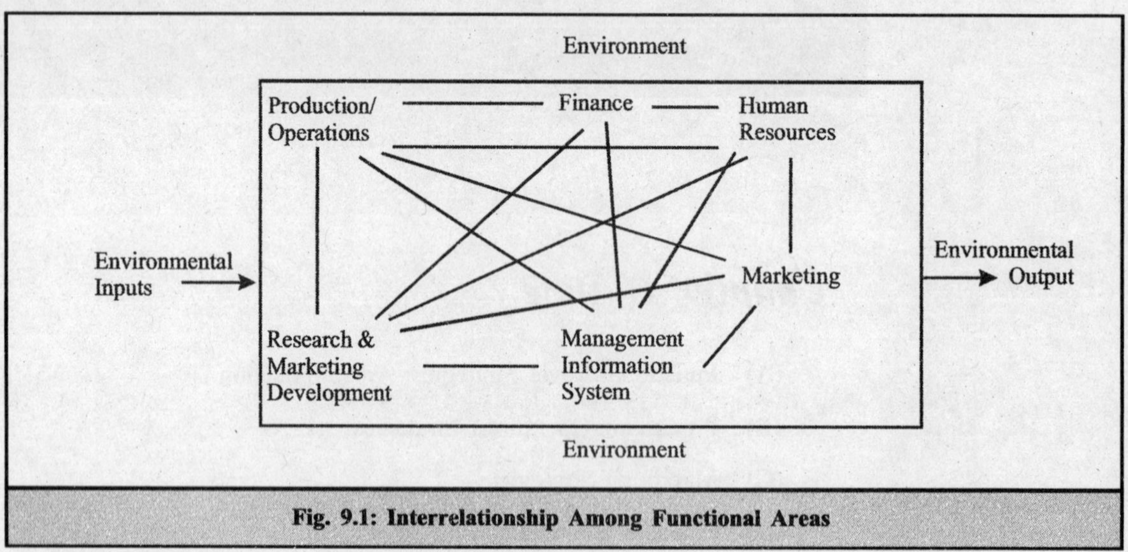

Fig. 9.1: Interrelationship Among Functional Areas

(B) PRODUCTION/OPERATIONS STRATEGIES

The important production and operations management strategies include:

Decision-making in Operations: The firm before starting the manufacturing/operations makes specific decisions with regard to cost, quality, dependability and flexibility. A firm can have the low cost of production strategy when it targets the market for the poor income group. In contrast, it can have a high quality product for upper income group. Singapore Airlines target upper income group and hence, does not concentrates on cost, but Tiger Airways concentrates on cost and focus, on lower-income air travelers.

Firms can select the flexibility strategy in contrast to fixed product strategy. Modern airlines like Tiger Airways and Virgin follow flexible product strategy in the sense that the price varies with the service options of the traveler including the weight of booked luggage, cabin luggage, food in the flight, etc.

Product design strategies include market driven product design strategies,technology driven product design strategies, and inter-functional driven product design strategies.

Product Design: Product design strategies include market driven product design strategies, technology driven product design strategies, and inter-functional driven product design strategies. Market driven product design strategies target the changing customer preferences and products are designed to satisfy such needs. These strategies provide and a competitive advantage to the firm over its rivals who follow technology driven product driven strategies. For example, Andhra Bank introduced mobile banking, evening and Sunday banking and opened the branches in residential areas. These strategies helped the bank to compete even with big banks. Introduction of new software by Microsoft and adding of new functions to mobile phones are some other examples of market driven product design strategies.

Products under technology-driven product design strategies are produced based on the existing technology. Firms adopting this strategy take less risk, spend less on research and development. Bharat Sanchar Nigam Limited used to adopt this strategy. In fact, most of the public sector undertakings across the globe including Telekom (PNG) adopt this strategy. Firms experiencing the problems with investment and talented human resources and enjoying monopolistic advantage go for this strategy. But, they can't continue with this strategy due to the globalisation and privatisation of business across the globe and mounting competition thereafter.

Inter-functional product design involves the technology, market conditions, human resource capabilities, financial position and outcome of research and development. These strategies are designed and based on a coordinated and balanced approach. Tata's 'Nano' car is the best example for the inter-functional product design.

Process Strategies: Basically, there are three process strategies, *viz.,* line process, intermittent process and project process. Most of the firms producing products involving linear or sequence of operations craft line process strategy. For example, automobile companies, TV companies and computer manufacturing companies design line process strategy.

Firms producing customised products like make-to-order furniture, cook-to-order food and delivering educational programmes based on a particular group of students craft intermittent process design strategy. However, the increased competition due to globalisation and strides in production technology enabled even line production process companies to produce customised products by crafting intermittent process strategy. For example, Toyota automobiles crafted intermittent process to produce customised cars based on the specific needs of customers. Similarly, companies producing progressive lens craft intermittent strategies to produce lens exactly the same power as that of the customer.

The remaining process strategy is a project process. Building construction companies, moviemaking companies, shipbuilding companies and the like craft project process strategy.

Technology Strategy: Technology strategy is related to set of processes, tools, methods, machinery and equipment that are used to convert raw material into finished goods and services. Technology strategy is related to the selection of state-of-the-art technology or appropriate technology or moderate and tested technology or outdated technology. Firms under severe competitive situation as well as catering to the fast changing consumer needs like information processing, and entertainment industry craft the strategies involving state-of-the-art technology.

Firms operating in developing countries normally craft appropriate technology strategy as the technology of the firm should be integrated with that of other firms whose production depends on that of the former. The software companies and computer service companies select the technology that is compatible with that of the computer manufacturing companies. Similarly, automobile spare parts manufacturing firms should select the technology based on the automobile companies for whose cars the spare parts are produced. Automobile companies producing cars for developing countries should select the appropriate technology that helps to produce cars for the road conditions of the developing country concerned.

Plant location is influenced by a variety of factors that includes government policies of various countries, availability of qualitative inputs at a less price including human resource, power, material and the like.

Similarly, firms located in highly populated countries like India and China select labour-intensive technology to make use of cheap labour.

Plant Location Strategy: Plant location is influenced by a variety of factors that includes government policies of various countries, availability of qualitative inputs at a less price including human resource, power, material and the like. Globalisation, strides in transportation technology and information technology and enhanced international competition forced the firms to craft split location strategy and global location strategy. Most of the automobile companies located their manufacturing facilities in more than 20 countries and assembled in the 21st country. Thus, the transnational companies split their production process and locate the units in different countries. The split location strategy enables the firm to get the advantage of large sale economies by taking the advantages of each location. Online technology solves the problems of co-ordination and exact fitness of the parts.

Facilities Strategy: Facilities strategy is concerned with the capacity of production. This strategy crafted taking the marketing strategies into consideration. Crafting facilities strategy takes into consideration, the firm's ability to fulfill the existing and future gap between demand and supply of the product. The firm formulates the strategy of fulfilling the part of the gap between demand for and supply of the product rather than the total in view of associated risks of entry of new companies. Firms even in the small markets like Caribbean and Pacific Rim markets prefer to craft this strategy.

Chase Strategy and Level Strategy in Aggregate Planning: Aggregate planning is concerned with matching supply and demand over the medium term range. Chase strategy aims at chasing demand with the workforce. In other words, this strategy aims at increasing the demand or reducing the demand based on the workforce and its ability to produce a certain quantity of output. Level strategy aims at increasing or decreasing the workforce based on the level of demand.

Inventory Strategies: Inventory strategies cover what to carry, how much to order, when to order and the type of control system to be used. Inventory strategy aims at reducing the cost of inventory carrying cost, by carrying the least possible volumes of material and supply of the material uninterruptedly. However, inventory strategy varies from one item to the other depending up on the criticality of the item in the production process. For example, in case of critical item, firms follow uninterrupted supply strategy like diesel in case of transportation industry.

Quality Strategy: Quality is the conformance to the customer needs. However, level of the quality varies from customer to customer based on ability to pay and the degree of requirement of the product/service. Quality strategies include zero defect, a certain degree of perfectness of the product/service, say 98% perfectness, 'make it perfect at the first time', and total quality. Total quality includes quality of the product, pre-sales and post-sales service, perfect contribution from all resources including human resources.

Exhibit 9.1 presents the key strategies areas in production/operations management.

Exhibit 9.1: Key Strategic Areas in Production/Operations Management

Cost	:	Low cost products vs. high price products
Quality	:	Zero defect vs. 98% Perfect
Flexibility	:	Fixed Package vs. Adaptable to customer convenience
Product Design	:	Market driven strategy, technology driven strategy and interfunctional design strategy
Process Design	:	Line, intermittent, project, customised strategies
Technology	:	state-of-the-art technology strategy, appropriate technology strategy, moderate technology strategy, outdated technology strategy
Plant Location Strategy	:	Single location, multiple location and split location strategies
Facilities and Equipment Strategies	:	Integrated vs. Separate process, Equipment strategies Centralised vs. Decentralised facilities, Peak capacity vs. Normal capacity, Level of mechanisation and integration, Demand chasing strategies vs. Demand leveling strategy
Sourcing Strategies	:	Single Source vs. Multiple Source for each item of raw material, Supplier Selection Mode, Supplier Relationship Management Forward buying/credit buying
Scheduling Strategies	:	Scheduled to order vs. Scheduled to stock
Inventory Strategies	:	Low inventory cost vs. Uninterrupted supply Prevention of failure vs. Resolving crisis

Now, we shall discuss marketing strategies.

(C) MARKETING STRATEGIES

Marketing strategies along with production strategies form the primary strategies. Marketing strategies are primarily based on business unit level strategies like production strategies. Du Pont's successful European marketing strategy for its elastic fiber, Lycra shows the close relationship between business and marketing strategies. The chief marketing manager's strategic planning responsibilities include: Participating in corporate and business unit level strategy and formulating and developing marketing strategies that follow business unit strategies.

Marketing strategy involves analysis, development and implementation of activities.

Exhibit 9.2: Business Unit and Marketing Strategies: A Comparison

	Business Strategies	*Marketing Strategies*
• Perspective	Organisational and/or competitive focus, often industry orientation.	Customer and/or product focus, often with a heavy end-user orientation
• Decisions	• Mission Determination • Allocation of resources to business units • Acquisition/diversification • Product Development • Selection and development of SBU strategies	• Identification of market opportunities • Choice of target markets • Marketing Programmes • Product, Price, Promotion and distribution strategies
• Strategic Focus	• Gain and keep strategic advantages • Craft business strategies • Business organisation Planning and control	• Divide markets into segments • What segments to serve • Position for each segment
• Information Needs	• Financial performance • Business opportunity Assessment • Market performance and Forecasts	• Financial performance by market target and product type • Customer/prospect description and requirements • Market position and Forecasts • Competitor's marketing strategies and performance

Source: David W. Cravens, "Strategic Marketing", Irwin, Sydney. p. 92.

Marketing strategies can be studied under the following areas:

- Product Strategies
- Place/Distribution Strategies
- Pricing Strategies, and
- Promotion Strategies

Product Strategies

Improving product/service quality is a critical competitive challenge that the companies across the world face.

Quality Improvement Strategy: Quality improvement is an organisational responsibility. Essential managerial style and leadership characteristics in developing a quality oriented culture include attention to detail, complete planning, problem monitoring, high personal standards, ongoing commitment to quality improvement, responsive and participative management style and trustworthiness.

Under product development strategies, companies develop product for the existing markets or develop new products for new markets. For example, Microsoft concentrated on the development of new products whereas HP concentrated on the development of products for the new markets like hospitals. Gujarat Co-operative Milk Marketing Federation concentrated on the development of new products like ice creams, deserts and health drinks to its existing customers. Similarly, Coca-cola developed new products like soft drinks with lemon flavour (Sprite), orange flavour (Fanta) and mineral water.

Under product differentiation strategy, companies produce different models, sizes and features of the same product.

Product Differentiation: Under product differentiation strategy, companies produce different models, sizes and features of the same product. Procter and Gamble produces laundry detergent of different brands with varied features. Colgate Palmolive produces different brands of toothpaste. McDonald has added toys to attract kids and playing cards to cater to the young customers.

Service Differentiation: Similar to product differentiation, companies providing service also adopt service diffractions strategy. These service differentiation include speed of delivery, installation, customer training, customer consulting, maintenance and repair and other services. Nandi Pipes of Nandyal in Andhra Pradesh delivers the pipes to the fields of the farmers. Cemex — a giant cement company of Mexico delivers cement faster than 'masala dosa' by a local hotel. Hewlett-Packard provides the installation services to the colleges and universities. General Electric sells x-ray machines to hospitals and trains the x-ray machine operators of the hospital. Modi Xerox and Canon sells photo copying machines and also provide maintenance and repair facilities. Hewlett-Packard sells personal computers which provides online technical support to its customers.

Now, we shall discuss place/channel of distribution strategies.

Place/Channel of Distribution Strategies

Place/channel of distribution strategies basically depend upon whether the company prefers to sell directly to the customer or outsource its distribution function. Strides in information technology enable the companies to opt for direct marketing through electronic marketing.

However, most of the companies still prefer to distribute the product through market intermediaries like wholesalers, retailers, agents, dealers, etc.

Channel differentiation can be a distinctive competitive advantage. Caterpillar's construction equipments are available in many locations, than that of its competitors, due to development of market intermediaries even in small locations. Bharat Sanchar Nigam Limited's success is due to location of pay phone/STD outlets even in the corners of even small towns and the villages throughout India by appointing commission agents.

Promotion Strategies

Promotion mix includes advertising, personal selling and sales promotion. Companies should have a large advertising budgets during product introduction stage in order to create consumer acceptance. The companies whose brand is enjoying a high market share can have a less advertising budget. However, in a highly competitive environment, companies should spend more on advertising. Similarly, the consumer and consumer durable goods industry needs to advertise frequently and as such, such an industry should have large advertising budgets.

Consumer and consumer durable goods industry mostly depends on advertising while the industrial goods industry depends on personal selling.

Online advertising started assuming greater significance and as such, all kinds of industries formulate promotion strategies around online advertising.

Now, we shall study the pricing strategies.

Pricing Strategies

Price and quantity of the product compete with each other in setting the price. High quality products compete with each other in setting the price. Companies go for good value strategy by fixing low price for medium quality products. Companies craft a super value strategy by fixing a low price for high quality products.

Price and quality of the product compete with each other in setting the price. High quality products compete with each other in setting the price.

Common pricing strategies are markup pricing, target return pricing, perceived value pricing, going rate pricing, psychological pricing, geographical pricing, price discounts, discriminatory pricing, and product-mix pricing.

Markup Pricing Strategies: Companies fix a price by adding a certain percentage to the cost of manufacturing or services in order to earn a desired return on invested capital.

Target Return Pricing: Firms fix the price after adding desired return on invested capital to the cost of manufacturing or service per unit.

Perceived Value Pricing: Companies determine the price of a product or service based on the customer's perceived value of the product or service. Customer's perceived value of the product is influenced by the customer's image of the product performance, the warranty, quality, customer's support, and trustworthiness, supplier reputation, esteem and the like. Caterpillar fixes the price for its construction equipment based on perceived value. The perceived value of the Caterpillar's customer is based on the superior durability, reliability, service, value and longer warranty on parts.

Value Pricing: Companies under value pricing strategy fix the price at low level for a high quality product or service in order to win the loyalty of the customers. Tiger Airways, Air India Express and KingFisher Airlines charge lower price for their services compared to the similar services offered by their competitors. LG offers its TVs at as low price compared to its competitors.

Going Rate Pricing: Companies adopting going rate pricing strategy fix the price based on the price of their competitors. Companies charge more or less the same price as that of the competitors charge. For example, different cement companies charge more or less similar price. Mobile companies in India also charge a more or less the same price.

Group Pricing: Internet is providing an opportunity for the buyers and sellers to form into groups either to buy at a low price or to sell at a higher price. Amazon.com is an example for grouping the sellers.

Psychological Pricing: High price is viewed as a reflection of high quality of the product by many of the upper income group customers. High priced cars, pharmaceuticals, TVs, refrigerators and other consumer durables are viewed as high quality products while the low priced products are viewed as low quality products. Bata shoes are viewed as high quality as their prices are high compared to the shoes produced by local companies in India as they are priced at low price.

In fact, shoes produced by local companies in India are branded as Bata Shoes. Similarly, Nike shoes are produced in Vietnam and are sold at a high price in the departmental stores in USA while the same shoes without Nike brand are sold at a very low price in Vietnam.

Geographical Pricing: Companies fix different prices for the same product in different geographical regions. For example, Sony TVs are sold at different prices in different countries.

Price Discounts and Allowances: Companies adopt another strategy to sell the product at different prices to different customers by offering discounts and allowances. These discounts include:

Cash Discount: Cash discount allows the customers to buy the products at the price less than the quoted price, when the customers pays the bills on or before due date.

Quantity Discount: Companies sell the product at less price to those customers who buy the product in larger quantities.

Functional Discount: Discount offered to wholesalers, retailers, and the commission agents by the manufacturers is called functional discount.

Seasonal Discount: Some businesses experience peak seasons as well as slack season for sales. For example, railways, airlines and road transport organisations experience peak season in sales mostly during summer/vacation season for educational institutions and slack season during other seasons. Companies reduce the price during the slack season. Hotels, companies producing air-conditioners and refrigerators fix a low price for their products during the winter season.

Allowance: Companies offer discounts for clearance sales, festive sales like Dussera, Pongal, Christmas, Ramzaan, etc.

(D) FINANCIAL STRATEGIES

Finance is the fundamental resource for starting and conducting of a business. In fact, companies need finance to implement their strategies. Financial strategies are centred around acquiring capital, reducing cost of capital, making complex investment decisions through capital budgeting, financing and dividend decisions, capital structure, working capital strategies in terms of accounts receivables, inventory, cash management, etc.

Acquiring Capital: Capital can be equity capital and loan capital/debt capital. Equity capital provides security, and free from paying interest and financial risk. Debt capital though, requires the payment of a fixed interest regularly, provides huge surplus during the periods of business boom. Therefore, companies prefer to have both equity capital and debt capital.

Capital Structure Strategy: Capital structure is the mix of equity capital, preference capital, retained earnings and debt capital. Companies formulate optimum capital structure strategy in order to balance the advantages and disadvantages/risks of various kinds of capital like equity capital, preference capital and debt capital. Optimum capital structure possess the following features:

- Generation of maximum rate of return on capital employed for the purpose of maximisation of wealth of equity shareholders.
- Excessive debt capital results in risk of solvency of the company. Hence, companies should limit the debt capital at a point where the risk begins.
- Companies should adopt a flexible structure in order to adapt the structure to the economic situations.
- The amount of debt capital should be within the capacity of the company to generate future cash flows.
- Capital structure of the company should result in control of risk involved in debt capital.

Thus, an appropriate capital structure strategy helps the firm in reducing the cost of capital, risks involved in debt capital management and enchasing the equity shareholder's wealth.

Dividend Strategy: Dividend strategy is to decide the amount of profits to be distributed to the shareholders after retaining certain amount of profits as a surplus for the future investment of the company and earning benefit to the shareholder. This in turn enables the company to generate the capital for future investment purpose which involves the least cost of capital as well as risk. As such, L&T follows the balanced dividend and retained earnings/surplus strategy.

Dividend strategy is to decide the amount of profits to be distributed to the shareholders after retaining certain amount of profits as a surplus for the future investment of the company and earning benefit to the shareholder.

Dividend strategy is to maximise the shareholder's return in the long run by maximising the value of investment. Thus, dividend strategy balances the current return and capital gains. Dividend strategy balances the current return and capital gains. Dividend strategy enables the shareholders to satisfy their desire for steady income and reduces the tax burden on income in addition to meet the company's goal of less costly capital structure. Thus, appropriate dividend's strategy enables the firm to reduce the cost of capital, minimise risk, and enhance the shareholders' value.

Long-term Investment/Capital Budgeting Strategy: After acquiring the capital, through capital budgeting strategy, companies invest capital, capital investment is also called capital budgeting. Capital budgeting is concerned with the investment in fixed assets or long-term assets. Companies make capital budgeting decisions for the establishment of the business, expansion, diversification, and modernisation, replacement of long-term assets, acquisition, merger and amalgamation strategies of the company.

Companies sometimes sell the long-term assets in order to replace the old assets, to tide over the financial difficulties due to recession in the business, or decline in the sales of the company and the like. Sale of assets involves disinvestment decisions. Capital budgeting involves disinvestment decisions.

Capital budgeting strategies are affected by the corporate strategies like expansion, diversification, takeover, merger, amalgamation as well as retirement like disinvestment, turnaround and liquidation of the business.

Capital budgeting strategy enhances the productivity of the business, returns, profitability, and shareholders' wealth. Capital budgeting decisions influences the —

- Growth rate and direction of the business;
- Risk element involved in the business due to the commitment of funds for long-term;
- The commitment of large amount of funds; and
- Fixation of funds in particular asset permanently, making the irreversible of the decision impossible.

Capital budgeting strategy involves the following phases:

- Identification or origination of investment opportunities based on corporate strategy and business unit level strategies;
- Forecasting the costs and benefits of the investment opportunities over the long run;
- Evaluation of the net benefits from each of the opportunity;
- Authorisation for progressing and spending capital expenditure;
- Control of capital projects.

After formulating of long-term investment strategies, companies craft short-term capital/working capital strategies. Now, we shall discuss working capital strategies.

There are two aspects of working capital, *viz.*, gross working capital and net working capital.

Working Capital Strategies: There are two aspects of working capital, *viz.*, gross working capital and net working capital. Company's investment in current assets is called gross working capital. Current assets include cash, accounts receivables, short-term securities, bills receivables and inventory. Difference between current assets and current liabilities is called net working capital. Current liabilities include accounts payable, bills payable and outstanding expenses.

Companies should maintain an adequate working capital to operate the daily and routine activities of the business. The shortage of working capital affects the creditworthiness of the companies and results in failure to pay even employees salary. In contrast, excessive working capital results in idle funds and in turn leads to high cost of capital.

Now, we shall discuss the strategies relating to each aspect of working capital strategies, *viz.*, cash management, accounts receivables and inventory management.

Cash Management: Management of cash brings into sharp focus on the trade-off between risk and return. Cash management deals with cash flows into and out of the company, cash flows among different departments of the company and cash balances held by the company to finance the deficits or to invest the surplus. Continuous deficit of cash creates risks and problems to the company while continuous surplus of cash result in high cost of capital. The companies have to plan for optimum cash and maintain it in order to prevent the possible problems of deficit as well as surplus of cash.

Cash should be managed efficiently. The surplus or deficit of cash can be managed through float of cash represented by incoming collections, payment made sooner than necessary, scattered deposit balances and excessive and unrewarding balances in checking accounts. This stage includes efficient management of near-cash in order to produce the highest return consistent with a low risk.

Companies prefer cash budgets to control cash flows. Cash budgets serve the purpose, only when the company accelerates its collections and postpones payments within allowed limits.

Accounts Receivables: Companies sell on credit due to a competition, bargaining power of the buyer/market intermediaries, relationship and network with the market intermediaries/manufacturer's, practices within the industry and requirements of the buyer. Companies make optimum credit policy in order to maximise the operating profit and reduce incremental cost. Amount of accounts receivables depends a volume of credit sales and collection period. Credit policy determines the volume of credit sales, credit period, credit standards, terms and collection efforts.

All customers may not pay during the credit period. Hence, companies make efforts to accelerate the collection in order to reduce bad debt losses. Companies, in addition, monitor receivables based on the average collection period and ageing schedules. When companies fail to collect the receivables, sells such receivables to specialised firms. This practice is called 'factoring'. Factors or companies involved in factoring advance cash against receivables to solve the problem of shortage of cash, for a certain rate of commission.

Inventory Management: Inventories constitute raw materials, work-in-progress and finished goods. Inventories constitute more than 60% of current assets. Efficient inventory management is essential in order to operate the production process uninterruptedly, to guard the production process against the risks involved in the supply of raw material and in the price fluctuations of raw material. At the same time, the cost of inventory should be minimised to the greatest extent possible in order to contribute to the low cost of production.

There are two conflicting objectives of inventory management. A production manager prefers less quantity of inventory in order to reduce the cost of inventory whereas the marketing manager prefers larger quantity of inventory in order to have uninterrupted supply of finished products. The finance manager balances these conflicting objectives of inventory management. Therefore, the efficient inventory management should:

- ensure continuous supply of raw materials to facilitate uninterrupted production;
- maintain sufficient quantity of raw materials in times of short supply and anticipate price changes;
- maintain finished goods of sufficient quantity for continuous sales operation and efficient customer service;
- minimise the carrying cost and time, and
- control investment in inventories and keep it at an optimum level.

(E) HUMAN RESOURCE STRATEGIES

Having discussed the finance function strategy, now we shall study the human resource management strategies.

Human Resource Management Strategies

Human resource is the critical, dynamic and living resource of an organisation unlike other resources. Human resource management strategies percolate into other functional strategies and integrates all of them towards corporate and business unit level strategies.

Human resources (HR) can be thought of as *the total knowledge, skills, creative abilities, talents and aptitudes of an organisation's workforce,* as well as *the values, attitudes and beliefs of the individuals involved.* Human resources management (HRM) is managing (planning, organising, directing and controlling) the functions of employing, developing, compensating and utilising human resources, resulting in the creation and development of human and industrial relations which would shape the future policies and practices of human resource management with a view to contribute proportionately (due to them) to the organisational, individual and social goals.

Objectives of Human Resources Management

Objectives are predetermined goals to which an individual or a group activity in an organisation is directed. Objectives of HRM are influenced by social objectives, organisational objectives, functional objectives and individual objectives. Institutions are instituted to attain certain specific objectives. The objectives of the economic institutions are mostly to earn profits, and that of educational institutions are mostly to impart education and/or conduct research so on and so forth. However, the fundamental objective of any organisation is survival. Organisations are not just satisfied with this goal. Further, the goal of most of the organisations is growth and/or profits.

The objectives of HRM may be as follows:

(i) To create and utilise an able and motivated workforce and to accomplish the basic organisational goals.

(ii) To establish and maintain a sound organisational structure and desirable working relationships among all the members of the organisation.

(vi) To secure the integration of an individual and groups within the organisation by co-ordination of the individual and group goals with those of the organisation.

(iv) To create facilities and opportunities for an individual or group development so as to match it with the growth of the organisation.

(v) To attain an effective utilisation of human resources in the achievement of organisational goals.

(vi) To identify and satisfy individual and group needs by providing adequate and equitable wages, incentives, employee benefits and social security and measures for challenging work, prestige, recognition, security, status, etc.

Organisation Structure and HRM Strategies

There are several types of organisation structures. The recent development in the organisation structure is virtual structure. Virtual organisation, according to Biswajeet Pattanayak, is a "social network in which all the horizontal and vertical boundaries are removed. It consists of individuals working out of physically dispersed workspaces, or even individuals working from mobile devices and not tied to any particular workspace. It is the co-ordinated intense structure, consisting primarily of patterns and relationships, and this form needs the communication and information technology to function.

Limited number of executives and employees co-ordinate the functions and activities of various outsourced agencies, combine the human skills, financial resources, marketing/customer needs, advertising agencies, innovations, etc. with the help of communication and information technology. A network of relationships coordinates the manufacturing, financing, human resourcing, marketing and other activities.

There are partial virtual organisations. These organisations physically perform certain activities and outsource the remaining activities. Bata physically markets its products and out sources the manufacturing activities.

Characteristics of virtual organisations: Characteristics of virtual organisations include:

- Flexi-work, Flexi-time and Flexi-work place
- Part-time work
- Job sharing
- Home-based working
- Dependency on information technology like e-mail integration, voicemail, mobile phone network, computer-telephony integration, etc.
- Loose organisational boundaries
- De-jobbing
- Multi-skilling
- Flexibility in power, work, etc
- Goal directed
- Customer centred.

Human Resource Trends in Virtual Organisations:

Human resource trends in virtual organisations include:

- Organisation's human resources are the loose web of people;
- Knowledgeable people are hired for short-term projects depending upon market demand;
- Employees have autonomy at work but are accountable to the targets, performance, etc.;

- Employees can work from their homes (home-cum-office) or from any other place as such social and work environment do not draw much attention of HR Manager.
- Career planning and development are based on projects;
- Employees are selected based not only on technical skills but also on their ability to work in teams; and
- Emotional and attitudinal quotient (EAQ) is the prime factor in employee selection rather than intelligence quotient (IQ).

Employment: It is the first operative function of Human Resources Management (HRM). Employment is concerned with securing and employing the people possessing the required kind and level of human resources necessary to achieve the organisational objectives. It covers functions such as job analysis, human resources planning, recruitment, selection, placement, induction and internal mobility.

Job Enrichment

Job enrichment loads the job vertically. Job enrichment means adding duties and responsibilities that will provide for skill variety, task identity, task significance, autonomy and feedback on job performance. It tries to deal with dissatisfaction by increasing the job depth as work activities from a vertical slice of the organisational unit are combined in one job.

Job enrichment means adding duties and responsibilities that will provide for skill variety, task identity, task significance, autonomy and feedback on job performance.

Job Analysis to Team Analysis

Most of the recent organisations have realised that teamwork produces better results than the performance of individual work. In fact, the practices of Enterprise Resources Planning (ERP), Business Process Reengineering (BPRE) and Supply Chain Management require teamwork. The impact of synergy results in high productivity of teamwork than that of the total of individual employees.

As such, most of the organisations in the 21st century shifted to teamwork and team analysis rather than job analysis. The aspects of team analysis include team description and team specification.

Team Description: Team description is an organised, factual statement of the duties and responsibilities of a complete team.

Team Specification: Team specification pertains to minimum acceptable human qualities and relationships necessary to perform all kinds of activities of the team.

The concept of the team analysis is of recent origin and it is still in the process of conceptualisation. The relevance of job analysis gets eroded slowly with the increase in the applicability of team analysis.

Job Sharing

A job is normally done by one full time employee. The arrangement of sharing one job by two or more part-time employees is called job sharing. Job sharers may work during different shifts or days without overlapping. However, they meet either face-to-face or virtually to discuss and arrange for work schedules, performance and targets. Companies like advertising, accounting, legal, health and financial services adopt job sharing. Apollo Hospitals, Care Hospitals, PricewaterCoopers, Mudra Communications, and Karvy Consultants adopt job sharing.

Telecommuting

Information technology and globalisation brought the flexible work place concept in human resource management. The number of telecommuting employees has been increasing year by year. Telecommuting is the use of personal computers, networks and other communication technology like fax, telephones and e-mail to do work in the home that is traditionally done in the work place. Telecommuting does not involve geographic relocation of employees quite often, but simply involves working at home at least part of the time.

Employee Empowerment

Empowerment refers to enabling a lower level employee to make all the decisions required/relevant for carrying out his duties or discharge his responsibilities, on his own and implement them.

Empowerment refers to enabling a lower level employee to make all the decisions required/relevant for carrying out his duties or discharge his responsibilities, on his own and implement them. Organisational restructuring/reorganisation through Business Process Re-engineering can be possible only with employee empowerment. The liberalisation, globalisation and privatisation resulted in severe competition. The competition forced the companies to serve and satisfy mostly the customer. Therefore, the organisations started empowering the employees to serve the customers better without any loss of time and inconvenience of going around various departments like finance, production and marketing/commercial. Empowerment enables the customer to get the better service/products without the loss of any time and at one point of contact. Thus, the satisfied customer will not only be loyal to the company but acts as a link in the chain of advertisements without any cost.

The recruitment strategies formulated by the companies include:

In-sourcing or Outsourcing: Companies recruit the candidates, employ them, train and develop them and utilise the human resources of these candidates. This strategy is called 'in-sourcing'. Companies formulate and implement this strategy when the corporate strategy shows stable growth. Some organisations employ and develop the candidates with a view to provide the human resources to other companies which concentrate on manufacturing, servicing and such other activities. Some manufacturing and service companies depend for their human resource requirements on such external organisations whose core business is to provide human resources. This strategy is called *'outsourcing'*. Most of the IT companies follow this strategy. Even manufacturing companies also depend on outsourcing for the running of canteens, hospitals, office maintenance, security, housekeeping, plant maintenance, etc. Outsourcing strategy is more suitable for both the fast growing and diversifying companies.

Vast and Fast Source: The fast developing IT industry and high technology oriented industry invariably requires vast human resources within a short span of time. The best strategy to get vast human resources immediately is Internet.

Strategic Management and Performance Appraisal

HRM practices mostly depend upon the strategy adopted by the company. Similarly, performance appraisal practices also depend upon the strategy. Traditional techniques of performance appraisal are appropriate for the stability and sustainable growth strategies.

Similarly, appraisal by the superior is appropriate for these strategies. Modern performance appraisal techniques are suitable for growth strategies like expansion, diversification, joint ventures, mergers and acquisitions. These strategies help the company to meet competition, build competencies, acquire strengths, enhance market share, innovate and create new markets, new products and new technologies. Performance appraisal by the customers, subordinates and peers in addition to the superiors, help the employees to have a feedback from multiple directions, identify their deficiencies and acquire competencies through training and development. In addition, the modern techniques of performance appraisal and 360^0 performance appraisal enhance employee creativity which in turn contributes for the achievement of strategies like new product development, low cost leadership and differentiation strategies.

Team Training

Organisations, today, mostly rely on teamwork and team management to achieve goals. Teamwork is more prevalent in all kinds of activities including production, marketing, customer relationship, supply chain and finance. Teamwork results in synergy and produces greater efficiency for organisational success.

Diversity Training

The number of employees from varied ethnic groups as well as diverse backgrounds has been increasing. In fact, diverse backgrounds bring varied knowledge that helps the organisation in making accurate and efficient decisions. Organisations need to provide diversity training in order to get the advantages of diversity.

(i) Retention Management: Employers prefer to retain more talented employees while they retrench less talented employees. Employers modify the existing human resource strategies and craft new strategies in order to pay more salaries, provide more benefits and create high quality of work life to retain the best employees.

Total Quality Human Resources

Total Quality is defined as, "a... people focused management system that aims at continual increase in customer satisfaction at continually lower cost. Total Quality (TQ) is a total system approach (not a separate area or programme), and an integral part of high level strategy. It works horizontally across functions and departments, involving all employees, top to bottom, and extends backwards and forwards to include the supply chain and customer chain."

Total Quality Management (TQM) is a continuous process of improvement for individuals, groups of people and the total organisation. Unlike other methods, TQM is the concentrated focus on continuous improvement. TQM is about changing the way things are done within the organisation's lifetime. People must know what to do, how to do it, have the right methods to do it and be able to measure the improvement of the process and the current level of achievement in order to improve the process.

Employer's Brand: In view of the scarcity of talent, companies have been formulating strategies to attract talent. One of these strategies is creating and establishing 'employer brand,' in the home and global labour markets especially in the minds of present and prospective employees and employment agencies. Product brand creates, attracts and retains the customers, and similarly, employer brand helps for creating, attracting, developing, utilising and retaining the employees for a particular employer. Employer branding is a critical input in HR marketing. Employer brand is defined as an emotional bond among the employer, the present and prospective employees and various organs of the labour market that creates and builds an organisation's reputation as the most preferred employer.

Employer brand is an emotional bond among the employer, the present and prospective employees and various organs of the labour market that creates and builds an organisation's reputation as the most preferred employer.

Competency Mapping

Competency mapping is the process of identification, evaluation of employees' competencies and organisational requirements and establishing perfect collaboration among them. Competency mapping also includes development and sustainability of competencies based on the changing organisational requirements.

Objectives: Objectives of competency mapping are:

- to align competencies with the strategies of the business
- to select the employees based on job and culture fit
- to plan for career and succession
- to train and develop employees
- for individual and organisational growth.
- **Employment:** The strategic human resource choices in employment include: internal sources or external sources or outsourcing some employees or certain functions like canteen, accounting, security, office maintenance and house keeping. HCL Technologies preferred broad banding to narrow banding in job design and also flat organisation structure to tall structure. The broad jobs at HCL technologies forced the HR Manager to plan for the employees with multi-skills rather than a few skills.

  Another strategic issues involved are long range human resource plan or short range human resource plan, employee selection based on skills or aptitude and extensive socialisation or limited socialisation.

Employee Referrals

Another strategic issue is employee referrals. Traditionally, employee selection process includes; application blank, written test, preliminary interview, group discussion, psychological tests, final interview, line manager's decision and offering employment. This process was necessary in order to know the candidate's skills, knowledge, etc.

Recently, organisations started to enquire the present employees to suggest the candidates with positive attitude, emotional involvement in the company issues and activities, emotional stability, etc. Organisations employ the candidates suggested by the present employees as the present employees judge the candidates' suitability to the job in terms of attitude and emotions. This practice is called employee referrals.

- **Development:** Employee training and executive development choices include: in house training or external training, competency building training or *ad-hoc* training, etc.
- **Performance Appraisal:** Polaris Software Lab appraises the employees based on behaviour whereas Bajaj Auto appraises based on results. The other choices include group criteria or individual criteria, developmental oriented or remedial oriented, use the results for pay or for promotion based on performance, etc.
- **Compensation:** Reliance prefers high base salaries whereas Infosys prefers low base salaries and high perks. Other choices are: fixed package or flexible package, long-term incentives or short-term incentives, equal pay or discriminated pay, etc.
- **Industrial Relations:** Infosys technologies prefer individual negotiation whereas L&T follows collective negotiations. Other choices are: broad employee participation or limited employee participation, partial employee ownership or no employee ownership, employee compliance or employee empowerment, etc.
- **Work Systems:** Zee Telefilms prefers job enrichment whereas Bharat Petroleum Corporation prefers simplified jobs. Wipro follows implicit job analysis while Nirma follows explicit job analysis. Teamwork is practised in Satyam Computer Services whereas individual orientation is preferred in Punjab Tractors. The other choices are: specialised jobs or rotation among jobs, self/peer supervision or close supervision.

- **Organisational Culture:** Organisational cultural choices include creation and maintenance of multi-culture or single culture. Creation of multi-culture includes: employing the candidates with various social, regional and ethnic backgrounds, tolerance for the differences, managing the diversities, etc. Organisational cultural choices are significant today in view of globalisation of business.

Knowledge Management

Most of the software companies have been contributing to knowledge management. First, we discuss the meaning of knowledge and knowledge creation process before we study knowledge management.

What is Knowledge?: Knowledge is the power/capacity for an effective action. The organised data is information. The processed information in the actionable form is referred to as knowledge. The knowledge becomes wisdom when it is used for a good cause for a large number of people. Fig. 9.1 presents the hierarchy of the knowledge.

However, it would be very difficult to make distinctions among data, information and knowledge as one person's data is another person's information. Further, it may be another person's knowledge.

Corporate and Human Resource Strategies

Management should formulate an appropriate human resource strategy for each of the corporate level and SBU level strategies. A number of research studies concluded that HRM activities can be and should be matched or aligned to the corporate and SBU level strategies. Now, we shall discuss human resource strategies appropriate to corporate level and SBU level strategies.

Corporate level Strategies *vis-a-vis* HR Strategies

Stability strategy: The stability strategies include maintenance of *status quo* and sustainable growth. Companies with stability strategy maintain the similar pattern of production, sales and profits. But the other companies in the industry grow during the same period. Therefore, employees may prefer to change the organization or may be frustrated as they carry out same or similar activities.

Appropriate HR strategies in this regard include motivation and retention of skilled employees. Job rotation, job enrichment and empowerment are appropriate HR practices to motivate the frustrated employees. Bajaj Auto followed the job rotation and job enrichment strategies in order to retain the talented employees.

Growth strategies: Organisations select the growth strategies to increase their profits, sales and/or market share and reduce the cost of production per unit. One of the growth strategies is internal growth.

Internal growth is achieved through increasing the firm's production capacity, employees and sales. This strategy preserves the company's efficiency, quality and image. The appropriate HR strategies in this regard include: training the existing employees and promote them to the higher levels, employ the new candidates at the lower level and outsourcing some employees.

Concentration Strategies are achieved through concentrating the firm's efforts on a limited combination of customer groups, customer functions and alternate technologies. Dabur India follows this strategy and concentrates on certain customer functions. It develops the specialised skills of employees through training. Bata India follows the strategy of outsourcing in producing shoes targeted to rich income brackets. Thus, the relevant HR strategies in this regard are training and developing employees and outsourcing specialised skills.

Merger and Acquisition Strategies

A merger is a combination of two or more businesses in which one acquires the assets and liabilities of the other in exchange for stock or cash or both.

Firms prefer to grow through mergers and acquisitions. "A merger is a combination of two or more businesses in which one acquires the assets and liabilities of the other in exchange for stock or cash or both. Companies are dissolved and assets and liabilities are combined and new stock is issued." Examples of merger include merger of Reliance Petroleum with Reliance Industries, Compaq with HP and ICICI Bank with ICICI, etc. Acquisitions/takeovers is defined as "the attempt of one firm to acquire ownership or control over another firm against the wishes of the latter's management." But in practice, takeover can be hostile (against the wishes of the acquired firm) or friendly (through mutual consent of buyer and seller like in merger). For example, merger of VSNL by Tata and CMC by TCS. Though there is the conceptual difference between mergers and acquisition, their effect regarding human resource strategies is the same.

HR managers play significant role in Mergers and Acquisition (M&A) strategy. They help top management in assessing pension, provident fund and other liabilities, labour contracts of the proposed target company, skill, attitude and culture base of the target company. HR strategies include:

- improving the employee morale, managing and unifying the cultural diversity, counselling the employees regarding resistance to change, and adoption to the new system and procedures which help the employees in allaying the fears of losing jobs,
- work pressures through counseling and open communication.

Other strategies are integrating the two wage structures, benefit programmes, seniority, etc. In case of retrenchment of surplus staff (which is mostly necessary in M&A), HR managers prepares an equitable and severance package and arrange outplacement assistance. HR managers also establish career and succession plans, clarify leadership style and cultural issues, etc.

- Create a new organisation structure that does not exist in either of the company.
- Assess the HR strengths of both the organisations and strengthen them further.
- Try to convert the HR weaknesses of both the companies into strengths, if possible, otherwise get rid of them. Exhibit 9.3 presents guidelines for HR professionals for dealing with mergers and acquisitions.

Exhibit 9.3: Guidelines for HR Professionals for Dealing with a Merger or Acquisition

1. Insist on early involvement, even as the combination is being considered. This allows a preventive rather than a curative stance.
2. Document everything – Record as much as possible in writing and ahead of time.
3. Learn the other company's personality and plan for any possible cultural mismatch.
4. As planning progresses, adopt a "plan, announce, act", pattern, using thought-out and deliberate actions, always announced beforehand.
5. Inform those employees who will lose their jobs as soon as possible so they can plan accordingly, but also induce them to stay as long as they are needed by the organisation.
6. Eliminate the "we/they' attitude by mixing employees as much as possible at all levels in the newly combined organisation.
7. Realize that staff areas are affected especially hard, and spend time accordingly. As duplications occur, safety valves such as early retirement should be available.
8. Communicate in all organizational directions, through all media to formal and informal leaders and to work groups. Communications enhance a feeling of security and reduce rumours.

Source: David Robino and Kenneth DeMuse, *"Corporate Mergers and Acquisitions: Their Impact on HRM."*

Horizontal Integration: Horizontal integration strategy aims at related diversification. For example, Coca-cola diversified to produce mineral water 'Kinley'. BPL producing TV's diversified to produce washing machines. L&T constructions diversified to produce cement. Relevant human resources strategies are to train and develop the existing employees to provide the skills necessary in the area of new businesses. Other strategies are employing the new candidates for the diversified business, formulation of performance appraisal schemes and compensation and industrial relations schemes slightly different from those of the existing business.

Conglomerate Diversification: Conglomerate diversification is diversification into unrelated activity to the original business of the company. For example, Gujarat Gas Ltd., created another business unit, *i.e.*, Gujarat Finance Company Ltd. The company should perform HRM functions altogether different from those of the existing company. However, the company may adopt the strategy to train the existing employees in the new business areas, skills, etc., and transfer them to the diversified business area.

Joint Ventures: Joint ventures are partnerships in which two or more firms carry out a specific project. Joint ventures can be temporary, complete or partial. For example, Maruti and Suzuki, Modi and Xerox, Tata and Corus, etc. As in case of M&A, this strategy also brings the cultural diversity as a major HR issue. The HR manager, therefore, should formulate the programme for management of cultural diversity. Another HR strategy is to train the existing employees in the new technologies and systems of the partner company. Other HR strategies include compensation package, agreements, etc., with the employees deputed by the partner company.

Retrenchment Strategies: The third major class of strategic alternatives available to a firm is retrenchment strategies. Retrenchment strategies include: turnaround strategies, captive company strategy, divestment strategy and liquidation strategy. Companies like HCL, State Bank of India, Polaris Software Lab, Visakha Steel Plant of SAIL, etc., adopted turnaround strategies.

Retrenchment strategies include: turnaround strategies, captive company strategy, divestment strategy and liquidation strategy.

Bokaro Steel Plant and Andhra Pradesh Paper Mills Ltd. adopted the turnaround strategy through HRD approach. They employed the HR strategies like open communication, employee counselling, reduction in the labour cost (without employee retrenchment) by enhancing labour productivity, attitudinal change, etc.

HR Strategies for liquidation and divestment strategies include retrenchment, outplacement assistance, cut in salaries, perks, long leave without pay, train the employees and re-deploy them in sister organisations, reduce the managerial staff, delayering, downsizing of the organisation and the like. Other HR strategies include: conducting companywide and departmentwise open meetings in order to create the awareness of the strategies, establish the climate acceptable to employees, provide incentives to the employees seeking to leave the company, etc.

Now, we shall discuss the HR strategies appropriate for SBU Level strategies.

SBU Level Strategies and Relevant HR Strategies

SBU level generic strategies are low cost leadership, differentiation and focus.

- **Low Cost Leadership:** Companies pursuing low cost leadership aggressively seek efficiencies in all operations including human resources to gain an edge over the competitors. For example, Dr. Reddy's Lab and Ranbaxy adopt low cost strategy.

Low cost does not mean cost controls and cost cuts including operating with fewer employees. The HR strategies those fit cost leadership include: enhancing labour productivity, improving skills, reducing movement time of the employee at work place, etc. Other HR strategies include: Low participation, explicit job criteria, mostly internal sources, narrow career paths, results criteria, short-term criteria, mostly individual criteria, little employment security, few incentives, hierarchical pay, little training and traditional labour/management relations.

- **Differentiation Strategy:** This strategy involves an attempt of the company to produce the product or render the services different from its competitors. The relevant HR strategies include developing creative skills of the employees through training, providing freedom to the employees, empowering the employees, etc.

- **Focus/Niche Strategy:** This strategy focuses or concentrates on a specific market or customer group. The relevant HR strategies include: high employee participation, narrow career paths, etc. Other HR strategies in this regard include: High participation, explicit job criteria, some external sources, narrow career paths, mostly results criteria, mostly short-term criteria, some group criteria, some employment security, some incentives, egalitarian pay, extensive training, and co-operative labour/management relations.

Human Resource Matrix

Human resource management functions can't be performed in isolation. They have to be aligned horizontally with the other functions like production and operations, marketing, finance and research and development. Similarly, they have to be aligned vertically with the policies and strategies formulated by the top level of the organisation to serve the current and future customers.

HR matrix looks like business process reengineering around the customers or clients rather than following superior-subordinate relationship in the traditional organisational chart. HR matrix first considers the priorities of the customers and expects all functions of all departments to align their functions around customer needs. Then, it aligns its functions and activities around customer expectations and other departments' activities in order to optimise the performance and outcome in achieving company's strategies and in serving the customer. This in turn, structures the teams from across the organisation based on the client's interest and to serve the client at a fast rate. In fact, organisations reengineer their business processes to suit the customers as well as to fit the strategic requirements.

e-Business and HRM Strategy

e-business is about using the convenience, availability and worldwide reach to enhance the existing business or to create new virtual business. According to the concept developed by the IBM, E-business combines the traditional information system with the vast reach of the web and connects critical business systems directly to critical business constituencies, *viz.*, production, marketing, finance, customers, suppliers and employees via, internets, extra nets and the World Wide Web.

e-business within the organisation uses the Intranet. Business-to-business (B2B) dealings take place over the extranet. Extranet consists of two or more Intranets connected via the Internet whereby two organisations are allowed to have access to the information of each other and to interact with each other.

Aspects of e-HRM

Thus, the electronic aspect of e-business processes transmits the information in the original form and/or in the processed form to all the parties concerned. Now, we shall discuss the electronic aspect of human resource management, i.e., e-HRM.

Electronic aspect is embodied in all the areas of HRM where there is transmission of information from one employee to another employee and from one client to other both internally and in the processed form are highly essentials in most of the functions and activities of HRM. Now, we shall discuss each of the important aspects of e-HRM.

e-Job Design and Job Analysis

Job Design and Job Analysis: Most of the organisations tended towards 'de-jobbing' environment and introduced alternative work schedules, flexi-work, broad job banding, employee empowerment, multi-skilling, etc.

HR Manager's job under this environment is identifying the skill requirements of the company, identifying the employee skills and matching these two. HR managers do these activities through 'listing skills' and 'competency mapping'. The information of listing skills and competency mapping are placed on the net. Then, the system matches the listing skills and competency mapping and produces the output of identifying the employee suitable for a particular task/activity. Thus, the EHR plays a vital role in de-jobbed environment.

e-Human Resource Planning

Computer programmes are developed and used extensively for the purpose of planning human resource requirements based on the data and information. These programmes indicate the number of employees required at each level for each category of the jobs based on sales and production forecasts. The extranet which connects the intranets of different organisations identifies the suitable people from other organisations for the purpose of outsourcing and also to draw them where and when contingency situations arise.

e-Recruitment

Organisations advertise the job vacancies through the World Wide Web (www) or send the information directly to the most competent people through e-mail. The job seekers send their applications through e-mail using the Internet. Alternatively, job seekers place their CVs in the World Wide Web through various sites like hot jobs.com and jobs.com, which can be drawn by the prospective employers depending upon their requirements.

e-Selection

e-selection has become popular with the conduct of various tests through online, contacting the candidates through e-mail and conducting the preliminary interviews and the final interview through audio-conferencing and videoconferencing. Further, the employers get the reference letters/ opinions from the referees through e-mail.

e-Performance Management

Further, organisations use computer networks, sophisticated telephone systems, and video equipments to monitor and record the employee work activities.

Several software packages are developed to measure employee performance and offer suggestions for improvement of employee performance. Many employers tend towards using these software packages and computerise the employee performance appraisal systems.

The software on employee performance appraisal provides a number of statements and sub-statements on each of the performance categories. The appraiser selects and clicks the appropriate rating for each statement. The system generates a detailed report, by the time the appraiser has moved all the performance categories and sub-factors. This report can be modified, comments can be added or deleted by the appraiser and a final report can be prepared by the manager.

e-Training and Development

Companies started providing online training and online executive development. Employees learn various skills by staying at the place of their work. Participants complete course work from wherever they have access to computer and Internet.

e-learning via intranet (Internet is now a global phenomenon and is central to training and development to many companies.

e-learning represents the total category of technology based learning while online learning is synonymous with web based learning. The term e-learning covers a wide set of applications and processes, including computer based learning, web-based learning, virtual classrooms and digital collaboration.

e-learning is enabled by the delivery of content via all electronic media, including the Internet, intranets, extranets, satellite broadcast, audio/video tape, interactive TV and CD-ROM.

Now, we shall study the research and development strategies.

(F) RESEARCH AND DEVELOPMENT STRATEGIES

Research and development include transfer of technology, adjusting production process to the local raw materials, adopting product ingredients and features to the tastes and preferences of local customers/target markets.

Research and development include transfer of technology, adjusting production process to the local raw materials, adopting product ingredients and features to the tastes and preferences of local customers/target markets. Research and development also include new product development modification/improvement of existing products, market penetration and market segmentation. R&D link the internal strengths with the opportunities provided by the external environment. In addition, they minimise internal weaknesses based on external opportunities.

Further R&D strategies improve implementation efforts to:

- enhance product and process improvements
- stress basic and applied research
- become leaders and/or followers in research and development
- develop robotics and/or manual-type process
- spend a high, average or low amount of money and R&D
- perform R&D within the firm or to outsource R&D activities
- use university/college/professional researches.

R&D department continuously interacts with other departments like production, marketing, human resource and finance for matching the departmental requirements with the results of R&D. Exhibit 9.4 Presents the linkages of R&D activities with the strategies.

Exhibit 9.4: Linkage between Strategy and R&D Activity

Type of Organisation	Strategy	R&D Activity
Pharmaceutical Company	Product Development	Test the efforts of new drug or different sub-groups
Boat Manufacturer	Concentric Diversification	Test the performance of various keel designs under various conditions
Plastic Container Manufacturer	Market Penetration	Develop biodegradable container
Electronics Company	Market Development	Develop a telecommunication System in a foreign country

Source: Fred R. David, "*Strategic Management*", Pearson, 2003 p. 291.

(G) INFORMATION STRATEGIES

Management Information System

Management requires accurate and timely information relating to a problem or an issue to make effective decisions at the right time. Management Information System (MIS) is a formal method of making available to management accurate and timely information necessary to facilitate the decision-making process and enable the organisation's planning, control and operational functions to becarried out effectively.

MIS strategies aim at providing accurate, relevant and timely information for making effective decisions, by eliminating duplication of work. Further, they aim at:

- Saving time by using more efficient methods;
- Establishing uniform procedures;
- Identifying responsibility for work and performance;
- Improving service, including providing necessary training for all who operate within the system;
- Promoting acceptance both of the system and of possible changes;
- Addressing the primary needs of management function;
- To contain sufficient and relevant information to minimise uncertainty in a format that can be easily understood and be usable without further modification.

A computer based decision support system that contains a central database, permits each functional area to access information it needs and to communicate electronically with the other functional departments as necessary. This facility helps each department to keep abreast of what other departments do and co-ordinate its efforts accordingly. MIS evolves through four stages, *viz.*, *(i)* At the first stage, companies use electronic data for cost reduction, accounting application, etc; *(ii)* Computer applications in the second stage spread into all functional areas; *(iii)* the third stage, focuses, on certain control activities such as purchasing and scheduling; *(iv)* the final stage is the most sophisticated, involving decision support applications such as planning models, simulations, online uses in human resources, cost analysis and order entries. This stage enables the company to develop competitive advantages.

Exhibit 9.5 presents the R&D strategies under different conditions.

Exhibit 9.5: R&D Strategies under Different Conditions

	Conditions	R&D Strategies
(1)	Low rate of technical progress, moderate growth of market, significant entry barriers for new entrants.	In-House R&D
(2)	Rapid technological change, market growth is slow.	Low R&D effort
(3)	Slow technological change, fast market growth.	Outsource R&D activity
(4)	Fast technical growth and fast marketing growth acquiring expertise from outside	Concentrate on R&D by acquiring expertise from outside

Source: Adapted from John Brown and Neil Agnew, "Corporate Agility", *Business Horizons*, 25, no.2, March-April 1982, p. 29.

R&D Approaches: R&D approaches towards strategy crafting are:

- **First Mover:** The first mover approach is to be the first company to market the technology in the industry. This is more or less like the first mover. This approach enjoys the advantages of the first mover and suffers from the limitations of the first mover strategy. 3M and General Electric were successful with this strategy implementation.

- **Imitator:** The second approach is imitating the successful technologies and products. This strategy is like the follower strategy. Under this strategy, a pioneer firm develops the technology/new products, implements it and once it is successful, other firms in the industry imitate the innovations.
- **Low-cost Strategy:** Under this strategy, once the innovation of technology/product is successful, the firm concentrates on reducing the cost of production as the new product's price normally would be very high. For example, the cost of a mobile phone was above Rs. 10,000 when it was introduced in India. Many firms later concentrated on cost and reduced the cost as low as Rs. 600 per piece. Similarly, the mobile phone call service initially was priced at Rs. 60 per minute of an outgoing call and it is reduced to as low as Re. 0.50. Thus, companies adopt various R&D strategies to reduce cost. (See Box 9.1).

BOX 9.1 JAPAN TRIO TO MERGE MOBILE UNITS

Japanese electronics groups Hitachi, Casio and NEC have announced plans to merge their mobile phone operations to cut costs and become more competitive.

The three companies, which are relatively small players in the mobile phone market, will share both technology and resources. By next year, NEC will own 71% of the new business, with Casio owning 20% and Hitachi holding a 9% stake. The merger will create Japan's second largest mobile phone maker. Analysts say there could be further consolidation in the competitive Japanese mobile phone market.

Record loss

Casio and Hitachi created a joint mobile phone venture in 2004. It makes handsets for Japanese mobile carriers KDDI Corp and Softbank Mobile Corp, while NEC makes phones for NTT Docomo and Softbank. All three companies have suffered badly during the downturn.

NEC is in the process of cutting 20,000 jobs worldwide, while Hitachi recently announced that it expects to make a loss of 270bn yen ($3bn; £1.8bn) this year. The firm made a loss of 787.3bn yen last year - a record for a Japanese manufacturer.

Source: http://news.bbc.co.uk/2/hi/business/8254135.stm (16/09/09)

Integrating the Functional Areas Further

All functional areas must be executed in perfect co-ordination to implement the generic strategy successfully. However, strategy issues depend upon tight integration of all functional strategies discussed so far. Tight integration requires perfect interweaving of one functional area/strategy with all functional areas/strategies. Companies can achieve a competitive advantage by accomplishing complete functional co-ordination and collaboration. Companies achieve superior efficiency, superior quality, superior product design, superior speed and superior guarantee, through functional coordination.

Now, we shall discuss each of these aspects.

(H) INTEGRATED FUNCTIONAL STRATEGIES: SUPERIOR EFFICIENCY

Efficiency means doing things right. In other words, efficiency is achieving a higher output for a given input. Prime activity of business organisations is conversion of inputs into output. Efficient business produce more for a given input compared to other businesses. In other words, the efficient businesses achieve higher productivity. Higher productivity indicates that the companies produce more for a given input compared to other firms. This in turn results in reduction in cost of production per unit. Thus, higher efficiency or higher productivity leads to reduction in cost of production per unit of output. Economies of scale are the major factor that contributes for the lower cost of production per unit.

Economies of Scale: Increase in the volume of production up to a certain stage would be possible without the increase in the investment in fixed assets. Therefore, the fixed cost per unit of production is reduced up to that stage. This reduction in the fixed cost per unit of production is a source of large scale economies. Reliance Petroleum produces larger volumes and enjoys lower cost of production per unit of output.

Division of labour and specialisation contribute for increased efficiency, higher productivity, better quality and lowest breakage and spoilage of the production process. Thus, they contribute for lowering the cost of production per unit. Thus, division of labour and specialisation contribute for the large-scale economies. Ford Motor Company by introducing greater division of labour and specialisation could produce cars on mass production. This in turn, contributed to the reduction of cost of production per car by US $1958.

Companies select the merger strategy in order to increase the volume of their business operations and enjoy the economics of scale. This in turn helps them to achieve the low cost leadership strategy. The merger of PNG Banking Corporation with the South Pacific Bank helped the bank to open more number of branches, reduce the costs of human resource, rent, equipment, etc., per unit and serve the customer at a less cost and at the same time increased its total profits.

Diseconomies: Companies enjoy the economies of scale up to a certain stage as increase in production beyond that stage results in disappearance of economies. This is due to the fact that production starts increasing after that stage as the company invests in additional capacities. This increase in cost of production per unit is due to the association of diseconomies.

Companies should know the stage of operation up to which they earn economies of scale and beyond which the diseconomies associate. Companies should stop their operation at this stage to maximise their large scale economies and minimise the diseconomies. Point Q1 in Fig. 9.2 is the stage where economies of scale disappear and diseconomies of scale start. Companies should stop their production/operations at this stage.

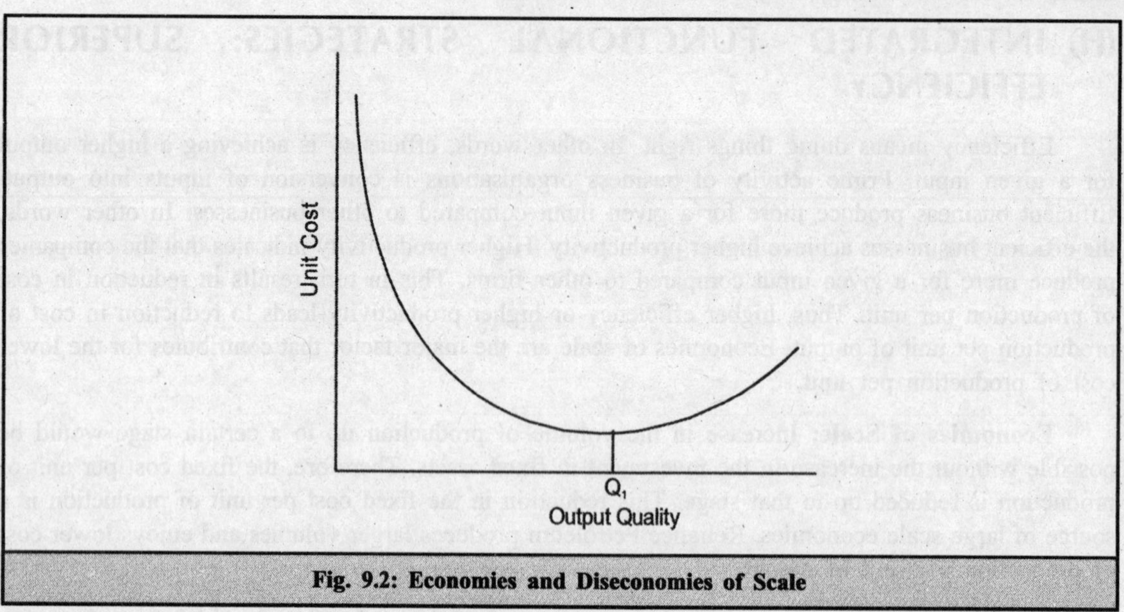

Fig. 9.2: Economies and Diseconomies of Scale

Learning Effects and Efficiency

Today, most of organisations prefer to be learning organisations. Organisations become learning organisations when their employees learn continuously. In fact, change and competition drive organisations and the individuals to be the life long learners. Individual employees exert superior performance when they learn higher level knowledge and acquire upper level skills, which in turn reduces the cost per unit of output. In fact, the impact of learning along with economies of scale would reduce the cost of production/operation more than that of economies of scale alone as depicted in Fig. 9.3.

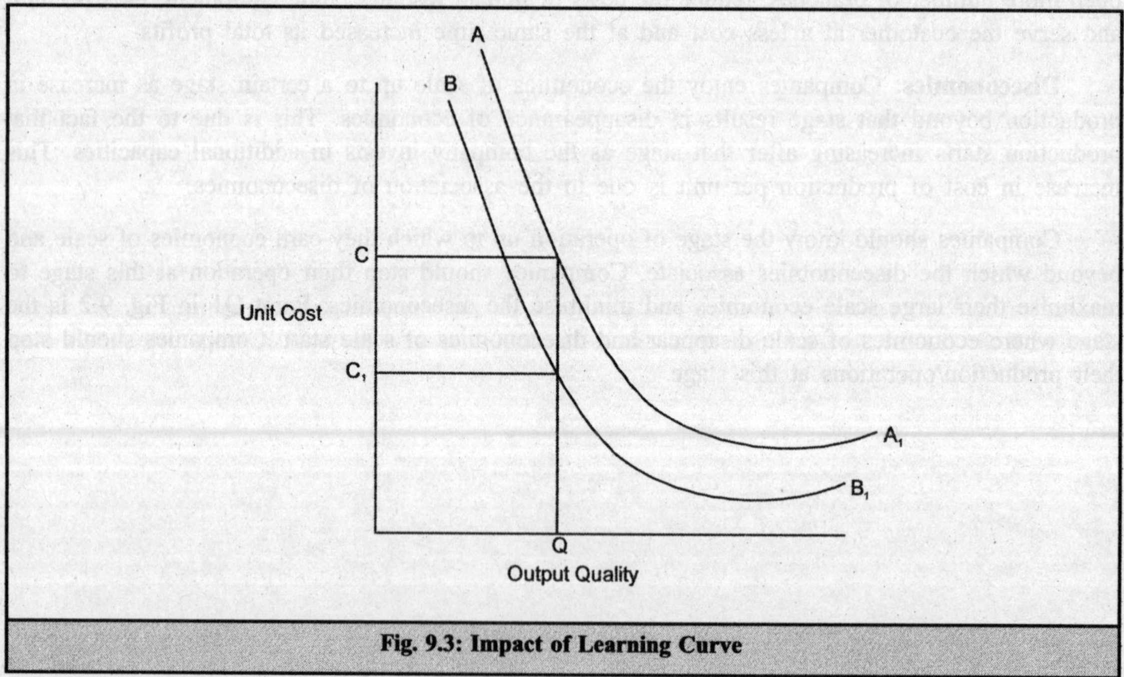

Fig. 9.3: Impact of Learning Curve

Curve AA_1 indicates the unit cost due to economies of scale whereas curve BB_1 indicates the unit cost due to economies of scale along with the learning effects. Unit cost is C with economies of scale and C_1 with economies of scale along with learning effects at the same level of output at 'Q'.

Experience Curve and Efficiency

When the employees do the same work continuously for quite a long period, they acquire experience, which in turn enhances the employee's efficiency. Similarly, when firms produce the same product continuously for a quite longer period, their efficiency increases along with the increase in experience. Thus, the increase in efficiency along with increase in experience result in reduction in cost per unit. The firms enjoying the benefits of experience curve along with learning curve effects and scale of economies reduce the cost much more than that of other organisations which enjoy the scale of economies along with learning curve effects and those enjoy only scale of economies. Fig 9.4 predicts the impact of the experience curve along with the learning curve effects and economies of scale.

Increase in efficiency along with increase in experience result in reduction in cost per unit.

Curve XX_1 indicates the unit cost due to economies of scale, curve YY_1 indicates the unit cost due to economies of scale and learning curve effects whereas ZZ_1 indicates unit cost due to economies of scale along with learning cure and experience curve effects. Unit cost is C_1 with economies of scale, C_2 with economies of scale and learning effects and C_3 with economies of scale, learning curve effects along with experience curve effects at the same level of output at 'Q'.

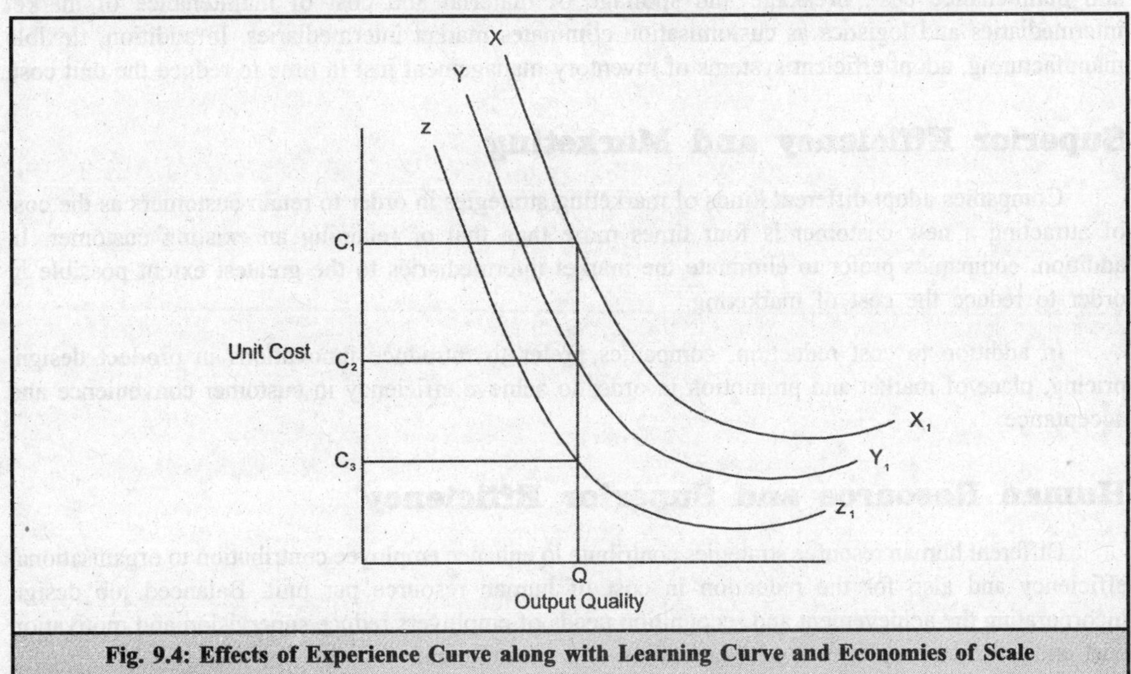

Fig. 9.4: Effects of Experience Curve along with Learning Curve and Economies of Scale

Thus, the firms enjoying the benefits of large scale economies along with the benefits of learning curve and experience curve produce at the lowest cost per unit compared to their competitors.

Caution: However, too much experience sometimes may produce negative results of increase in unit costs. Too much experience sometimes drive the firm to produce based on the same procedure without thinking innovatively. For example, Texas Instruments which enjoyed the benefits of experience curve during 1960 and 1980 habituated to have single-minded focus on cost reduction and failed to understand customer needs and market trends after 1982. Consequently, competitors like Casio and Hewlett-Packard gained the market share for the Texas Instruments. Therefore, companies should not excessively rely on the benefits of experience curve. They should also focus on other areas of strategy like technology, customer, political, social and economics factors.

Superior Efficiency vs. Customisation

Globalisation, liberalisation and privatisation led to severe competition, which in turn resulted in customisation of production and services. But, as we discussed earlier, firms can achieve efficiency and thereby low unit cost owing to large scale economies, learning curve effect and experience curve effect.

However, the development of a flexible manufacturing technology or lean production could meet the challenges of customisations and the probability of increase in unit cost. Flexible manufacturing technologies designed, "to reduce set up times for complex equipment, increase the use of individual machines through better scheduling and improve quality control at all stages of the manufacturing process." Research also suggests that low unit cost of production like that of standardised and mass production could be achieved with customisation. As such, the term mass customisation has been coined. The once upon a time's conflicting objectives, *viz.*, low cost and differentiation, became harmonious and compatible objectives with the help of flexible manufacturing technology.

Customisation also contributes to the low unit cost as the firms can reduce inventory handling and maintenance cost, breakage and spoilage of material and cost of maintenance of market intermediaries and logistics as customisation eliminates market intermediaries. In addition, flexible manufacturing, adopt efficient systems of inventory management just in time to reduce the unit cost.

Superior Efficiency and Marketing

Companies adopt different kinds of marketing strategies in order to retain customers as the cost of attracting a new customer is four times more than that of retaining an existing customer. In addition, companies prefer to eliminate the market intermediaries to the greatest extent possible in order to reduce the cost of marketing.

In addition to cost reduction, companies prefer to introduce innovations in product design, pricing, place of market and promotion in order to achieve efficiency in customer convenience and acceptance.

Human Resource and Superior Efficiency

Different human resource strategies contribute to enhance employee contribution to organisational efficiency and also for the reduction in cost of human resource per unit. Balanced job design incorporating the achievement and recognition needs of employers reduce supervision and motivation cost and enhance employee's self motivation and commitment.

- Employee referrals and online recruitment enhance recruitment effectiveness and reduce the cost.
- Self managed teams would result in synergy which contributes to the higher productivity, lowering unit cost, quality improvement and reduction in the need for supervision and control.
- Employer branding inspires the best of the prospective employees to seek employment in the company, which in turn results in the employment of more qualified and competent human resources.
- Employee empowerment enables the employers to make use of the best potentialities, reduce the organisational hierarchies, speed up the decision-making and implementation process.
- Employee competency mapping allows the managers at various levels, in various departments and locations to spot out and utilise the competencies of employees.

- Employee training strategies enable the employees to develop their skills and knowledge in tune with organisational strategies. This in turn makes the skills readily available for implementation of strategies.

- Discriminative remuneration enables the high performers to contribute significantly for the enhancement of productivity as well as quality. This in turn motivates other employees to, enhance commitment and organisational loyalty. To sum up, it contributes to employee job satisfaction.

- Online training strategies as well as collaborative efforts for training reduces cost, increases benefits and conveniences and augment the fit between organisational training needs and performance.

- Variety of benefits improves employee's sense of belongingness, enhances employee's commitment to the jobs and organisation, which in turn contributes for the cost reduction and quality improvement.

- The strategies of flextime, flexi-workplace and flexible work provide convenience to employee, enhance innovation and reduce cost.

Information System and Efficiency

Information technology including Internet brought paradigm shifts in all functional areas of businesses like manufacturing, marketing, finance and human resources. Information technology enables the companies to locate the manufacturing facilities in a number of locations across the world. These enabled the companies to increase productivity and reduce the cost. Cisco, Dell and IDBI Bank use web-based information for efficient and low cost coordination. Web-based programmes provide easy interaction with the suppliers of raw material, marketing intermediaries and customers.

Web-based programmes provide absolute co-ordination among various machines, production processes, and warehouses, reducing the processing time, deviations from standards and breakage/ wastage. Thus, information technology and internet enhance efficiency.

Now, we shall study the contribution of functional strategies for achieving a superior quality.

Superior Quality

Various functional strategies contribute to the product reliability and product attributes. Product reliability as promised contributes to product quality. Total Quality Management (TQM) is a continuous process of improvement for individual, groups and the total organisation. TQM works horizontally across functions and departments, involving all employees from top to bottom and extends backwards and towards to include the supply-chain and customer-chain.

The quality emphasis, initially, was on quality control as a defensive mechanism. However, today, the emphasis is shifted to strategic quality management. The dimensions of quality of products include:

- Performance of the products in terms of operating characteristics.

- Product features, though they are not as vital as product primary operating characteristics, are important.

- Reliability: Reliability is the successful functioning of the product uninterruptedly for a particular span of time.

- Durability: Durability is the expected operational life of the product.
- Conformance is meeting of the established standards by the process and individual components of the product.
- Serviceability: Serviceability is related to the ability to be repaired at a fast rate, availability of spare parts, competence to undertake repair and courtesy to carry out the repair.

The dimensions of quality in services include: reliability, tangibles, responsiveness, assurance and empathy.

Why superior quality? Achieving efficiency in superior quality is essential due to the cost of poor quality. Costs of poor quality include cost of prevention, cost of detection/appraisal and cost of failure. Cost of failure can be internal failure costs and external failure costs. Internal failure costs are those associated with producing defective products that are identified prior to shipment. External failure costs are those associated with producing defective products that are identified after deliverey to the customer.

Organisations initiate total quality management (TQM) in order to avoid the costs of quality failure.

Total Quality Management

As mentioned earlier, total quality management is a continuous process and an organization-wide approach that focuses on producing superior quality products and services. TQM is an integral part of an organisation and encompasses all the functional areas and levels in an organisation including input suppliers.

The primary element of TQM are leadership, employee involvement, products/process excellence and customer focus. TQM in its turn enable for achieving all-round superior quality.

Leadership: TQM process involves vision, mission, and strategy communication which are the functions of an efficient leadership. A leader can formulate and implement quality strategy with full commitment by involving and inspiring the employees and suppliers.

Employee Involvement: Employee involvement is the entire TQM process. The employees should be involved in data and information gathering, decision-making, problem identification, idea generation, development of viable solutions and the like.

Product/Process Excellence: Product or process excellence includes quality in product design, analysis of field failures, statistical process quality and other analytical tools.

Customer Focus: Customer focus is in Quality, which means conformance to the customer needs. Therefore, customers' demand and views should be taken into account in quality design and maintenance.

Six Sigma: Motorola introduced quality improvement programme in order to produce very high quality programmes. This quality improvement programme is known as "Six Sigma", whose goal is to reduce process variation to the point where the defects rate is only 3.4 per million products.

Deming suggests TQM philosophy on the following five-step reaction:

- TQM reduces/avoids the costs of poor quality and thus, reduces/costs of production.
- Improvement in productivity;
- Improved quality enables market share and enjoys a high margin or higher price and high profit.

- Improvement in market share and stability in business.
- Company can create more employment opportunities.

Advantages of superior quality: Achieving superior quality and total quality brings the following advantages:

- Producing a qualitative product reduces the quantity of defects, which causes the yield to increase,
- Producing the right product the first time reduces the number of rejects and time and money spent on network,
- Making the production employees responsible for quality, eliminates the need for inspection
- Improvement of quality converts the wastage of employee hours and machine time into the manufacturing of good products and better service. Improvement in quality naturally and inevitably begets improvement of product.

Superior customer service: Pre-sales and post-sales customer service assume greater significance in an integrated approach of all functions and in formulating the overall functional strategies. Customer service also differentiates product from that of the competitor. Customer service also includes product serviceability. Therefore, product features, durability, conformance, and technical compatibility in terms of availability of spare parts and technical skills, competence of service employees and courtesy of the service employees carry out the maintenance activities of the product functioning.

The company should focus on customer's current and prospective needs, design and develop products based on such needs. Customers, themselves may not know their needs in most cases.

Therefore, company based on its innovations, research and development efforts should identify such needs. Company leadership should also focus on customer needs. In addition, the leader should inspire employees to develop a positive attitude and mindset of employees towards customer focus.

As we discussed in production strategies, and low cost strategies, customization of products also brings a low cost owing to flexible manufacturing technology or lean production and flexible machine calls. Customization of products/services enhances the quality of customer service.

Recession and Customer Service: Superior Customer Service helps the company particularly during recession by enhancing customer retention In addition, superior customer services and customization divert the customer's mind low priced products to the products of the company that renders superior customer service during the boom and recessionary periods.

Superior Customer Service

Pre-sales and post-sales customer service assume greater significance in an integrated approach of all functions and in formulating overall functional strategies. Customer service differentiates the product from that of the competitor. Customer service also includes product serviceability. Therefore, product features, durability, conformance, and technical compatibility in terms of availability of spare parts and technical skills, competence of service employees and courtesy of the service employees to carry out the maintenance activities of the product functioning.

Pre-sales and post-sales customer service assume greater significance in an integrated approach of all functions and in formulating overall functional strategies.

Company should focus on customer's current and prospective needs, design and develop products based on such needs. Customers, themselves may not know their needs in most cases.

Therefore, company based on its innovations, research and development efforts should identify such needs. Company leadership should also focus on customer needs. In addition, leader should inspire employees to develop positive attitude and mindset of employees towards customer focus.

As we discussed in production strategies, and low cost strategy, customisation of products also brings low cost owing to flexible manufacturing technology or lean production and flexible machine cells. Customisation of products/services enhances the quality of customer service.

Recession and Customer Service: Superior customer service helps the company particularly during recession by enhancing customer retention. In addition, superior customer service and customisation diverts the customer's mind from low price requirement, infrequent purchases, postponement of purchase, shift to low priced products to the product of the company that renders superior customer service during the boom and recessionary periods.

Superior Guarantee

Problems of functioning, quality, etc., occasionally arise and result in less than acceptable product/services. Companies, in order to avoid the consequences of these problems to customers, guarantee the customer against acceptable quality and functioning gains, which provides a competitive advantage over the competitors. A service guarantee is more challenging to provide than a product guarantee. There are five desirable characteristics that are to be included in a service guarantee. They are:

(i) The guarantees should be unconditional, with no exceptions.

(ii) It should be easily understood and written in simple language.

(iii) The guarantee should be meaningful by guaranteeing what is important to the customer and making it worth the customer's time and effort to invoke the guarantee, should he or she be dissatisfied.

(iv) The guarantee should be convenient to invoke and not require the customer to appeal to several layers of bureaucracy.

(v) The customer should be satisfied promptly, without a lengthy waiting period.

Conclusion: Strategies at functional level, *viz.*, production/operations, marketing, finance, human resource and information bring integrated strategies. These strategies include achieving superior efficiency that results in producing at the lowest cost, superior quality, superior customer service and superior guarantee. Theses strategies enable the company to achieve its business unit level and corporate level strategies efficiently.

POINTS TO BE REMEMBERED

- Product design strategies include market driven product design strategies, technology driven product strategies and inter-functional strategies.
- Marketing strategy is the analysis, strategy development and implementation of activities.
- Finance is the fundamental resource for starting and conducting of a business.
- Human resource strategies bring the efficient management of people which in turn influence the people to take care of the customers and thus, the business of the company.
- Integration of all functional strategies enables the company to achieve a superior efficiency that result in superior quality, customisation of products, superior customer service and superior guarantee.

KEY WORDS

- Production Strategies
- Marketing Strategies
- Finance Strategies
- Human Resource Strategies
- Research Strategies
- Information Strategies
- Superior Efficiency
- Superior Quality
- Low Cost
- Economies of Scale
- Superior Performance
- Superior Customer Service
- Superior Guarantee
- Customisation

QUESTIONS FOR DISCUSSION

(1) Discuss the significant production and operation strategies.

(2) State the financial management strategies that affect the company's operations.

(3) What are the marketing strategies? How do they influence business unit level strategies?

(4) Discuss the human resource management strategies. Why do these strategies influence the organisational strategies?

(5) What are the information strategies?

(6) How do the functional strategies result in superior efficiency?

(7) How do the learning curve and experience curve result in low cost of operations?

(8) What is superior quality? How do the companies achieve it?

(9) Discuss the significance of superior customer service.

REFERENCES

1. David W. Cravens, "*Strategic Marketing*", Irwin, Sydney, p. 90.
2. Frank Leonard, *et.al.*, "The Incline of Quality", *Harvard Business Review*, September-October 1982, pp. 163-171.
3. Philip Kotler, "*Marketing Management*", Pearson, New Delhi, 2003, pp. 322-324.
4. Johnson R.L., "*Financial Decision Making*", Good year, 1973.
5. J.M Pandy, *Financial Management*," Vikas Publishg House Pvt.Ltd; New Delhi, 2005, pp.618-619
6. L.M. Payday, *op.cit.*, p 934
7. I M pandy , *op.cit.*, p.879
8. L.M. Pandey, *op.cit.*, p. 887.
9. G. Stalk and T. M. Hout, "Competing Against Time", *Free Press*, New York 1990 and D. Miller, "The Icarus Paradox", *Harper Business*, 1990. Quoted in Charles W.L. Hill and Gareth R. Jones, "Strategic Management", *Biztantra*, New Delhi, 2004, p. 116.
10. Quoted in Charles W.L. Hill and Gareth R. Jones, *op. cit.*, p.118.
11. Mark M. Davis and Janalle Heineke, "*Operations Management*", MCGraw-Hill, Boston, 2005, pp. 285- 286.
12. Quoted in Charles W. L. Hill and Gareth R. Jones, "Strategic Management", *Biztantra*, New Delhi, 2004, p. 128.

✦ ✦ ✦

10 CHAPTER STRATEGIC ANALYSIS AND CHOICE

Chapter Outline

(A) Introduction

(B) Criteria for Evaluating Strategic Alternatives

(C) The Input Stage

(D) The Matching Stage Corporate Portfolio Analysis

(E) Selection of the Matrix

(F) The Decision Stage

Learning Objectives

After studying this chapter, you should be able to:

- Study the criteria for evaluating strategic alternatives;
- Analyse and match strengths and opportunities and weaknesses and threats;
- Discuss the criteria for analysing strategic alternatives by using various matrices like BCG, GE Nine-Cell matrix and the directional policy matrix;
- Study the selection of matrix in terms of industry attractiveness and business unit strength;
- Analyse the decision-making stage in terms of qualitative matrix.

(A) INTRODUCTION

The strategy formulation process involves environmental analysis, organisational analysis, development of strategic alternatives and analysis and selecting the most appropriate strategy from the alternatives developed. (Fig. 10.1) We have discussed, in Chapter 7, various strategy alternatives at corporate level. The corporate level strategies include:

(i) stability strategies,

(ii) growth strategies, *viz.,* internal growth strategies, mergers, takeovers, horizontal integration, conglomerate diversification, vertical integration, joint ventures,

(iii) retrenchment strategies, *viz.,* turn around strategy, captive company strategy, transformation strategy, divestment strategy and liquidation strategy, and

(iv) combination strategy or portfolio restructuring. We have also discussed, in Chapter 8, business unit strategies. These strategies include: *(i)* the Generic strategies, *viz.,* a low-cost leadership strategy, differentiation strategies, focus and specialisation strategies, *(ii)* offensive strategies, *(iii)* defensive strategies, *(iv)* functional strategies, and *(v)* matching strategy to situation.

The logical next step is analysing these strategy alternatives both at corporate level and business unit and functional level and choosing/selecting an appropriate strategy. At this, situation, we should recall the business mission, objectives and goals. This is because, the strategy, we select should contribute for the achievement of organisation's mission and objectives. We also recall the objectives and goals of strategic business units and functional levels as the strategies we select also contribute to the achievement of objectives of these levels.

The process of analysis is concerned with understanding of what the future holds and how the company can sustain and grow. The process should analyse all types of strategies as in reality, low priority strategies, may be employed. The process should also identify the probable hurdles of strategy implementation, likely consequences or results of the plans. The firm's attitude towards risk plays an important role in the analysis and selection of a strategy.

(B) CRITERIA FOR EVALUATING STRATEGIC ALTERNATIVES

There are a number of different criteria for evaluating strategic alternatives. It would be very difficult to use all these criteria to get a satisfactory result simultaneously. However, to make the evaluation practically possible, all the criteria can be classified into three groups, *viz.,* criteria of suitability, criteria of feasibility and criteria of acceptability.

(i) Criteria of Suitability: These criteria attempt to measure the extent to which the proposed strategies fit the situation identified in the strategic analysis. The situation should indicate the list of the important opportunities and the threats that the firm faces and the particular strengths and weaknesses of the firm.

Criteria of suitability attempt to measure the extent to which the proposed strategies fit the situation identified in the strategic analysis.

The evaluation should measure the suitability of the strategy to the situation. The evaluation of suitability is also called the criteria of consistency. The strategy to be selected should meet the following criteria:

- To what extent, the strategy can overcome the difficulties identified in the strategic analysis? For example, can the strategy increase the market share of the company?
- To what extent the strategy can exploit the environmental opportunities by using the company's strengths? For example, can the strategy provide the status of leader in introducing the new product, under the stable market conditions?

- Does the strategy fit in with the company's objectives and values? For example, would the strategy fit in the recently signed agreement with the members of the Chamber of Commerce and Industry in the country?

(ii) Criteria of Feasibility: These criteria, assess the practical implementation and working of the strategy. For example, will the strategy of price-cut result in hike in profits under the competitive environment? The following questions need to be assessed at the evaluation stage:

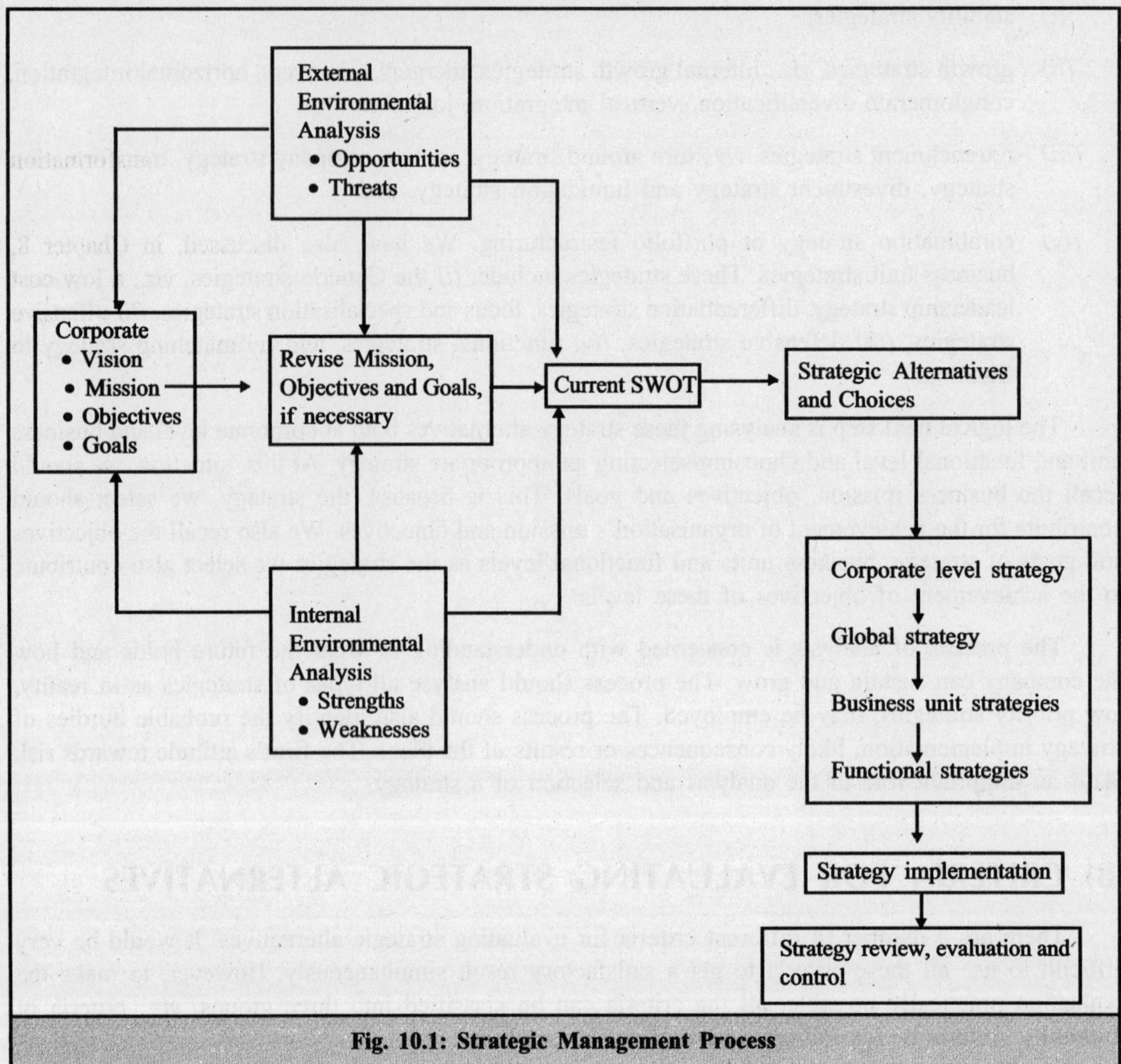

Fig. 10.1: Strategic Management Process

- Can the company provide enough financial resources to implement the strategy? This can be examined by analysing future cash flows, company's commitments, ability and willingness of the management to budget the funds.
- Is the company capable of performing to the required level?
- Can the necessary market position be achieved? Will the necessary marketing skills be available?
- Can competitive reactions be coped with?
- How will the company ensure that the required managerial and operative skills be available?
- Will the technology be available to compete effectively?
- Can the necessary materials and services be procured?

(iii) Criteria of Acceptability: The third measurement is acceptability of the strategy. The firm should assess the strategy to decide whether the consequences of proceeding with a strategy are acceptable. The strategy should be acceptable to the strategy decision-maker in the company. Therefore, acceptability involves not only the consequences of the strategy, but also the personal considerations like values of the strategy decision-maker. The following factors will help to identify the likely consequences of the strategy after its implementation:

- What will be the financial performance of the firm in terms of profitability?
- How will the financial problems (like liquidity) be solved?
- What will be the effect on capital structure?
- Will any proposed changes be acceptable to the general cultural expectations within the organisation?
- Will the function of any department, group or individual change significantly?
- Will the company's relationship with outside stakeholders (like suppliers, bankers, customers) need to change?
- Will the strategy be acceptable to the company's environment (like local community)?
- Will the proposed strategy fit existing systems or will it require major changes?

Framework for Evaluating Strategic Alternatives

After developing a number of strategic alternatives, they should be evaluated against the criteria, in order to select the best strategy. The process of evaluation is discussed below. Fig. 10.2 depicts the proposed framework for undertaking a strategic evaluation. The steps in the process of strategic evaluation are:

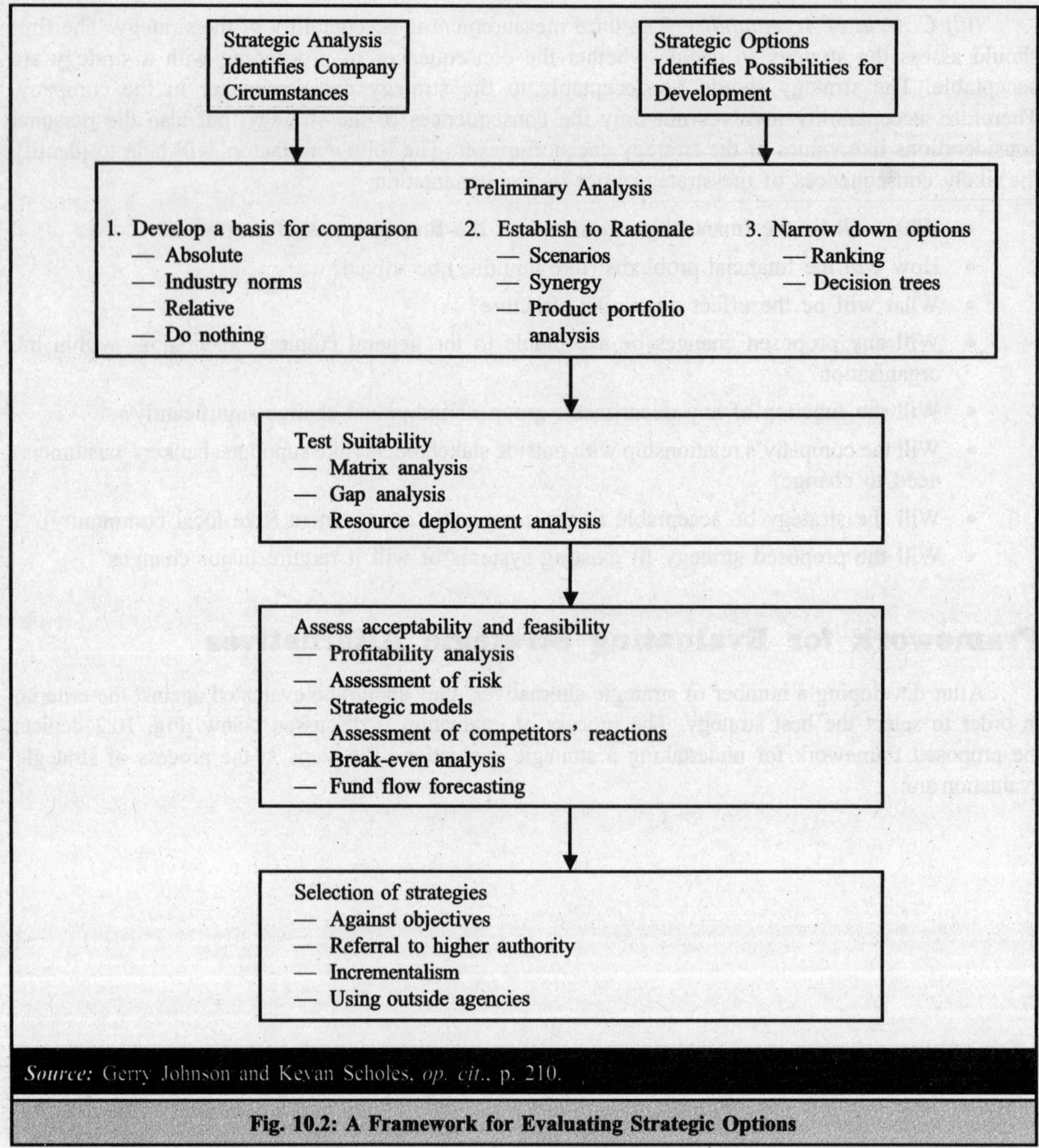

Source: Gerry Johnson and Kevan Scholes, *op. cit.*, p. 210.

Fig. 10.2: A Framework for Evaluating Strategic Options

(i) The first step is a strategic analysis in order to gain a clear understanding of the circumstances affecting the organisation's strategic situation.

(ii) The second step is to produce a range of strategic options.

(iii) The third step is to develop a basis of comparison. This may be available from the strategic analysis or may need to be specially developed.

(iv) It is helpful to establish the underlying rationale for each strategy by explaining why the strategy might succeed. This is often done in qualitative terms and by using techniques like scenario building product portfolio analysis and the assessment of synergy.

(v) At this stage, the large number of strategic alternatives may be narrowed down, before a more detailed analysis is undertaken. Strategic alternatives may be ranked, based on their relative merits and demerits.

(vi) Suitability of each alternative should be tested. There are a number of techniques for testing. The specific choice of technique will depend upon the circumstances.

(vii) The next stage is assessing the feasibility and acceptability of strategies which appear reasonably suitable based on the analysis. The choice of the technique should be based on the circumstances of the company.

(viii) Finally, the company will need some system for selecting future strategies as a result of these evaluations.

A Strategy Analysis Framework

According to Fred D. David, significant strategy analysis techniques can be integrated into three-stage decision-making framework as presented in Fig. 10.3. The first stage of analytical frame work consists of the Internal Factor Evaluation (IFE) Matrix, the External Factor Evaluation (EFE) Matrix and Competitive Profile Matrix. These three techniques summarise the basic input information needed to generate feasible alternative strategies. Hence, this step is called input stage.

Strategy analysis techniques summarise the basic input information needed to generate feasible alternative strategies.

The second stage of analytical framework consists of Threats-Opportunities-Weaknesses-Strengths (TOWS) Matrix, Strategic Position and Action Evaluation (SPACE) Matrix, Boston Consulting Group (BCG) Matrix, General Electric (Nine-Cell Matrix), Directional Policy Matrix, Hofer's Life Cycle Matrix, Internal-External (IE) Matrix and Grand Strategy Matrix. This stage of analytical framework focusses on generating feasible alternative strategies. Key internal and external factors are matched in this stage. Hence, it is called 'matching stage.' The third stage of the analytical framework is the decision stage. This stage helps to select specific strategies.

(C) THE INPUT STAGE

1. The Internal Factor Evaluation (IFE) Matrix

The Internal Factor Evaluation (IFE) Matrix summarises an organisation's key general management, marketing, finance, human resource, production/operations and research and development strengths and weaknesses. This technique is useful in answering four major questions about a firm's internal strategic position. They are:

The Internal Factor Evaluation matrix summarises an organisation's key general management, marketing, finance, human resource, production/operations and research and development strengths and weaknesses.

(a) What are the company's key strengths and weaknesses?

(b) What is the relative significance of each strength and weakness to the company's overall performance?

(c) Does each factor represent a major weakness, a minor weakness, a minor strength and a major strength?

The weightages to the factors may be assigned as follows:

Factor	*Weightage*
A major weakness	–2
A minor weakness	–1
A minor strength	+1
A major strength	+2

(d) What is the company's total weighted score resulting from the internal factor evaluation matrix? Is the score above or below +0.10?

The internal factors should be stated in objective terms to the possible extent. The factors selected, would represent the internal bases from which an organisation's strategies will be formulated. The strategists should assign appropriate weights and ratings to each factor. An example of IFE Matrix is presented in Table 10.1.

Table 10.1 An Example of the Internal Factor Evaluation Matrix

Key Internal Factor	Weight	Rating	Weighted Score
1. The company's level of productivity has dropped to 65 percent	0.20	–2	–0.40
2. The company's organisational structure is being totally revamped	0.05	–1	–0.05
3. The company's earning per share (EPS) was lowest in the industry in 1992	0.10	–1	–0.10
4. The company's return on investment (ROI) was only 2.2% in 1992, second lowest in the industry	0.10	–1	–0.10
5. The company is boosting R&D expenditure to 20% of sales in 1993	0.15	+1	+0.15
6. The company through 21 plant locations offers excellent customer service	0.15	+1	+0.15
7. The company has established a reputation for technical excellence	0.25	+2	+0.50
Total weighted score	1.0		+ 0.15

Source: A modified version from: Reichhold's *Annual Report*, 1984. Quoted in Fred R. David, p. 201.

The company in example, has scored slightly more than the average in terms of overall internal strategic position.

2. The External Factor Evaluation (EFE) Matrix

External Factor Evaluation technique summarises an organisation's opportunities provided and threats posed by the external environmental factors.

The second technique of input stage of strategy formulation analytical framework is the External Factor Evaluation Matrix. This technique summarises an organisation's opportunities provided and threats posed by the external environmental factors, *viz.*, economic, political, technological, social, cultural, governmental, competitors and international. The External Factor Evaluation Matrix answers four questions. They are:

(a) What are the company's environmental opportunities and threats?

(b) What is the relative significance of each opportunity and threat to the company's overall performance?

(c) Does each factor represent a major threat, a minor threat, a minor opportunity or a major opportunity? The weightages to the factors may be assigned as follows:

Factor	*Weightage*
Major Threat	–2
Minor Threat	–1
Minor opportunity	+1
Major opportunity	+2

(d) What is the company's total weighted score resulting from the External Factor Evaluation Matrix? Is the score above or below the average of +0.10?

Table 10.2 presents an example of preparing the External Factor Evaluation Matrix. It is observed from the exhibit that the company has scored +0.25. Therefore, it can be viewed as the company has a strong external strategic position.

Stage 1: THE INPUT STAGE

1. Internal Factor Evaluation (IFE) Matrix	2. External Factor Evaluation (EFE) Matrix	3. Competitive Profile Matrix

Stage 2: THE MATCHING STAGE

1. Threats — Opportunities — Weaknesses — Strength (TOWS) Matrix	2. Strategic Position and Action Evaluation (SPACE) Matrix	3. Boston Consulting Group (BCG) Matrix	4. GE Nine Cell Matrix	5. Directional Policy Matrix	6. Hofer's Life Cycle Matrix	7. Internal-External (IE) Marix	8. Grand Strategy Matrix

Stage 3: THE DECISION STAGE

Quantitative Strategic Planning Matrix (QSPM)

Source: Modified version from: Fred R. David., *op. cit.*, p. 199.

Fig. 10.3: The Strategy Formulation Analytical Framework

The strategists should quantify subjectivity during the early stages of strategy formulation process. The strategists should have good judgement skills to determine appropriate weights and ratings. However, an absence of objective input information often results in biases, politics etc., in the strategy formulation process.[5]

Table 10.2: An Example of the External Factor Evaluation Matrix

Key External Factor	*Weightage*	*Rating*	*Weighted Score*
1. Due to heavy competition in the international markets, nearly 90% sales of the company were within India in 1996	0.25	–2	–0.50
2. Due to the entry of many new firms into the industry, the company's market share has declined by 10%	0.15	–1	–0.15
3. The Government, in its recent budget offered incentives to this industry	0.10	+1	+0.10
4. The changing culture, will result in the increase in the total industry's sales	0.15	+1	+0.15
5. The company's diversification into the new operations will increase the income by 30%	+0.25	+2	+0.50
6. The decline in input prices will reduce the cost of production by 15%	+0.10	+1	+0.10
Total Weighted Score	1.00		+0.25

3. The Competitive Profile Matrix

The Competitive Profile Matrix summarises significant information about competitors. Strategists should use only the factual information about competitors in strategy formulation.

As analysed in the earlier chapter, identifying and analysing competitor's strengths, weaknesses and strategies are useful in the strategy formulation process. The Competitive Profile Matrix summarises significant information about competitors. Strategists should use only the factual information about competitors in strategy formulation. A Competitive Profile Matrix should answer the following questions:

(a) Who are our major competitors?

(b) What key factors are most important to being successful in the industry?

(c) What is the relative importance of each key factor to success in the industry?

(d) To what extent is each competitor strong or weak on each key success factor? (Where –2 = major weakness, –1 = minor weakness, +1 = minor strength and +2 = major strength)

(e) Overall, how strong or weak is each major competitor?

Table 10.3 presents an example of Competitive Profile Matrix.

Table 10.3: Competitive Profile Matrix: An Example					
Key Success Factors		*Competitor 1*		*Competitor 2*	
	Weight	*Rating*	*Weighted Score*	*Rating*	*Weighted Score*
Customer service	0.22	+2	+0.44	+1	+0.22
Price	0.20	+1	+0.20	–1	–0.20
Product Quality	0.18	+1	+0.18	+1	+0.18
Technological Superiority	0.11	+1	+0.11	+2	+0.22
Dealer Relations	0.10	+2	+0.20	-1	–0.10
Financial Strength	0.10	+1	+0.10	+2	+0.20
Advertising Effectiveness	0.09	+2	+0.18	+1	+0.09
Total Weighted Scores	1.00	+1.41			+0.61

Source: Modified version from: Fred R. David, *op. cit.*, p. 204.

It is observed from the table 10.3 that both the competitors are strong and competitor 1 is more stronger than the competitor.

(D) THE MATCHING STAGE CORPORATE PORTFOLIO ANALYSIS

The matching stage of the analytical framework for strategy formulation is also called corporate portfolio analysis. Corporate portfolio analysis or the matching stage is a set of techniques useful in strategy formulation relating to individual products or business in a company's portfolio. The matching stage or the corporate portfolio analysis techniques include:

Corporate portfolio analysis or the matching stage is a set of techniques useful in strategy formulation relating to individual products or business in a company's portfolio.

(a) The Threats-Opportunities-Weaknesses-Strengths (TOWS) Matrix

(b) The Strategic Position and Action Evaluation (SPACE) Matrix

(c) The Boston Consultancy Group (BCG) Matrix

(d) The General Electric Nine-Cell Matrix

(e) Hofer's Product Market Evolution Matrix

(f) Directional Policy Matrix

(g) The Internal-External (IE) Matrix, and

(h) The Grand Strategy Matrix

Matching means aligning internal factors with external factors to generate alternative strategies.

1. The Threats-Opportunities-Weaknesses-Strengths (TOWS) Matrix

All firms must formulate appropriate strategies to win. A good offence strategy without a good defense strategy and *vice versa*, most often leads to defeat. Firms should use their strength to exploit the opportunities and/or to overcome the threats. Alternatively, companies may pursue defensive strategies to overcome weaknesses and avoid threats.

A good offence strategy without a good defense strategy and *vice versa*, most often leads to defeat.

It is disastrous for the firm to face the threats posed by the environment, if it is already suffering from its weaknesses. However, a company can overcome its weaknesses, if the environment provides opportunities to it. It is rather difficult, but quite important to match key internal and external factors.

The TOWS Matrix helps to match the internal and external factors.

The TOWS Matrix tool results in the development of four types of strategies. They are:

(i) Strengths-Opportunities Strategies (SO),

(ii) Weaknesses-Opportunities Strategies (WO),

(iii) Strength-Threats Strategies (ST), and

(iv) Weaknesses-Threats Strategies (WT).

Companies would like to be in strengths-opportunity situation to exploit the opportunities provided by the external environment. Companies generally pursue WO, ST and WT strategies with a view to move to SO strategy. The TOWS Matrix is shown in Fig. 10.4.

Always leave blank	Strengths-S 1. 2. 3. 4. 5. 6. List strengths 7. 8. 9. 10.	Weaknesses-W 1. 2. 3. 4. 5. 6. List weaknesses 7. 8. 9. 10.
Opportunities-O 1. 2. 3. 4. List opportunities 5. 6. 7. 8. 9. 10.	SO Strategies 1. 2. 3. 4. Use strengths to take advantage of opportunities 5. 6. 7. 8. 9. 10.	WO Strategies 1. 2. 3. 4. Overcome weaknesses by taking advantage of opportunities 5. 6. 7. 8. 9. 10.
Threats - T 1. 2. List threats 3. 4. 5. 6. 7. 8. 9. 10.	ST Strategies 1. 2. Use strengths to avoid threats 3. 4. 5. 6. 7. 8. 9. 10.	WT Strategies 1. 2. Minimise weaknesses and avoid threats 3. 4. 5. 6. 7. 8. 9. 10.

Source: Fred R. David., *op. cit.*, p. 207.

Fig. 10.4: The TOWS Matrix

Steps Involved in Constructing a TOWS Matrix

1. List the company's key strengths.
2. List the company's key weaknesses.

3. List the company's key opportunities.
4. List the company's key threats.
5. Match the strengths with opportunities and record the resultant SO strategies in the appropriate cell.
6. Match weaknesses with opportunities and record the resultant WO strategies.
7. Match strengths with threats and record resultant ST strategies.
8. Match weaknesses with threats and record the resultant WT strategies.

2. The Strategic Position and Action Evaluation (SPACE) Matrix

The Strategic Position and Action Evaluation (SPACE) Matrix is an important matching tool. Fig. 10.5 presents SPACE Matrix. SPACE Matrix is a four quadrant framework and it suggests whether aggressive, conservative, defensive or competitive type strategies are more appropriate for a given company. The SPACE Matrix axes are: Financial Strength (FS), Competitive Advantage (CA), Environmental Stability (ES), and Industry Strengths (IS). The two internal dimensions, Financial Strength (FS) and Competitive Advantage (CA) and two external dimensions, Industry Strength (IS) and Environmental Stability (ES) can be considered the most important determinants of an organisation's overall strategic position.

There are a number of variables that could comprise each of the dimensions represented on the axes of the SPACE Matrix. Some example of variables, often included are presented in Exhibit 10.1. The recommended strategies for the four dimensions are presented in Fig. 10.6.

3. The Boston Consulting Group (BCG) Matrix

Autonomous divisions or profit centres of a company comprise what is called a business portfolio. The Boston Consulting Group — a leading management consulting firm devised a four-square grid. This grid was first portfolio matrix to be widely used. The BCG — type matrix is presented in Fig. 10.7. The matrix is formed using industry growth rate on the vertical axis and relative market share on the horizontal axis. Each business unit appears as a circle on the four cell matrix with the size of each circle scaled to the per cent of revenues it represents in the overall corporate portfolio.

BCG matrix is formed using industry growth rate on the vertical axis and relative market share on the horizontal axis.

Relative market share is the ratio of business's market share to the market share held by the largest rival company in the industry, with market share measured in terms of quantity of sales but not value of sales. In other words, relative market share is calculated by dividing a business's percentage share of total industry's sales volume by the percentage share held by its largest rival. For example, if business X has a 20 per cent share of the industry's total sales volume and its largest rival is business Y. Company Y's market share is 60 per cent. Then, the relative market share of business X is 20 ÷ 60 = 0.33. Alternatively, if X has a 40 per cent share of the industry's sales volume and Y has a 20 per cent share of the industry's sales volume, X's relative marketshare is 20 ÷ 40 = 2.00. It is clear from this definition that, only market-share leader businesses in their respective industries will have relative market share values greater than 1.0 and businesses with market share less than that of one or more rivals will have ratios below 1.0.

The border between high and low relative market shares is at 1.0, as shown in Fig. 10.7. Circles in the two left side cells (upper cell and lower cell), the matrix represent businesses that are market share leaders in their industry as the boundary is set at 1.0. Thus, the circles in the right side cells (upper cell and lower cell) of the matrix represent the portfolio members that are in runner-up positions in the industry. The size of the circle shows the degree to which the businesses trail is indicated by the size of the relative market share. A ratio of 0.20 indicates the business has a market share of 2/10 or 1/5 that of the largest business in the market and a ratio of 0.80 indicates a market share 4/5 of the largest business in the industry.

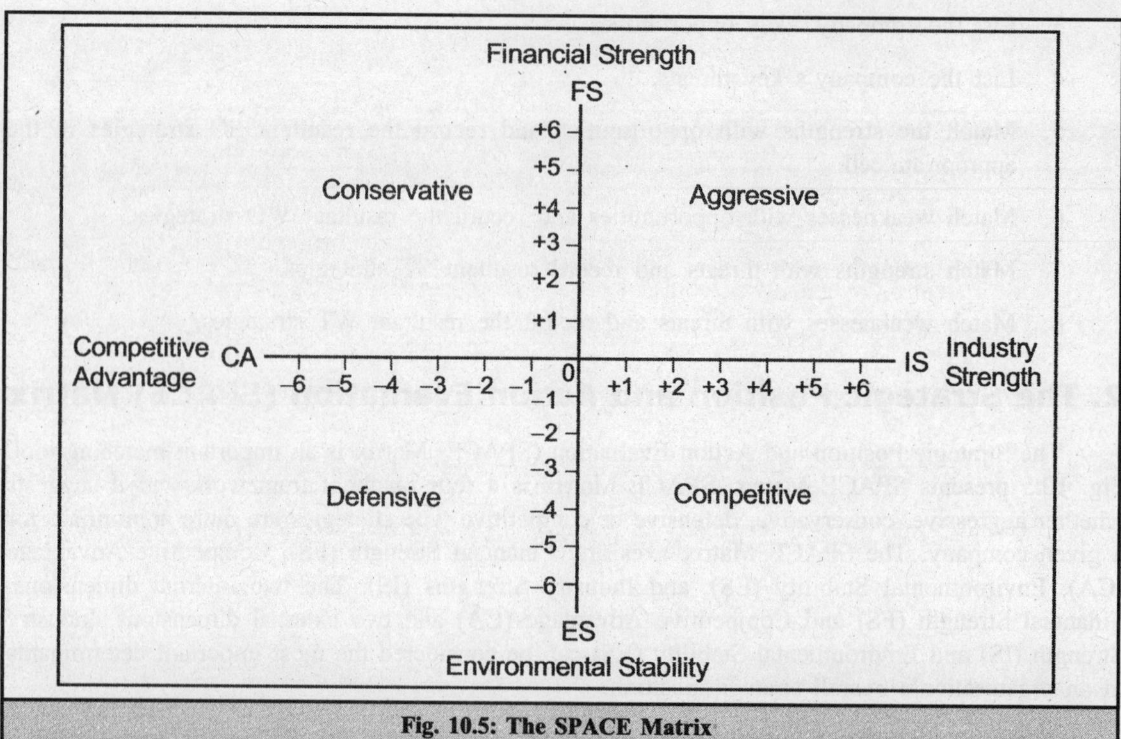

Fig. 10.5: The SPACE Matrix

Exhibit 10.1: Some example of factors that comprise the SPACE Matrix Axes

INTERNAL STRATEGIC POSITION	EXTERNAL STRATEGIC POSITION
Financial Strength (FS)	**Environment Stability (ES)***
Return on investment	Technological changes
Leverage	Rate of inflation
Liquidity	Demand variability
Working capital	Price range of competing products
Cash flow	Barriers to entry into market
Ease of exit from market	Competitive pressure
Risk involved in business	Price elasticity of demand
Competitive Advantage (CA)	**Industry Strength (IS)**
Market share	Growth potential
Product quality	Profit potential
Product life cycle	Financial stability
Customer loyalty	Technological know-how
Competition's capacity utilization	Resource utilization
	Capital intensity
Technological know-how	Ease of entry into market
Control over suppliers and distributors	Productivity, capacity utilization

Source: H. Rowe, R. Mason, and K. Dickel, *Strategic Management & Business Policy: A Methodological Approach* (Reading, Mass: Addison-Wesley Publishing Company, Inc., 1982), 155-156.

* A stable environment represents a better strategic position than an unstable environment.

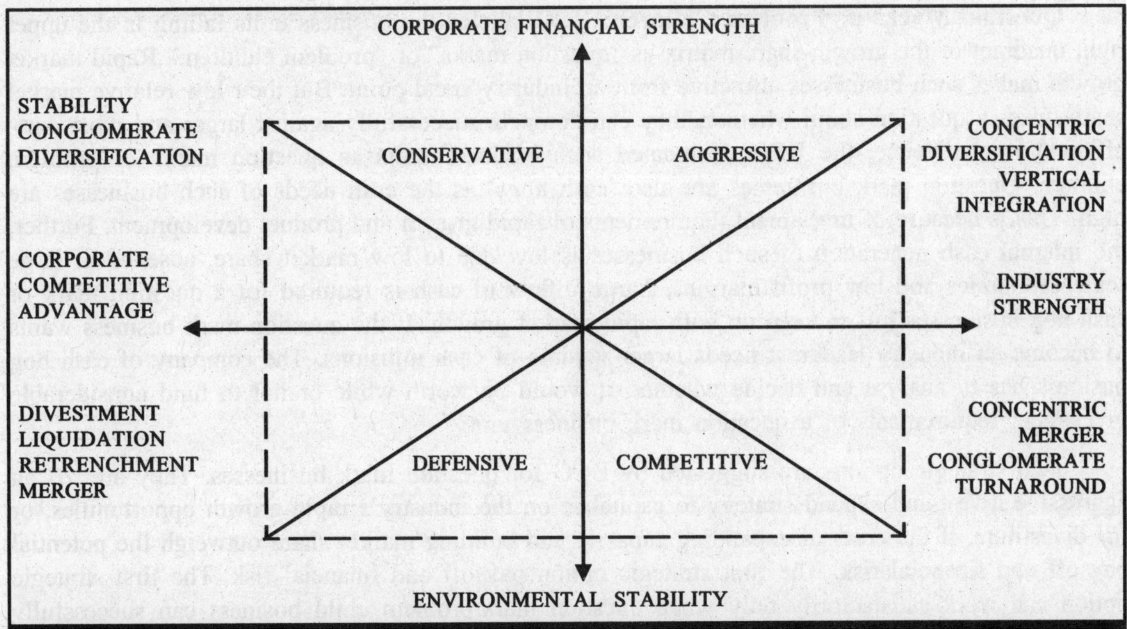

Source: A.J. Rowe, R.O. Mason and K. Dickel. *"Strategic Management and Business Policy — Methodological Approach."* Addison-Wesley, Reading, Mass. 1982, p. 164.

Fig. 10.6: SPACE Diagram: Recommended Strategies

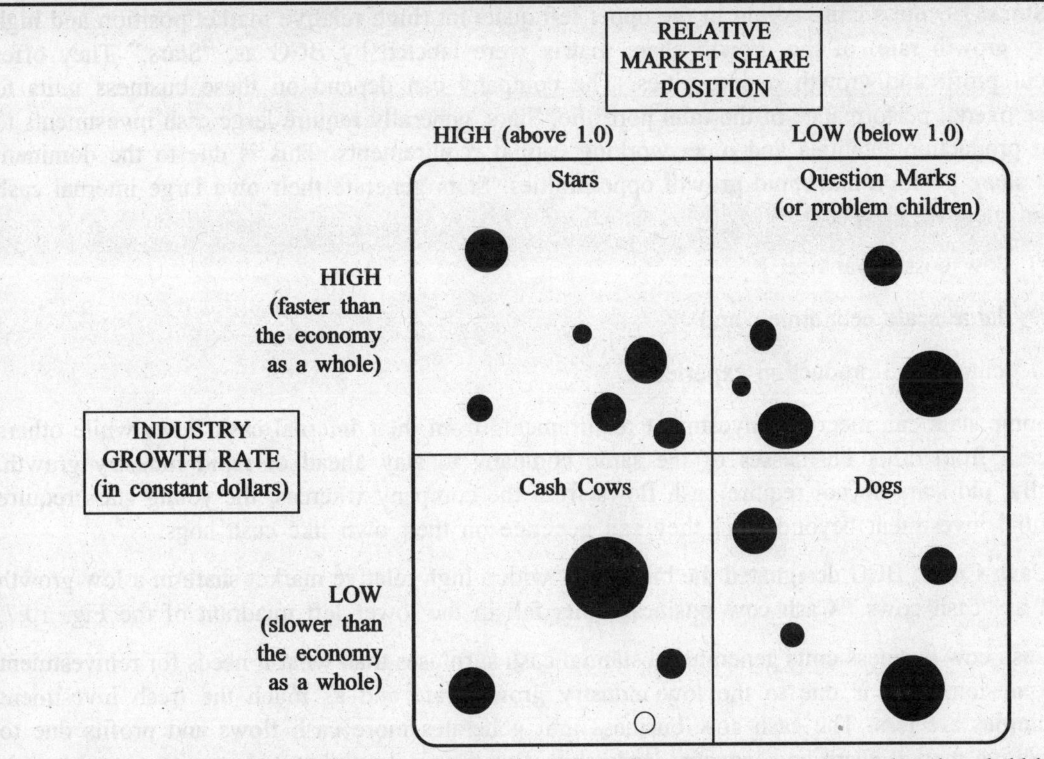

Note: **Relative market share is defined by the ratio of one's own market share to the market share held by the largest rival firm. When the vertical dividing line is set at 1.0, the only way a firm can achieve a star or cash cow position in the growth-share matrix is to have the largest market share in the industry. Since this is a very stringent criterion, it may be "fairer" and more revealing to locate the vertical dividing line in the matrix at about 0.75 to 0.80.**

Source: Arthur A. Thompson and A.J. Strickland. *op. cit.*, p. 194.

Fig. 10.7: The BCG Growth-Share Business Portfolio Matrix

Question mark businesses are also 'cash hogs' as the cash needs of such businesses are high.

Question Marks or Problem Children: BCG labeled the business units falling in the upper right quadrant of the growth-share matrix as "question marks" or "problem children." Rapid market growth makes such businesses attractive from an industry stand point. But their low relative market share raises a question about whether, they can compete successfully against larger and most cost-efficient rivals. Hence, the BCG designated such business units as question marks or problem children. Question mark businesses are also 'cash hogs' as the cash needs of such businesses are high. This is because of investment requirements of rapid growth and product development. Further, the internal cash generation of such businesses is low due to low market share, absence of large scale economies and low profit margins. Large inflow of cash is required for a question mark or cash hog businesses just to keep up with rapid market growth. If the question mark business wants to become an industry leader, it needs larger volume of cash infusions. The company of cash hog business has to analyse and decide whether, it would be worth while or not to fund considerable investment requirements of a question mark business unit.

Two strategic options are suggested by BCG for question mark businesses. They are: *(i)* an aggressive invest-and-expand strategy to capitalise on the industry's rapid-growth opportunities, or *(ii)* divestiture, if the costs of expanding capacity and building market share outweigh the potential pay off and financial risk. The first strategic option pay off and financial risk. The first strategic option can work satisfactorily only when question mark/problem child business can successfully pursue a fast growth strategy and earn major market share. If it is not feasible, the only long run alternative strategic option available is divestment. The viable strategy for question mark business is that: divest the weaker businesses that have less chance to catch the leaders and invest heavily in high potential problem children and groom them to become tomorrow's 'stars'.

Stars require large cash investments to expand production facilities and meet working capital requirements. This is due to the dominant market share position and rapid growth opportunities.

Stars: Business units falling in the upper left quadrant (high relative market position and high industry growth rate) of the growth share matrix were labeled by BCG as, "Stars." They offer excellent profit and growth opportunities. The company can depend on these business units to increase overall performance of the total portfolio. Stars, generally require large cash investments to expand production facilities and meet working capital requirements. This is due to the dominant market share position and rapid growth opportunities. Stars generate their own large internal cash flows in view of:

(i) low cost advantage,

(ii) large scale economies, and

(iii) cumulative production experience.

Some stars can meet the investment requirements from their internal cash flows while others need cash from other businesses of the same company to stay ahead of rapid industry growth. Normally, old stars do not require cash flows from the company whereas, the young stars require substantial investment beyond what they can generate on their own like cash hogs.

Cash cow business units generate substantial cash surpluses than what it needs for reinvestment and expansion. This is due to the low industry growth rate and as much the fresh investment opportunities are less.

Cash Cows: BCG designated the businesses with a high relative market share in a low growth market as "cash cows." Cash cow business units fall in the lower left quadrant of the Fig. 10.7.

Cash cow business units generate substantial cash surpluses than what it needs for reinvestment and expansion. This is due to the low industry growth rate and as much the fresh investment opportunities are less. The cash cow business unit generates more cash flows and profits due to high relative market share and industry leadership. But the reinvestment opportunities are less.

Due to the maturity of the industry demand, many of the yesterday's stars dropped into the lower cell of the left side area of the Fig. 10.7. Since the reinvestment opportunities are stagnated, the surpluses generated by the cash cows may be used to cover:

- Dividend payments
- Finance acquisitions
- Investing in emerging stars
- Investing in problem children that can be groomed as future stars.

The health and the efficiency to generate cash surplus of cash cows should be protected. However, weakening cash cows may be harvested and eventually disinvested.

Dogs: Business units falling under the lower right quadrant of the growth share matrix were labeled by BCG as "Dogs." Dogs are the businesses with a low relative market share in a slow growth industry. These business units are called dogs because of:

(i) their dim growth prospects,

(ii) their trailing market position,

(iii) squeeze that being behind the leaders.

These business units fail to generate cash flows on long-term basis. These units, sometimes fail even to generate cash flows that are necessary for working capital requirements. Therefore, BCG suggests that weak dog businesses be harvested, divested or liquidated depending upon the ability of the strategy to yield more cash.

BCG Matrix and Corporate Strategy: The important contributions of BCG Matrix are:

(i) It draws the attention to the cash flow and investment characteristics of various types of businesses.

(ii) It indicates how the company's financial resources can be shifted between/among businesses to optimise the returns/performance of the entire company portfolio.

According to BCG analysis, a sound long-term corporate strategy should utilise the surplus cash generated by cash cow businesses to:

(i) Finance market share increases for cash hog businesses.

(ii) Finance the young stars unable to generate cash to finance their own growth.

(iii) Finance the problem children having potentiality to grow into stars.

This strategy will help the cash hogs to become self-supporting stars. When the business of the stars reach the maturity stage, they become cash cows. The cash cows, when weaken will turn into dogs. Further the problem children without potentiality for growth will also turn into dogs. Dogs should be retained as long as they contribute duly to the overall performance of the company. The strong dogs which are close to '+1' may generate average cash flow and make average profits. BCG Matrix suggest harvest strategy for weakening or already weak dog businesses. A weak dog should be eliminated from the portfolio, if harvesting strategy is not attractive.

Disaster Sequences: There are two disaster sequences in BCG Matrix. They are: *(i)* when a star's relative market share is declined below +1 the star will be dragged to the position of a problem child. Further, if the situation of negative industry growth is added to the problem, the business will be dropped in the cell of dog. *(ii)* When the cash cow's relative market share declines below +1, the cash cow will turn into a dog.

There are two disaster sequences in BCG Matrix. They are: *(i)* when a star's relative market share declines below +1 and *(ii)* when the cash cow's relative market share declines below +1, the cash cow will turn into a dog.

The Possible Mistakes: Companies may commit the following mistakes in adopting strategies:

(i) Over-investing in a safe cash cow.

(ii) Under-investing in question marks.

(iii) Investing resources in all question marks rather than concentrating on the potential ones.

Strengths and Weaknesses of the BCG Matrix Approach

The BCG business portfolio matrix has the following strengths:

(i) It makes definite contribution to the strategist's tool kit.

(ii) It provides strategy-situation match by prescribing broad guidelines and providing direction to the companies.

(iii) It provides guidelines for maximising the financial performance of a diversified company.

(iv) It highlights the interaction within a corporate portfolio.

(v) It helps for fixing priorities for corporate resource allocation.

(vi) It provides rationalisation for both invest, expand and divest strategies.

However, the BCG Matrix has certain shortcomings.

Weaknesses of BCG Matrix

The legitimate shortcomings of the BCG Matrix are:

(i) This matrix based on high-low classifications ignores many businesses with an average growth rate.

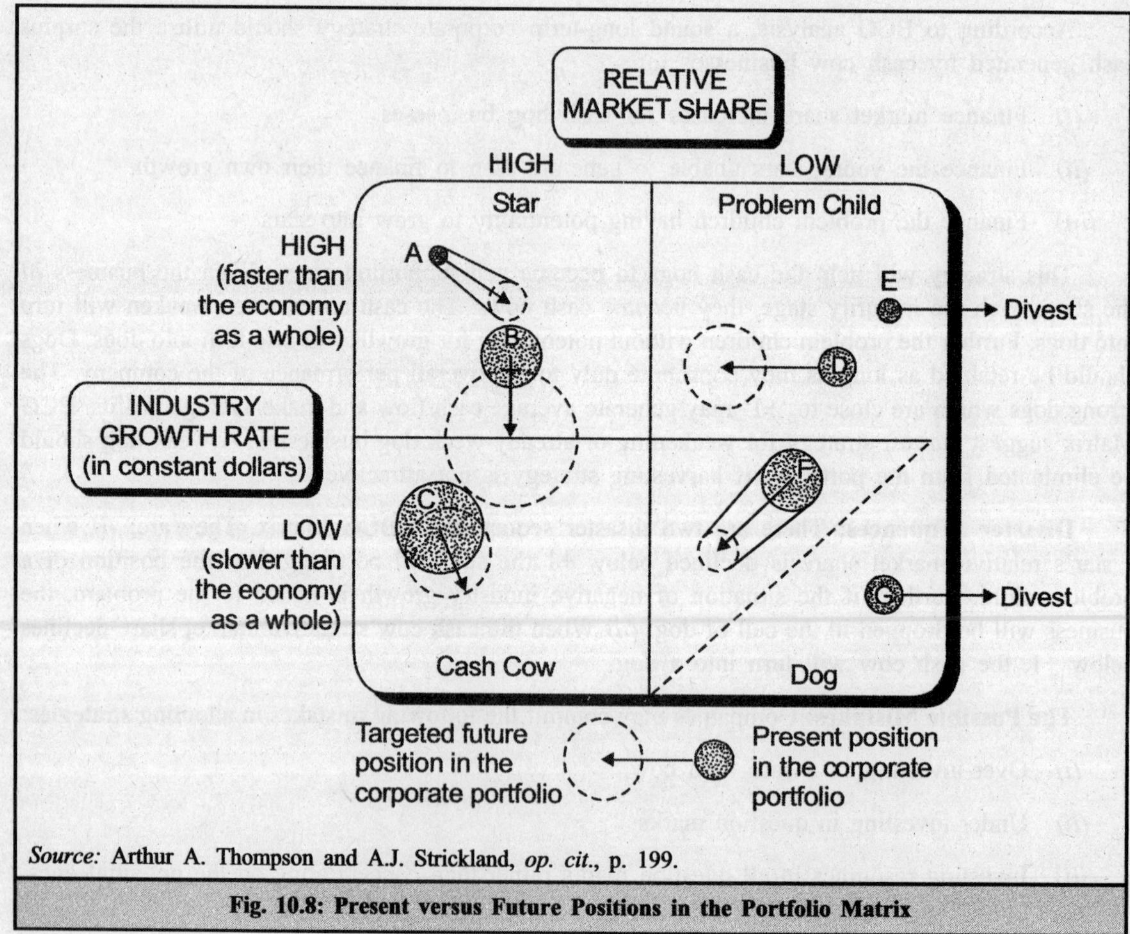

Source: Arthur A. Thompson and A.J. Strickland, *op. cit.*, p. 199.

Fig. 10.8: Present versus Future Positions in the Portfolio Matrix

(ii) The matrix has classified all businesses into four categories, *viz.*, stars, problem children, cash cow and dog. But, some market share leaders have never really been stars in terms of profitability. All businesses with low relative market shares are not dogs or question marks. In many cases runner-up firms have proven track records in terms of growth, profitability and competitive ability. Therefore, a key characteristic to assess a firm is the trend in a firm's relative market share. Is the firm gaining ground or losing ground and why? This shortcoming can be overcome by placing directional arrows on each of the circles in the matrix as shown in Fig. 10.8.

(iii) The BCG Matrix is not a reliable indicator of relative investment opportunities across business units. For example, investing in a star is not necessarily more attractive than investing in a lucrative cash cow.

(iv) Being a market leader in a slow growth industry does not guarantee cash cow status.

(v) Strategists should examine more than just industry growth and relative market share variables to assess the long term attractiveness of the portfolio's business units.

(vi) The relationship between relative market share and profitability is not as tight as the experience curve effect implies. The significance of length production experience in lowering production cost per unit varies from industry to industry. Sometimes, the large market share is due to cost advantage and sometimes it is not.

4. GE Nine-Cell Matrix

Some of the shortcomings of BCG Matrix are avoided in an alternative approach. The alternative approach is the nine-cell matrix, based on the two dimensions of long-term industry attractiveness and business strength/competitive position. This approach is pioneered by General Electric as a way to analyse its own portfolio. This analysis was developed with the help of the consulting firm of Mckinsey and Company. The dimensions of the matrix, *viz.*, long-term industry attractiveness and business strength/competitive position are a composite of several considerations as opposed to a single factor.

The nine-cell matrix, based on the two dimensions of long-term industry attractiveness and business strength/competitive position.

The factors that influence the criteria for determining long-term industry attractiveness include:

(i) market size and growth rate,

(ii) technological requirements.

(iii) the intensity of competition,

(iv) entry and exit barriers,

(v) seasonality and cyclical influences,

(vi) capital requirements,

(vii) emerging industry threats and opportunities,

(viii) historical and projected industry profitability,

(ix) social, environmental and regulatory influences.

The selected measures are assigned weights based on their significance to management and their role in the diversification strategy. The sum of the weights must be 1.00. Use the 1-10 rating scale and assign appropriate weights to each factor. Then multiply the weights with the rating concerned. The product will be the weighted industry rating. Then add the weighted industry ratings of all the factors. The sum will be the industry attractive rating. Table 10.4 presents the procedure for calculation of industry attractiveness rating. Attractiveness ratings are calculated for each industry represented in the corporate portfolio. The position of each industry based on the industry's attractiveness score is placed on the vertical scale of Fig. 10.9.

The factors that influence the business strength/competitive position include:

(i) market share,

(ii) relative cost position,

(iii) ability to match rival firms on quality and service,

(iv) knowledge of customers and markets,

(v) possession of desirable core competencies,

(vi) adequacy of technological know-how,

(vii) caliber of management,

(viii) profitability relative to competitors.

The approach followed for the calculation of long term industry attractiveness, is followed for the calculation of business strength/competitive position. The analytical issue is whether to rate each business unit on the same generic factors or on each unit's strength on the factors most pertinent to its own industry. Each business's strength/position rating determines its position along the horizontal axis of the matrix — that is whether it merits a strong, average or weak designation.

Table 10.4: Calculation of Industry Attractiveness Rating

Industry/Attractiveness Factor	*Weight*	*Rating*	*Weighted Industry Rating*
Market size and projected growth	0.15	5	0.75
Seasonality and cyclical influences	0.10	8	0.80
Technological considerations	0.10	1	0.10
Intensity of competition	0.25	4	1.00
Emerging opportunities & threats	0.15	1	0.15
Capital requirements	0.05	2	0.10
Industry profitability	0.10	3	0.30
Social, political, regulatory and environmental factors	0.10	7	0.70
Industry attractiveness rating	1.00		3.90

The industry attractiveness and business strength scores provide the basis for placing a business in one of the nine cells of the matrix. The area of the circles is proportional to the size of the industry and the pie slices within the circles reflect the business's market share in the GE attractiveness strength matrix. The long-term industry attractiveness is shown on vertical axis and from low to high. (*i.e.*, low, medium and high). Business strength/competitive position is shown on horizontal axis and presented from weak to strong (*i.e.*, weak, average and strong). Thus, three on horizontal and three on vertical lines make the total cells 3 × 3 = 9. Three cells are shown in vertical lines, three cells are shown in horizontal lines and the remaining three cells are shown in white colour in Fig. 10.9.

Corporate Strategy Implications: The attractive strength matrix helps in deciding investment priorities in different businesses of a company. The important strategic implications of the matrix are:

(i) Industry attractiveness and business strength/competitive positions are high in the upper left three cells. Top investment priority should be given to the businesses in these three cells. Therefore, the strategic prescription for the business in these three cells is "grow and build."

(ii) The second priority comes to the three diagonal cells stretching from the lower left to the upper right (*i.e.,* the lower-left cell, the middle cell and the upper right cell). Medium priority should be given to the businesses falling in these cells. Funds should be invested steadily in these businesses to protect and maintain their industry position. If any business in these three cells has high attractiveness, it should be given top priority in investment and be given go-ahead to employ a more aggressive strategic approach.

(iii) The business in the three cells in the lower-right corner do not receive any investment decisions. Rather, the strategies of harvest or divest may be employed for these businesses. However, if there are any exceptional cases for turnaround, the strategy of turnaround may be employed.

Strengths and Weaknesses of GE Matrix

Strengths: This matrix has three strengths:

(i) It allows for intermediate ranking between high and low and between strong and weak.

(ii) It incorporates a much wider variety of strategically relevant variables, whereas the BCG Matrix is based totally on two considerations — industry growth rate and relative market share.

(iii) It stresses the channeling of corporate resources to businesses with greatest probability of achieving competitive advantage and superior performance. That is top investment priority for the businesses in the three upper left cells, medium priority for the businesses in the three diagonal cells stretching from the lower left to the upper right and adopting turnaround, harvest and divest strategies for the businesses in the three lower right cells.

Weaknesses: Though the GE Matrix is better than the BCG Matrix, it also suffers from some weaknesses. They are:

(i) The nine-cell GE Matrix provides no real guidance on the specific business strategy. This matrix also suggests general strategy like — aggressive expansion, fortify-and-defend or harvest divest. These strategies do not address the issue of strategic coordination between businesses, specific competitive approaches and strategies to be adopted at the business unit level.

(ii) The GE method tends to obscure business that are about to become winners because their industries are entering the take off stage.

5. Directional Policy Matrix

The directional policy matrix uses two parameters, *viz.*, business sector prospects and company's competitive abilities. Business sector prospects are rated on the basis of market growth, market supply and the like.

The directional policy matrix (DPM) was developed by Shell Chemicals, U.K. This matrix uses two parameters, *viz.*, business sector prospects and company's competitive abilities. Business sector prospects are rated on the basis of market growth, market supply and the like. Business sector prospects are judged as attractive, average and unattractive. Company's competitive abilities are judged as strong, average and weak. Business sector prospects represent vertical axis of the diagram of the directional policy matrix. Fig. 10.10 presents the directional policy matrix. There are 9 cells in the diagram. The business in the right lower cells deserve top priority for investment whereas, the business falling in the left upper cells deserve for divestment, withdrawal, etc. The businesses positioned in the three diagonal cells stretching from the lower left to the upper right are usually given medium priority. They merit steady reinvestment to maintain and protect their industry positions. However, the business with unusual attractiveness in these cells, should win higher investment priority.

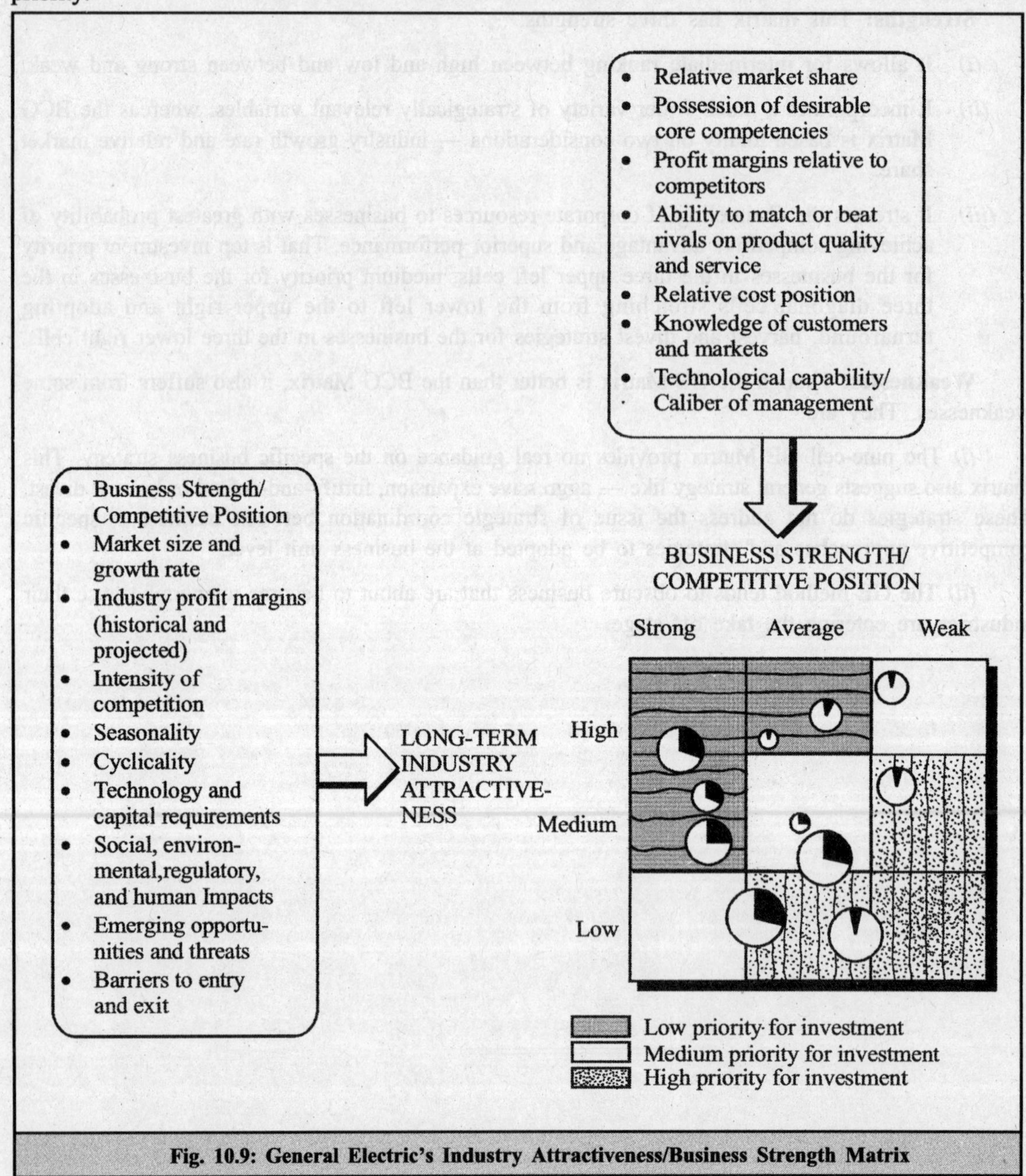

Fig. 10.9: General Electric's Industry Attractiveness/Business Strength Matrix

Business Sector Prospects

Company's Competitive Abilities	*Unattractive*	*Average*	*Attractive*
Weak	Divestment	Imitation/Phased withdrawal	Phased Withdrawal/Cash generation
Average	Phased Withdrawal/ Merger	Maintenance of position/market penetration	Expansion/Product differentiation
Strong	Diversification/ Cash generation	Growth/market segmentation	Market leadership Innovation

Sources: Adopted from D.E. Hussey, "*Portfolio Analysis: Practical Experience with the Directional Policy Matrix,*" *Long Range Planning*, August 1978, p. 3 and A.J. Rowe, R.O. Mason and K. Dickel, "*Strategic Management and Business Policy — A Methodological Approach*," Addison-Wesley, Reading, Mass, 1982, p. 154.

Fig. 10.10: The Directional Policy Matrix

6. Hofer's Life Cycle Matrix

Hofer developed a 15-cell matrix. In this matrix, businesses are plotted in terms of the industry's stage in the evolutionary life-cycle and the business unit's competitive position as shown in Fig. 10.11. The industry's stage in the evolutionary life cycle consists of the following stages: early development, industry takeoff, rapid growth, competitive shake-out, maturity, market saturation and stagnation, industry decline. The business unit's competitive position consists of strong, average and weak. The industry's stage in the evolutionary life cycle represents the vertical axis whereas the business unit's competitive position represents the horizontal axis. The circles in the matrix represent the sizes of the industries involved, and pie wedges denote the business's market share. The businesses shown in Fig. 10.11 could be labeled as follows:

In Hofer's 15-cell matrix businesses are plotted in terms of the industry's stage in the evolutionary life-cycle and the business unit's competitive position.

Business 'A' could be labeled as: developing winner

Business C " a potential loser

Business E " an established winner

Business F " a cash cow

Business G " a loser/dog.

The life cycle matrix has 15 cells and tells about the distribution of the company's business across the stages of industry evolution.

7. The Internal-External (IE) Matrix

The internal-external matrix is based on two dimensions *viz*., *(i)* Internal Factor Evaluation Matrix and *(ii)* External Factor Evaluation Matrix. IFE matrix and EFE matrix were explained at the beginning of (in Input Stage) this chapter. The Internal-External Matrix is presented in Fig. 10.12. The IFE total weighted scores are plotted on the horizontal axis and the EFE total weighted scores are plotted on the vertical axis. Each business of the company should construct an IFE Matrix and EFE Matrix. Corporate level IE can be constructed based on the total weighted scores of all businesses of a company.

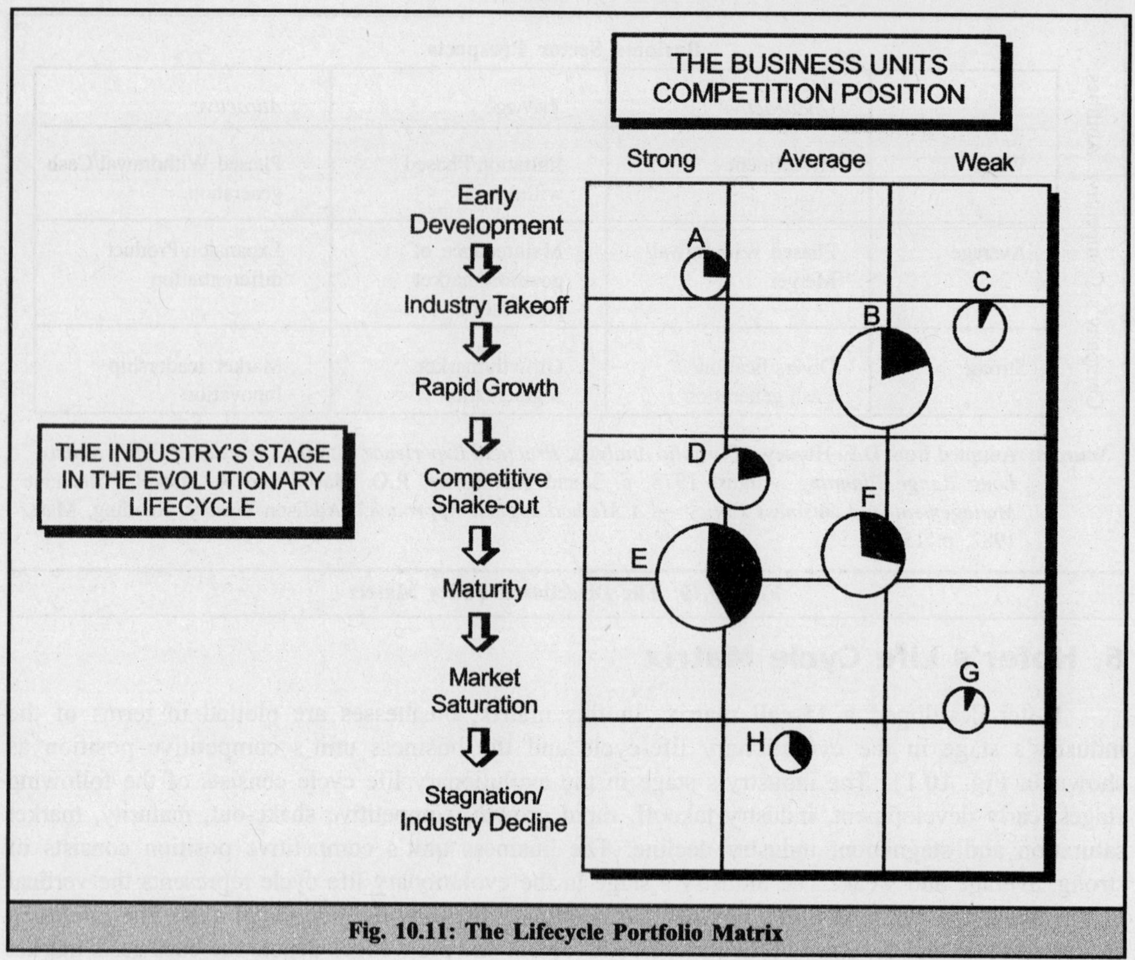

Fig. 10.11: The Lifecycle Portfolio Matrix

On the horizontal axis of the IE matrix, the IFE total weighted scores of –2 to –1 represent weak internal position, scores of –1 to +1 represent average position and scores of +1 to +2 represent strong position. Similarly, on the vertical axis an EFE total weighted scores of –2 to –1 represent low position, scores of –1 to +1 represent medium position and scores of +1 to +2 represent high position.

Strategy Implications: The IE matrix have nine-cell (3 × 3 = 9) display. The business falling in the left upper three cells (*i.e.,* cells I, II and IV) are accorded top investment priority. Therefore, the strategic prescriptions for these businesses can be 'Grow and Build'. Intensive (market penetration, market development and product development) or integrative (forward integration, backward integration and horizontal integration).

Next in priority come business positioned in the three diagonal cells stretching from the lower left to the upper right (businesses VII, V and III). These businesses are usually given medium priority. The strategic prescriptions for these businesses can be steady reinvestment to maintain and protect their industry positions. Market penetration and product development are two commonly adopted strategies for these types of businesses. However, if there is any business in these three cells, with an unusually attractive opportunity, it can be given higher investment opportunity and be allowed to go ahead to adopt a more aggressive strategic approach. The strategy prescription for businesses in the three cells (VIII, IX and VI) in the lower right corner is typically harvest or divest. In exceptional good business cases the strategy of turnaround can be employed.

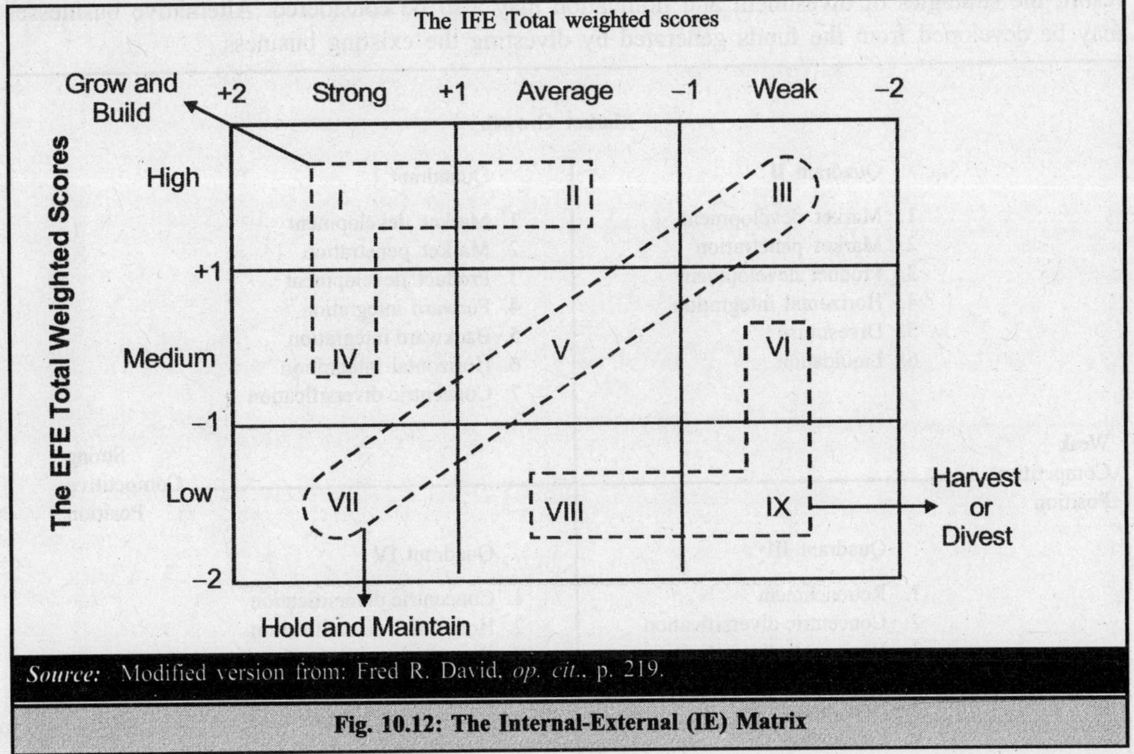

Source: Modified version from: Fred R. David, *op. cit.*, p. 219.

Fig. 10.12: The Internal-External (IE) Matrix

The IE Matrix vs the BCG Matrix

The IE matrix seems to be similar with the BCG matrix.

(i) The tools involve in plotting businesses of a company in a schematic diagram

(ii) the size of each circle represents the percentage sales contribution of each business and

(iii) the pie slices reveal the percentage profit contribution of each business are similar.

There are some deviation between IE matrix and BCG matrix. The axes are different. The IE matrix is built with the help of more information about the businesses composed to that of BCG matrix. Further, the strategic implications of each matrix are different.

8. The Grand Strategy Matrix

The Grand Strategy Matrix has become a popular tool for formulating corporate strategy. The Grand Strategy Matrix is shown in Fig. 10.13. There are four quadrants in the matrix. All companies can be positioned in one of four quadrants of the matrix. The businesses of the company can also be positioned on the similar ones. The matrix is based on two evaluative dimensions, *viz.*, competitive position and market growth. Appropriate strategies for a company to consider are presented in the quadrant concerned in the order of attractiveness.

Businesses/companies falling in the quadrant I are in the excellent strategic position. The firm in this quadrant may go for backward, forward or horizontal integration when they have excessive resources. These firms may also go for concentric diversification strategy in order to reduce the risks of narrow product line. These forms can also adopt aggressive strategies and exploit the opportunities provided by the external environment.

The businesses/firms falling in the quadrant II, *i.e.*, rapid market growth and weak competitive position, are unable to compete effectively at market place and exploit the opportunities offered by the external environment. These firms can employ the strategy of horizontal integration. As a last resort, the strategies of divestment and liquidation may also be considered. Alternative businesses may be developed from the funds generated by divesting the existing business.

Quadrant II	Quandrant I
1. Market development 2. Market penetration 3. Product development 4. Horizontal integration 5. Divestiture 6. Liquidation	1. Market development 2. Market penetration 3. Product development 4. Forward integration 5. Backward integration 6. Horizontal integration 7. Concentric diversification
Quadrant III	**Quadrant IV**
1. Retrenchment 2. Concentric diversification 3. Horizontal diversification 4. Conglomerate diversification 5. Divestiture 6. Liquidation	1. Concentric diversification 2. Horizontal diversification 3. Conglomerate diversification 4. Joint ventures

Rapid Market Growth (top); Slow Market Growth (bottom); Weak Competitive Position (left); Strong Competitive Position (right)

Source: Adapted from Roland Christensen, Norman Berg and Malcolm Sulter, *"Policy Formulation and Administration,"* Richard D. Irwin, Homewood Ill., 1976, pp. 16-18.

Fig. 10.13: The Grand Strategy Matrix

The businesses/firms falling in quadrant III, *i.e.,* slow-market growth and weak competitive position, must make drastic and quick changes to avoid further loss and extinction. As a first step, these firms may reduce costs and assets. As a second step, the firms may shift resources away from the existing businesses to new businesses.

The business firms falling in quadrant IV, *i.e.,* slow market growth and strong competitive position — have strength to launch diversified programmes into more promising growth areas. These firms have more cash flows but less external opportunities to grow. These firms/businesses can successfully pursue concentric, horizontal or conglomerate diversification. Another strategic option available for these firms is 'joint venture'.

(E) SELECTION OF THE MATRIX

Each matrix has its own strengths and weaknesses. It would be better to construct all the eight matrices, provided, adequate data is available. It will help to assess the company's portfolio from different perspectives.

Each matrix has its own strengths and weaknesses. It is not wise to restrict the analysis to one type of portfolio matrix. Therefore, it would be better to construct all the eight matrices, provided, adequate data is available. It will help to assess the company's portfolio from different perspectives. This process enables to achieve the analytical objective. The analytical objective is to understand:

(i) The portfolio's mix of industries.

(ii) The strategic position each business has in its industry.

(iii) The portfolio's performance potential.

(iv) The kind of financial and resource allocation considerations that have to be dealt with.

1. Comparing Industry Attractiveness

Judging the attractiveness of the industries in which the business is the central issue in evaluating a diversified company's strategy. Industry attractiveness can be judged from three perspectives:

(i) The attractiveness of each industry represented in the portfolio. The important consideration is that, "Is this a good industry for the company to have its business in?"

(ii) Each industry attractiveness is relative to the others. The company should find itself. "Which industries in the portfolio are the most attractive and which are the least attractive?" The allocation of resources will become easy by ranking the industries from the most attractive to the least attractive.

(iii) The attractiveness of all industries as a group. The company should find, "how appealing is the mix of industries?"

All the industries represented in the business portfolio should be judged on the following attractive factors:

(a) *Market size and projected growth rate:* Generally, faster growing industries are more attractive than slow growing industries.

(b) *The intensity of competition:* Industries with less competitive pressure are more attractive than industries with strong competitive pressure.

(c) *Technological and production skills required:* Industries where the skill requirements are closely matched to company capabilities are more attractive.

(d) *Capital requirements:* Industries with low or procurable capital requirements are more attractive.

(e) *Seasonal and cyclical factors:* Industries where demand is relatively stable, dependable and continuous are more attractive than that of industries whose demand is seasonal and/or cyclical.

Industry Profitability: Industries with high rates of return are more attractive than industries with low profit margins.

Social, political regulatory and environmental factors: Industries with fewer problems in these areas are normally more attractive.

Strategic fits with other industries with the firm has diversified into. The industries with valuable strategic fit relationship with other industries in the portfolio are more attractive.

Industries should be ranked from most to least attractive based on the calculation of industry attractiveness ratings for all industries in the corporate portfolio. A diversified company to be a strong performer, should get a substantial portion of its revenue and profits from businesses in attractive industries. The core businesses of the company should be attractive, good outlook for growth and above average profitability industries.

2. Comparing Business Unit Strength

Appraising each business unit's strengths and competitive position in its industry helps managers to judge a business unit's chance for success in its industry. Assessment of how a company's business compares in competitive strength should be based on the following factors:

(i) *Relative Market Share:* Business units with higher relative shares have greater competitive strengths.

(ii) *Ability to Compete on Price and/or Quality:* Business units that have cost advantage and have established brand names for quality will be more strongly positioned.

(iii) *Technology and Innovation Capabilities:* Business units with advanced technology and track record in innovations will be strong competitors.

(iv) *How well the business unit's skill and competences match industry key success factors:* The business units would be stronger, if their skills and competencies match with industry's key success factors, most exactly.

(v) *Profitability Relative to Competitors:* The business units that earn high rate of return consistently compared to the competitors will compete more strongly.

(vi) *Other factors include:* Knowledge about customers and markets, production capabilities, marketing skills, reputation and brand awareness and efficiency of management.

Shareholders' interests are normally served better, by concentrating company resources on business that can contend for market leadership in their industry.

3. Comparing Business-Unit Performance

After the businesses have been rated based on industry attractiveness and competitive strength, the business should be evaluated to know their performance prospects ranging from the best to the worst. The factors that should be considered in this respect are: sales growth, profit growth, contribution to corporate earnings, rate of return on the capital employed, cash flow generation, etc.

4. Strategic Fit Analysis

The strategic fit analysis studies, how well each business unit fits into the company's overall portfolio of business.

The strategic fit analysis studies, how well each business unit fits into the company's overall portfolio of business. This can be analysed from two angles:

(i) Whether a business unit has valuable strategic fit with other businesses the firm has diversified into.

(ii) Whether a business unit meshes well with corporate strategy or adds a beneficial dimension to the corporate portfolio.

The best strategic fit business in the overall corporate portfolio makes valuable financial contributions. It also contributes to the achievement of corporate objectives.

Ranking the Business Units on Investment Priority

Managers should rank the businesses in terms of priority for new capital investment based on the analysis given so far. First, the strategists should decide, whether the company will be investing additional funds or not? Once, it is decided that the business will invest additional funds, the strategist should rank the businesses based on their significance, competence, ability to generate cash flows, earn high rate of return, etc. They should rank the business from good to excellent prospects and investing minimally. Strategists should consider whether and how corporate resources and skills can be used to enhance the competitive standing of particular business units.

5. Formulating a Corporate Strategy

Strategist should, move to formulate a strategy to improve the performance of a diversified company. This is based on the overall mix of businesses in the portfolio. Key considerations in this regard include:

(i) Does the portfolio contain enough business in attractive industries?

(ii) How many businesses are question marks?

(iii) What is the proportion of mature businesses in the portfolio?

(iv) Does the portfolio contain enough cash cows to finance the stars and emerging winners?

(v) Does the core businesses of the company earn enough profits?

(vi) Seasonality and cyclical factors.

(vii) Are there too many weak portfolios?

(vii) Does the new corporate strategy improve the overall performance of the company?

The strategist should evaluate the company in terms of performance objectives with its current line of business in order to know the financial viability of the strategy. The strategist can pursue any five basic options to avoid a probable shortfall in financial performance:

(i) Alter the strategic plans for some or all of the businesses.

(ii) Add new business units. Strategists must decide about:

(a) Acquiring related/unrelated businesses. *(b)* Size of acquisitions. *(c)* Specific features of acquisition of business units. *(d)* Pattern of investing the new acquisitions.

(iii) Divest weak performing or money losing businesses.

(iv) Form alliances to try to alter conditions responsible for sub-par performance potentials.

(v) Lower corporate performance objectives.

Deploying Corporate Resources

Strategists must find the sources to finance the strategy. The funds from divestment, cash cows and harvest can be the sources of funds for the corporate treasury. Options for allocating these funds include:

(i) Invest in maintenance and expansion of existing businesses;

(ii) Invest in acquisitions;

(iii) Invest in long-range R&D;

(iv) Paying off existing long-term debt;

(v) Pay higher dividends; and

(vi) Repurchase of company's stock.

(F) THE DECISION STAGE

1. The Quantitative Strategic Planning Matrix (QSPM)

After the input stage and the matching stage, the decision stage follows. The QSPM is an important technique in the third stage strategy formulation analytical framework. This matrix suggests which alternative strategies are best. QSPM is the most current of the strategy formulation analytical techniques. QSPM utilises input information, matching results and analyses to evaluate alternative strategies quantitatively, based on specific organisational capabilities and limitations. It requires subjective decision in assigning weights and ratings. Table 10.5 presents the basic format of QSPM. The left column of the table consists of internal and external factors and the top row consists of feasible alternative strategies. The ratings of key factors are also recorded. Alternative strategies that are desired from TOWS Matrix, SPACE Matrix, BCG Matrix, GE Matrix, Directional Policy Matrix, IE Matrix and Grand Strategy Matrix are also considered. These matching tools, normally, generate feasible alternative strategies similar to each other.

Table 10.5: The Quantitative Strategic Planning Matrix — QSPM — Basic Format

Key Factors	Strategic Alternatives			
	Ratings	Stage 1	Stage 2	Stage 3
Internal Factors:				
Management				
Marketing				
Finance				
Human Resource				
Production/operations				
Research & Development				
External Factors:				
Economy				
Political				
Social				
Technological				
Competitive				

Source: Fred R. David., *op. cit.*, p. 224.

The relative attractiveness of various strategies is determined by QSPM. It uses key internal and external factors in determining relative attractiveness. Though any number of sets of alternative strategies can be included in a QSPM and any number of strategies can comprise a given set, only strategies within a given set are evaluated relative to each other by QSPM. In other words, strategies in each set (like centric, horizontal and conglomerate diversification) are evaluated against each other. Therefore, strategies of the same set should be included in the table for the purpose of evaluation. Table 10.6 presents a sample and a more detailed example of QSPM.

Appendix 10.1 presents a direct application of QSPM.

Table 10.6: A Sample Quantitative Strategic Planning Matrix

		Strategic Alternatives				
Key Factors	*Rating*	*Acquire Financial Services, Inc.*		*Acquire Food Services, Inc.*		*Rationale for Attractiveness Score*
		*AS**	*TAS**	*AS**	*TAS**	
Internal Factors						
Top management team has fifteen years' experience	3	4	12	2	6	Fifteen years' experience is in financial services
We have excess working capital of $2 million.	4	2	8	3	12	Food Services is valued at $2 million.
All of four twenty plants are located in the Northeast United States.	1	2	2	4	4	Food Services is located in the Sun-belt.
Our R&D department is outstanding.	3	—	—	—	—	This item does not affect the strategy choice.
Our Return on Investment (ROI) ratio of .12 is lowest in the industry.	1	2	2	3	3	ROI at Food Services is higher than at Financial Services.
External Factors						

Interest rates are expected to rise to 15 percent in 1987.	2	3	6	4	8	Rising rates will hurt the financial services business.
Population of the South is expected to grow by 15.3 million between 1980 and 2000.	3	4	12	2	6	Many new houses and apartments will be built and financed.
The financial services industry is expected to grow by 40 percent in 1986.	4	4	16	2	8	This 40 percent growth is in financial services.
Two major foreign competitors are entering the industry.	1	1	1	3	3	Food Services, Inc. is not affected by this entry.
President Reagan is expected to deregulate the industry.	2	—	—	—	—	This item does not affect the strategy choice.
SUM TOTAL ATTRACTIVENESS SCORE					59	50

*AS = Attractiveness Score; TAS = Total Attractiveness Score
Attractiveness Score: 1 = not acceptable; 2 = possibly accepted 3 = probably acceptable; 4 = most acceptable
Internal Ratings: 1 = major weakness; 2 = minor weakness; 3 = minor strength: 4 = major strength
External Ratings: 1 major threat; 2 = minor threat; 3 = minor opportunity; 4 = major opportunity

Note: Multiplying the rating times the attractiveness score is based upon the premise that to capitalize on strengths and take advantage of opportunities is more important for firms than improving weaknesses and avoiding threats. Some strategies do not agree with this premise and therefore, do not compute the total attractiveness score. They simply sum the attractiveness scores to determine the relative attractiveness of strategies using the QSPM.

Source: Fred R. David., *op. cit.*, p. 225.

2. Guidelines for Strategy Formulation Process

Strategy formulation is not a simple process. Moreover, it is not purely a quantitative analysis. Quantitative analysis aid the process to some extent. Strategies in major diversified enterprises emerges incrementally over a period of time based on internal and external situations and experiences. This process is also the result of

(a) probing the future,

(b) experiments,

(c) gathering additional information from time to time,

(d) sensing problems,

(e) building awareness of various options,

(f) developing *ad hoc* responses to unexpected crisis,

(g) communicating partial consensus as it emerges and

(h) acquiring a "feel" for all the strategically relevant factors, their importance and their interrelationships.

Executives of major diversified companies do not formulate strategies all at once in comprehensive fashion. The strategic decisions in such organisations emerge gradually but not at one time in a full scale analysis. Top strategists make strategic decisions, "a step at a time, often starting from broad, intuitive conceptions and then embellishing, fine tuning and modify their original thinking as more information is gathered as formal analysis confirms or modifies emerging judgments and as confidence and consensus build for what strategic moves need to be made."

Politics and Strategy Formulation

Often, politics affect the strategy formulation.

Often, politics affect the strategy formulation. The following factors are responsible for politics:

(i) The organisational hierarchy, levels of authority and command.

(ii) Career goals of employees at different levels.

(iii) Problem of allocation of scarce resources.

(iv) Formation of coalitions and groups of individuals.

(v) Superiority of individual goals and group goals over organisational goals.

(vi) Ego clashes of top and middle level executives and line and staff executives.

Strategists have to spend most of their time and energy in nurturing the team concept and gain the support of key individuals and key groups. Internal support is crucial for strategists to manage the external forces. Sometimes, strategic decisions are based on the politics of the moment, when major groups of individuals do not support the best strategic alternative. Managing organisational politics is an integral part of building enthusiasm and team work. Strategists should ensure that all major power bases within an organisation have representation in or access to top management.

Board of Directors and Strategy Formulation

Often, the managing director of the company, in the capacity of chief executive officer and chief strategist, formulate the strategies without consulting the Board of Directors. The businesses to-day are more diversified, large in size and involve large amounts of financial resources. In view of these factors and also due to protecting the rights of shareholders, the board of directors should be informed and involved in the strategy formulation process. Exhibit 10.2 presents Board of Directors strategy audit framework.

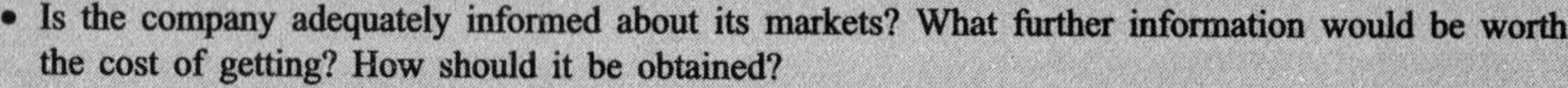

Exhibit 10.2: A Board of Directors Strategy Audit Framework

- Is the company adequately informed about its markets? What further information would be worth the cost of getting? How should it be obtained?
- How well informed is the company about its competitors? How well is it able to forecast what competitors will do under various circumstances? Is there a sound basis for such competitive appraisals? Is the company underestimating or overestimating its competitors?
- Has management adequately explored various ways of segmenting its market? To what extent is it addressing market segments in which the company's strengths provide meaningful advantages?
- Are the products and services the company proposes to sell, ones that it can provide more effectively than competitors? What is the basis for such a belief?
- Do the various activities proposed in the strategy provide synergistic advantages? Are they compatible?
- Does the proposed strategy adequately address questions of corporate objectives, financial policy, scope of operations, organisation, and integration?
- What specific resources (personnel, skills, information, facilities, technology, finances, relationships) will be needed to execute the strategy? Does the company already possess these resources? Has management established programmes for building these resources and overall competence which will provide telling competitive advantages over the long run?
- To what extent does the strategy define a unique and appropriate economic rule for the company? How different is it from the competitor's strategy?
- Has the issue of growth rate been raised? Are there good reasons to believe that investment in growth will pay off? Does the company's track record support such a conclusion?
- Does the proposed dividend policy reflect the company's growth policy, based on a demonstrated

ability or inability to reinvest cash flow advantageously? Or is it just a "safe" compromise, conforming to what others usually do?

- Is the management capable of implementing the strategy effectively? What leads to this conclusion?
- How and to what extent is the strategy to be communicated to the organisation? Is it to be distributed in written form? If competitors are aware of the company's strategy, will that help or hurt?
- What provision is to be made for employing the strategy as a guide to operating decisions? To what extent is it to be used by the board? How?
- How is it to be kept up-to-date? Are there to be regular reviews? How often and by whom?
- Has a set of long-range projections of operations following the strategy been prepared? Have the possible results of following alternative strategies been prepared?
- Does the strategy focus on the few really important key issues? Is it too detailed? Does it address genuine business questions (as opposed to "motherhood" statements)?
- In its strategic thinking, has management avoided the lure of simplistic approaches such as:

  Growth for growth's sake?

  Diversification for diversification's sake?

  Aping the industry leader?

  Broadening the scope in order to secure "incremental" earnings?

  Assuming it can execute better than the competitors without objective evidence that such is the case?
- Are there other issues, trends, or potential events that should have been taken into account?

Source: Milton Lauenstein, "Boards of Directors: The Strategy Audit," *Journal of Business Strategy* 4, No. 3 (Winter 1984): 90, 91.

POINTS TO BE REMEMBERED

- Strategic alternatives at all levels, *viz*; corporate, strategic business unit level and functional level should be analysed and evaluated to rank them and to select the best strategy.
- The evaluation should measure the suitability of the strategy to the situation.
- The internal factor evaluation matrix summarises an organisation's key strengths and weaknesses.
- The matching stage of the analytical framework for strategy formulation attempts to match strengths with the opportunities and threats with the weaknesses
- Boston Consultancy Group's matrix evaluates based on industry growth rate and reactive market share position of the company.
- GE nine-cell matrix examines in terms of long-term industry alternativeness and business strength/competitive position.
- Selection of the matrix involves the portfolio mix of industries and portfolio performance potential

KEY WORDS

- Internal Factors
- Competitive Profile
- GE Nine-Cell Matrix
- Hofer's Life Cycle Matrix
- External Factors
- Boston Consultancy Group
- Directional Policy Matrix
- Internal-External Matrix

- Grand Strategy Matrix
- Strategic Fit Analysis
- Industry Attractiveness
- Busines Unit Strength

QUESTIONS FOR DISCUSSION

1. What type of criteria do you adopt to evaluate strategic alternatives?
2. Discuss the framework for evaluating strategic alternatives.
3. What is external factor evaluation matrix?
4. What is the matching stage corporate portfolio analysis?
5. How do you evaluate the strategic alternatives using the BCG criteria?
6. How do you evaluate the strategic alternatives using GE Nine-Cell matrix?
7. What is the internal-external matrix? Explain its strengths over other criteria.
8. What is selection of the matrix?
9. What is the decision stage? How do you use the quantitative strategic planning matrix to make a decision with regard to strategy selection?

REFERENCES

1. Gerry Johnson and Kevan Scholes, "*Exploring Corporate Strategy*", Prentice-Hall, Englewood Cliffs, NJ, 1984, pp. 206-207.
2. S. Tilles, "How to Evaluate Corporate Strategy", *Harvard Business Review,* July-August 1963.
3. Gerry Johnson and Kevan Scholes, *op. cit.*, p. 211.
4. Fred R. David, *op. cit.*, pp. 198-200.
5. *Ibid*., pp. 200-201.
6. *Ibid*., pp. 202-203.
7. *Ibid*., p. 203.
8. Heinz Weihrich, "The TOWS Matrix: A Tool for Situational Analysis", *Long Range Planning*, Vol. 15, No. 2, April 1982, p. 61.
9. Fred R. David, *op. cit.*, p. 208.
10. A Rowe, R. Mason and K. Dickel, "*Strategic Management and Business Policy, A Methodological Approach*", Addison-Wesley Publishing Co., Reading, Mass, 1982, pp. 155-164.
11. Arthur A. Thompson Jr., and A.J. Strickland III, *op. cit.* pp. 194-195.
12. *Ibid*., p. 195.
13. *Ibid*., p. 196.
14. *Ibid*., p. 197.
15. *Ibid*., p. 198.
16. Derek F. Abell and John S. Hammond, "*Strategic Market Planning*", Prentice-Hall, Englewood Cliffs, NJ, 1979, p. 212.
17. Michael G. Allen, "Diagramming G.E.'s Planning for What's WATT", in "*Corporate Planning: Techniques and Applications*", Robert J. Allio and Malcolm W. Pennington, AMACOM, New York, 1979.
18. Arthur A. Thompson and A.J. Strickland III, *op. cit.*, pp. 200-201.
19. Charles W. Hofer and Dan Schendel, "*Strategy Formulation: Analytical Concepts*", West Publishing, St. Paul Minn., 1978, p. 33.
20. *Ibid*., p. 34.
21. Fred R. David, *op. cit.*, pp. 218-220.
22. Arthur A. Thompson and A.J. Strickland III, *op. cit.*, pp. 205-206.

23. *Ibid*., pp. 206-207.

25. *Ibid*., p. 209.

26. Hofer and Schendel, "*Strategy Formulating: Analytical Concepts*," p. 80, Quoted in *Ibid*., p. 210.

27. Barry Hedley, "Strategy and the Business Portfolio," *Long Range Planning*, Vol. 10, No. 1, February 1977, p. 13.

28. Fred R. David, "Evaluating Alternatives Growth Strategies – An Analytical Approach," *Long Range Planning*, Spring 1986.

29. Fred R. David, *op. cit*., pp. 223-224.

30. Michael E. Porter, "*Competitive Advantage*," p. 58 and p. 196. Quoted in Thompson and Strickland, *op. cit*., p. 213.

31. Arthur A. Thompson and A.J. Strickland, *op. cit*., p. 213.

32. Fred R. David, *op. cit*., pp. 230-231.

33. *Ibid*., p. 232.

✦ ✦ ✦

11 CHAPTER STRUCTURAL IMPLEMENTATION

Chapter Outline

(A) Analysing Strategic Change
(B) Managing Strategic Change
(C) Issues in Strategy Implementation
(D) Organisational Structure
(E) Approaches to Organisation Structure
(F) Matching Structure and Strategy
(G) Assessment of Organisational Structure
(H) Perspectives on the Methods of Organising

Learning Objectives

After studying this chapter, you should be able to:

- Analyse the need for strategic change;
- Study various issues in strategy implementation like project, procedural implementation and organisation implementation;
- Discuss strategy and structure relationship and Structure-follow-strategy thesis;
- Analyse different approaches to organisational structure like product, geographic and strategic business unit structures;
- Explain various approaches match the structure to the strategy;
- Study the assessment of organisational structures.

(A) ANALYSING STRATEGIC CHANGE

The strategist should find out to what extent the organisation will have to change in order to succeed in the strategic implementation. Different kinds of strategies require different change in the business process, nature and size. For example, a stability strategy affects the present business and organisation to the least extent. Similarly, a new pricing strategy affects only the people in the marketing department and brings a few changes in the day-to-day business operations. In fact, the joint venture strategy brings radical changes in the organisation, *viz.*, replacing the existing organisational structure, introducing a more flexible, cross-functional organisational structure based on team building, new production process, technology, new markets and market practices, dropping existing products and adding new products and/or services.

Different kinds of strategies require different change in the business process, nature and size.

Strategic change can be a continuum varying from no variation in strategy to a complete and radical change in the project procedure, organisational mission, objectives and organisational structure. Samuel C. Certo and Paul Peter divide strategic change into five discrete stages. They are stable strategy, routine strategy change, limited strategy change, radical strategy change and organisational redirection. Exhibit 11.1 presents levels of strategic change.

Exhibit 11.1: Levels of Strategic Change

Strategic Change	*Industry*	*Organisation*	*Products*	*Market Appeal*
Stable Strategy	same	same	same	same
Routine Strategy Change	same	same	same	new
Limited Strategy Change	same	same	new	new
Radical Strategy Change	same	new	new	new
Organisational Redirection	new	new	new	new

Source: Samuel C. Certo and J. Paul Peter, *op. cit.*, p. 113.

The implementation process of strategy involves many people, tasks, business units and products when it moves from stable strategy to organisational redirection. The implementation process becomes more complex when it moves towards organisational redirection.

Stable Strategy

Stable strategy is continuation of stability in all aspects of the business. Therefore, mostly, it requires continuation of strategy from the previous planning period. It requires running of the business and performing the same tasks with the same skills. Successful implementation of stability strategy requires monitoring the activities to ensure that the objectives are achieved. The learning from previous experiences (experiences curve effects) will help to achieve the objectives effectively.

Stable strategy is continuation of stability in all aspects of the business.

Routine Strategy Change

In the routine strategy change, a firm seeks to attract customers, by making normal, predicted adjustments in the methods. The strategy changes include: Changing advertising appeals, update packaging, using different pricing tactics, change the distributors, distributing channels and methods, adding gifts, etc. Managers should integrate and coordinate the activities with various agencies and intermediaries in order to implement the strategies successfully. Similarly, the strategists should also co-ordinate the activities within the company. For example, the strategy of price reduction will enhance the demand for the product. Hence, the strategist should coordinate the activities of marketing department and production department to increase production, capacities of distribution channels and distributors. This strategy does not require major efforts and major changes for its successful implementation.

In the routine strategy change, a firm seeks to attract customers, by making normal, predicted adjustments in the methods.

Limited Strategy Change: This strategy involves offering new products to new markets within the same general products class. Products are new, though, they belong to the same general class. Hence, the managers have to perform many new activities. These activities include: designing the new products, procurement of new kinds of inputs, new machinery, producing new products, arranging new market intermediaries (if necessary), new market channels and the like.

Radical Strategy Change: This strategy involves a major shift for the firm. The radical strategy change is necessary, when the firm adopts the strategies like mergers and acquisitions in the same basic industry. These strategies create complex problems in integrating the two firms into one firm. These complex problems include: restructuring the organisation, organisational change, change in the organisational culture, change in the positions of key personnel, change in the distributors and distributing channels, etc.

Organisational Redirection

This strategy involves mergers and acquisitions of firms in different industries. The magnitude of strategic change depends on the degree of variation of the nature of industries and the degree of centralisation of the new firm. Another form of organisational redirection involves when a firm leaves one industry and enters a new one. For example, a firm enters the hot drinks industry by leaving the soft drinks industry.

(B) MANAGING STRATEGIC CHANGE

The board of directors should actively involve like catalyst (See Exhibit 11.2) in the implementation process. The managing director can get a sense of the magnitude of a newly implemented change from the broad categories of change discussed above. However, these strategies will not provide the details of actually managing a strategic change effort. James Brian Quinn provides an outline of the steps that effective leaders often use to manage strategic change. Exhibit 11.3 presents three major sequential steps, along with the specific activities in each. Quinn's approach emphasises the essential analytical and political roles of the executives in managing strategic change. Effective leaders also need political and leadership skills to sell those interpretations to others.

Formulation and Implementation of Strategy

The strategy formulation and the relationship between strategy formulation and strategic implementation should be studied. This is because, the formulation and implementation process are intertwined in real life. The two linkages exist between strategy formulation and strategy implementation are: *(i)* forward linkage, and *(ii)* backward linkage. The forward linkage deals with preparing the organisational activities including organisational structure, leadership, culture, etc., necessary for the strategic implementation.

The backward linkage deals with the influence of implementation on strategy formulation. In other words, once the strategy is selected and implemented, it is found in the reality that there are certain deviations due to the different ground realities. These deviations force the strategist to reformulate the strategy based on the ground realities. Therefore, the past strategic actions and experiences should be taken into consideration in formulating strategies.

(C) ISSUES IN STRATEGY IMPLEMENTATION

A number of issues are normally involved in strategy implementation. The important issues are: project, procedural, organisational structural, behavioural considerations, production/operations, human resources, financial and marketing.

1. Project Implementation

Project is defined by the Project Management Institute of the US as, "a one-shot, time limited, goal-oriented, major undertaking, requiring the commitment of varied skills and resources." Thus, a project is a highly specific programme for which the time schedule and specific costs are determined in advance. Projects create all necessary conditions and facilities for the strategy implementation.

Exhibit 11.2: Degree of Involvement of Board of Directors in Strategy Implementation

Low (Passive) → *High (Active)*

Phantom	*Rubber Stamp*	*Minimal Review*	*Nominal Participation*	*Active Participation*	*Catalyst*
Never knows what to do, if anything, no degree of involvement.	Permits officers to make all decisions. It votes as officers recommend on action issues.	Formally reviews selected issues that officers bring to its attention.	Involved to a limited degree in the performance of review of selected key decisions, indicators, or programmers of management.	Approves, questions, and makes final decisions on mission, strategy, policies and objectives; Has active Board committees. Performs fiscal and management audits.	Takes the leading role in establishing and modifying the mission objectives, strategy and policies. It may have a very active strategy committee.

Source: Adapted from P.K. Ghosh, "*Business Policy*," Sultan Chand & Sons, New Delhi, 1994, p. 288.

Exhibit 11.3: Managing Strategic Change

INITIATING STRATEGIC CHANGE

- Build networks to sense needs
- Improve and lead the formal information system
- Amplify understanding
- Build awareness
- Change symbols
- Legitimise new viewpoints
- Develop partial solutions
- Broaden support

MOVE FROM CONCEPT TO STRATEGY

- Overcome opposition to change by finding zones of indifference and no loss situations
- Building comfort levels; change perceived risks
- Structure flexibility
- Test trial concepts

SOLIDIFY COMMITMENT

- Create key pockets of commitment
- Keep political exposure low
- Eliminate options
- Crystalize focus and consensus; management coalitions
- Formalise commitment, empower champions
- Design continuous strategic change process.

Source: Samuel C. Certo and J. Paul Peter, *op. cit.*, p. 116.

2. Procedural Implementation

Strategy implementation also requires executing the strategy, based on the rules, regulations and procedures formulated by the government. Though, many procedures are simplified with the liberalisation, privatisation and globalisation of Indian economy, certain procedures are still applicable in the process of strategy implementation. Therefore, the strategists should study the following procedural aspects before implementing the strategy. They are: licensing procedures, foreign collaboration procedures, Foreign Exchange and Regulation Act requirements, environmental requirements, Monopolies and Restrictive Trade Practices requirements, import and export requirements, incentives and benefits, requirements of labour laws and other legislations (See Box 11.1).

BOX 11.1 SHELL OFFERS BUSINESS MODEL ON PROFIT-SHARING TO ONGC

In order to overcome any bottlenecks on their joint co-operation in exploration and production (E&P) activities Royal Dutch Shell has offered ONGC a business model of profit sharing for any enhancement in productivity. Sources told *Business Line* that ONGC is considering Shell's proposal based on a framework outlined by the latter. The two companies have been holding high-level discussions on the issue. Indications are that ONGC was not open to going beyond Government prescribed norms on making joint investments and giving operatorship of the fields. However, ONGC has said that it was ready to share any enhancement made on planned profile of a field with Shell. Opportunities The steering committee set up by the two entities to manage co-operation between the two companies, following a memorandum of understanding inked between the oil sector behemoths, is looking into these aspects. Opening the doors for a possible participation in overseas projects as well as domestic ventures, earlier this year ONGC and Shell Exploration Company B.V. (subsidiary of the world's third largest petroleum group Royal Dutch Shell) had inked an understanding to examine significant opportunities for future co-operation both in India and other countries. The MoU covered wide areas of cooperation across the full range of upstream and downstream activities, including exploration and production, coal gasification, natural gas, oil products, refining and petrochemicals. The areas of cooperation in the upstream sector included investigation of increasing and enhancing production from existing producing fields in the country, joint bidding in exploration acreage rounds in India. The cooperation also includes farming into existing, but undeveloped Indian exploration blocks, investigation of opportunities for cooperation and joint participation in international upstream ventures from Shell and ONGC's portfolios, and evaluation of a joint project for coal gasification facilities in the country.

Source: http://www.blonnet.com/2006/09/29/stories/2006092904270200.htm

3. Organisational Growth

Organisational structure is a means to an end of achieving organisational mission and objectives.

Organisational structure is a means to an end of achieving organisational mission and objectives. Thus, it is an important means for strategic implementation. Organisational structure refers to the methods of allocating duties and responsibilities to individuals, and the ways that individuals are grouped together into units, departments and divisions. The formal organisational structure represents the relationships between people and functions as designated by management and conveyed in the organisation chart. It also defines the number of levels in the organisational hierarchy. The informal organisational structure represents the web of social relationships among various members of a company.

4. Organisational Structures and Strategies

Companies build structures for their organisations based on their strategies. There are a number of methods/ways that the organisations can be structured. The simple strategies require simple structures whereas the growth strategies require flexible structure and complex strategies necessarily influence to build matrix structures. In fact, the stable strategies require a mechanistic organisation and a growth strategy require an organic structure.

5. Entrepreneurial Structure

Generally, the small businesses and businesses when they are started consist of an owner-manager and few employees. (Fig. 11.1) These types of organisations do not require an organisational chart and formal assignment of responsibilities. Organisation structure is fluid with each employee often knowing how to perform more than one task and with owner-manager involved in all aspects/areas of business.

Generally, the small businesses and businesses when they are started consist of an owner manager and few employees.

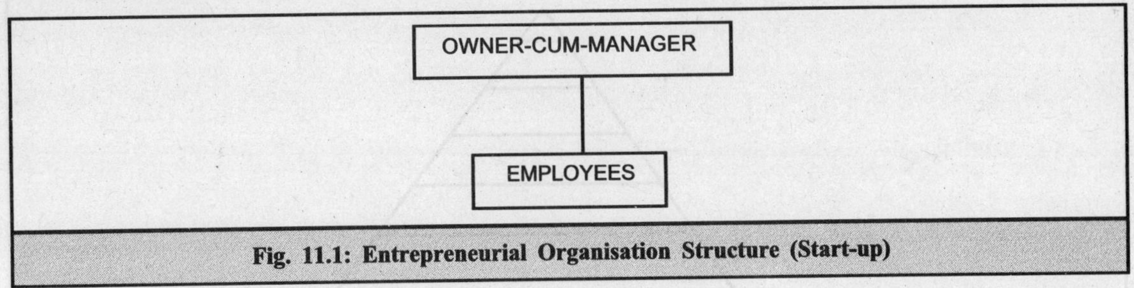

Fig. 11.1: Entrepreneurial Organisation Structure (Start-up)

The small firms, if, they are successful during the first years of crucial periods, it would be due to the increased demand for products or services. The entrepreneurs develop the business and increase the size of the firm to meet the increased demand. The business begins to evolve from fluidity to a status of more permanent division of labour due to the growth. The owner-manager, who was performing all functions in the initial stage now finds that he has to perform more managerial activities than operational activities. The growth demands the owner to employ new candidates and this results in assignment of specialised functions to these employees.

The business growth results in expansion of organisational structure both vertically and horizontally. The entrepreneurial organisational structure with growth is depicted in Fig. 11.2. As can be seen from this figure, the operative functions of manufacturing are assigned to manufacturing manager and the operative functions of marketing are assigned to the marketing manager. These two managers perform the activities with the help of employees. The owner-manager performs managerial and strategic functions.

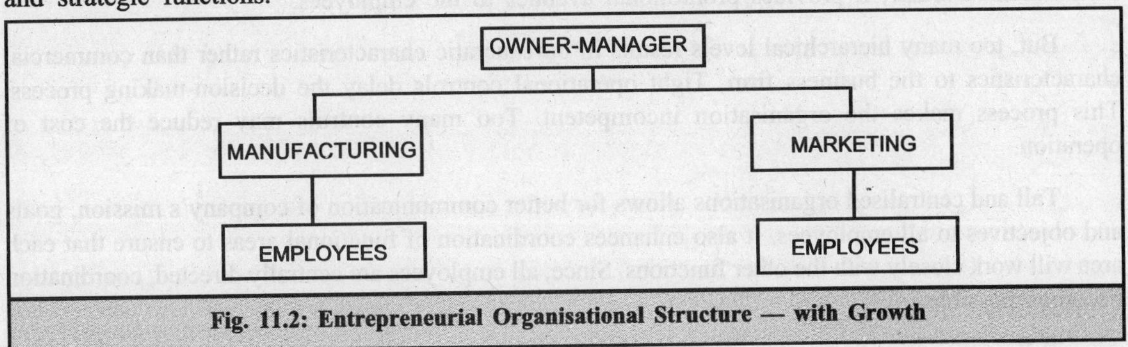

Fig. 11.2: Entrepreneurial Organisational Structure — with Growth

Strategic Indication: The entrepreneurial structure is simple and it offers some advantages like: timely decision-making, sensitive to environmental demands and operational flexibility. But, this structure results in excessive dependence on owner-manager who is normally not a professional manager. This structure cannot respond to the increasing demand beyond a point. Thus, this structure is mostly suitable to the strategy catering to the needs of a local market by being small.

6. Vertical/Tall Organisations

Vertical/Tall organisations refer to increase in the length of the organisation's hierarchy chain of command.

Vertical/Tall organisations refer to increase in the length of the organisation's hierarchy chain of command. The hierarchical chain of command represents the company's authority – accountability relationship between superiors and subordinates. Authority and responsibility flows from the top to the bottom through all the levels of the hierarchy. Accountability flow from the lowest level to the highest level. Fig. 11.3 shows the vertical/tall organisation. Employees at each level should report to their superior, who in turn should report to boss. Thus, the activities are reported to the top. Authority is more centralised in tall organisation.

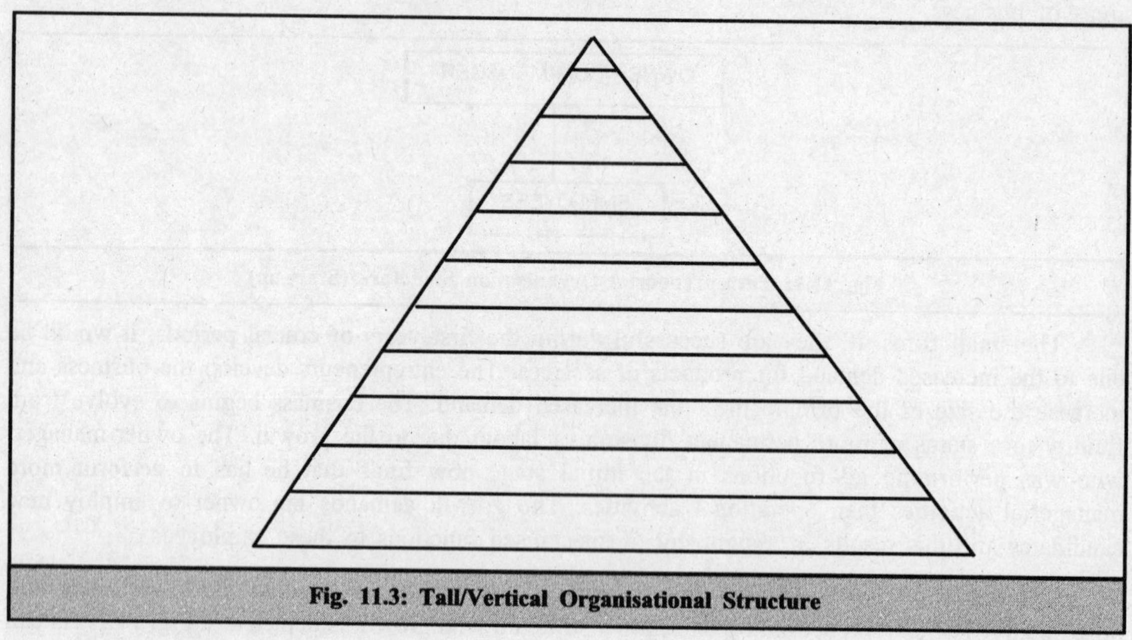

Fig. 11.3: Tall/Vertical Organisational Structure

Strategic Implication: The advantage of tall organisation include: effective analysis of factors and efficient decision-making are possible as a number of managers at different levels supervised and check the activities. The organisation can formulate effective policies, programmes and control mechanisms. Further, it provides promotional avenues to the employees.

But, too many hierarchical levels results in bureaucratic characteristics rather than commercial characteristics to the business firm. Tight operational controls delay the decision-making process. This process makes the organisation incompetent. Too many controls may reduce the cost of operation.

Tall and centralised organisations allows for better communication of company's mission, goals and objectives to all employees. It also enhances coordination of functional areas to ensure that each area will work closely with the other functions. Since, all employees are centrally directed, coordination becomes possible.

Tall organisational structure is appropriate for the firms having bleak growth opportunities, problem children and dogs. Further, firms with cost minimisation strategy and firms in maturity stage can adopt tall organisations. Thus, this type of structures are well suited for environments that are relatively stable and predictable.

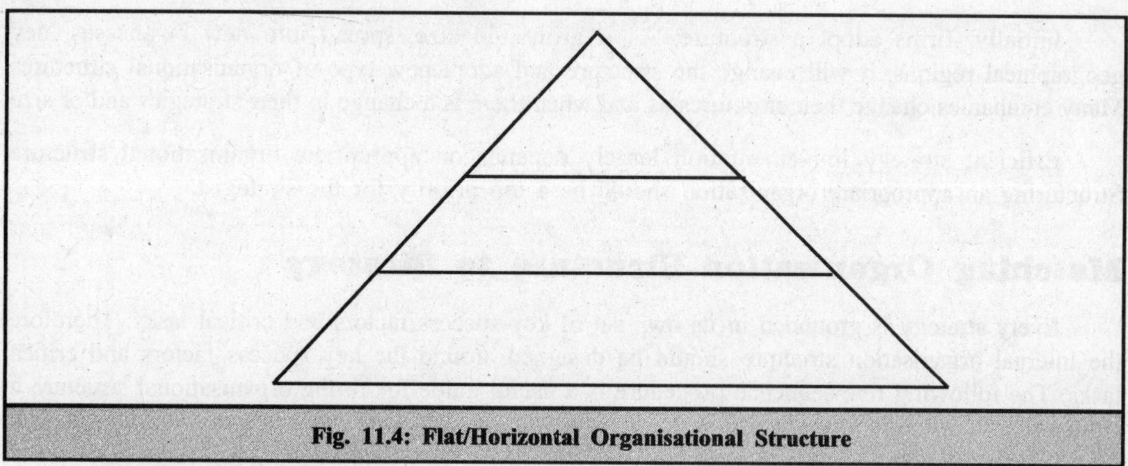

Fig. 11.4: Flat/Horizontal Organisational Structure

Horizontal/Flat Organisations: Horizontal/flat organisations refer to an increase in breadth of an organisation's structure. Fig. 11.4 presents the model of horizontal/flat organisation. The number of levels in the organisational hierarchy are a few. The span of control is relatively large.

The increasing bio-professionalisation and multi-professionalisation and wide acceptance for empowerment allowed even the large business firms to reduce the number of hierarchical levels of their organisations. Consequently, large sized firms also started adopting horizontal/flat organisation by delayering. In fact, this structure is well suited for the small size business firms.

Authority is more decentralised in relatively flat structures. Managers with broad span of control must grant more authority to his subordinates. Decisions are more likely to be made by the employees who are at the helm of affairs and more familiar with the situations and ground realities. Organisational activities are mostly performed informally. Professional managers are treated as real professionalists.

Strategy Implications: The major advantage of flat structure is quick decision-making. Thus, it enables the management to take decisions in right time. Other advantages of this structure include: low administrative costs, freedom and autonomy to the managers to operate, decision-making by the managers who are at helm of affairs and empowerment of managers. These benefits motivate the managers to accept responsibility and commit themselves towards organisational objectives. Further, these characteristics enable the organisation to be duly sensitive to the environmental demands. The employees also become innovative and creative.

The horizontal/flat organisational structure are appropriate for the organisations with horizontal and vertical growth strategies, stars and cash cows. Thus, these structures are useful for competitive and dynamic business firms.

(D) ORGANISATIONAL STRUCTURE

Organisational structure is an established pattern of relationships among the component parts of an organisation. Structure is made up of three component parts, *viz.*, complexity, formalisation and centralisation. Complexity refers to horizontal differentiation, vertical differentiation and locational differentiation. Horizontal differentiation is horizontal separation between units based on occupations and specialisations. Vertical differentiation is the potential for communication distortion. Locational differentiation refers to the degree to which the location of an organisation's offices, plants and personnel are geographically spread.

Organisational structure is an established pattern of relationships among the component parts of an organisation.

Formalisation refers to the degree to which the jobs within the organisation are standardised. High standardisation of jobs results in less freedom and discretion. Centralisation refers to the degree to which decision-making is concentrated at a single point in an organisation.

Initially, firms adopt a structure. As it grows, in size, spread into new businesses, new geographical regions, it will change the structure and adopt new type of organisational structures. Many companies change their structures as and when there is a change in their strategies and/or size.

Efficient strategy implementation largely depends on appropriate organisational structure. Structuring an appropriate organisation should be a top priority for the strategist.

Matching Organisation Structure to Strategy

The internal organisation structure should be designed around the key success factors and critical tasks.

Every strategy is grounded in its own set of key success factors and critical tasks. Therefore, the internal organisation structure should be designed around the key success factors and critical tasks. The following five-sequence procedure is a useful guide for fitting organisational structure to strategy.

1. Pinpoint the key functions and tasks necessary for successful strategy execution.
2. Reflection on how strategy-critical functions and organisational units relate to those that are routine and to those that provide staff support.
3. Make strategy-critical business units and functions of the main organisational building blocks.
4. Determine the degrees of authority needed to manage each organisational unit bearing in mind both the benefits and costs of decentralised decision-making.
5. Provide the coordination among the various organisational units.

1. Strategy-critical Activities

Some activities and skills are generally critical in the execution of a strategy. In fact, much of the activities are performed in a routine manner even in the process of strategy implementation. The critical tasks to be performed only for strategy implementation include: tight cost control when the firm adopts the strategy of low-cost producer, special promotional appeal, tight quantity control to produce zero defect products, critical skills to produce distinctly qualitative products, and special design of the produce, when the company adopts the strategy of market leader. The critical activities in high-tech industries include: research and development, product innovation, developing new products, developing new uses of existing products, taking the laboratory results into the market quickly, testing the new products in the market, etc. Thus, the strategy-critical activities vary according to the nature of the firm and competitive situation of the firm.

The firm in order to decide on the type of organisation structure should know the special tasks/functions to be performed and the right time for effective strategy execution. Further, the firm should also find out the vulnerable areas where malperformance of the tasks/functions seriously endanger strategic success. This effort will enable the management to concentrate on the crucial areas in organisation building efforts.

Understanding the Relationships among Activities

The strategic relationship among the critical, supportive and routine activity groups should be analysed and scrutinised. Activities or functions can be related by the flow of material, production process, types of customers served, distribution channels used, the intermediaries used, technical skills and know-how necessary to perform the activities, sequence or the order in which the activities must be performed, geographical location help in grouping and regrouping of activities in the organisation restructuring or redesigning process.

Grouping Activities into Organisation Units

The strategy critical activities should be used as the main building blocks in structuring the organisation. The strategy-critical activities must receive the attention and be the prominent parts in the organisation rebuilding scheme. The role and power of the key and critical groups should be duly recognised. Further, adequate resources should be allocated to these critical activities. All this would be possible by grouping the key and strategy-critical areas. Top management should be informed about the significance of the strategy-critical areas in the strategy execution. The managers in charge of these areas should be given influential position in the newly built organisational structure.

Determining the Degree of Authority and Independence to Each Unit

The tall organisations are normally centralised. The decision-making authority in these firms is highly centralised. The strategies are formulated by only top management. Even the policy decisions are made at top management level. The lower level managers are delegated with the limited authority to make operational decisions.

The tall organisations are normally centralised. The decision-making authority in these firms is highly centralised.

The flat organisations are highly decentralised. Enough authority to formulate strategies, modify strategies, make policy and operational decisions is delegated to the managers at all levels. In fact, some organisations empower their managers to function independently, with little direct authority exerted by corporate staff.

Guidelines for Delegating Authority: Strategies have to be implemented by the managers at different levels, but not only by the top management. In fact, the middle and lower level managers play a key role in strategy implementation. Hence, adequate authority should be delegated to the middle and lower level managers. The guidelines include:

(i) Activities and organisational units with a crucial role in strategy implementation process should not be subordinate to routine and non-key activities.

(ii) Revenue-producing and results producing activities should not be subordinate to internal support or staff functions.

(iii) Authority to make strategic and policy decisions should be delegated to the level of helm of affairs, particularly, when lower level managers can make better decisions, in right time than high level managers.

(iv) However, the final authority to make strategic decisions should rest with the top management for consistency and uniformity.

(v) Select the key jobs and competent managers and appoint the right and competent manager as head of each unit.

(vi) Delegate enough authority to these competent managers to formulate and implement strategies.

(vii) Do not delegate authority to incompetent managers, managers who consistently produce unsatisfactory results and managers who have a poor track record in strategy formulation and implementation.

(viii) Centralise the authority of strategy formulation, cxccution and decision-making in diversified companies with related businesses in their portfolio.

Coordination among Units

Coordination among key units and between key units and other units is important in the process of strategy execution. Generally, the managers with authority should perform this task. The chief executive, the chief operating manager, the strategic business unit level managers should perform the coordination tasks as their positions have enough authority over the entire unit. The strategy formulation procedure should take care of coordination among all the units and/or managers. The functions of coordination should be centralised even in case of diversification strategies into related and unrelated areas.

2. The Structure-Follows-Strategy Thesis

The practice of matching organisation structure to the particular needs of strategy is a fairly recent and research based management development.

The practice of matching organisation structure to the particular needs of strategy is a fairly recent and research based management development. Alfred Chandler, in his research study found that changes in a company's strategy bring about new administrative problems, which in turn, require a new or refashioned structure for the new strategy to be successfully implemented. A company's internal organisation should be reassessed whenever strategy changes. Otherwise, internal problems would crop-up and result in failure in strategy implementation. Structure follows strategy as organisational structure is only a means to an end rather than end itself. Organisational structure is a managerial tool in the process of achievement of organisational objectives. It is easy to coordinate strategic moves across functional areas, if functions, activities and responsibilities are efficiently organised to link strategy and structure.

(E) APPROACHES TO ORGANISATION STRUCTURE

There are six approaches to structure the organisation. They are: (1) Functional organisation structure, (2) Product organisation structure, (3) Geographical organisation structure, (4) Decentralised business divisions, (5) Strategic business units, (6) Matrix organisational structure, (7) Team Structure and (8) Virtual Structure.

1. Functional Organisation Structure

Each functional department consists of those jobs in which employees perform similar jobs at different levels.

Functional organisation structure is most widely used structure. Each functional department consists of those jobs in which employees perform similar jobs at different levels. The commonly used functions are: marketing, finance and accounting, human resources, manufacturing, research and development and engineering. Fig. 11.5 illustrates a typical functional structure.

Strategic Advantages:

(i) A functional structure would be effective in single bųsiness firms where key activities revolve around well defined skills and areas of specialisation.

(ii) Indepth specialisation and focussed concentration on performing functional tasks can enhance operating efficiency and the development of core competencies.

(iii) This type of structure promotes maximum utilisation of up-to-date technical skills and enables the firm to capitalise on specialisation and efficiency. These are strategically important considerations for single business companies, dominant product companies and vertically integrated companies.

(iv) The functional structure is most appropriate when firms compete on the basis of technical specialisation or efficiency in a relatively stable environment.

(v) This structure promotes common values and goals among employees of the department, facilitating co-operation and collaboration within the functional department.

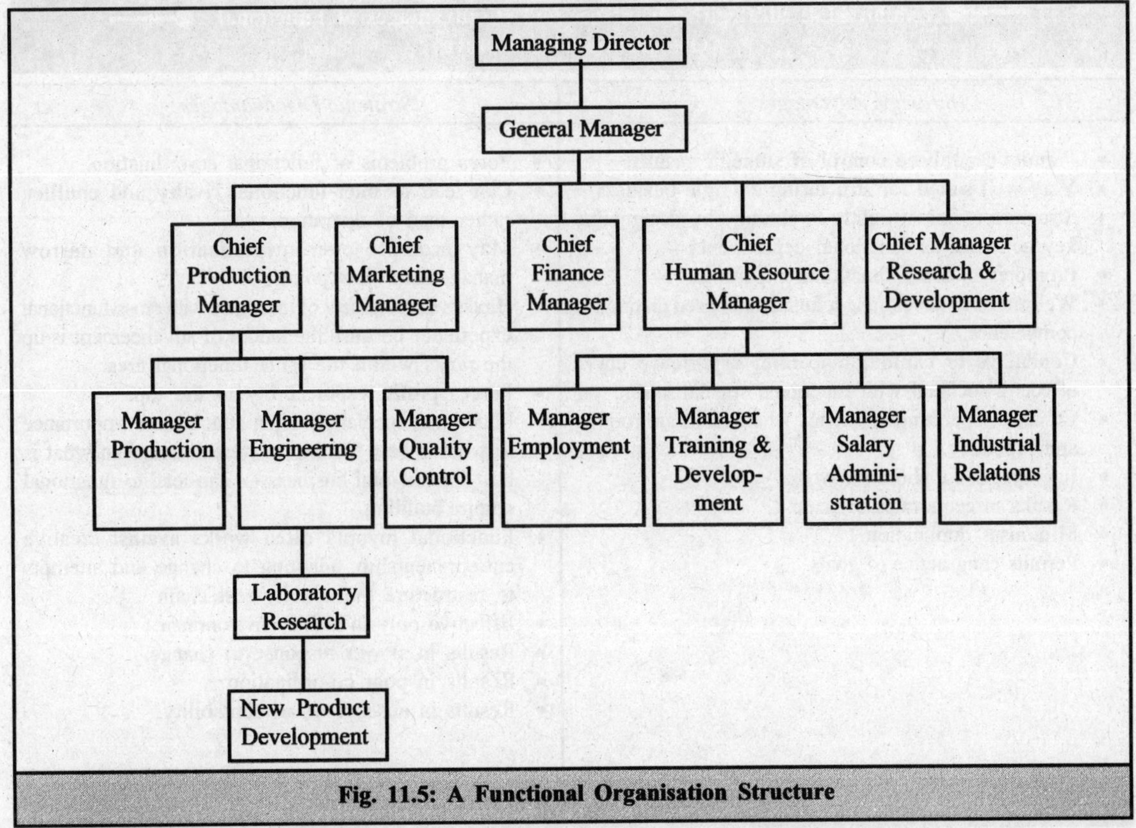

Fig. 11.5: A Functional Organisation Structure

Strategic Disadvantages:

(i) The horizontal diversification of the business reduces the efficiency of the functional structure.

(ii) The departmental members may see the activities from the narrow view point of the department rather than the total organisation. This aspect results in absence of inter-departmental coordination and cooperation.

(iii) Interdepartmental policies further result in conflicts. This situation leads to indecision, delay in decision-making or ineffective decision-making.

(iv) Further, the narrow specialisations kill the initiative of entrepreneurs and the zeal of innovativeness and creativeness. Consequently, the firm may lose sensitiveness to the customer demands, technological changes and environmental demands. These limitations of functional structure may make the firm to reassess the suitability of the structure to the strategy and decide accordingly. Exhibit 11.4 present strategic advantages and disadvantages of functional organisation structure.

Exhibit 11.4: Strategic Advantages and Disadvantages of Functional Organisational Structure

Strategic Advantages	*Strategic Disadvantages*
• Permits centralised control of strategic results. • Very well suited for structuring a single business. • Structure is linked tightly to strategy by designating key activities as functional departments. • Promotes in-depth functional expertise. • Well suited to developing a functional based distinctive competence. • Conducive to exploiting learning/experience curve effects associated with functional specialisation. • Enhances operating efficiency where tasks are routine and repetitive. • Encourages collaborative work. • Results in economies of scale. • Minimises duplication. • Permits congruence of goals.	• Poses problems of functional co-ordination. • Can lead to inter-functional rivalry and conflict, rather than co-operation. • May promote over-specialisation and narrow management view points. • Hinders development of managers with cross-functional experience because the ladder of advancement is up the ranks within the same functional area. • Forces profit responsibility to the top. • Functional specialists often attach more importance to what is best for the functional area than what is best for the total business — can lead to functional empire building. • Functional myopia often works against creative entrepreneurship, adapting to change and attempts to restructure the activity-cost chain. • Effective only in stable environment. • Results in slower response to change. • Results in poor co-ordination. • Results in absence of accountability.

Source: Modified version: Thompson and Strickland, *op. cit.*, p. 225.

2. Product Organisation Structure

Activities are divided on the basis of individual products, product line, services and are grouped into departments in product organisation structure.

Activities are divided on the basis of individual products, product line, services and are grouped into departments in product organisation structure. All important functions, *viz.*, marketing, production, finance and human resource are contained within each department. This type of organisation structure overcomes many of the major limitations of functional organisational structure. Fig. 11.6 presents the product organisation structure.

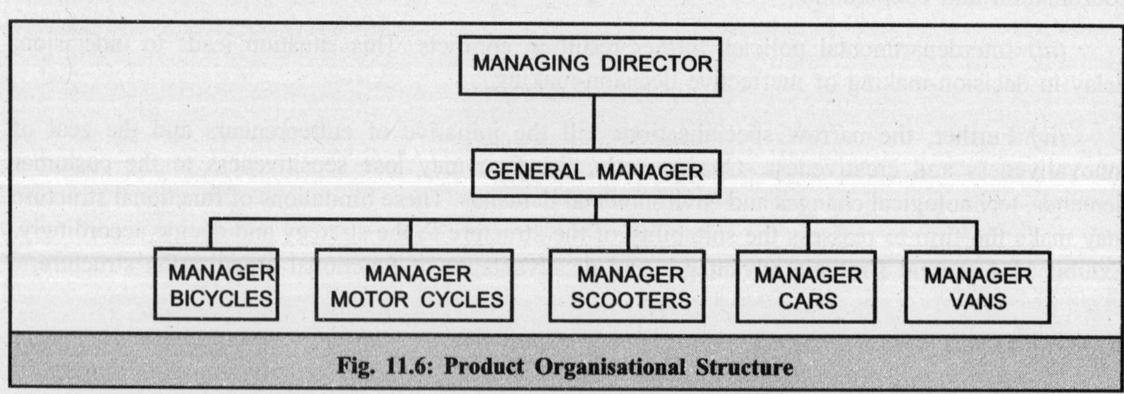

Fig. 11.6: Product Organisational Structure

Strategic Advantages:

(i) The product organisation structure is more appropriate than the functional form of organisation for firms producing multiple products.

(ii) Coordination among functional areas like product design, producing, distributing, marketing is effective as all functions are performed in each department.

(iii) Since, each department is independent, most of the decisions can be made at departmental level without involving the top management in this process. It will result in fast decisions, enhancement of organisational competency to compete in rapidly changing environment.

(iv) Responsibility and accountability for market share, sales, profit/loss is clearly fixed. Thus, either the credit for the success or blame for the failure of a product can be clearly attributed to a particular department. This advantage cannot present in case of functional organisation structure. Exhibit 11.5 present strategic advantages and disadvantages.

Exhibit 11.5: Strategic Advantages and Disadvantages of Product Organisation Structure

Strategic Advantages	*Strategic Disadvantages*
• Appropriate for organisations with multiple products.	• Result in inconsistent decisions from one department to another.
• Improves coordination across functions.	• Involves difficulty in allocating overheads.
• Suited to a more dynamic environment.	• Results in duplication of equipment and personnel.
• Moves decisions close to the problem.	• Encourages dysfunctional competition for resources.
• Release Managing Director's time	• Results in loss of specialisation.
• Clarifies profit/loss accountability.	• Emphasises departmental rather than organisational goals.

Source: Modified Version: Joe G. Thomas, op. cit., p. 266.

Strategic Disadvantages: Product organisational structure is also not free from limitations:

(i) One of the major limitation is that unnecessary duplication of equipment and personnel among various departments. This results in loss of specialisation.

(ii) Each department will have production, marketing, human resource, finance managers, secretarial and support staff, computers and testing equipment. As such specialised personnel and equipment cannot be procured.

(iii) Some decisions like pay, promotion, product quality, design and pricing strategy may be inconsistent between departments.

(iv) Interdepartmental conflicts arise regarding sharing of common resources, allocation of common and overhead expenses, etc.

3. Geographical Organisation Structure

The activities or functions are grouped into departments based on the activities performed in the geographical areas/regions. Each geographical unit includes all functions required to produce and market the products in a particular geographical area. Figure 11.7 presents a geographical organisation structure. Multinational organisations, enterprises operating in diverse geographic markets or serving an expansive geographic area are organised based on the geographic structure. This structure is also used by chain stores, power companies, restaurant chains, dairy products, banking companies, insurance companies, etc.

The activities or functions are grouped into departments based on the activities performed in the geographical areas/ regions.

Strategic Advantages: The advantages of this type of organisational structure are:

(i) Products and services are better designed to the climatic and cultural needs of specific geographical regions.

(ii) A geographical structure allows a firm to respond to the technical needs of different international area.

(iii) Producing and distributing products in different national or global locations may give the organisation to serve better the consumer needs of various nations.

(iv) This organisation structure enables a company to adapt to varying legal systems.

(v) It also allow firms pinpoint the responsibility for profits or losses.

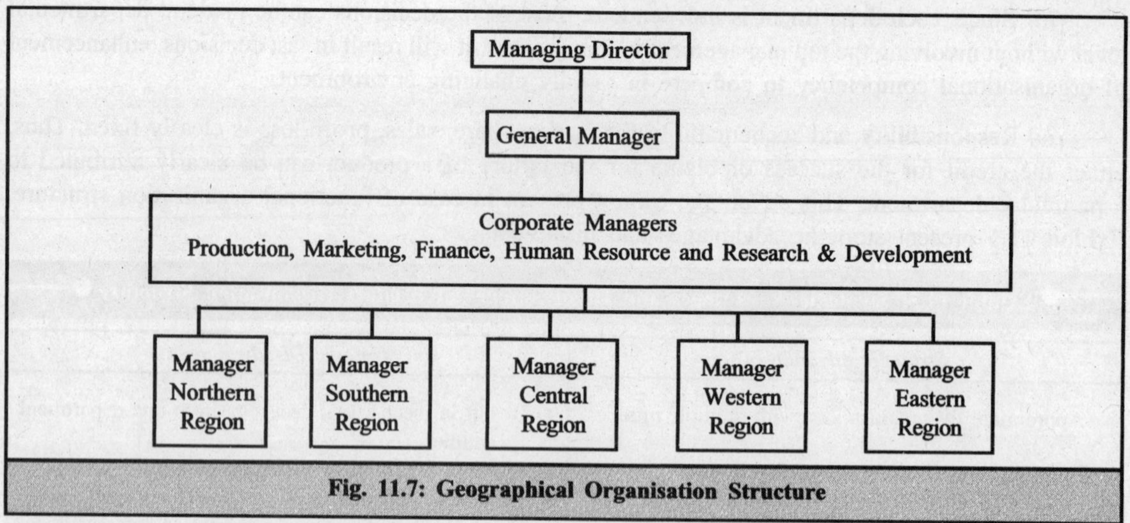

Fig. 11.7: Geographical Organisation Structure

Strategic Disadvantages: This organisational structure is also not free from limitations. The limitations of this structure are similar to those of product structure.

(i) Often more functional personnel are required. The firm cannot appoint specialists unlike in functional structure due to duplication of personnel.

(ii) There would be duplication of equipment and facilities.

(iii) Coordination of company-wide activities would be difficult.

(iv) There would be a problem of imposing a degree of uniformity and diversity.

(v) It is difficult to maintain consistent company image or reputation.

(vi) This structure adds another layer of management to run the geographic units. Strategic advantages and disadvantages are presented in Exhibit 11.6.

Exhibit 11.6: Strategic Advantages and Disadvantages of Geographical Organisation Structure

Strategic Advantages	*Strategic Disadvantages*
• Allows tailoring of strategy to needs of each geographical market. • Delegates profit/loss responsibility to lowest strategic level. • Improves functional coordination within the target market. • Takes advantages of economies of local operations. • Area units make an excellent training ground for higher level general managers. • Clarifies profit/loss accountability. • Results in good functional co-ordination.	• Poses a problem of how much geographic uniformity headquarters should impose versus how much geographic diversity should be allowed. • Greater difficulty in maintaining consistent company image/reputation from area to area when area managers exercise much strategic freedom. • Adds another layer of management to run the geographic units. • Can result in duplication of staff services at headquarters and regional levels, creating a relative cost disadvantage. • Results in inconsistent decisions from one region to another region. • Results in duplication of equipment and personnel. • Encourages dysfunctional competition for resources. • Results in loss of specialisation. • Emphasises regional rather than company goals.

Source: Thompson and Strickland, *op. cit.*, p. 226 and Joe. G. Thomas, *op. cit.*, p. 267.

4. Decentralised Business Unit Structure

Grouping activities based on product lines has been a trend among diversified companies since 1920. In a diversified firm, the basic organisational building blocks are its business units, each business is operated as a stand-alone profit centre. Fig. 11.8 presents decentralised line of business type of organisational structure.

In a diversified firm, the basic organisational building blocks are its business units, each business is operated as a stand-alone profit centre.

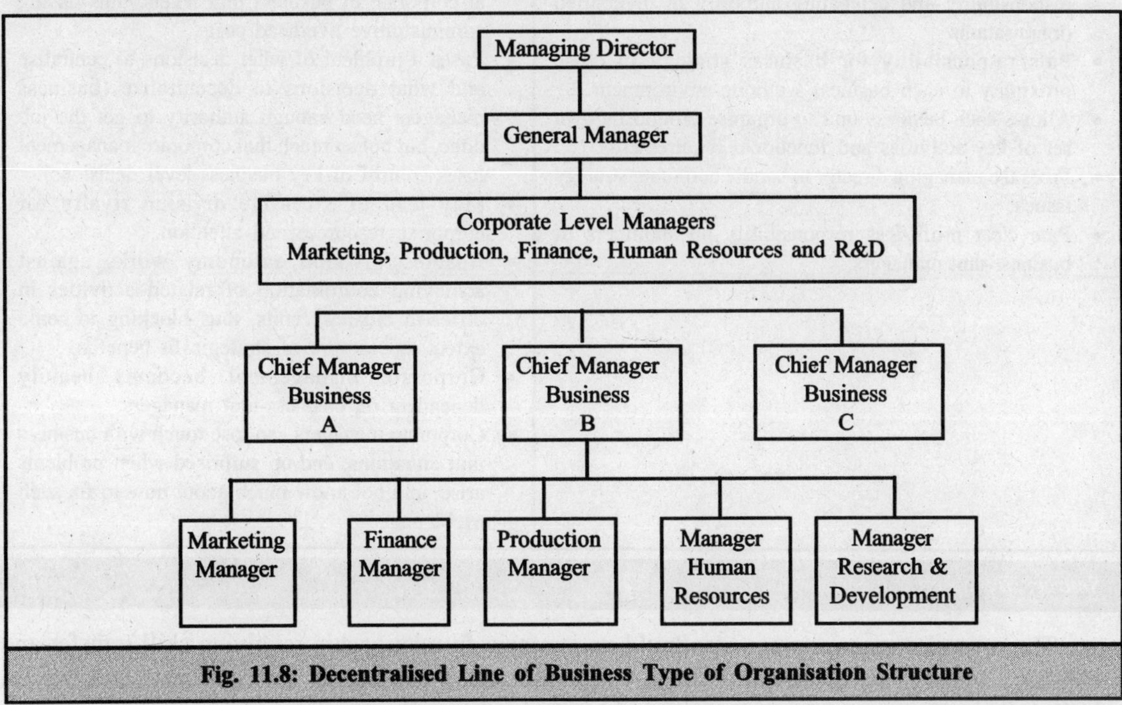

Fig. 11.8: Decentralised Line of Business Type of Organisation Structure

Strategic Advantages: Functional structure and geographic structure are standard organisational building blocks in a single business firm. But, in multi-business firms, the businesses are diversified.

(i) Diversification is generally managed by decentralised decision-making and delegating authority and responsibility to a manager at each business unit.

(ii) Each business unit should be managed by an entrepreneurially oriented general manager who is delegated with authority to formulate and execute business strategies.

(iii) Each business unit operates as a stand-alone profit centre. Each business unit is structured on the basis of either functional structure or geographic structure depending upon strategy, key activities and operating requirements.

Strategic Disadvantages: The strategic advantages and strategic disadvantages of a decentralised line-of-business type of organisation structure are presented in Exhibit 11.7. The disadvantages are:

(i) The major problem of this type of organisation structure is absence of mechanism for coordinating related activities across business units.

(ii) General manager in-charge of each business unit functions independently. It makes coordination a complicated task. Therefore, corporate headquarters must devise some internal mechanism for achieving strategic coordination and to capture strategic benefits. Co-ordination can be achieved by developing corporate R&D department, corporate sales force, sales force of closely related businesses, merging the order processing and shipping functions of businesses with common customers and consolidating the production of related parts.

Exhibit 11.7: Strategic Advantages and Disadvantages of Decentralised Line of Business Type of Organisation Structure

Strategic Advantages	*Strategic Disadvantages*
• Offers a logical and workable means of decentralising responsibility and delegating authority in diversified organisations. • Puts responsibility for business strategy in close proximity to each business's unique environment. • Allows each business unit to organise around its own set of key activities and functional requirements. • Frees the managing director to handle corporate strategy issues. • Puts clear profit/loss responsibility on shoulders of business-unit managers.	• May lead to costly duplication of staff functions at corporate or business unit levels, thus raising administrative overhead costs. • Poses a problem of what decisions to centralise and what decisions to decentralise (business managers need enough authority to get the job done, but not so much that corporate management loses control of key business-level decisions). • May lead to excessive division rivalry for corporate resources and attention. • Business/division autonomy works against achieving coordination of related activities in different business units, thus blocking to some extent the capture of strategic fit benefits. • Corporate management becomes heavily dependent on business-unit managers. • Corporate managers can lose touch with business unit situations, end-up surprised when problems arise, and not know much about how to fix such problems.

Source: Thompson and Strickland, *op. cit.*, p. 229.

The corporate managers can also build up strategic fit relationship involving skill transfer and technology transfer across business units. Corporate office can set up inter-business task forces, standing committees, or project teams for the purpose of skills transfer and technology transfer.

5. Strategic Business Unit Structure

A strategic business unit is a grouping of business subsidiaries based on some important strategic elements common to each.

A single chief executive cannot control a number of decentralised units of a broadly diversified company. The business can be effectively controlled, if the related businesses are grouped into strategic units and the efficient and senior executive is delegated with the authority and responsibility for its management. The senior executive will in turn report the matter to the chief executive. This arrangement will improve strategic planning and implementation, though, it adds one layer in the organisational hierarchy. Top management coordinates the interests of the diversified business units.

A strategic business unit is a grouping of business subsidiaries based on some important strategic elements common to each. The common or related elements could be an overlapping set of competitors, a closely related strategic mission, a common need to compete globally, an ability to accomplish integrated strategic planning, common key success factors and technologically related growth opportunities. Fig. 11.9 presents SBU type of organisation structure.

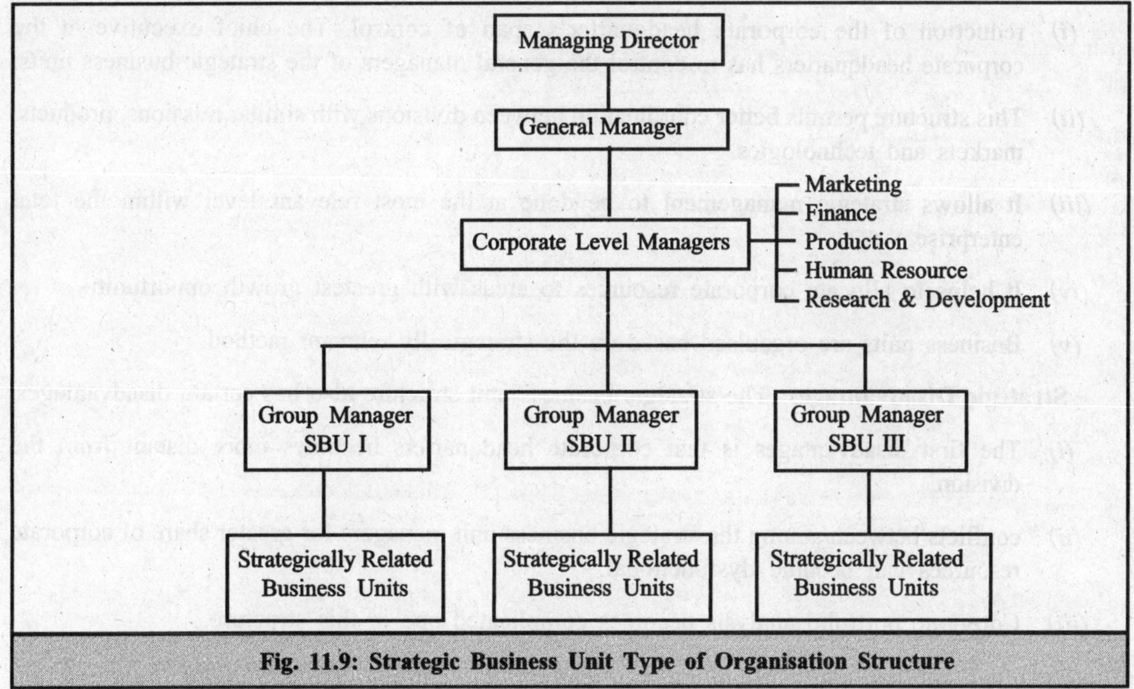

Fig. 11.9: Strategic Business Unit Type of Organisation Structure

Exhibit 11.8: Strategic Advantages and Disadvantages of Strategic Business Unit (SBU) Type of Organisation Structure

Strategic Advantages	*Strategic Disadvantages*
• Provides a strategically relevant way to organise the business unit portfolio of a broadly diversified company. • Facilitates the coordination of related activities within an SBU, thus helping to capture the benefits of strategic fit in the SBU. • Promotes more cohesiveness among the new initiatives of separate but related businesses. • Allows strategic planning to be done at the most relevant level within the total enterprise. • Makes the task of strategic review by top executives more objective and more effective. • Helps allocate corporate resources to areas with greatest growth opportunities. • Improves coordination among businesses facing similar strategic issues.	• It is easy for the definition and grouping of business into SBUs to be so arbitrary that the SBU serves no other purpose than administrative convenience. • If the criteria for defining SBUs are rationalisations and have little to do with the nitty-gritty of strategy coordination, then the groupings lose real strategic significance. • The SBUs can still be myopic in charting their future direction. • Adds another layer to top management. • The roles and authority of the managing director, general manager, SBU level managers have to be carefully worked out. • Unless the SBU head is strong willed, very little strategy coordination is likely to occur across business units in the SBU. • Performance recognition gets blurred; credit for successful business units tends to go to corporate managing director, then to business unit head, last to group manager. • Increases layers of management. • May result in SBU goals that differ from corporate goals.

Source: Thompson and Strickland, *op. cit.*, p. 231.

Strategic Advantages: The strategic advantages and disadvantages of the strategic business unit structure are presented in Exhibit 11.8. The advantages of this structure include:

(i) reduction of the corporate headquarter's span of control. The chief executive at the corporate headquarters has to control the general managers of the strategic business units.

(ii) This structure permits better coordination between divisions with similar missions, products, markets and technologies.

(iii) It allows strategic management to be done at the most relevant level within the total enterprise.

(iv) It helps to allocate corporate resources to areas with greatest growth opportunities.

(v) Business units are organised based on the strategically relevant method.

Strategic Disadvantages: The strategic business unit structure also has certain disadvantages.

(i) The first disadvantages is that corporate headquarters becomes more distant from the division.

(ii) conflicts between/among the strategic business unit managers for greater share of corporate resources can become dysfunctional.

(iii) Corporate portfolio analysis becomes complicated one in this structure.

6. Matrix Organisation Structure

Both functional and project managers exercise authority over organisational activities, in matrix structure.

Organisational structures discussed earlier have possessed a single chain of command. In other words, employees in those structures reports to only one manager. But, the organisation structure possesses a dual chain of command. Both functional and project managers exercise authority over organisational activities, in matrix structure. Thus personnel in this structure have two superiors *viz.*, a project manager and the manager of the functional department. Fig. 11.10 presents the matrix organisational structure.

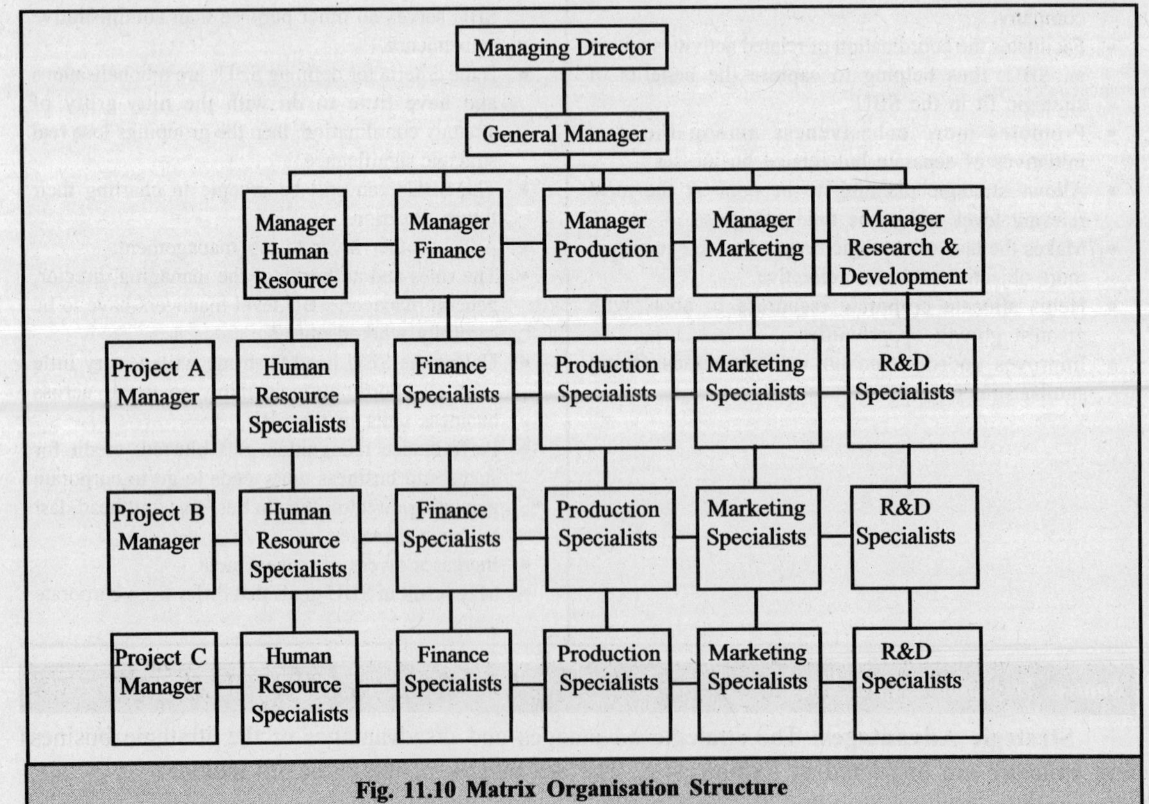

Fig. 11.10 Matrix Organisation Structure

A matrix organisational structure is appropriate when:

(i) Management attention must be focussed on two or more key issues (technical issues, consumer needs, functional efficiency).

(ii) Large amounts of diverse information need to be processed.

(iii) Problem solving is complex (environmental uncertainty, interdependence among organisational units, complex products or technology).

(iv) Economies of scale require the sharing of human resource expertise to achieve high performance.

Strategic Advantages: The matrix structure is commonly used in the firms whose technological change is rapid. The advantages of matrix structure include:

(i) the company can have the advantages of both project type of organisational structure and functional organisation structure.

(ii) Functional personnel are paid for their services whenever they are used by project managers. This practice enables the management to reduce the cost.

(iii) This structure has considerable flexibility. The personnel can be transferred from one project to the other depending upon the need of the project.

(iv) The lower level functional employees are highly motivated and satisfied with their job as they are involved in decision-making.

(vi) Each project manager is in-charge of a unit. Therefore, he can be developed as a general manager through performing general managerial functions. Exhibit 11.9 presents the strategic advantages and strategic disadvantages of matrix organisational structure.

Exhibit 11.9: Strategic Advantages and Disadvantages of Matrix Organisation Structure

Strategic Advantages	*Strategic Disadvantages*
* Gives formal attention to each dimension of strategic priority. * Creates checks and balances among competing viewpoints. * Facilitates capture of functionality based strategic fits in diversified companies. * Promotes making trade-off decisions on the basis of, "What is best for the organisation as a whole." * Encourages cooperation, consensus-building, conflict resolution and coordination of related activities. * Permits focus of attention on more variables and encourages generation of new ideas. * Makes efficient use of functional expertise. * Facilitates operation in complex and dynamic environment. * Encourages optimisation of organisational goals. * Managers are aware of strategic issues.	* Very complex to manage * Hard to maintain balance between the two lines of authority. * So much shared authority can result in a transactions log jam and disproportionate amounts of time being spent on communications. * It is hard to move quickly and decisively without getting clearance from many other people. * Promotes an organisational bureaucracy and hamstrings creative entrepreneurship. * Violates unity of command. * Managers should have interpersonal skills. * Requires too much time for meetings and collaboration. * Requires decision-making input from many sources. * May result in conflict between functional and project managers.

Source: Thompson and Strickland. *op. cit.*, p. 232 and Joe G. Thomas *op. cit.*, p. 269.

Strategic Disadvantages: The significant strategic disadvantages of matrix organisational structure include:

(i) greater administrative costs associated with its operation. Personnel spend much of their time in meetings and exchanging of information to coordinate functional areas with projects.

(ii) In view of the two forms associated in this structure, they are characterised by conflicts. The most critical conflict is between functional managers and project managers.

(iii) Functional employees experience stress by working in matrix structure. Reporting to two bosses, creates role ambiguity and role conflict. Some companies reverted their organisational structures back to traditional structures from matrix structures due to these problems.

7. Team Organisation Structure

Strategies of business are not always static. They go on changing depending upon internal and external environmental factors. Hence, a single type of organisational structure is not suitable for all situations. Blending the basic forms of organisation to match the structure to strategy in the units concerned in essential. Another option is to supplement special situation devices to the basic organisational structure. This option is Team structure.

Team structure takes three forms, *viz., (i)* Project Team, *(ii)* Task Force Team, and *(iii)* Venture Team.

(i) *Project Team:* Project teams are created to handle special kind of situations with a finite life expectancy. Project teams are self-sufficient work groups. These are created to supervise the completion of a special activity. The special activities include: setting up a new technological process, starting up a new venture, producing a new product, initiating and completion of a joint venture and the like.

(ii) *The Task Force Team:* Interdisciplinary assignments necessitate the formation of task force team. A task force team consists of top level executives and specialists in different areas from the organisation. The advantages of special task force team include: increased opportunity for creativity, open communication, cross-functional authority, effective integration of talents, quick conflict resolution, collaborative approach for problem solving.

(iii) *The Venture Team:* Venture team is a group of individuals. The purpose of forming this team is to bring a specific product or a new business into being. The problems of venture team are: *(i)* Difficulty of deciding the manager to whom the report should be made, *(ii)* Source of funding to the venture, *i.e.*, is the source from department or business or corporation *(iii)* problem of coordinating large number of different ventures.

Virtual organisation is a "social network in which all the horizontal and vertical boundaries are removed. It consists of individuals working out of physically dispersed workspaces, or even individuals working from mobile devices and not tied to any particular workspace. It is the coordination intense structure, consisting primarily of patterns and relationships, and this form needs the communication and information technology to function."

8. Virtual Organisational Structure

There is a Footwear Company. But it does not produce footwear. Small industries in Kanpur, Kharagpur, TamilNadu, etc., produce shoes for this company. Shoe Design and Quality Company's executives prescribe the shoe designs, models, specifications, etc., and communicate the same to the small industries through internet. Shoe Design and Quality Company's quality control inspectors inspect the quality of the shoes produced by the small industries and certify them. This company does not sell the shoes to the customers. But the shoe retailing shops throughout the country sell this company's shoes. Transport Corporation of India transports the shoes for this company from the manufacturing points to the retailing outlets. Commuiq Ads advertises for this company. Thus several agencies perform various business functions relating to shoe company, i.e., design, production, logistics and marketing of sales which are connected through a social network which operate in physically dispersed locations by different electronic devices like phones, mobile phones, internet, etc. This company is called virtual organization.

Virtual organisation, according to Biswajeet Pattanayak, is a "social network in which all the horizontal and vertical boundaries are removed. It consists of individuals working out of physically dispersed workspaces, or even individuals working from mobile devices and not tied to any particular workspace. It is the coordination intense structure, consisting primarily of patterns and relationships, and this form needs the communication and information technology to function."

Virtual organization is an organization that exists in the minds of stakeholders, as a network or alliances of independent companies that collaboratively pursue a particular business.

Business Week describes virtual organization as follows:

Technology: Virtual partnerships are based on electronic network among independent companies, some times located in different places.

Excellence: Virtual partnerships draw on the core competencies of each member to create and deliver the best final product and/or service like medical services.

Opportunism: Virtual organization is based on opportunities available. Once, the opportunities disappear some or all the partners may separate from the network/strategic alliance.

Trust: Partner companies of virtual organization build and maintain network based on mutual trust and confidence.

No Borders: Partners of the virtual organization, with their complex network of relationships, make it hard to identify the boundaries among themselves.

Virtual Workplace: People/employees of various partners of virtual organization, some time may not have a common workplace. They can work from any place and coordinate their activities through internet. Telecommuting/tele-work is quite common in virtual organizations.

Characteristics of virtual organisations: Characteristics of virtual organisations include:

- Flexi-work, Flexitime and Flexi-work place
- Part-time work
- Job sharing
- Home-based working
- Dependency on information technology like e-mail integration, voice-mail, mobile phone network, computer-telephony integration, etc.
- Loose organizational boundaries
- De-jobbing
- Multi-skilling
- Flexibility in power, work, etc
- Goal directed
- Customer centred.

Virtual Organisations and Behavioural Implications:

Behavioural implications trends in virtual organisations include:

- Organisation's human resources are the loose web of people;
- Knowledgeable people are hired for short term projects depending upon market demand;

- Employees have autonomy at work but are accountable to the targets, performance, etc.;
- Employees can work from their homes (home-cum-office) or from any other place as such social and work environment do not draw much attention of HR Manager;
- Career planning and development are based on projects;
- Employees are selected based on not only technical skills but their ability to work in teams; and
- Emotional and attitudinal quotient (EAQ) is the prime factor in employee selection rather than intelligence quotient (IQ).

Employees' features in virtual organisations include:

- Self-motivation, adaptability, self-commitment, effective communication, goal/result-orientation, technical competency, multi-skills, etc.;
- Employee performance is managed based on three dimensions *viz.*;
  (i) Setting performance standards/requirements;
  (ii) Facilitating performance by providing required facilities, resources, eliminating obstacles, etc.;
  (iii) Encouraging the employees to perform successfully; and
- Create a network of employees and enable them to create and share information and knowledge.

Advantages:

(i) These structures enable for doing business with less capital, less human resources and other inputs

(ii) These structure provide for flexibility of operations

(iii) These structures react to the environment demands most efficiently

(iv) These structures develop the ancillary industries.

Disadvantages:

(i) Companies do not have strong foundations or strengths in their operations,

(ii) Organisations have to heavily depend on outsourcing,

(iii) Failure in the network results in the failure of the entire organisation.

(F) MATCHING STRUCTURE AND STRATEGY

The suitability of structure to strategy is dependent on a number of situational factors. Absence of fit between strategy and structure leads to inefficient functioning of the company. The stages of organisation development is an important factor that influence the match between strategy and structure.

Stages of Organisation Development

Generally successful companies grow larger in size and diversify their activities. The growth of the company brings a number of changes. These changes include:

(i) Increase in financial resources (gross profits and investments)

(ii) Increase in resource needs (human resources, financial resources, material resources).

(iii) Increase in number of products and markets.

(iv) Increase in operating and managerial specialisation.

(v) Increase in size, complexity and risk of operating and managerial problems.

As organisations develop, the dominant strategic issues change with organisation's developmental changes. The three most frequently discussed stages of development models are those developed by Thain, Cannon and Greiner.

1. Cannon's Stages of Development Model

Cannon developed comprehensive stages of development model. His model consists of five stages of development. He argues that firms are found in one of these five stages of development. Though, Cannon does not contend that firms move through stages, strategic issues facing a firm move with each stage.

Stage I: The Entrepreneurial Stage: As discussed earlier, this stage represents the small business, generally operated by the owner-manager. The market of the firm in limited to a specific geographical area.

Stage II: When the company grows in size, the owner-manager cannot perform increased volume of managerial functions. Therefore, the owner-manager, hires an accountant, sales representatives and other agents. The other functional managers will also be hired with the further increase in the organisational size. A functional form of organisation structure will be adopted. But the problems of functional structure will come to the surface with the further increase in the company's operations. These problems include: delay in getting approval for new products and other innovations. These problems may push the company to the next stage.

Exhibit 11.10: Summary of Cannon's Stages of Development

Characteristics	*Entrepreneurial* I	*Functional Development* II	*Decentralisation* III	*Staff Profiteration* IV	*Recentralisation* V
Strategic decisions	Made mostly by the top person	Made more and more by other managers	May have loss of control	Corporate staff assists in decisions	Corporate management makes decisions
Organisation structure	Informal operations	Specialisation based on functions	To cope with problems of functionalisation	Corporate staff assists chief executive	Similar to Stage 1
Communication and climate	From leader down. Informal communication	Internal communication is important, is difficult	By industry or product division	Conservatism may result in slower communications	
Control system	Minimal need for coordination and control	Concerned with everyday situations	Problems with control	May be problems between line and staff	Tightening of control

Source: Adapted from J. Thomas Cannon. *op.cit.*. pp. 525-528. Quoted in P.K. Ghosh. *op. cit.*. p. 302.

Stage III: Organisation will be restructured either based on product or geographic or customers. Control may become difficult when each division develops its own view of product quality, pricing, etc.

Stage IV: To regain control of the organisation, management may employ additional human resources to assist top management.

Stage V: This stage involves increasing involvement of top management in strategic decision making. This move to recentralisation may be as part of a cutback and turnaround strategy.

Exhibit 11.10 depicts Cannon's stages of development model.

2. Thain's Stages of Corporate Development Model

Thain proposed a different conceptualisation of organisational stages of development. Exhibit 11.11 presents Thain's model. It identifies three stages of organisational development with different factors relevant to top management in each stage.

Stage I: Stage of Thain is similar to Cannon's entrepreneurial stage. The manager maintains absolute ownership and control. The company's strengths, weaknesses, and performance are shaped by the owner-manager's personality, ability and style. The increase in the size of the business forces the owner to appoint managers for different functions.

Stage II: In this stage, there is the existence of a management team built around one business and selling primarily to one market. The company in this stage specialises in one product and concentrates in one area. These characteristics, may threaten the survival of the firm consequent upon changes in consumer preferences or ability to buy. Companies try to overcome this danger by diversifying the activities.

Stage III: The firms in this stage are conglomerate diversified with multiple operating units controlled by corporate office. Companies in this stage can often operate independently of outside resources. But the organisation adopts a bureaucratic structure to manage and control a large size and diversified business.

3. Greiner's Phases of Organisational Growth

Greiner explains how growth affects management style. There are two stages in each phase of Greiner's model. Those stages are: evolution-steady organisational growth period and revolution periods upheaval or turmoil. The accumulated problems in each phase will be solved only when a breaking point is reached. This breaking point causes revolutionary change in organisational structure. Managers should prepare revolutionary change by identifying the phase through which the organisation is passing. Exhibit 11.12 presents the five phases and organisational issues in each phase of Greiner's model.

Phase 1: in this phase, creativity centres around the development of products and markets. Management spends most of the time in solving operating problems, rather than in managing the company. Organisational structure is mostly informal and authority for decision-making is centralised. The growth of the company in size makes the informal organisation ineffective and crisis in management and leadership. The revolution ends this phase by employing functional specialists.

Phase 2: Functional managers improve the organisational efficiency and performance. However, decision-making is centralised among the functional managers. The absence of strategic decision-making authority among the lower level managers results in revolution in autonomy.

Phase 3: This phase is concerned with delegation. Lower-level managers are delegated with strategic decision-making authority for particular products or markets. Top level management concentrates on business growth and diversification. Absence of coordination among business units relating to products or markets creates revolution. This revolution leads to Phase 4.

Exhibit 11.11: Thain's Key Management Factors by Stage of Development

Key Factors	*Stage I*	*Stage II*	*Stage III*
1. Size up major problems.	Survival and growth, dealing with short-term operating problems.	Growth, rationalization, and expansion of resources, providing for adequate attention to product problems.	Trusteeship in management and investment and control of large, increasing, and diversified resources. Also important to diagnose and act on problems at division level.
2. Objectives.	Personal and subjective.	Profits and meeting functionally oriented budgets and performance targets.	ROI, profits, earnings per share.
3. Strategy.	Implicit and personal; exploitation of immediate opportunities seen by owner-manager.	Functionally oriented moves restricted to "one-product" scope; exploitation of one basic product or service field.	Growth and product diversification; exploitation of general business opportunities.
4. Organization, major characteristic of structure.	One-unit "one-man show."	One-unit functionally specialized group.	Multi-unit general staff office and decentralized operating divisions.
5. *(a)* Measurement and control.	Personal, subjective, control based on simple accounting system and daily communication and observation.	Control grows beyond one man, assessment of functional operations necessary, structured control systems evolve.	Complex formal system geared to comparative assessment of performance measures, indicating problems and opportunities and assessing management ability of division managers.
(b) Key performance indicators.	Personal criteria, relationships with owner, operating efficiency, ability to solve operating problems.	Functional and internal criteria such as sales, performance compared to budget, size of empire, status in group, personal relationships, etc.	More impersonal application of comparisons such as profits, ROI, P/E ratio, sales, market share, productivity, product leadership, personnel development, employee attitudes, public responsibility.
6. Reward-punishment system.	Informal, personal, subjective; used to maintain control and divide small pool of resources to provide personal incentives for key performers.	More structured, usually based to a greater extent on agreed policies as opposed to personal opinion and relationships.	Allotment by "due process" of a wide variety of different rewards and punishments on a formal and systematic basis. Company-wide policies usually apply to many different classes of managers and workers with few major exceptions for individual cases.

Source: D.H. Thain, "Stages of Corporate Development," *Business Quarterly*, Winter 1969.

Phase 4: Improvement and maintenance of coordination is the main concern in this phase. Co-ordination systems are introduced. Decentralised units are combined into strategic business units. The coordination efforts will result in formalised communication system, centralised decision-making, formulation of rules, regulations and controls. These factors result in a bureaucratic organisation, which causes a crisis and brings Phase 5.

Phase 5: This phase strives to enhance collaboration. Behavioural orientation, group working, project teams and matrix structures are adopted to improve problem solving.

Greiner argues that only a limited number of firms have reached Phase 5. Phase 5 brings organisational changes due to the emphasis on behavioural skills and behavioural modification.

Exhibit 11.12: Greiner's Five Phases of Growth

Category	*Phase 1*	*Phase 2*	*Phase 3*	*Phase 4*	*Phase 5*
Management focus	Make and sell	Efficiency of operations	Expansion of market	Consolidation of organisation	Problem solving and innovation
Organisation structure	Informal	Centralized and functional	Decentralised and geographical	Line-staff and product groups	Matrix of teams
Top management style	Individualistic entrepreneurial	Directive	Delegative	Watchdog	Participative
Control system	Market results	Standards and cost centres	Reports and profit centres	Plans and investment centres	Mutual goal setting
Management reward system	Ownership	Salary and merit increases	Individual bonus	Profit sharing and stock options	Team bonus

Source: Quoted in Joe G. Thomas, *op. cit.*, p. 277.

4. Leontiades Stages of Growth Model

Leontiade's growth model is one of the recent model. Leontiades states that growth is best understood by examining single business and multi-business firms. Two sub-categories of strategies exist within each classification as presented in Exhibit 11.13.

Exhibit 11.13: Leontiades' Stages of Growth

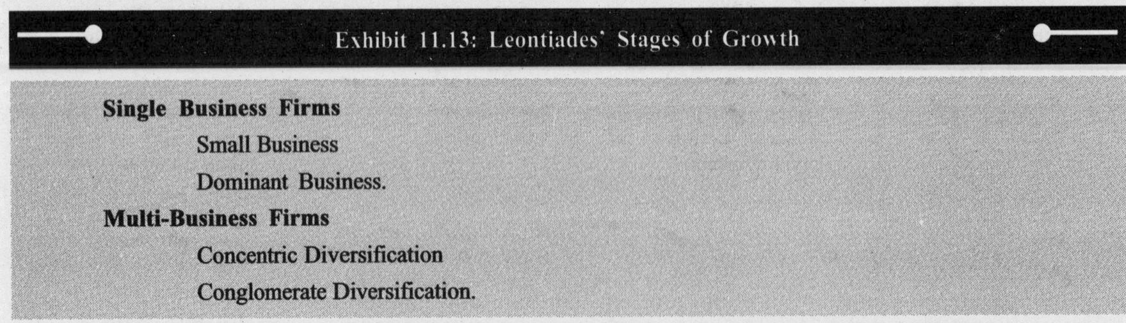

Single Business Firms

Small Business

Dominant Business.

Multi-Business Firms

Concentric Diversification

Conglomerate Diversification.

Organisational structure appears to vary between single-business and multi-business firms. Single business firms follow a functional design and multi-business firms use a divisional structure.

(G) ASSESSMENT OF ORGANISATIONAL STRUCTURE

The crucial question is: how a company can implement its strategy by designing appropriate organisational structure. There are no hard-and-fast rules for evaluating the appropriateness of a company's organisation structure. However, the following questions (as presented in Exhibit 11.14) will help in assessing the organisation structure.

Exhibit 11.14: Checklist for Determining Appropriateness of Organisational Structure

1. Is the structure compatible with the corporate profile and the corporate strategy?
2. At the corporate level, is the structure compatible with the firm's business units?
3. Are there too few or too many hierarchical levels at either the corporate or business unit level of analysis?
4. Does the structure promote coordination among its parts?
5. Does the structure allow for appropriate centralisation or decentralisation of authority?
6. Does the structure permit the appropriate grouping of activities?

Source: Peter Wright, Charles D. Pringle and Mar J. Kroll, *op. cit.*, p. 165.

1. *Is the structure compatible with the corporate profile and the corporate strategy?*

Companies may be in one business or several related businesses or several unrelated businesses. Functional structure may be viable for single business firms but not viable to the multi-business firms. For the multi-business firms, product or divisional and multi-divisional structure may be appropriate. Therefore, the company should adopt the suitable structure based on its corporate profile.

If the company wants to remain small, a functional structure may be suitable. Alternatively, the multi-divisional structure is appropriate for the continuously growing companies. Therefore, the company's structure should also be compatible with its corporate level strategy.

2. *At the corporate level, is the structure compatible with the firm's business units?*

The firms producing different technical products, should opt for the organisational structure based on product divisional structure. Each division produces the distinct products and markets them. However, the firm producing related products in terms of production and/or marketing, can go for geographic organisational structure. Thus, the structure should be compatible with the firm's business units.

3. *Are there too few or too many hierarchical levels at either the corporate or business unit level of analysis?*

Flat organisations with a few hierarchical levels and wider spans are suitable for dynamic and fast changing firms. Tall organisations with more hierarchical levels and narrow spans are suitable for the stable firms or stable and predictable environments. Different business units of the same company operate in different environments like dynamic and stable. Therefore, different business units of the same company can have different types of organisational structures.

4. *Does the structure promote coordination among its parts?*

Different divisions of the organisation need coordination at varying degrees. If the company has diversified and unrelated businesses, the minimum level coordination among these units is necessary. However, high degree of coordination is essential within each business unit. Similarly, high degree of coordination is necessary, if the company's has related diversified business units. The co-ordination may become difficult in the complex business organisations. Special permanent co-ordinating units may be established in such organisations.

5. *Does the structure allow for appropriate centralisation or decentralisation of authority?*

The delegation of authority of decision-making depends upon a number of factors. One among them is organisation size. Authority is delegated downward in large organisations compared to the small organisations. The second factor is the number and types of business units. If the company has a number of unrelated business units, the authority is delegated downward compared to that of the company with a number of related business units. The third factor is the type of environment. Companies in relatively changing environments decentralise the authority compared to the companies in relatively stable environment. Therefore, depending upon the environment, the strategy should allow the centralisation or decentralisation.

6. *Does the structure permit the appropriate grouping of activities?*

Structure may be appropriately designed to group the activities appropriately. It facilitates the implementation of the strategy successfully.

(H) PERSPECTIVES ON THE METHODS OF ORGANISING

The above analysis brings two aspects, *viz., (i)* there is no perfect or ideal organisational design, and *(ii)* there are no universally applicable rules for matching strategy and structure. Further, it can be concluded that, two or more organisational structures can be used for different business units of the same company at the same time like functional, geographic and product structures. "The best organisational structure is the one that fits the firm's situation at the moment."

Peter F. Drucker sums up the intricacies of organisation design as:

"The simplest organisation structure that will do the job is the best one. What makes an organisation structure "good" are that it does not create. The simpler the structure, the less that can go wrong.

Some design principles are more difficult and problematic than others. But none is without difficulties and problems. None is primarily people-focussed rather than task-focussed, none is more "creative", "free" or "more democratic". Design principles are tools and tools are neither good nor bad in themselves. They can be used properly or improperly, and that is all. To obtain both the greatest possible simplicity and the greatest "fit", organisation design has to start out with a clear focus on key activities needed to produce key results. They have to be structured and positioned in the simplest possible design. Above all, the architect of organisation needs to keep in mind the purpose of the structure he is designing."

POINTS TO BE REMEMBERED

- Firms seek to attract customers by making normal predicted adjustment in the methods
- Organisational structure is to be adjusted or modified according to the strategy requirements.
- Structural systems include entrepreneurial, tall and horizontal structures.
- Structural approaches include: product, functional, geographic, matrix, team, virtual, etc.
- Organisational structure should be assessed in order to know its comparability with the strategy.

KEY WORD

- Routine Strategy Change
- Radical Strategy Change
- Project Implementation
- Procedural Implementation
- Entrepreneurial Structure
- Vertical Strategy
- Horizontal Structure
- Functional Structure
- Geographic Structure
- Decentralised Structure
- Strategic Business Unit Structure
- Matrix Structure
- Team Structure
- Virtual Structure

QUESTION FOR DISCUSSION

1. What is strategy implementation?
2. What is strategic change? How do you manage it?
3. What is project? How do you implement it as a part of strategy implementation?
4. What are the systems of organisational structure?
5. What is procedural implementation?
6. What are the strategic advantages of:
   (a) Product structure
   (b) Strategic business unit structure
   (c) Matrix structure
   (d) Virtual structure
7. Discuss structure-follows-strategy theory.
8. How do you match structure to the strategy?
9. Discuss the assessment of organisation structure.

REFERENCES

1. Samuel C. Certo and J. Paul Peter, "*The Strategic Management Process*", Richard D. Irwin Inc., Homewood, Illinois, 1995, p. 113.
2. *Ibid.*
3. *Ibid.*, p. 114.
4. James Brian Quinn, "*Strategies for Change*," Richard D. Irwin, Homewood III, 1980.
5. Michael Beer, Russel Eisenstat and Bert Spector, "*The Critical Path to Corporate Renewal*", Harvard Business School Press, Boston, 1991.
6. K. Andrews, "*The Concept of Corporate Strategy*," Taraporevala & Sons, Bombay, 1971, p. 179.
7. *Project Management Journal*, Project Management Institute, USA, August, 1984.
8. Azhar Kazmi, *op. cit.*, p. 213.
9. J. Child, "*Organisation: A Guide for Managers and Administrators*," Harper & Row, New York, 1977, p. 10.

10. Peter Wright, Charles D. Pringle and Mark J. Kroll, *op.cit.*, p. 149.
11. La Rue T. Hosmer, "*Strategic Management: Text and Cases on Business Policy*," Prentice Hall, Englewood Cliffs, NJ., 1982 and J. Thomas Cannon, "*Business Strategy and Policy*," HarCourt Brace Jovanovich, New York, 1968, p. 316. Quoted in Thompson and Strickland, p. 220.
12. Arthur A. Thompson and A.J. Strickland, *op. cit.*, p. 220.
13. Peter F. Drucker, "*Management: Tasks, Responsibilities, Practices*," Harper & Row, New York, 1974, pp. 530, 535.
14. Arthur A. Thompson and A.J. Strickland, *op. cit.*, pp.220-221.
15. *Ibid.*, p. 222.
16. Alfred Chandler, "*Strategy and Structure*," MIT Press, Cambridge, Mass, 1962. Quoted in Ibid.
17. Raymond Corey and Steven H. Star, "*Organisational Strategy: A Marketing Approach*," Harvard Business School, Boston, 1971.
18. Arthur A. Thompson and A.J. Strickland, op. cit., p. 223.
19. R. Duncan, "*What is the Right Organisation Structure*?" Organisational Dynamics, Winter 1979, pp. 59-80, J.W. Lorsch and A.H. Walker, "*Organisational Choice: Product Vs. Function*," Harvard Business Review, November/December 1968, pp. 129-138.
20. Joe G. Thomas, *op. cit.*, pp.265-266.
21. Arthur A. Thompson and A.J. Strickland, *op. cit.*, pp.227-228.
22. *Ibid.*, p. 228.
23. Peter Wright, Charles D. Pringle and Mark J. Kroll, *op.cit.*, p. 160.
24. S. Davis and P.R. Lawrence, "*Matrix*," Addison Wesley, Reading, Mass, 1977, pp. 11-24.
25. Arthur A. Thompson and A.J. Strickland, *op. cit.*, pp.233-235.
26. P.R. Lawrence and J.W. Lorsch, "*Organisation and Environment*," Richard D. Irwin, Homewood III, 1967, p.138.
27. D.H. Thain, "*Stages of Corporate Development*," Business Quarterly, Winter 1969, p. 34.
28. M. Leontiades, "*Strategies for Diversification and Change*," Little Brown, Boston, 1980, Chapter 2. Quoted in Joe G. Thomas, *op. cit.*, p. 271.
29. J.T. Cannon, "*Business Strategy and Policy*," HarCourt Brace Jovanovich, New York, 1968, pp. 525-528.
30. Joe G. Thomas, *op. cit.*, pp. 272-273.
31. D.H. Thain, "*Stages of Corporate Development*," Business Quarterly, Winter, 1969, pp. 33-45.
32. *Ibid.*, pp. 39-40.
33. Joe G. Thomas, *op. cit.*, p. 273.
34. L.E. Greiner, "*Evolutions and Revolutions as Organisations Grow*," Harvard Business Review, July-August 1972, pp. 37-46.
35. Joe G. Thomas, *op. cit.*, pp. 227-278.
36. Leontiades, "*Strategies for Diversification and Change*," pp. 36-46.
37. *Ibid.*, p. 39.
38. Peter Wright, Charles D. Pringle and Mark J. Kroll, *op. cit.*, pp. 164-166.
39. Arthur A. Thompson and A.J. Strickland, *op. cit.*, p. 236.
40. *Ibid.*
41. Peter F. Drucker, "*Management*," pp. 601-602.

✦ ✦ ✦

12

CHAPTER

BEHAVIOURAL IMPLEMENTATION

Chapter Outline

(A) Positive Attitude and Mindset

(B) Leadership

(C) Corporate Culture

(D) Values

(E) Power

(F) Organisational Changes

(G) Organisational Development

Learning Objectives

After studying this chapter, you should be able to:

- Analyse the positive attitude and discuss the approaches to enhance positive attitude among employees to smoothen the strategy implantation process;
- Study the leadership styles and to develop and use the appropriate leadership style based on the strategy;
- Discuss the corporate culture that is appropriate for the chosen strategy;
- Explain values in different countries and values appropriate for the strategy;
- Discuss power and methods of assessing power;
- Analyse the process of organisational change and development.

(A) POSITIVE ATTITUDE AND MINDSET

Attitude and mindset are evaluative statements — either favorable or unfavourable — concerning objects,people or events.

Attitude and mindset are evaluative statements — either favorable or unfavourable — concerning objects, people or events. They reflect how one feels about something. Belief is the cognitive component of an attitude. Emotional or feeling segment is affective component of an attitude. Behaviourial component of an attitude is an intention to behave in a certain way towards someone or something.

Positive attitude is viewing and thinking realistically or positively with regard to strategy implementation. Positive attitude helps to cope more easily with the daily affairs of strategy implementation. It brings optimism into strategy implementation process and makes it easy to overcome all kinds of obstacles in the strategy implementation process. Employees see the bright side of the strategic change, become optimistic and expect the best to happen. Positive attitude is a state of mind that is worth developing and strengthening for efficient strategy implementation.

Therefore, organisations before implementing strategies should develop and strengthen positive attitude and mindset. Organisations can manifest positive attitude in the following ways:

- Understanding the situations positively
- Creative thinking
- Thinking optimistically
- Try again and again until succeed
- Anticipating success
- Foreseeing the possible problems
- Develop all possible solutions to solve the possible anticipated obstacles
    - Thinking and acting proactively
    - Anticipate and chase opportunities
    - Create opportunities
    - Minimise/avoid threats
    - Inspire subordinates, customers and all other stakeholders
    - Energise the employees
    - Develop the attitude of 'I Can Do!
    - Communicate most effectively and frequently
    - Open communication
    - Enable the subordinates, customers and all other stakeholders
    - Motivate employees towards their goals
    - Eliminate all kinds of deviations of employees in the process of strategy implementation
    - Inspire the existing abilities and skills of employees
    - Empower employees toward strategy implantation.

Development of positive attitude and mindset of the employees enable companies to seek unsolicited cooperation and collaboration of employees. In addition, employees think and take care of strategy implementation. Further, all kinds of hurdles in the process of strategy implementation are removed. In addition, employees stop resisting the strategic changes.

(B) LEADERSHIP

Leadership is the relationship in which one person (the leader) influences others to work together willingly on a related task to attain goals devised by the leader and/or group. Leadership is the key factor in strategy implementation. Some people equate leadership with management. But these two concepts are not synonymous. In fact, leadership is a part of management, but not all.

Leadership is the relationship in which one person (the leader) influences others to work together willingly on a related task to attain goals devised by the leader and/ or group.

Leaders require and use three different skills in influencing and interacting with people to attain goals, *viz.*, technical skills, human relations skills and conceptual skills. Manager exhibits leadership when he or she secures the cooperation of others in accomplishing objectives. Organisational leadership plays a significant role in the changing business environment.

The competitive environment and remaining competitive require an organisation to develop an appropriate leadership. The changing business and its consequences for the leadership factor are presented in Fig. 12.1. Leadership can be felt throughout an organisation. It provides pace and energy to the work and empowers the employees. Though efficient leadership is essential for organisational success, it is not just sufficient to achieve the organisational effectiveness. This is because of the fact that organisational effectiveness depends on several factors. However, the appropriate style of the leader helps for successful implementation of the strategy.

1. Leadership Styles

Leadership is practised by its styles which may be positive or negative. The way in which a leader uses power also establishes leadership styles. There are three popularly known styles, *viz.*, free-rein, autocratic, participative and democratic.

There are three popularly known styles, *viz.*, free-rein, autocratic, participative and democratic.

Free-rein or *Laissez-faire* Style: The leaders, in this style, avoid authority and responsibility. They mostly depend upon the group to establish objectives and goals, formulate policies and programmes. The group members train and motivate themselves. Contrary to autocratic style the leader plays minor or negligible roles and depends upon the group. It is, however, concluded that there is no direction and control by the leader.

Autocratic Style: Autocratic leader or leaders in the autocratic style centralise power of decision-making in themselves. The followers have no say either in decision-making or implementation. They have to completely obey and follow the instructions of the autocratic leaders. The leaders take full authority and responsibility. Autocratic leaders are classified into:

(i) Strict autocrat who follows autocratic style completely where the method of influencing subordinates is thoroughly negative.

(ii) Benevolent autocrat typically gives awards to subordinates and motivates them to achieve the goals.

(iii) Incompetent autocrat, who adopts autocratic style with a view to hide his/her incompetency.

Participative Style: Participative leaders decentralise authority and encourage subordinates to express their opinion in decision-making as well as in implementing decisions. Leaders solicit the opinions and idea of the subordinates and make the decisions by themselves. Thus, the authority to make decisions is reserved by the leaders. However, decisions are arrived at by consultation.

Democratic Style: Democratic leaders decentralise authority and encourage subordinates to participate and involve in decision-making and implementation process. Decisions are made jointly by the leader and subordinates as a group.

It is, however, concluded that there is no clear-cut and single leadership style which is applicable universally and in all circumstances. Leaders adopt different styles in different situations depending upon situational requirements.

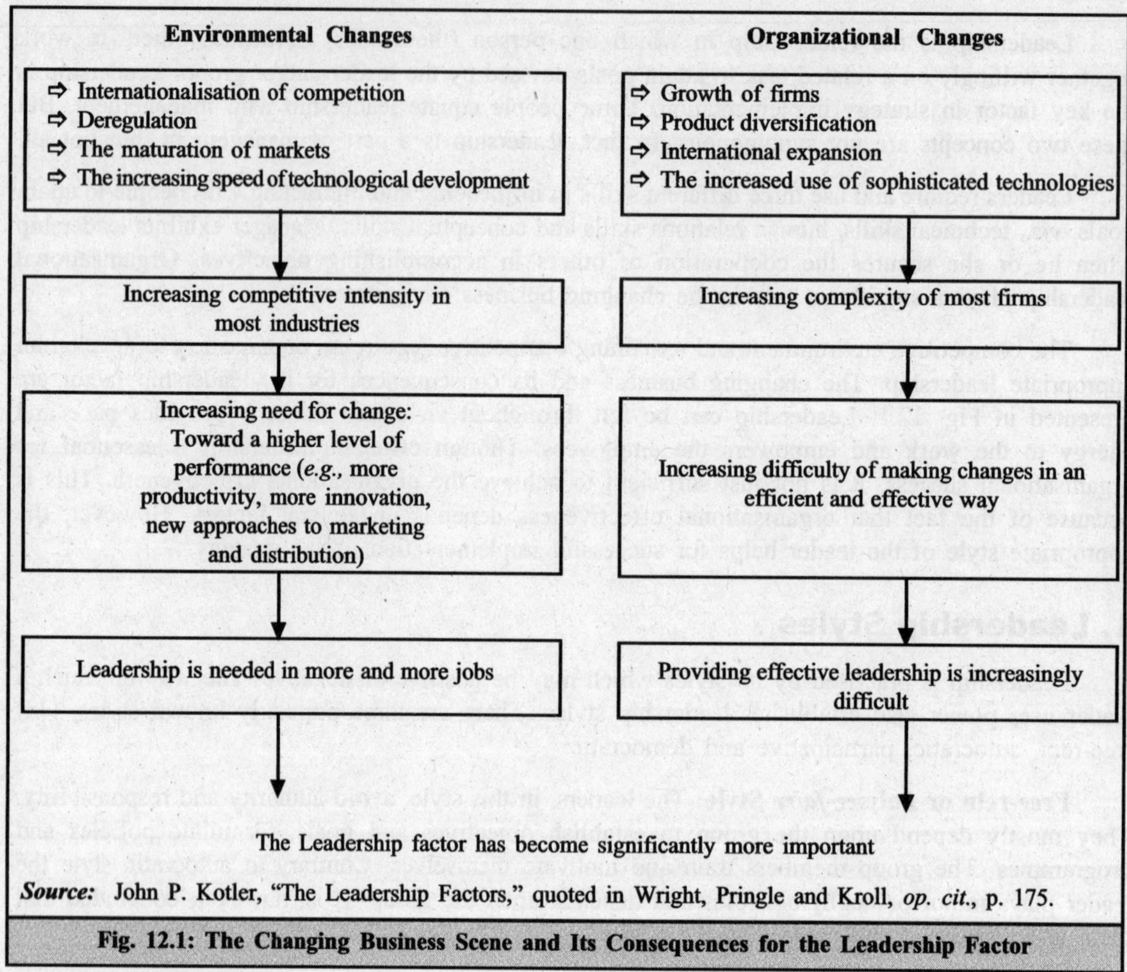

Source: John P. Kotler, "The Leadership Factors," quoted in Wright, Pringle and Kroll, *op. cit.*, p. 175.

Fig. 12.1: The Changing Business Scene and Its Consequences for the Leadership Factor

Situational Approach: Hersey and Blanchard's approach identifies two major styles, *viz.*, tasks style and relationship style. Hersey and Blanchard incorporated the maturity of the followers into their model. The level of maturity is defined by the degree of achievement motivation, willingness to take responsibility and amount of education and/or experience. The key for leadership effectiveness in this model (Fig. 12.2) is to match up the situation with the appropriate style.

The four styles are:

(i) **Telling Style:** This is a high task, low relationship style, it is effective when followers are at low level of maturity.

(ii) **Selling Style:** This is a high task, high relationship style. It is effective when followers are on the low side of maturity.

(iii) **Participative Style:** This is a low task, high relationship style. It is effective when followers are on high side of maturity.

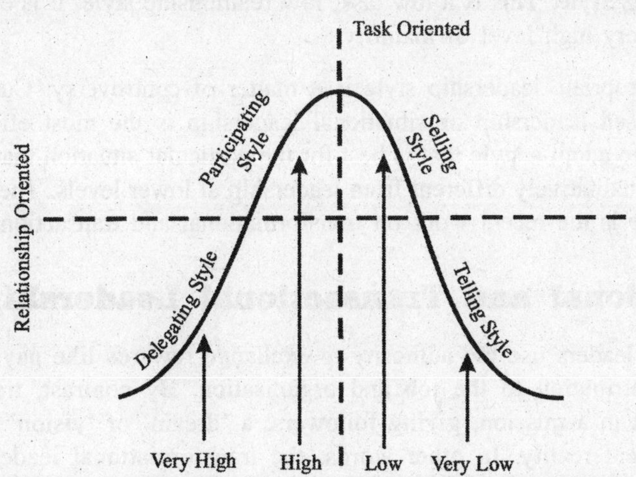

Maturity Level of followers (need for achievement, willingness to accept responsibility, and education/experience)

Source: Paul Hersey and Kenneth Blachard, *Management of Organisational Behaviour: Utilisation of Human Resources*, Prentice Hall, Englewood Cliffs N.J., 1977, p. 170.

Fig. 12.2: Hersey and Blanchard's Situational Leadership Model

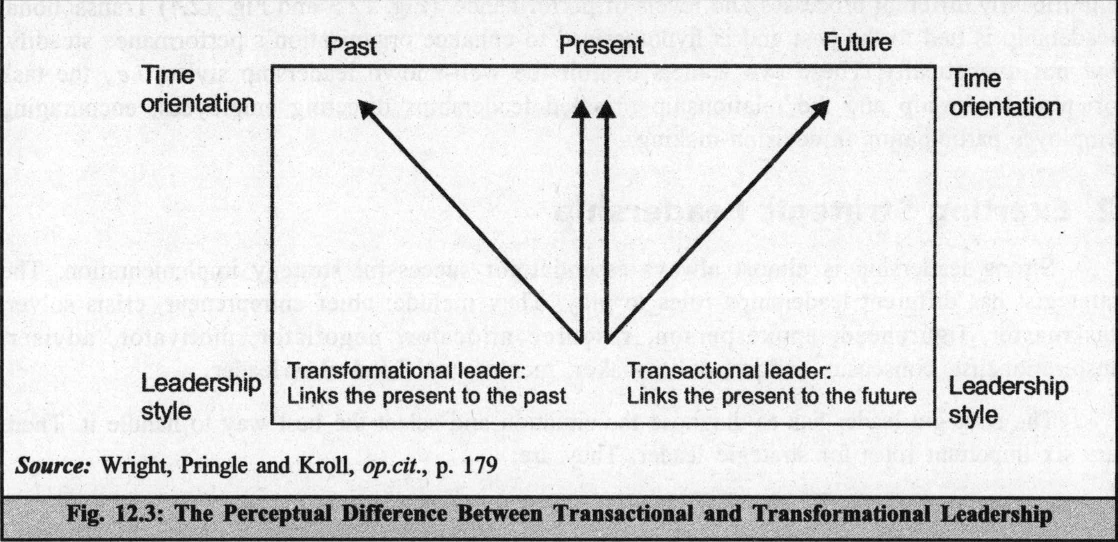

Source: Wright, Pringle and Kroll, *op.cit.*, p. 179

Fig. 12.3: The Perceptual Difference Between Transactional and Transformational Leadership

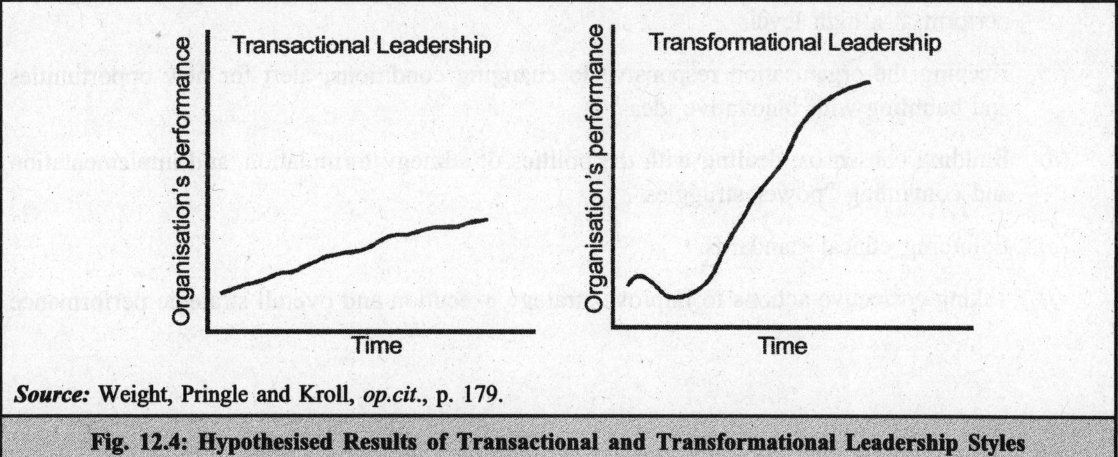

Source: Weight, Pringle and Kroll, *op.cit.*, p. 179.

Fig. 12.4: Hypothesised Results of Transactional and Transformational Leadership Styles

(iv) **Delegating Style:** This is a low task, low relationship style. It is effective when followers are at a very high level of maturity.

The most appropriate leadership style is a matter of controversy. Current research indicates that contingency-based leadership or situational leadership is the most effective. In other words, leaders are advised to adopt a style that is best for the particular situation that they are facing. Upper level leadership is qualitatively different from leadership at lower levels. The most pertinent body of knowledge available is the recent work on transformational and transactional leadership styles.

Transformational and Transactional Leadership Styles

Transactional leaders use the authority to exchange rewards like pay, fringe benefits, status for employees' contribution to the job and organisation. By contrast, transformational leaders, inspire involvement in a mission, giving followers, a 'dream' or 'vision' of a higher order than the followers' present reality.

Transactional leaders use the authority to exchange rewards like pay, fringe benefits, status for employees' contribution to the job and organisation. By contrast, transformational leaders, inspire involvement in a mission, giving followers, a 'dream' or 'vision' of a higher order than the followers' present reality. In other words, the transformational leaders inspire followers to contribute more than they originally expected to do by stretching their abilities and increasing their self-confidence. Employees are 'transformed' by becoming more aware of the significance of their contribution and by being helped to transcend their own self-interest for the sake of organisational mission.

Bernard M. Bass proposes that most leaders exhibit both transactional and transformational styles. But they do so in different amounts. Transactional leaders improve their organisations step-by-step. Transformational leaders lead their organisations toward a future that may result in significantly different processes and levels of performance. (Fig. 12.3 and Fig. 12.4) Transactional leadership is tied to the past and is hypothesised to enhance organisation's performance steadily, but not dramatically. These two leaders exhibit the well-known leadership styles, *i.e.,* the task oriented leadership and the relationship oriented leaderships directing employees, encouraging employee participation in decision-making.

2. Exerting Strategic Leadership

Strong leadership is almost always essential for successful strategy implementation. The strategist has different leaderships roles to play. They include: chief entrepreneur, crisis solver, taskmaster, figurehead, spokesperson, resource allocator, negotiator, motivator, adviser, inspirationalist, consensus builder, policymaker, mentor, and head cheerleader.

The strategic leader has to diagnose the situation and select the best way to handle it. There are six important roles for strategic leader. They are:

(a) Staying on top of what is happening and how well things are going.

(b) Promoting a culture in which the organisation is "energised" to accomplish strategy and perform at a high level.

(c) Keeping the organisation responsive to changing conditions, alert for new opportunities, and bubbling with innovative ideas.

(d) Building consensus, dealing with the politics of strategy formulation, and implementation, and containing "power struggles".

(e) Enforcing ethical standards.

(f) Taking corrective actions to improve strategy execution and overall strategic performance.

3. Managing by Walking Around

The leader, to stay on top of how well the implementation process is going on, should develop a broad network of contacts. The methods of networking include: talking with key subordinates, reading written reports, and latest operating results, getting feedback from customers, watching the competitive reactions of rivals, tapping into grapevine, listening to rank-and-file employees, etc. These methods have their own limitations. The leader, in order to overcome the limitations may visit the field regularly and talk with many different people at different levels. The leaders normally attach great importance to informal communication to gain quick and easy access to information. The leaders tend to become isolated if they stay in their offices.

Fostering a Strategy-Supportive Climate and Culture

The leader should spend much of his time in personally leading the major strategic changes. The leaders should play a leading role in pushing ahead and prodding for continuous improvements in values and culture into in tune with strategy. Leaders should convince people that the selected strategy is right and it should be implemented to the best of the company's ability. Words inspire people, infuse spirit and drive, define strategy. Supportive cultural norms and values. Deeds add credibility to the words, create strategy-supportive symbols and set example. The leader's role depends on the degree of strategic shift in cultural norms. Walking around gives the leader a feel for how things are progressing, opportunity to encourage employees, lift spirits, shift attention from the old to new priorities, etc.

Keeping the Internal Organisation Responsive and Innovative

Though, the strategy implementation is the responsibility of the leader, it is difficult to one person to generate fresh ideas, identify new ideas, identify new opportunities and respond to changing conditions etc. Therefore, the leader should develop dependable supply of fresh ideas from rank-and-file, managers at different levels, entrepreneurs, etc. A flexible, responsive, innovative internal environment is essential as is fast moving high technology industries. The leader should take special pains to develop, nourish and support employees who come forward with new ideas, better services, new product ideas and product applications, ideas of new divisions, new industries, etc.

Empowering Champions

The leaders need to do the following things where champions can blossom and thrive, in order to promote organisational climate. They are:

The leaders need to inspire the champions who can blossom and thrive, in order to promote organisational climate.

(i) encouraging the individuals and groups to bring their ideas forward, be creative and exercise initiative.

(ii) the champion's maverick style has to be tolerated. Do not look at people with creative ideas, as disruptive or troublesome.

(iii) leaders should induce and promote attempts and be willing to tolerate mistakes and failures.

(iv) leaders should use different kinds of *ad hoc* organisational forms like venture teams, task forces, groups, etc., to support ideas and experimentation, and

(v) leaders should ensure the champions should be rewarded adequately.

Dealing with Company Politics

A leader cannot formulate and implement strategy successfully in view of organisational politics. The leader should be perceptive about company politics and adopt to political manoeuvring.

Organisational politics play a dominant role in strategy formulation and implementation. Groups and their coalitions press for modification of strategic plan. Internal politics influence in selecting a strategy against the other. Organisational politics also affect organisational structure, staffing decisions and budget allocations. The politics affect primarily the strategy in stimulating options, nurturing support for strong proposals and killing weak proposals, guiding the formulation of coalitions on particular issues and achieving consensus and commitment.

According to a research study, successful executives used the following political tactics:

(i) Letting weakly supported ideas and proposals die through inaction.

(ii) Establishing additional hurdles or tests for strongly supported ideas that the manager views as unacceptable but that are best not opposed openly.

(iii) Keeping a low political profile on unacceptable proposals by getting subordinate managers to say no.

(iv) Letting most negative decisions come from a group consensus that the manager merely confirms, thereby, reserving personal veto for big issues and crucial moments.

(v) Leading the strategy but not dictating it — giving few orders, announcing few decisions, depending heavily on informal questioning and seeking to probe and clarify until a consensus emerges.

(vi) Staying alert to the symbolic impact of one's actions and statements best a false signal stimulate proposals and movements in unwanted directions.

(vii) Ensuring that all major power bases within the organisation have representation in or access to top management.

(viii) Minimising political exposure on issues that are highly controversial.

4. Enforcing Ethical Behaviour

Strategic manager must exercise ethical leadership in different aspects. They are:

(i) He/she must set an excellent ethical example in his/her own behaviour and establish a tradition of integrity.

(ii) He/she must educate the managers and employees about what is ethical and what is not,

(iii) top management should clearly refer to the company's ethical code and take a strong stand on ethical issues.

Leading the Process of Making Corrective Adjustments

Making adjustments or "mid-course" corrections is a normal and necessary part of strategic management. Corrective adjustments in the company's approach to strategy implementation should be made on an "as-needed" basis strategy. Leaders should be proactive as well as reactive in reshaping strategy and how it is implemented.

5. Leadership Implementation

According to Lawrence R. Jauch and William F. Glueck, organisations accomplish leadership implementation in several ways:

(i) Through changes in current leadership at appropriate levels;

(ii) By developing appropriate leadership style and climate;

(iii) By getting involved in career development of future strategists; and

(iv) By adopting organisation development techniques to effect changes.

Leader Choice and Assignment

After selecting the strategies at different levels, the top management should place the right strategists at right places including at SBU levels. The questions relating to leadership are:

(i) Who holds the current leadership positions?

(ii) Do they have the right characteristics to assure that the strategy will work well?

(iii) Who should be assigned what and which type of tasks?

The company must examine the strategist's education, abilities, experience, and personality to implement the selected strategy. The firm must examine the match between the new strategy and the chief executive officer.

Style and Climate

Leadership style is one of the important aspects of leadership implementation. The questions relating to leadership style include:

(i) Can the strategist lead the SBU efficiently with his or her present style?

(ii) Can the strategist change the leadership style if that is necessary to make the new strategy work?

(iii) Can the strategist develop the right climate and culture for the strategy?

There should be the match between the strategy and the climate of managerial values and leadership style. Fig. 12.5 suggests that different managerial skills appear to be relevant depending on the job requirements for a given strategy and SBU. A SBU in the cash cow stage require leadership styles and characteristics different from that of another SBU in the significant expansion stage. Leader is responsible for developing a climate conducive for the implementation of the strategy. Climate can be viewed from the point of the nature of leadership, motivation, decision, communication and control process. Review of these aspects is presented in Exhibit 12.1. The aspect of corporate culture is a dimension of climate that leaders help to develop. These aspects of leadership implementation are essential components of the administrative system which can make or break a strategy. They can be used to engender commitment and loyalty to the organisation and its strategies.

Career Development

The top management of the organisation should plan for the career of strategic leaders and develop them in view of the significant role played by them. The following elements should be taken care of in the development of leaders:

(i) Plan for the number and kind of leaders necessary for the implementation of the future strategies.

(ii) Review of present inventory in terms of skills, talents, knowledge, aptitude and values.

(iii) Preparation of promotion, transfer and employment schedules.

(iv) Development of individual leaders in anticipation of future vacancies at higher levels.

(v) Reward system to attract and retain competent managers/leaders.

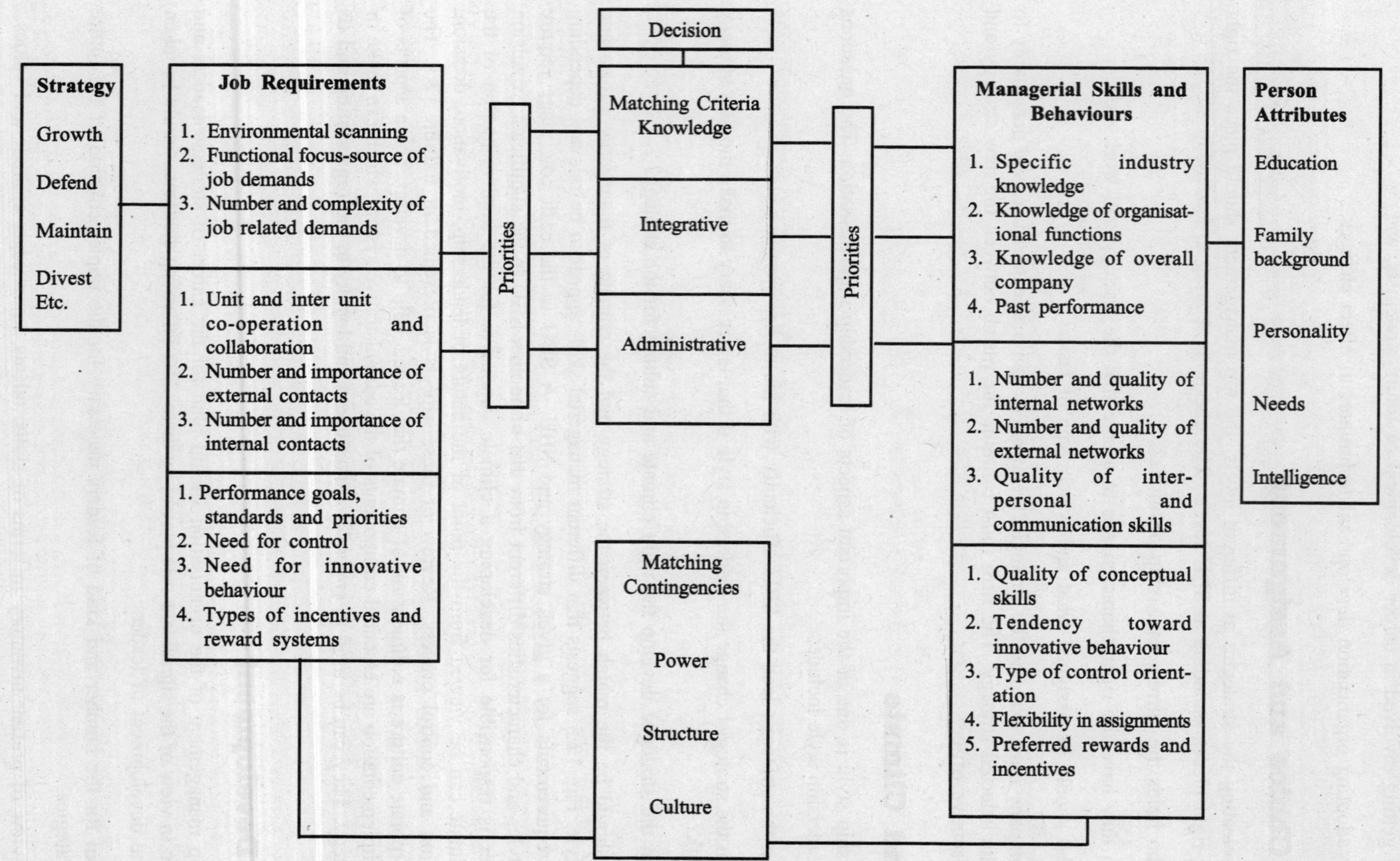

Source: Lawrence R. Jauch and William F. Glueck, *op. cit.*, p. 356.

Fig. 12.5: A Suggested Framework for Strategy-Manager Matching

Exhibit 12.1: Development of Conducive Climate for Strategy Implementation by the Leader — Ways of Viewing it

Leadership processes as a component of climate refer to the following types of questions:

1. To what extent do superiors have confidence in and trust subordinates? (No confidence to complete trust.)
2. To what extent do superiors behave in a manner that encourages subordinates to feel free to discuss important matters their jobs? (No discussion to full discussion.)
3. To what extent do superiors try to get ideas and opinions from subordinates and use them constructively? (Never or seldom to always.)

Motivational processes as a component of climate can be represented by the following:

1. What types of motives are used? (Fear, threats, punishment, economic rewards, noneconomic rewards.)
2. How much responsibility do various managerial levels assume for goal achievement? (Attempts to sabotage at some levels to high responsibility at all levels.)
3. What types of interactions occur? (Little interaction and distrust to extensive friendly interaction with confidence and trust.)
4. To what extent is there is a feeling of teamwork? (None or damaging competitiveness to substantial cooperation and cohesiveness.)

Decision process as a dimension of climate can be characterised as follows:

1. At what level are decisions formally made? (Bulk at the top and centralised to decentralised spread of decision authority and delegation.)
2. To what extent are decision-makers aware of lower-level problems? (Unaware to fully aware.)
3. To what extent is technical and professional knowledge used in making decisions? (No extent to great extent.)
4. To what extent do subordinates get involved in decisions related to their work? (No participation to high participation.)

The communication process component of climate includes these questions:

1. In what manner are orders issued or goals set? (Orders issued from above to goals established by means of group participation.)
2. How does communication primarily occur? (Formal written memos to informal verbal exchanges.)
3. How does communication flow? (Primarily downward to laterally to primarily upward.)

The control process dimension of climate is characterised as follows:

1. The extent to which review and control is concentrated. (Highly concentrated at the top to widespread responsibility for control.)
2. The extent of controls and standards. (Loose to tight.)
3. The extent to which control data are used for self-guidance. (Data used for policing to co-ordinated problem solving.)

Source: Lawrence R. Jauch and William F. Glueck, *op. cit.*, pp. 357-358.

Organisation Change and Development: The next aspect of leadership implementation deals with change process. The successful implementation of new strategies requires change in the present policies, plans, people and organisational climate. Organisational development techniques help to implement the new strategies through behavioural change. The organisation development techniques include: survey feedback, confrontation meeting, team building, transactional analysis, managerial grid approach, etc.

(C) CORPORATE CULTURE

An organisation's culture may be weak and fragmented, if most of the employees have no deeply felt sense of company purpose, view their jobs as a source of income and have divided loyalties.

Every company has its own history, own methods of solving problems, organising activities, composition of managerial personalities and styles. An organisation's culture may be weak and fragmented, if most of the employees have no deeply felt sense of company purpose, view their jobs as a source of income and have divided loyalties. Culture of some companies may be strong and cohesive in the sense that most of the people understand the company's objectives and strategy, and know what their individual roles are. A strong culture is powerful lever for channelling behaviour and helping employees in doing their jobs in a more strategy-supportive manner. This occurs in the following ways:

(i) Employees in strong culture companies, are provided with a system of informal rules and peer pressures regarding how to behave or do the work most of the times. The absence of strong company identity and purposeful work climate in weak culture companies, results in substantial employee confusion and wasted effort.

(ii) A strong culture provides structure, standards, and a value system and provides strong company identification among employees. Thus, a strong culture turns a job into a way of life and motivates the employees to contribute effectively to the company.

Therefore, to implement a strategy, an organisation's culture must be closely fit with the strategy.

What is Corporate Culture?

Corporate culture refers to the values and patterns of beliefs and behaviour that are accepted and practised by the members of a company. Companies within the same industry and companies within the same city exhibit distinctly different ways of operating and working as each company develops its own unique culture. Impact of culture on two different types of organisations is presented in Exhibit 12.2.

Exhibit 12.2 Impact of Culture on Two Different Groups of Organisations

	Dimensions of corporate culture	*Multinational subsidiaries and professionally managed companies*	*Family business and non-resident Indian companies*
1.	Nature of desired managerial skills and capabilities	Emphasis on professional qualifications and rank	Emphasis on demonstrated skills, depth and quality of knowledge
2.	Actual performance or results achieved	Emphasis on seniority, conformity to organisational values, loyalty, and relative fit between desired managerial behaviour and position in hierarchy	Emphasis on originality of action and thinking, innovation, and upgradation of knowledge and skills by personal efforts
3.	Managerial style of planning and decision-making	Emphasis on information gathering, bureaucratic mode of functioning, risk aversion and non-entrepreneurial decision-making	Emphasis on selective information usage, intuitive and qualitative decision-making of an entrepre-eurial nature
4.	Management systems adopted	Emphasis on use of elegant, scientific, sophisticated and rational systems which degenerate due to low usage	Emphasis on reliance on business sense and "no-frills" systems geared to quick action
5.	Nature of management control	Emphasis on comprehensive, formal and written reporting and rationalisation of failures rather than resolution of problems	Emphasis on primary use of verbal reporting and remedial action

Source: M.Rokeach. *The Nature of Human values*. (NewYork: Free Press).

To manage human resources of a company effectively and efficiently, it is necessary for bringing a close culture-strategy match. Culture with a perfect match with the strategy energises employees significantly to the power and helps for effectiveness of strategy implementation. Strategy-culture mismatch results in conflict and weakens the company's performance. Therefore, the culture should be changed as quickly as possible to bring culture-strategy fitness.

1. Impact of Culture on Strategy

Culture reflects the past and environmental change. These changes bring significant modifications in corporate culture. Corporate culture in turn affects the strategy implementation either positively or negatively. Changes in strategy must be accompanied by corresponding alternations in corporate culture to implement the strategy successfully. Conservative organisations follow the controlling approach even though they have formulated new goals and plans. Exhibit 12.3 presents the impact of corporate culture on strategy formulation.

Even though, firms formulate effective strategy, the strategy may fail, if it is not accompanied by assumptions, values and ways of working that are at variance with the organisation's culture. The employees may follow the same old methods of doing the jobs, even if the strategy and organisation structures are changed, unless the culture is not modified.

2. How Leaders Shape Culture?

Leaders can shape the corporate culture. Transactional leaders are less influential in modifying the company's culture than transformational leaders. "The transactional leader works within the organisational culture as it exists, the transformational leader changes the organisational culture."

Exhibit 12.3: Impact of Corporate Culture on Strategy Formulation

Organisation type	*Dominant objectives*	*Characteristics of policy-making Preferred strategies*	*Planning and control systems*
1. Defenders	Desire for a secure and stable niche in market	Specailisation; cost-efficient production; marketing emphasises price and service to, defend current business, tendency to vertical integration.	Centralised detailed control. Emphasis on cost efficiency. Extensive use of formal planing.
2. Prospectors	Location and exploitation of new product and market opportunities	Growth through product and market development (often in spurts). Constant monitoring of environmental change. Multiple technologies.	Emphasis on flexibility, decentralised control, use of *ad hoc* measurements.
3. Analysers	Desire to match new ventures to present shape of business	Steady growth through market penetration. Exploitation of applied research. Followers in the market.	Very complicated. Coordinating roles between functions (*e.g.* product managers). Intensive planning

Source: R.E. Miles and C.C. Snow, "*Organizational Strategy, Structure and Process*," McGraw-Hill, 1978.

According to Schein, leader can change the organisational culture in five ways. They are:

(i) By systematically paying attention to certain areas of business. These areas including controlling costs, improving employee productivity, improving sales, etc.

(ii) By reacting to critical incidents and organisational crises. The crises include declining sales, employee unrest, technological change, etc. The way leader deals with crisis can emphasise norms, values and working procedures etc.

(iii) By serving as a deliberate role model, teacher or coach.

(iv) By allocating rewards and status to the employees.

(v) By adopting the procedures through which a company selects, employs, and promote, retrenches and dismisses the employees. Corporate culture can be perpetuated by employing and promoting employees whose values are similar to the company's values.

Schein, also identifies primary embedding mechanisms and secondary articulation and reinforcement mechanisms. (Exhibit 12.4). The secondary reinforcement mechanisms include: organisation design and structure, organisational systems and procedures, design of physical space, stories about important events and people and formal statements of organisational philosophy etc.

Exhibit 12.4: Mechanisms for Embedding and Reinforcing Organizational Culture 

Primary Embedding Mechanisms

1. What leaders pay attention to, measure, and control
2. Leader reactions to critical incidents and organizational crises
3. Deliberate role modelling, teaching, and coaching
4. Criteria for allocation of rewards and status
5. Criteria for recruitment, selection, promotion, retirement, and ex-communication

Secondary Articulation and Reinforcement Mechanisms

1. Organisation design and structure
2. Organisational systems and procedures
3. Design of physical space, facades, buildings
4. Stories about important events and people
5. Formal statements of organisational philosophy, creeds, charters

Source: E.H. Schein, *Organisational Culture and Leadership* (San Fransisco: Jossey-Bass, 1985). Chap. 10.

3. Match Between Strategy and Culture

Some parts of corporate culture may be unchangeable. The strategy-maker, in such cases should select the strategy which fits in the existing corporate culture. Once the strategy is selected, the strategy implementer should bring corporate culture into close alignment with the strategy and stabilise it there.

Aligning culture with strategy requires:

(i) Diagnosing the facets of existing culture which are strategy supportive;

(ii) Identifying the facets of present culture which are to be modified to bring match with the strategy; and

(iii) Deciding the actions to be taken by the management to modify the cultural environment and create a stronger match with the strategy.

Symbolic Actions and Substantive Actions

Managerial actions to bring the match between culture and strategy include symbolic and substantive. Symbolic actions provide the indication about the kind of behaviour and performance, strategy implementers wish to encourage. The common symbolic actions include: honouring the employees whose actions and performance serve as role models, awarding the employees for their significant contributions to the organisations and the like. Awards, rewards, ceremonies, role models are a fundamental part of a strategy implementer's culture modifying effort. Strategy implementer use symbols to build and nurture the culture. They personally conduct ceremonial events and publicly congratulate individual employees. They use every ceremonial function and every conversation to implant values, send reinforcing signals and praise good deeds.

Chief strategy implementers must be careful to lead by example. The chief executive's sincere and committed effort is necessary for reinforcing the culture through both words and deeds. Further, the task of making culture supportive of strategy is not a short term exercise. It takes time for a new culture to emerge and prevail.

Establishing Ethical Standards and Values

It is essential for a company to build a strong corporate culture on ethical principles and sound values. An ethical corporate culture has a positive impact on company's long-term strategic success. Strong values and high ethical standards nurture the corporate culture in a very positive way. Companies set forth their values and code of ethics in written documents. The kind of topics covered in these documents are presented in Exhibit 12.5. The values and code of ethics can be implemented in the following ways:

It is essential for a company to build a strong corporate culture on ethical principles and sound values.

Exhibit 12.5: Topics Covered in Value Statements and Code of Ethics

Topics covered in values statements	Topics Covered in Codes of Ethics
• Importance of customers and customer service • Commitment to quality • Commitment to innovation • Respect for the individual employee and the duty the company has to employees • Importance of honesty, integrity and ethical standards • Duty to shareholders • Duty to suppliers • Corporate citizenship • Importance of protecting the environment	• Honesty and observance of the law • Conflicts of interest • Fairness of selling and marketing practices • Using inside information and securities trading • Supplier relationship and purchasing practices • Payment to obtain business • Acquiring and using information about others • Political activities • Use of company assets, resources and property • Protection of proprietary information • Pricing, contracting and billing

Source: Thompson and Strickland. *op. cit.*, p. 258.

(i) Incorporating the statement of values and the code of ethics into employee training and educational programmes.

(ii) Giving explicit attention to values and ethics in recruiting and employing to screen out applicants who do not exhibit compatible character traits.

(iii) Communicating the values and ethics to all employees and explaining compliance procedures.

(iv) Management involvement at all levels.

(v) Strong endorsement by the top management.

(vi) Word-of-mouth indoctrination.

4. Spirit of High Performance and Culture

Successful strategy implementation requires the spirit of high performance on the part of employees. Development of strong individual commitment and spirit of high performance, is therefore, essential for strategy implementation. The spirit of high performance culture results in improvement in organisational performance and organisational excellence. Organisations with a spirit of high performance are intensely human resource oriented. They treat the people with dignity and respect, encourage employees to use their potentialities, initiatives and creativity to the maximum extent in performing their work. Further, the employees are empowered in discharging their responsibilities. The companies set reasonable and clear performance expectations, use rewards and punishments, encourage the managers to develop the subordinates and grant autonomy to employees to contribute to the goals excellently. Companies must develop champions out of the people who turn in winning performances in order to create a result-oriented corporate culture.

Shared Values

The values widely shared by managers and employees are the core of the corporate culture. Fits with strategy should be created internally regarding structure, organisational skills and distinctive competence, budgets, support systems, rewards and incentives, policies and procedures and culture. The strategy can be implemented powerfully, if the fit among the administrative activities and the characteristics is strong.

McKinsey & Co., a leading consulting firm, has developed a framework for examining the fits in seven broad areas, *viz.*,

(i) strategy,

(ii) structure,

(iii) shared values, attitudes and philosophy,

(iv) approach to staffing the organisation and its overall "people-oriented",

(v) administrative systems, practices and procedures used to run the organisation, including the reward structure, formal and informal policies, budgeting and programmes, training, cost accounting and financial controls,

(vi) the organisation's skills, capabilities and core competencies, and

(vii) style of top management including how they allocate their time and attention, symbolic actions, their leadership skills, how the top management team comes across to the different levels and areas of the organisations.

McKinsey has diagrammed these seven elements which is called McKinsey 7-S framework. (Fig. 12.6). These seven elements are: strategy, structure, systems, style, staff, skills and shared values. The shared values are the core of the 7-S framework. They bond the corporate culture and give it energy.

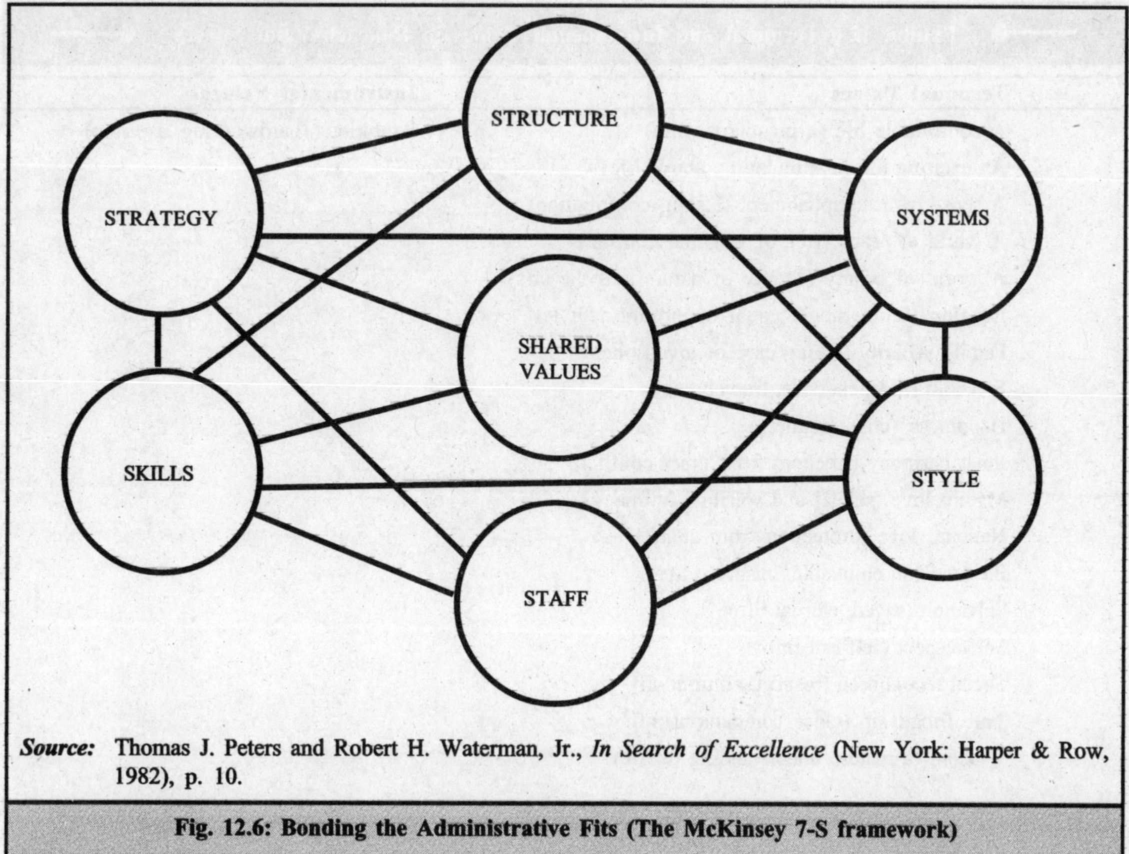

Source: Thomas J. Peters and Robert H. Waterman, Jr., *In Search of Excellence* (New York: Harper & Row, 1982), p. 10.

Fig. 12.6: Bonding the Administrative Fits (The McKinsey 7-S framework)

(D) VALUES

Values influence attitudes and behaviour. 'Normally employees view that' promotions are based on either merit or seniority or merit-cum-seniority. But the employees tend to be frustrated when they know that the promotions in an organisation are based on reservations.

Values influence attitudes and behaviour. 'Normally employees view that' promotions are based on either merit or seniority or merit-cum-seniority.

Thus, the values help to form attitudes, perceptions, morale and determine employee behaviour in an organisation.

Types of Values

Values which influence different areas of behaviour are classified into terminal values and instrumental values by Milton Rokeach in his Rokeach Value Survey.

- Terminal values refer to desirable end-states of existence. Individuals would like to achieve these values during his/her life time.
- Instrumental values refer to preferable modes of behaviour or means of achieving the terminal values.

Exhibit 12.6 presents the terminal and instrumental values in this survey.

Exhibit 12.6 Terminal and Instrumental Values in Rokeach Value Survey

Terminal Values	Instrumental Values
A confortable life (a prosperous life)	Ambitious (hardworking, aspiring)
An exciting life (a stimulating, active life)	
A sense of accomplishment (lasting contribution)	
A world at peace (free of war and conflict)	
A world of beauty (beauty of nature and the arts)	
Equality (brotherhood, equal opportunity for all)	
Family security (taking care of loved ones)	
Freedom (independence, free choice)	
Happiness (contentedness)	
Inner harmony (freedom from inner conflict)	
Mature love (sexual and spiritual intimacy)	
National love (protection from attack)	
Pleasure (an enjoyable, leisurely life)	
Salvation (saved, eternal life)	
Self-respect (self-esteem)	
Social recognition (respect, admiration)	
True friendship (close companionship)	
Wisdom (a mature understanding of life)	

(*Source:* M. Rokeach, The Nature of Human Values (New York: The Free Press.

It is confirmed by different studies that Rokeach Value Survey's values vary among groups, People in the same occupations or categories tend to hold similar values. Exhibit 12.6 presents mean value ranking of executives, union members and activists.

Values in Different Cultures

Cultures vary from country to country due to variations in climatic conditions, economic conditions, physical security issues and the like. Culture, in turn, influences the formation, development and maintenance of values. Since the cultures vary across the globe, so is the case with values.

Exhibit 12.7: Mean Value Ranking of Executives, Union Members, and Activists
(Top Five Only)

Executives		Union Members		Activists	
Terminal	Instrumental	Terminal	Instrumental	Terminal	Instrumental
1. Self-respect	1. Honest	1. Family security	1. Responsible	1. Equality	1. Honest
2. Family	2. Responsible	2. Freedom	2. Honest	2. A world of peace	2. Helpful
3. Freedom	3. Capable	3. Courageous	3. Family Security	3. Courageous	3. Happiness
4. A sense of accomplishment	4. Ambitious	4. Self-respect	4. Independent	4. Self-respect	4. Responsible
5. Happiness	5. Independent	5. Mauter love	5. Capable	5. Freedom	5. Capable

(*Source:* M. Rokeach, The Nature of Human Values (New York: *The* Free Press.

Geert Hofstede surveyed more than 116,000 IBM employees in 40 countries about their work related cultures. He classified the values into five categories based on his survey. They are: power distance, individualism vs. collectivism, quantity of life vs. quality of life, uncertainty avoidance and long-term vs. short-term orientation.

- ***Power Distance:*** It is a national culture attribute describing the extent to which a society accepts that power is distributed unequally in institutions and organisations. Equal power distribution is called low power distance and extremely unequal power distribution is called high power distance.
- ***Individualism vs. Collectivism:*** Individualism is the degree to which people in a country prefer to act as individuals rather than a member of a group. Low individualism is collectivism.
- ***Quantity of life vs. Quality of life:*** Quantity of life is the degree to which values like assertiveness, the acquisition of money and material goods and competition. Quality of life is the degree to which people value relationships and show sensitivity and concern for the welfare of others.
- ***Uncertainty Avoidance:*** It is the degree to which people in a country prefer structured over unstructured situations. People with high score on uncertainty avoidance have increased level of anxiety resulting in greater nervousness, stress and aggressiveness.
- ***Long-term vs. short-term orientation:*** Long term orientation is a national culture attribute that emphasises the future, thrift and persistence. Short-term orientation is a national culture attribute that emphasises the past and present, respect for tradition and fulfilling social obligation. People with short-term orientation emphasises on tradition and fulfilling social obligations. Exhibit 12.7 presents rating of these five dimensions in different countries.

Individual values influence the organisations as well as the strategy. Organisations consist of a large number of individuals with a variety of values. The values are shaped by the organisational environment and nature of the business. Individuals will share interests and values with others within the organisations. The mode of influence of values on strategy is presented in Fig. 12.7.

Factors that Shape and Change Values: The major sources of influence of an individual's values include; external influences, the nature of business and the company culture. Fig. 12.7 shows the facts which shape and change values.

External Influences: External influences include: *(i)* values of society, and *(ii)* organised groups.

***(i)* Values of Society:** Various issues like attitudes to work, authority, and equality are constantly shaped by society at large. This process should be understood from the point of corporate strategy due to the following reasons:

(a) values of society change and adjust over time

(b) multinational and transnational companies have the added problem of coping with the different standards and expectations of different countries.

***(ii)* Organised Groups:** Individuals very often have allegiances to other groups which are very influential on their values. These allegiances are directly related to working situations like membership of trade unions or more informal like membership in clubs and social organisations.

Nature of Business

The issues concerning the nature of a business include market situation, and product/technology. These two factors are more specific to the particular circumstances of a company.

***(i)* Market Situation:** Different companies face different market situations like recession, and boom. The values of the people within the company will change depending upon the market situation. Strategic decisions, in turn, are influenced by these changed values of the people, and values of the employees.

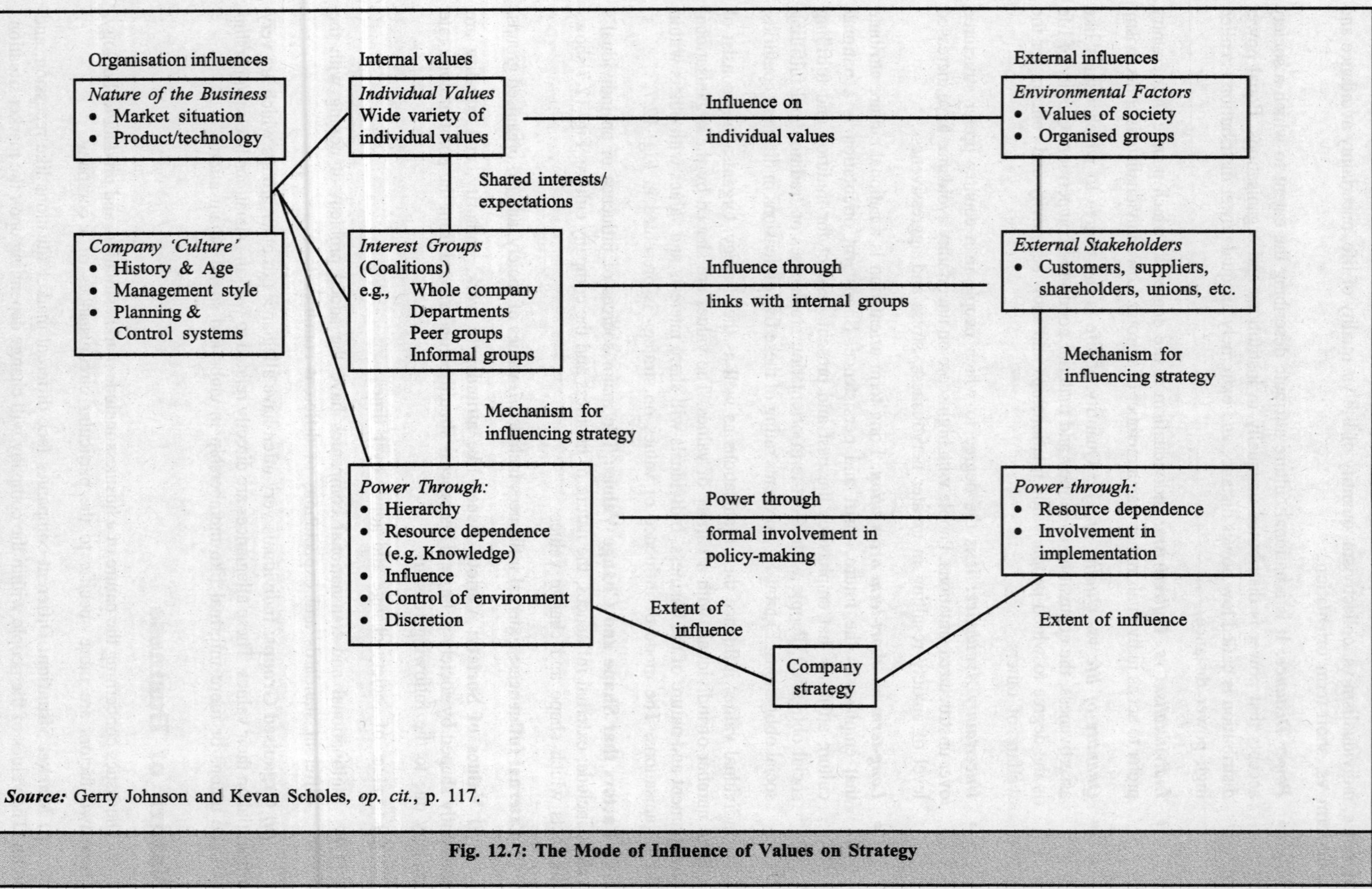

Source: Gerry Johnson and Kevan Scholes, *op. cit.*, p. 117.

Fig. 12.7: The Mode of Influence of Values on Strategy

(ii) **Products/Technology:** Technology influences values through the product, systems of production, distribution, etc. The influence of technology on values would be in two ways *viz., (i)* The company's ability to compete in the market is determined by various factors including technology. Technology determines methods of operating and tasks to be performed by employees *(ii)* The skills required by the company are determined by the nature and level of technology. This in turn determines the kind of people required to operate the technology and their values.

(E) POWER

Power, from the view point of strategic management is extent to which individuals or groups are able to persuade, induce or coerce others into following certain courses of actions. It is helpful to know the sources of power to understand and assess the importance of power in relation to strategic management. A clear distinction should be made between the authority and power in assessing the impact of power on strategic management. It is necessary to know the sources of power to understand its impact on strategic management.

Power, from the view point of strategic management is extent to which individuals or groups are able to persuade, induce or coerce others into following certain courses of actions.

1. Sources of Power

The sources of power can be divided into two categories *viz., (i)* internal sources, and *(ii)* sources for external stakeholders as shown in Fig. 12.8.

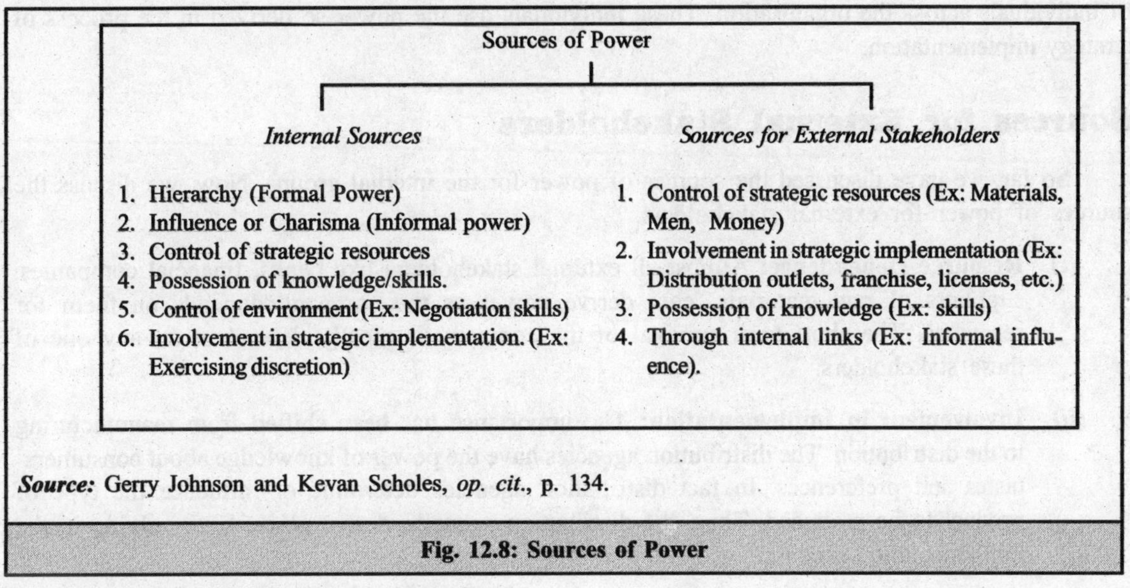

Source: Gerry Johnson and Kevan Scholes, *op. cit.*, p. 134.

Fig. 12.8: Sources of Power

Internal Sources of Power

(i) **Hierarchy:** Hierarchical positions in the organisational structure provide formal authority to the managers at higher levels. The managers with more formal authority influence the policy formulation and implementation extensively. Managers should use this power along with other types of power to make their influence efficient.

(ii) **Influence/Charisma:** Influence is an important source of power. This arises from personal qualities like charisma of the leader. Charisma is the leader's ability to influence others through his/her personal magnetism, enthusiasm and strongly held convictions. Leaders communicate these convictions and their vision for the future through a dramatic, persuasive manner of speaking. Charismatic leaders create an image of competence and success. Their personal magnetism make them role models for their employees. The more the followers admire their leaders, the more likely they are to accept their leaders' values and beliefs. This acceptance makes the leaders to exert

significant influence over their follower's behaviours. The charismatic leaders are more powerful during the periods of organisational crisis and transition.

***(iii)* Control of Strategic Resources:** Control of strategic resources is an important source of power. The relative importance of different resources change depending upon the strategy and situation. The leader can gain power by possessing or controlling the strategic resources.

***(iv)* Expertise or Knowledge or Skill:** Expertise or knowledge is a crucial source of power for top management. Managers acquire power through achievement and performance. The better the achievement and performance, the greater will be the power of the managers. Expertise refers to a manager's ability to influence the behaviour of others. The subordinates follow the managers as they believe that their managers have command and knowledge of the problems.

***(v)* Control of the Environment:** Normally, events in the company and company's internal environment affect the company's performance. Some groups or individual employees have more influence over events and company's internal environmental factors. This can be a source of power within the company. Marketing and finance managers can control the important internal environmental factors. Therefore, they play a dominant role in the strategic management whereas, the human resource manager and production manager take a back seat.

***(vi)* Exercising Discretion:** Exercising discretion is a most significant source of power within an organisation. Individuals due to the nature and level of their jobs, derive power. These individual employees occupy different positions in the organisation. Strategy is to be implemented by a number of individuals across the organisation. These individuals use the power so derived in the process of strategy implementation.

Sources for External Stakeholders

So far, we have discussed the sources of power for the internal groups. Now, we discuss the sources of power for external stakeholders.

(i) **Resource Dependence:** Almost all external stakeholders like banks, financial companies, suppliers of raw materials, etc., derive power as the company depends on them for resources. The short term survival of the company is mostly dependent on any one of these stakeholders.

(ii) **Involvement in Implementation:** The importance has been shifted from manufacturing to the distribution. The distribution agencies have the power of knowledge about consumers' tastes and preferences. In fact distribution agencies determine or influence the type of product to be produced. Thus, the distribution agencies derive power by involving in the implementation process.

(iii) **Expertise:** The agencies having specialised skill or expertise that is demanded by the company derive the power for their expertise knowledge.

(iv) **Internal Links:** Internal links can provide a way for external stakeholders to influence the company's strategy. Highly authoritarian organisation normally does not provide inter links and give chance to external stakeholders to influence the strategic management process.

2. Methods of Assessing Power

It is rather very difficult to assess the power of internal individuals or groups and external stakeholders. Preffer suggests that the best way of assessing the power is to depend on indicators of power.

Indicators within Organisations: There are four indicators of power within organisations. They are:

(i) **The Status of the Individual or Group:** The position of the individual in the organisational hierarchy, and the job grade work as an indicator to assess the power. The reputation of individual or group compared to others can also be used to assess the power.

(ii) **The Claim on Resources:** The claim of the individual or group for resources in terms of share in budget, number of employees, etc., can be used to measure the power. The resources of the least powerful group normally are eroded by the more powerful group.

(iii) **Representation in Powerful Positions:** The power of the individuals and groups can be assessed by their representation in boards, committees, groups, teams, etc.

(iv) **Symbols of Power:** Power of individuals and groups can also be assessed through various physical symbols like size and location of offices, facilities like secretary, telephone, carpet, meeting tables, etc.

Indicators for External Stakeholders: The indicators to assess the power of external stakeholders are:

***(i)* The Status:** The status of the external stakeholders like suppliers of raw materials, distributors can be assessed through, how quickly and to what extent their demands are met by the company.

***(ii)* Resource Dependence:** Resource dependency can be measured by the proportion of the company's business with a single distributor, proportion of the raw material supplied by a supplier to the total raw materials required by the company, etc.

***(iii)* Negotiating Arrangements:** The power of the external stakeholder can be assessed through whether the stakeholder invited for negotiation is allowed to interact closely or treated at arm's length.

***(iv)* Symbols:** Symbols are equally valuable clues. The symbols that are used to assess the power of external stakeholders include the level of manager that deals with the stakeholder, whether, the management team wine or dine with the stakeholder, etc.

The power can be assessed relatively as high, medium and low.

(F) ORGANISATIONAL CHANGE

Change is the law of nature.

Change is the law of nature. It is a necessary way of life in most organisations for their survival and growth. The term organisational change implies the creation of imbalances in the present pattern or situation. Adjustment among people, technology and structural set-up is established when an organisation operates for a long time. Change could be both reactive and proactive. A proactive change has necessarily to be planned to attempt to prepare for anticipated future challenges.

Approaches to organisational change include:

- Employee participation in decision-making relating to changes
- Advanced planning and preparing all the parties for change
- Protecting employees' interests
- Encourage team work
- Cautious and phase-wise introduction of change
- Motivating the employees to welcome the change
- Sharing the benefits of change between employees and management.

1. Planning and Implementing the Change

The strategist is often called a 'change agent' as his role is to initiate the change, and help make it work successfully. Employee's support is most essential in implementing the change successfully as they are at the helm of affairs, though the strategist is an agent of change. Change is typically viewed as the required three steps, *viz.,* unfreezing, changing and refreezing. Unfreezing means that old ideas and practices need to be cast aside so that, new ones can be learnt. Change is the step in which the new ideas and practices are learnt, so that an employee can think and perform in new ways. Refreezing means that what has been learnt is integrated into actual practice.

Implementation is the institutionalisation and internalisation of a change after it has been accepted by an organisation and a decision has been taken to accept and make it part of the on-going activity. Implementation may be seen as multidimensional process. The end result of implementation is the institutionalisation and stabilisation of change. Institutionalisation is making the change permanent part of organisation and internalisation means stabilisation of the change. The implementation process should start with planning. The three important stages of implementation of change processes (See Fig. 12.9) are:

(i) Monitoring the change;

(ii) Taking action in relation to the change; and

(iii) Making necessary adjustments in the programme accepted for implementation.

1. Planning: The main objective of planning, is to have an overall understanding of the nature of implementation. Planning process refers to determining in advance the entire process of implementation of change phasing. Planning may be focussed on phasing. Phasing may be either temporal (in terms of time) or spatial (in terms of various units or the locations of the organisation).

2. Processes: Various processes involved in implementation should be decided in advance. Various stages of the process include: initiation, motivation, diagnosis, information collection, deliberation, action proposal, implementation and stabilisation (See Fig. 12.10). Attention should be paid to the process of collaboration, increasing the capability of the organisation to face the problems of change, establishing the norms and values.

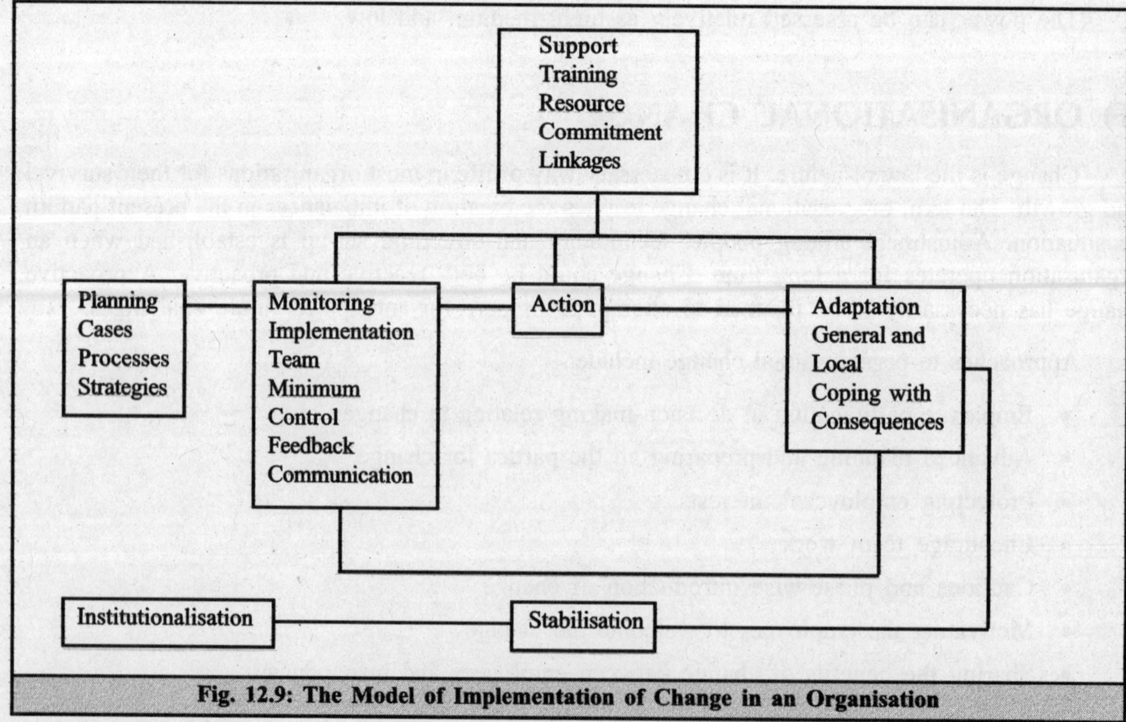

Fig. 12.9: The Model of Implementation of Change in an Organisation

3. Strategies: Management should formulate various strategies for implementation. These strategies should focus on taking outsider's help, change agents, designing permanent organisational structures, unit/location of the organisation to be selected for initial process, openness with the environment, etc.

4. Monitoring: It is the process of "routine periodic measurement of programme inputs, activities and outputs undertaken during programme implementation. Monitoring is normally concerned with the procurement, delivery and utilisation of programme resources, adherence to work schedule or progress made in the production of outputs." Monitoring is essential to make implementation effective. Monitoring/control is to ensure that a plan proceeds according to the original design. A broader group of people should be involved in monitoring function. An independent team without having interest in change may be entrusted with the task. This team may have a continuous status.

5. Implementation Team: A broad based task group of implementation should be set-up to look after the implementation of the change programme and monitor such programme. HRD department of the organisation may be asked to take up this responsibility.

6. Minimum Control: Controls should be minimum in order to make the monitoring effective. It is a delicate issue. On one hand it is a control function and on the other it also attempts to develop new norms of creativity, diversity and experimentation. Key roles involved in the implementation process are task force, implementation team, chief implement or counterpart consultant and corporate management.

7. Review and Feedback: Implementation requires reviewing various process and provide feedback. It involves getting data, information and experiences and providing feedback to the people on how they are implementing compared to the design and plans.

8. Dissemination of Information: The data, information and experiences collected in the various units/processes of the organisation may be provided to all the parties of change implementation with a view to reinforce a sense of success amongst various people.

9. Action: Action covers all the minute details of what is to be implemented at different stages. This process involves various phases and steps for people and various group tasks in relation to change programme.

10. Adaptation: Adaptation is the combination of two main criteria of effectiveness of implementation. Adaptation may be both general in the sense that some modifications may be made in the original plan and some may be developed at later stage.

11. Support: Various types of support from all concerned will be required for the implementation of change.

12. Human Resource Development: Effective implementation of change requires new and varied technical, managerial and behavioural skills and knowledge. Human Resource development department can contribute for the enhancement of these skills through training, executive development and organisation development programmes.

13. Resources: Implementation requires support in the form of various fields like financial resources, human resources, technological support, etc.

14. Linkages: Support may also be required in terms of building linkages both with external experts, various external agencies and internal departments. Linkage among departments, implementation teams, line management and top management is essential.

Change before change changes you.

15. Top Management Commitment: The most important aspect of support essential for implementing change is the support and commitment of top management. Top management should involve itself in the process of change implementation, encourage the implementation team, provide all types of resources.

Management has to get the support from employees through the following means: *(a)* Encouraging and using group force; *(b)* Development of leadership for change; *(c)* Encouraging participation and sharing views; *(d)* Maintenance of employees' security; *(e)* Effective communication; *(f)* Participation and working with the unions; *(g)* Working with the total system of the organisation which requires adopting useful and necessary changes; *(h)* Changing by evolution but not by revolution; *(i)* Adopting the change with adequate attention to human relations; *(j)* Identifying and taking care of post-change problems.

(G) ORGANISATION DEVELOPMENT

Change and Development

As discussed earlier change is a must. Change occurs not only in technology, marketing but also in human values, attitudes, relationships, social system, organisational climate, culture, etc. Hence, all are aware of and are concerned with change. Changes in values, etc., have tremendous impact on organisation as changes in technology and marketing. As such the management has to meet the challenges of change. Management can effectively meet these challenges through a systematic and planned change effort. Organisation development (OD) has emerged to help the planned change for organisational effectiveness. Thus, it is said that the organisational development is the modern approach to management of change and human resource development. Organisation development (OD) concentrates on people dimensions like norms, values, attitudes, relationships, organisational climate, etc.

History of Organisation Development

Douglas McGregor served as resource person to help Union Carbide Corporation to create an OD capability where OD department was set up in 1962. French and Bell who have done most of the work on OD feel that laboratory training and survey feedback are the main stems of OD. Sensitivity training programmes were conducted to managers under the OD movement. OD is still developing and evolving as a technique.

1. What is OD?

OD is a complex educational strategy designed to increase organisational effectiveness and wealth through planned inventions by a consultant using theory and techniques of applied behavioural science.

Warren G. Bennis defines OD as, "a complex educational strategy to change the beliefs, attitudes, values and structure of organisations so that they can better adapt to new technologies, markets and challenges and the dizzying rate of change itself."

Dale S. Beach defines OD as, "a complex educational strategy designed to increase organisational effectiveness and wealth through planned inventions by a consultant using theory and techniques of applied behavioural science."

2. OD Interventions/Techniques

Organisation development interventions techniques are the methods created by OD professionals and others. Single organisation or consultant cannot use all the interventions. They use these interventions depending upon the need or requirement. The most important interventions are: Survey feedback, process consultation, sensitivity training, the managerial grid, goal setting and planning, team building and management by objectives. Other interventions are job enrichment, changes in organisational structure and participative management and quality circles.

(1) Survey Feedback: This intervention provides data and information to the managers. Attitudes of employees about wage level, and structure, hours of work, working conditions and relations are collected and the results are supplied to top executive teams. These teams analyse the data, find out the problems, evaluate the results and develop the means to correct the problems identified. The teams are formed with the employees at all levels in the organisational hierarchy, *i.e.,* from rank and file to the top level.

(2) Process Consultation: Under this method, the process consultant meets the members of department in work teams, observes their interactions, problem identification skills, problem solving procedures, etc. He feeds back the team with the information collected through observation, coaches and counsels individuals and groups in moulding their behaviour.

(3) Goal Setting and Planning: Each divisions in an organisation or branch/zonal office sets the goals or formulates the plans relating to profitability, markets share, human resources productivity, etc. These goals are sent to the top management, which in turn sends them back to the divisions/zones/branches after modifications. A set of organisation-wide goals thus, emerge thereafter.

(4) Managerial Grid: Industrial psychologist Blake and Mouton developed the managerial grid basing it on the Ohio State Study. The managerial grid identifies a range of management behaviour based on the different ways that how production/service-oriented and employee-oriented states interact with each other.

(5) Sensitivity Training: The most commonly used OD intervention is sensitivity training. It is also called laboratory training. It is called laboratory training as it is conducted by creating an experimental laboratory situation in which employees are brought together, in groups, to interact in an unstructured environment. The members are encouraged to interact with new members and new individual behaviours.

The objectives of laboratory training are:

(i) To help people understand themselves better; *(ii)* To create better understanding of others; *(iii)* To gain insight into the group process; and *(iv)* To develop specific behavioural skills.

Some people never understand why they feel and act as they do and how the others feel about them. Some people are insensitive to the effects of their behaviour upon others and their orders upon subordinates. Laboratory training helps such people to understand the impact of their behaviour on others. Most of the people concentrate on what they are going to say rather than what the others are saying. This training develops the communication skills of the employers and develops them as good listeners. It also helps the participants to form into informal groups and teams and work more effectively.

Modus Operandi of Sensitivity Training

Sensitivity training provides face to face interaction. This training is carried out by largely unstructured groups without an agenda, leader and predetermined goals. The group is given complete freedom in developing their own devices, interactions and on-going process for interaction. Sometimes, the trainer introduces certain planned activities involving one or two professional trainers set in with each "T" group. The emphasis in this training is not upon learning specific facts but upon gaining understanding of feelings, gestures, attitudes and emotions, *i.e.,* sensitivity to oneself and others.

Another type of group is encounter group. These groups involve unstructured small group interaction under stress in a situation that requires people to become sensitive to one another's feelings in order to develop group activity. These groups seek to improve understanding of self and others, group process, culture and general behaviour skills.

(6) Team Building: Most of the laboratory training takes place among the employees of the same department. These employees work together as a team. Team building is nothing but application of various techniques of sensitivity training to the actual work groups in various departments. These work groups consists of peers and a supervisor. Laboratory techniques are also applied to short-term work teams. The technique, like laboratory training, aims at improving inter-group relations. This technique is designed to improve the ability of the employees to work together as teams.

(7) Job Enrichment: Job enrichment as is currently practised all over the world, is a direct outgrowth of Herzberg's two factor theory of motivation. It is therefore based on the assumption that in order to motivate workers, the job itself must provide opportunities for achievement, recognition, responsibility, advancement and growth. The basic idea is to restore to jobs the elements of interests that were taken away under the intensive specification. However, job enrichment is significantly different from horizontal loading, referred to earlier. Horizontal loading does not enrich the task. Washing dishes, then silver ware, and then pots and pans does no more to satisfy and provide an opportunity to grow than washing only dishes. Under job enrichment there is a conscious effort to build into jobs a higher sense of challenge and achievement. In a job enrichment programme, the worker decides how the job is performed, planned, and controlled, and makes more decisions concerning the entire process. The job enrichment approach to boring jobs is to give the individual employee more autonomy in that job. Employees decide how the job will be performed and receive less direct supervision on the job. Consequently, the employee receives a greater sense of accomplishment as well as more authority and responsibility, job satisfaction. This in turn contributes for better employee performance and higher productivity.

(8) Changes in Organisational Structure: Various models of organisational structure, particularly matrix organisation, improves intergroup interaction and relations. Further, changes may be introduced in organisational structure to provide the scope for team work, group interaction and increased inter-personal relations.

(9) Participative Management and Quality Circles: Participative management and quality circles are extension to team work. They provide for voluntary formation of groups/teams, association, interaction etc. They encourage open discussion on various problems and arriving at a commonly agreed solutions and execution of the agreements by the members themselves.

Use of a Consultant

Top managements engage a consultant or a change agent to help in establishing OD programmes when the qualified, competent and professional employees are not available within the organisation. OD professionals generally possess advanced qualifications in behavioural science and knowledge and experience in designing and conducting laboratory training programmes. The consultant examines the routine activities, provide information, help the management in designing and administering the OD programme. He also helps and trains the members to become self-sufficient in problem solving. The consultant prepares the report and submits to the top management regarding OD policy and programmes on the basis of data and information collected by him from various sources of the organisation. He also helps the organisation in executing the OD programmes. The consultant helps much in developing the members to become more effective in dealing with one another.

3. Benefits of OD

Individual employees, groups/teams and the organisations are benefited by the OD programmes. The benefits of OD include performance improvements, job specification and self-change.

OD programmes contribute to the increase in the job performance of individual employees, groups and the organisation. Impact of OD can be measured by comparing the performance of controlled group with that of non-controlled group. Group performance will be enhanced much as OD emphasises on group activity.

OD programmes encourage team work, communication skills, cooperation, interpersonal relations, openness, etc. Employees with these changing behavioural dimensions feel happy have a sense of satisfaction about the job and organisation.

OD programmes contribute to the change in behaviour, values, attitudes, perceptions, etc., by enabling the employees to understand about themselves and others in the group and organisation. This results in self-change of the employees.

POINTS TO BE REMEMBERED

- Positive attitude is viewing and thinking realistically and positively with regard to strategy implementation.
- Leaders influence the followers through various styles all of which are oriented to strategy implementation direction.
- Corporate culture builds appropriate systems, relationships and climate necessary for efficient implementation of the strategy.
- Values influence the organisation as well as strategy.
- Power is extent to which individuals or groups are able to persuade, induce or coerce others into strategy implementation process.
- Change is the law of nature. Change before change, changes you.
- Organisation development is the behavioural changes towards the organisational and strategy implementation requirements.

KEY WORDS

- Positive Attitude
- Positive Mindset
- Leadership
- Transformational Leader
- Democratic Leader
- Autocratic Leader
- Power
- Organisational change
- Organisational Development
- Values
- Strategic Leadership
- Organisational climate

QUESTION FOR DISCUSSION

1. What is the positive attitude? Discuss the approaches to develop positive attitudes.
2. What is leadership? Explain different kinds of leadership that are appropriate for various strategies
3. What are organisational change? How do you bring the strategic change?
4. What is organisational development? How do you use it for strategy implementation?
5. What is corporate culture? Discuss appropriate culture for strategy implementation.
6. What is power? How do you exert power in the process of strategy implementation.

REFERENCES

1. W. Bennis, "*Why Leaders Can't Lead: The Unconscious Conspiracy Continues,*" Jossey-Bass, San Fransisco, 1989, p. 22.
2. P. Subba Rao, "*Essentials of Human Resource Management and Industrial Relations,*" Himalaya Publishing House, Mumbai, 1996, pp. 338-339.
3. Fred Luthans, "*Organizational Behaviour,*" p. 398.
4. F.E. Fidler, "A *Theory of Leadership Effectiveness,*" McGraw-Hill New York, 1967 and V.H. Vroom and A.G. Jago, "*The New Leadership: Managing Participation in Organisations*", Prentice-Hall, Englewood Cliffs, N.J. 1988.
5. Day and Lord, "*Executive Leadership,*" p. 459.
6. J.N. Burns, "*Leadership*", Harper & Row, New York, 1978.
7. B.M. Bass, "*Leadership and Performance Beyond Expectations,*" Free Press, New York, 1985.
8. *Ibid.*, p. 29.
9. B.M. Bass, "Leadership: Good, Better, Best," *Organisational Dynamics*, 13, Winter 1985, pp. 26-40.
10. Thompson and Strickland, *op. cit.*, p. 266.
11. *Ibid.*, pp. 268-269.
12. *Ibid.*, p. 270.
13. Abraham Zaleznik, "Power and Politics in Organisational Life," *Harvard Business Review*, Vol. 48, No. 3, May-June 1970, pp. 47-60.
14. Quinn, "*Strategies for Change,*" p. 68.
15. Thompson and Strickland, *op. cit.*, p. 271.
16. Quinn, "Strategies for Change," pp. 128-145. Quoted in *Ibid.*, pp. 271-272.
17. Thompson and Strickland, *op. cit.*, p. 273.
18. *Ibid.*, pp. 273-274.
19. Lawrence R. Jauch and William F. Glueck, *op. cit.*, p. 353.
20. *Ibid.*, pp. 357-358.
21. *Ibid.*, p. 360.
22. Terence F. Deal and Allen A. Kennedy, "*Corporate Cultures,*" Addison-Wesley, Reading, Mass, 1982, p. 4.
23. *Ibid.*, pp. 15-16.
24. *Ibid.*
25. C.D. Pringle, D.F. Jennings and J.G. Longencker, "*Managing Organisations: Functions and Behaviour,*" Merrill, Colombus, Ohio, 1988, p. 594.
26. Pringle *et. al.*, "*Managing Organisations,*" p. 309.
27. Schein, "*Organisational Culture,*" p. 30.
28. *Ibid.*, p. 33.
29. Bass, "*Leadership and Performance,*" p. 24.
30. Schein, "*Organisational Culture,*" pp. 224-237.
31. Thompson and Strickland, *op. cit.*, p. 257.
32. *Ibid.*, p. 258.
33. *Ibid.*, pp. 259-260.
34. Peters and Waterman, "*In Search of Excellence,*" pp. 240 and 269.
35. Robert H. Water, Jr., Thomas J. Peters and Julien R. Phillips, "Structure is not Organisation," *Business Horizons*, Vol. 23, No.3, June 1980, pp. 14-26. and Robert H. Waterman, Jr., "The Seven Elements of Strategic Fit," *Journal of Business Strategy*, Vol. 2, No.3, Winter 1982, pp. 68-72.
36. Gerry Johnson and Keven Scholes, *op. cit.*, pp. 121-122.
37. I.C. MacMillan, "*Strategy Formulation: Political Concepts,*" West, 1978, p. 15.
38. D.E. Berlew, "*Leadership and Organisational Excitement,*" in D.A. Kolb, I.M. Rubin and J.M. McIntyre (Eds.) "*Organisational Psychology,*" Prentice-Hall, Englewood Cliffs, N.J., 1974.

39. Yukl, "*Leadership in Organisations*," p. 206.
40. J.R.P. French, Jr., and B. Raven, "*The Bases of Social Power*," pp. 150-167.
41. J.M. Godiwala, W.A. Meinhart and W.D. Warde, "*Corporate Strategy and Functional Management*," Praeger, 1979.
42. Samuel C. Certo and J. Paul Peter, *op. cit.*, p. 219.
43. *Ibid.*, p. 224.
44. *Ibid.*
45. T.M. Garrett, "Business Ethics," *The Times of India Press*, Mumbai, 1970.
46. Samuel C. Certo and J. Paul Peter, *op. cit.*, p. 231.
47. Gene R. Laczniak, "Framework for Analyzing Marketing Ethics," *Journal of Macromarketing*, Spring, 1983, pp. 7-18.
48. Samuel C. Certo and J. Paul Peter, *op. cit.*, p. 231.
49. D. Thakore, "How corrupt is Indian Industry," *Business World*, May 11-24, 1987, pp. 58-67, Quoted in Azhar Kazmi, *op. cit.*, p. 297.
50. Warren G. Bennis, "*Organisational Development*" Addison Wiley, Reading Mass, 1969, p. 2.
51. Dale S. Beach, "*Personnel*," MacMillan Publishing Co., New York, 1985, p. 426.
52. Stephen P. Robbins, "*Organisational Behaviours*," Prentice-Hall, New Delhi , 2007, p.62.

13

CHAPTER

FUNCTIONAL IMPLEMENTATION: FUNCTIONAL ISSUES

Chapter Outline

(A) Operational/Production Policies

(B) Marketing Policies

(C) Financial Policies

(D) Human Resource Policies

(E) Management Information System

Learning Objectives

After studying this chapter, you should be able to:

- Study different kinds of functional activities for implementation of strategies;
- Discuss production/operational issues and activities that affect strategy implementation;
- Explain marketing policies/issues and activities that affect strategy implementation;
- Analyse financial policies/activities that affect strategy implementation;
- Discuss human resource policies and activities that affect strategy implementation;
- Analyse information system policies and activities that affect strategy implementation.

(A) OPERATIONAL/PRODUCTION POLICIES

1. The Operations Function

In the broad sense, operations management is concerned with the production of goods and rendering of services. Therefore, the general term operations management is used to denote production of goods and rendering of services. Operations management is defined as decision-making for operations functions and systems which produce goods and/or services. The focus in operations management is primarily on decision-making responsibility and secondarily on methodology. Managers in the production process manage the transformation process which supplies goods and services. The transformation process converts inputs, *i.e.,* materials, energy, capital, human resources, components and information into output, *i.e.,* goods, services and information. The five key decisional areas of operations management include: Process, capacity, inventory, human resources, and quality. These five decisional areas are useful for describing an existing operation or identifying the decisions required to establish a new operation. Exhibit 13.1 shows strategic and routine decisions in production/ operations management.

In the broad sense, operations management is concerned with the production of goods and rendering of services.

Exhibit 13.1: Strategic and Routine Decisions in Production/Operations Management

Decisional Area	*Strategic (Design) Decisions*	*Routine (Utilisation) Decisions*
Process:	Select process type choose equipment	Analyse process flows. Provide for maintenance of equipment
Capacity:	Determine materials size. Determine facilities, location. Set workforce levels.	Decide overtime. Arrange for subcontracting. Determine scheduling.
Inventory:	Set overall inventory size. Design inventory control system.	Decide when to order and how much to order
Human Resource:	Design jobs. Design Training policies and methods. Select compensation system.	Provide supervision. Set work standards. Appraise performance. Improve performance. Maintain sound industrial relations.
Quality:	Set Quality Standards Design on Quality Organisation.	Decide an amount of inspection control on quality to meet the standards.

Source: Modified version from: Roger G. Schroeder, *Operations Management*, p. 16.

Operations management in a service organisation is different from a manufacturing organisation. A service is produced and consumed more or less simultaneously. The differences between a service and a manufacturing organisation include: Services are intangible, service can be viewed as an extremely perishable product, it can't be stored as inventory for future use. Therefore, the delivery of services presents a special problem for inventory and capacity planning. Quality of services cannot be readily assessed. Service organisations are often dispersed geographically. As a service can't be stored and shipped, it should be produced at the point of consumption or the customer must be brought to the place of service. The marketing and operations functions in service organisations tend to be closely related. This is due to the fact that, services are consumed at the same time and place that they are produced. The opposite is true in manufacturing organisations.

2. Decision-Making in Operations

Decision-making is the act of choosing among alternatives. In the broad sense, decision-making is a process which includes problem definition, generation of alternatives, evaluation of alternatives choose the best solution and implementation of the solution. Decisions are often made in the face of imperfect information, this results in bounded rationality. Therefore, the decision maker seeks a satisfactory solution rather than an optimal or best solution. The criteria for evaluating operations decisions include: cost, quality, dependability and flexibility.

Cost: The cost plays a significant role in operations decisions. The strategist should include all relevant costs. The strategist should identify and include all costs affected by the decisions and ignore the costs not affected by the decisions.

Quality: The quality objective is concerned with the quality of the product and service. This objective is influenced by the product/service design and process design. Quality is affected by the strategic decisions like product design, process design, human resources, quality of inputs and approach and system of quality control.

Dependability: Dependability is concerned with the dependability of the supply of the goods and/or services. Dependability may be measured by the percentage of stock-out, the percentages of delivery promises met, etc. Dependability is affected by the strategic decisions like scheduling, aggregate planning inventory management, process design, etc.

Flexibility: Flexibility is concerned with the ability of operations to make changes in product design, volume of product, delivery, etc. Flexibility may be measured by the amount of time it takes to change from one product design to the another form, level of output, quality of output, etc.

Fig. 13.1 shows the interaction among operations objectives.

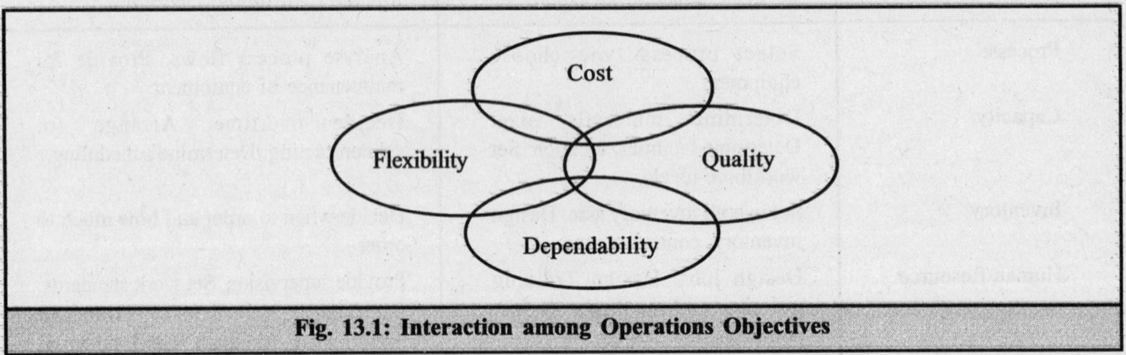

Fig. 13.1: Interaction among Operations Objectives

Trade-offs in Production/Operations Decisions

Evaluating decision in operations management require numerous trade offs among the decision criteria. The strategists should understand the nature of these trade-offs. Many failures in operations management is due to the absence of awareness of important trade offs or a faulty analysis of the trade-offs available. Exhibit 13.2 depicts some important trade-off decisions in manufacturing or "You can't have it both ways."

3. Product Design

New product design plays a crucial role in the survival and development of most of the firms. New product introduction is a way of life in fast-changing industries. The strategist is expected to play a vital role in the new product design and/or product redesign.

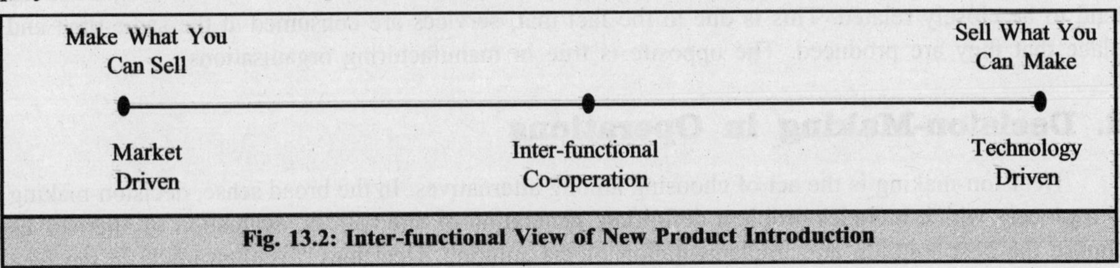

Fig. 13.2: Inter-functional View of New Product Introduction

Exhibit 13.2: Some Important Trade-off Decisions in Manufacturing — Or "You Can't Have it Both Ways"

Decision Area	*Decision*	*Alternatives*
Plant and equipment	Span of process	Make or buy
	Plant size	One big plant or several smaller ones
	Plant location	Locate near markets or near materials
	Investment decisions	Invest mainly in buildings, equipment, inventories, or research
	Choice of equipment	General-purpose or special-purpose equipment
	Kind of tooling	Temporary, minimum tooling or "production tooling"
Production planning and control	Frequency of inventory taking	Few or many breaks in production for buffer stocks
	Inventory size	High inventory or lower inventory
	Degree of inventory control	Control in great detail or in lesser detail
	What to control	Controls designed to minimize machine downtime, labour cost, or time in process or to maximize output of particular products or usage of certain materials
Labour and staffing	Quality control	High reliability and quality or low costs
	Use of standards	Formal, informal, or none at all
		Highly specialized or not highly specialized
		Technically trained first-line supervisors or supervisors who are not technically trained
		Many job grades or few job grades; incentive wages or hourly wages
		Close supervision or loose supervision
Product design engineering	Job specialization	Many or few such engineers
	Supervision	
	Wage system	Many customer specials, few specials, or none at all
	Supervision	Frozen design or many engineering change orders
	Industrial engineers	Use of new processes unproved by competitors or follow-the-leader policy
	Size of product line	Complete packaged design or design as you-go approach
Organization and management	Design stability	Few or many manufacturing engineers
	Technological risk	Functional or product focus; geographical or other
	Engineering	High involvement in investment, production planning, cost control, quality control or other activities
	Use of manufacturing engineering	Decisions based on much or little information
	Kind of organization	Large or small staff group
	Executive use of time	Much or little involvement in detail; authoritarian or nondirective style; much or little contact with organization
	Degree of risk assumed	
	Use of staff	
	Executive style	

Source: Wickham Skinner, "Manufacturing — Missing Links in Corporate Strategy," *Harvard Business Review*, May-June, 1969.

The new-product development process consists of six stages. They are: idea generation, product selection, preliminary design, prototype construction, testing and final design. (Fig. 13.3).

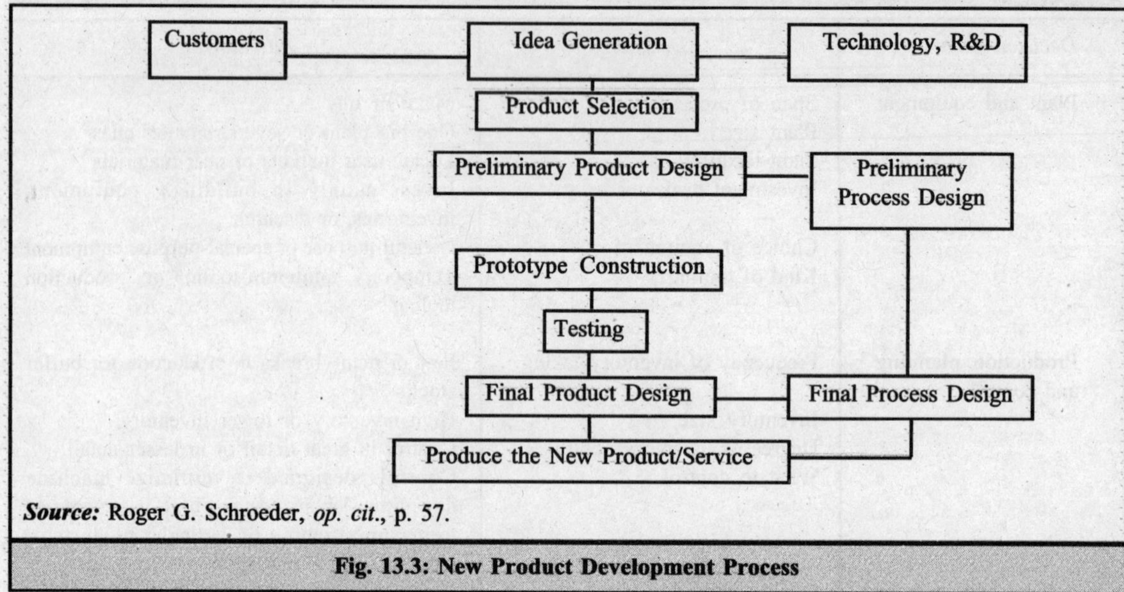

Source: Roger G. Schroeder, *op. cit.*, p. 57.

Fig. 13.3: New Product Development Process

The strategist should be aware that all the ideas generated will not reach the final stage. The ideas should be filtered based on their evaluation. David Uman's study indicates that one out of 60 new product idea results in a successful product. The greatest reduction takes place before preliminary product design. Therefore, the strategist must place great weight on the initial product selection phase and the associated analysis.

It is important to specify the bundle of goods and services desired in defining products. The bundle includes facilitating goods like food items, tables, chairs, etc., explicit services like the server serving the food and implicit services or psychological benefits like the taste of the food, satisfying the need of hunger, etc., in case of a hotel industry.

There are three stages of product-process interaction during the life cycle of a product. They are: the fluid stage, the semi-automated stage and the fully automated stage. There is a great deal of interaction between product and process during these stages of life cycle of a product. The product greatly affects the objectives of operations, *viz.,* cost, dependability, quality and flexibility. Flexibility may be the first important objective when the product is first introduced. Cost reduction may be the important objective when the price competition develops. The strategist should remember that either too little variety or too much variety result in low profit. Therefore, the strategist should select an optimum amount of product variety. Modular production is an approach used to produce a wide variety of products from a limited number of product components. This approach can be used to control product proliferation by limiting the number of components or modules available by producing standard components.

4. Process Selection

There are three types of process flow, *viz.,* line flow, intermittent flow or job shop and project.

Process selection decisions determine the type of productive process to be used and appropriate span of that process. There are three types of process flow, *viz.,* line flow, intermittent flow or job shop and project. Line flow is characterised by a linear sequence of operations used to make the product or render service. Line operations are extremely efficient and also extremely inflexible — processes utilise specialised equipment. An intermittent-flow process is characterised by production in batches at intermittent intervals. Equipment and labour are organised into work centres by similar types of skill or equipment. A product or job then will flow to those work centres that are required and will skip the rest. Therefore, the resulting flow pattern is jumbled. Intermittent operations are highly flexible but less efficient than line operations. The project flow is used to make a unique product.

Operations processes can also be classified as make-to-order and make-to-stock. The make-to-order process is set in motion by customer orders and geared to delivery performance. The make-to-stock process is geared to the replenishment of inventory; it does not respond to specific customer orders.

The combination of product flow with type of customer order yields six types of operations processes. Various factors like capital, market conditions, human resources, management skills, raw materials, components, technology should be considered in making a selection from the three processes.

The process-product matrix describes stages in the life cycles of products and processes. It is suggested that process and product be viewed as two sides of a matrix. A company should define its distinctive competence in terms of both process and product by selecting a path on the matrix. The matrix helps relate process-selection decisions to product decisions and the market. A change in the product strategy may move the company to the right, off the diagonal, if the old process remains in effect. The competitors operating on the diagonal can produce at lower costs. It will force to change the process technology to move the firm back down to the diagonal or below it. The strategy of moving down the diagonal ahead of the competition has cost advantages. The firm adopting this strategy suffers from absence of flexibility.

Choice of Technology

Technology is that set of processes, tools, methods, procedures and equipment which is used to produce goods and/or rendering services. The decisions of technological choice are of extreme importance. Technology is one component of a decision which involves economics, strategy, products and all aspects of management responsibility. Further, the choice of technology is never neutral with respect to society and the human resources. Therefore, it is essential to consider the joint social and technical consequences through the concept of socio-technical design. Technologies are chosen to optimise both social and technical variables. The choice of technology should not be based solely on return on investment (ROI). The effect of technology on operations should also be considered.

Process-Flow Analysis

Both materials flow and information flow can be analysed by a common framework and common procedure. The results of this analysis may lead to changes in any or all elements of the process. A socio-technical approach is needed to consider physical flow design result in processes which are both economically and humanly rewarding.

Plant Location: Plant location has direct impact on the cost of production/operations and on the marketing efficiency. The company remains in the same locations for many years. Therefore, the strategist should make an effective decision regarding plant location. The plant location is influenced by various factors like nearness to markets, availability of transportation facilities, availability of human resources, nearness to raw materials, climate conditions, government factors, etc. There are three models of plant location, *viz.,* critical model, objective model and subjective model. Critical model is based on the availability of critical factors like raw materials, energy, etc., objective model is based on the cost factor, *i.e.,* cost of raw materials, cost of human resources, etc. The subjective model is characterised by a qualitative type of measurement like the influence of trade unions, political factors, cultural factors and community services (See Box 13.1).

BOX 13.1 PRODUCTION RESUMES AT LONGBRIDGE

Car production has restarted at the former MG Rover plant in Longbridge, Birmingham

Shanghai Automotive (SAIC) said it had sold 70% of the orders for its new model, the MG TF LE500. However, it has been suggested the production is not "full scale" as the engines and bodies are being shipped over from China for hand finishing. An MG UK spokeswoman said Longbridge did have a "full-on" production line with 180 workers on site. Eleanor de la Haye, of MG UK, said: "We have 180 workers on site working, not necessarily on that line but on support services as well. "We are hand building cars. We are producing them in the same way we would expect from any other manufacturing facility." Former Jaguar chief executive Sir Nick Scheele said this could damage the brand for anyone wanting to buy a "British" car. He said: "The brand must elicit trust and trustworthiness from potential customers."

Owners SAIC say 700 MG TFs will be produced by the end of the year

The company has 55 dealers across the UK and believes the first cars will be with customers by next month. MG Rover collapsed in 2005 with the loss of about 6,000 jobs. It was bought by Nanjing Automobile Corporation for £53m but they were taken over by SAIC.

'Looking forward' SAIC said it hoped to produce 700 of its sports cars by the end of the year. The model will cost nearly £16,500. Ms de la Haye said: "We are delighted to have reached this important point and are looking forward to seeing the cars in showrooms shortly." Birmingham City Council leader Mike Whitby said: "This is truly an historic day for our city and our region and it points towards a much brighter future. "Combined with Tata's recent collaboration with Jaguar and Land Rover this is bringing the rebirth of our automotive industry one step closer to reality." Longbridge was opened in 1905 by motoring legend Herbert Austin. As well as producing cars, it was used as a munitions factory during both world wars and began production of the iconic Mini in 1959. It also produced the popular Metro and Rover 200 models before the Rover company was bought by BMW in 1994. BMW subsequently sold the firm to the Phoenix Consortium, under whom it went into administration in 2005.

Source: http://news.bbc.co.uk/2/hi/uk_news/england/west_midlands/7536527.stm (02/08/08)

Facilities Decisions

The procedure for analysing facilities decisions includes: measurement of capacity, forecasting of demand, determination of capacity needs, generation of alternatives, evaluation of alternatives, and deciding. Facilities decisions are often taken by the chief executives and the board of directors as these decisions are encompassing. Managers should determine the role of process, volume or capacity economies in any given decisions. Facilities locations issues include: single facility location, plant and warehouse location, retail store location, and emergency service location. Each of these issues has different criteria and utilises different modelling approach.

Aggregate Planning

Aggregate planning is concerned with matching supply and demand over the medium time range. The overall input level is planned so as to use the best possible mix of resource inputs. Supply variables which may be changed by aggregate planning are hiring, firing, overtime, idle time, inventory, subcontracting, part time labour and cooperative arrangements. Variables which influence demand are pricing, promotion, backlog, or reservations, or complementary products. When demand is given, two pure strategies are available for adjusting supply, *viz.,* the chase strategy and the level strategy. The chase strategy aims at chasing demand with the workforce. The level strategy aims at increasing or decreasing the workforce. With a perfectly level strategy, the rate of regular-time out put will be constant. Changes in demand must be absorbed by using inventories, overtime, part-time employees, sub contracting, cooperative arrangements, etc. These two strategies are extreme. In practice, many combinations are also possible in between them.

Aggregate planning is concerned with matching supply and demand over the medium time range.

Scheduling Operations: Scheduling seeks to satisfying the conflicting objectives of low inventories, high efficiency, and good customer service within the available resources. Trade-offs are made whenever, a schedule is developed. Scheduling differs between line, intermittent and project flow of operations.

8. Inventory Management

The role of inventory management is to balance the conflicting objectives among the marketing, finance and operations functions in the best interest of the company as a whole. Inventory is a stock of materials used to facilitate production or to satisfy customer demands. Inventories include raw materials, work in process and finished goods. Decision problems in inventory management include: what to carry, how much to order, when to order, and type of control system to use. The inventory management should aim at reducing the cost of inventory and to provide uninterrupted flow of materials for production.

Managing Human Resources: Managing human resources is explained in the section on "Human Resource Management.".

The strategist should design the jobs incorporating skill variety, task identity, task significance, autonomy and feedback. Such design results in employee self motivation, interest in the job, high commitment and productivity. Similarly, job enrichment also contributes to such results. Other strategies include. Selecting and retaining competent people, developing them continuously, maintaining a competitive compensation system and sound industrial and human relations.

9. Quality Planning and Control

Quality is fitness for use by customer. The dimensions of quality include: quality of design, quality of conformance, the abilities and field service. Management should set an overall quality policy and it should be implemented through specific objectives set by managers at different levels. The consumer movement, increasing competition based on quality and the increasing significance of total quality management necessitate the management to formulate strategies relating to quality. The total quality concept utilises a systems approach to quality by integrating quality programmes and objectives across organisational lines. The strategy of, "Make it perfect at the first time," serves to prevent defects from occurring.

Quality control is the conformance to given product or service specifications. It can be achieved through the design of quality control systems. This system design should specify where inspection takes place, what types of measurements are used, how much inspection is done and who does the inspecting.

Conclusion

The method of policy and strategy determination for operations is summarised and presented in Fig. 13.4. Skinner has identified four factors to design and manage from top down. These four factors area: *(i)* Develop an explicit, brief statement of corporate objectives and strategy, *(ii)* translate the objectives and strategy statement into operations, *(iii)* carefully examine each element of the operations system for consistency with the stated policy, and *(iv)* recognise the structure of operations to provide a congruent focus.

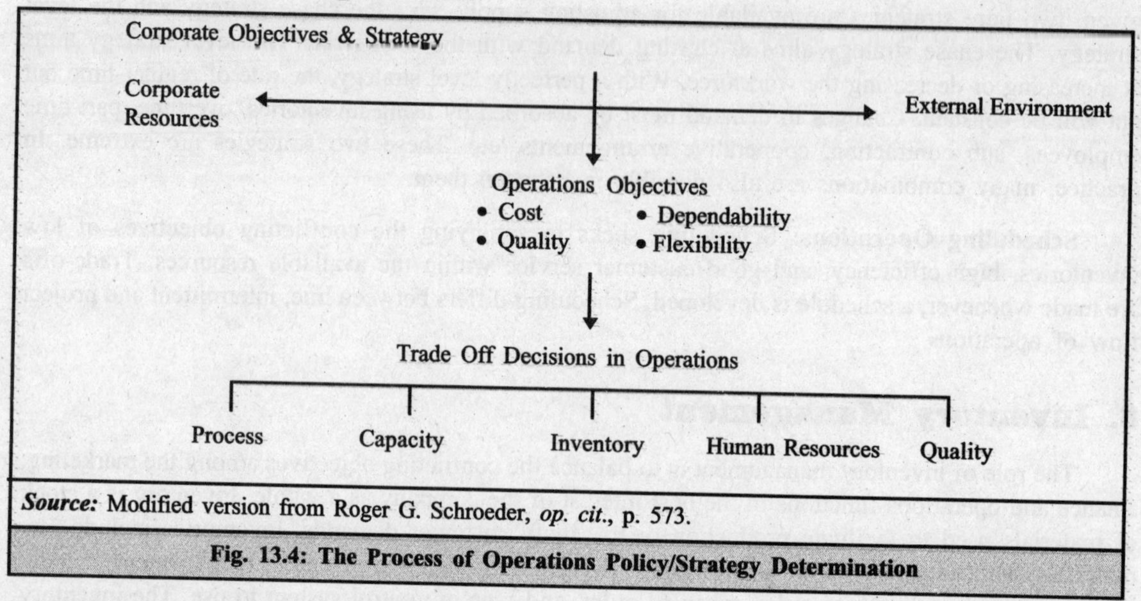

Source: Modified version from Roger G. Schroeder, *op. cit.*, p. 573.

Fig. 13.4: The Process of Operations Policy/Strategy Determination

(B) MARKETING POLICIES

Marketing is a social and managerial process by which individuals and groups obtain what they need and want through creating, offering and exchanging products of value in the market. Marketing management is the process of planning and executing the conception, pricing, promotion and distribution of goods, services, and ideas to create exchanges with target groups that satisfy customer and organisational objectives.

Customers are value maximisers. A customer's satisfaction is a function of the product's perceived performance and the buyer's expectations. Strong companies manage the four core business processes efficiently. They are: the new product realisation process, the inventory management process, the order-to-remittance process, and the customer service process. Customer influence the company's profitability significantly. Therefore, companies can not afford to lose a customer. It is estimated that the cost of attracting a new customer is five times the cost of keeping a current customer satisfied. Therefore, the marketers want to retain the customer by adding financial and social benefits to the product. However, unprofitable customers can be avoided. Quality of the product plays a vital role in retaining the customer. Firms, today, have no choice whether to implement or not to implement the Total Quality Management programmes.

1. Market-Oriented Strategic Planning

Market-oriented strategic planning is the managerial process of developing and maintaining a viable fit between the organisation's objectives, skills and resources and its changing market opportunities. The purpose of strategic planning is to shape and reshape the company's business and products so that they yield target profits and growth.

Marketing Information System: The marketing system plays a vital role in the modern organisations due to the growth of global marketing, the new emphasis on buyers' wants and the increasing trend toward non-price competition. Marketing managers need a marketing information system (MIS) to carry out the analysis, planning, implementation and control responsibilities. The purpose of marketing information system is to provide accurate information to the marketing managers in right time. The four important components of marketing information system are: an internal record system, a marketing intelligence system, a marketing research system and a computerised marketing division support system. The company conducts marketing research to discover market opportunities. Company decides which markets to enter based on the market research analysis. The company also forecasts the sales. These forecasts are based on estimates of demand. The two types of demand are industry demand and company demand. Company determines total market potential, area market potential, industry sales and market share.

Market Environment: Marketing environment presents a never-ending series of opportunities and threats. The major responsibility for identifying significant changes in the macro-environment falls to a company's marketers. Marketing opportunities are found by identifying trends, megatrends (large social, economic, political and technological changes). Marketers should monitor environmental factors like: demographic, economic, natural, technological, political, legal, social and cultural.

Consumer Behaviour

The marketers have to study consumer markets and consumer behaviour. The companies have to understand who constitutes the market (occupants), what the market buys (objects), why the market buys (objectives), who participates in the buying (consumers and organisations), how the market buys (operations), when the market buys (occasions), and where the market buys (outlets). Model of consumer behaviour is presented in Fig. 13.5.

Marketing Stimuli	*Other Stimuli*	*Consumer's Characteristics*	*Consumer's Decision Process*	*Consumer's Decisions*
• Product • Price • Place • Promotion	• Economic • Technological • Political • Cultural	• Cultural • Social • Personal • Psychological	• Problem Recognition • Information Search • Evaluation • Decision • Post Purchase Behaviour	• Product Choice • Brand Choice • Dealer Choice • Purchase Timing • Purchase Amount

Source: Philip Kotler, *op. cit.*, p. 172.

Fig. 13.5: Model Consumer Behaviour

Consumer behaviour is influenced by various factors like cultural, social, personal and psychological. Fig. 13.6 presents the factors influencing consumer behaviour. Marketers should do research into these factors to find how to reach and serve consumers more effectively.

The marketers should understand who makes buying decisions, who are the initiators, influencers, deciders, buyers or users in order to target the different market campaigns. They should also know the buyer's level of involvement and the number of brands available in order to know whether consumers are engaging in complex buying behaviour, dissonance-reducing buying behaviour, habitual behaviour, or variety-seeking buying behaviour.

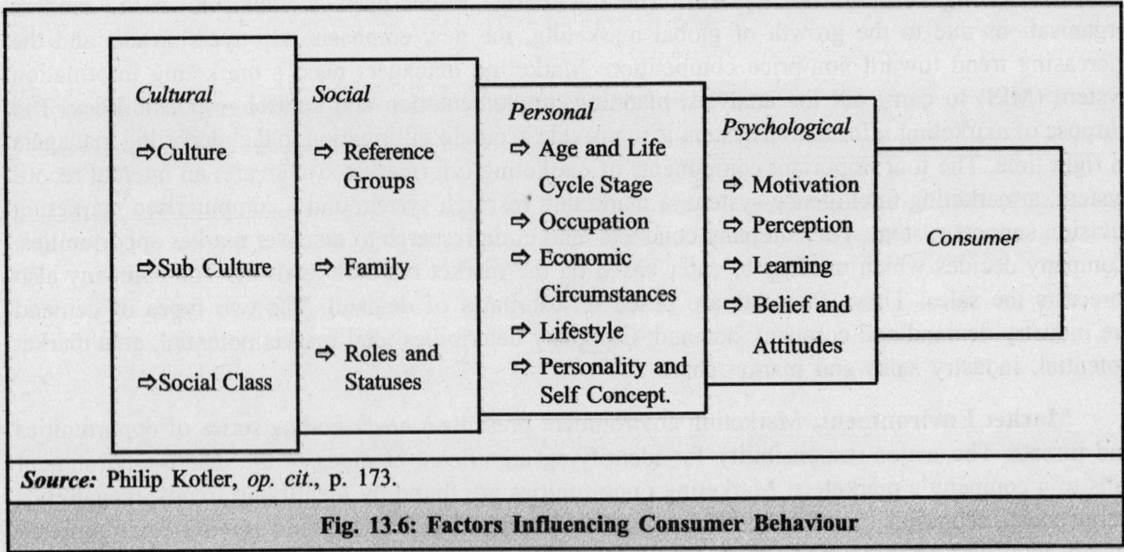

Source: Philip Kotler, *op. cit.*, p. 173.

Fig. 13.6: Factors Influencing Consumer Behaviour

Analysing Industries and Competitors

Companies must study its competitors and its potential customer in order to prepare an effective marketing strategy. For this purpose, the companies should identify its competitors' strategies, objectives, goals, strengths, weaknesses and reaction patterns. They should formulate to attack specific weakness or strength of the competitors and to balance a competitor orientation with a customer orientation.

Companies must pay attention to the closest and latent competitors. Company should use competitive intelligence to analyse the competitors. Marketers should conduct a customer value analysis to reveal company's strengths and weaknesses in comparison with those of competitors. However, the company should not overact in this regard.

Identifying Market Segments and Selecting Market Targets

Target marketing involves — *(i)* market segmentation, *(ii)* market targeting, and *(iii)* market positioning. Companies must target their markets in order to choose their markets and serve them efficiently. Companies are increasingly turning to micromarketing at four levels *viz.,* segments, niches, local areas and individuals due to various problems. The future is likely to see more self-marketing — a form individual marketing in which individual consumers decide which products and brands to buy. Consumer markets can be segmented based on consumer characteristics and consumer responses. The major segmentation variables include geographic, demographic (age, family, family lifecycle, gender, income, occupation, education, religion, race, generation, nationality, social class) psychographic (lifestyle, personality) and behavioural (occasions, benefits, user status, usage rate, loyalty status, buyer-readiness stage, attitude). Market segments should be measurable, substantial, accessible, differentiable and actionable.

The firm has to evaluate various segments and decide how many and which ones to target after identifying its market-segment opportunities. The firm can target single segment, several segments, a specific product or a specific market or the full market. Marketers must choose target markets in a socially responsible manner.

2. Differentiating and Positioning the Market Offering

The key to competitive advantage in a competitive industry is product differentiation. A market offering can be differentiated along five dimensions, *viz.,* product, services, personnel, channel and image. A difference is worth establishing to that extent that is important, distinctive, superior, communicable, preemptive affordable and profitable.

Many marketers promote only one product benefit, thus, creating a unique selling proposition as they position their product. However, double-benefit position and triple-benefit position can also be successful. The position strategy should be communicated effectively via marketing mix.

3. Developing New Products

Successful new product development requires the firm to establish an effective organisation for managing and development process. The stages of new product development process include: idea generation, idea screening, concept developing and testing, marketing strategy development, business analysis, product development, market testing and commercialisation. New product idea should be evaluated in terms of the product meeting the needs, product's ability to meet superior profitability, etc.

The stages of new product development process include: idea generation, idea screening, concept developing and testing, marketing strategy development, business analysis, product development, market testing and commercialisation.

Product Life Cycle Strategies: Companies find it necessary to reformulate their strategies several times during a product's life cycle. This is due to the changes in the economic conditions and thereby changes in the competitive situations. Technologies, product forms and brands also exhibit life cycles with distinct stages. The general sequences of the stages of the life cycle are: introduction, growth, maturity and decline.

Introduction Stage: The marketing strategies during the introduction stage of a product are: *(i)* a rapid skimming strategy consists of launching the new product at a high price and high promotion level, *(ii)* low skimming strategy consists of launching the new product at a high price and low promotion, *(iii)* a rapid penetration strategy consists of launching the product at a low price and high promotion level, and *(iv)* a slow penetration strategy consists of launching the new product at a low price and low level of promotion.

Growth Stage: The growth stage is marked by a rapid increase in sales. Many consumers start buying the product. Prices remain where they are or fall slightly, depending on how fast demand is increasing. The strategies in the growth stage include: *(i)* improving product quality and adding new product features, *(ii)* adding new models and flanker products (*i.e.,* products of different sizes and flavour), *(iii)* entering new market segments, *(iv)* increasing its distribution coverage and entering new distribution channels, *(v)* shifting from product awareness advertising to product preference advertising, *(vi)* lowering prices to attract the next layer of price sensitive buyers.

Maturity Stage: At the maturity stage, rate of sales growth will slow down and product reaches relative stability stage. This stage poses challenges to marketing managers. The maturity stage can be divided into three phases, *viz.,* growth maturity — the sales growth rate starts to decline, stable maturity, there is more or less stability in the volume of sales and decaying maturity, the absolute level of sales starts declining.

Marketing strategies in maturity stage include: *(i)* abandoning the weaker products, *(ii)* concentrating the resources on more profitable and new products, *(iii)* expanding the market for the mature brand by converting non-users into users, entering new market segments, winning competitors' customers, by motivating the existing customers to use the product more frequently, by increasing the usage of the product per occasion, and by increasing new and more varied uses of the product, *(iv)* stimulate the sales by modifying the product's characteristics through quality improvement, feature improvement, and style improvement. *(v)* Stimulate the sales by modifying marketing mix like price, distribution, advertising, sales promotion, personal selling and services.

Declining Stage: During this stage, the sales of the most product forms and brands eventually decline. The sales decline may be slow or rapid. The sales decline may be due to change in consumer taste and preference, technological advancements and increased domestic and foreign competition.

The marketing strategies during this stage include: *(i)* increasing the firm's investment, *(ii)* maintaining the firm's investment level until the uncertainties about the industry are resolved, *(iii)* decreasing the firm's investment level selectively by dropping unprofitable customer groups, *(iv)* harvesting the firm's investment to recover cash quickly, *(v)* divesting the business quickly by disposing of its assets as advantageously as possible. Companies that successfully restage or rejuvenate a mature product often do so by adding value to the original, declining product. Fig. 13.7 depicts summary of product lifecycle characteristics, objectives and stra-tegies.

Designing Marketing Strategies for Market Leaders, Challengers, Followers and Nichers

Market Leader Strategies: Market leading firm has the largest market in the relevant product market. Market leading firm leads the other firms in price changes, new product introductions, distribution coverage and promotional intensity. The other firms in the industry acknowledge the dominance of the leader, though they may not admire or respect the leader. The strategies of the leader firm include: *(i)* expanding the total market by adding new users, new uses to the product, and more usage of the product. *(ii)* Depending market share through position defense, flank defense (erect outposts to protect a weak front or possibly serve as an invasion base for counterattacking in addition to guarding its territory), *(iii)* Preemptive defense (preemptive defensive believes in prevention rather than cure) is launch an attack on the enemy before the enemy starts its offence against the leader, *(iv)* Counter Offensive Defense: It is responding with a counter attack when attacked. The leader reacts to the strategies of price-cut, promotion blitz and product improvement of the competitors, *(v)* Mobile Defense: In mobile defense, the leader stretches its domain over new territories that can serve as future centres for defense and offense. *(vi)* Contraction Defense: Sometimes, large companies find that they can no longer defend all their territories. Then the best course of action is planned contraction (or strategic withdrawal).

Market-Challenger Strategies

Firms that occupy second, third and lower ranks in an industry are often call runner-up or trailing firms.

Firms that occupy second, third and lower ranks in an industry are often call runner-up or trailing firms. These firms can attack the leader and other competitors. Strategic objective of market challengers is to increase their market share. Market challengers can attack the market leader, firms of its own size that are doing the job and are underfinanced and small, local and regional firms that are not doing the job and are underfinanced.

4. Choosing a General Attack Strategy

Five options are available to attack an enemy after knowing the opponent and their objectives clearly. These attacks are:

***(i)* Frontal Attack:** An aggressor launches a frontal attack when it masses its forces right up against its opponent. It attacks the opponent's strengths rather than weaknesses.

***(ii)* Flank Attack:** An enemy's army is strongest where it expects to be attacked. Its weak spots are natural targets for attack. This attack can be directed along two strategic dimensions, *viz.*, geographical and segmental.

***(iii)* Encirclement Attack:** This attack is an attempt to capture a wide slice of the enemy's territory through a comprehensive blitz attack (See Box 13.2).

BOX 13.2 WHAT IS MICROSOFT SO AFRAID OF?

It is hardly news when the Redmond software giant behaves a little oddly. But usually that behavior takes the form of bullying competitors or the self-delusion of believing that it is a major technology innovator.

Microsoft's strange actions of late show a company that isn't just scared but fears for its very existence.

But Microsoft's unusual behavior over the last few weeks has taken a different form: for the first time, perhaps since the Netscape threat arose in the early 1990s, Microsoft is acting scared. First, of course, there was the still-unsettled attempt at a hostile takeover of Yahoo. Microsoft may still win that one in the end; but in the meantime, despite roaring into the negotiations full of sound and fury, Microsoft ended up being a cat's paw for both the woefully out-of-his-depth Yahoo CEO Jerry Yang and for rogue buyout master Carl Icahn. Then Microsoft, either desperately on the rebound or in a ham-fisted move to make Yahoo jealous, starting making advances at pitiful old AOL instead. Whatever the strategic advantages of these acquisitions — and frankly, it's hard to see how bolting one failing search company to another is going to compete any more effectively against a drag racer like Google — it is hardly the behavior of a company that's sure of its own capabilities and confident in its future. The old, swaggering Microsoft would have decided that it could win this battle against Google on its own, through a combination of a perpetually upgraded search engine, questionable linkages to existing MS products (such as Vista), raiding talent from Google and Yahoo and strong-arming everyone up and down the distribution and retail chains. That's how Microsoft used to rule the tech world, and it left both enemies and friends quaking in their boots. It wasn't pretty — and some of it might not even have been legal — but that was how MS rolled when it was on top … not groveling to buy some other also-ran. Ever since the Yahoo debacle, Microsoft has been acting strangely, and one can only conclude that the two events are somehow connected.

Vista Implementation Issues

Microsoft's suddenly transformed manner first appeared last week after a report, by the systems management appliance company KACE, saying that 60 percent of the administrators it surveyed had no intention of ever implementing Microsoft's year-old flagship operating system Windows Vista — up 10 percent from last November. Potentially even more devastating was the fact that more than 40 percent of the respondents said they were actively looking at other platforms, from the Apple Mac OS X to Linux — while the remainder had either already abandoned Vista or were sticking with Microsoft's older Windows XP.

Source: http://abcnews.go.com/Business/IndustryInfo/story?id=5444215&page=1(02/08/08)

(iv) **By Pass Attack:** This attack aims at by passing the enemy and attacking easier markets to broaden one's resource base. This strategy consists of diversifying into unrelated products, diversifying into new geographical markets and leap-fogging into new technologies to supplement existing products.

(v) **Guerrilla Attack:** Guerrilla warfare consists of waging small, intermittent attacks on an enemy's different territories.

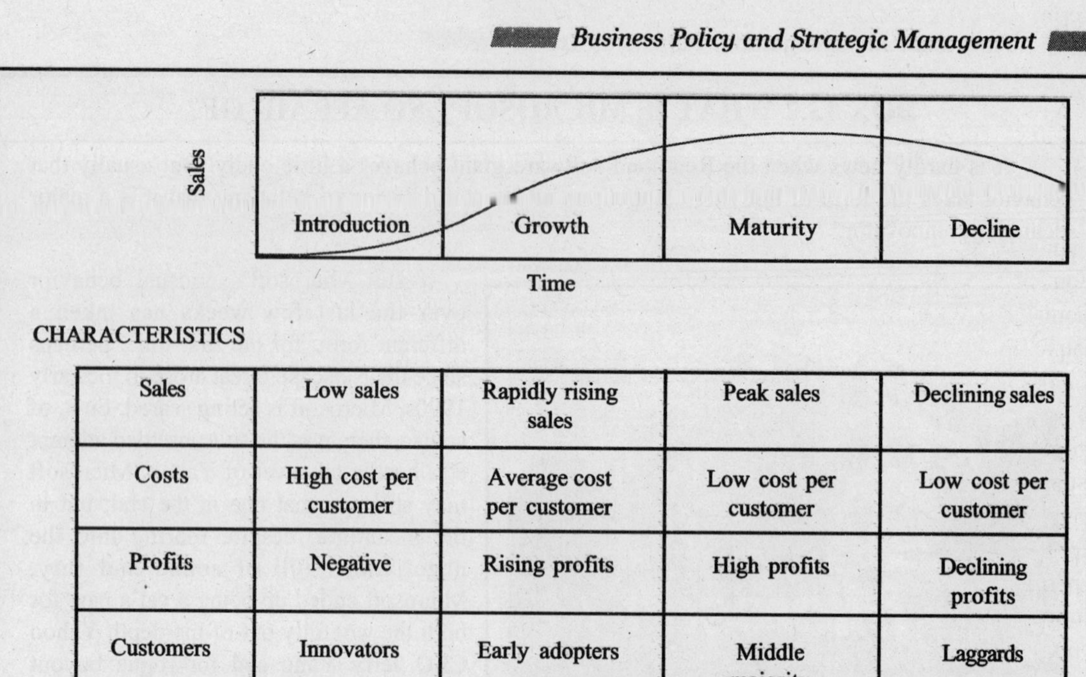

CHARACTERISTICS

Sales	Low sales	Rapidly rising sales	Peak sales	Declining sales
Costs	High cost per customer	Average cost per customer	Low cost per customer	Low cost per customer
Profits	Negative	Rising profits	High profits	Declining profits
Customers	Innovators	Early adopters	Middle majority	Laggards
Competitors	Few	Growing number	Stable number beginning to decline	Declining number

MARKETING OBJECTIVES

	Create product awareness and trial	Maximize market share	Maximize profit while defending market share	Reduce expenditure and milk the brand

STRATEGIES

Product	Offer a basic product	Offer product extension, service, warranty	Diversify brands and models	Phase out weak items
Price	Charge cost-plus	Price to penetrate market	Price to match or best competitors	Cut price
Distribution	Build selective distribution	Build intensive distribution	Build more intensive distribution	Go selective: phase out unprofitable outlets
Advertising	Build product awareness among early adopters and dealers	Build awareness and interest in the mass market	Stress brand differences and benefits	Reduce to level needed to retain hard-core loyals
Sales Promotion	Use heavy sales promotion to entice trial	Reduce to take advantage of heavy consumer demand	Increase to encourage brand switching	Reduce to minimal level

Source: Quoted in Philip Kotler, *op. cit.*, p. 363.

Fig. 13.7: Summary of Product Life-Cycle Characteristics, Objectives, and Strategies

Fig. 13.8 presents different attack strategies.

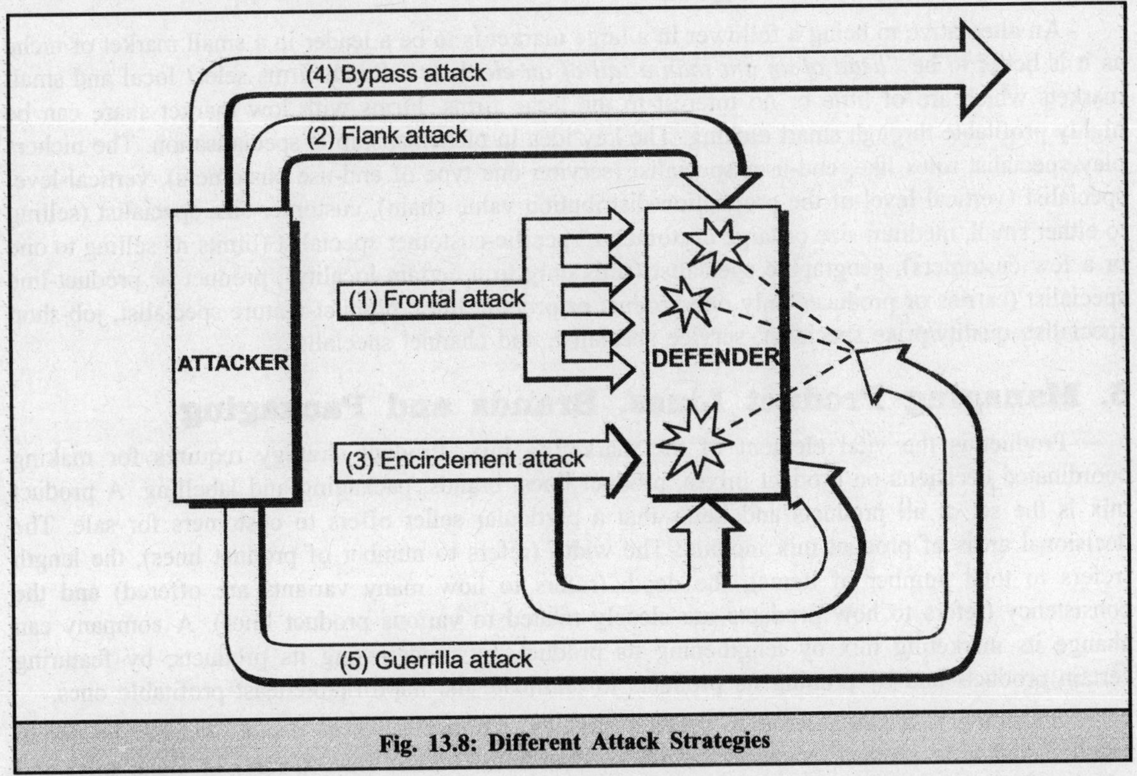

Fig. 13.8: Different Attack Strategies

The marketer should choose a specific strategy from the different strategies. They are: Price discount strategy, cheaper goods strategy, prestige goods strategy, product-proliferation (large product variety) strategy, product-innovation strategy, improved services strategy, distribution innovation strategy, manufacturing cost reduction strategy, intensive promotion strategy, etc.

Market-Follower Strategies

Theodore Levitt argued that a strategy of product imitation might be as profitable as a strategy of product innovation. For example, Sony innovates new products and Panasonic copies from Sony and sells the products at lower price. Panasonic, thus, earns more profit. Sony treats Panasonic as a bitter enemy.

A strategy of product imitation might be as profitable as a strategy of product innovation.

Runner-up/follower firms prefer to follow rather than challenge market leader. But leaders never take the actions of the followers lightly. Leader quickly matches the strategies of the follower to diffuse the attack. The followership strategies are:

***(i)* Counterfeiter:** The counterfeiter duplicates the leader's product and package and sells it on the black market or disreputable dealers.

***(ii)* Cloner:** The cloner emulates the leader's products, distribution, etc. The cloner's products and packaging may resemble the leader's while the brand name might be slightly different.

Imitator: The imitator copies some things from the leader and maintains differences in other areas like packaging, brand, advertising, etc.

Adaptor: The adaptor takes the leader's products and adapts or improves them. He may choose different markets to avoid direct confrontation with the leader.

Market-Nicher Strategies

An alternative to being a follower in a large market is to be a leader in a small market or niche as it is better to be *"head of an ant than a tail of an elephant"*. Small firms select local and small markets which are of little or no interest to the large firms. Firms with low market share can be highly profitable through smart niching. The key idea in nichemanship is specialisation. The nichers play specialist roles like: end-user specialist (serving one type of end-use customers), vertical-level specialist (vertical level of the production-distribution value chain), customer-size specialist (selling to either small, medium-size or large customers), specific-customer specialist (limits its selling to one or a few customers), geographic specialist (sells only to a certain locality), product or product-line specialist (carries or produces only one product or product line), product-feature specialist, job-shop specialist, quality/price specialist, service specialist, and channel specialist.

5. Managing Product Lines, Brands and Packaging

A product mix is the set of all products and items that a particular seller offers to customers for sale.

Product is the vital element of the marketing mix. Product strategy requires for making coordinated decisions on product mixes, product lines, brands, packaging and labelling. A product mix is the set of all products and items that a particular seller offers to customers for sale. The decisional areas of product mix include: The width (refers to number of product lines), the length (refers to total number of items), the depth (refers to how many variants are offered) and the consistency (refers to how products are closely related to various product lines). A company can change its marketing mix by lengthening its product, by modernising its products, by featuring certain products and by pruning its products to eliminate the unprofitable/least profitable ones.

Branding is a major issue in product strategy. Companies must decide whether or not to brand, whether to produce producer brands or distributor brands (like Godrej or Bajaj oils) and whether to use line extensions, brand extensions, multibrands, new brands or co-brands. Well-designed packages can create convenience value for customer and promotional value for producers. Thus, they act as "five-second commercials" for the product. Marketers should develop packaging concept and test it functionally and psychologically (See Box 13.3).

BOX 13.3 WORLD'S 2 MOST VALUABLE BRANDS: COCA-COLA, IBM

Consumers lost trust in brands amid downturn, but Coca-Cola, IBM remain world's most valuable Consumers lost trust in brands this year as the recession deepened, according to an industry report released Thursday, although longtime staples Coca-Cola and IBM retained their spots as the world's two most valuable brands.This is the first time the combined value of the world's top 100 brands as ranked by Interbrand, a branding agency, has fallen in the 10 years Interbrand has assessed them.The list's total value, including brands like Google Inc., Nintendo and Sony, fell 4.6 percent to $1.15 trillion, Interbrand estimates. "That says something about the environment that we're in, especially when you consider that brands are by nature less volatile than business valuations," said Interbrand CEO Jez Frampton, who called a company's brand its most valuable asset. The environment — a recession the likes of which the world hasn't seen for decades — has eaten away at people's trust in specific brands, starting with financial companies, he said. Consumers even started to question retail brands as stores slashed prices to get sales, leading consumers to wonder about pricing, and why they had to pay so much before. "All of these things lead you to re-evaluate the nature of the relationships that we have with brands and indeed how confident we feel in brands to live up to the promises they make," he said. "Brands are promises which we value and are prepared to pay for and if we feel those promises have been broken we're less likely to trust." Brands are more than just names, colors or logos — think Coca-Cola's red or McDonald's golden arches. A brand includes all the elements of a product or service from its design, ingredients and manufacture to its marketing, advertising and logo. A well-honed brand evokes in consumers an emotion and a promise of what it will deliver, without the consumer having to do much — if any — research, said Allen Adamson, managing director at branding firm Landor Associates. Brands are important for all businesses, and critical in categories that have direct consumer contact, like autos, he said. "In a cluttered world where people are time-compressed, brands are short cuts to help them make decisions," he said. Each year, Interbrand ranks companies by the amount of their revenue that is attributable to their brands, using a formula that takes into account the brand's future strength and its role in creating demand, whether among consumers or business customers or both. The firm assigns a monetary value to each brand and measures annual growth, in this case from July 1, 2008, to June 30, 2009. Given the recession, it was not surprising to see financial companies posting the steepest decline in their brands' values this year, with drops by American Express (now number 22, down from 15), HSBC (now 32, down from 27), Citi (now 36, down from 19), and UBS (now 72, down from 41). Merrill Lynch and AIG both dropped off the list. Automakers also dropped in the rankings as their sector's sales slumped in the recession. In addition, major U.S. automakers General Motors Corp. and Chrysler Group LLC received government aid to stay afloat, which generated negative feelings among consumers. Neither of those brands made the top 100 Interbrand list. Even Toyota's brand — top-ranked among auto companies at number eight, down from 6 in 2008 — suffered, while BMW went from 13 to 15, and Ford was unchanged at 49. Honda edged up two slots to 18. Despite the economic uncertainty, the top 10 brands this year stayed relatively stable, with Coca-Cola Co. in the first slot, a place it has held since the rankings started in 2000. The soft-drink maker retains its recognition around the world, Frampton said, and it has been releasing new products as it hopes to woo consumers shifting to healthier juices and teas. Coca-Cola's brand value rose 3 percent in 2009 to $68.73 billion, while IBM's gained 2 percent to $60.21 billion. The technology giant, often known as "Big Blue," also rolled out new products that increased the value of its brand in 2009, according to the report. The company — which sells computer servers, software and technical services to businesses — received more than 4,000 U.S. patents during the period, marking the 16th straight year it has received the most. Rolling out new products keeps customers interested and spending, even in a recession, Frampton said. Companies can't be idle when times are tough, he warned." Innovation is the bedrock of any successful company in the future," he said. "Nobody can stand still nowadays." The remaining brands in the top five all lost value but retained their ranks from last year. Microsoft's brand value fell 4 percent to $56.64 billion to take third, while General Electric's value fell 10 percent to $47.77 billion for fourth. Nokia lost 3 percent to place fifth at $34.86 billion.The value of online giant Google's brand grew the fastest in the world again, rising 25 percent to $31.98 billion to place seventh, up from 10th place last year and 20th the year before. Frampton said the company's brand growth is "miraculous," though the report notes that as it gets bigger, "it has to deal with the inevitable mistrust and ugliness ascribed to being a very large, diversified and very profitable company." But Deborah Mitchell, executive fellow at the Center for Brand and Product Management at Wisconsin School of Business, thinks Google already has found balance by earning consumers' trust even as it becomes nearly omnipresent in their lives.That's partly due to Google's value statement — "Do no evil" — which resonates with consumers, especially in a downturn, she said. Mitchell said consumers are increasingly focusing on a company's values and don't want to associate with businesses whose values they question."There's been a shift in the focus on values and not just economics to consumers," she said. "They're looking more closely at who is selling them what."

Source: http://finance.yahoo.com/news/Worlds-2-most-valuable-brands-apf-3039041815.html?x=0

6. Designing Pricing Strategies and Programmes

Price plays a phenomenal role in marketing mix even though the role of the non-price factors increased in recent years. The only revenue earning "P" out of the "4P"s is price whereas the other three Ps incur the cost.

The company should formulate the pricing objectives, like survival, maximum current profit, maximum current revenue, highest sales growth, highest market skimming or product-quality leadership. Then the company estimates the demand for the product. Next it estimates the cost behaviour at different levels of output. Then it examines the competitors costs, prices and offers. Next it selects a pricing method. The pricing methods include: Cost plus or Mark up pricing, target-return pricing, perceived value pricing, value pricing, going-rate pricing, and sealed-bid pricing. Then the company selects the final price taking into account psychological pricing, the influence of other three Ps, influence of the non-price factors, etc.

Companies normally set more than one price taking the geographical demand, costs, market segment requirements, purchase timing, order levels, etc., into consideration. The price-adaptation strategies include: *(a)* geographical pricing, *(b)* price discounts and allowances, *(c)* promotional pricing like loss-leader pricing (super markets reduce the price on well-known brands to stimulate additional traffic), special event pricing, cash rebates, low-interest rate financing, longer payment terms, warranties/guarantees and service contracts and psychological discounts (fixing an artificially high price on a product and then offering at reduced price), *(d)* discriminating pricing (different prices in different market segments based on customer, segment, product form, image, location, etc., *(e)* product-mix pricing (setting prices for product lines, by products, product bundles, etc.).

The strategy of price decrease might be brought about by excess plant capacity, declining market share, dominating the market through lower costs. The strategy of price increase might be brought about by cost inflation or over-demand. The alternatives to price increase are reducing the size of the product or quality of the product, substituting the cheap material, reducing product features, etc.

The firms should understand the competitor's intent to and duration of price change. The firm's strategy depends on whether it is producing homogeneous or non-homogeneous products. Market leaders who are attacked by competitors with the strategy of low-price, can choose to maintain price, increase the perceived quality, increase or decrease price, improve quality or launch a low-price fighter-line.

7. Market Channels/Place

Most of the firms sell the products through middlemen, agents, dealers etc. rather than selling the product directly to the end user. The host market intermediaries perform a variety of functions and help the manufacturer. The company's decision of selecting channels affect other decisions.

Companies usc intermediaries in the following cases: When they do not have financial resources to sell directly to the ultimate user, when direct marketing is not feasible, when they want to concentrate on the production etc. The intermediaries perform important functions like collection of information, promotion, negotiation, ordering, financing, risk taking, physical possession, payment, customer service, etc.

There are different types of marketing channels as presented in Fig. 13.9. Channel decision is based on analysing customer needs, establishing channel objectives and identifying and evaluating the benefits of major channels. The manufacturer's strategy should be developing long-term relationships with the market intermediaries (See Box 13.4).

BOX 13.4 BA BUYS UP FRENCH RIVAL CARRIER

British Airways has bought L'Avion - a French business-class only airline that flies between Paris and New York. The £54m deal increases the number of flights BA runs between the two cities - weeks after BA launched OpenSkies, which also serves the route. L'Avion flies two Boeing 757 jets - each with 90-seats. The move comes after the collapse of several business-class only carriers operating between London and New York - including, most recently, Silverjet. Maxjet and EOS have also fallen by the wayside after failing to make the business-only model work successfully. **'Many synergies'** L'Avion flies between Paris Orly and Newark airport, while OpenSkies goes between Orly and JFK Airport. The French carrier will be integrated into the BA subsidiary - with the combined airline running up to three daily flights "L'Avion is a successful airline that has built up a premium business between Orly and New York in a relatively short period of time," said BA chief executive Willie Walsh. "It has many synergies with OpenSkies and buying it provides OpenSkies with a larger schedule and an established customer base in the Paris-New York market." Christophe Bejach, co-founder and chairman of L'Avion, said he was happy with the merger. "This transaction will strengthen our current base and enable the combined airline to grow faster and stronger," Mr Bejach said. "Our staff will benefit from the ambition and recognised expertise of the buyer and our customers will have access to an even better service, on a larger scale." OpenSkies became possible thanks to a transatlantic air agreement between the European Union and the US, which came into force in March.

Source: http://news.bbc.co.uk/2/hi/business/7485263.stm

7. Promotion/Marketing Communications

Modern marketing requires that companies should communicate with their present and potential customers, intermediaries, and other stakeholders. The marketing communication mix consists of advertising, sales promotion. Personal selling, public relations, publicity and direct marketing. Developing effective communication involves: identifying the target audience, determine the communication objectives, design the message, select the communication channels, establish the total promotion budget, decide on the promotion mix, measure the promotion's results and manage and coordinate the integrated communication process.

8. Electronic Markets

Electronic markets are sponsored information utilities that describes the product and services offered by marketers and allow customers to get information, identify their needs, and place order. Then the product is delivered to the customer. Electronic markets permit fast price changes based on yield management and change the role of place in market mix.

9. Online Marketing

There are two types of online marketing channels, *viz.,* commercial online channels and the internet. Customers can order for products 24 hours a day just from home or office.

Customers can have information about the different competitive products. Companies can quickly add products, change prices. The cost of marketing is less to the online marketers. Online marketers build and develop relationships directly with the customers.

Marketers can conduct their marketing on online by creating an electronic storefront, participating in forums, new groups, bulletin boards, placing advertisements online and using e-mail.

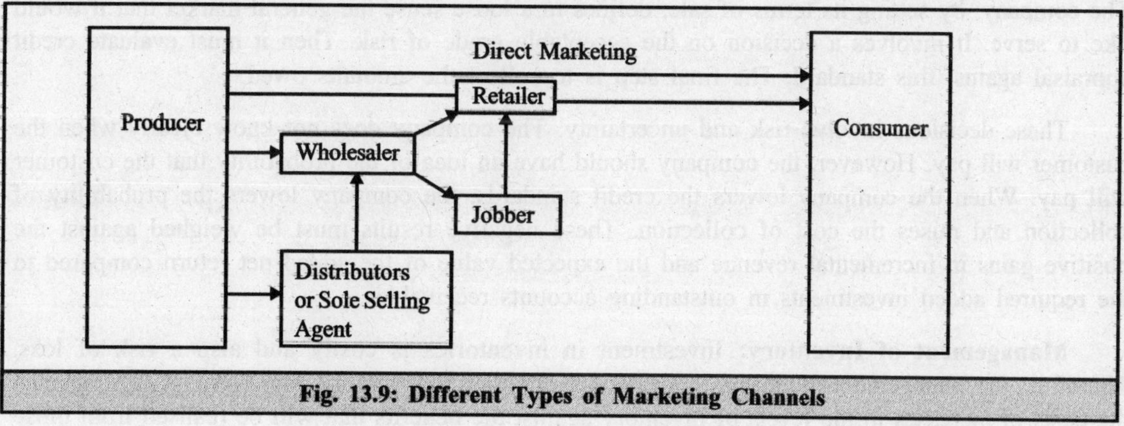

Fig. 13.9: Different Types of Marketing Channels

(C) FINANCIAL POLICIES

A financial manager must adjust his function to his environment or attempt to change it in order to contribute to the achievement of organisational objective, *i.e.,* maximise owner's wealth. The value of the owners' wealth depends upon *(i)* their expected future cash flows, and *(ii)* the dispersion of possible flows around the expected value-return versus risk. Decisions that affect earning power and financial leverage may affect both these factors.

The financial manager must balance the chance of making maximum profits for the owners against the greater variability of returns and greater danger of bankruptcy.

Planning and Managing Assets

Planning and managing assets include management of cash, management of accounts receivables, management of inventory, management of fixed assets and capital budgeting and preparation of budgets.

1. Management of Cash

Management of cash brings into sharp focus on the trade-off between risk and return faced by the financial manager.

Management of cash brings into sharp focus on the trade-off between risk and return faced by the financial manager. The financial manager will face the ultimate risk, if cash is not available to meet bills as they are presented on due date. It is necessary to have a clear understanding of how cash flows are measured and why reported earnings do not match cash flows, as the financial statements prepared by accountants are used frequently.

There are two stages of the cash management, *(i)* cash should be managed and near-cash efficiently. The waste can be reduced by the float of cash represented by incoming collections, payments made sooner than necessary, scattered deposit balances and excessive and unrewarding balances in checking accounts. This stage include efficient management of near-cash in order to produce the highest return consistent with a low risk. In the second stage, given efficient handling of cash flows and balances, the principal task of cash management can be taken up. It includes: maximisation over some planning horizon of the technical value of the accumulated returns from payments and investments, less the interest cost of short-term financing.

2. Management of Accounts Receivables

The management of accounts receivables involves many complex and interrelated decisions. The company, by setting its terms of sale, defines in a loose sense the general market that it would like to serve. It involves a decision on the acceptable grade of risk. Then it must evaluate credit appraisal against this standard. The final step is to collect the amounts owed.

These decisions involve risk and uncertainty. The company does not know clearly when the customer will pay. However, the company should have an idea of the probability that the customer will pay. When the company lowers the credit standards, the company lowers the probability of collection and raises the cost of collection. These negative results must be weighed against the positive gains in incremental revenue and the expected value of the added net return compared to the required added investments in outstanding accounts receivables.

Management of Inventory: Investment in inventories is costly and also a risk of loss. Therefore, the management should pay considerable attention to inventory. Management must balance the costs of increases in the levels of inventory against the benefits that will be realised from those increases. The management should not reduce the idle stocks to zero levels. Some stocks must be maintained to allow for unforeseen changes like failure of a supplier to deliver on schedule and a sudden increase in demand. Some stocks are maintained to meet forthcoming demand. Development of a system to make optimal inventory decisions and to facilitate detailed management of inventory is greatly aided by the use of computers.

Capital Budgeting

Capital budgeting probably spells the difference between success and failure for many business firms. Evaluation of the desirability of a particular project requires that the company gives greater weight to income that is to be received in the near future. The company should consider the time value of money. The methods of capital budgeting are net present value and discounted rate of return. The company should consider the rate of return and risk associated with the project.

Major Policies: The major financial policy issues are:

(1) Sources of Finance and

(2) Capital Structure Decisions;

(3) Dividend Policy.

Sources of Finance

Strategy implementation, fundamentally requires financial resources. The management should take steps to procure finance. The sources of finances are broadly divided into external sources and internal sources. *(i)* The external sources of finance include: equity capital, preference capital, debenture capital, public deposits, long-term loans from development banks. These are the external sources for long term finances. The external sources for short term finance include loans and advances from commercial banks, short-term public deposits, bill discounting, overdrafts and cash credits, factoring issues of commercial paper, loans from non-banking financial companies, etc. *(ii)* The internal source of finance include reserves of the company for long-term purposes and bank balances and cash on hand with the company for short-term purposes.

Capital Structure Decisions

The capital structure decisions are concerned with the optimum mix of equity capital and debt capital. These decisions take into account the interest payment burden, risk of excessive borrowing and the company's objective of maximisation of owners' wealth. Another factor to be taken into consideration is the operating leverage or the proportion of fixed costs in the operating cost structure. The factors like *(a)* overall weighted cost of capital, *(b)* the debt capacity of the firm in terms of adequacy of cash flows to meet the fixed interest rate burden and principal amount, and *(c)* the need for flexibility in the capital structure should also be considered in deciding the capital structure. The desirable debt-equity ratio for private sector firms is 2:1.

The capital structure decisions are concerned with the optimum mix of equity capital and debt capital.

Dividend Policy

The policy regarding the proportion of profit to be distributed to shareholders as dividend and the proportion of the profit retained in the company as reserves is the crucial one. This decision is affected by the factors like:

(a) The shareholders' preference as to current dividend income against capital gains.

(b) The reinvestment opportunities and financial needs of the company.

(c) Need for stability of dividend distribution.

(d) Advantages and disadvantages of cash dividend and stock dividend.

The priorities of the management of the companies and the stakeholders vary. Exhibit 13.3 presents the differences in priorities of management and shareholders and the probable areas of conflict.

Exhibit 13.3: Differing Priorities of Management and Shareholders and the Probable Areas of Conflict

Financial policy area	*Management priorities*	*Shareholder's priorities*	*Probable area of conflict*
1. Sources of funds	— Retained earnings — Long-term debt — New common stock	— Debt — Retained earning — New common stock	— Extent of use of these resources in financing growth
2. Usage of funds (investment proposals)	— Internal rate of return on the basis of past performance	— External as well as internal investment opportunity rates including competing business organisations of comparable risk	— Cut-off rate of acceptable investment opportunities and amounts committed to perpetuate existing investments
3. Management of funds	— Measuring financial performance on the basis of anticipated changes in specific cash flows in the foreseeable future - amount, certainty and timing	— Anticipated changes in share values as measured by trends in earnings per share and dividends	— Ranking of investment alternatives depreciation policy, stock option, acquisition, mergers, etc.
	— Acceptable risk on the basis of preserving the individual corporate entity and management goals.	— Acceptable risk on the basis of a portfolio of investment over several companies.	— Diversification of products and markets; debt-equity proportions.

Source: Adapted from DB. Ekpenyong: "Strategic Financial Planning for Emergencies" in *The Chartered Accountant*, Mar. 1989, p. 799. Quoted in Azhar Kazmi, *op. cit.*, p. 268.

(D) HUMAN RESOURCE POLICIES

1. Employment

The term human resources can be thought of as, "the total knowledge, skills creative abilities, talents and aptitudes of an organisation's workforce as well as the value, attitudes and beliefs of the individuals involved." Objectives of human resources management are influenced by organisational objectives, individuals and social goals. Human resources are managed to direct and utilise their resources towards and for the accomplishment of organisational objectives. The objectives of the human resources management include contributing to the organisational objectives and also to meet the needs, aspirations, values and dignity of individual employees and having due concern, for socioeconomic problems of the community.

The objectives of HRM may be as follows:

(i) to create and utilise an able and motivated workforce, to accomplish basic organisational goals.

(ii) To establish and maintain sound organisational structure and desirable working relationships among all the members of the organisation.

(iii) To secure the integration of individual and groups within the organisation by co-ordination of the individual and group goals with those of the organisation.

(iv) To create facilities and opportunities for individual or group development so as to match it with the growth of the organisation.

(v) To attain an effective utilisation of human resources in the achievement of organisational goals.

(vi) To identify and satisfy individual and group needs by providing adequate and equitable wages, incentives, employee benefits and social security and measures for challenging work, prestige, recognition, security, status, etc.

(vii) To maintain high employee morale and sound human relations by sustaining and improving the various conditions and facilities.

(viii) To strengthen and appreciate the human assets continuously by providing training and developmental programmes.

(ix) To consider and contribute to the minimisation of socio-economic evils such as unemployment, under-employment, inequalities in the distribution of income and wealth and to improve the welfare of the society by providing employment opportunities to women and disadvantaged sections of the society, etc.

(x) To provide an opportunity for expression and voice in management.

(xi) To provide fair, acceptable and efficient leadership.

(xii) To provide facilities and conditions of work and creation of favourable atmosphere for maintaining stability of employment.

After the establishment of human resource objectives, human resource policies are to be formulated. Human resource policies are a set of proposals and actions that act as a reference point for managers in their dealings with employees. Human resource policies constitute guides to action. They furnish the general standards or bases on which decisions are reached. Human resource policies guide the course of action intended to accomplish human resource objectives.

Job Design & Analysis: The strategy of the job design includes designing the jobs to the possible maximum extent by incorporating core job dimensions, *viz.,* skill variety, task identity, task significance, autonomy and feedback. Job analysis information should include role analysis also as it contributes for the team work and interacting with the environment efficiently. Thus, these strategies of job design and job analysis help the organisation to make the people to commit and contribute to the job and organisation.

Recruitment and Selection: The strategies in these areas include identifying the best possible sources and techniques of recruitment, like campus recruitment head hunters, body shoppers, scouting the efficient employees from other organisations, employing agencies, executive search consultants, etc. However, other sources may be used particularly for lower level jobs. However, recruitment strategies are to be formulated within the limitations imposed by the external factors like government regulations and laws, internal environmental factors like promotional policies of the organisation. Recruitment policy should take into consideration the government's reservation policy, policy regarding sons of soil, etc., internal sources for promotions, social responsibility in absorbing minority sections, women, etc. Recruitment policy should commit itself to the organisation's personnel policy like enriching the organisation's human resources, motivating the employees through internal promotions, improving the employee loyalty to the organisation by absorbing the retrenched or laid off employees, casual/temporary employees and dependants of present and former employees.

Recruitment is searching and inspiring prospective employees to apply for a job in a company.

The selection strategies should include the appointment of external consultants for conducting tests and interviews or the entire selection process, designing selection tests, deciding the issue of job for the candidate or candidate for the job, choosing the criteria of profile matching, successive hurdles or multiple correlation. Conducting of selection tests is a crucial step in the selection process.

The type of selection tests include:

(i) *Aptitude Tests*

(a) Intelligence test

(b) Mechanical Aptitude

(c) Psychomotor tests

(d) Clerical aptitude tests

(ii) *Achievement Tests*

(a) Job Knowledge Test

(b) Work Sample Test

(iii) *Situational Tests*

(a) Group Discussion

(b) In Basket

(vi) *Personality Tests*

(a) Objective Tests

(b) Projective Tests

(v) *Personality Tests*

(a) Objective Tests

(b) Projective Tests

The strategists should remember that the tests predict the candidate's failure on the job rather than success. Therefore, excessive dependence on selection tests is not viable. The human resource strategists may depend on the techniques like role play, group discussion, etc. for the selection of executives. Assessment centre's score may be used for this purpose.

2. Human Resource Development

Human resource development (HRD) assumes significance in view of the fast changing organisational environments and need of the organisations to adopt new techniques in order to respond to the environmental changes.

HRD from organisation point of view is a process in which the employees of an organisation are helped/motivated to acquire and develop technical, managerial and behavioural knowledge, skills and abilities, and mould the values, beliefs, attitudes necessary to perform present and future roles by realising highest human potential with a view to contribute positively to the organisational, group, individual and social goals.

Human resources development plays a crucial role in market economies. HRD to be effective should essentially have a strong base of human resource planning, recruitment and selection based on effective HRD requirements. The base factors enable the organisation to develop its human resources effectively. The strategist can use the HRD process and techniques before the implementation of strategies.

The implementation of various strategies like mergers, take over, absorptions, turn around, expansion, diversification, etc., require the development of human resources. In fact, successful implementation of all strategies depends on the human resource development.

Performance Analysis and Development

Appraising the performance of individuals, groups and organisations is a common practice of all societies. Performance appraisal is a method of evaluating the behaviour of employees in the work-spot, normally including both the quantitative and qualitative aspects of job performance.

Traditionally, the purposes of performance appraisal were to guide to the job changes and salary changes. Today, performance appraisal techniques are used for a wider purpose including analysing the performance without hurting the employees' feeling, and to develop the employees' skills and knowledge, Hence, the term performance appraisal is used in the modern organisations as 'Performance Analysis and Development.' Further, traditionally, performance had been appraised by the superior of the employee only. But performance of the employees in the contemporary organisations is appraised by not only by superiors, but also by the peers, subordinates, employees themselves (self appraisal), users of services (customers) and consultants. Performance appraisal by all these parties is called "360° Performance Appraisal".

Methods of Performance Appraisal

The important methods of performance appraisal include:

(1) Graphic Rating Scales
(2) Ranking Method
(3) Paired Comparison Method
(4) Forced Distribution Method
(5) Checklist Methods:
  (a) Simple Checklist
  (b) Weighted Checklist
  (c) Forced Choice
(6) Critical Incident Method
(7) Essay or Free from Appraisal
(8) Group Appraisal
(9) Behaviourally Anchored Rating Scales
(10) Assessment Centres
(11) Human Resource Accounting
(12) Management by Objectives/Appraisal by objectives.

The strategist should create the view to the employees that the performance appraisal is for employee development rather than a employee punishment technique. Appropriate techniques of performance analysis are to be applied to the jobs. There is no single technique suitable to all types of jobs. The strategist should get the cooperation and support of trade unions to implement the performance appraisal techniques sincerely and seriously.

System of Performance Appraisal

Performance appraisal is a nine-step process. At the first stage, performance standards are established based on job description and job specification. The standards should be clear, objective and incorporate all the factors.

The second stage is to inform these standards to all the employees including appraisers.

The third stage is following the instructions given for appraisal, measurement of employee performance by the appraisers through observation, interview, records and reports.

Fourth stage is finding out the influence of various internal and external factors on actual performance. The influence of these factors may be either inducing or hindering the employee performance. The measured performance may be adjusted according to the influence of external and internal factors. The performance derived at this stage may be taken as actual performance.

Fifth stage is comparing the actual performance with that of other employees and previous performance of the employee and others. This gives an idea where the employee stands. If performance of all the employees is ranked either too high or too low, there may be something wrong with the standards and job analysis.

Sixth stage is comparing the actual performance with the standards and finding out deviations. Deviations may be positive or negative. If employee's performance is more than the standards, it is positive deviation and *vice versa* is negative deviation.

Seventh stage is communicating, the actual performance of the employee and other employees doing the same job and discuss with him about the reasons for positive or negative deviations from the preset standards as the case may be.

Eighth stage is suggesting necessary changes in standards, job analysis, internal and external environment.

Ninth stage is follow-up of performance appraisal report. This stage includes guiding, counselling and directing the employee or making arrangements for training and development of the employee in order to ensure improved performance. If the actual performance is very poor and beyond the scope of improvement, it may be necessary to take steps for demotion or retrenchment or any other suitable measure.

Counselling

Counselling is a planned, systematic intervention in the life of an individual who is capable of choosing the goal and the direction of his own development.

After the performance of the employee is appraised, the superior should inform the employee about the level of the his performance, the reason for the same, need for the methods of improving the performance. The superior should counsel the employee about his performance and the methods of improving it.

Counselling is a planned, systematic intervention in the life of an individual who is capable of choosing the goal and the direction of his own development. Thus, the purpose of counselling is to help the employee to be aware of his own performance, his strengths and weaknesses, opportunities available for performance development and the threats in the form of technological change etc. Performance counselling can be done in the form of performance interview by the superior.

The Post Appraisal Interview

The post appraisal interview has been considered by most of the organisations, as well as by employees, as the most essential part of appraisal system. This interview provides the employee the feedback information, and an opportunity to the appraiser to explain the employee his rating, the traits and behaviour he has taken into consideration for appraisal, etc.

It also gives the opportunity to employee to explain his views about the rates, standards or goals, rating scale, internal and external environmental causes for low level of performance, his resources responsible for performance, etc. Further, it helps both the parties to review standards, set new standards based on the reality factors, and helps the appraisers to offer his suggestions, help, guide and coach the employee for his advancement. Thus, the post appraisal interview is designed to achieve the following objectives:

(1) To let employees know where they stand;

(2) To help employees do a better job by clarifying what is expected of them;

(3) To plan for employee development and growth;

(4) To strengthen the superior-subordinate working relationship by developing a mutual agreement of goals;

(5) To provide an opportunity for employees to express themselves on performance related issues.

Thus, post appraisal interview is most helpful to the employee as well as his superior.

Training and Development

Organisation and individual should develop and progress simultaneously for their survival and attainment of mutual goals. The management should develop the individuals and the organisation through training and development. The changing governmental policies, trends towards globalisation, changes in technology and increasing competition make the training a crucial and significant function of human resource management.

Management can use the training to increase productivity, improve the quality of the product, improve organisational climate, prevent obsolescence and minimise resistance to change. The training objectives formulated by the strategist include:

Training Objectives

Generally, line managers ask the personnel manager to formulate the training policies. The personnel manager formulates the following training objectives in keeping with the Company's goals and objectives:

(a) To prepare the employee both new and old to meet the present as well as the changing requirements of the job and the organisation.

(b) To prevent obsolescence.

(c) To impart the new entrants the basic knowledge and skill they need for an intelligent performance of definite job.

(d) To prepare employees for higher level tasks.

(e) To assist employees to function more effectively in their present positions by exposing them to the latest concepts, information and techniques and developing the skills they will need in their particular fields.

(f) To build up a second line of competent officers and prepare them to occupy more responsible positions.

(g) To broaden the minds of senior managers by providing them with opportunities for an interchange of experiences within and outside with a view to correcting the narrowness of outlook that may arise from over-specialisation.

(h) To develop the potentialities of people for the next level job.

(i) To ensure smooth and efficient working of a department.

(j) To ensure economical output of required quality.

(*k*) To promote individual and collective morale, a sense of responsibility, co-operative attitudes and good relationships.

Management development is a systematic process of growth and development by which managers develop their abilities to manage. The strategist uses the management development to achieve the following objectives:

Objectives of Management Development

The management development programmes are organised with a view to achieving specific objectives. They are:

(1) To overhaul the management machinery.

(2) To improve the performance of the managers.

(3) To give the specialists an overall view of the functions of an organisation and equip them to co-ordinate each other's efforts effectively.

(4) To identify the persons with the required potential and prepare them for senior positions.

(5) To increase the morale of the members of the management group.

(6) To increase the versatility of the management group.

(7) To keep the executives abreast with the changes and developments in their respective fields.

(8) To create the management succession which can take over in case of contingencies.

(9) To improve thought process and analytical ability.

(10) To broaden the outlook the executive regarding his role position and responsibilities.

(11) To understand the conceptual issues relating to economic, social, and technical areas.

(12) To understand the problems of human relations and improve human relations skills.

(13) To stimulate creative thinking.

Career Planning and Developments

Individual career planning assumes greater significance with the unparallel growth of knowledge, educational and training facilities and widespread increase in job opportunities. The strategist uses the career planning in order:

— To attract competent persons and retain them in the organisation.

— To provide suitable promotional opportunities.

— To enable the employees to develop and make them ready to meet the future challenges.

— To reduce employee dissatisfaction and turnover.

— To improve motivation and morale.

Promotions: Promotion is an advancement of an employee to a better job — better in terms of greater responsibility, more prestige or status, greater skill and especially increased rate of pay or salary. The purposes of promotion include: to utilise the employee's skill and knowledge at the appropriate level, to develop competitive spirit and inculcate the zeal in the employees to acquire additional skill, knowledge, etc.

Organisations adopt different bases of promotion depending upon their nature, size, management, etc. These bases include seniority, merit and seniority-cum-merit.

Promotion Policy: Every organisation has to specify clearly its policy regarding promotion based on its corporate mission, objectives, policy and goals.

Transfer

Organisations resort to another type of mobility of employees in order to place the right employee in the right job. This type of mobility is restricted to movement of an employee from one job to another in the same level of organisational hierarchy is termed as transfer.

Transfer is also defined as, "... the moving of an employee from one job to another. It may involve a promotion, demotion or no change in job status other than moving from one job to another." However, transfer is viewed as change in assignment in which employee moves from one job to another in the same level of hierarchy requiring similar skill involving approximately same level of responsibility, same status and same level of pay. Thus, promotion is upward reassignment of a job, demotion is a down ward job reassignment whereas transfer is a lateral or horizontal job re-assignment.

Transfer Policy: Organisations should clearly specify their policy regarding transfer. Otherwise superiors may transfer their subordinates arbitrarily if they do not like them. It causes frustration among employees. Similarly subordinates may also request for transfer even for the petty issues. Most of the people may ask for transfer to riskless and easy jobs and places. As such organisation may find it difficult to manage the transfer policy.

4. Wages and Benefits

Wage and Salary: One of the important factors in human resource management is wage and salary administration. Wage or salary is significant to most of the employees as it constitutes a major share of their income. The strategist can achieve the following goals through sound wage and salary policies:

— Acquiring qualified and competent personnel
— Retain the competent and efficient employees
— Secure internal and external equity
— Ensure desired employee behaviour
— Utilise human resources to the maximum extent
— Convert the employee potentialities into realities.

A strategy of product imitation might be as profitable as a strategy of product innovation

The strategist while formulating the wage policy, should take the following factors into consideration.

- Remuneration in comparable industries
- Company's financial position
- Cost of living
- Employees skill, knowledge, potentialities, etc.
- Productivity
- Union pressure and strategies
- Government legislations.

Fringe Benefits: Fringe benefits are those which are provided by an employer to or for the benefit of an employee and which are not in the form of wages, and salaries. The strategist can provide the benefits with a view to

- Create and improve sound industrial relations
- Boost up employee morale

- Motivate the employees by identifying and satisfying their unsatisfied needs
- Provide qualitative work environment and work life
- Provide security to the employees against social risks
- Protect health of employees and their family members
- Create a sense belongingness among employees and retain them.

(E) MANAGEMENT INFORMATION SYSTEMS

Management requires complete information relating to a problem or issue in right time in order to make effective decision. The proper collection, handling and providing the right information to the right manager in right time not only reduce the risk of wrong decisions but also work as an effective controlling technique. Complexities involved in business and economic activities and voluminous government regulation create the need for supply of right information to the right manager in the right time.

Management Information System (MIS) is defined as, "a formal method of making available to management accurate and timely information necessary to facilitate the decision-making process and enable the organisation's planning, control and operational on the past, present and projected future and on relevant events inside and outside the organisation."

Generally, an organisation's MIS consists of a series of information system of varying degrees of complexity, competence and scope. They are:

(i) Transaction processing and inquiry response;

(ii) Management information for operational planning, decision-marking and control:

(iii) Management information for tactical planning and decision-marking; and

(iv) Management information system for strategic planning and policy planning and decision-making.

An orgasnisation's information system must provide the various types of information required by managers at the various levels of organisational hierarchy with different levels of operational responsibilities, operational control, management control and strategic planning.

The number of computer based information systems in private and public sector organisations has grown exponentially during the past two decades. To build computer based information systems, new computer products and service industry has developed to supply the necessary tools. While a large number of people are employed to design and operate information systems, many more individuals are involved as users or "consumers" of information system. Users include individuals from a broad spectrum of occupations ranging from workers in a factory to the top management of a corporation. Use of an information system includes the receipt of a report, the submission of input for a system and the operation of a terminal or a similar activity. Most individuals encounter these systems in other activities, in addition to work experiences with computer based information systems. Credit and users of a bank, travelers making reservations and many other confront computer based systems directly or indirectly.

In today's complex society, a knowledge of computer based information systems is vital for an educated individual, particularly for the professional manager. It has been estimated that 1/3rd or 1/2 of the gross national income of the United States is currently attributed to the production and distribution of information. This trend is a departure from a traditional economy based on the production and distribution of tangible goods. This clearly shows that we are entering an "Information Age." For most organisations in the future if not already the determining factor in competition will be the processing and analysing of information.

Information System

An information system is a set of organised procedures which when executed, provides information to support decision-making. Information can be defined as a tangible or intangible entity which serves to reduce uncertainty about some future state or event.

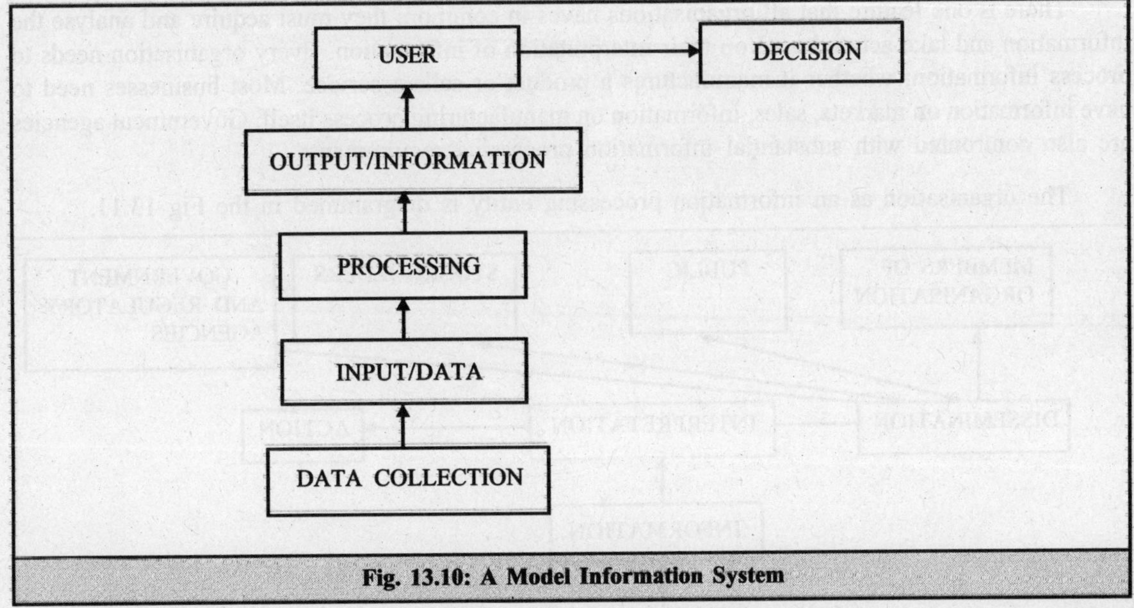

Fig. 13.10: A Model Information System

A schematic representation of an information system is diagrammed in Fig. 13.10. We should note that information is not just raw data. Rather, data are processed in some way, for example, collected and summarised to produce output which is interpreted as information by the user decision-maker.

Formal organisations, from the stage of their inception, require information systems in order to operate successfully. Deposits, advances, economic development, financial, personnel and external data on consumer and markets are vital to the successful operation of most modern banks.

Essential Features of an Information System

An information system combines related operations and procedures to perform a major organisation and management activity (such as document production). The efficiency and success of the system depend on careful planning, organisation, and control by the supporting staff of a bank. The objectives of an information system include:

(i) Decision-making by supplying the best possible current information to management.

(ii) Eliminating duplication of work.

(iii) Saving time by using more efficient methods.

(iv) Establishing uniform procedures.

(v) Identifying responsibility for work and performance.

(vi) Improving service, including providing necessary training for all who operate within the systems.

(vii) Promoting acceptance both of the system and of possible change (resulting from feedback on the system's effectiveness).

To achieve these objectives, a system must be flexible enough to allow revisions and for interaction with additional sub-systems.

The Organisation as an Information Processing Entity

There is one feature that all organisations haves in common: they must acquire and analyse the information and take action based on their interpretation of information. Every organisation needs to process information; whether it manufactures a product or sells a service. Most businesses need to have information on markets, sales, information on manufacturing process itself. Government agencies are also confronted with substantial information processing requirements.

The organisation as an information processing entity is diagrammed in the Fig 13.11.

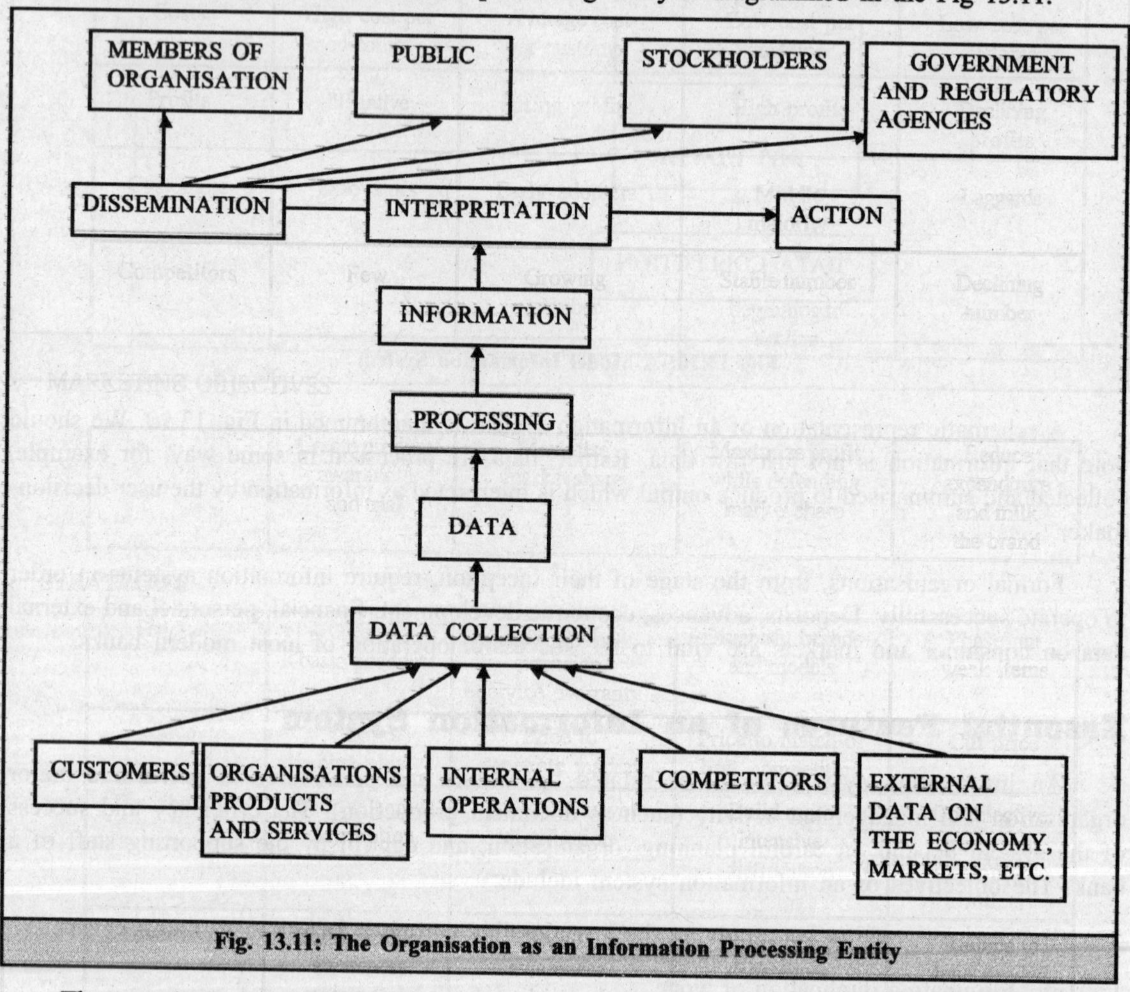

Fig. 13.11: The Organisation as an Information Processing Entity

The organisation collects data from a number of sources, including its own internal operations and customers. Most organisations also attempt to gather data on their competition and on other phenomena external to the organisation, such as the economy. Many government prepared statistics are used by organisations, and these data are classified as externally derive.

The organisation must process all these data and the output may take many forms, such as tabular reports or graphic displays. It is likely that the output is interpreted and action is taken on the basis of information. For example, a bank might offer a new service based on the information derived from its market research study.

Most of this interpreted information is disseminated within the organisation for use by its members; production control, accounting and budgeting information fall into this category. Many banks must make information available to the public despositors as well, for example, to stock holders.

Though, processing information clearly is not the ultimate goal of most organisations, it is one vital component of their operations. Individuals who are or will become the members of organisations need to understand the importance of information. In a modern organisation, the processing of information contributes about information processing tools, techniques and concepts

Decision-making, including the process leading up to the decision, can be termed as planning, and management can be defined as the planning and control of the physical and human resources of the company in order to achieve the objectives of the company. Referring back to the MIS definition, we can simplify it by saying that "MIS is a system that aids management in performing its jobs."

The term MIS is well conceived in that if one understands the three words that comprise it, one can have a basic understanding of the whole.

Management

Management has been defined in many ways, but for our purpose we define it as the process of planning, organising and controlling of the physical and human resources in order to achieve the objectives of the company. Managers plan by setting objectives and goals and selecting the best course of action to achieve the plan. The task, necessary for operational plans are organised and set up into homogeneous groups. The performance of the work is controlled by setting performance standards and avoiding deviations from standards.

As the decision-making is such a fundamental prerequisite to each of the foregoing processes, the job of an MIS becomes that of facilitating decisions necessary for planning, organising and controlling the work and functions of the business.

The Management Triangle

The Fig.13.12 indicates the three levels of business activities carried out in operating a company.

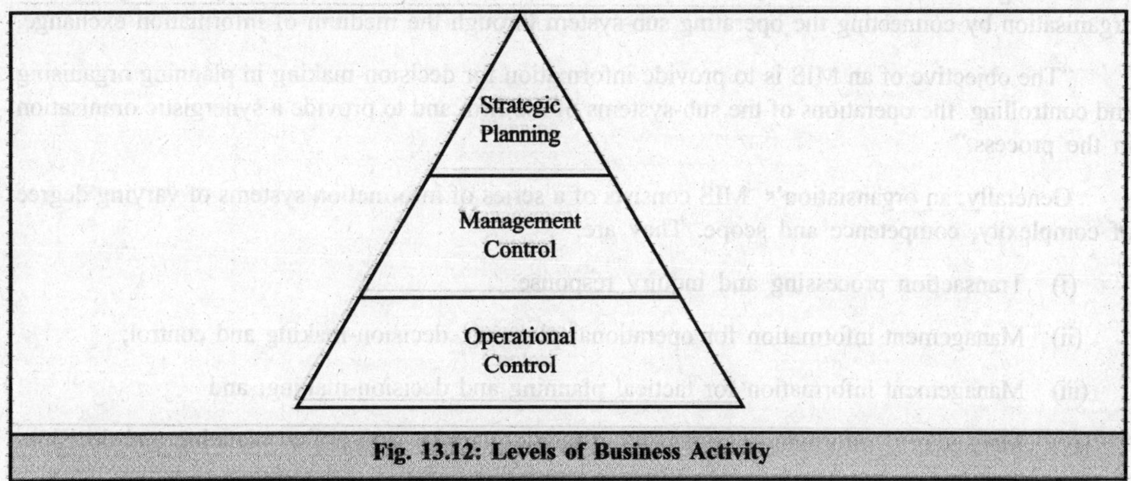

Fig. 13.12: Levels of Business Activity

The process performed to control the basic products or services produced by the company are indicated by the first level, *i.e.*, operational control. In a bank, operational control includes the physical sorting, recording and posting of checks, etc.

Management control, being at the second level indicates processes or functions that facilitate the management of those processes delegated to the operational control level.

The top level of the triangle represent strategic planning process, the processes that determine what products to produce or what to provide in the first place or, even more broadly what markets or businesses the company should be in currently or plan to be in the future.

Top management establishes the policies, plans and objectives of the company, as well as a general budget framework under which the various departments will operate. These factors are passed down to middle management, where they are translated into specific revenue, cost and profit goals. Once these are reviewed, analysed and modified in accordance with the overall plans and policies, the middle management issues the specific schedules and measurement yardsticks to operating management. The lowest level, operation control, has the job of producing goods and services required to meet the revenue and profit goals, which in turn will enable the company to achieve its overall objectives.

Information, the second term in "Management Information System," is recognised as an increasingly valuable commodity required by management to plan and control business operations effectively. Information can be defined as a tangible or intangible entity which serves to reduce uncertainty about some future state or event.

Data must be distinguished form information. Data are facts and figures that are not currently being used in a decision process. An example of data would be: number of deposits and total number of accounts in a bank. On the other hand, information is used for informative purpose or as a basis for forecasting or decision-making.

System

A system can be defined as a set of interrelated elements working towards a common purpose. A subsystem is part of a larger system with which we are concerned and all system are parts of larger system.

While we have achieved a very high degree of automation and joining together of sub-system in scientific, mechanical and factory manufacturing operation, we have hardly applied the systems' principles to business systems. The concept of synergism applies to the integration of the subsystems through information interchange. This concept of synergism has not generally been applied to business organisation. "The system concept of MIS is therefore one of optimising the output of the organisation by connecting the operating sub-system through the medium of information exchange.

"The objective of an MIS is to provide information for decision-making in planning organising and controlling the operations of the sub-systems of the firm and to provide a synergistic oranisation in the process."

Generally, an organsiation's MIS consists of a series of information systems of varying degree of complexity, competence and scope. They are:

(i) Transaction processing and inquiry response;

(ii) Management information for operational planning, decision-making and control;

(iii) Management information for tactical planning and decision-making; and

(iv) Management information system for strategic planning and policy planning and decision-making.

An organisation's information system must provide the various types of information required by managers at the various levels of organisational hierarchy with different levels of operational responsibilities, operational control, management control and strategic planning.

Information requirements of the various managerial levels must be considered in the design of an MIS. Generally, the information sources for operational control are based largely within an organization while the information sources for strategic planning are outside the organisation, whereas sources for management control are more evenly distributed among internal and external origins.

MIS Goals

The goals of an ideal MIS are to relieve management from converting data into information, provide relevant information to each management level for effective decision-making and the effective conduct of the job function, and present information that is current and in a readily usable and easily understood format. To meet these goals, the MIS would possess the following attributes;

(i) It would address the primary needs of the management function and not the needs of person.

(ii) It would address the underlying problem, not just the symptoms.

(iii) It would present a maximum of information and a minimum of data

(iv) It would be reliable.

(v) The outputs would be timely.

(vi) The output would contain sufficient and relevant information to minimize further modification.

Stages of MIS Development

(i) Strategic and projects planning stage.

(ii) Conceptual system design stage.

(iii) Detailed system design stage.

(iv) Implementation, evaluation and maintenance stage.

Guidelines for Effective Design

(i) The user of the information should be included on the design team.

(ii) Cost of money and time of the system should be taken into account, ands match them with the benefits derived from the system.

(i) Weightage should be given to relevance and selectivity over sheer quantity.

(ii) The system should be tested before it is installed.

(iii) Adequate training and documentation should be provided for the operations and users of the system.

(iv) Information should be disaggregated and similar decision should be aggregated.

(v) The actual mechanical methods for information processing are deigned and controls for the systems developed.

The decisions system must be thoroughly analysed.

POINTS TO BE REMEMBERED

- Operation management is concerned with the production of goods and rendering of services.
- Process selection decisions determine the type of production processes to be used.
- Marketing is a social and managerial process by which individuals and groups obtain what they need.
- Successful new product development requires the firm to establish an effective organisation for managing and development process.
- Financial manager must adjust his/her function to the strategic needs.
- Human resources are the vibrant resources that contribute effectively and efficiently for strategy implementation.

KEY WORDS

- Marketing Policies
- Production Policies
- Market Driven
- Technology Driven
- Production Process
- Product Design
- Process Selection
- Consumer Behaviour
- Maturity Stage
- Niche Market
- Electronic Markets
- Cash Management
- Accounts Receivables
- Inventory Management
- Employment
- Training
- Recruitment
- Management Development
- Salary Administration
- Motivation
- Management Information System

QUESTIONS FOR DISCUSSION

(1) What are the different kinds of functional strategies? How do you implement them?

(2) What are the production/operational issues that contribute to strategy implementation?

(3) What are the marketing issues that contribute to the strategy implementation?

(4) What are the financial issues that contribute to the strategy implementation?

(5) Discuss various human resource activities that contribute to the strategy implementation

(6) Discuss various information system issues that contribute to the strategy implementation.

REFERENCES

1. Roger G. Schroeder, "*Operations Management*," McGraw-Hill Book Company, New York, 1981, pp. 19-20.
2. *Ibid*., pp. 27-28.
3. *Ibid*., pp. 69-70.
4. Roger G. Schroeder, "*Operations Management*," McGraw-Hill Book Company, New York, 1981.
5. Kathryn Rudie Harrigan, "Strategies for Declining Industries," *Journal Of Business Strategy*, Fall 1980, p. 27.
6. Theodore Levitt, "Innovative Imitation," *Harvard Business Review*, September-October 1966, p. 63.
7. Philip Kotler, "*Marketing Management*," Prentice-Hall International Inc. New Jersey, 1997.
8. P. Subba Rao, "*Essentials of Human Resource Management and Industrial Relations*," Himalaya Publishing House, Mumbai, 1996.

14

CHAPTER

STRATEGIC EVALUATION AND CONTROL

Chapter Outline

(A) Introduction
(B) Process of Strategic Control
(C) Reluctance to Use Strategic Control
(D) Strategic Control and Environmental Factors
(E) Information for Strategic Control
(F) Implementing Strategic Control
(G) Successful Maintenance of Strategic Control

Learning Objectives

After studying this chapter, you should be able to:

- Understand the concepts of control, strategic control and the purpose of strategic control;
- Explain the process of strategic control;
- Understand why some managers are reluctant to use strategic control;
- Discuss various factors that affect the strategic control environment;
- Know the kinds of information necessary for strategic control;
- Understand how to implement strategic control;
- Know how to maintain strategic control successfully.

(A) INTRODUCTION

Once the strategy is formulated and implemented, there is no guarantee that the strategy is implemented as it is designed and the strategy generates the results as aimed at. Therefore, the strategist has to evaluate the strategy and its programme to assess whether the implementation of the strategy is as per the strategic plan. Further, a number of deviations either in the external environment or in organisational environment may take place. These deviations, may necessitate a change in the strategy. These changes also require a strategic evaluation and control.

1. Definition of Control

Control consists of making something happen the way it was planned to happen. According to Henri Fayol, control consists in verifying whether everything occurs in conformity with the plan adopted, the instructions issued and principles established. It's objective is to point out weaknesses and errors in order to rectify them and prevent recurrence. It operates on everything, things, people, actions. The control function includes three procedures, *viz.*, *(i)* measuring actual performance, *(ii)* comparing actual performance to standards, and *(iii)* taking corrective action to ensure that planned events actually occur. Fig.14.1 shows the model of control process.

Control consists in verifying whether everything occurs in conformity with the plan adopted, the instructions issued and principles established.

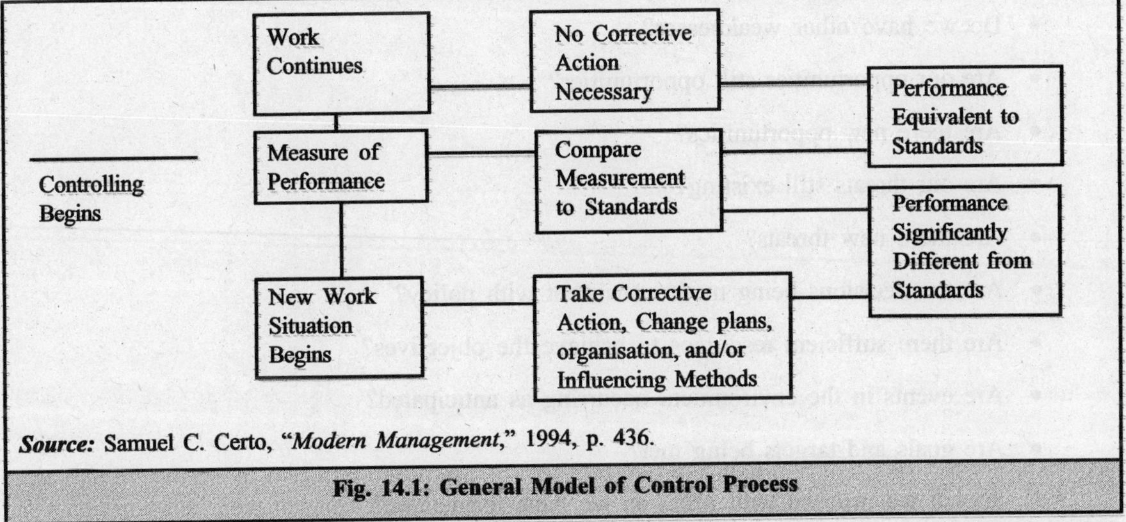

Source: Samuel C. Certo, *"Modern Management,"* 1994, p. 436.

Fig. 14.1: General Model of Control Process

Three Types of Control: There are three types of managerial control, *viz.*, preliminary control, concurrent control and feedback control. These three types of managerial control are presented in Fig. 14.2.

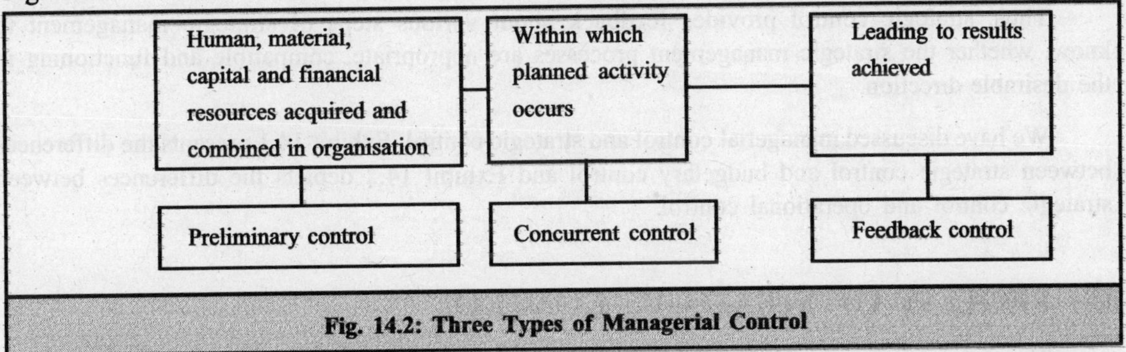

Fig. 14.2: Three Types of Managerial Control

Preliminary control focuses on preventing the possible deviations in the quality and quantity of resources. Human resources must meet the job requirements. The materials must meet acceptable levels of quality and other specifications. Financial resources must be available at reasonable cost in the right time. Concurrent control monitors ongoing operations to ensure that objectives are pursued.

Feedback control methods focus on end results. Corrective action is directed at improving either the resource acquisition process or the actual operations.

2. Strategic Control

Strategic control focuses on monitoring and evaluating the strategic management process to ensure that it functions in the right direction. The strategic control aims at achieving the results planned at the time of strategy formulation. Strategic control is a special type of organisational control.

3. Purposes of Strategic Control

The basic purpose of strategic control is to help top management to achieve strategic goals as planned. To be specific, the purposes of strategic control are to answer the questions such as:

- Are our internal strengths still holding good?
- Have we added other internal strengths?
- Are our internal weaknesses still holding good?
- Do we have other weaknesses?
- Are our opportunities still opportunities?
- Are there new opportunities?
- Are our threats still existing?
- Are there new threats?
- Are the decisions being made consistent with policy?
- Are there sufficient resources to achieve the objectives?
- Are events in the environment occurring as anticipated?
- Are goals and targets being met?
- Should we proceed with plans as we have formulated?
- Are the organisational vision, mission and objectives appropriate to the changing environment factors?

Thus, strategic control provides feedback about various steps of strategic management to know, whether the strategic management processes are appropriate, compatible and functioning in the desirable direction.

We have discussed managerial control and strategic control. Exhibit 14.1 presents the differences between strategic control and budgetary control and Exhibit 14.2 depicts the differences between strategic control and operational control.

(B) PROCESS OF STRATEGIC CONTROL

The strategic control process consists of six steps (Fig. 14.3). Top management, initially must decide what elements of the environment and the organisation need to be monitored, evaluated and controlled. The three key areas to be monitored and controlled are: the macro-environment, the industry environment and internal operations.

Exhibit 14.1: Differences Between Strategic Control and Budgetary Control

Strategic Control	*Budgetary Control*
Time period is lengthy — ranging from a few years to over ten years.	Time period is usually one year or less.
Measurements are quantitative and qualitative.	Measurements are quantitative.
Concentration is internal and external.	Concentration is internal.
Corrective action is on-going.	Corrective action any be taken after budget period has elapsed.

Source: Wright, Pringle and Kroll, *op. cit.*, p. 202.

Exhibit 14.2: Differences Between Strategic Control and Operational Control

	Attribute	*Strategic Control*	*Operational Control*
1.	Basic question	"Are we moving in the right direction?"	"How are we performing?"
2.	Aim	Pro-active, continuous questioning of the basic direction of strategy	Allocation and use of organisational resources
3.	Main concern	"Steering" the organisation's future direction	Action control
4.	Focus	External environment	Internal organisation
5.	Time horizon	Long-term	Short-term
6.	Exercise of control	Exclusively by top management, may be through lower-level support	Mainly by executive or middle-level management on the direction of top management
7.	Main techniques	Environmental scanning, information gathering, questioning and review	Budgets, schedules and MBO

Source: Adapted from J.A. Pearce III and R.B. Robinson, *Jr. Strategic Management: Strategy Formulation and Implementation* (3rd edn.). (Homewood, Ill. Richard D. Irwin.), pp. 404-419. Quoted in Azhar Kazmi, *op. cit.*, p. 319.

Step 1: Key Areas to be Monitored

Macro-environment: As stated earlier, one of the key areas to be monitored is the macro- environment of the company. This area should be focussed first. Normally, individual companies cannot influence the environment significantly. But, the external environmental forces must be continuously monitored as the changes in the environment influence the strategic implementation process of the company. As discussed in the earlier chapters, continuous strategic fit between the company and its external environment is necessary. Therefore, strategic control is essential.

Strategic Monitoring and Control Includes: Modifying any one or more of the areas like company's mission, objectives, goals, strategy formulation and strategy implementation. The modification depends upon the nature and degree of changes and shifts in the environment.

Strategic monitoring and control includes modifying any one or more of the areas like company's mission, objectives, goals, strategy formulation and strategy implementation.

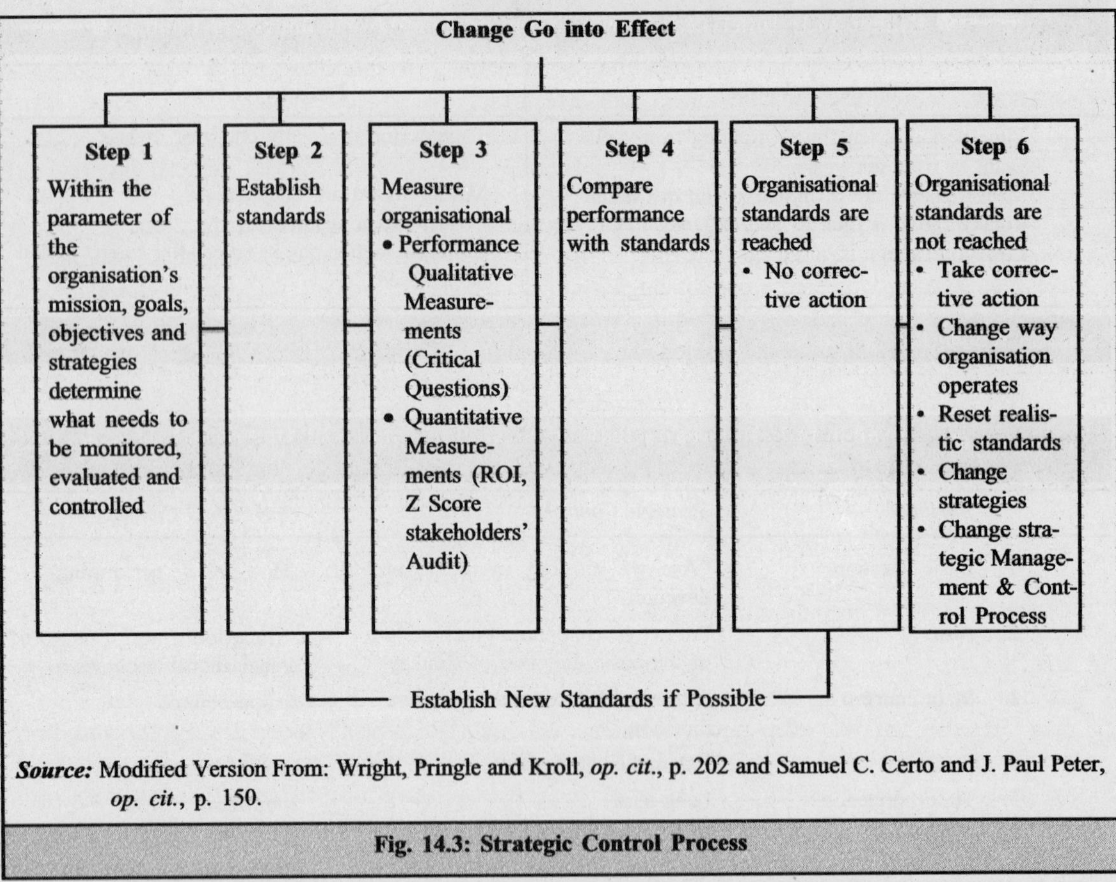

Source: Modified Version From: Wright, Pringle and Kroll, *op. cit.*, p. 202 and Samuel C. Certo and J. Paul Peter, *op. cit.*, p. 150.

Fig. 14.3: Strategic Control Process

Industry Environment: The strategist also monitors and control the industry related environment. The environmental forces may not be as they were planned. The changes in the environment may provide new opportunities or pose new threats. The strategy, therefore, should be modified accordingly. Thus, the purpose is to modify the company's strategy, goals and operations in order to capitalise the new opportunities and defend against the new threats effectively. The industry environment of the future should be considered by the top management for the purpose of strategic evaluation and control (See Box 14.1).

BOX 14.1 STARBUCKS ROLLS OUT VIA INSTANT COFFEE NATIONWIDE

Starbucks releases Via instant coffee nationwide, stocks store shelves and other retailers

The company that added "venti" and "frappuccino" to American vocabularies is making a push throughout North America to convince connoisseurs to sample what many see as a down-market drink — instant coffee.

Nearly eight months after Starbucks Corp. began selling its Via instant coffee in Seattle and Chicago, the company on Tuesday will begin offering the dissolvable drink to the rest of the country and in its Canadian stores. Backed by the company's first-ever television ads, along with large-scale distribution to about 1,500 sites outside its stores, the Via launch shows just how determined Starbucks is to own a stake in the $21 billion worldwide instant coffee market.

"Based on the success we've had, we feel strongly that we're sitting on a very big opportunity," said Starbucks CEO Howard Schultz said during a conference call with journalists. "What's going to sell Via at the end of the day is that (it) delivers in the cup. Most people will not be able to tell the difference." While instant coffee is pervasive throughout Europe — accounting for as much as 80 percent of coffee sales in the U.K. — the insta-brews haven't won over American taste buds, in large part because of their image as an inferior knock-off of drip-brewed beverages. But it's that perception that Starbucks executives are trying to change. They hope the skinny cylindrical 3-packs ($2.95) and 12-packs ($9.95) of coffee that dissolve in water will eventually be as prevalent on store shelves as its packaged coffee is now. The coffee is available in Colombia and Italian Roast flavors, and more varieties are expected to be introduced in the future. While experts see opportunity for Starbucks, they also see challenges.

Bob Goldin, an analyst at the Chicago-based food consultant Technomic Inc., said Starbucks faces twin hurdles of perception and price. The Starbucks instant comes in just shy of a dollar a cup, compared with the pennies it costs for a cup of home-brewed joe. Marshaling vendors like camping store chain REI and office supply chain Office Depot Inc., will help the company get the product in the hands of new customers. Via also will be sold inside Costco Wholesale Corp. and Target Corp., stores and to big food vendors like Compass and Aramark. The offensive is also taking to the air, where passengers onboard certain United flights on Tuesday will be able to sample the drinks. In late October, United travelers will be able to buy 3-packs of the coffee from flight attendants while cruising at 30,000 feet. Vendors will be able to set their own prices for Via, but the company recommends similar prices to what the product will be sold for in Starbucks stores. Next year, Via will appear on grocery store shelves, which along with bulk stores account for roughly two-thirds of Starbucks' packaged coffee sales. Executives wouldn't release data on how Via's performed during its eight months on the market, but said early sales in the two U.S. cities — as well as in London — have exceeded expectations.

Among the surprises so far are the various uses of the drink discovered by consumers, executives said. Some people are buying the ground coffee to cook and bake with, while others are mixing it with cold water or milk. Schultz said it's also being bought by teachers to keep in lunchrooms and desks and by physicians who want a quick cup of coffee in a hospital. The introduction of Via comes at a particularly trying time for Starbucks, which has seen its revenue slide for the last three consecutive quarters. Meanwhile, profits have fallen in five out of the past six quarters.

Hit by increasing competition and a recession that's caused caffeine addicts to switch to cheaper drinks, the gourmet chain's also had to close hundreds of stores and lay off workers as it tries to regain its financial swagger. Whether or not Via will be a home run remains to be seen, particularly as competitor Nestle SA ramps up marketing of its own single-serve instant Nescafe coffee. Goldin said the product will need more widespread sales than vendors such as Office Depot, REI and United can offer. If Starbucks can get Via in front of enough consumers, then it could have a chance for the beverage to succeed. "They're trying to find a breakthrough and I give them credit for that," he said. "But it's easier said than done. I think they're going to have some challenges."

Source: http://finance.yahoo.com/news/Starbucks-rolls-out-Via-apf-273848205.html?x=0

Internal Operations: The strategist has to evaluate the internal operations continuously in view of the changes in the macro-environment and industry environment. The strategist has to introduce changes in internal operations when the changes in the environment affect the strategy.

Step 2: Establishing Standards

Evaluating an organisational performance is normally based on certain standards. These standards may be the previous year's achievements or the competitor's records or the fresh standards established by the management. Qualitative judgements like the qualitative features of the product or service in

Evaluating an organisational performance is normally based on certain standards.

the last year may be used. Quantitative measures like return or investment, return on sales may also be used for judging the performance. Companies should establish the standards for evaluating the performance of the strategies taking several factors into consideration (See 14.2).

BOX 14.2 VOLKSWAGEN L1 CONCEPT: 240 MILES PER GALLON

A one-liter car? This moniker describes a car that uses one liter of fuel—about a quarter of a gallon—to propel a car for 100 kilometers, or 62 miles. The one-liter car's fuel economy translates to almost 240 mpg, and VW has had such a car in its sights for some time now. In 2002, outgoing VW CEO Ferdinand Piëch, now head of the company's supervisory board, drove a cigar-shaped prototype from VW headquarters in Wolfsburg to a shareholders' meeting in Hamburg.

Now the idea of the one-liter car has been resurrected. VW's biggest news at the Frankfurt auto show was the L1 concept, a prototype that "is close to production" and "will be developed," the company says. Three ingredients were needed to make it happen: a supremely efficient powertrain, great aerodynamics, and lightweight engineering.

As to the powertrain, VW has opted for a two-cylinder, 39-hp turbo-diesel engine combined with a 14-hp electric motor. There is a stop/start system and a seven-speed dual-clutch transmission. The L1 can reach 100 mph, but fuel economy at that speed drops to a shameful 1.38 liters per 100 kilometers, or 170 mpg.

The front-wheel-drive L1's aerodynamics are optimized by the two-seat layout with the occupants sitting in a row. The result is a car that is relatively long, quite low, and extremely slim. The monocoque and body is made of carbon fiber, and total weight of the L1 is a mere 838 pounds. We think that the seating configuration will likely be changed as development progresses; two people sitting behind each other is too unusual for prospective buyers.

Even so, the L1 looks refined and close to series production, which couldn't be said of the 2002 concept. It could be on the market as soon as 2013, Volkswagen sources tell us. The L1 may seem ironic to those who remember that VW is also responsible for Bugatti, which makes the fastest production car in the world, the Bugatti Veyron, and which just unveiled the W-16 Galibier sedan concept. But if you think about the styles of both Piëch and current VW chairman Martin Winterkorn, this contradiction seems logical: These guys both tend to go to extremes. And we submit that the Volkswagen L1 is a more significant step in saving resources than are heavy gasoline-electric hybrids.

Source: http://autos.yahoo.com/auto-shows/frankfurt_auto_show_2009/1106/Volkswagen-L1-Concept

The standards may include:

- Quality of Products/Services.
- Quantity of Products to be Produced.
- Quality of Management.
- Innovativeness/Creativity.
- Long term investment value.
- Volume of sales and/or market share.
- Financial soundness in terms of return on investment, return on equity capital, market price of the share, earnings per share, etc.
- Community and environmental responsibility in terms of amount spent on community development, variety of facilities provided to the community, programmes undertaken for the environmental protection and ecological balance, etc.

- Soundness of human resource management in terms of number of employee grievances, employee satisfaction rate, employee turnover rate, industrial relations situation, etc.
- Ability to attract, develop and retain competent and skilled people.
- Use of company's assets.
- Production targets, rate of capacity utilisation, design of new products, new uses of existing products, rate of customer complaints about the product quality, suitability of ingredients, etc.
- Corporate image among the customers and general public.
- Market place performance.
- Standards relating the organisational variables include freedom and autonomy, level of control, responsibility, formal organisation and degree of formality, informal organisation.

Step 3: Measuring Performance

The strategist has to measure the performance of various areas of the organisation before taking an action. Strategic audits and strategic audit measurement methods are useful to measure the organisational performance.

Strategic Audit

A strategic audit is an execution and evaluation of organisation's operations affected by the strategy implementation. Strategic audit may be very comprehensive, emphasising all facets of a strategic management process. It may also be narrowly focused, emphasising only on a single part of the process such as environmental process. Strategic audit may be quite formal adhering to organisational rules and procedures. It may be quite informal providing freedom and autonomy to the managers to take decisions. The strategic audit must work to integrate related functions. Hence, the strategic audits are carried out by cross-functional teams of managers.

A strategic audit is an execution and evaluation of organisation's operations affected by the strategy implementation.

There are no universally accepted single method of strategic audit. Each organisation can formulate its own method depending upon its need. Exhibit 14.3 presents a worth while set of general guidelines on how to conduct a strategic audit.

Exhibit 14.3: How to Conduct a Strategic Audit

A strategic audit is conducted in three phases: diagnosis to identify how, where, and in what priority in-depth analyses need to be made; focussed analysis; and generation and testing of recommendations. Objectivity and the ability to ask critical, probing questions are key requirements for conducting a strategic audit.

Phase One: Diagnosis

1. Review key documents such as:
   (a) Strategic plan
   (b) Business or operational plans
   (c) Organisational arrangements
   (d) Major policies governing matters such as resource allocation and performance measurement
2. Review financial, market, and operational performance against benchmarks and industry norms to identify key variances and emerging trends.
3. Gain an understanding of:
   (a) Principal roles, responsibilities and reporting relationships
   (b) Decision-making process and major decisions made

(c) Resources, including physical facilities, capital, management and technology

(d) Interrelationships between functional staff member and businesses or operating units

4. Identify strategic implications of strategy for organisation structure, behaviour patterns, systems, and processes — define interrelationships and linkage to strategy.
5. Determine internal and external perspectives.
   (a) Survey the attitudes and perceptions of senior and middle managers and other key employees to assess the extent to which they are consistent with the strategic direction of the firm. One way to accomplish this task is through carefully focused interviews and/or questionnaires to ask employees to identify and make trade-offs among the objectives and variables they consider most important.
   (b) Interview a carefully selected sample of customers and prospective customers and other key external sources to understand their view of the company.
6. Identify aspects of the strategy that are working well. Formulate hypotheses regarding problems and opportunities for improvement based on the findings above. Define how and in what order to pursue each.

Phase Two: Focussed Analysis

1. Test the hypotheses concerning problems and opportunitists for improvement through analysis of specific issues. Identify interrelationships and dependencies among components of the strategic system.
2. Formulate conclusions as to weaknesses in strategy formulation, implementation deficiencies, or interactions between the two.

Phase Three: Recommendations

1. Develop alternative solutions to problems and ways of capitalising on opportunities. Test these alternatives in light of their resource requirements, risks, rewards, priorities, and other applicable measures.
2. Develop specific recommendations to produce an integrated, measurable, and time-phased action plan to improve strategic results.

Source: Adapted from A.J. Prager and M.B. Shea, "*The Strategic Audit*," in The Strategic Management Handbook. ed. K.J. Albert (New York: McGraw-Hill.), pp. 8-14.

Strategic Audit Measurement Methods

Generally accepted methods may be used to measure organisational performance. These methods can be broadly divided into two categories, *viz., (i)* Qualitative Methods and *(ii)* Quantitative Methods. Exhibit 14.4 presents Key Strategy Evaluation Questions.

Exhibit 14.4: Key Strategy-Evaluation Questions

1. Do you feel that the strategic-management system exists to provide service to you in your day-to-day work? How has it helped you in this respect?
2. Has the strategic-management system provided the service that you feel was promised at the start of its design and implementation? In which areas has it failed and excelled, in your opinion?
3. Do you consider that the strategic-management system has been implemented with due regard to costs and benefits? Are there any areas in which you consider the costs to be excessive?
4. Do you feel comfortable using the system? Could more attention have been paid to matching the output of the system to your needs and if so, of, in what areas?
5. Is the system flexible enough in your opinion? If not, where should changes be made?
6. Do you still keep a personal store of information in a notebook or elsewhere? If so, will you share that information with the system? Do you see any benefits in so doing?
7. Do you think that the strategic-management system is still evolving? Can you influence this evolution and, if not, why not?
8. Does the system provide you with timely, relevant, and accurate information? Are there any areas of deficiency in this respect?

9. Do you think that the strategic-management system makes too much use of complex procedures and models? Can you suggest areas in which less complicated techniques might be used to advantage?
10. Do you consider that there has been sufficient attention paid to the confidentiality and security of the information in the system? Can you suggest areas for improvement of these aspects of its operation?

Source: K.J. Radford, *Information Systems for Strategic Decisions*, 1978, pp. 220-21.

Qualitative Organisational Measurements

Qualitative measurements are in the form of non-numerical data that are subjectively summarised. These measurements are organised and provided to the strategists for decision-making and strategy control action. Critical questions are designed to reflect important facets of organisational operations. Answers to these questions form as the basis for measurements. There are no universally acceptable list of questions by all companies. However, Exhibit 14.5 presents a list of useful questions of quantitative organisational measurements.

Seymour Tilles in his paper on, "How to Evaluate Corporate Strategy," mentioned several important questions to measure organisational performance qualitatively. These questions include:

1. *Is organisational strategy internally consistent?* Internal consistency is concerned to the cumulative impact of various strategies on organisation. Are strategies conflicting with each other. Strategies should also be judged by their relationship with other organisational initiatives.
2. *Is the organisation's strategy consistent with its environment?* Normally, organisational strategies are formulated based on the industry's environment and general environment.

Similarly, the strategies are modified based on the environmental changes. The strategist should see, whether the strategies are consistent with the present and future environmental factors or not? These environmental factors include: Present and future regulations of the Government, Customers taste and preferences, trends of labour supply, technology changes, competitors products and demand. Many organisational problems can be solved easily, if the management brings the balance between the strategy and the environment.

Exhibit 14.5: Sample Questions for Qualitative Organisational Measurement

- Are financial policies with respect to investment, dividends, and financing consistent with the opportunities likely to be available?
- Has the company defined the market segments in which it intends to operate specifically with respect to both product lines and market segments? Has it clearly defined the key capabilities it needs to succeed?
- Does the company have a viable plan for developing a significant and defensible superiority over competitors based on these capabilities?
- Will the business segments in which the company operates provide adequate opportunities for achieving corporate objectives? Do they appear attractive enough to draw an excessive amount of investment to the market from potential competitors? Is the company providing adequately for developing attractive new investment opportunities?
- Are the management, financial, technical, and other resources of the company really adequate to justify an expectation of maintaining superiority over competitors in key capabilities?
- Does the company have operations in which it cannot reasonably expect to outperform competitors? If so, can managers expect these operations to generate adequate returns on invested capital? Is there any justification for investing further in such operations, even just to maintain them?

- Has the company selected business segments that can reinforce each other by contributing jointly to the development of key capabilities? Do competitors combine operations in ways that give them superiority in the key resource areas? Can the company's scope of operations be revised to improve its chances against competitors?
- To the extent that operations are diversified, has the company recognized and provided for the special management and control system this requires?

Source: Milton Lauenstein. "Keeping Your Corporate Strategy on Track." *Journal of Business Strategy* 2. No. 1 (Summer 1981). p. 64.

3. Is organisational strategy appropriate, given organisational resources? Strategy implementation invariably requires the allocation of sufficient resources. Therefore, the strategist should enquire, whether the existing organisational resources are sufficient to carry out a proposed strategy? The strategist should not implement the strategy, without the allocation of sufficient money, material, machines/technology and human resources.

4. Is the time horizon of the strategy appropriate? Organisational strategies are formulated to achieve specific goals within a time framework. The strategist should require whether the time framework, under the existing circumstances is realistic and acceptable? Organisational goals cannot be achieved satisfactorily, if there is inconsistency between these two variables:

Qualitative measurement methods are efficient and are useful. But applying them relies mostly on human judgement. Conclusion based on such methods should be drawn carefully due to the subjectivity of the judgement.

Quantitative Organisational Measurements: Under quantitative organisational measurements of the performance of strategy implementation is taken place in the form of numerical data. The numerical data can be summarised and organised to draw conclusions and to recommend strategic action. Quantitative measurements can be used to evaluate:

(i) number of units produced per time period,

(ii) cost of production, cost of marketing,

(iii) productivity and production efficiency levels,

(iv) Employee turnover, absenteeism levels,

(v) sales and sales growth market shares,

(vi) Profit-gross, net, earning per share, dividend rate, return on equity, market price of the share,

(vii) Cost of production,

(viii) cost of marketing, etc.

Organisations design and use their own methods to evaluate the performance quantitatively. The commonly used methods include:

1. Return on Investment: Return on Investment is widely used as a measure of organisational performance

$$\text{Return on Investment (ROI)} = \frac{\text{Amount of Income per year}}{\text{Total Investment during that year}}$$

Management calculates the return on investment for consecutive years or consecutive quarters and compares the values over the period to measure the performance. ROI as a measure of organisational performance. It has its advantages and limitations (Exhibit 14.6). Managers can use the ROI alongwith other measures of organisational performance in view of its limitations.

Exhibit 14.6: Advantages and Limitations of ROI Performance Measures

Advantages

1. ROI is a single comprehensive figure influenced by everything that happens in a firm.
2. It measures how well the division manager uses the assets of the company to generate profits. It is also a good way to check on the accuracy of capital investment proposals.
3. It is a common denominator that can be compared among many entities.
4. It provides an incentive to use existing assets efficiently.
5. It provides an incentive to acquire new assets only when doing so would increase the firm's return.

Limitations

1. ROI is very sensitive to depreciation policy. Variances in depreciation write-offs between divisions affect their ROI performance. Accelerated depreciation techniques reduce ROI, conflicting with capital budgeting discounted cash flow analysis.
2. ROI is sensitive to book value. Older plants with more fully depreciated assets have relatively lower investment bases than newer plants, increasing ROI. (Note also that inflation can skew asset values and ROI.) Managers might be tempted to hold down asset investment or dispose of assets in order to increase ROI performance.
3. In many firms that use ROI, one division sells to another, so transfer pricing affects the measure. Expenses incurred affect profit. Since, in theory, the transfer price should be based on the total impact on firm profit, some investment center managers are bound to suffer. Equitable transfer prices are difficult to determine.
4. If one division operates in favourable industry conditions and another division operates in an industry with unfavourable conditions, the former division will automatically look better than the other.
5. ROI reflects a short time span. The performance of division managers should be measured in the long run. This is top management's time-span capacity.
6. The business cycle strongly affects ROI performance, often despite managerial performance.

Source: Excerpt from James M. Higgins, *Organisational Policy and Strategic Management: Text And Cases.*

2. Weighted Performance: This quantitative measure numerically weights and sums five performance measures to arrive at an overall score.[10] The score becomes a basis for classifying companies as healthy and unlikely to go bankrupt or as sick and likely to go bankrupt.

The formula is $Z = 1.2 \times 1 + 1.4 \times 2 + 3.3 \times 3 + 0.6 \times 4 + 1.0 \times 5$.

Z = Index of overall financial health. The five variables are explained in the Exhibit 14.7.

Exhibit 14.7: Variables for Z Score

X_1 = Working capital/Total assets	Frequently found in studies of corporate problems, this is a measure of the net liquid assets of the firm relative to its total capital. Working capital is the difference between current assets and current liabilities. This variable explicitly allows for liquidity and size characteristics. Ordinarily, a firm experiencing consistent operating losses will have shrinking current assets in relation to total assets.
X_2 = Retained earnings/Total assets	This measure of cumulative profitability over time relies on balance sheet figures. It implicitly considers the age of a firm. For example, a relatively young firm will probably show a low RE/TA ratio because it has not had time to build up its cumulative profits. Therefore, this analysis may seem to discriminate against the young firm, since its chance of being classified as likely to go bankrupt is relatively higher than another, older firm. This is precisely the situation in the real world, though. Failure is much more likely in a firm's earlier years; over 50 per cent of firms that fail do so in the first five years of existence. Note, however, that the retained earnings account is subject to manipulation via

	corporate quasi reorganisations and stock dividend declarations. A basis could be created by a substantial reorganization or stock dividend.
X_3 = Earnings before interest and taxes/total assets	In essence, this ratio measures the true productivity of the firm's assets, abstracting from any tax or leverage factors. Since firm's ultimate existence is based on the earning power of its assets, this ratio appears to be particularly appropriate for studies dealing with corporate failure. Furthermore, insolvency occurs when total liabilities exceed a fair valuation of the firm's assets, with value determined by the earning power of the assets.
X_4 = Market value of equity/ Book value of total liabilities	Equity is measured by the combined market value of all shares of stock, preferred and common, while liabilities include both current and long-term debt. Book values of preferred and common stockholders' equity may be substituted for market values. The substitution of book values, especially for the common stock component, should be recognized as a proxy without statistical verification, however, since the model was built using market values (Price × Shares outstanding). The measure shows how much the firm's assets can decline in value (measured by market value of equity plus debt) before the liabilities exceed the assets and the firm becomes insolvent. For example, a company with equity worth $1,000 and debt worth $500 could experience a two-thirds drop in asset value before insolvency. However, the same firm with $250 in equity would be insolvent after a drop of only one-third in value.
X_5 = Sales/Total assets	This capital-turnover ratio is a standard financial ratio that illustrates the sales-generating ability of the firm's assets. It is one measure of management's capability in dealing with competitive conditions.

Note that variables X_1, X_2, X_3, and X_4 should be inserted into the model as decimal fractions; for example, a Working capital/Total assets ratio of 20 percent should be written as 0.20. The variable X_5, however, is usually a ratio greater than unity; for example, where sales are twice as large as assets, the ratio is 2.0.

Source: Adapted from Edward I. Altman and James K. LaFleur, "Managing a Return to Financial Health," *Journal of Business Strategy*, 2, No. 1 (Summer 1981), pp. 31-38.

3. Stakeholders' Audit: Stakeholders are the people who have a stake in the company. They are interested in the company's activities as they are significantly affected by the company's objectives. The organisational stakeholders include:

(i) shareholders or owners of the company who are interested in dividend, market price, the share,

(ii) Trade unions and employees interested in favourable wages, benefits, conditions of employment and better quality of work life,

(iii) creditors interested in company's liquidity position and ability to repay the debts with interest in right time,

(iv) suppliers interested in retaining the organisation as a good customer,

(v) government interested in keeping the organisation as a good tax payer, maintaining the congenial industrial relations, maintaining the ecological balance, and contributing to solve the social and economic problems of the country,

(vi) social interest groups such as consumer protection associations and environmental protection associations

(vii) customers who expect a qualitative product/service at a reasonable price, prompt service and favourable conditions of sales.

Stakeholders audit is one of the measures of organisational performance. Exhibit 14.8 provides stakeholder groups and measures to assess both the short run and long run impact they may have on organisational performance.

Step 4: Compare Performance with Standards

Once the performance of the different aspects of the organisation is measured, it should be compared with the predetermined standards. Standards are set to achieve the already formulated organisational goals and strategies. Organisational standards are yardsticks and benchmarks that place organisational performance in perspective. The strategists should set standards for all performance areas of the organisation based on the organisational goals and strategies. Normally, the standards vary from one company to the other company. Further, they also vary from time to time in the same company. The standards developed by General Electric can be used as model standards. These standards include.

1. Profitability Standards: These standards include how much gross profit, net profit, return on investment, earning per share, percentage of profit to sales the company should earn in a given time period.

2. Market Position Standards: These standards include total sales, sales-region-wise and product-wise, market share, marketing costs, customer service, customer satisfaction, price, customer loyalty shifts from other organisations' products etc.

3. Productivity Standards: These standards indicate the performance of the organisation in terms of conversion of inputs into outputs. These standards include capital productivity, labour productivity, material productivity, etc.

4. Product Leadership Standards: These standards include the innovations and modifications in products to increase the new uses of the existing product, developing new products with new uses, etc.(See Box 14.2).

BOX 14.2 WORLD'S LARGEST PASSENGER JET MAKES U.S. DEBUT

Some of my earliest childhood memories involve my tiny face pressed up against the inside of an airplane, looking down at the passing land below. While flying these days is often a hassle with long lines, frustrating security and a complete lack of service, there is still that little kid in me pressed up against the window. Today that little kid got a big treat: A close look at the first U.S. landing of the A380, the world's largest commercial airplane.

The double-decker plane flown by Emirates Airlines touched down at New York's JFK airport at 4:29 p.m.. Crowd of reporters and VIPs cheered and then eagerly waited as the mammoth plane taxied to the terminal. More than 70 ground crew were on hand to quickly unload and then reload the plane for its return to Dubai. Many had cell phone cameras out to capture the moment. The plane was escorted in by police cars and dwarfed everything along its way. The A380 was also greeted by two airport firetrucks with water cannons that gave it a ceremonial wash. The A380 is unlike any other plane before.

The average first class ticket on the route goes for $14,635, business for $9,571 and coach for $1,477. While that is the same as the service on the airline's Boeing 777 routes, there are substantially more of these high-end seats to sell. The four-engine jumbo jet can carry up to 850 passengers, although most airlines plan to fly closer to 500. This plane put an end to the Boeing 747's astonishing 40-year reign as the world's largest passenger jetliner.

Emirates configured its A380 for 489 passengers. Most are in coach but there are 76 business-class seats and 14 private suites in first-class with electronic doors for privacy. They also get showers, their own mini-bar, a 23-inch high-definition TV screen, your own wardrobe and meals on demand. Singapore Airlines was the first to fly the A380, launching service in October. It now flies the planes between Singapore and London and Sydney and Tokyo. Dubai-based Emirates is the second to fly the jet, but the largest of Airbus' 17 customers. By the way, not one of them is an American airline.

Source: http://news.bbc.co.uk/2/hi/uk_news/england/west_midlands/7536527.stm (02/08/08)

5. Human Resource Standards: Human resource standards include providing competitive salaries, benefits and different aspects of quality of work-life. These standards also include human resource performance, productivity, turnover rates, absenteeism rates, etc.

Exhibit 14.8: Stakeholder Groups and their Impact on Organizational Performance

Stakeholder Category	Near-Term Performance Measures	Long-Term Performance Measures
Customers	Sales (value and volume) New customers Number of new customer needs met	Growth in sales Turnover in customer base Ability to control price
Suppliers	Cost of raw material Delivery time Inventory Availability of raw materials	Growth rates of Raw materials costs Delivery time Inventory New ideas from suppliers
Financial Community	EPS[a] Stock price Number of "buy" lists[b] ROE[c]	Ability to sell strategy to Wall Street Growth in ROE
Employees	Number of suggestions Productivity Number of grievances	Number of internal promotions Turnover
Congress	Number of new pieces of legislation that affect the firm Access to key members and staff	Number of new regulations that affect the industry Ratio of cooperative to competitive encounters
Consumer advocates	Number of meetings Number of hostile encounters Number of coalitions formed Number of legal actions	Number of changes in policy due to consumer advocates Number of calls for help initiated by consumer advocates[d]

Environmentalists	Number of meetings Number of hostile encounters Number of coalitions formed Number of Environmental Protection Agency complaints Number of legal actions	Number of changes in policy due to environmentalists Number of calls for help initiated by environmentalists

a Earnings per share.

b Lists from which financial brokers recommend stock purchases for their clients.

c Return on equity.

d Calls in which consumer advocates attempt to enlist others in action against a company.

Source: Adapted from Edward Freeman *Strategic Management: A Stakeholder Approach*. Boston: Pitman-Publishing.

6. Employee Attitude Standards: Employee attitude standards include employees' favourable attitude towards the nature of work, organisation, salaries, benefits, working environment, quantity of work-life, treatment by superiors, etc.

7. Social Responsibility Standards: All organisations discharge their responsibilities towards different sections of the society. These standards are related to the services of the organisations towards community, government, employees, suppliers, creditors, etc.

8. Standards Reflecting Balance between Short-range and Long-range Goals: Short-range and long-range strategies should be balanced successfully. Standards in these areas should bring balance between short-range and long-range goals.

Step 5: Take No Action if Performance is in Harmony with Standards

If the performance of various organisational areas match with the standards, the strategist need not take any action. He should just allow the process to continue. However, he can try to improve the performance above the standards, if it would be possible, without having any negative impact on the existing process.

Step 6: Take Corrective Action, if necessary

Strategist should take necessary corrective action, if performance is not in harmony with standards.

The strategists compare the performance with standards. If they find any deviation between the standards and performance, they should take corrective action to bridge the gap between the standards and performance.

Causes of Deviations: It is very easy to conclude that someone made a mistake, when deviations are identified. But, the deviation may be the result of an unexpected move by a competitor, a typical whether patterns or changes in external environment. Therefore, the strategist should consider the following before making a decision, in this regard:

- Was the cause of deviation internal or external?
- Was the cause random, or should it have been anticipated?
- Is the change temporary or permanent?
- Are the present strategies still appropriate?
- Does the organisation have the capacity to respond to the change needed?

Corrective Action: Corrective action may be defined as change in a company's operations to ensure that it can more effectively and efficiently reach its goals and perform up to its established standards.

Strategies that do not achieve standards produce three possible responses, *viz.*, *(i)* to revise strategies, *(ii)* to change standards, and *(iii)* to take corrective action in the existing process without changing standards and strategies. Strategy change may require a 'fine tuning' of the existing strategy or complete changes in strategies. If it is realised that the existing standards are unrealistic under the present conditions, the strategist should reset the standards taking the existing conditions into consideration.

Corrective action may be as simple as increase in the price or may be as complex as change the chief executive officer. Deviations require re-examination of the company's mission, objectives, relationship to its environment, internal strengths, weaknesses and strategies (See Box 14.2).

BOX 14.2 WHERE WAL-MART WENT WRONG

Late 2006, Mukesh Ambani-promoted Reliance Retail opened its first store in Hyderabad. Around the same time, Wal-Mart Stores Inc., the world's largest retailer in terms of sales, announced its partnership with Bharti Enterprises to begin operations in India. Eighteen months hence, Reliance Retail is a 600-store chain, while Wal-Mart, which had planned to start operations by the year-end, has deferred the launch to 2009. Our August announcement (to start by 2008-end) was a statement of intent," said a Bharti Wal-Mart spokesperson. "As we get closer to execution, we are investing significant resources to better understand the nuances of the market and closely studying the existing supply chain infrastructure." In fact, Wal-Mart showed extreme alacrity when it overtook British supermarket chain Tesco Plc., which was earlier in talks with Bharti. In November 2006, the US retailer was able to clinch the deal with the Indian business house in a record three months, rendering Tesco's over a year-long talks futile. Nonetheless, it took the two companies 10 months just to decide the formats in which the joint venture would roll out the operations. Ambani opened its first retail store five months after the initial announcement. Ending the speculation of Bharti being the franchisee for Wal-Mart's front end operations, the companies signed an agreement to establish Bharti Wal-Mart Private Ltd, an equal joint venture for wholesale cash-and-carry and back end supply chain management operations in India in August 2007. "In the case of one or two clients, we saw that it takes a long time in such joint ventures to even synchronise the calendar for every one for discussions," said Arvind K Singhal, chairman of Technopak, a business consulting firm. "These international retailers are also facing some degree of crisis in some of their markets, which would take away their attention," he added. Wal-Mart argues that the delay is because India is the first market that it is entering organically in the last 10 years. "It took us time to understand the nuances of the market through customer research and get our agreements in place," said the Bharti Wal-Mart spokesperson. However, analysts have a different opinion about the slow pace of Bharti Wal-Mart's rollout plan. "It took time because Wal-Mart was evaluating if it could be brought to the front end," said an analyst with a leading domestic brokerage. Wal-Mart inked the pact with Bharti when the industry was expecting some amount of foreign direct investment (FDI) in multi-brand retailing and Tesco was seen taking the lead from Wal-Mart. The government allowed 51 per cent FDI in single brand retail stores in 2006 and some amount of FDI was also expected in multi-brand retail. However, FDI in multi-brand retailing was not allowed amidst opposition from political parties expressing concern of negative impact on small kirana shops. However, 100 per cent FDI in the wholesale cash-and-carry model remained intact. This left only one route for multi-brand international retailers, such as Wal-Mart, Tesco, and Carrefour, to open its stores under own brand name: to find a franchise. The franchise route has been open for the foreign retailers. However, it did not attract Wal-Mart and it chose to partner Bharti for the cash-and-carry operation, which it could have gone alone under government guidelines. However, Wal-Mart insists that its India joint venture is out of choice and not compulsion. Bharti Enterprises, through a separate subsidiary, also moved into front end retailing under the brand name Easy Day, which opened its first store only last month in Ludhiana. It has got three stores now and more will follow.

Source: http://www.rediff.com/money/2008/jun/02walmart.htm(Accessed on 02/06/2008)

Further questions useful in establishing reasons for deviations and in identifying possible actions are depicted in Fig. 14.4.

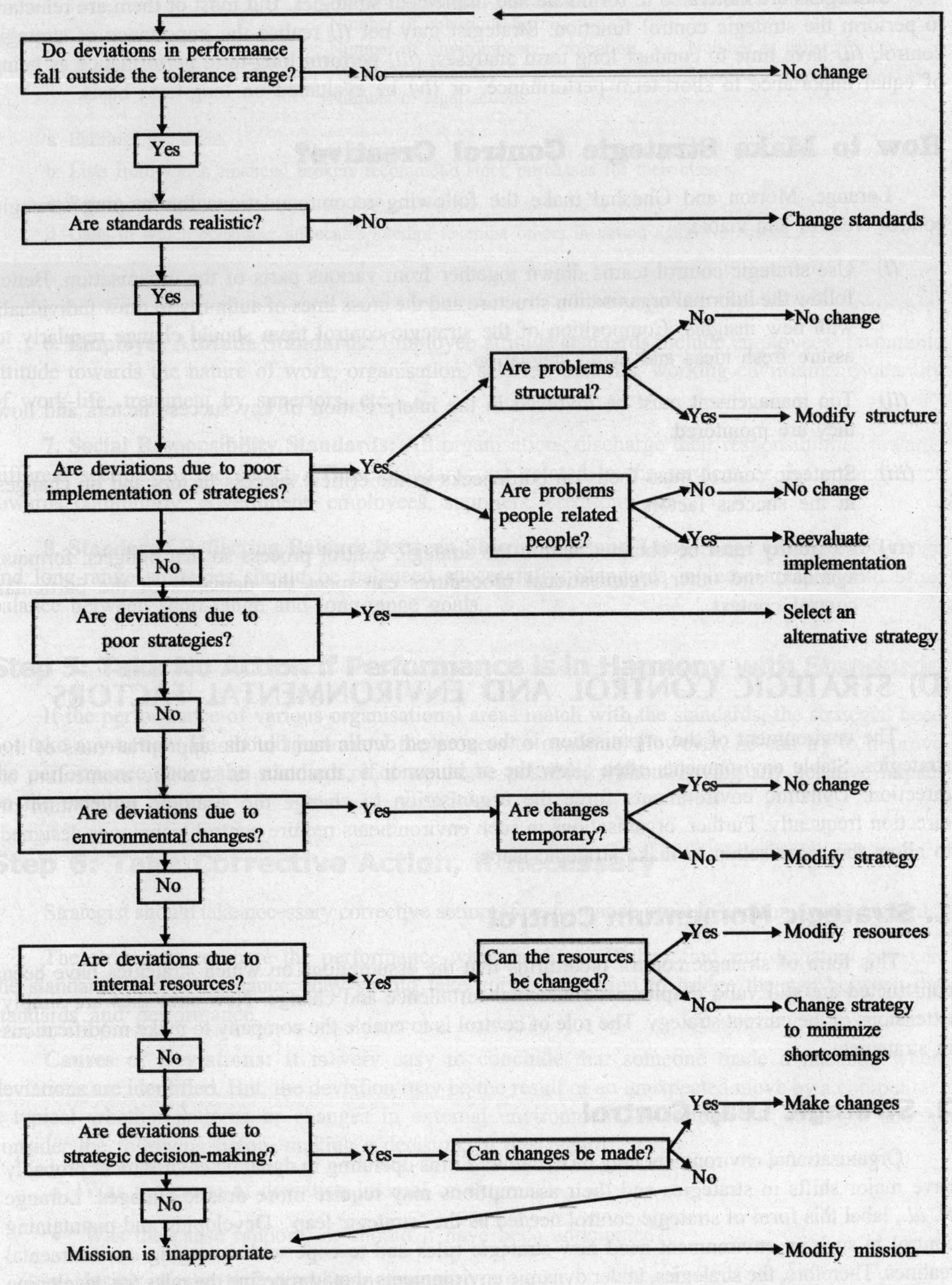

Source: Joe G. Thomas, *op. cit.*, p. 340.

Fig. 14.4: Determining Reasons for Deviations

(C) RELUCTANCE TO USE STRATEGIC CONTROL

Strategists are motivated to formulate and implement strategies. But most of them are reluctant to perform the strategic control function. Strategist may not *(i)* realise the importance of strategic control, *(ii)* have time to conduct long term analyses, *(iii)* perform long-term performance as being of equal importance to short-term performance, or *(iv)* be evaluated on long-term basis.

How to Make Strategic Control Creative?

Lorange, Morton and Ghoshal make the following recommendations for keeping strategic control creative and viable.

(i) Use strategic control teams drawn together from various parts of the organisation. Better follow the informal organisation structure and the cross lines of authority to draw individuals with new insights. Composition of the strategic control team should change regularly to assure fresh ideas and avoid stagnation.

(ii) Top management must be involved in the interpretation of key success factors and how they are monitored.

(iii) Strategic control must focus on bottlenecks in the critical success factors and on changes in the success factors.

(iv) Flexibility must be obtained within the strategic control process so that budgets, formats, agendas, and other organisational procedures can meet the demands of the particular control context.

(D) STRATEGIC CONTROL AND ENVIRONMENTAL FACTORS

Stable environments often allow the organisation to maintain its strategic momentum or direction.

The environment of the organisation is the greatest determinant of the appropriateness of the strategies. Stable environments often allow the organisation to maintain its strategic momentum or direction. Dynamic environments force the organisation to change the strategic momentum or direction frequently. Further, organisations in such environments require control techniques designed to allow the organisation to make strategic leaps.

1. Strategic Momentum Control

This form of strategic control reconfirms that the assumptions on which strategies have been constructed are still valid despite environmental turbulence and change. New strategies are simply extensions of the current strategy. The role of control is to enable the company to make modifications in strategies.

2. Strategic Leap Control

Organisational environment may be dynamic. Firms operating in dynamic environment probably have major shifts in strategies and their assumptions may require more drastic changes. Lorange *et. al.*, label this form of strategic control needed as the 'strategic leap'. Developing and maintaining control in such an environment need new strategic rules and to cope with emerging environmental realities. Therefore, the strategies, under dynamic environments should redefine the rules for developing and operationalising strategies. There are four forms of strategic leap control, *viz.*, *(i)* strategic issue management, *(ii)* strategic field analysis, and *(iii)* systems modelling, and *(iv)* scenarios.

***(i)* Strategic Issue Management:** Strategic issue management involves the identification of one or a few key issues that are perceived as crucial to an organisation to achieve its performance objectives. Strategic issue management is designed to reduce the chances of an organisation being caught unaware by a major environmental change. These control techniques encourage the company to remain sensitive to potential environmental changes, plan appropriate actions for changes and avoid becoming locked into a particular course of action.

***(ii)* Strategic Field Analysis:** It is a way of examining the nature and extent of synergies that exist or are lacking between/among components of an organisation. This examination allows the managers to exploit the opportunities provided by the environment.

***(iii)* Systems Modelling:** Systems models are typically computer-based models trying to capture the administrative realities of an organisation and how it interfaces with its environment.

***(iv)* Scenarios:** Scenario planning focuses on qualitative aspects of the organisation broad trends, describing alternative major scenarios and developing an assessment of which scenario is most likely.

Moving from Momentum to Leap and *Vice Versa*

The environmental factors may change from stable to dynamic and *vice versa*. The strategist should also change from momentum to leap control and *vice versa* depending upon the nature of the environment.

(E) INFORMATION FOR STRATEGIC CONTROL

Accurate and reliable information about various measures of organisational performance is highly essential for successful strategic control. Organisations should develop and implement formal system to collect valid, reliable and timely information. There are two information systems, *viz.*, Management Information Systems (MIS) and Management Decision Support Systems (MDSS).

1. Management Information System (MIS)

A management information system is a formal computer-assisted organisational function designed to provide managers with information to help their decision-making. The important use of such information is to support strategic control. There are six steps in the operation of MIS (Fig. 14.5).

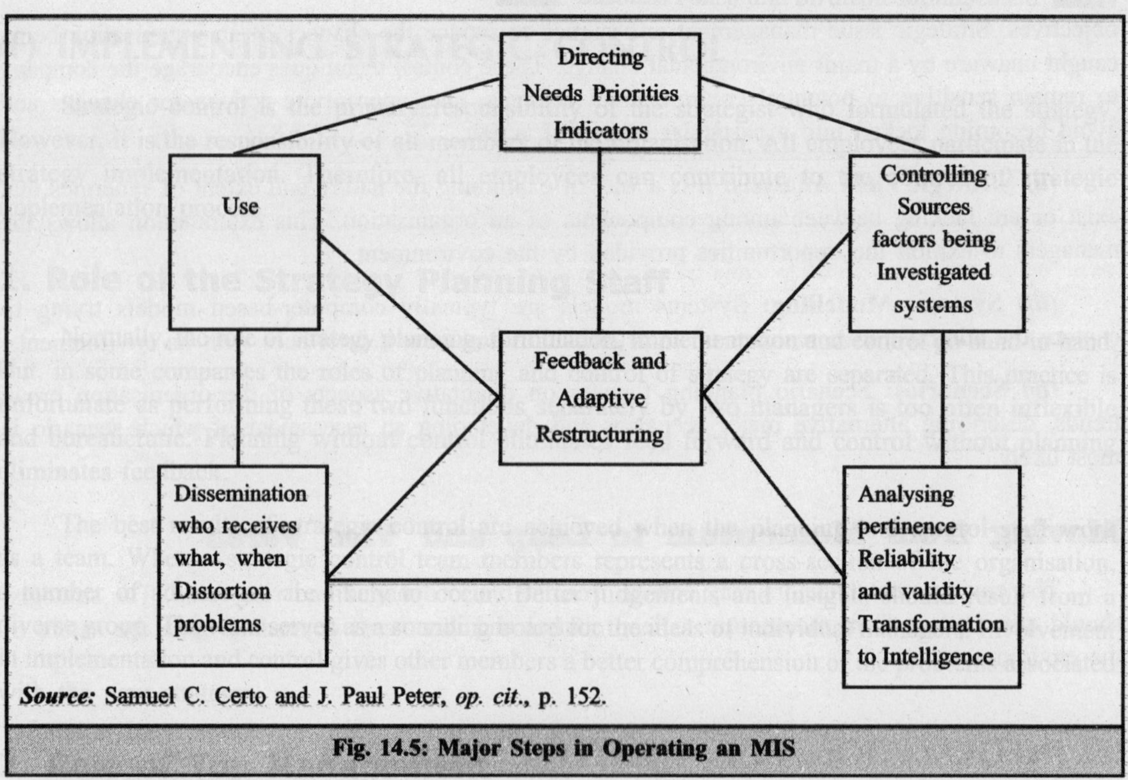

Source: Samuel C. Certo and J. Paul Peter, *op. cit.*, p. 152.

Fig. 14.5: Major Steps in Operating an MIS

Managers at different levels of the organisation perform different functions and therefore, they need different kinds of information. MIS should be flexible to provide different kinds of information to the managers at various levels. Exhibit 14.9 presents typical activities performed by top management, middle management and junior management.

Exhibit 14.9: Typical Activities of Managers at Various Organizational Levels

Organisational Level	*Characteristics of Activities*	*Sample Activities*
Top management	Future oriented Significant uncertainty Significant subjective assessment Strategic management emphasis	Establishing organizational direction Performing environmental analysis Developing organisational strategies
Middle management	Somewhat future oriented (less than top-management activities) Emphasis on implementation of strategies Emphasis on daily production	Marking short-term forecasts Budgeting Human resource planning
Supervisory management	Emphasis on daily performance that reflects organizational strategy and contributes to attaining long-term goals	Assigning jobs to specific workers Managing inventory Supervising workers Handling worker complaints Maintaining organisational procedures and rules

Source: Samuel C. Certo and Paul Peter. *op. cit.*, p. 153.

Since the success of the strategic control depends on the efficient functioning of MIS, the strategists should monitor the functioning of MIS continuously. The strategists should be aware of the symptoms of a malfunctioning MIS (Exhibit 14.10) and set the MIS in the right direction and in right time.

Exhibit 14.10: Symptoms of a Malfunctioning MIS

Operational Symptoms	*Psychological Symptoms*	*Report Content Symptoms*
Large physical inventory adjustments	Surprise at financial results	Excessive use of large tables of numbers
Capital expenditure overruns	Poor attitude of executives about usefulness of information	Multiple preparation and distribution of identical data
Unexplained changes from year to year in operating results	Lack of understanding of financial information by nonfinancial executives	Disagreements among information from different sources
Uncertain direction of company growth		
Unexplained cost variances	Lack of concern for environmental changes	Lack of periodic comparative and trend information
No order backlog awareness		
No internal discussion of reported data	Excessive homework	Late information
		Too little or excess detail
Insufficient knowledge about competition		Inaccurate information
Purchasing parts from outside vendors that the firm could make itself		Lack of standards for comparison
		Failure to identify variances by cause and responsibility.
Failure of investments in facilities, or in programs such as R&D and advertising		Inadequate externally generated information

Source: Institute for Practitioners in Work-Study, Organization, and Methods, Middlesex, England, Management Sciences 4, No. 5 pp. 15-24.

2. Management Decision Support System

A management decision support system is an independent set of decision aids that helps managers make relatively unstructured, perhaps non-recurring decisions. Fig. 14.6 presents information needs of executives responsible for strategic control in their firms and the internal functions responsible for finding, interpreting and passing on critical information to top managers.

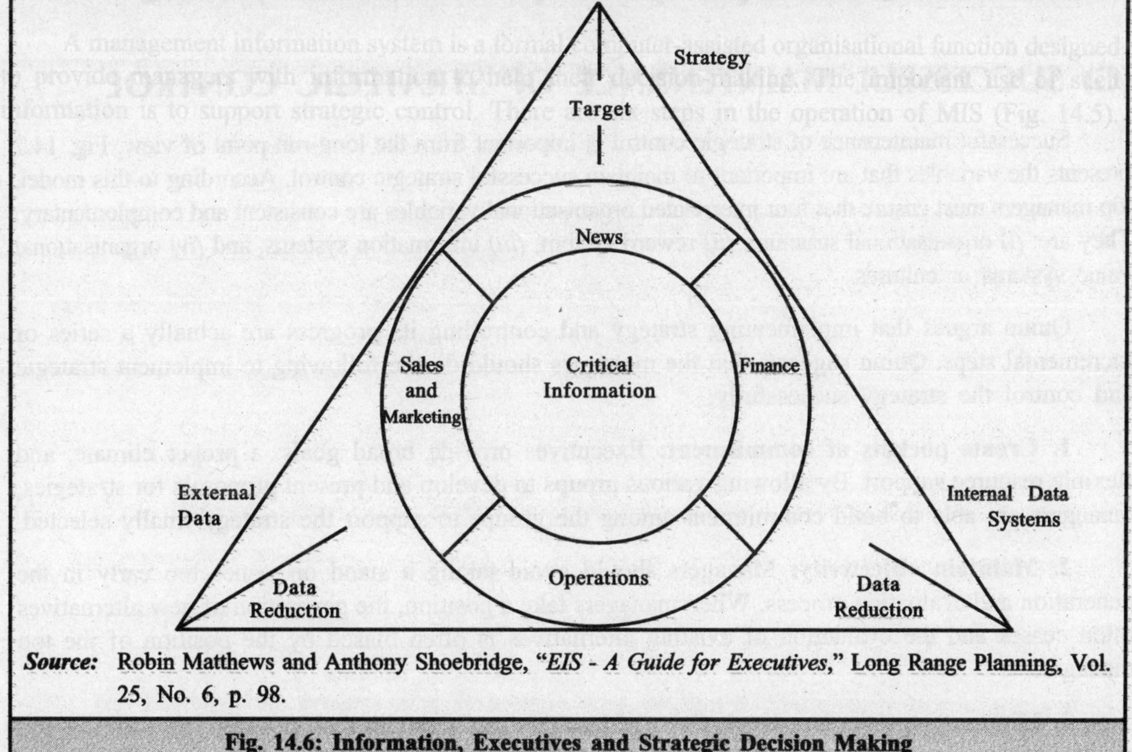

Source: Robin Matthews and Anthony Shoebridge, "*EIS - A Guide for Executives,*" Long Range Planning, Vol. 25, No. 6, p. 98.

Fig. 14.6: Information, Executives and Strategic Decision Making

(F) IMPLEMENTING STRATEGIC CONTROL

Strategic control is the primary responsibility of the strategist who formulated the strategy. However, it is the responsibility of all members of the organisation. All employees participate in the strategy implementation. Therefore, all employees can contribute to the control of strategic implementation process.

1. Role of the Strategy Planning Staff

Normally, the role of strategy planning, formulation, implementation and control go hand-in-hand. But, in some companies the roles of planning and control of strategy are separated. This practice is unfortunate as performing these two functions separately by two managers is too often inflexible and bureaucratic. Planning without control eliminates feed forward and control without planning eliminates feedback.

The best results of strategic control are achieved when the planning and control staff work as a team. When a strategic control team members represents a cross-section of the organisation, a number of advantages are likely to occur. Better judgements and insights should result from a diverse group. The team serves as a sounding board for the ideas of individual managers. Involvement in implementation and control gives other members a better comprehension of the problems associated with the new strategy.

2. Role of Top Management

Top level managers are primarily responsible for strategy formulation, analysis and implementation. Therefore, they should understand strategic control and take actions implies in the control process. Top managers should have a vision about the possible changes in the environment and their possible affect on the current strategy and feed this information forward to the staff at the ground. They must be committed to the strategic control process. Top managers are in leadership position and as such they should influence the organisational members in strategic control process.

(G) SUCCESSFUL MAINTENANCE OF STRATEGIC CONTROL

Successful maintenance of strategic control is important from the long-run point of view. Fig. 14.7 presents the variables that are important to maintain successful strategic control. According to this model, top managers must ensure that four interrelated organisational variables are consistent and complementary. They are: *(i)* organisational structure, *(ii)* reward system, *(iii)* information systems, and *(iv)* organisational value systems or cultures.

Quinn argues that implementing strategy and controlling its progress are actually a series of incremental steps. Quinn suggests that the managers should do the following to implement strategic and control the strategy successfully.

1. Create pockets of commitment: Executives provide broad goals, a proper climate, and flexible resource support. By allowing various groups to develop and present proposals for strategies, managers are able to build commitment among the groups to support the strategy finally selected.

2. Maintain objectivity: Managers should avoid taking a stand on issues too early in the generation and evaluation process. When managers take a position, the generation of new alternatives often ceases and the evaluation of existing alternatives is often biased by the position of the top manager.

3. Eliminate options two levels down: Managers can maintain their position of neutrality and avoid rejecting proposals by encouraging, discouraging, or killing options through subordinates.

4. Crystallize focus and consensus: By controlling membership on committees, managers are able to influence, and if desired, receive the proposals wanted. Properly selected committees can broaden support for and increase commitment to new strategies.

5. Empower champions: Managers are given responsibility for developing new ideas and programmes early. As the programme is evaluated and gains support, these individuals tend to become committed to the programme or strategy. Once it is given final approval, these managers are then willing to champion the strategy and to guide it through whatever hurdles are necessary to get it operating effectively.

6. Develop strategies incrementally, but not piecemeal: Part of management's responsibility is to make certain that strategies are integrated and appropriate for the environment in which the firm is operating. Strategies may be developed in incremental steps, but they must be made to fit together in a unified, integrated, and cohesive whole.

7. Recognise continuing dynamics: Strategies do not remain constant and fixed for long periods. Part of the executive's responsibility is to gain consensus and support for the new strategy, but at the same time room must be maintained to modify or terminate the strategy. Managers should use discretion in making certain that the organisation does not become overcommitted to the new strategy and unwilling to change at some future point.

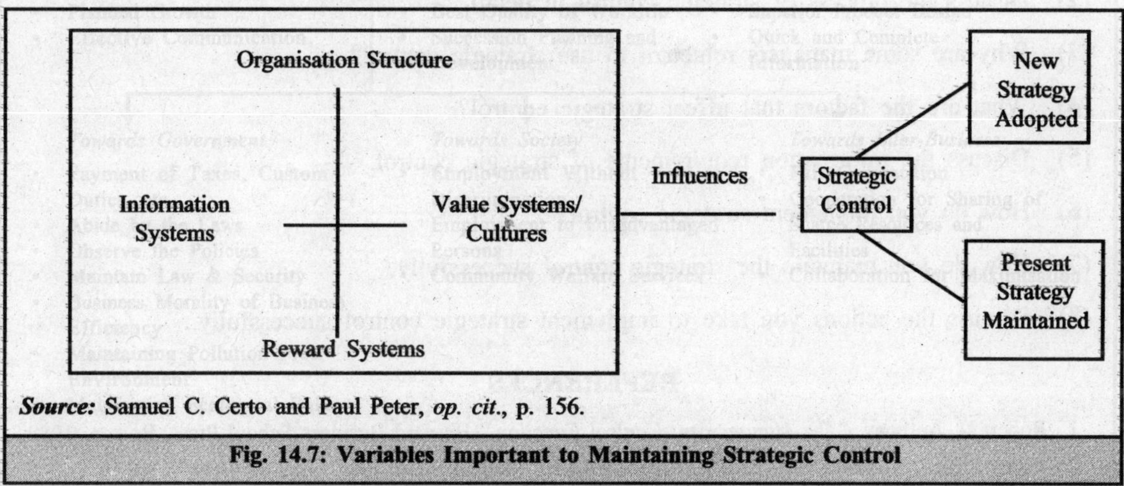

Source: Samuel C. Certo and Paul Peter, *op. cit.*, p. 156.

Fig. 14.7: Variables Important to Maintaining Strategic Control

POINTS TO BE REMEMBERED

- Control consists of making something happen the way it was planned to happen.
- Strategic control focusses on monitoring and evaluating the strategic management process to ensure that it functions in the right direction.
- The three key areas to be monitored and controlled are the microenvironment, the industry environment and internal operations.
- Strategic audit is an execution and evaluation of organisation's operations affected by the strategy implementation.
- Performance should be compared with predetermined standards.
- Take no action, performance is in harmony with standards
- Take appropriate correction action, when the performance is inferior to the standards.
- Strategies are motivated to formulate and implement strategies.
- The environment of the organisation is the greatest determinant of the appropriateness of the strategies.

KEY WORDS

- Control
- Standards
- Corrective Action
- Microenvironment
- Strategic Audit
- Stakeholder's Audit
- Strategic Momentum Control
- Strategic Control
- Quantitative Measures
- Microenvironment
- Qualitative Standards
- Weighted Performance
- Strategic Leap Control
- Management Information System

QUESTIONS FOR DISCUSSION

(1) What is strategic control? Discuss the purpose of strategic control.

(2) Discuss the process of strategic control in detail.

(3) Why are some managers reluctant to use strategic control?

(4) What are the factors that affect strategic control?

(5) Discuss the information requirements of strategic control.

(6) How do you implement strategic control?

(7) How do you maintain the strategic control successfully?

(8) Discuss the actions you take to implement strategic control successfully.

REFERENCES

1. Robert N. Anthony, "*The Management Control Function,*" Harvard Business School Press, Boston, 1988.
2. Henry Fayol, "*General and Industrial Management,*" Pitman Publishing, London, 1949, p. 107.
3. Peter Lorange, M.F.S. Morton and S. Ghoshal, "*Strategic Control,*" West Publishing, St. Paul, Minn, 1985.
4. Lawrence L. Steinmetz and H. Ralph Todd Jr., "*First Line Management,*" Richard D. Irwin, Homewood, 1986.
5. Fred R. David, *op. cit.*, p. 325.
6. Lawrence R. Jauch and William F. Gleuck, *op. cit.*, p. 377.
7. Samuel C. Certo and J. Paul Peter, *op. cit.*, p. 139.
8. Peter Wright, Charles D. Pringle and Mark J. Kroll, *op. cit.*, p. 203.
9. Samuel C. Certo and J. Paul Peter, *op. cit.*, pp. 139-140.
10. Seymour Tilles, "*How to Evaluate Corporate Strategy,*" Harvard Business Review, July-August 1963, pp. 111-121.
11. R.E. Freeman, "*Strategic Management: A Stakeholder Approach,*" Pitman, Boston, 1984, p. 25.
12. R. Kaufman, "*Preparing Useful Performance Indicators,*" Training and Development Journal, September 1989, pp. 80-83.
13. Robert W. Lewis, "*Measuring Reporting, and Appraising Results of Operations with Reference to Goals, Plans and Budgets,*" in Planning, Managing and Measuring the Business: A Case Study of Management Planning and Control at General Electric Company, Controllership Foundation, New York, 1955.
14. Joe G. Thomas, *op. cit.*, pp. 338-339.
15. Samuel C. Certo and J. Paul Peter, *op. cit.*, p. 149.

16. R. Hodgetts and M. Wortman, "*Administrative Policy,*" Wiley, New York, 1980, p. 128.
17. Lorange, Morton and Ghoshal, "*Strategic Control,*" p. 138.
18. *Ibid*., pp. 10-11.
19. *Ibid*., p. 11.
20. Joe G. Thomas, *op. cit.*, p. 346.
21. Lorange, Morton and Ghoshal, *op. cit.*, pp. 104-106.
22. *Ibid*., p. 112.
23. Samuel C. Certo and J. Paul Peter, *op. cit.*, p. 153.
24. Lorange, Morton and Ghoshal, *op. cit.*, p. 139.
25. Samuel C. Certo and J. Paul Peter, *op. cit.*, p. 156.
26. J.B. Quinn, "*Strategies for Change,*" Irwin, Homewood, 1980, pp. 126-138.

15

CHAPTER

STRATEGIC MANAGEMENT IN NON-PROFIT ORGANISATIONS

Chapter Outline

(A) Introduction

(B) Categories of Non-Profit Organisations

(C) Mission, Objectives and Goals

(D) Strategy Formulation and Implementation

(E) Popular Strategies of Non-Profit Organisations

(F) Strategic Evaluation and Control

(G) Measures to Control the Constraints

Learning Objectives

After studying this chapter, you should be able to:

- Understand different categories of non-profit organisations;
- Discuss the mission, objectives and goals of non-profit organisations;
- Analyse the process of strategy formulation and implementation of non-profit organisations;
- Discuss various popular strategies of non-profit organisations;
- Explain the strategic evaluation and control in non-profit organisations;
- Identify the measures to control the constraints.

(A) INTRODUCTION

Traditionally, studies in strategic management have dealt with profit making business organisations engaged in manufacturing and/or service. They neglected the non-profit organisations. The basic concepts of strategic management discussed in the earlier chapters are applicable to profit and nonprofit organisations. All organisations formulate the MOST, *i.e.*, Mission, Objectives, Strategies and Tactics. In fact, they analyse their environments — internal and external, formulate strategies, analyse and select the appropriate strategies, implement the strategies and evaluate and control the strategies. However, there are distinct differences between profit and non-profit organisations.

All organisations including non-profit formulate the MOST, *i.e.*, Mission, Objectives, Strategies and Tactics.

(B) CATEGORIES OF NON-PROFIT ORGANISATIONS

Non-profit organisations can be basically classified into two groups, *viz.*, *(i)* private non-profit organisations, and *(ii)* public non-profit organisations. Significant differences among profit organisations and non-profit private organisations are presented in Exhibit 15.1.

Exhibit 15.1: Differences between Profit and Non-Profit/Private Organisations

	Profit Organisations	*Non-profit/Private Organisations*
Ownership	Private	Private
Funding	Sales revenue	Membership fee, contributions from public and/or private sources, sale of products or services
Types	Single proprietorship, partnership, corporation	Floated by members
Activities	Production and/or Marketing of goods and/or services	Educational, charitable, social service, Health service, foundation, cultural, religious, and recreational
Main objective	Profit maximisation	Service maximisation

Significant differences between business and non-profit government organisations are presented in Exhibit 15.2.

Though, the public organisations like central government, state governments and local governments are also included under non-profit organisations, typically the term non-profit includes private non-profit organisations such as hospitals, private universities, private colleges, recreational societies, etc. Public utilities like transportation corporation, water supply corporations, dairy corporations are in a grey area somewhere between profit and non-profit organisations. Non-profit organisations assumes importance as the society particularly the low-income people depend on these organisations. Further, they provide services, which cannot be provided by the profit-making organisations.

1. Types of Non-Profit Organisations

The different types of non-profit organisations include:

(i) Private educational institutions like private universities, colleges, and schools

(ii) Charities.

(iii) Social service organisations.

(iv) Health service organisations like Sri Venkateswara Institute of Medical Sciences.

Exhibit 15.2: Significant Differences between Business and Public (Government) Organisations

	Business	*Public Non-Profit Organisations*
Main Objective	Profit	Public service
Economic Objectives	Profit required bankruptcy possible	No profit required bankruptcy unlikely
Structure	Frequently decentralised into profit centres	Usually a centralised bureaucracy
Accountable to	Shareholders	Representative of the people
Control of Strategy	Management	Representatives of the people
Scope of Activity	Unlimited, no monopoly	Limited, State monopoly
Major Sources of Funds	Shareholders, banks, financial companies	Government Taxation

Source: A. Waldansky. "The Politics of Budgetary Process." Little Brown and Company. Boston.. 1964.

(v) Foundations.

(vi) Cultural organisations.

(vii) Religions organisations like Tirumala-Tirupati Devasthanams and Shirdi Sai Samsthanams.

(viii) Social organisations.

Importance of Sources of Revenue

The sources of revenue is one of the important factors which differentiates the profit organisations and non-profit organisations. The profit organisations mainly depend upon the revenue of sales of goods and/or services. Their sources of income is the customer who buys and uses the product and/ or service, and who pays for it when received. Profit results when the revenue is more than the costs of producing and distributing the product. Profit is the main measure of the corporation's effectiveness.

The non-profit organisations depends on membership dues, assessments, donations, funding from sponsor agencies, subscriptions to the periodicals published by the organisations. Thus, revenue for these organisations comes from a variety of sources.

Strategic Issues in Non-profit Organisations

Strategic management is applicable for both profit-making organisations and non-profit organisations. Now, we discuss various issues of strategic management concerning to non-profit organisations. These issues include: formulation of mission, goals and objectives, environmental analysis, strategy formulation and implementation and strategic control.

(C) MISSION, OBJECTIVES AND GOALS

Even, non-profit organisation should have mission, objectives, and goals.

1. Mission

Formulation of well defined mission is important to non-profit organisations to have a clear direction. In fact, the major non-profit organisations formulate mission. According to Peter F. Drucker, "the best non-profits devote a great deal of thought to defining their organisation's mission."

The non-profit organisations while formulating the mission should consider the questions like: What is our business? Or what are our activities? Who is the customer? Or who are our clients? What does our customer (or client) consider the value? As Hesselbein explained, "more than any one thing, that made the difference. Because when you are clear about your mission, corporate goals and operating objectives flow from it."

As an example, the mission statement of one non-profit medical institute is:

"Our mission shall be the promotion of human knowledge within the field of the basic sciences (principally in the field of medical research and medical education) and the effective application thereof for the benefit of mankind."

The mission statement of a management educational institute is:

The establishment of a full-fledged management institute as an international centre of excellence for education, research and consultancy in all the areas of management.

2. Objectives and Goals

The non-profit organisations based on their mission statement, should formulate objectives and goals. But many non-profit organisations fail in this regard. Profit organisations can easily measure their production, sales, turnover, profits, market share, etc. But the non-profit organisations cannot have such clear goals. The reasons for the absence of clarity in goals are:

(i) Many goals of the non-profit organisations are value-laden.

(ii) Non-profit goals often involve important trade-offs.

(iii) Goals may often be deliberately vague, broad and general like. "Protect our environment," or "provide high quality education."

Goals in non-profit organisations are often vague because leadership is subject to frequent changes and it leads to change in direction.

Goals in non-profit organisations are often vague because leadership is subject to frequent changes and it leads to change in direction.

Goals may sometimes not reflect the needs of the organisation's customers/clients as much as they reflect the wishes of the organisations' financial donors. Some non-profit organisations, may not turn down substantial donations, if the donors insists that the funds be used for a purpose other than the basic mission of the organisation. In view of these observations, though, it is difficult to formulate goals compared to that in business firms, non-profit organisations should formulate goals. Formulation of objectives and goals will help the organisation to have a clear direction.

The non-profit organisations may formulate objectives and goals by considering the interests of all the stakeholders. They should bring balance among the conflicting interests of different stakeholders. The organisations can define specific, if not quantifiable objectives and goals. Methods of determining cost-benefit ratios and standards are essential. The standards like expenditure per client, norms for defining a deserving client may be determined. Such standards act as a surrogate performance measure when profit figures are not applicable.

The goals of the non-profit health organisation include:

(i) Community services like health, educational and environmental protection.

(ii) A centre for prevention of ill health, community problems.

(iii) Education for the community regarding health, sanitation, cleanliness, consumerism, etc.

(iv) Training and education of volunteers who will carry out the mission of the organisation like instructors, medical practitioners, religious priests, etc.

(v) Providing facilities for physicians, teachers, etc.

Determining the goals of a temple or church is equally perplexing. The goal to provide: *(i)* worship facilities, *(ii)* religious education, *(iii)* evangelical effort, *(iv)* missionary effort, *(v)* opportunities for members to fulfill social and psychological needs, *(vi)* fund raising for charitable organisations, *(vii)* contribution to the identification and solution of societal problems, *(viii)* contribution to the develoment of educational and health facilities like Sri Satya Sai Central Trust, *(ix)* revival of the ruined temples like Tirumala Tirupati Devasthanams. Exhibit 15.3 shows the objectives and goals of a management institute.

Exhibit 15.3: Objectives and Goals of a Management Institute 

Objectives:

To pursue the stated mission, the Institute strives to achieve the following objectives.

(i) To train young students, add the value, develop their competency and inculcate professionalism among them in order to prepare appropriate managers and entrepreneurs for Eritrean economy.

(ii) To undertake research studies with a view to provide inputs to the policy makers of the Government, and business.

(iii) To organize management development and training programmes with a view to equip practicing managers with latest skills and techniques of management profession.

(iv) To organize seminars and conferences in order to disseminate the advanced managerial knowledge to the practicing managers.

(v) To provide consultancy services with a view to solve the managerial and operational problems of Eritrean business.

(vi) To undertake any related activities to pursue the mission.

Strategies:

To achieve the above mentioned objectives, the following strategies are formulated.

(i) Strengthening teaching facilities like curriculum revision, preparation of qualitative course material and teaching aids.

(ii) Human resource development. It includes the development of junior staff through Ph.D., programmes of linkage Universities.

(iii) Secondment of senior faculty.

(iv) Support the library in the process of procurement of books and journals.

Goals:

Our goals during 1997-98 Academic Year are:

(i) Educate the students towards their M.B.A., degree with conceptual, practical skills and knowledge.

(ii) Modify the curriculum incorporating the courses relevant to Eritrean business.

(iii) Carryout the research studies in the areas of

- *(a)* Human Resource Management and
- *(b)* International marketing

(iv) Provide Tutorial classes for the government officers who are pursuing Certificate course in Management of the Open University UK.

(v) Provide consultancy services.

(vi) Organisation of National and International Seminars and Conferences.

(vii) Conduct Management Development and Training Programmes.

(D) STRATEGY FORMULATION AND IMPLEMENTATION

The strategies of non-profit organisations complement the strategies and services of governmental agencies.

Strategy formulation is more or less the same in non-profit organisations compared to that of profit organisations. In general most of the organisations attempt to satisfy specific social needs. The strategies of non-profit organisations complement the strategies and services of governmental agencies. For example, the strategies of Ministry of Health, Government of India and the non-profit health organisations strategies are more or less similar. They include: providing medical and health facilities to the people, development of hospitals and health clinics, development of doctors and para-medical personnel etc. Some non-profit organisations have the distinct strategies. However, they are comparable with the corporate strategies. Exhibit 15.4 shows the growth strategies for churches.

Exhibit 15.4: Growth Strategies for Churches

One of the nation's largest churches is Willow-creek Community Church in South Barrington, illinois, a Chicago suburb. Although the church was founded only in 1974, it now has over thirteen thousand parishioners. Its founder and pastor, Bill Hybels, adopted the growth strategy, based on business fundamentals. He originally went door to door asking people why they did not attend church. From this market research, he began to offer services that catered to the needs of his "customers." For instance, he holds full services on Wednesday evenings because some working parents prefer to spend Sundays with their children. And for those unable to attend any of the services, he provides his sermons on cassette tapes.

Another huge religious institution following a growth strategy is Houston's Second Baptist Church. With a Sunday morning attendance of twelve thousand, the church complex covers 32 acres. In 1984, however, the church was simply a conventional church on a large plot of land. Its incoming pastor, H. Edwin Young, was familiar with the demographics of the area: thousands of young families and single people new to Houston. He sold his vision of a growing church to his congregation and persuaded them to pledge over $1 million needed for new physical facilities while the church borrowed over $26 million for additional construction costs.

Pastor Young dispatched church members to study office management techniques at Xerox and IBM and parking and people skills at Disney World. He varied religious services to fit particular needs. In addition to the traditional Sunday morning service, there is a Sunday evening servicc that catcrs to a mostly singles crowd; and on Wednesday nights, separate services are offered, one traditional and one with religious rock music.

Today, computers regulate mood lighting during church services; shuttle buses bring latecomers in from outlying parking decks; parking attendants empty the church's numerous parking lots every Sunday in half an hour; billboards and television ads invite people to visit this "Fellowship of Excitement"; an information desk is staffed with cheerful beginning at 6:00 A.M.; and a restaurant offers two types of menus: "saints" for those who prefer a low-calorie meal and "sinners" for those who desire richer food.

Sources: R.G. Niebuhr. "Megachurches Strive to Be All Things to All Parishioners." *The Wall Street Journal*. 13 May 1991: P.F. Drucker. "What Business Can Learn from Non-profits." *Harvard Business Review* 67. No. 4 (1989): 89.

Sometimes, the strategies of non-profit organisations particularly government agencies differ from those of corporate strategies. One of the important reasons for the difference is the presence of greater political constraints upon their strategic choices. Most of the decisions in public organisations are to be approved by the ministers, parliaments or the legislative assemblies. These bodies politicalise the strategic decisions by their public visibility in the press. The rules, regulations, procedures and formalities of public organisations complicate the process of strategy formulation.

1. Constraints on Strategic Management

Though, there are some common features of the strategic management in profit and non-profit organisations, non-profit organisations are different from profit-making organisations. There are a number of characteristics peculiar to the non-profit organisations that constrain their behaviour and affect their strategic management. Newman and Wallender list the following five constraining characteristics:

(i) Service is often intangible and hard to measure. This problem is compounded by the existence of multiple service objectives developed in order to satisfy multiple sponsors.

(ii) Client influence may be weak. Often the organisation has a local monopoly, and payments by customers may be a very small source of funds.

(iii) Strong employee commitment to profession or to a cause may undermine their allegiance to the organisation employing them.

(iv) Resource contributors — notably fund contributors and government — may intrude upon the organisation's internal management.

Stakeholder Constraints on Public Organisations are shown in Fig 15.1.

In view of these constraints, the strategic management process for any given situation will be different in a non-profit organisation than in a profit making organisation.

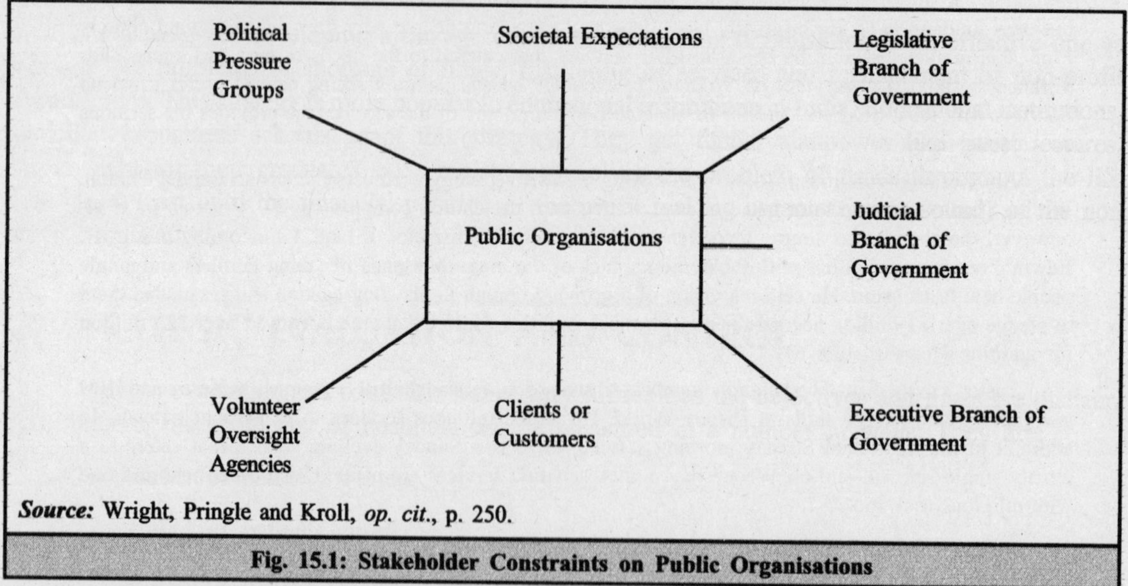

Source: Wright, Pringle and Kroll, *op. cit.*, p. 250.

Fig. 15.1: Stakeholder Constraints on Public Organisations

2. Impact of Constraints on Strategy Formulation

The above mentioned constraints affect the long-range planning and decision-making. The complications arise in strategy formulation are:

(i) **Goal Conflicts Interfere with Rational Planning:** Divergent goals and objectives are likely as the non-profit organisations typically lacks a single and clear-cut goal. Different interests of the sponsors may prevent the management from formulating the goals. The low influence of the clients permits the organisation to have diversified values and goals to occur. This goal conflicting situation interfere with rational planning of the organisation.

(ii) **An Integrated Planning Focus Tends to Shift from Results to Resources:** There is almost no net bottom line as non-profit organisations tend to provide services that are hard to measure. Therefore, planning is concerned with the resource inputs than the service outcomes.

(iii) **Ambiguous Operating Objectives Create Opportunities for Internal Politics and Goal Displacement:** The combination of vague objectives and resource concern give a room for more self interest than the organisational interest. There is a scope to ignore the clients as the organisation concentrates on satisfying the sponsors than the clients. Even the Board of the Trustees are selected on the basis of their ability to mobilise funds rather than managerial experience. These factors result in goal displacement and creation of politics.

(iv) **Professionalisation Simplifies Detailing Planning but Adds Rigidity:** The professional employees contribute to the detailed planning. But the systematic and scientific operations as applicable to business organisations are applied by the professionals to the strategic planning. This adds rigidity.

3. Impact of Constraints on Strategy Implementation

The constraining characteristics affect the organisation structure and job design of the non-profit organisation. The complications are:

***(i)* Decentralisation is Complicated:** Decentralisation and delegation of decision-making authority is complicated due to the absence of clear cut goals and hard to measure output *i.e.,* service. Therefore, the decision-making is centralised. Further, the defensive centralisation is necessary to avoid the objections of the sponsors.

***(ii)* Linking Pins for External-Internal Integration become Important:** As indicated earlier, the non-profit organisations excessively depend upon the external sources for funds particularly the sponsors, and donors. Some employees should act as linking pins between the internal operations and external sponsors. Some organisations employ public relations officers or fund raising officers.

***(iii)* Job Enrichment and Executive Development:** Job enrichment and executive development may be restrained by professionalism. Employment of Professionals at various levels will restrain job enrichment as it is viewed as encroachment into the authority of the next higher level professional.

(E) POPULAR STRATEGIES OF NON-PROFIT ORGANISATIONS

The general objective of non-profit organisations is to satisfy an ultimate need of a segment of a general public. The organisation expands its activities, if the revenue is more than the cost. In contrast, the organisations reduces its activities, if the expenses are more than the revenue. Some organisations change their missions in order to attract new sponsors and carry out activities different from the existing ones. But more organisations rejects such donations and they stick to their missions. Such organisations impose pressure on their members to increase membership contributions and enable the organisations to carry out their activities successfully. Three popular strategies are: (1) Strategic piggybacking, (2) inter-organisational linking, and (3) Linkage with a profit making organisation.

Three popular strategies of non-profit organizations are: (1) Strategic piggybacking, (2) inter-organisational linking, and (3) Linkage with a profit making organisation.

1. Strategic Piggybacking

The term strategic piggybacking is coined by Neilsen. This term refers to the development of a new activity for the non-profit organisations for the purpose of generating funds needed to make-up the deficits in the budget. The new activity is taken up primarily to subsidise the primary service activities. Further, the new activity may be somewhat related to the existing activities even, indirectly. Top management invests in new, safe cash cows to fund its current cash-hungry stars, question marks and stars, in an inverted use of portfolio analysis.

Strategic piggybacking refers to the development of a new activity for the non-profit organisations for the purpose of generating funds needed to makeup the deficits in the budget.

Edward Skloot, President of the New York Consulting firm New Ventures suggests that a non-profit organisation have five resources before beginning a revenue-earning activity. They are:

(i) *Something to sell:* The organisation should see whether it can find a market for its goods or services.

(ii) *Critical mass of management talent:* There must be enough people available to nurture and sustain an income venture over the long haul.

(iii) *Trustee support:* Trustees may actively or passively resist commercial involvement, if they do not like earned-income ventures.

(iv) *Entrepreneurial attitude:* Management must be able to combine an interest in innovative ideas with business like practicality.

(v) *Venture capital:* Engaging a joint venture with a business organisation can provide necessary funds to initiate the activities as well as marketing and management support.

2. Inter-Organisational Linkage

A major strategy often employed by non-profit organisations to increase their ability to serve clients efficiently or to acquire resources is developing cooperative ties with other organisations. Non-profit hospitals increasingly use this strategy as a way to cope up with raising costs or declining revenues. Through the co-operation with other hospitals, services can be purchased and provided more efficiently than if done alone.

3. Linkage with a Profit-Making Organisation

The strategy of developing a linkage with a profit making organisation is an effective one as it solves the problems of shortage of funds, marketing of services and management of non-profit organisations. This strategy is more popular in educational institutions in India. Educational institutions, particularly business schools adapt this strategy. They get funds, manpower like guest lectures, employment for their graduates etc. This strategy solves the problem of funds throughout the life time (or at least until the financial position of the profit making organisation is sound) of the non profit organisation.

(F) STRATEGIC EVALUATION AND CONTROL

Strategic evaluation and control is rather very difficult as the objectives and goals are unclear. For example, the efficiency of hospitals can be measured in a number of ways. They are:

(i) number of patients treated,

(ii) number of patients cured,

(iii) number of medical doctors,

(iv) number of total staff,

(v) number of beds, etc. These controls may not be effective without formulating goals clearly.

Similarly the efficiency of educational institutions can also be measured in a number of ways. They are:

(i) number of and level of courses the institutions is offering,

(ii) number of and level of staff,

(iii) number of students registered,

(iv) number of students successfully completing their courses every year,

(v) number of students getting placements, etc. These standards are also not effective unless the goals are clearly stated.

Obviously, control is more difficult, when goals are not clear or when goals are conflicting. Some non-profit organisations have literally no goals.

However, the strategies of non-profit organisations may be evaluated in one aspect. This approach to evaluation in the absence of quantifiable objectives, is being cost-aware and concentrating upon making the operation efficient, *i.e.,* to achieve the same output with less input. However, if the organisation does not have objectives/goals, the importance of a budget-based organisation is determined by the size of its staff and the size of its budget.

1. Impact of the Constraints on Evaluation and Control

There are two problems caused by the constraints discussed earlier. They are:

***(i)* Rewards and Penalties have Little or no Relation to Performance:** When the objectives and goals are unclear or conflicting, the results expected are vague. Under such situations, judgement about performance is subjective. Performance is judged either intuitively or on the basis of those small aspects of a job that can be measured. Therefore, the rewards and punishments have little or no relation to performance.

***(ii)* Control the Inputs Heavily Rather than Output:** The non-profit organisations may control the in puts heavily rather than out put, as inputs can be measured than output as stated earlier. Therefore, more emphasis may be laid on controlling costs and expenses.

(G) MEASURES TO CONTROL THE CONSTRAINTS

The non-profit organisation can deal with the complications arising from the constraints to some extent through the following measures.

***(i)* Select a Dynamic and Forceful Leader:** The leader should be selected based on values to be used in decision-making, enough power to make important choices, be influential to make the others to accept his/her decisions. The leader can formulate appropriate mission, objectives and goals and raise to approach that the decisions are pushed from top to the down. Therefore, the lower level managers should adapt the approaches of 'play it safe,' 'await the guidance', etc.

***(ii)* Develop a Mystique:** The non-profit organisation can be integrated toward efficient goal accomplishment by developing a 'mystique' that dominates the enterprise and attracts the likely sponsors. The shared value about the important mission by the employees and sponsors can serve to motivate unusually high performance and client satisfaction. Once established, the mystique sets the character and values to decision-makers and others are expected to follow.

***(iii)* Generate Rules and Regulations:** The non-profit organisations suffer from the absence of objectives and goals and concentrating on the sponsors rather than clients. Hence, the top management should formulate rules and regulations so that the employees will pay enough attention towards the clients.

***(iv)* Appointment of a Strong Board:** Appointment of a strong board of trustees will help the organisation in funds raising, formulation of mission and objectives. Then the employees can concentrate on the clients. The board can concentrate on strategic issues as well as on the operational issues like hiring, directing and developing the budget.

***(v)* Establishment of Performance-based Budgets:** Establishment of performance-based budgets is the fifth approach in dealing with complications of non-profit organisations. This approach is to institute an information system that ties measurable objectives to budget line items. One such system is planning, programming and budgeting system. It includes five steps:

(a) Specify objectives as clearly as possible in quantitative measurable terms.

(b) Analyse the actual output of the non-profit organisation in terms of the stated objectives.

(c) Measure the cost of the particular programme.

(d) Analyse the alternatives and search for those that have the greatest effectiveness in achieving the objectives.

(c) Establish the process in a systematic way, so that it continues to occur over time.

POINTS TO BE REMEMBERED

- Non-profit organisations are of two groups, *viz.*, private non-profit organisations and public non-profit organisations.
- Types of non-profit organisations are educational institutions hospitals, charities, social service organisations, foundations, cultural organisations and social organisations.
- Goals of non-profit organisations are value-laden, trade-offs and provide high quality service.
- Strategy formulation is more or less the same in non-profit organisations compared to that of private and profit oriented organisations.
- There are certain constraints on strategy formulation and implemetation of non-profit organisations.
- Popular strategies of non-profit organisations include strategic piggybacking, inter-organisational linkage, and linkage with other non-profit organisations.
- Non-profit organisations deal with the complications arising from the constraints to some extent.

KEY WORDS

- Non-profit Organisations
- Constraints
- Inter-organisational Linkage
- Strategic Piggybacking
- Mission
- Objectives
- Strategy
- Goal
- Charities
- Social Organisations
- Structure
- Educational institutions
- Hospitals
- Religious organisations

QUESTIONS FOR DISCUSSION

1. What are non-profit Organisations? Discuss various types of non-profit organisations.
2. Discuss mission, objectives and goals of non-profit organisations.
3. How do you formulate strategies for non-profit organisations?
4. How do you implement strategies for non-profit organisations?
5. What are the popular strategies for non-profit organizations?
6. Discuss the process of strategy evaluation and control in non-profit organisations?
7. Suggest measures to control the constraints of strategic management in non-profit organisations.
8. Describe the strategic management process in non-profit organisations.

REFERENCES

1. Peter F. Drucker, "*What Business can Learn from Non-profits,*" Harvard Business Review, vol. 67, No. 4, 1989, p. 89.
2. Brayne, "*Profiting from the Non-profits,*" p. 72.
3. The Annual Report of the Howard Hughes Medical Institute 1989.
4. P.D. Harvey and J.D. Synder, "*Charities Need a Bottom Line Too,*" Harvard Business Review, Vol. 65, no. 1, 1987, pp. 14-22.
5. David E. Hussey, "*Corporate Planning for a Church,*" Long Range Planning, April 1974, p. 63.
6. W.H. Newman and H.W. Wallender III, "*Managing Non-profit Enterprises,*" Academy of Management Review, January 1978, p. 26.
7. P.C. Nutt, "*A Strategic Planning Network for Non-Profit Organisations,*" Strategic Management Journal, January-March, 1984, p. 57.
8. R.P. Nilsen, "*SMR Forum: Strategic Piggybacking — A Self Subsidising Strategy for Non-profit Institutions,*" Sloan Management Review, Summer 1982, pp. 65-69.

   R.P. Nilsen, "*Piggybacking for Business and Non-Profits: A Strategy for Hard Times,*" Long-Range Planning, April 1984, pp. 96-102.
9. Thomas L. Wheeler and J. David Hunger, *op. cit.*, p. 304.
10. E. Skloot, "*Should Non-profits Go into Business,*" Harvard Business Review, January-February 1983, pp. 20-26.
11. *Ibid.*, p. 24.
12. K.C. Provan, "*Inter-organisational Co-operation and Decision Making Autonomy in a Consortium Multi-hospital System,*" Academy of Management Review, July 1984, pp. 494-504.
13. Thomas L. Wheeler and J. David Hunger, *op. cit.*, p. 305.
14. Peter F. Drucker, "*Management: Tasks, Responsibilities and Practices,*" p. 142.
15. W.H. Newman and H.W. Wallender III, *op. cit.*, p. 28.
16. E.H. Fram, "*Changing Expectations for Third Sector Executives,*" Human Resource Management, Fall 1980, p. 9.
17. Keating B.P. and Keating M.O., "*Not For Profit,*" *Thomas Horton and Daughters, New Jersey,* 1980, pp. 140-141.

◆ ◆ ◆

16 CHAPTER SOCIAL RESPONSIBILITIES AND ETHICS OF BUSINESS

Chapter Outline

(A) Introduction
(B) Social Responsibilities of Business
(C) Business Ethics
(D) Value-Based Management

Learning Objectives

After studying this chapter, you should be able to:

- Understand the rationale behind the traditional view of social responsibility of business;
- Evaluate why the modern view of social responsibility of business has emerged;
- Discuss the arguments for and against social responsibilities of business;
- Discuss the social responsibilities of business towards consumers/customers, employees, shareholders/stockholders, Government, other business firms and community;
- Scan the external environment and analyse its impact on business;
- Understand the meaning of ethics and business ethics;
- Discuss the need for business ethics with practical incidents;
- Evaluate the ethical principles need to be followed in business organisations;
- Discuss the ethical climate and need for following the ethical principles in business;
- Know some of the unethical practices that the business organisations resort to;
- Appraise the code of business ethics;
- Discuss the values that form the basis for conduct of business under value-based management;
- Understand Dharmic principles, Indian ethos and Principles from Bhagavat Gita and other Indian Texts;
- Appreciate the relevance of values drawn from Indian Texts to modern management.

(A) INTRODUCTION

From the above case incident, it creates a curiosity in our cognition to know what is social responsibility? Now, shall we discuss the concept of social responsibility?

Traditional View of Social Responsibility

Traditional view: Business's business is business.

In traditional societies, the prime purpose of business was profit maximisation. Even as late as 1970, Milton Friedman stated that '*the business of business is business*'. In other words, the only objective of business is the making of profits. Friedman argues that the profit earned by business belongs exclusively to the shareholders of the business and these profits cannot be diverted to any other social purpose. He defended his argument by saying that "if the executive uses corporate resources for social ends, he is using the money for the purposes for which it was not intended... " He further states that "there is one and only one social responsibility of business – to use its resources and engage in activities designed to increase its profits..." John Lodd expressed a similar opinion in 1970, saying "it is improper to expect organisational conduct to conform to the ordinary principles of morality..."

However, most academicians, economists, socialists, philosophers, politicians and even businessmen and bankers do not compromise with these opinions. It is doubtful whether these opinions hold good today, especially during the post liberalisation era. T.A. Mathias felt that "moral behaviour pays….at least in the long run." An enlightened approach aims at long-run objectives and not mere short-run gains. The days of traditional views are gone. Now, we shall study the modern view towards social responsibilities.

Modern View of Social Responsibility

Modern view: Business is not an end in itself.

It is now being increasingly recognised that business is not an end in itself. It is only a means to an end. That end is man, be it a worker, customer, consumer or any member of society. It is also recognized that business is a social and economic institution which cannot live in isolation.

The establishment and development of business is dependent on the contributions made by society. Society has to bear the cost and consequences of the establishment and operation of business. It has to allot land, supply water and other materials, provide infrastructural facilities and develop and provide human resources. In addition to this, consumers who are members of society, allow the business to continue its operations by creating effective demand for the goods and services produced/rendered or distributed by the business.

Thus, business is mostly dependent upon society. Realising this, most of the businessmen today, feel that their objective is not merely profit maximisation but it also consists of contributing something towards solving the problems of their employees, consumers and society at large. Here it is appropriate to state that, "a socially and ethically conscious firm and its managers should, therefore, look upon profits not as the be-all and end-all of their operations.." '*Social Audit*' is one such technique used to measure performance. Exhibit 16.1 presents the summary of major arguments for and against social responsibilities of business.

Exhibit 16.1: Summary of Major Agruments for and against Social Responsibility for Business For Social Responsibility

- It is in the best interest of a business to promote and improve the communities where it does business.
- Social action can be profitable.
- It is an ethical thing to do.
- It improves the public image of the firm.
- It increases the viability of the business system. Business exists because it gives society benefits. Society can amend or take away its charter. This is the 'iron law of responsibility.'
- It is necessary to avoid government regulation.
- Socio-cultural norms require it.
- Laws cannot be passed for all circumstances. Thus, business must assume responsibility to maintain an orderly legal society.
- It is in the stockholders' best interest. It will improve the price of stock in the long run as the stock market will view the company as less risky and open to public attack.
- Society should give business a chance to solve social problems that the government has failed to solve.
- Business is considered by some groups to be the institution with the financial and human resources to solve social problems.
- Prevention of problems is better than cures-so let business solve problems before they become critical.

Against Social Responsibility

- It might be illegal.
- Business plus government equal monolith.
- Social actions cannot be measured.
- It violates profit maximisation.
- The cost of social responsibility is too great and would increase prices too much.
- Business lacks social skills to solve societal problems.
- It would weaken the balance of payments because price of goods will have to go up to pay for social programs.
- Business already has too much power. Such involvement would make business too powerful.
- Business lacks accountability to the public.
- Such business involvement lacks broad public support.

(***Source:*** Adapted from R.Joseph Monsen, Jr., *The Social Attitudes of Management*, in Joseph W.McQuire, ed., *Contemporary Management (Englewood Cliffs,N.J.:Prentice Hall, 1974)*, p. 616. Quoted in Certo and Peter, p. 222.)

Thus, it is accepted today that the business has to discharge its responsibility towards society. The concept of 'Social Responsibility of Business' includes responsibilities towards itself, shareholders, employees, other business firms, government, customers/consumers, creditors and the society.

This declaration also emphasised certain main features of Social Responsibility of Business, *viz.*,

- In addition to making a fair and adequate return on capital, business must be just and humane, as well as efficient and dynamic.
- The social responsibilities of business can best be assumed in an atmosphere of freedom with the least possible restraint on healthy competition.
- Every business has an overriding responsibility to make the fullest possible use of its resources, both human and capital.

- It highlights the respective roles of the enterprises, the shareholders, the workers, the customers, the management and the community.
- It laid emphasis on the reciprocal duties between business and the community.

(B) SOCIAL RESPONSIBILITIES OF BUSINESS

The social responsibilities of Business, in the Indian context are presented in Fig. 16.1

Now, we shall study the social responsibilities of business towards different stakeholders, *viz.*, consumers/customers, employees, shareholders/stockholders, other business firms, state and community.

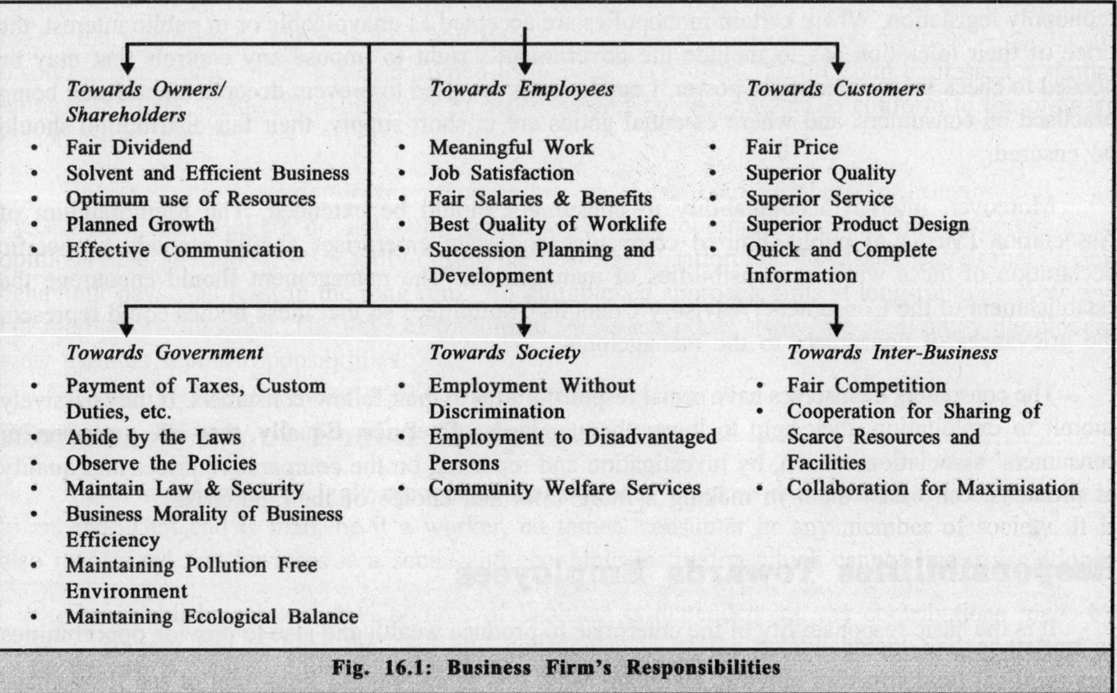

Fig. 16.1: Business Firm's Responsibilities

Responsibilities Towards Consumers/Customers

Consumer satisfaction is the ultimate aim of all economic activity. This includes:

- the goods must meet the needs of the consumers of different classes, tastes and the purchasing power;
- they must be reasonably priced, be of a dependable quality and of sufficient variety;
- the sale of such goods must be followed by after sales service to ensure advice, guidance and maintenance;
- there should be a fair and wide spread distribution of goods and services among all the sections of consumers and community, and
- there should be prevention of concentration of goods in the hands of a limited number of producers, purchasers or groups.

In other words, business owes to itself the primary obligation to give a fair and square deal to its customers and consumers. They should be charged a fair and reasonable price which should

Business owes to itself the primary obligation to give a fair and square deal to its customers and consumers.

be well within their reach. The supply of goods should be of uniform standard and of reasonably good quality. Their distribution must be widespread as to be within the easy reach of the consumer. No business should directly or indirectly indulge in profiteering, hoarding or creating artificial scarcity. Business should not mislead the consumer and community by false, misleading and exaggerated advertisements, because obscene advertisements are demoralizing the society and a danger to public morals.

Consumer satisfaction is the ultimate aim of all economic activity. But adulteration of goods, poor quality, failure to give fair measure, lack of service and courtesy to the customer, misleading and dishonest advertising, are all examples of violation of its obligations by a business enterprise towards the consumers.

Therefore, free competition must be allowed to operate and should be encouraged by anti-monopoly legislation. Where certain monopolies are accepted as unavoidable or in public interest, the price of their toleration has to include the government's right to impose any controls that may be needed to check undue monopoly power. Legislation is required to prevent deception and fraud being practised on consumers, and where essential goods are in short supply, their fair distribution should be ensured.

Moreover, internal accountability to consumers should be extended. The Memorandum of Association (MoA) of public limited companies and state enterprises should embody a specific declaration of these wider responsibilities of management. The management should encourage the establishment of the Consumers' Advisory Councils/Committees so that these bodies could represent the grievances of consumers to the management.

The consumers themselves have social responsibilities to their fellow-consumers. If they passively submit to exploitation, they help to lower the standards of service. Equally, they are a support to consumers' associations which, by investigation and reporting on the comparative prices and quality of products, can assist them in making a more informed choice of their purchases.

Responsibilities Towards Employees

The management should develop its administration in such a way so as to promote a spirit of cooperative endeavour between employers and employees.

It is the basic responsibility of the enterprise to produce wealth and also to provide opportunities for meaningful work. The management should develop its administration in such a way so as to promote a spirit of cooperative endeavour between employers and employees. There should be a sense of participation between capital, on the one hand, and labour and skill, on the other, in their objective towards prosperity and progress. The cooperation of workers can be won by creating conditions in which workers are enabled to put forward their best efforts in the common task as free men. This means recognition:

- of the workers' right to a fair wage;
- of the right to participate in decisions affecting their working life;
- to membership of the trade union;
- to collective bargaining and
- to the right to strike.

Management should give workers opportunity to develop their capabilities through training, education and enjoyment of freedom to the greatest possible extent. Management should develop among workers a sense of belonging to the business and provide them with healthy living conditions, cheap houses, leisure and amenities, profit-sharing and an efficient system of communication.

The business or a plant is a community and justice should be its rule. This means there should be a company code of conduct with a recognised procedure for settling grievances which result in improved performance. The code should guarantee religious, political and social independence of the workers and make reasonable provisions for them to take part in civic activities which benefit the community.

The image of business should be improved in the eyes of the workers so that persons of high calibre and capacity could be drawn to it. Routine monotony and boredom should be broken by job enrichment and job enlargement programmes. Finally, industrial peace and new techniques of professional management must be ensured within the precincts of the industry itself.

Likewise, workers should realise their moral duty to do a good day's job for a good day's salary, to cooperate in increasing productivity, to come forward with suggestions and to participate in discharging their responsibility to the life of the plant and the community.

Responsibilities Towards Owners/Shareholders

Management's first duty is to see that enterprise is stable, enterprising and actively engaged in accomplishing its objectives. It would then be capable of providing those who commit their capital to it with such a fair and adequate reward for risk taken. It permits the company to attract the necessary capital from the market. This capital is raised by the owners (proprietors, retailers, wholesalers, sole-traders) owning business, its property and looking after its management; the share of stockholders who contribute to the shares and debentures of the company or the partners (if there are any).

Responsibility towards Owners: a fair and reasonable return on the capital invested by them.

The expectations of these types of owners are:

- a fair and reasonable return on the capital invested by them;
- a part in profit, if the Memorandum so specifies, in the shape of profit-sharing or bonus payment schemes;
- political and economic security for investment through a stable government, good law and order situation and stable tax policies and fiscal measures;
- knowledge about the working of the enterprise, its periodical progress report, so that they may be satisfied that their capital has been faithfully and usefully employed;
- a fair amount of dividend or retained earnings; and
- profiteering, black-marketing, cornering of supplies, unfair trade practices are curbed and legally prohibited.

The shareholders also have their obligations. Shareholders in the General Meetings should question the Directors on the accounts and discuss policy matters and make their representation more effective through their associations. They can thus ensure that the company is pursuing a dynamic policy and that sufficient profit is laid aside for innovation and expansion. They should play a constructive role in encouraging the directors to pursue a responsible policy towards the company, its obligations to the community, employees and customers, upon which in the long run, the company's reputation and future prospects depend.

Responsibilities Towards Inter-Business

The social responsibilities of business include a healthy co-operative business relationship between different businesses. Businessmen must resist unfair and unethical competition and avoid unfair interference in their rival's business such as price-rigging, undercutting, patronage, unfair canvassing, supply of substandard goods, application of undue financial, legal and political pressure; spreading false rumours/statements about the rival's products, creating labour troubles for the competitors' industry or launching a boycott campaign of their products, employing unethical advertisements and controlling the supply of particular goods/services produced by them only so that an artificial scarcity is created in the market, giving rise to monopolistic conditions, artificial high prices as per quality of goods, etc.

Destructive competition is always harmful, as it destroys confidence in business and introduces chaos instead of order and discipline. Therefore, the correct solution is not retaliation but the development of true ideas among the business community and to secure such legal regulation as is necessary to protect businessmen. A good businessman should adopt fair means to meet his rival's competition. This may be by adopting better designs, good advertisements, quick and safe delivery with after-sales service, reasonable price, etc.

It is needless to say, that unfair competition enters with extortion, bribery, kick backs and granting of discriminatory advertising allowances or brokerage fees and these should be avoided at all costs.

Responsibilities Towards the State

Responsibility towards State: be a law-abiding citizen.

The social responsibilities of business towards the state (government) demands that:

It will: —

- be a law-abiding citizen;
- pay its dues and taxes to the state fully and honestly;
- not corrupt public servants and the democratic process for his selfish ends;
- not purchase political support by unfair means;
- strive fairly and honestly to stimulate economic growth even by making reasonable sacrifices on occasions of national need;
- participate in the public life of the country in helping to make policies, fair legislation and working on advisory bodies;
- sell his goods, commodities and services without adulteration at fair and reasonable prices; and
- maintain fair trade practices and refrain from activities like restraint of trade and will not take recourse to hoarding, cornering and profiteering and other such unfair practices.

The government has also some obligations towards business, such as to provide:

- a clean, prompt and efficient administration;
- intelligent, practical laws, easily understood and easily applied;
- reasonable political and social stability without frequent changes in legislative, administrative and fiscal policies;
- law and order ensuring safety of life, property and continuing business;
- a dynamic framework for rapid economic growth (infrastructure, legal aid);
- rule of law;
- holding of scales evenly between groups and sections in society;
- political and social stability where business can grow and develop;
- reasonable legislation for protecting units of business against monopoly; and
- healthy atmosphere to industrial peace.

Unfortunately, both have failed to fulfil their reciprocal obligations because of the following causes (See Box 16.1).

BOX 16.1 PALIN ATTACKS FED ON HONG KONG VISIT, WANTS 'RESPONSIBLE CHINA'

Former Republican vice-presidential candidate Sarah Palin used her first trip to Asia to attack the Federal Reserve for creating asset bubbles and encouraging excessive risk-taking that hurt working-class Americans. In a wide-ranging, 80-minute speech to fund managers in Hong Kong today, Palin spoke about issues ranging from Alaskan fishing to energy independence to U.S.-Sino ties. She repeated calls for "market-oriented" health-care reform and said governments shouldn't regulate executive compensation.

The Fed and the government sent a message to companies that "the bigger that you are, the more problems that you get yourself into, the more likely the government is to bail you out," Palin said in the closed door speech, according to a tape of the event given to Bloomberg News. "Of course the little guys are left out then. We're left holding the bag, all the moms and pops all over America." The speech was Palin's first major public appearance since quitting as Alaska governor on July 26, less than a year after she ran with John McCain in an unsuccessful campaign against now-President Barack Obama. People at the event said she focused on a wide range of global and domestic issues rather than her own political future. "It was a very safe speech," said Suyeon An of RCM Asia Pacific Ltd, who left before Palin stopped talking. "Boring I have to say."

Palin, 45, spoke to a full house in the main ballroom of Hong Kong's Grand Hyatt hotel. Reporters were kept out of the investor forum organized by CLSA Asia-Pacific Markets, the regional brokerage unit of Paris-based Credit Agricole SA. "It was a great speech," Jonathan Slone, CLSA's chief executive officer, said. "People got a lot of information" and "are now fully informed on Sarah Palin's views."

Palin criticized Obama's plan to give the Fed powers to monitor risks to the financial system. A meltdown last year led to $1.6 trillion of bank losses and writedowns and triggered a global recession. "How can we think that setting up the Fed as monitor of systemic risk in the financial sector will result in meaningful reform," she said. "The words 'fox' and 'henhouse' come to mind." Palin, who only obtained a passport in 2007, faced criticism last year after saying her state's proximity to Russia and Canada bolstered her foreign-policy credentials. CLSA has declined to say if or how much Palin was paid. The speech may augment both her bank account and overseas profile ahead of a possible 2012 White House bid, said Charlie Cook, publisher of the nonpartisan Cook Political Report in Washington. "When Palin resigned her governorship, it was assumed that it was in part to make more money, build a nest egg and lay the groundwork for a 2012 presidential race," he said prior to the speech. "This trip is simply an example of her doing so." Little-known outside Alaska before McCain picked her as his running mate, Palin has largely kept a low public profile since stepping down as governor. Citing a scheduling conflict, she didn't appear at a Sept. 19 "Values Voter Summit" in Washington that brought together some of the most ardent social conservatives in the U.S. Palin remains on most lists of potential candidates for the 2012 Republican presidential nomination, along with former Arkansas Governor Mike Huckabee and former Massachusetts Governor Mitt Romney, two 2008 contenders, among others. She hasn't said whether she would pursue a campaign. In a Bloomberg News poll this month, Palin had the highest unfavorable ratings among a list of public figures, at 55 percent. Asked about the difficulties of balancing her political career with her home life, Palin said today: "I have a husband. I could have used a wife."

Source: http://news.yahoo.com/s/bloomberg/20090923/pl_bloomberg/adptsoiuwheu

- **Economic-Political and Organisational Factors**
  - breach of law by employers;
  - monopolism/groupism among all sectors;
  - business's apathy to change for lack of time and unwillingness;
  - ideological and methodical conflicts and differences between different states;
  - existence of price-cutting, malpractices and unfair trade practices;
  - division of management and labour into two warring groups, one endeavouring to win over the other; and
  - technological changes, rationalisation, modernisation, leading to false notions of mass employment among labour.
- **Government Administrative Factors**
  - discriminatory authority vested in government officials;
  - excessive political bias in the formulation of targets, policies and procedures without regard to basic economic laws;
  - loose, short-lived uncoordinated administrative structure;
  - multiplicity and complexity of laws;
  - frequent changes in laws and policies;
  - absence of integrated economy linking the private-public, large-medium, small and tiny sectors;
  - administrative delays and red-tapism; and
  - unstable law and order situation.

What is, therefore, needed is that the government should adopt progressive legal tax policies, and to ensure their strict observance; reduction in tax burden; careful planning, keeping in view the economic principle; strict supervision of and penalty for defaulters; easily understandable laws which are not frequently changed.

Responsibilities Towards the Community

The business owes great responsibility to the community in various directions. Some of the major areas where business can and does contribute towards community welfare as part of its social responsibility are:

(i) **In the field of Industry:** Industry/business can help rural areas by introducing 'self- help' and 'earn-while-you-learn' programmes. Initially, such programmes may be labour-intensive in areas like carpentry, pottery, spinning, weaving, agro-based industry, farming, dairy farming, poultry and pig rearing, storage, etc., so that increasing employment could be provided in rural areas. For this purpose, identification of areas needing improvement, facilities, skill requirements and financial assistance may be surveyed by business experts.

(ii) **In the field of Agriculture:** As a social responsibility, a large business house can play an important role in agricultural development, to provide full-time employment to the vast unemployed rural labour force. For this purpose, the business should get the survey done by its experts in the field of climate, soil conditions, breeding of livestock facilities for irrigation, proper water supply and actual supply of fertilizers, seeds, pesticides, expertise, and finances. Non-agricultural activities seeking linkage with the agricultural sector and the industrialised sector can also be developed.

(iii) **Housing Facilities:** The social responsibility of business in this sphere is great, specially because a major proportion of the rural population is doomed to illnesses, squalid existence in techniques ill-planned and filthy houses. Business can, therefore, play its role in changing house-building, extending loans and financial-aid facilities, providing material and manpower support. In the urban areas, slum clearance schemes, one or two room tenements with facilities for sanitation should be provided in labour colonies.

(iv) **Transportation:** Business and other agencies can help the government by undertaking studies and programmes of technical and financial assistance for the development of cheap public transport and distribution systems through improved journey planning and traffic regulation, increased operational efficiency and utilisation of road capacity, improved systems and procedures of granting licenses, more rational and scientific estimates for vehicle fleet size and man power for different modes of transport, improved maintenance and replacement policy for the spares and structural changes in urban and rural layouts.

(v) **Health and Education:** Business organisations also hold a responsibility towards improvement of the quality of life the people in the community. They can and should be engaged in works like providing water sources for drinking and bathing, improving sewage disposal system, cleaning dirty areas of the solid waste, reducing pollution (caused by soot of chimneys, and crowded industrial units, disposal of waste water and other residues; noise, etc.), improving sanitary facilities (through construction of underground drains, cleaning of existing foul water and waste-carrying open drains, improving roads by filling pits and giving them a regular slope, provision of public toilets and bathrooms and maintaining their cleanliness). Such measures would reduce preventable and water-borne diseases. They can also distribute free medicines, nutritious food to school-going children and pregnant mothers, the aged and the sick. Holding of open camps for operation of minor ailments, eye diseases, family planning (vasectomy or tubectomy) can also be arranged by them. The explosion in population can be held in check by making available cheap contraceptives and advice for their use.

The problems responsible for ill-health in the rural areas need solution, for they result from no proper health education, unhealthy environment, unclean habits of living, poverty, poor diet and the social culture. These problems can be solved through medical help, and the help of social workers. Besides, rural education could provide individuals with knowledge and skills to enable them to manage their families, to participate in cultural and economic life and to sharpen problem-solving capabilities.

(vi) **Industrial Aid to Education in Urban Areas:** Progressive individual businessmen and individual business houses (such as Birlas, Tatas, Modis, Ruias, Lalbhais, Shreerams and others) are running and supporting schools, colleges and technical/professional educational institutions. In fact, it is a part of modern social responsibility of business that it should support educational programmes, more particularly technical education. In some cases, they help by lending the services of their specialists (as visiting experts) and giving financial help.

The National Industrial Conference Board of America in its Report on '*Industrial Aid to Education*' has suggested five different forms of educational aid which business can render to the community;

— cash contribution to educational institutions;

— scholarship and loans to undergraduate students;

— contribution of material and equipments to educational institutions;

— teaching aids for students and teachers and

— contribution of company manpower.

(vii) **Social Audit on Factual Assessment:** This should be done by trained and professional personnel to show the social performance of business. The team 'social audit' generally means a comprehensive evaluation of the way a company discharges all its responsibilities to shareholders, customers, employees, community and the government. A social audit should generally adopt a four-step process, *viz.*,

- firm must itemise all the activities that have a potential social impact;
- the circumstances leading to these actions or activities must be explained;
- some evaluation of the performance must be conducted; and
- the company must examine the relationship between the goals of the firm and those of society to see how the programmes relate to one another.

In brief, it may be said that "business must accept responsibility to the society and its various constituents as a trustee for the goods and services that it produces, consumes, saves and reinvests." Such responsibilities extend beyond the business to the lives of the people and the community and as such they should endeavour to:

– play a proper role in civil affairs within the goals of the business;

– promote amenities and help, create better living conditions;

– help in making people law-abiding and improving legislation and administration in municipal and industrial affairs; and

– set up socially desirable standards of living, themselves avoiding ostentatious, wasteful expenditure and improvident display in weddings, festivities and parties.

Towards Input Suppliers: The business owes responsibility towards input suppliers and ancillary industries. They include:

(i) Providing technical know-how and assistance

(ii) Providing fair price

(iii) Assuring continuous purchase of inputs

(iv) Helping them in expansion and development

Towards Bankers and Financial Institutions: Responsibilities towards bankers and financial institution include:

(i) Providing correct data and information for project appraisal.

(ii) Prompt payment of interest.

(iii) Clearance of the principal amount on or before due date.

Towards Market Intermediaries: Business should render its responsibilities towards wholesalers, retailers and franchises. They include:

(i) Providing products quiet in advance.

(ii) Providing freedom to have price margins.

(iii) Taking back poor quality products.

(iv) Providing technical managerial know-how.

(v) Training the personnel.

(vi) Providing freedom in promotional programmes.

Business is continuously influenced by the environment. In fact, business also influences and manipulates the environment. Now, we shall study the business environment.

(C) BUSINESS ETHICS

Need for Ethics in Business

The erstwhile regulated economies necessitated their governments to regulate and control business organisations and economic institutions through law and government mechanisms to enable them to play their role in contributing to the growth and well being of their stakeholders in a balanced way such that the interest of the majority of the people was protected. Governments which were hitherto discharging the responsibilities of safeguarding the customers, interest in respect of quality, price, safe and timely delivery of the product, etc., protecting the companies from unhealthy competition, restricting the concentration of economic power in the hands of a few which should be otherwise enjoyed by the majority of the population and the like relegated and shifted them to the shoulders of the international business organisations by creating competition via globalisation, liberalisation and privatisation. Many social scientists felt that the deregulation of business wouldencourage the business to reverse to its orthodox objective of profit maximisation by all means including practising unethical methods. But sooner or the later, many incidents took place in the business scenario across the globe proving that international businesses should carry out their operations ethically for their basic survival. A worthwhile incident that needs mention at this juncture is the lowest price car project of the Ford Motor Company (See Box 16.2).

BOX 16.2: BUSINESS ETHICS: CASE OF THE FORD MOTOR COMPANY

The Ford Motor Company decided to produce the first lowest priced car in the USA. The Company President Mr. Lee Iacocca wanted to rush the development of a car costing less than $2,000, as he promised the public that his company will bring out the car at that price (as low as $2,000) and also fight the growing popularity of Volkswagen's Beetel. Preliminary tests showed that it involved an additional cost of $11 to enhance the safety of the car. Then he organised the meeting of the executives of the company to decide how to reduce the cost below $2,000. Many executives suggested that the company should sell the car at $2,011 by including the safety features. But some executives viewed that the company should sell the car at $2,000 as was promised by excluding the safety feature. However, the company decided to go ahead without the safety feature. The car was released and sold at $2,000. After six months of release, one of the cars met with an accident killing all the passengers travelling in it. The competitors influenced the newspapers to publish this accident significantly and the newspapers in the U.S.A. highlighted the absence of the safety features. This incident resulted not only in the loss of sales but also in the closure of the unit resulting in a loss of $250 million to the company.

Source: *The Economic Times*, Mumbai, 23rd November, 2003.

This case indicates that a business should consider the ethical principles while making decisions in order to achieve its basic objective of survival. Thus, widespread and intensified competition forces a business to conduct its business ethically. Increasing literacy, widespread use of information technology, and vanishing sellers' markets leave little scope for debating on the need for conducting business ethically.

The problem regarding ethics over the period has not been due to lack of information and knowledge or due to the non-acceptance of principles of ethical behaviour underlying such knowledge, but due to avoiding the attitude developed by business people towards law consequent upon the opportunity provided by the sellers' market. The issue, now, is to treat ethics as a part of human behaviour naturally and part of making business decisions individually and collectively. In fact, many businessmen are extremely religious as individuals, but their business suit makes them blind towards human sufferings, which are the results of their actions, of course, under the sellers' market conditions. In fact, the buyers' market environment caused the international businessmen to realise that behaving ethically not only in personal life but in business life is in their own interest in the long run.

What is Ethics?

The word ethics is derived from the Greek word 'ethos', which means character. Ethics is a branch of philosophy that is concerned with human character and conduct. It is a discipline dealing with that which is good and bad and with moral duty and obligation. Ethics is the embodiment of moral values, which describes what, is 'right' and what is 'wrong' in human behaviour and what 'ought to be'. Thus, ethics refers to good character and morality and to generally accepted human character and behaviour considered as desirable by the contemporary society. The same action or practice is viewed as ethical or unethical depending upon the school of moral thought to which one subscribes. Further, the perceptions of ethical or unethical change at times because some values are dropped and some values are added over the period.

What is Business Ethics?

What is ethical and unethical in general society may not be the same in business as the latter operates in different environments and with different objectives that are centred on profit and wealth maximisation. Business ethics is "concerned primarily with the relationship of business goals and techniques to the specific human needs. It studies the impact of acts on the good of the individual, the firm, the business community and the society as a whole. Business ethics studies the special obligations that a man and a citizen accept when he becomes a part of the world of commerce".

Normative Philosophy and Business Ethics

Normative Philosophy is the study of proper thought and conduct. All hard ethical decisions are compromises between the economic and social performance in case of business and between wants and duties in case of individuals. Normative Philosophy provides clues in making those compromises. Morality refers to the standards of behaviour by which people are judged, and particularly to the standards of behaviour by which people are judged in their relationship with others. Moral standards of behaviour vary between groups within a single culture, between cultures, and between times. However, certain common principles can be drawn even in differential standards. Otherwise, if everyone acts on the basis of his/her own self-interest and ignores the well being of others, life would be "solitary, nasty, brutish and short."

All hard ethical decisions are compromises between the economic and social performance in case of business and between wants and duties in case of individuals.

Utilitarianism

Utilitarianism – a teleological theory – states that moral worth of personal conduct can be determined by the consequence of that behaviour. An action is right, if it benefits larger number of people. Moral values contribute to the greatest degree of benefits for the largest number of people while incurring the least amount of damage/harm. The rule of Utilitarianism states that 'act in accordance with rules fashioned on utility.' Utilitarianism is close to cost-benefit analysis and also to distribution that is a political process. It may be different from economic concert to some extent as the greatest good for the 'greatest number' takes precedence in utilitarian theory over 'greatest good for smaller but more elite'.

Deontological Approach

Deontological approach to business ethics is the reverse of the teleological theory. This approach states that moral worth of an action is to be decided based on the intentions of the persons making decisions or performing acts but not the actions or their consequences, as actions are uncertain. Immanuel Kant (1985) proposed a simple test for personal duty and goodwill to eliminate self-interest and to ensure regard for moral worth. The test states as follows:

'Ask ourself whether you would be willing to have everyone in the world, faced with similar circumstances, forced to act in exactly the same way you act.'

This test indicates that is it right and proper, if every one performs the same act and it would be unfair to everyone to do something that others do not do or won't do. Thus, Immanuel Kant's moral action is based on rational decision and logical consistency and general rights based approaches, *i.e.*, individuals have rights to autonomy, privacy, dignity, respect, self-esteem, authenticity, etc. Kant tells us to treat people as ends in themselves, not merely as means to an end, and to behave with integrity, enacting virtues and values in all that we do. However, these approaches are criticized on the ground that they cannot be used to judge all moral actions under all circumstances.

Theory of Distributive Justice

John Rawls proposes a theory of distributive justice that states that the benefits are to be distributed based on justice, but not equally. According to him, distributive justice is that which ensures equal distribution of public education, need-based distribution of welfare payments, effort based distribution of sales commission, conferring public honours based on contributions and payment of salaries based on competence. An institution of law that violates individual liberty, even though it may result in greater happiness and increased benefits for others, has to be rejected as being unjust. In fact, the law guides ethical choice.

Law and Business Ethics

Law is a consistent set of universal rules that are widely published, generally accepted and usually enforced. Thus, law is a set of rules established by the society to govern behaviour within the society. These rules are often complex, occasionally obsolete, and continually changing. Laws are negative commandments while the standards of ethics are more often positive. Rules of the law overlap the ethical standards of a society to a considerable extent, but do not contradict them. Many times it is viewed that law is a subset of ethics. Further, rules of law tend to lag behind the apparent ethical standards of a society.

The gap between law and ethics is owing to the process of formation of law. Each individual has a set of norms, beliefs and values that subjectively determine his/her moral standards that are based on emotional rather than rational thinking process. Norms, values, and beliefs of the individuals in the groups and in society interact with those of others and turn into social values, norms and beliefs, and ultimately ethics. Formation of law is both social as well as a political process. Sometimes, it is more of a political process than a social one. This is the basic reason for the existence of gap between law and ethics.

However, law is a guiding factor of ethics.

Scope of Business Ethics

Business organisations have to perform a variety of activities. In fact, their activities include production and marketing of goods and services, rendering service to customers, procuring the required finance to carry out activities, managing human resources in the process, maintaining contacts with the suppliers of inputs, contributing to the goals of the society and the like. Thus, business interacts with various sections of the economy and the society. It has to follow ethics in interaction with these sections having conflicting interests. As such, these interactions may involve ideological conflicts.

Business houses produce goods/render services of large quantities contributing to the Gross Domestic Product. The Gross Domestic Product is not an end by itself. It is a means to an end, in the sense that it contributes to the satisfaction of human needs. Business allocates scarce resources among various production means based on priorities.

Therefore, it has to perform the activities more ethically, judiciously and wisely. Business has the responsibility of product selectivity in the sense that it has to produce the goods and render the services that contribute to the welfare and well being of the people at large. According to Eells, (1900), responsibility of product selectivity may mean the exclusion of product lines that promise large returns, but would require the use of capital for socially dubious purposes. A company may choose among alternatives, none of which will result in socially deleterious products and services, but some of which may contribute more substantially to the building up of the kind of community a responsible executive wants to see.

Principles of Business Ethics

The basic principles of business ethics include:

(i) Human values grow with the increase in the size of business.

(ii) The purpose of all economic activities is to meet the consumer needs and to contribute to the well-being of the community.

(iii) Business should produce products that will not harm the customer's health. It must protect the customer's health in the long run rather than meet the immediate pleasures of the customers.

(iv) Business should be based on the theory of trusteeship. Business should give top priority to service and only the next priority to profits.

(v) Business must be conducted trustfully, legally and morally for the benefit of the people whom it serves.

(vi) Business must not only be efficient and dynamic but also be just and humane.

(vii) Business should reconcile and harmonize the separate and conflicting responsibilities towards customers, employees, shareholders, Government, suppliers, bankers and the community.

(viii) Business should not contribute to the concentration of economic power and monopolistic trends.

(ix) Every business has an overriding obligation to make the fullest and maximum possible use of its inputs – both material and human.

Ethical Values in Global Business

The ethical issues involved in the international business include:

- Utilisation of the natural resources of the host country appropriately and in an optimum way.
- Utilisation of the natural resources for the production of goods for the consumption in the domestic country. If these goods are exported, the benefit of foreign exchange should be provided to the host country.
- Do not use the ingredients in the production which harm the basic health of the customers of the host country. (See Box 16.3).

BOX 16.3: MORE PESTICIDES FOUND IN COCO-COLA, PESPI CO DRINKS

All 57 drinks, samples tested by the Centre for Science and Environment (CSE) contained residues of three to five different pesticides, calling for stricter standards to be enforced in India.

The findings, which were spread over 11 soft drinks brands, add to the public relations, problems facing Coca-Cola and PepsiCo in India, and threaten to knock their sales in a soft drinks market growing by seven to eight per cent per year.

The new CSE report echoes a similar study by the same group in 2003, which also found soft drinks in Delhi contaminated with pesticides at levels above the international standards.

Soft drinks firms questioned the study's accuracy, but it was endorsed by India's Parliament, which asked for standards to be set on pesticides in fizzy soft drinks. These have now been drafted by the Bureau of Indian Standards, but continued debate and lobbying has kept them from being fully implemented.

CSE has warned consumers to avoid Coca-Cola and Pepsi Co drinks. It claimed to have found one drink containing the neurotoxin Chlorpyrifos at 200 times above the proposed safety limit.

Soft drinks makers in India rejected the findings. *"Consumer safety is paramount to us. The soft drinks manufactured in India comply with stringent international norms and all applicable national regulations,"* said the Indian Soft Drinks Manufacturers' Association.

The association said it had spent three years working with the government, scientists and campaign groups to establish *"stricter norms"* for pesticide traces in drinks that complied with international standards.

Coca-Cola has stated previously that its drinks in India were confirmed safe by the Ministry of Health and Family Welfare in 2003. *"In India, as in the rest of the world, our plants use a multiple barrier system to remove potential contaminants and unwanted natural substances, including pesticides."*

CSE, however, said it was *"even more confident"* about its findings this time because its lab was accredited by the international quality standard ISO 9001:2000.

The lab also contained GC-MS testing equipment, a detection method used by many food scientists including those at the US Food and Drug Administration.

The Bureau of Indian Standards has set provisional limits of 0.1 parts per billion for individual pesticides in fizzy drinks and 0.5 parts per billion for total pesticide content.

Source: Adapted from http://www.nutraingredients-usa.com

- Enter the foreign country mostly through a joint venture with the business firms of the host countries.
- Transfer of technology to the developing countries.
- Develop the managers and human resources of host countries and particularly of the developing host countries.
- Discharge the responsibilities to various social segments of the host country. These responsibilities include: development of medical facilities, construction of hospitals, educational institutes, public utilities, water, roads etc.
- Donate medicines, books, computers and the like to the people, educational institutes of the host country.
- Market qualitative and economically appropriate goods to the customers. Avoid marketing of outdated and spoiled products.
- Avoid marketing of those products which harm the health of the citizens of the host country.
- Avoid marketing of those products/services which do not have the compatibility with the culture of the host country.
- Employ the local people to the largest extent possible and give them the opportunity to earn income and develop the skills.
- Treat the foreign employees and local employees equally in offering salary, career advancement and providing the working life.
- Non-involvement in political affairs of the host country.
- Help the host Government during the periods of natural calamities like floods, droughts, earth quakes, cyclones, etc.
- Avoid bribing or corrupting the government officials of the host country *(See Exhibit 13.1)*.
- Pay the taxes to the government of the country accurately.
- Maintain the accounts ethically as per the accounting standards of the host country.
- Maintain sound business relations with the market intermediaries, suppliers of raw materials and other inputs, bankers and financial institutions.

(D) VALUE-BASED MANAGEMENT

The process of globalisation of business and management requires adaptation of most desirable concepts, theories and principles by the management for the long run survival and development of business. Most of the principles of management are developed by the Westerns. Therefore, the western religious texts and social values might have influenced the development process of management principles.

Indian religious texts and social texts also have rich values based on which management styles and principles can be developed and modified. In fact, Indian managers and academicians started thinking in this direction. But no concrete efforts have been made so far. However, there are a few books and published papers towards this direction. Now, we shall discuss human values during early days in India.

Human Values During the Early Days in India

Industry and business operations during and before 15th century were limited to cottage and small industries and mostly to local markets. Business operations were tuned to customer-orientation. Under this approach, products were produced based on the needs of the individual customers separately. In fact, the producers used to suggest modifications in the needs of the customers in terms of health, convenience, comfort, dignity and prestige. Sometimes, the suggestions of the producers caused reduction in profits but more customer value and satisfaction.

Further, the traders and industrialists used to give emphasis on quality, delivery, etc. The industrialists used to design the products that help in the maintenance and improvement of human health, provide/offer comfort and convenience to the customers, enhance the human dignity and prestige and do not widen the gap between rich and poor. Thus, the producers and marketers used to give emphasis on the human values rather than on the materialistic values.

Similar approach of human values had been followed between 18th and 19th centuries with certain exceptions regarding robbery in the process of transportation of products both in domestic and international trade.

The human orientation drawn from the society had been extended to business and politics. Mahatma Gandhi had given human orientation to Indian politics and to the national life of India.

Standard and Customisation: The population explosion led to the phenomenal increase in human needs. These factors led to the industrial revolution and mass production. The producers under these circumstances standardized the human needs based on various factors like age, sex, income, geographical area, religion, community and other social segments. The standardized human needs had been the basis for producing standard goods and rendering services. Thus, the 1900s witnessed a significant shift from the standardization to customisation.

Shift in Human Values

The shift from standardization to customisation of production of goods and rendering of services undermined the individual human needs. Further, this shift helped the producers and traders to reduce the cost of production and sales and increase the sales revenue through price hike. Producers tended to view maximisation of profits by reducing cost of production per unit and by increasing the price. This process led the business people to emphasise on economic values rather than human values. Thus, the approach of profits through human service shifted to the approach of profits by all means.

Humanistic vs. Poverty

India is endowed with human resources. India is rich in scientific, technical and software human resources. But, the problem of unemployment and under-employment are quite rampant. More than half of our population are sunk in poverty, ignorance and suffering. Science and technology in our country could not achieve human justice of taking care of basic human needs.

The purpose of advancement of science and technology should also be the alleviation of human sufferings in addition to advancement of knowledge. Education of science and technology should be associated with humanistic impulse. Most probably, the reason for this situation would be absence of association among education, politics and administration with the human pulse. Hence, our ability to alleviate human suffering has been reduced.

The human unconcern in various social, political and economic activities resulted in social and economic unethical practices like bribery, corruption, tax-avoidance, smuggling, absence of duty-mindedness, punctuality, honest work for the salaries received and public spirit.

Rights vs. Duties

Every citizen including the corporate citizens in India should be responsible to stop down ward trend and rebuild the nation. Every citizen should participate in the nation-building process instead of working in isolation and staying/remaining in isolation. In fact, the Constitution of India mentioned the ideas of human values and also expressed the desire to implement them. People of the country should feel the duty of implementing the human values rather than stressing their fundamental rights.

Corporate citizens along with the citizens of the country should be humanistic and should have ethical values in discharging their duties and responsibilities. The citizens of the country should work hard and work together through team spirit to build the nation. The egos and profits and pleasures of individuals should be sacrificed to some extent in order to contribute to the development and progress of the country.

Along with the social responsibilities, the freedom of the corporate citizens needs to be enriched with the democratic virtues of self-discipline and a humanly oriented will. Mostly common people have learned the work ethic. But the educated intelligentsia are mostly self-centred and self-interested. They exploit common people. They may be lazy or work hard for their self advancement. According to Bhagavad Gita and Swami Vivekananda, no nation can become great or achieve prosperity, without its people developing a sense of self-discipline, social-responsibility and capacity and willingness to work smartly and efficiently in a cooperative and collaborative approach.

Bhagavad Gita and Human Values

Most important ideas relating to work ethics are found in Bhagavad Gita. Bhagavad Gita is the most prominent book of Hindu religion. Its main theme is work, man at work, and the dual benefits to the man from the work, *i.e.*, social welfare outside and spiritual growth within one self (See Box 16.4).

BOX 16.4 BASIC PRINCIPLES OF INDIAN ETHOS FOR MANAGEMENT

(1) Immense potential energy and talents for perfection as human being has the spirit within his heart. (2) Holistic approach indicating unity between the Divine, individual self and the universe. (3) Subtle, intangible subject and gross tangible objects are equally important. One must develop one's Third Eye, Jnana Chakshu, the Eye of Wisdom, Vision, Insight and Foresight. Inner resources are much more powerful than outer resources. Divine virtues are inner resources. Capital, materials and plant and machinery are outer resources. (4) Karma Yoga offers double benefit, private benefit, self-purification and public benefit. (5) Excellence at work through self-motivation and self-development is the best means of Total Quality Management. (6) Co-operation is a powerful instrument for team work and success in any enterprise involving collective work.

(***Source:*** S.A.Sherlekar, *op.cit.*, p.95.)

Bhagavad Gita unlike other Indian or foreign religious books, deals with the increasing work efficiency, leading to social welfare, increasing the individual capability and collective human welfare. Lord Sri Krishna represents the energy of Yoga and the energy of vision. These two energies are needed to achieve total human welfare. Writing Philanthropic energy with Philosophic calm is true education. Managements of all companies will achieve the highest level of efficiency when the people of these companies achieve the true education.

- The first fruit of confluence is economic prosperity, which solves the problems of mass poverty, unemployment, etc. Eradication of poverty needs knowledge, hard work, capacity for dedication and team work, which is the gift of character and energy. The knowledge accompanied by character is called true knowledge. The true knowledge produces economic prosperity, when it is applied to work. The economic prosperity, in its turn achieves human welfare.
- The second fruit of confluence is success in every project. It is possible through hard work, character and energy with knowledge.
- The third fruit of confluence is general welfare.
- The fourth front of confluence is 'dharma.' This fourth value is more crucial to achieve the first, second and third confluences. In other words, the character, knowledge, prosperity and general social welfare can be achieved only when the citizens of the country practice the fourth value, *i.e.*, 'dharma.' Dharma awakens moral sense, ethical values and human values in the citizens. Then the citizens, follow the rules, regulations and laws effectively. (See Box 16.5).

BOX 16.5: DHARMA AND MANAGEMENT

1. Virtues and values should never be weighed against profits. Profitability shall not be justified by lying, harassment, cheating, fraud, and such other vices (asuric actions).
2. Each employee adheres to the set values even at the cost to himself as a demonstration of his/her dharma or integrity.
3. Such fearless adherence must be encouraged by public appreciation and the ethico-moral oriented fair reward structure.
4. All managers must practise these same values in leading by example.

(***Source:*** S.A.Sherlekar, "*Global Dharmic Management,*" Himalaya Publishing House, Mumbai, 2001, p.33.)

Morality and purity are the only strengths. They are above the law. Religion goes to the root of the matter. If it is right, all is right... Swami Vivekananda said, "the basis of all systems, social or political... rests upon the goodness of men." Management concepts are redefined in the wake of Indian Values. (See Exhibit 16.2).

Exhibit 16.2: Management Concepts Redefined in Wake of Indian Values

Term	General Definition *(At Present)*	Definition of *Indian Ethics Management*
1. Management	Gettings things done. Emphasis only on output and turn over.	Helping other people to produce extraordinary results. Emphasis on human response.
2. Productivity	Related to plant capacity	Related to men's capability unlimited potential.
3. Planning	Management by results.	Management by strategy.
4. Leadership	Produce results at lower cost to achieve maximum motivators.	Produce performers. Help the subordinates to develop leadership quality.
5. Motivation of People	Maslow's theory of needs with some modifications.	Emphasis on self-motivation by subordinates to have creative joy and autonomy.
6. Resources	Reliance almost on external resources.	Reliance almost on Internal resources.
7. Health of the Company	Balance Sheet and Profit/ Loss A/c money-oriented.	People oriented performance, environment friendly. Private Public benefit.
8. Profitability	In terms of money. Social costs nct included in Balance Sheet.	In terms of good public image. Social costs internalised. Trust of customers and society.
9. Hygiene factor	Attention only on job enrichment.	Primary emphasis on mind enrichment. Total quality mind.
10. Rights and duties	Emphasis on taking not on giving rights become primary duties become subsidiary.	Emphasis on giving not on taking. Duties given great importance and Rights assume secondary value.
11. Marketing	Keen competition to capture and retain demand: market driven economy.	Through co-operation by playing complementary role. Social awareness in marketing.
12. System	Set of inter-related elements working as a whole. Hardware aspect. More emphasis on quantity and objective aspect.	Pattern of particular response expressed through organisational functioning. Software aspect. Equal emphasis on quality/quantity with emphasis on subjective spect. Holistic.
13. Structure	Hierarchical.	Organic evolution, autonomous.
14. Growth	Ultimately dependent on turn over of goods.	Co-ordinating private and public benefit.
15. Job satisfaction	Hygiene factor. Creativity ignored.	Through innovation uniqueness, extraordinary result, trouble shooting.
16. Training	Functional skill Efficiency on orientation in values or Effectiveness.	Value-based skill develop good character education in Ethics Healthy Philosophy of Life, emotional stability. Holism.
17. Man-Machine Equation	Machine dominates man as human being receives lip sympathy.	Man behind the machine given due regard. Healthy philosophy of life. Emotional stability.
18. Man Placement	Academic qualification experience in the job values not stressed.	Equal stress given on academic degrees and ethico-moral Values. Dalvi sammpati — Divine qualities.
19. Quality	Product quality by I.S.O., TQM, Q.C., Human value, quality plays minor role. We have crises of Values, Adulteration is widespread.	Human quality, values, character, mind-enrichment, whole-man approach. Mind and matter are given equal treatment.

(*Source:* S.A.Sharlekar, op.cit., pp.108-109.)

POINTS TO BE REMEMBERED

- In traditional societies, prime purpose of business was profit maximisation.
- Modern view: Business depends on society for input acquisition and output marketing.
- Business discharges social responsibilities to shareholders/owners employees, customers, Government, society and other businesses.
- Ethical issues are above the legal issues.
- Business ethics refers to application of moral values and moral principle to business.
- Business ethical principles/policies and practices influence and shape the individual ethics, characteristics and behaviour.

KEY TERMS

- Social Responsibility
- Customers
- Consumers
- Shareholders
- Stockholders
- Ethics
- Rights
- Code of Conduct
- Human Development
- Employees
- Inter-Business
- Government
- Fair Wage
- Fair Prices
- Bhagavat-Gita
- Ethical Climate
- Dharma
- Dharmic-Management
- Transportation
- Health
- Education
- Community
- Social-Audit
- Business Ethics
- Duties
- Values
- Human Values

QUESTIONS FOR DISCUSSION

1. What is social responsibility of business? Explain the arguments for and against responsibilities of business towards the society.
2. Compare and contrast the traditional view and modern view of social responsibility of business.
3. "The business of business is business." Critically comment.
4. List out the responsibilities of business towards various stakeholders.
5. What is external environment? State the impact of external environment on business.
6. Define the terms ethics and business ethics.
7. Explain the ethical climate of a country. Discuss how does the ethical climate of country affect the business.
8. Discuss the ethical principles that applicable to business.
9. Why should business follow ethical principles during the days of deregulations, globalisation and capitalistic trends?

10. Illustrate some unethical practices that the business adopted and their consequences.
11. Explain the principles of business ethics and code of business ethics.
12. What are the human values according to Bhagavat Gita?
13. What is Dharma? Indicate the principles of Dharma. How is Dharma superior to Law?
14. Discuss the applicability of Indian ethos to modern management.

REFERENCES

1. Milton Friedman, *The Social Responsibility of Business to Increase Profits*, New York Time Magazine, September 13, 1970, p. 32.
2. Milton Friedman, *The Social Responsibility of Business*, in Tom,L:. and Norman (Eds.), *Ethical Theory and Business*, Prentice Hall Inc., New Jersery, 1979, p. 136.
3. John Lodd, *Morality and the Ideal Rationality in Formal Organisations*, October 1970, p. 499.
4. T.A.Mathias, *Profits or People — Business and Society*, Indian Management, June 1984, p. 4.
5. *Ibid.*
6. Chambers Twentieth Century Dictionary, 1976, p. 448.
7. Banmhart, R., *Ethics in Business*, Holt, Reinhart and Winston, New York, 1968, p. 10.
8. Garrett Thomas, M., *Business Ethics*, The Times of India Press, Bombay, 1970, p. 4.
9. *Ibid.*
10. Eells Richard, *The Meaning of Modern Business*, Columbia University Press, New York, 1900, pp. 230-31.
11. Clarence, C. Walton, *Corporate Social Responsibilities*, Wordsworth Publishing Co., Belmont, 1967, pp.122-41.
12. *Ibid.*, p. 84.
13. Peter F. Drucker, *Concept of the Corporation*, Beacon Press, Boston, 1962, p. 140.
14. Sherlekar, S.A., "*Global Dharmic Management*", Himalaya Publishing House, Mumbai, 2001, p. 3.

✦ ✦ ✦

17 CHAPTER

CORPORATE GOVERNANCE: A STRATEGY FOR SUSTAINABLE DEVELOPMENT

Chapter Outline

(A) Introduction

(B) Why Corporate Governance?

(C) Corporate Governance and Strategic Management

(D) Parties to the Corporate Governance

(E) Principles of Good Corporate Governance

(F) Mechanisms and Controls To Ensure Good Corporate Governance

Learning Objectives

After studying this chapter, you should be able to –

- Understand the meaning of corporate governance;
- Analyse the need for corporate governance;
- Explain the role of corporate governance in the process of strategic management;
- State various parties to corporate governance;
- Discuss various principles of corporate governance;
- Study the mechanism and controls to ensure good corporate governance;
- Discuss internal and external parties and measures of corporate governance.

(A) INTRODUCTION

The basic purpose of most of the business organizations is to maximize the shareholder's wealth. However, there has been paradigm shifts in the approach towards the basic purpose of business organizations. Some organizations view that meeting the customer's needs is the purpose of an organization as customers take care of the organization's business and in turn maximizing the shareholders' wealth. Of late, there has been a dramatic change in the approach of the basic purpose of the business organizations. Business organizations like Virgin Blue and Virgin Atlantic view that their basic purpose is to satisfy employees' needs as employees take care of customers' needs and customers take care of business and in turn business takes care of shareholders' wealth. Thus there are varied views towards the approach towards the purpose of business organizations that covers more or less all kinds of stakeholders. Now, we shall discuss the meaning of corporate governance.

Meaning

Corporate Governance is a voluntary code of conduct that the board of directors particularlythe chief executive officer of the business organisation is expected to follow in operating the business.

Corporate Governance is a voluntary code of conduct that the board of directors particularly the chief executive officer of the business organisation is expected to follow in operating the business. The code contains expectations and provisions that are more extensive than any statutory, professional or capital market requirements.

Corporate Governance is the framework of rules, relationships, systems and processes within and by which authority is exercised and controlled in corporations. Thus corporate governance deals with – not only rules, laws and regulations but also the moral and ethical code that the officers concerned are expected to follow.

For example, Mr Ramalinga Raju and other executives of System Computers Limited are expected to operate the business transparently and invest the money in the business operations not in the real estate. Therefore, it is felt that Mr Ramalinga Raju and other executives failed to follow the expected code of conduct of business.

Thus the important aspect of corporate governance is to follow the rules, regulations. code of conduct, laws, and morals to operate the business in the best interest of all of its stakeholders. Therefore, the derivative and second aspect of corporate governance is the relationship among the stakeholders of the company like shareholders, board of directors, employees, directors, banks and financial institutions, suppliers of inputs, market intermediaries, the government and the community at large.

Corporate governance thus is the set of policies, rules and code of conduct designed to ensure the creation of long-term sustainable value of the firm to meet the integrated and balanced interests of all concerned.

Securities Exchange Board of India Committee on Corporate Governance defines corporate governance as the "acceptance by management of the inalienable rights of the shareholders as the true owners of the corporation and of their own role as trustees – on behalf of the shareholders. It is about commitment to values, about ethical business conduct and about making a distinction between Gandhian principle of trusteeship and the Directive Principles of the Indian Constitution. Corporate Governance is also viewed as ethics and moral duty.

(B) WHY CORPORATE GOVERNANCE?

There were the failure of banks as well as insurance companies in India as well as in other countries during the early 1900s. These failures were mostly due to the unethical practices by their managing agents. Consequently the managing agency system was abolished. In fact, the first documented bank failure of corporate governance was the South Sea Bubble in 1700s in UK. It led to the improvement of business laws in UK. Similarly many of the Securities Acts were amended in USA after the capital market collapse in 1929. In addition, the concerns of shareholders with regard to executive pay and continuously declining share prices created the necessity for corporate governance.

Economists suggested the need for changing role of modern corporation in society due to the wall street crash of 1929. Multinational corporations have been established after World War II led to the creation of new managerial class. Most of these MNCs have dominant control over business affairs without sufficient accountability or monitoring by their board of directors. Large US companies like General Motors, General Electric, AT &T, Texas Instruments and IBM dominated US economy in particular and the World economy in general particularly before 1970s. These companies had an integrated approach to all the stakeholders of the business like customers, employees and society in addition to the shareholders owing to the stable business environment. They also emphasized on research and development.

But the developments in the post 1970s period disturbed the 1970s stable business environment. The factors responsible for this trend include: increased competition from the emergence of new MNCs from Japan, technological revolution and emergence of new and low cost products and turbulences in the oil prices and the prices of significant inputs. These factors created vibrations in managing large corporations on ethical grounds.

The further and significant development in this direction is deregulation of economics, opening up of almost all World economies in the name of globalization. Globalization and deregulation led to serve competition and liberalization of laws and regulation over business in India as well as in other countries. Amendment of Monopolies and Restrictive Trade Practice Act and Foreign Exchange Regulation Act in favour of private business is examples at this juncture. Such amendments provided freedom to business in India that led to misuse of funds and rights by the credit rating agencies, regulating firms, CEOS and Board of Directors. Ramalinga Raju of Satyam computers misused the rights and the credit rating agencies and accounting firms helped him in misusing the rights in investing company's funds in real estate. Similarly, the massive bankruptcies of Enron and dotcom companies and lesser corporate debacles like Adelphia communications, AOL, Arthur Anderson, Global Grossing and Tyco during 2008 led to the need for efficient corporate governance.

(C) CORPORATE GOVERNANCE AND STRATEGIC MANAGEMENT

Corporate Governance is highly essential from the point of view of the shareholders, customers, employees and company and society at large for the survival and sustainable growth of the company. Strategic management is the process of formulating and implementing strategies. Strategy is an integrated course of action/plan. Thus, strategy integrates internal environment including corporate governance and external environment. But the Strategy aims at maximizing organizational interest, sometimes at the cost of competitor's (other organizations in the economy and the society), customers, employees, and the society.

Strategy integrates internal environment including corporate governance and external environment.

Strategy achievement of a company may adversely affect the competitors' interest in the forms of price war, product imitations, grabbing market share and the like resulting in wastage of competitors/ other organization's resources. Efficient strategy achievement of more companies, some times also adversely affect the customer's interest. Companies in the process of luring the customers provide misleading information and false guarantees to the customers. Consequently, customers may fail to receive the value for their money that result in wastage of economy's resources.

Some companies pay excessive salaries and provide benefits to the C.E.O. and other executives which would be at the cost of lower level employees as well as customers. This factor, some times would result in inflation. Similarly, strategy implementation would affect adversely the society of large as well as various stakeholders.

Therefore, strategy achievement would sometimes adversely affect all stakeholders including the company. The crazy strategies of the CEOs would result in bankruptcy of the company itself. But, the corporate governance meets the interests all the stakeholders including the long-run interest of the company itself in a more balanced way, by regulating and controlling the misleading, immoral and unethical ideas and acts of CEO, Board of Directors and other strategists.

Thus, strategic management should be under the preview, control of and the provisions of corporate governance provisions and practices of a company.

(D) PARTIES TO THE CORPORATE GOVERNANCE

Parties to the corporate governance are broadly divided into two groups viz., direct parties and indirect parties.

Parties to the corporate governance are broadly divided into two groups viz., direct parties and indirect parties. Direct Parties are shareholders, CEO, Board of Director and the Senior Management.

Individual and Institutional Shareholders: Shareholders initially were individuals. These individuals were wealthy individuals or families. Thus small individual investors were deprived of the opportunity of investing in large companies.

Over the time, small investors became institutional investors. Thus the concept of institutional investors has emerged. Institutional investors include mutual funds, hedge funds, pension funds, exchange traded funds, insurance companies, brokers, financial institutions and investor groups.

These institutional investors are managed by professionals. Thus, the self management of own finances is absent in institutional investors as in case of company management. The management of institutional investors is highly professionalized, not necessarily on the interest of the small investors. Some times, they efficiently perform their activities in the interest of either the fund manager or in the interest of the company in which the money is invested. Despite, individuals prefer to invest in mutual funds and the other institutional investment than in bank deposits.

The managers of the institutional investments by virtue of its larger stake in the company's equity are elected/nominated as the directors of the board. The CEO of the company and the mangers of the institutional investment help each other at the stake of the interest of the small investors as well as the company's interest. Thus mutual help affect the company as well as the economy of the country due to failure of such companies. In addition, institutional investors fail to support the resolutions of executive pay, takeover, merger etc., though they are against the shareholders' interest. Managers of the institutional investments are not the real owners and as such, they sometimes fail to act in good faith to protect the interests of their members.

Individual shareholders hold negligible share of the stock and as such they can not influence the decision of the CEO. Further, most of the individual shareholders are interested in the dividend and/ or growth in the market price of the share; as such they may not concentrate on the long run sustainable growth of the company. This approach of the individual shareholders provides freedom to the CEO as well as the Board of Directors to craft strategies and make decision that would result in maximizing the short run gains. These short run gains help the company to increase dividend rate as well as to influence the market price of the share positively. Further the CEO and Board of Directors make use of this freedom for increasing their pay, benefits and perks in addition to misusing the office for their personal gains.

The next significant party to corporate governance is the Board of Directors. Now, we shall discuss how the Board of Directors contributes to create hurdles in the process of achievement of strategies.

Board of Directors

Most of the corporate governance issues are centred on Board of Directors. The functions of Board of Directors include:

- Reviewing corporate mission, guiding on corporate strategies, policies, philosophies and major business plans and budgets;
- Monitoring the corporate performance continuously;
- Monitoring the implementation of fraud corporate strategies like mergers, acquisitions, absorptions and diversifications;
- Monitoring the major issues of conflicts of managing director/CEO, Board of Directors and shareholders and misuse of corporate assets;
- Examine the processes of disclosers and communication; and
- Selection of key executives, career planning and succession planning of senior executives.[5]

Board of Directors is the representatives of shareholders and it is in between the CEO and the shareholders as shown in Fig 17.1. If the Board of Directors does not function in good faith the and seriously, it contributes for the failure of the corporate governance.

Board of Directors in different companies contributes differently to the corporate governance due to variations in goals and duties, structure, composition, size of the board, board leadership and board committees.

The board of directors should be effective in order to contribute for efficient corporate governance. An effective Board of Directors is:

- **Heterogeneous**–consisting of people with significantly varied backgrounds, managerial experience at different levels in different fields and geographical locations.
- Free of non-combatants or non-contributing members,
- Small in size
- Free of "Yes-Men"
- **Task-oriented:** Its discussions should centre on achieving specific and common objectives and not reaching broad-brush political or policy conclusions.
- Performance oriented with regular analysis, explanation and redirection of achievement.
- **Flexible:** Its members are not bound to the boss or to a friend or loyal subordinates. There is no permanent majority in supporting the causes. So, board supports the cause, whichever case makes the best sense.
- **Lead democratically:** Each director's opinion is freely presented and impartially judged.

Board Committees

Normally various directors of different boards are not the employees of the company for which they act as directors of the board and they may be employed somewhere else. Board committees are formed to deal with various issues including confidential issues in depth.

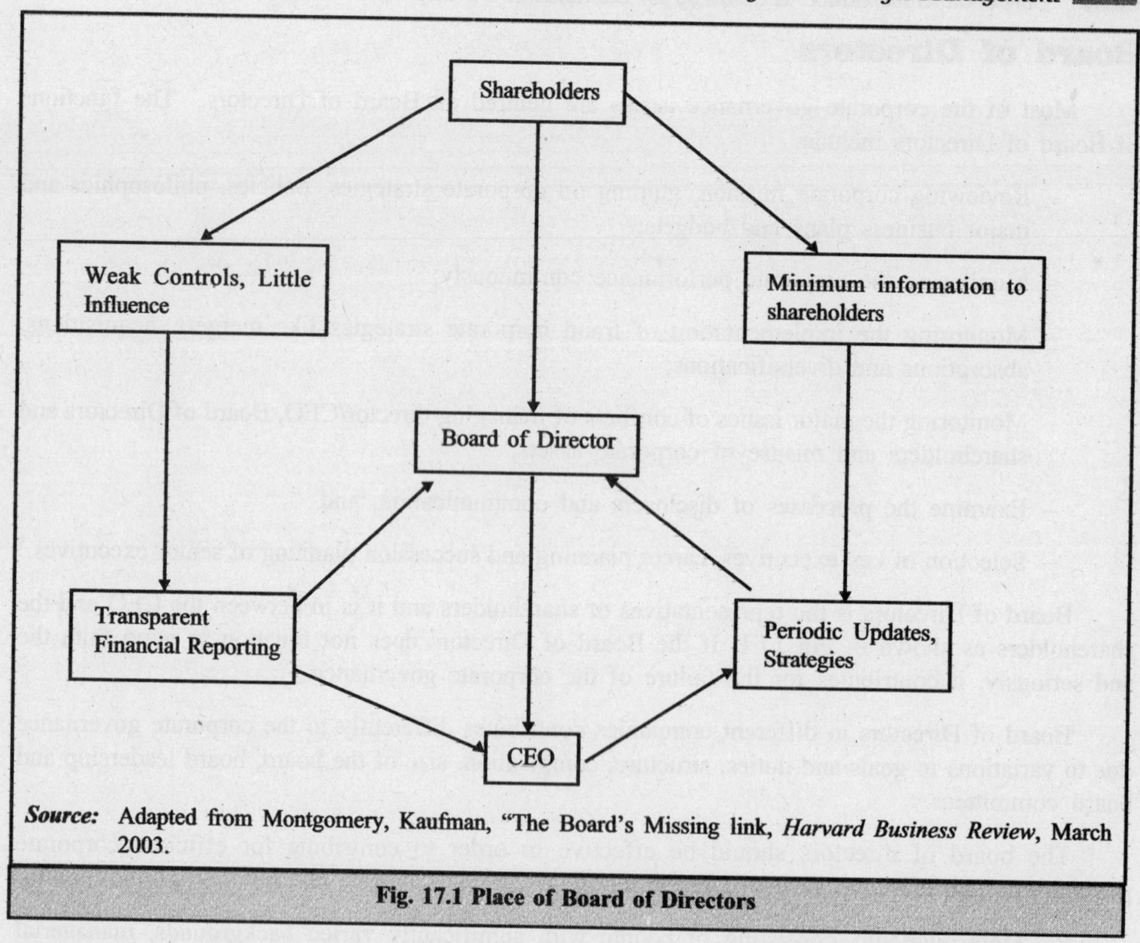

Source: Adapted from Montgomery, Kaufman, "The Board's Missing link, *Harvard Business Review*, March 2003.

Fig. 17.1 Place of Board of Directors

These Committees consist of specialists in the area concerned who can discuss the issues in detail. Members of these committees reduce burden on board of directors and are useful to the board on sensitive and confidential issues.

Other parties

Other parties for the corporate governance include company secretary, senior executives, and employees. All these parties have direct and in bearing on the company's performance as well as long run sustainable growth of the company. In addition, these parties are also interested in the efficient working of the company. Secretary, senior executives and employees receive salaries and benefits.

The other parties are customers, banks and financial companies, suppliers of material, market intermediaries and the society at large. Customers receive goods, banks receive interest, suppliers receive price, market intermediaries receive commission and the society receive certain benefits like infrastructural facilities and boom of the economic activities.

If any party receives the benefits in the share of other parties of the corporate governance or stakeholders, that issue would invariably lead to the problem of corporate governance. In addition, any decision of the CEO or board of directors, if result in inappropriate distribution of benefits/ shares, those issues also lead to the problems of corporate governance.

Good corporate governance should be maintained by avoiding the problems, by following certain principles. Now, we discuss these principles.

(E) PRINCIPLE OF GOOD CORPORATE GOVERNANCE

Good corporate governance can be achieved when the parties to governance perform their respective functions in honesty, trust, integrity, openness, greater responsibly and accountability, performance orientation, mutual respect and commitment to the company's goals. The principles of good corporate governance include:

Good corporate governance can be achieved when the parties to governance perform theirrespective functions in honesty, trust, integrity, openness, greater responsibly and accountability, performance orientation, mutual respect and commitment to the company's goals.

Rights and Equitable Treatment of shareholders: Shareholders are the real owners of the company. Therefore they have the rights for not only getting just dividend, but for ensuring proper functioning of the company. All other parties take the benefits from the sacrifices of the shareholders. Therefore, all other parties should treat the shareholders fairly and ethically. They should provide true and accurate information to the shareholders.

Obligations of all stakeholders: All other stakeholders of the company like board of directors, CEO, senior executives, bankers and suppliers should discharge their obligations properly towards the company. This ensures that company receives its share from all the stakeholders.

Role and Responsibilities of the Board: As presented earlier, the board is the representative of the shareholders. The board is in between the shareholders and the CEO. The board has to play its role in good faith and discharge its responsibilities towards the shareholders and other stakeholders. Board has to ensure disclosers, transparency of the business and efficient achievement of strategies ethically.

Integrity and Ethical Behaviour: All the stakeholders of corporate governance should make decisions, implement them, perform their functions and activities with integrity. They should behave ethically with all parties as well as in all issues.

Disclosures and Transparency

Companies should disclose all the relevant data and information accurately to the parties concerned and investing public. Further, all the officers of the company should maintain transparency in their activities including major strategy implementations, agreements, understandings and joint ventures.

Understandings and Joint Ventures

Corporate governance can't be achieved on its own despite the proposition of various principles. There should be mechanisms and controls. Now, we shall discuss the mechanisms and controls to ensure good corporate governance.

(F) MECHANISMS AND CONTROLS TO ENSURE GOOD CORPORATE GOVERNANCE

The parties to corporate governance sometimes fail to follow the principles of corporate governance either voluntarily or involuntarily. Therefore corporate governance control mechanisms are developed in order to minimize the inefficiencies of the system. These controls are classified into internal corporate governance controls and external corporate governance controls.

Internal Corporate Governance Controls

Internal corporate governance controls are those designed within the company to check the actions and set them in the right direction. These controls include:

Monitoring by the Board of Directors

Board of directors are authorized to safeguard the interest of the shareholders by reviewing and safeguarding corporate strategy formulation and implementation, monitoring corporate performance and overseeing major capital expenditure.

Boards to monitor the activities of the CEO and the senior executives should consist of heterogeneous group, free from non-combatants, small in size and oriented towards the task and the organizational good of long-term growth and sustainability.

Qualities of Directors for Efficient Governance

The directors with the following qualities can monitor the actions of CEO and other senior executives:

- confidence,
- courage,
- free standing posture,
- free thinking, ability to avoid conflict of interest,
- respect for confidentiality matters,
- ability to ask the CEO and senior executives probing questions,
- enthusiasm,
- constructive use of ability and influence,
- commitment,
- making penetrating suggestions for innovation, and
- strategic direction and planning.

Composition of the Board

The size of the board should be optimum of around six directors to monitor the corporate governance principles efficiently. The board should consist of outsider lead directors, who in turn assist in selection of members in board committees, agendas of meetings checking the disclosure information etc. Such a lead director will monitor the unethical and immoral actions of CEO and other senior executives. In addition, boards should consist of independent directors who can control the unethical practices without bias as they do not have any vested interests.

Evaluating Directors' Performance

Directors should be held greater accountability to the shareholders as well as other stakeholders. To ensure this, the voting pattern and decision-making pattern of the directors should be recorded, and analyzed along with the output/consequences of the decisions and fed it to all the parties concerned including the directors. This evaluation would help the directors to improve their performance in monitoring internal control procedures.

Procedures for Governance

Internal control procedures are the rules and regulations formulated by the Board of Directors, CEO and senior management to ensure the conduct of the business on sound business principles and to avoid all kinds mishandling of business dealings. Those procedures include finance regulations, human resource policies, and procedures with regard agreements and understandings with external agencies.

Internal Auditors

Almost all major companies appoint internal auditors in order to ensure that financial transactions are in accordance with the accepted and established financial prudential norms. Internal auditors check the financial transactions and report the deviations to the board of directors. Internal auditors ensure the reliability of financial statements, results and reporting. They also ensure that the financial transactions are in accordance with the established and accepted norms.

Balance of Power

Every major decision of the company should be appraised critically by other individuals or group. This practice ensures the thorough analysis of the decision making events, and processes, identify the possible hindrances, plan for overcoming such deviations and thereby improve the effectiveness of the decision/possible action. These checks of balance of power would arrest the possible unethical and immoral acts and possible failures of the decision when implemented.

Remuneration

Remuneration package of the board of directors, CEO and the senior executives should ensure the performance of the activities ethically. It does mean that the remuneration package should include ethical performance-based pay plus benefits. In addition, certain portion of the remuneration should be in the form of ethical performance-based gratuity. This amount would be paid after the completion of term of office, if no act of the officer concerned is found to be unethical. Similarly, certain portion of the remuneration should be in the form of pension, which would be paid monthly after the expiry of the term of office until the death of the officer concerned or detection of any unethical act while he/she was in the term of office, which ever is earlier. Now, we shall discuss the external corporate governance controls.

External Corporate Governance Controls

There are a variety of external corporate governance controls. The significant among them include:

- Competition
- Government Regulations
- Managerial labour market
- Media Pressure
- Role of Universities and Business Schools
- Takeovers

External corporate governance controls include:
- Competition
- Government Regulations
- Managerial labour market
- Media Pressure
- Role of Universities and Business Schools
- Takeovers

Competition

Threats of competition not only with regard to marketing and attracting best employees but also in attracting investors, suppliers and market intermediaries force the companies to be honest and truthful in providing accurate information and make ethical decisions.

Government Regulations

Governments impose regulations with regard to disclosures, norms to be followed and regulations to be addressed to the Government. These regulations should ensure the effective implementation of these controls as the failure of the enforcement machinery of the government has been the main reason for failure of corporate governance in the past.

Managerial Labour Market

Adequate supply of qualified and talented human resources for managerial jobs would provide an opportunity to the company to employ qualified people. In addition, adequate supply would set the mind of the company to adequately control and otherwise dispense with the services of the unethical executives.

Role of Universities and Business Schools

Universities and other management/business schools should incorporate corporate governance and managerial ethics courses in their programmes in order to ensure that executives set their minds towards ethical behaviour rather than thinking of short run credit/gains and short-cuts for efficient performance.

Media Pressure

Media should investigate into the corporate activities and publish widely the unethical practices. Media can provide information to the parties concerned and alert them from making a wrong decision and act based on the misleading information provided by the corporations.

Takeovers

Companies that are poor in corporate governance should be taken over by or absorbed by the major corporations that are good in corporate governance. Such takeovers would alert the companies from misconducts. Further, government should encourage such takeovers.

Other Measures

There are certain other measures that can ensure corporate governance like small shareholders' network, gaining voting strengths, supply of accounting information and external auditing firm, and enforcement of rules and laws. Now, we shall discuss these measures.

Small shareholders' Network

Providing information to small shareholders is costly to the organizations. In addition, companies take small shareholders for free ride on the judgments of large professional investors. Organization of small shareholder's network would solve this problem to a greater extent.

Gaining voting strengths

Network of small shareholders would gain significant voting strength, which can check and pose threat to the unethical resolutions including of appointment of directors.

Supply of Accounting Information and External Auditing firm

Information with regard to accounting and financial position is most essential for the investing public, bankers, creditors and other stakeholders. The financial manager of the company should be ethical in providing accurate information without incorporating any misleading clauses.

Accountant/financial manager and auditors provide financial information to the capital market. The directors of the company should ensure and monitor that the financial information to be provided should be in compliance with the statutory and ethical obligations and rely on auditor's competence.

Accounting firms should act as an independent organization in auditing the accounts as well as in reporting and providing accounting information. Further, the companies should not follow any creative accounting concepts which are in conflict with the statutory and ethical requirements.

USA enacted changes in the form of Sarbanes – Oxley Act in response to Enron's failure for maintaining good corporate governance, prohibiting accounting firms from providing auditing and management consulting services. Similar provisions are incorporated under clause 49 of Securities and Exchange Board of India Act in India. Collapse of Enron and Satyam Computers are the examples for providing misleading accounting and financial information to the investors and creditors.

Enforcement of Rules and Laws

It would be easy to formulate rules as well as enactment of laws. The most difficult one is their enforcement. In fact, poor enforcement leads to poor corporate governance. Weak enforcement encourages corruptive and unethical practices on the part of executives. Therefore, governments should have efficient machinery to ensure strict enforcement.

Enlightened Directors

Enlightened directors think and act beyond the rules, laws and regulations. Such directors think more ethically and from an "integrative approach".

Conclusion

Companies should view the corporate governance as a strategy for long run sustainable growth and survival. They should also ensure that the boards should be structured appropriately to ensure the implementation of rules, regulations, ethical and moral principles and obligations. In addition, the governments should strengthen their machineries for perfect implementation of laws in addition to enacting the appropriate laws to ensure that the corporate governance is followed. The accounting and auditing firms should follow ethical and code of conduct that ensure fair profession rather than running profession like an unethical business to help the corporations to govern their organizations ethically for the balanced interest of all their stakeholders.

POINTS TO BE REMEMBERED

- The basic purpose of most of the business organizations is to maximize the shareholder's wealth.
- Corporate Governance is a voluntary code of conduct that the board of directors particularly the chief executive officer of the business organisation is expected to follow in operating the business.
- Corporate Governance is highly essential from the point of view of the shareholders, customers, employees and company and society at large for the survival and sustainable growth of the company.
- Parties to the corporate governance are broadly divided into two groups viz., direct parties and indirect parties. Direct Parties are shareholders, CEO, Board of Director and the Senior Management.

- Corporate governance principles include: Rights and Equitable Treatment of shareholders, obligations to shareholders and other stakeholders, role and responsibilities of the board and the like.
- Mechanisms and controls to ensure corporate governance include internal and external measures.

KEY WORDS

- Corporate Governance
- Board of Directors
- Enforcement Rules
- External measures
- Transparency
- Disclosures
- Strategy
- Takeovers
- Media Pressure
- Social Organisations
- Structure
- Internal Auditors
- Universities
- Competition

QUESTION FOR DISCUSSION

- What is corporate governance?
- What is the need for corporate governance?
- Explain the role of corporate governance in the process of strategic management.
- State and discuss different parties to corporate governance.
- What are the principles of corporate governance?
- What are the mechanism and controls available to ensure good corporate governance?
- Discuss internal and external parties and measures of corporate governance.

REFERENCES

1. wps.pearsoned.co.uk/wps/media/objects/1065/1090612/glossary/htm (Accessed on 12/04/2009).
2. www.quantum3.co.za/c1%20 Glossary.htm.
3. Robert A. Pitts and David Lei, "*Strategic Management*", Thomson, 2006, p.486.
4. Vasudha Joshi, "*Corporate Governance*", Foundation Books, new Delhi, 2004, p.4.
5. Ibid., p.95.
6. Mills Geoffery, "*On the Board*", Gower Publishing Limited, in association with the Institute of Directors, Aldershot, UK, 1981.
7. Denis D.K. and J.J. Mc Connell, "Internal Corporate Governance", *Journal of Finance and Quantitative Analysis*, 38(1), 2003.
8. http://en.wikipedia.org.

18 CHAPTER

CORPORATE STRATEGIC FAILURES

Chapter Outline

(A) Introduction

(B) Enron Scandal

(C) Strategic Failure of Satyam Computer Services

(D) Failure of Dot.Coms

(E) Sony's Strategic Failures

(F) Conclusion

Learning Objectives

After studying this chapter, you should be able to –

- Understand the reasons for failure of Enron;
- Analyse the reasons responsible for the failure of Satyam Computer Services;
- Find the circumstances responsible for the failure of Dot.Coms

(A) INTRODUCTION

Managements of almost all the companies make strategic decisions systematically and yet some of the companies fail to achieve their basic purpose of survival while other companies fail to achieve the objectives like earning profits as well as maximizing shareholders' wealth. Though the managements make all possible efforts with utmost care and formulate and implement strategies with utmost seriousness, companies declare bankruptcy that leads to the loss of all capital as well as colossal waste of nation's economic and other resources.

Around 30,000 companies were established in USA in 2003, but about 95% collapsed in the following year itself.

Around 30,000 companies were established in USA in 2003, but about 95% collapsed in the following year itself. Success is transient, and sustained superior performance can be claimed by just a few companies. Strategy deals with achieving sustained superior performance with an integrated approach which cuts across functional domains and looks at the organization in a holistic sense. A significant portion of the literature dwells on the success stories - Southwest, Toyota, Nucor, Dell... And yet, in sheer statistical terms, there is perhaps more to be learned from the failures than from the few successes. what can we learn from the failures? Can smart managers frequently overlook the dangers lurking round the corner? What are the pitfalls to avoid? Can we develop the concept of avoiding failure? How can organizations overcome strategic equilibrium?

Therefore, one should understand not only the strategies of successful companies, but also the strategies of failed companies in order to prevent the possible failure of achievement of strategic goals. Now, we shall study various cases of failed companies in order to draw lessons.

(B) ENRON SCANDAL

Kenneth Lay founded Enron in 1985 by merging Houston Natural Gas and InterNorth. Enron was the largest merchant of natural gas in North America by 1992, and the gas trading business became the second largest contributor to Enron's net income. Enron pursued a diversification strategy with a view to grow at a fast rate. Consequent upon its diveersification strategy, Enron had become a conglomerate that both owned and operated gas pipelines, pulp and paper plants, broadband assets, electricity plants, and water plants internationally by 2001. The corporation also traded in financial markets for the same types of products and services.

Strategic Failures

Enron's executives followed non-transparent accounting and financial system.

Strategic failiures of Enron include mark-to-market accounting, special purpose entities,

Mark-to-market Accounting: However, the company's executives followed non-transparent accounting and financial system. In addition the company followed a complex business model that stretched the limits of accounting, requiring that the company use accounting limitations to manage earnings and modify the balance sheet to portray a favorable depiction of its performance. Enron executives concentrated on managing accounts based on the stock market requirements of increasing the market value of share through the use of mark-to-market accounting that found new ways to hide its debt.

Thus, the executives of the company were able to hide billions in debt from failed deals and projects by making use of accounting loopholes, special purpose entities, and poor financial reporting. Enron's board of directors and audit committee were misled by the Chief Financial Officer Andrew Fastow and other executives of high-risk accounting issues. "The Enron scandal grew out of a steady accumulation of habits and values and actions that began years before and finally spiralled out of control.

The U.S. Securities and Exchange Commission (SEC) began an investigation when the stock price of Enron phenomenally came down from $90 in mid 2000 to $ 1 by the end of November 2001. Finally Enron filed for bankruptcy on 2nd December 2001.

Special purpose entities: Enron used special purpose entities to fund or manage risks associated with specific assets. The company elected to disclose minimal details on its use of special purpose entities. For financial reporting purposes, a series of rules dictates whether a special purpose entity is a separate entity from the sponsor. In total, by 2001, Enron had used hundreds of special purpose entities to hide its debt.

Enron used special purpose entities to fund or manage risks associated with specific assets.

Enron created special purpose entities like Chewco Investments L.P. which raised debt guaranteed by Enron and was used to acquire CalPER's joint venture stake for $383 million. Because of Fastow's organization of Chewco, JEDI's losses were kept off of Enron's balance sheet.

Corporate Governance on Paper: Enron had a good corporate governance model including outside board of directors, audit committee on paper only. Consequently, Enron Enron had a good corporate governance model including outside board of directors, audit committee on paper only could "attract large sums of capital to fund a questionable business model, conceal its true performance through a series of accounting and financing maneuvers, and hype its stock to unsustainable levels." Enron's high-risk accounting practices were not hidden from the board of directors. The board knew of the practices of accounting and creation of special purpose entities and took no action to prevent Enron from using them.

Enron had a good corporate governance model including outside board of directors, audit committee on paper only.

Executive Compensation: Employees had large expense accounts and many executives were paid sometimes twice as much as competitors. In 1998, the top 200 highest-paid employees earned $193 million from salaries, bonuses, and stock. Two years later, the figure jumped to $1.4 billion.

Failure of Financial Audit: Enron's auditor firm, Arthur Andersen, was also responsible and as such it was accused of applying reckless standards in their audits because of a conflict of interest over the significant consulting fees generated by Enron. In 2000, Arthur Andersen earned $25 million in audit fees and $27 million in consulting fees (this amount accounted for roughly 27% of the audit fees of public clients for Arthur Andersen's Houston office). The auditors' methods were questioned as either being completed for conflicted incentives or a lack of expertise to adequately evaluate the financial complexities Enron employed.

Lessons: Lessons from the strategic failure of Enron are man-made particularly its CEOs, board of directors (see Box 18.1) and financial executives. These are manipulating accounts, creation of special purpose entities, complex business model and on paper corporate governance measures.

Thus, failure to honour corporate governance measures is the major reason for the failure of Enron. Having learnt lessons from Enron, now we shall study failure of Satyam Computers

BOX 18.1 STRATEGIC PLANNING: WHAT IS THE BOARD'S ROLE?

How should the Board be involved in strategic planning? This is a frequently asked question. The key objective of strategic planning is to identify the sound course and direction for the organization that optimizes the organization's future potential. Setting the strategy is the responsibility of the senior management team — the team is responsible for the success or failure of the strategy. This team is close to both the customers and the internal workings of the company and is best suited to determine the course and direction for the company.

How can the Board play a role? While the Board is not responsible for setting strategy it can often give valuable input before the strategic planning process begins and act as a sounding board as part of a review process. Hence, the Board can play an important role during several steps of the strategic planning process:

1. Before the process starts – the Board gives guidance including an overview of future environment along with specific opportunities and issues to be considered during the strategic planning process. The Board will often have a broader vision, enabling the team to consider more choices before selecting the optimal course and direction.

2. After strategy development – the Board provides a review function; review of the strategy to make sure that it is internally consistent and that there are concrete implementation plans for key strategic objectives.

3. During the year – the Board should monitor progress to ensure the strategy stays on track or changes when business conditions necessitate change. Some Boards participate in all three steps — others in steps two and three. In the case where the Board is not close to the business then the process should include just steps two and three. If the Board has members who do have broad business experience and understand the industry than participation upfront is often beneficial. ***Board Involvement before the Strategic Planning Process Begins*** **Typically Board members work through the following steps:**

1. Industry Scenario – this allows Board members to give the strategic planning team their insight into industry trends.

2. Winner's Profile – Board members may see characteristics of the winner that team members may not see (Board members may have a better understanding of what a company will look like at $100 million than the team members of a $50 million company looking to grow to $100 million.).

3. Opportunities – to be evaluated — the broader make-up of the Board may uncover additional opportunities to be researched.

4. Threats/Issues – the Board members may have a broader vision of what the risks are in the business. The Board should be providing guidelines and suggestions rather than edicts. The senior management team should then use the input as they work on the strategic plan. Some ideas may be incorporated into the strategic plan — others, while considered, may not make it into the plan. This does not mean that the ideas were not good, it just means that with limited resources the team had to select the few items to work on rather than choosing a large number and becoming unfocused.This is a general format for Board involvement before the process begins — however, due to the individual nature of a Board's relationship with the senior management team we continue to work with companies to design programs that work for their specific requirements. The key thought is that Board members often have wide ranging experience and you need to ask yourself the question: How can we best leverage their expertise when developing a strategic plan?

Source: http://www.cssp.com/strategicplanning/blog/?p=261

(C) STRATEGIC FAILURE OF SATYAM COMPUTER SERVICES

The saga of Satyam Computers will go down as the worst episode of corporate governance failure in corporate India. The fraud which is in excess of Rs 7,000 crore, is unfortunately of a truly global scale. Post the aborted merger with Maytas, many had suspected that Ramalinga Raju and family were heavily leveraged at a personal level, stuck in property and thus, needed a bail-out. Nobody, however, I think suspected that Satyam itself was a fraud, with no cash and a non-existent margin structure. Raju's letter implies that the company is basically unprofitable at a net level, and made no money over the last few years. How can Satyam, with 50,000 employees and global scale, make no money at all, when even mid-tier mediocre IT companies make at least 10 per cent operating margins? How can this fraud be going on for years? How can the auditors not have confirmed cash balances, and that too of Rs 5,000 crore? Cash is supposed to be real, profit an accounting fiction, but here the cash itself was fraudulent. Raju goes on to state that he was going to merge Maytas Infra and his privately-held property company to bail out Satyam, and not use

Satyam's cash to bail himself out (as assumed by most who opposed the merger). Raju also writes that he pledged all his shares to raise cash to pump into Satyam, to keep the charade going.

Post Enron in the US, we saw a slew of regulations culminating in the Sarbanes-Oxley Act. In India, we have by and large adequate laws and disclosure standards, though we can improve disclosure in areas like promoters-pledged shares or detailing the bank accounts where the company's cash is parked. Our framework of a majority of independent directors, minimum frequency of board meetings, shareholder approval needed for major decisions etc is of global standards. We also force our CEO and CFO to certify the accuracy of the published accounts. We can tinker with new disclosures but it is unlikely to make much difference. Satyam after all reported its results in Indian GAAP, IFRS and US GAAP, and even gave audited half-yearly statements. With a US listing it was also under the jurisdiction of the SEC, but none of this made any difference.

The ultimate defense against poor governance is the market itself. It was well-known that Satyam had a suspiciously high and growing current account balance, as well as nearly Rs 400 crore interest accrued but not received on deposits. Why will a company keep Rs 2,000 crore in a current account? Why will the bank not credit interest to a deposit for multiple quarters? While investors can legitimately claim that they were relying on a PriceWaterhouse-signed balance sheet, one of the lessons of the sub-prime debacle is that investors cannot rely blindly on external service providers.

Investors should exercise proper due diligence, and not allocate capital to companies with poor disclosure or governance practices. Investors cannot allow large companies to have unknown auditors, or rubber-stamp boards and must force them to split the CEO/chairman role in substance. If investors refuse to back poor managements, you will see large valuation gaps for companies in the same industries. If poor governance attracts poor valuations, it will incentives shareholder-friendly behaviour and marginalize companies with weak corporate governance. Investor memory also cannot be short, poor governance has to attract a permanent de-rating.

Lessons: Unethical practices of auditors, accountants, management and credit-rating firms together contributed for the failure of Satyam Computer Services Limited.

(D) FAILURE OF DOT.COMS

A dot.com company, (or simply a dot.com) does its business on the Internet. Many dot.coms were formed to take advantage of the surplus of venture capital funding. Some were launched with very thin business plans. The stated goal was often to "get big fast", The exit strategy usually included an IPO and a large payoff for the founders. With the stock market crash around the year 2000 that ended the dot.com bubble, many failed and failing dot.com companies were referred to punningly as dot.bombs, Many of the surviving firms dropped the .com suffix from their names.

Reasons for Failure

One of the biggest mistake early dot com businesses made was that they were more interested in attracting visitor to their website but not necessarily winning them over to customers. Early dot com businesses also failed to take the time to properly researching the situation before starting their business. There are thousands of failed companies from the dot-com bubble of the late 1990s. Some companies like Kozmo.com failed to adopt full price strategy that includes only operational cost. The business plan of one dot.com specified 12x as many sales as actually occurred in the first 12 months of operations. The cheap plastic, easily breakable HandSpring devices, sold directly by YadaYada via a reseller agreement, accounted for 96% of support calls vs. the magnesium cased Palm devices, despite the latter's market predominance at the time, and the resulting consumer discontent resulted in many returns and cancelled contracts.

One of the biggest mistake early dot. com businesses made was that they were more interested in attracting visitor to their website but not necessarily winning them over to customers.

Lessons

Failure of most of the dot.coms was due to lack of business plans and strategic approach to establishment and growth of a business organization and a goal of earning fast money.

Now, we shall study a few strategic failures in case of corporate level strategies and functional level strategies.

(E) SONY'S STRATEGIC FAILURES

Sony's reluctance to compete with products such as Apple's iPod music players, mainly due to resistance from the firm's music and movie divisions.

Sony Computer Entertainment boss Ken Kutaragi has lashed out at Sony's failure to compete in key sectors such as the MP3 player market in the past, in an unusually direct statement where he claimed that the firm is "growing up". Company's reluctance to compete with products such as Apple's iPod music players, mainly due to resistance from the firm's music and movie divisions. Until recently, Sony has insisted on sticking doggedly to proprietary formats such as the ATRAC music format, instead of using popular open formats such as MP3 which have been embraced by competitors.

According to Kutaragi, this approach - recently addressed by products such as PlayStation Portable, which supports open standards such as MP3 for music and MP4 for video - was driven by concerns over piracy from the media divisions. In a rare admission of mistakes and an unusually direct criticism of the company's management, Kutaragi said that Sony's innovation had been "diluted", but promised that these problems had now been identified. "It's just starting," he told reporters at the club; "we're growing up." Kutaragi is pushing the PlayStation Portable as a combined platform for games, music and movies, and the forthcoming PlayStation 3 home console is also expected to offer significant media functionality as well as a powerful videogames platform.

(F) CONCLUSION

Strategic failure of companies and lessons learnt indicate that corporate governance as well as business ethics play a vital role for preventing failure and help for sustainable growth.

POINTS TO BE REMEMBERED

- Though the managements make all possible efforts with utmost care and formulate and implement strategies with utmost seriousness, companies declare bankruptcy that leads to the loss of all capital as well as colossal waste of nation's economic and other resources.
- Failure to honour corporate governance measures is the major reason for the failure of Enron.
- Unethical practices of auditors, accountants, management and credit-rating firms together contributed fro the failure of Satyam Computer Services Limited.
- Failure of most of the dot.coms was due to lack of business plans and strategic approach to establishment and growth of a business organization and a goal of earning fast money.

KEY TERMS

- Strategic Failure
- Corporate Governance
- Audit Committees
- Enron
- Dot.Com
- Satyam Computers
- Business Ethics
- Credit Rating Firms

QUESTIONS FOR DISCUSSION

1. Discuss the reasons for strategic failure of different companies.
2. To what extent the failure to implement corporate governance is responsible for corporate governance?
3. Explain the reasons for the failure of dot.coms.

REFERENCES

1. http://www.bettermanagement.com/
2. Healy, Paul M.; Krishna G. Palepu (Spring 2003). "The Fall of Enron" (PDF). *Journal of Economic Perspectives* **17** (2): 5. http://www-personal.umich.edu/~kathrynd/JEP.FallofEnron.pdf.
3. Healy, Paul M.; Krishna G. Palepu (Spring 2003). "The Fall of Enron" (PDF). *Journal of Economic Perspectives* **17** (2): 9. http://www-personal.umich.edu/~kathrynd/JEP.FallofEnron.pdf. Retrieved 2009-08-04.
4. McLean, Bethany; Peter Elkind. *The Smartest Guys in the Room*. pp. 132–133.
5. Healy, Paul M.; Krishna G. Palepu (Spring 2003). "The Fall of Enron" (PDF). *Journal of Economic Perspectives* **17** (2): 10. http://www-personal.umich.edu/~kathrynd/JEP.FallofEnron.pdf.
6. Healy, Paul M.; Krishna G. Palepu (Spring 2003). "The Fall of Enron" (PDF). *Journal of Economic Perspectives* **17** (2): 11. http://www-personal.umich.edu/~kathrynd/JEP.FallofEnron.pdf.
7. Healy, Paul M.; Krishna G. Palepu (Spring 2003). "The Fall of Enron" (PDF). *Journal of Economic Perspectives* **17** (2): 4. http://www-personal.umich.edu/~kathrynd/JEP.FallofEnron.pdf.
8. McLean, Bethany; Peter Elkind. *The Smartest Guys in the Room*. p. 401.
9. McLean, Bethany; Peter Elkind. *The Smartest Guys in the Room*. p. 241.
10. Healy, Paul M.; Krishna G. Palepu (Spring 2003). "The Fall of Enron" (PDF). *Journal of Economic Perspectives* **17** (2): 15. http://www-personal.umich.edu/~kathrynd/JEP.FallofEnron.pdf.
11. http://www.business-standard.com/india/news/akash-prakash-indias-enron/00/09/345660/
12. http://www.usatoday.com/money/dotcoms/dot039.htm
13. Glasner, Joanne (2001-08-31). "*Dot's In A Name No More*". Wired news. http://www.wired.com/news/business/1,46403-0.html.
14. http://www.gamesindustry.biz/articles/father-of-playstation-slams-sonys-strategic-failures

✦ ✦ ✦

GAMES AND CASES

(A) Game- Strategic Planning-Made Easy

(B) Method of Case Analysis

(C) Case Study-1: Bright Lightings Limited

(D) Case Study-2: Artos Industries Limited

(E) Case Study-3: Microsoft

(F) Case Study-4: Sony

(G) Case Study-5: Xerox Corporation

(A) GAME

STRATEGIC PLANNING*

MADE EASY

Strategic planning can be a powerful tool for organization effectiveness. Here's a simple model to get you started.

Strategic planning is a familiar buzzword in most organizations, but it can mean many different things — from long-range daydreams to tediously detailed quarterly objectives.

However, the term is interpreted, there's a need for some kind of strategic planning in organizations of all sizes and cultures. A plan and the process of developing it can be powerful tools for making organizations more effective. Here's a simple planning model to get you started.

Who, What, and Why

The first step is deciding who, what, and why. the planning process will work best if the following questions are answered in the beginning.

- Who will be included in the process and at what point? (Usually, the more the better)
- What will the process focus on? Next year's goals? Mission changes? Internal reorganization?
- Why have a plan? To increase competitiveness? To satisfy customers? To improve the work climate?

Spending some time answering those basic questions sets the stage for good planning. (See the sidebar for more questions to consider.)

A Simple Framework

A simple framework can help you organize the elements of the plan and know what questions need to be answered. The figures below illustrates a framework built around the following planning elements:

- Mission
- Key results areas
- Critical issues
- Goals
- Objectives
- Srategies.

Mission

It may sound simple, but can you exactly define the true "business" of your organization? The planning group should understand and agree on that definition before going any further.

A good mission statement can help. It clarified what the organization provides, who its customers are, and what the products or services do for those customers. The mission statement should also describe how the organisation differs from its competition.

The first step in writing the mission is to make three lists: products and services, customers, and a description of what the products and services do. Try composing a sentence that combines the essence of each list. Keep boiling it down until that sentence represents the key ideas from each area, in the fewest possible words.

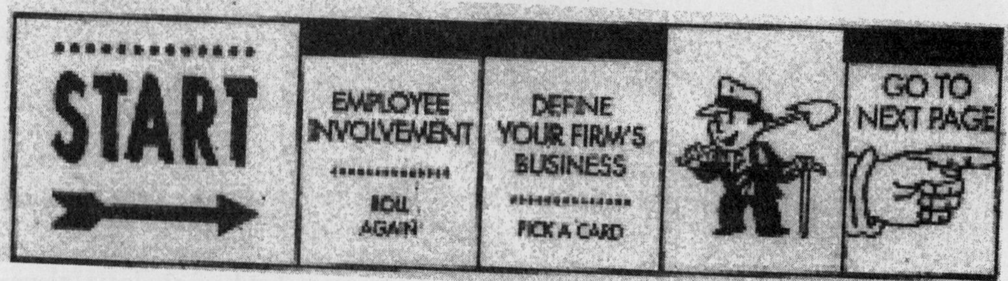

Key Results Areas

The next step is to decide what results will indicate success. A key results area is any area in which you must be successful in order to accomplish your mission. It can be anything from the number of widgets produced to the level of customer satisfaction. Your final list of key results areas should have five to ten major headings.

The best way to go about defining those areas is to list all the stakeholders in your business. They may be customers, employees, stockholders, or other community members. It's important to identify what each of them expects of your organization. Most likely, you'll find many different expectations among them.

Put all the ideals that you can think of on the list. Then group them into major headings. Try to reduce the number of headings to between five and ten. Combine your final list and your mission statement to spell out your organisational goals.

Critical Issues

What's going on, inside and outside the organisation, is the real stuff of planning. In particular, look at the issues that may affect your ability to deliver on the key results areas and accomplish the mission.

Defining critical issues can be overwhelming. They can be almost anything — for example, competition, product or service offerings, government regulations, new technologies, and staff skills.

A simple but effective approach is to ask all members of the planning group to write down on 10 critical issues that they believe will be the most instrumental to organisational success in the next three years.

Group members should also write down what they think are the organisation's primary strengths, weaknesses, opportunities, and threats. Ask everyone to be as specific as possible.

When the lists are complete, make a group list. Go around the table asking each member to name one item until everyone has exhausted his or her list. Don't spend any time on discussion at this point, and don't list any item more than once, even though, several people may have mentioned it.

When the group list is complete, you'll probably have 30 to 40 very different items. The next step is to sort and organise them. Before you do that, you may choose to set priorities by having the group select the five items it thinks are the most critical, or simply by identifying the issues that several members had on their individual lists.

To organise the items, group those that have something in common, such as issues about the internal organisation or about competition. Once you've determined a particular grouping, give it a heading and discuss other issues that might be included. Again, you should have five to ten headings.

UNCLEAR DEPARTMENTAL RELATIONSHIPS
GO TO COMMUNICATION
GO BACK TO EMPLOYEE INVOLVEMENT
O.D. CONSULTANT
PICK A CARD
GOAL STATEMENT
GOOD ACTION VERBS
GO AHEAD 2 SPACES
CRITICAL ISSUES
PICK A CARD
UNCLEAR MISSION STATEMENT
LOSE 1 TURN
NO AGREEMENT ON OBJECTIVES
GO BACK 4 SPACES

Goals

In the context of the planning process, a goal is a statement of long-range intentions for a specific aspect of the organisation. If you understand your mission and the primary results that you're trying to achieve — and you've identified the critical issues — the major goals should become evident.

To establish goals, consider each of the groups of critical issues and ask what has to be done to meet the challenge in each area. It usually takes some discussion to reach a resolution, but hang in there. If you've already identified the real issues, now's the time to define an initial plan of attack.

Depending on the size of your group, it may work well to divide into sub-groups of four to seven people. Each subgroup takes one set of issues. The assignment is to better define the issues, draft initial short-term or long-term recommendations, and prepare to lead a discussion in the large group on the first two tasks.

After about two hours, reconvene into one group. Now the assignment is to work through all the sets of issues. the objectives are to reach agreement on the issues and establish at least one long-term goal per set. Short-term items and other specific issues can be listed under subheads.

Some issues may seem to be controlled by outside forces. In such cases, ask what your roles should be. For goals that can't be accomplished at present, ask what planning should take place.

Avoid copping out. Determine your roles, regardless of who has responsibility or when something should happen. Use of the right verb in your goal statement can make it clearer. Examples of such "action" verbs: improve, expand, integrate, create, acquire, implement, and ensure.

For every critical issue heading, there should be at least one major goal that identifies what your organisation will be doing and why. the "what" involves the organisation's primary approach. The "why" relates to key result areas that may be affected.

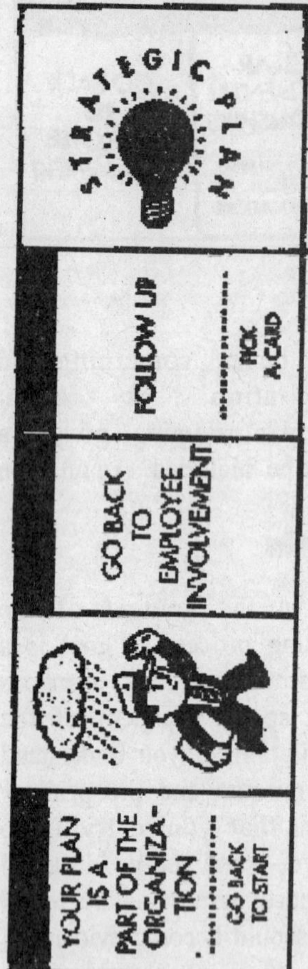

For example, the statement "We will improve our level of customer satisfaction by establishing and meeting service standards that exceed the industry in both quality and responsiveness", isn't a specific action an organisation will take, but it does point to a direction and an expected outcome.

The next step shows how you're going to get there.

Objectives

Simply stated, objectives are specific, short-range initiatives that support the goals. They are next year's projects and tasks for each of the major goal areas. Objectives involve who's going to do what and by when.

In organisations with different departments, each department should outline what it can do to support the goals, including the goals of other departments. That can lead to an exchange of ideas across the organisation as well as the creation of richer ideas. It also encourages collaboration between groups and may result in a unified, integrated organisational effort.

The process of developing objectives is usually best done away from the job at the department or project level. It can involve additional participants from the affected areas of the organisation. If strategic planning is conducted by the board of directors or top management, the objectives phase logically involves operational managers. In a very small organisation, it may simply be the agenda for a staff meeting.

No matter what the structure, the questions at this stage are the same — who, what, when, and how. Answering them should result in a set of clear, measurable objectives that collectively add up to a significant contribution to long-range goals.

QUESTIONS AND ISSUES

Purpose

Context

- Strategic (3 to 5 years). Looks at "blue sky" options. What do we want to look like?
- Operational (1 to 3 years). Looks at specific, measurable goals. Leads to department or individual objectives.

Focus

- Organisation. Who does what? What are our charter duties, and responsibilities? How should each department be evaluated?
- Objectives. What will we commit to achieving? Who will do it? How and when?

Participation

- Top-down. Senior management sets goals and objectives.
- Bottom-up. Every level of management is involved.

People

- Who are the key people to involve?
- Who will be involved at which stages?
- Are any outside perspectives needed?

Process

- How much time will it take? Is there a schedule? What is the meeting format? Will be held off-site?
- Who will facilitate?
- What about follow-up meetings? How can planners get the involvement of employees who aren't at the planning meetings?

Product

- What will it look like?
- Who will it be for?
- How will it be used?

Conceptual model of strategic planning and major components

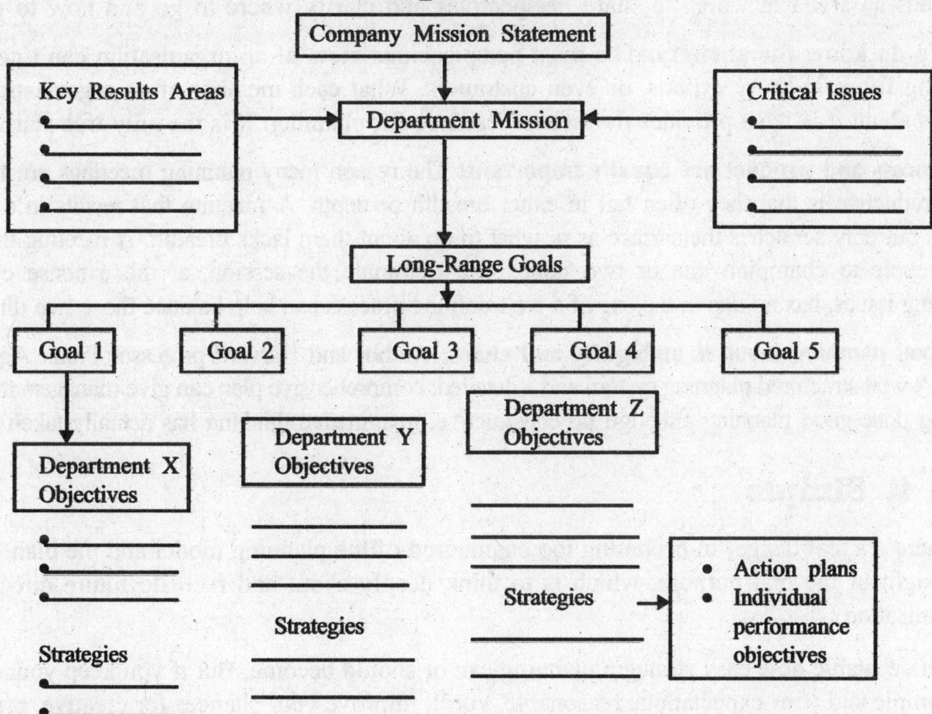

STRATEGIC PLANNING CAN BE FORMIDABLE TASK

Strategies

It's doubtful that any two planning models define strategies the same way. In this model, strategies is a catch-all category. It refers to any underlying assumptions, resource constraints, interdependencies, or other critical considerations that clarify the necessary conditions and requirements for achieving stated objectives.

In that context, strategies may be developed to support either a single objective or a set of objectives for a single goal. In both cases, strategies define how goals will be achieved.

Implementation and Communication

The final steps are implementation and communication. How will you track and follow up on the plan that you've created? How will employees who are not in the planning group learn about the plan and become involved?

The answers to those questions are critical. They ensure that the plan becomes a living part of the organisation and begins to repay the investment and effort that went into its development.

Four Underlying Principles

Strategic planning can be a formidable task. At one time or another, many of us have had tough experiences trying to devise reasonable plans for the future amid the chaos and uncertainty of the present.

As you go about your own planning, keep in mind the following statements. They seem to ring true, at least for the kind of strategic planning that's been described here.

Strategic planning is a myth: Even a very good planning meeting can't predict the future or serve as the sole guide to human resources work. A planning session is a communication event. It provides an arena in which to share perspectives and clarify where to go and how to get there.

We do know the answers: The most perspicacious view of an organisation can't come from consulting firms, industry experts, or even customers. What each member of an organisation knows and feels about it is what provides the richest resource for planning. It is the only true starting point.

Process and product are equally important: The reason many planning meetings are frustrating and unproductive is that they often fail in either breadth or depth. A meeting that results in a great list of issues but only scratches the surface as to what to do about them lacks breadth. A meeting that allows a few people to champion one or two issues that dominate the session, at the expense of equally compelling issues, has no depth. the use of a well-defined process can help balance those two dimensions.

Good planning involves ambiguity and chaos: Author and Harvard professor Frank Aguilar said it best: "A well-structured planning system and a detailed, comprehensive plan can give managers the illusion of having done good planning although no constructive, imaginative thinking has actually taken place."

Keep it Simple

There's a real danger in becoming too enamoured of the planning model and the plan. It's easy to lose sight of the real purpose, which is to think deeply about and recreate future directions for the organisation.

It's debatable how easy strategic planning can or should become. But if you keep your planning model simple and your expectations reasonable, you'll improve your chances for creative, productive, and even enjoyable planning.

✦ ✦ ✦

(B) METHOD OF CASE ANALYSIS

1. INTRODUCTION

Almost all business schools across the globe use the case method as the prime teaching technique for the course on Business Policy and Strategic Management. Students of strategic management practice business policy and strategic management through case analysis.

1. What is a Case?

A case is a description of management problem or situation as viewed or presented to a decision-maker. It is a pedagogical tool which involves a discussion centred around the case. It sets a situation with all the ancillary facts, figures, emotions, opinions, views, grapevine and the like.

A case presents facts, the events and organisational circumstances surrounding a particular managerial situation. It puts the readers at the scene of the action and familiarises them with all the relevant circumstances. The case method includes the special type of instructional material that is developed for the purpose and the special technique of using that material in the instructional process.

2. Need for Case Method

Professor Charles Gragg[3] observed that managerial skills and expertise cannot be acquired through mere listening to lectures and reading books. He suggested that readymade answers about the practice of management cannot be found in text books. This is because of the fact that each managerial situation is different from others with unique aspects, requiring its own diagnosis and judgement. Cases provide the tomorrow's managers with a valuable way to practice wrestling with the actual problems of actual managers in actual companies.

Most of the management students have no or limited knowledge about the practical aspects of management. Cases bridge this gap to some extent and help the students to substitute for practical knowledge by: *(i)* giving broader exposure to different types of situations, companies and industries, *(ii)* placing the students in different roles of case, *(iii)* providing an opportunity to apply principles, concepts and techniques of management to problem situations, and *(iv)* including the students to prepare managerial action plans and to deal with related issues.

3. Objectives of Case Analysis

The objectives of the case analysis are:

(i) To increase the understanding of the students of what managers should and should not do in guiding a business to success.

(ii) To build the students' skills in conducting strategic analysis in a variety of situations, companies and industries.

(iii) To provide the students valuable practice in diagnosing strategic issues, evaluating strategic alternatives with the help of SWOT analysis and formulating practicable plans of action based on the ground realities.

(iv) To enhance the students sense of business judgement as opposed to accepting the opinion of the teacher or "back-of-the-book" answers.

(v) To provide the students an in-depth exposure to a variety of companies and industries, thereby, gaining something close to actual business experience.

Thus, the purpose of the case method is to enhance the students' skills in sizing up situations and developing their managerial judgment about what needs to be done and how to do it. Case analysis helps the students to think actively, to offer critical analysis, to propose action plans based on ground realities, and to explain defend their assessments.

2. HOW TO ANALYSE A CASE?

Students who are habituated to lecture method of teaching are required to re-orient their study habits. A case assignment unlike lecture method of teaching, requires conscientious preparation before class. Student cannot get any benefit from case discussion or he/she can't contribute to the discussion unless, he/she prepares himself/herself thoroughly for the case discussion. The student has to prepare to reflect carefully on the situation presented, develop reasonable thoughts, write well-supported analysis of the situation and a sound, defensible set of suggestions and recommendations about the strategic actions need to be taken. The students can follow the approach discussed below.

1. *Read the case material quickly to get familiarity:* The first time reading of the case provide the students an initial understanding of the situations, issues involved in the case, etc.

2. *Read the case a second time:* This step provides a full command of the facts, information, opinions, views, company culture, values etc.

3. *Read the exhibits, appendices, etc., carefully:* This step provides full information about the case.

4. *Study the case:* The student should recall the difference between reading and studying. Read in-between the lines as the problems may not be apparent in the case material itself. Students have to prepare notes about facts, important situations, information, less important information, situations, etc.

5. *Identify the strategic issues:* Students have to identify the strategic issues in the case. It helps to identify the tools and techniques of analysis and process. As mentioned in step 4, some times the students are required to identify the strategic issues and problems by reading in-between the lines or by digging the information given.

6. *Diagnose the key issues:* The students should use their creative or innovative skills, analytical skills and application skills to diagnose the key issue or key problem in the case. This is the crucial step in the case analysis.

7. *Check the diagnosis:* Students have to check the diagnosis made with the help of questions given at the end of the case. The students should think repeatedly even, if the diagnosis matches with the questions. Students may move to the next step after confirming the diagnosis.

8. *Support diagnosis and opinions with reasons and evidence:* Students have to support their diagnosis and opinions with reasons and evidence.

9. *Checkout conflicting opinions and make some judgements about the validity of all the data and information provided:* Case material may provide contradicting opinions, views and information. Students have to evaluate the opinions, views, data and information provided with the help of their skills of inferences and judgement.

10. *Start analysis of the issues:* After diagnosing the basic issues all other issues relate to the basic issue should be analysed. These issues include calculation of financial ratios, production figures, sales figures, human resource costs and benefits, etc., Exhibit 1 presents the summary of key financial ratios.

Exhibit 1: A Summary of Key Financial Ratios, How They Are Calculated, and What They Show

Ratio	*How Calculated*	*What it Shows*
Profitability Ratios		
1. Gross profit margin	$\frac{\text{Sales} - \text{Cost of goods sold}}{\text{Sales}}$	An indication of the total margin available to cover operating expenses and yield a profit.
2. Operating profit margin (or return on sales)	$\frac{\text{Profits before taxes and before interest}}{\text{Sales}}$	An indication of the firm's profitability from current operations without regard to the interest.
3. Net profit margin (or net return on sales)	$\frac{\text{Profits after taxes}}{\text{Sales}}$	Shows after tax profits per dollar of sales. Subpar profit margins indicate that the firm's sales prices are relatively low or that its costs are relatively high, or both.
4. Return on total assets	$\frac{\text{Profits after taxes}}{\text{Total assets}}$ or $\frac{\text{Profits after taxes + Interest}}{\text{Total assets}}$	A measure of the return on total investment in the enterprise. It is sometimes desirable to add interest to after tax profits to form the numerator of the ratio since total assets are financed by creditors as well as by stockholders; hence, it is accurate to measure the productivity of assets by the returns provided to both classes of investors.
5. Return on stockholders' equity (or return on net worth)	$\frac{\text{Profits after taxes}}{\text{Total stockholders' equity}}$	A measure of the rate of return on the stockholders' investment in the enterprise.
6. Return on common equity	$\frac{\text{Profits after taxes} - \text{Preferred stock dividends}}{\text{Total stockholders' equity} - \text{Par value of preferred stock}}$	A measure of the rate of return on the investment which the owners of the common stock have made in the enterprise.
7. Earnings per share	$\frac{\text{Profits after taxes} - \text{Preferred stock dividends}}{\text{Number of shares of common stock outstanding}}$	Shows the earnings available to the owners of each share of common stock.
Liquidity Ratios		
1. Current ratio	$\frac{\text{Current assets}}{\text{Current liabilities}}$	Indicates the extent to which the claims of short-term creditors are covered by assets that are expected to be converted to cash in a period roughly corresponding to the maturity of the liabilities.
2. Quick ratio (or acid-test ratio)	$\frac{\text{Current assets} - \text{Inventory}}{\text{Current liabilities}}$	A measure of the firm's ability to pay off short-term obligations without

3. Inventory to net working capital	Inventory / (Current assets – Current liabilities)	relying on the sale of its inventories. A measure of the extent to which the firm's working capital is tied up in inventory.
Leverage Ratios		
1. Debt-to-assets ratio	Total debt / Total assets	Measures the extent to which borrowed funds have been used to finance the firm's operations.
2. Debt-to-equity ratio	Total debt / Total stockholders' equity	Provides another measure of the funds provided by creditors versus the funds provided by owners.
3. Long-term debt-to-equity ratio	Long-term debt / Total shareholders' equity	A widely used measure of the balance between debt and equity in the firm's long-term capital structure.
4. Times-interest-earned (or coverage) ratio	Profits before interest and taxes / Total interest charges	Measures the extent to which earnings can decline without the firm becoming unable to meet its annual interest costs.
5. Fixed-charge coverage	(Profits before taxes and interest + Lease obligations) / (Total interest charges + Lease obligations)	A more inclusive indication of the firm's ability to meet all of its fixed-charge obligations.
Activity Ratios		
1. Inventory turnover	Sales / Inventory of finished goods	When compared to industry averages, it provides an indication of whether a company has excessive or perhaps inadequate finished goods inventory.
2. Fixed assets turnover	Sales / Fixed Assets	A measure of the sales productivity and utilization of plant and equipment.
3. Total assets turnover	Sales / Total Assets	A measure of the utilization of all the firm's assets; a ratio below the industry average indicates the company is not generating a sufficient volume of business, given the size of its asset investment.
4. Accounts receivable turn-over	Annual credit sales / Accounts receivable	A measure of the average length of time it takes the firm to collect the sales made on credit.

5. Average collection period	Accounts receivable / Total sales/365 or Accounts receivable / Average daily sales	Indicates the average length of time the firm must wait after making a sale before it receives payment.
Other Ratios		
1. Dividend yield on common stock	Annual dividends per share / Current earnings per share	A measure of the return to owners received in the form of dividends.
2. Price-earnings ratio	Current earnings per share / After earnings per share	Faster-growing or less-risky firms tend to have higher price-earnings ratios than slower-growing or more risky firms.
3. Dividend payout ratio	Annual dividends per share / After tax earnings per share	Indicates the percentage of profits paid out as dividends.
4. Cash flow per share	After tax profits + Depreciation / Number of common shares outstanding	A measure of the discretionary funds over and above expenses that are available for use by the firm.

Source: Arthur A. Thompson and A.J. Strickland. *op. cit.*, pp. 284-285.

11. *Identify and make notes of data and information required to solve the problem diagnosed:* The students have to use the conceptual knowledge and skills of management in identifying the data and information required to develop solutions.

12. *Compare the data and information available in the case with the data required to offer recommendations:* If both these two do not match with each other and data available are not sufficient to solve the problem, the student has to identify the gaps in information available.

13. *Fill-in the gaps:* The student has to fill-in the gaps through inferences and assumptions with the help of information available, conceptual knowledge and by reading in between the lines of the case material.

14. *Re-check the diagnosis:* In view of the step (13), the student has to re-check the diagnosis and re-diagnose the basic problem, if necessary.

15. *Use tools and techniques of strategic analysis:* Strategic analysis is not just a collection of opinions and views. It has powerful tools and techniques as presented in the text. The students have to use these tools and techniques.

16. *Analyse the case:* Students have to analyse the case thoroughly with the help of strategic management tools, techniques, their opinions, judgement, etc.

17. *Generate alternative solutions:* The detailed case analysis normally pave the way to generate alternative solutions or recommendations to solve the basic problem diagnosed. The strategic management concepts should be inter-weaved with the issues identified, in developing alternative solutions.

18. *Evaluate the alternative solutions:* Student should evaluate each of the alternative solutions in terms of their strengths to implement, weaknesses, opportunities provided by the external environment for implementation and threats posed by the external environment in the

process of implementation. Further, the possible outcome of each solution should also be considered in the process of evaluation.

19. *Rank of Solutions:* The student has to rank the solutions on the basis of their score in SWOT analysis.

20. *Select the best solution:* The student should recognise that there is no single best solution for all situations. It varies from individual to individual and from situation to situation and based on judgment. However, the student can select the best solution based on the ranking of alternative solutions.

21. *Prepare an action plan:* The students have to prepare a detailed plan for executing the best solution. The possible hindrances should also be pointed out along with the means to overcome them in the plan of action.

22. *Communicate the results to parties concerned:* The student should prepare detailed communications and address them to the parties regarding the plan of action.

3. PARTICIPATING IN A CLASS DISCUSSION

Participating in a class room discussion of a case is different from participating in a lecture class. The students have to take active role in case discussion.

The role of the instructor includes: initiation of discussion, solicit student participation, keep the discussion on track, moderate the discussion, offer alternative views and ideas, inter-weaving the concepts and strategic management techniques in to the problem situations, play the devil's advocate (*i.e.*, if not students play active role jump into the discussion and offer opposing views), lead the discussion and the like.

The role of the students include: Analysing the situations, offering comments on reading in-between the lines, identifying the strategic issues, diagnose the key issues, using the strategic tools and techniques, identifying the gaps in data and information, fill-in the gaps, developing alternative solutions, preparing and presenting the recommendations and defending them etc. Students have to broaden their views and thinking when the fellow students offer criticism or suggestions or modifications to their ideas, as the old adage goes, "two heads are better than one." In view of the different views and lines of thinking and analysis, the class will do a more penetrating and searching work of case analysis than an individual student. Normally, group effort is effective and efficient than individual effort. Exhibit 2 presents the expectations from the student in a class room of case analysis.

Exhibit 2: Expectations from the Student in the Class-room of Case Analysis

1. Expect students to dominate the discussion and do most of the talking. The case method enlists a maximum of individual participation in class discussion. It is not enough to be present as a silent observer, if every student took this approach, there would be no discussion.
2. Expect the instructor to assume the role of extensive questioner and listener.
3. Be prepared for the instructor to probe for reasons and supporting analysis.
4. Expect and tolerate challenges to the views expressed. All students have to be willing to submit their conclusions for scrutiny and rebuttal. Each student needs to learn to state his or her views without fear of disapproval and to overcome the hesitation of speaking out. Learning respect for the views and approaches of others is an integral part of case analysis exercises. But there are times when it is OK to swim against the tide of majority opinion. In the practice of management, there is always room for originality and unorthodox approaches. So while discussion of a case is a group process, there is no compulsion for you or anyone else to cave in and conform to group opinions and consensus.
5. Don't be surprised if you change your mind about some things as the discussion unfolds. Be alert to how these changes affect your analysis and recommendations (in the event you get called on).
6. Expect to learn a lot from each case discussion; use what you learn to be better prepared for the next case discussion.

Source: Modified version from: Arthur A. Thompson and A.J. Strickland, *op. cit.*, pp. 286-287.

Exhibit 3 presents the activities that a student should do, to be an active participant in the class discussion.

Exhibit 3: Activities to be done by Students to be Active Participants

- Although, you should do your own independent work and independent thinking, don't hesitate before (and after) class to discuss the case with other students. In real life, managers often discuss the company's problems and situation with other people to refine their own thinking.
- In participating in the discussion, make a conscious effort to contribute, rather than just talk. There is a big difference between saying something that builds the discussions and offering a long wondering what the point was.
- Avoid the us of "I think," "I believe," I feel"; instead say, "My analysis shows.." and "The sampan should do... because.. " Always give supporting reasons and evidence for your views; then your instructor won't have to ask you "Why?" every time you make a comment.
- In making your points, assume that everyone has read the case and knows what it says; avoid reciting and rehashing information in the case instead, use the data and information to explain your assessment of the situation and to support your position.
- Always prepare good notes (usually two or three pages' worth) for each case and use them extensively when you speak. There's no way you can remember everything off the top of your head — especially the results of your number crunching. To reel off the numbers or to present all five reasons why, instead of one, you will need good notes. When you have prepared good notes to the study questions and use them as the basis for your comments, everybody in the room will know you are well prepared, and your contribution to the case discussion will stand out.

Source: Arthur A. Thompson, Jr., & A.J. Strickland III, *op. cit.*, p. 287.

4. METHODS OF CASE DISCUSSION

1. Individual and Syndicate Methods: Oral Discussion

There are two methods of case discussion *viz.*, *(i)* individual method and *(ii)* syndicate or group method. In case of individual method, the instructor opens the discussion in the class, all the students participate in the discussion. The instructor moderates and coordinates the discussion. In case of syndicate or group method, students are formed into syndicates or groups in one session of the class and each group analyses, discusses the case and prepares the written report and presents the same to the class in the next session for comments and further discussion. Then all the students listen to the reports of all groups and then further discuss the case based on the reports. Finally, the class will offer recommendations and plan of action.

2. Preparing a Written Case Analysis

A written case analysis is more or less similar to the class discussion of case analysis. As there is no role of instructor and classmates, the student has to think and analyse the case from all directions, criticise his own ideas and views, modify them. Student has to follow all the guidelines of case analysis presented earlier. Exhibit 4 presents the guidelines for written case analysis.

Exhibit 4: Guidelines for Written Case Analysis

1. Provide a sharply focussed diagnosis of strategic issues and key problems.
2. Offer analysis and evidence to back-up your conclusions. Do not rely on unsupported opinions and over generalizations. Present logical arguments backed up with facts and figures.
3. Use tables and charts to present the calculations clearly and efficiently, if analysis involves important qualitative calculations. Though, you present exhibits and annexures at the end of the report, cite important figures and calculations in the text of the report. Highlight the conclusions to be drawn from the exhibits.
4. Use the conceptual knowledge, inter-weave it with problem situations. Thus, demonstrate that you have the command on the strategic concepts and analytical tools you have been exposed.
5. Your interpretation of the evidence should be reasonable and objective. Don't prepare one-sided argument. Don't try to exaggerate or over dramatise. Inject balance into our analysis avoid emotional rhetoric. Write as "My analysis shows ... "Don't write," "I think...," "I feel..." or "I believe...".
6. Avoid recommending any thing you would not yourself be willing to do if you were in management's shoes.
7. State your recommendations in sufficient detail to be meaningful.
8. Be sure the company is financially able to implement your recommendations.
9. Your recommendations should be practically viable and feasible to implement.
10. Your report should be well organised and well-written.

Source: Modified Version From: Arthur A. Thompson and A.J. Strickland *op. cit.*, pp. 288-289.

3. Format of the Written Case Analysis Report

The first paper will be individual case analysis. The student's written report must be turned in during the class period in which it is presented. The package will begin with an executive summary that is at least half a page long, but no longer than one page. It will have three basic components.

1. Statement of the problem;
2. Brief discussion of the main considerations; and
3. Recommended action.

The purpose of the executive summary is to brief a busy upper-level decision-maker. It must stand alone, so that it could be used independently of the detailed analysis which follows in the package. It must give a clear picture of the problem in a nutshell, with a cognet recommendation. A recommendation of some kind must be made. Waffling will not be acceptable. If you cannot decide what to do, at least describe the additional information you would need in order to make a recommendation.

Next in the package will be a five-page case analysis which builds on the executive summary with a more thorough discussion. This portion is aimed at the decision-maker's aides. It should explain the logic of your recommendations, and fill in background on the points made in the executive summary. Since the audience of executive aides would not all be familiar with them, avoid using business jargon and technical business terms unless you give a plain language explanation along with them. In other words, you must convince the decision maker and his/her aides in plain English that you have gotten to the root of a problem that requires their attention and that your recommendation is the best alternative for solving it.

Each case analysis will be examined and presented based on the following format:

1. Brief resume of significant events
2. External analysis
3. Industry analysis
4. Internal analysis
5. Statement of the problem
6. Goals
7. Assumptions
8. For *each* of the alternatives:
   (a) Compare advantages/disadvantages or strength and weaknesses
   (b) Time factors — short-range considerations versus long-range factors — timing
   (c) Resources
   (d) Opportunities and threats.
9. Decision
10. Implementation
11. Feedback (control)
12. Communication to the parties concerned.

As you write the executive summary and case analysis, remember that the intended audience works for the company you are advising. They will already be familiar with the basic facts about the company. Instead, give them new insights into the situation, without simply repeating what they already know. Make it a point to get to the point.

5. CONCLUSION

Exhibit 5: Presents the summary of the guidelines of case analysis.

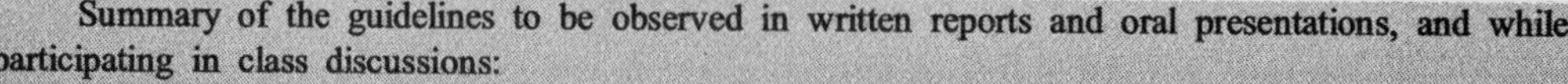

Exhibit 5: Summary of the Guidelines of Case Analysis

Summary of the guidelines to be observed in written reports and oral presentations, and while participating in class discussions:

1. Read the case twice, once for an overview and once to gain full command of the facts; then take care to explore every one of the exhibits.
2. Make a list of the problems and issues that have to be confronted.
3. Do enough number crunching to discover the story told by the data presented in the case.
4. Look for opportunities to use the concepts and analytical tools you have learned earlier.
5. Be thorough in your diagnosis of the situation and make at least a one-or two-page outline of your assessment.
6. Support any and all opinions with well-seasoned arguments and numerical evidence; don't stop until you can purge "I think" and "I feel" from your assessment and, instead, are able to rely completely on "my analysis shows."
7. Develop charts, tables, and graphs to expose more clearly the main points of your analysis.
8. Prioritise your recommendations and make sure they can carried out in an acceptable time frame with the available skills and financial resources.
9. Review your recommended action plan to see if it addresses all of the problems and issues you identified.
10. Avoid recommending any course of action that could have disastrous consequences if it doesn't work out as planned; therefore, be as alert to the downside risks of your recommendations as you are to their upside potential and appeal.

Modified version from: Arthur Thompson and A.J. Strickland, *op. cit.*, p. 290.

Fifty Tips for Success in Case Analysis

1. View your case analysis and presentation as a product that must have some competitive factor to differentiate it favourably from the case analysis of other students.
2. Prepare your case analysis far enough in advance of the due date to allow time for reflection.
3. Develop a mindset of "why," continually questioning assumptions and assertions (your own as well as others').
4. The best ideas are lost if not communicated to the reader, so as ideas develop, think of their most appropriate presentation.
5. Maintain a positive attitude about the class, working with problems rather than against them.
6. Keep in tune with your professor and understand his or her values and expectations.
7. Since business policy is a capstone course, seek the help of professors in other speciality areas as needed.
8. Other students will have strengths in functional areas that will complement your weaknesses, so develop a co-operative spirit that moderates competitiveness in group work.
9. Read your case frequently as work progresses, so that you don't overlook details.
10. When preparing a case analysis as a group, divide into separate teams to work on the external analysis and internal analysis. Each team should write its section as if it were to go into the paper; then give each group member a copy.
11. At the end of each group session, assign each member of the group a task to be completed for the next meeting.

12. Have a good sense of humour.
13. Capitalize on the strengths of each member of the group; volunteer your services in your areas of strength.
14. Set goals for yourself and your team; budget your time to attain them.
15. Become friends with the library.
16. Foster attitudes that encourage group participation and interaction. Do not be too hasty to judge group members.
17. Be creative and innovative throughout the case analysis process.
18. Be prepared to work. There will be times when you will have to do more than your "share." Accept it, and do what you have to do to move the team forward.
19. Think of your case analysis as if it were really happening; do not reduce case analysis to a mechanical process.
20. To uncover flaws in your analysis and to prepare the group for questions during an oral presentation, assign one person in the group to actively play the "devil's advocate."
21. Do not schedule excessively long group meetings; two-hour sessions are about right.
22. A goal of case analysis is to improve your ability to think clearly in ambiguous and confusing situations; do not get frustrated that there is no "single best answer."
23. Push your ideas hard enough to get them listened to but then let up; listen to others and try to follow lines of thinking; follow the flow of group discussion, recognizing when you need to get back on the track; do not repeat yourself or others unless clarity or progress demands repetition.
24. Do not confuse symptoms with causes; do not develop conclusions and solutions prematurely; recognize that information may be misleading, conflicting or wrong.
25. Work hard to develop the ability to formulate reasonable, consistent and creative plans; put yourself in the strategist's position.
26. Develop confidence in using quantitative tools for analysis; they are not inherently difficult; it is just practice and familiarity you need.
27. Develop a case-writing style that is direct, assertive, and convincing; be concise, precise, fluent and correct.
28. Have fund when at all possible. It is frustrating at times, but enjoy it while you can; it maybe several years before you are playing CEO again.
29. Acquire a professional typist and proof-reader. Do not perform either task alone.
30. Strive for excellence in writing and technical preparation of your case. Prepare nice charts, tables, diagrams, and graphs. Use colour and unique pictures. No messy exhibits!
31. In group cases, do not allow personality differences to interfere. When they occur, they must be understood for what they are and put aside.
32. Do not forget that the objective is to learn; explore areas with which you are not familiar.
33. Pay attention to details.
34. Think through alternative implications fully and realistically. The consequences of decisions are not always apparent. They often affect many different aspects of a firm's operations.

35. Get things written down (drafts) as soon as possible.
36. Read everything that other group members write, and comment on them in writing. This allows group input into all aspects of case preparation.
37. Provide answers to such fundamental questions as what, when, where, why and how.
38. Adaptation and flexibility are keys to success; be creative and innovative.
39. Do not merely recite ratios or present figures. Rather, develop ideas and conclusions concerning the possible trends. Show the importance of these figures to the corporation.
40. Support reasoning and judgement with factual data whenever possible.
41. Neatness is a real plus; your case analysis should look professional.
42. Your analysis should be as detailed and specific as possible.
43. A picture speaks a thousand words, and a creative picture gets you an "A" in many classes.
44. Let someone else read and critique your paper several days before you turn it in.
45. Emphasize the "Strategy Selection" and "Strategy Implementation" sections. A common mistake is to spend too much time on the external or internal analysis parts of your paper. Always remember that the "meat" of the paper or presentation is the strategy selection and implementation sections.
46. Make special efforts to get to know your group members. This leads to more open ness in the group and allows for more interchange of ideas. Put in the time and effort necessary to develop these relationships.
47. Be constructively critical of your group members' work. Do not dominate group discussions. Be a good listener and contributor.
48. Learn from past mistakes and deficiencies. Improve upon weak aspects of other case presentations.
49. Learn from the positive approaches and accomplishments of other classmates.
50. Be considerate, dependable, reliable, and trust worthy.

Source: Fred R. David, *op. cit.*, pp. 336-338.

REFERENCES

1. Arthur A. Thompson and A.J. Strickland, *op. cit.*, p. 280.
2. S. Venkatesh and Nina Jacob, "Case Method: An Effective Training tool," *Management Review*, April-June 1996, p. 54.
3. Charles I. Gragg, *"Because Wisdom Can't be Told,"* in M.P. McNair (ed.) *"Case Method at the Harvard Business School,"* New York, 194, p. 11.
4. Arthur A. Thompson and A.J. Strickland, *op. cit.*, p. 281.
5. Charles I. Gragg, *op. cit.*, pp. 12-14 and D.R. Schoen and Phillip A. Sprague, *"What is the Case Method?"* in M.P. Nair (ed.), *"The Case Method at the Harvard Business School,"* pp. 78-79.
6. Arthur A. Thompson and A.J. Strickland, *op. cit.*, pp. 282-283.
7. *Ibid.*, p. 286.
8. *Ibid.*, pp. 287-288.

✦ ✦ ✦

(C) CASE STUDY 1

BRIGHT LIGHTINGS LIMITED

Bright Lightings Limited was established in 1997 in Hyderabad for manufacturing general lightings service lamps in the joint sector by the A.P. Industrial Development Corporation and private individual investors. The company having been set up as an assembly unit without any captive units for components was totally dependent upon external sources of supply for component requirements. Indian Machine Tools and Bright Lightings Limited (BLL) signed an agreement. Under this agreement, Indian Machine Tools accepted to market the full production of BLL.

Personnel Policy: The company followed the Personnel Policy of public sector as it was under joint sector until 2009. It used to employ the workers based on the list of the candidates sent by the employment exchange. It also observed the reservation policy announced by the government from time to time strictly until 2009.

Production Policy: The company's policy regarding production was procuring materials from external sources, assemble the material into different kinds of electric bulbs. The company determined to maintain the quality as per the specifications imposed by the Indian Machine Tools.

Marketing Policy: The company's marketing policy was linked to the marketing policy of the Indian Machine Tools. Therefore, there was no separate marketing policy to the company. In fact, Indian Machine Tools acted as a sole marketer for BLL. Thus, the company did not establish a separate marketing department.

Financial Policy: Company's cash inflows/sales revenue was based on the production level. Therefore, the company concentrated on the production capacity utilisation. The company also concentrated on the working capital management for efficient management of finances.

Organizational Culture: The company has acquired the culture of a public sector industrial unit. The wages/salaries of employees were fixed on the basis of the scales of the employees of public sector industrial units. The company also started providing various fringe benefits to the employees like canteen facilities, medical facilities, conveyance allowance, etc. The workers used to get dearness allowance based on that of public sector.

Trade unions formed at the early stage of the company. Trade unions were active in regulating and controlling the management. They protected the workers to a greater extent. In this process, they did not take the financial position of the company into consideration. In fact, they view that the published financial accounts of the company were mostly mismanaged and misinterpreted.

After the company crossed the gestation period, the Industrial Development Corporation transferred the entire equity held by it to the private individual investors in 2002. Thus, the company's status has changed from a joint sector industrial unit to a private sector industrial unit. Another significant change during this year was, the Indian Machine Tools withdrew itself from the agreement with the company as the sole marketer of the company's products. At this juncture the company's management has been headed by a private individual investor-cum-politician. Some significant changes had taken place in the company and company's external environment including the changes in the economic directions of the country at large during this period.

Production/Operations Issues: The company expanded its capacity by installing the latest and automatic machinery in 2008. The company could achieve full capacity utilization during the period 2004-2008. However, the strikes organized by the workers a number of times disturbed the company in achieving full capacity in some years. Added to this, the company also declared lock-outs which affected the production levels. The product quality had been appreciated by the competing firms. The company's plant continued to be located in Hyderabad.

Marketing Issues: After the Indian Machine Tools, withdrew from the agreement, the company branded its products as "Lepakshi" (name of a well known tourist place in Andhra Pradesh). Company located its marketing department in New Delhi. It appointed its dealers in different places of the country and started marketing its own brand in 2003. Company could not succeed in selling the products through dealers even after a continuous and vigorous effort. The company's sales did not cross even 20 per cent of the output. The stores of the company was full with finished products in 2003 and 2004. It caused the company to stop the production for some time. Then the company searched for marketing alliance with the established brands like Phillips and Bajaj. The company could succeed in establishing the alliance with the established companies. The company agreed to produce and brand its products for the established companies and sell the products to them at an agreed price. The price is normally 50% lower than the retail market price of the products of market partners. Added to this, the company also accepted to maintain the quality of the product as per the specifications of the partner companies.

In addition to producing the product for the partners, the company continued its own brand of 'Lepakshi'.

Further, the Managing Director of the company also tried to boost-up the sales by getting the approval of government departments and organisations to buy the 'Lepakshi' brand bulbs. He could not succeed in this direction. The company, thus, could not increase the sales of its own brand. Therefore, it continued its alliance.

Personnel Issues: The company continued its personnel policies mostly based on public sector personnel policies even after it was converted into a private sector organization. The company continued paying higher salaries, better fringe benefits to employees, paying dearness allowance at the rate of public sector. Further, the company also continued the automatic promotion scheme which was introduced before 1982. This resulted in more number of operators at higher level than required and less number of operators at lower level than the specified number. However, all levels of operators were doing the same job irrespective of their levels. Added to this, the trade union of the company was more active in protecting the interests of the workers and regulating even the management. Trade union was successful in raising the wages from time to time and getting additional benefits. Consequently, the share of cost of wages and benefits in operational expenses increased from 48% in 2002 to 63% in 2003.

Financial Issues: The company's financial position was not sound from the beginning. The position had become more weak as the company could not sell its own brand. The market partners failed, many times to clear their dues in time. The wage/salary bill had serious working capital management problems, several times. The financial manager used to go after the banks frequently to adjust the money. The company could not pay dividend to its shareholders from the stage of its inception. The high growth rate of cost of raw materials, cost of wages and lower growth rate of per unit price of the product were responsible for the unsound financial position of the company.

Environmental Changes

The Government of India announced economic liberalisations in 2000. Those liberalisations include de-licencing for certain categories of industries seeking expansion. Before 1991, the government used to assess the supply of and demand for the products and used to issue the licences for the establishment and expansion of industrial units when demand was more than the supply. The de-licencing allow the industrial units to expand their capacities without seeking any licences/permission from the government. The marketing partner companies of the BLL could not get the licence for expansion from the government before economic liberalisations and, therefore, continued their tie-ups with BLL. The economic liberalisations helped these companies to expand their capacities without any difficulty. These companies could complete their expansion projects by the end of 2003.

There is no increase in overall demand for the general lightings services lamps in the country. The economic liberalisations announced by the government created a boom in the capital market. A number of new investors emerged. Having new companies as well as old companies had been successful in mobilising equity capital, the BLL had the idea of backward linkage and was preparing the documents to go for public issue. At that time, the managements of marketing alliance partners informed the BLL that, they had expanded their capacities, and therefore, they had decided to divorce the marketing alliance with BLL.

The management had called for an emergency meeting of the Board of Directors to decide the future strategies of the company on February 5th, 2009 at 10.00 a.m.

(D) CASE STUDY 2

ARTOS INDUSTRIES LIMITED

Artos Soft Drinks Limited, Ramachandrapuram, was one of the leading soft drinks industrial unit during 1960s in Andhra Pradesh. In fact, the variety of soft drinks available in the market were a few. The market in Andhra Pradesh was rather unorganised during 1960s. The transport facilities and other infrastructural facilities for marketing soft drinks were not developed. The culture of the customers was not in favour of consumption of soft drinks. In fact, consumption of soft drinks was a luxurious item for most of the consumers during this period in the region. Strategic themes of the company during this period include:

- Develop its brand as a major brand with market leadership.
- Sophisticated, yet efficient, operating systems.
- Create the awareness among consumers about soft drink consumption.

The company could implement the first strategy. It could become the leader in the area through its niche strategy with a few followers. The company's closest competitor was M/s Raju Soft Drinks Company, Vijayawada. This company could not perform well in the market due to low demand and as such, offered a merger proposal with Artos Soft Drinks Limited in 2001. The management of Artos Soft Drinks Limited accepted the proposal and executed the merger in 2002. The new company's product range include:

- Artos Orange
- Artos Lemon
- Artos Grape and
- Artos Pineapple

The company's capital went up from Rs. 1 lakh to Rs. 50 lakhs, the sales increased from Rs. 15 lakhs to Rs. 10 crores per year during the period between 1960 and 1975. The return on investment has gone up from 18 percent to 24 per cent during the period. Company also expanded its market to the neighbouring states during the period 1972 to 1975. During this period, environment was favourable to the company due to the economic growth, population growth, increased awareness of the soft drink consumption and the like. Moreover, the environment was marked by the negligible competition in the soft drink industry.

The new brands of soft drinks like Gold Spot (orange flavour), Limca (lemon flavour), Kismet (pineapple flavour) were introduced in 1976 in different sizes, attractive bottles and attractive flavour. Added to this, these new brands were advertised extensively. The high income bracket customers, who generally consume soft drinks frequently, shifted their loyalty to the new brands. The new company offered concessional price for bulk purchases for marriages and other functions.

These factors created threats to Artos Soft Drink Limited. The company's sales declined year by year and reached the lowest level of Rs. 2 lakhs during 1980. The cost of sales was more than the sales revenue. The company was unable to pay even the salaries of its employees during 1980. The management called for a meeting of its Board of Directors to decide upon the future strategy of the company. The Board of Directors considered several alternative strategies including:

- Conversion of soft drink manufacturing plant into beer manufacturing plant with additional investment.
- Turn around the existing company

- Divesting the present company as it is
- Merge with the new company

The Board of Directors, after considering SWOT analysis of each of the above strategies, selected the strategy of converting the existing plant and facilities to produce beer as the competition in beer industry was significantly less. The company mobilised the additional capital through loans and advances from the banks and the board of directors. The process of conversion was completed in 1982. The company changed its name as Artos Industries Limited in 1982.

The company followed the strategy of penetration pricing policy for the Artos Beer and advertised about the product extensively. The favourable marketing and environmental conditions and the companies strategies helped it to revive the company's financial position by 1988. The company could generate surplus cash reserves by 1989. The company, after the failure of its soft drinks products, was of the opinion that, it should have more than one type of business in its portfolio. The present cash surplus position of the company enabled the Board of Directors to plan about a new business in its portfolio. The board of directors met in April 1989 and discussed about the different portfolios including related and unrelated businesses.

Sri Ram Textiles, a loss-making company, offered itself for merger with Artos Industries. In fact, Sri Ram Textiles communicated the same offer to several profit-making and cash surplus companies in early 1989. The board of directors of Artos Limited discussed the offer and decided to accept it in June 1989. Sri Ram Textiles was merged with the Artos Industries in September 1989. The shareholders of Sri Ram Textiles were given one equity share in Artos Industries Limited of Rs. 10 fully paid for every three shares of Rs. 10 fully paid held by them in Sri Ram Textiles.

The management of Artos Industries invested all their cash surplus and turned around their textiles business. The textile business introduced a number of changes including new designs, improving the quality, extensive advertising and reducing the prices. These strategies of the company had started producing the results in the form of increase in sales, gross profit and net profit since 1991.

The competition in beer business started intensifying from the year 1990. It reached its peak level in 1995. Artos industries had been affected severely by the mounting competition. The company's beer unit's sales declined drastically by 1995. Operating expenses were in excess of sales revenue. The company's management could not estimate the situation and also could not come out of the shock. However, the management called for an urgent meeting of the Board of Directors to discuss the issue and formulate the future strategies.

Strategic Options Available

The strategic options to the Board of Directors were:

(i) Harvesting the assets of the beer business;

(ii) Turn around the beer business by investing additional finances generated by the textile unit;

(iii) Merging the beer unit with the competitor's units; and

(iv) Firing the chief executive of the beer unit and appointing the new chief executive.

✦ ✦ ✦

(E) CASE STUDY 3

MICROSOFT

Microsoft Corporation is an international computer technology corporation with 2005 global annual sales of close to $40 billion USD and about 64,000 employees in 85 countries and regions which develops, manufactures, licenses, and supports a wide range of software products for computing devices. Headquartered in Redmond, Washington, its most popular products are the Microsoft Windows operating system and the Microsoft Office suite of productivity software, each of which has achieved near ubiquity in the desktop computer market. Microsoft possesses footholds in other markets, with assets such as the MSNBC cable television network, the MSN Internet portal, and the Microsoft Encarta multimedia encyclopedia. The company also markets home entertainment products, such as the Xbox, Xbox 360 and MSN TV.

Microsoft's name, originally bicapitalized MicroSoft, is a blend of "microcomputer software", and is often abbreviated as MS. The company was founded in Albuquerque, New Mexico on April 4, 1975 by Bill Gates and Paul Allen to develop and sell BASIC interpreters for the Altair 8800. After the market saw a flood of IBM PC clones in the mid-1980s, Microsoft used its new position, which it gained in part due to a contract from IBM, to dominate the home computer operating system market with MS-DOS. The company later released an initial public offering (IPO) in the stock market, which netted several of its employees millions of dollars due to the ensuing rise of the stock price. The price of the stock continued its rise steadily into the early 2000s. In Microsoft Windows, the company was selling what would become the most widely used operating system in the world, which was originally an add-on for MS-DOS; Microsoft continued to push into multiple markets, such as computer hardware and television. In addition, Microsoft has historically given customer support over Usenet newsgroups and the World Wide Web, and awards Microsoft MVP status to volunteers who are deemed helpful in assisting the company's customers.

With what is generally described as a developer-centric business culture, Microsoft has become widely known for some of its internal codes of conduct for its employees. One example is the "eat your own dogfood" mantra, which describes the practice of using pre-release products inside the company to test them in an environment geared towards the real world. Microsoft has also become widely panned for its business practices—the U.S. Justice Department, among others, has sued Microsoft for antitrust violations and software bundling. In addition, Microsoft has been criticized for the insecurity of its software. Despite this, Microsoft has won several awards, such as the "1993 Most Innovative Company Operating in the U.S." by Fortune Magazine. The company is on the Fortune 500 list of companies as of 2005.

Product divisions

To be more precise in tracking the performance of each unit and delegating responsibility, Microsoft reorganized into seven core business groups—each an independent financial entity— in April 2002. Later, on September 20, 2005, Microsoft announced a rationalization of its original seven business groups into the three core divisions that exist today: the Windows Client, MSN and Server and Tool groups were merged into the Microsoft Platform Products & Services Division; the Information Worker and Microsoft Business Solutions groups were merged into the Microsoft Business Division; and the Mobile and Embedded Devices and Home and Entertainment groups were merged into the Microsoft Entertainment and Devices Division.

Microsoft Windows, the Company's best-known product

This division produces Microsoft's flagship product, the Windows operating system. It has been produced in many versions, including Windows 3.1, Windows 95, Windows 98, Windows 2000, Windows Millennium Edition, Windows XP and Windows Server 2003. Almost all IBM compatible personal computers designed for the consumer come with Windows preinstalled. The next planned desktop version of Windows is Windows Vista. The online service MSN, the cable television station MSNBC, and the Microsoft online magazine Slate are all part of this division. Slate was later acquired by The Washington Post on December 21, 2004. At the end of 1997, Microsoft acquired Hotmail, the first and most popular webmail service, which it rebranded as "MSN Hotmail". Later in 1999 Microsoft introduced MSN Messenger, an instant messaging client, to compete with the popular AOL Instant Messenger. Along with Windows Vista, MSN is to become Windows Live.

Microsoft Visual Studio is the company's set of programming tools and compilers. The software product is GUI-oriented and links easily with the Windows APIs, but must be specially configured if used with non-Microsoft libraries. The current version is Visual Studio 2005. The previous version, Visual Studio.Net 2003, was named after the .NET initiative, a Microsoft marketing initiative covering a number of technologies. Microsoft's definition of .NET continues to evolve. As of 2004, .NET aims to ease the development of Microsoft Windows-based applications that use the Internet, by deploying a new Microsoft communications system, Indigo. This will address some issues previously introduced by Microsoft's DLL design, which made it difficult to manage, install multiple versions of complex software packages on the same system (see DLL-hell), and provide a more consistent development platform for all Windows applications (see Common Language Infrastructure. In addition, the Company established a set of certification programs to recognize individuals who have expertise in its software and solutions. Similar to offerings from Cisco, Sun Microsystems, Novell, IBM, and Oracle Corporation, these tests are designed to identify a minimal set of proficiencies in a specific role; this includes developers ("Microsoft Certified Solution Developer"), system/network analysts ("Microsoft Certified Systems Engineer"), trainers ("Microsoft Certified Trainers") and administrators ("Microsoft Certified Systems Administrator"), ("Microsoft Certified Database Administrator").

Microsoft offers a suite of server software, entitled Windows Server System. Windows Server 2003, an operating system for network servers, is the core of the Windows Server System line. Another server product, Systems Management Server, is a collection of tools providing remote-control abilities, patch management, software distribution, and a hardware/software inventory. Other server products include: SQL Server, a relational database management system;

- Exchange Server, for certain business-oriented e-mail features;
- Small Business Server, for messaging and other small business-oriented features; and
- BizTalk Server, for employee integration assistance and other functions.

Business culture

Microsoft's RedWest campus

Microsoft has often been described as having a developer-centric business culture. A great deal of time and money is spent each year on recruiting young university-trained software developers who meet very exacting criteria, and on keeping them in the company. For example, while many software companies often place an entry-level software developer in a cubicle desk within a large office space filled with other cubicles, Microsoft assigns a private or semiprivate closed office to every developer or pair of developers. In addition, key decision makers at every level are either developers or former developers. In a sense, the software developers at Microsoft are considered the "stars" of the company in the same way that the sales staff at IBM are considered the "stars" of their company.

Employees of Microsoft are expected to be comfortable with ambiguity in that they may not, for example, know with any degree of certainty when a product will ship, what it will be called, or what features will be included. Managers at Microsoft are expected to have a general attitude of long-term strategic and to be ready for any challenge from the competition or the market, and to keep in mind that being the largest software company in the world is not seen as a form of safety or a guarantee of future success. For instance, future competitors could rise from other industries, or computer hardware companies could try to become less dependent on Microsoft, or consumers could decide not to upgrade their software as often.

Within Microsoft the expression "eating our own dog food" is used to describe the policy of using the latest Microsoft products inside the company in an effort to test them in "real-world" situations. Only prerelease and beta versions of products are considered dog food. This is usually shortened to just "dog food" and is used as noun, verb, and adjective. The company is also known for their hiring process, dubbed the "Microsoft interview", which is notorious for off-the-wall questions such as "Why is a manhole cover round?" and is a process often mimicked in other organizations, although these types of questions are rarer now then they were in the past. For fun, Microsoft also hosts the Microsoft Puzzle Hunt, an annual puzzle hunt (a live puzzle game where teams compete to solve a series of puzzles) held at the Redmond campus. It is a spin-off of the MIT Mystery Hunt.

User culture

Technical reference for developers and articles for various Microsoft magazines such as Microsoft Systems Journal (or MSJ) is available through Microsoft's MSDN site, short for Microsoft

Developer Network. MSDN also offers subscriptions for companies and individuals, and the more expensive subscriptions usually offer access to pre-release beta versions of Microsoft software. In recent years, Microsoft launched a community site for developers and users, entitled Channel9, which provides many modern features such as a wiki and an Internet forum.

Most free technical support available through Microsoft is provided through online Usenet newsgroups (in the early days it was also provided on Compuserve). There are several of these newsgroups for nearly every product Microsoft provides, and often they are monitored by Microsoft employees. People who are helpful on the newsgroups can be elected by other peers or Microsoft employees for Microsoft Most Valuable Professional (MVP) status, which entitles people to a sort of special social status, in addition to possibilities for awards and other benefits.

Corporate structure

The company is run by a Board of Directors consisting of ten people, made up of mostly company outsiders (as is customary for publicly traded companies). Current members of the board of directors of Microsoft are: Steve Ballmer, James Cash, Jr., Dina Dublon, Bill Gates, Raymond Gilmartin, Ann Korologos, David Marquardt, Charles Noski, Helmut Panke, and Jon Shirley. The ten board members are elected every year at the annual shareholders' meeting, and those who do not get a majority of votes must submit a resignation to the board, which will subsequently choose whether or not to accept the resignation. There are five committees within the board which have oversight over more specific matters. These committees include the Audit Committee, which handles accounting issues with the company including auditing and reporting; the Compensation Committee, which approves compensation for the CEO and other employees of the company; the Finance Committee, which handles financial matters such as proposing mergers and acquisitions; the *Governance and Nominating Committee*, which handles various corporate matters including nomination of the board; and the *Antitrust Compliance Committee*, which attempts to prevent company practices from violating antitrust laws.

There are several other aspects to the corporate structure of Microsoft. For worldwide matters there is the Executive Team, made up of sixteen company officers across the globe, which is charged with various duties including making sure employees understand Microsoft's culture of business. The sixteen officers of the Executive Team include the Chairman and Chief Software Architect, the CEO, the General Counsel and Secretary, the CFO, senior and group vice presidents from the business units, the CEO of the Europe, the Middle East and Africa regions; and the heads of Worldwide Sales, Marketing and Services; Human Resources; and Corporate Marketing. In addition to the Executive Team there is also the Corporate Staff Council, which handles all major staff functions of the company, including approving corporate policies. The Corporate Staff Council is made up of employees from the Law and Corporate Affairs, Finance, Human Resources, Corporate Marketing, and Advanced Strategy and Policy groups at Microsoft. Other Executive Officers include the Presidents and Vice Presidents of the various product divisions, leaders of the marketing section, and the CTO, among others.

(***Source:*** Adapted from http://en.wikipedia.org/wiki/Microsoft)

Questions

1. How do the business culture and user culture of Microsoft distinct from that of other companies?
2. Discuss the product division structure of Microsoft.
3. To what extent the corporate structure contributed for the strategic success of Microsoft?

✦ ✦ ✦

(F) CASE STUDY 4

SONY

Sony is a Japanese leading manufacturer of audio, video, communications, and information technology products for the consumer and professional market. Its music, motion picture, television, computer entertainment, and online businesses make Sony one of the most comprehensive entertainment companies in the world. Sony's principal U.S. businesses include Sony Electronics Inc., Sony Pictures Entertainment, Sony Computer Entertainment America Inc., and a 50% interest in Sony BMG Music Entertainment, the second-largest record company in the world. Sony recorded consolidated annual sales of approximately $67 billion for the fiscal year ended March 31, 2005, and it employs 151,400 people worldwide. Sony's consolidated sales in the U.S. for the fiscal year ended March 31, 2005 were $18.4 billion.

Short history

Shirokiya, which was one of Japan's oldest companies (founded 1662), operated department stores. Shortly after the original store was rebuilt in 1924, it featured a state-of-the-art research and development division that created rice cookers, tape recorders and electric cushions, all under the Shirokiya brand. However, as Shirokiya's fortunes waned, the head researchers, Masaru Ibuka and Akio Morita departed in 1946, taking all 20 employees with them. They then founded Sony on May 7, 1946 as the Tokyo Telecommunications Engineering. Their first consumer product, in the late 1940s, was a rice cooker, which was a spectacular failure. As it grew into a major international corporation, Sony acquired other companies with longer histories, including Columbia Records (the oldest continuously produced brand name in recorded sound, dating back to 1888). Today Norio Ohga is Honorary Chairman, Sir Howard Stringer is Chairman and CEO, and Ryoji Chubachi is President and Electronics CEO.

Brand change

When Tokyo Tsushin Kogyo was looking for a romanized name to use to market themselves, they strongly considered using their initials, TTK. The primary reason they did not, is that the railway company Tokyo Kyuko was known as TKK.

The name "Sony" was chosen for the brand as a mix of the Latin word sonus, which is the root of sonic and sound, the English word "sunny", and from the word Sonny-boys which is Japanese slang for "whiz kids". However "Sonny" seemed not to be appropriate since it sounds too much like the Japanese soh-nee which means "business goes bad", Akio Morita pushed for a word that does not exist in any language so that they could claim the word "Sony" as their own (which paid off when they sued a candy producer who also used the name who claimed that "Sony" was just an existing word in some language).

At the time of the change, it was extremely unusual for a Japanese company to use Roman letters instead of Chinese characters to spell its name. The move was not without opposition: TTK's principal bank at the time, Mitsui, had strong feelings about the name. They pushed for a name such as Sony Electronic Industries, or Sony Teletech. Akio Morita was firm, however, as he did not want the company name tied to any particular industry. Eventually, both Ibuka and Mitsui Bank's chairman gave their approval.

In August 1955, Sony produced its first coat-pocket sized transistor radio they registered as the TR-55 model. In 1956, Sony reportedly manufactured about 40,000 of its Model TR-72 box-like portable transistor radios and exported some of this model to North America, the Netherlands and Germany.

That same year they made the TR-6, a coat pocket radio which was used by the company to create its "SONY boy" advertising character. The following year, 1957, Sony came out with the TR-63 model, the then smallest (112 x 71 x 32 mm) set in commercial production. and a great sales success worldwide. The TR-63 was a shirt pocket transistor radio that was exported all over the world.

University of Arizona professor Michael Brian Schiffer, Ph.D., says, "Sony was not first, but its transistor radio was the most successful. The TR-63 of 1957 cracked open the U.S. market and launched the whatçver new industry of consumer microelectronics." By the mid 1950s, American teens had began buying portable transistor radios in huge numbers, helping to propel the fledgling industry from an estimated 100,000 units in 1955 to 5,000,000 units by the end of 1958. However, this huge growth in portable transistor radio sales, that saw Sony rise to be the dominant player in the consumer electronics field, was not because of the consumers who had bought the earlier generation of tube radio consoles, but was driven by a distinctly new American phenomenon at the time called Rock and Roll.

Management

On March 7, 2005, Sony Corp. announced that Nobuyuki Idei will step down as Chairman and Group CEO and will be replaced by Briton Sir Howard Stringer, current Chairman and CEO of Sony Corporation of America, Corporate Executive Officer, Vice Chairman and COO Sony Entertainment Business Group. Sony's decision to replace Idei with the British Howard Stringer will mark the first time that a foreigner will run a major Japanese electronics firm. Sony Corp. also announced on the same date that current president, Kunitake Ando, will step down and be replaced by Ryoji Chubachi.

Sony also owns television channels in India and channels aimed at Indian communities in Europe. In Latin America, it owns Sony Entertainment Television, a TV channel that broadcasts popular series from the major networks in the US with subtitles in Spanish and Portuguese (Brazil only).

Corporate Governance

Current members of the board of directors of Sony are: Peter Bonfeld, Ryoji Chubachi, Sakie Fukushima, Hirobumi Kawano, Yotaro Kobayashi, Göran Lindahl, Yoshihiko Miyauchi, Akishige Okada, Howard Stringer, Fueo Sumita, and Yoshiaki Yamauchi.

Proprietary formats

Sony has historically been notable for creating its own in-house standards for new recording and storage technologies instead of adopting those of other manufacturers and standards bodies. The most infamous of these was the videotape format war of the early 1980s, when Sony marketed its Betamax system for video cassette recorders against the VHS format developed by JVC. In the end, VHS gained critical mass in the marketplace and became the worldwide standard for consumer VCRs and Sony adopted the format. Since then, Sony has continued to introduce its own versions of storage technologies, with varying success. Examples include -

- **MiniDisc** was created by Sony for use in portable music players. They were designed to share the market of Walkman products. Low consumer adoption has seen the product fail outside of the Japanese market.
- Sony also makes heavy use of its Memory Stick flash memory cards for digital cameras and other portable devices; however, other manufacturers are also making use of this technology.

- One successful attempt was the introduction of the 90mm micro floppy diskettes (better known as 3.5inch floppy discs), which Sony had developed at a time when there were 4" floppy discs and a lot of variations from different companies to replace the then on-going 5.25" floppy discs. Sony had great success and the format became dominant; 3.5" floppy discs gradually became obsolete as they were replaced by more current media formats.

- The DVD format currently being used in households world wide was jointly developed by Philips and Sony to replace CD; the use of a shorter wavelength laser beam sees the higher storage capacity of 4.7-17+GB as opposed to 640-700MB on a single disc.

- Sony attempted, unsuccessfully, to compete with the Iomega Zip drive and Imation SuperDisk with their HiFD.

- In 1993 Sony challenged the industry standard Dolby Digital 5.1 surround sound format with its newer and more advanced proprietary motion picture digital audio format called SDDS (Sony Dynamic Digital Sound). This format employed eight channels (7.1) of audio opposed to just six used in Dolby Digital 5.1 at the time. Unlike Dolby Digital, SDDS utilized a method of backup by having mirrored arrays of bits on both sides of the film which acted as a measure of reliability in case the film was partially damaged. Ultimately, SDDS has been vastly overshadowed by the preferred DTS (Digital Theatre System) and Dolby Digital standards in both the motion picture industry and home audio formats.

- Since the introduction of the MiniDisc format, Sony has attempted to promote its own audio compression technologies under the ATRAC brand, against more widely-used formats like MP3. Until late 2004, Sony's Network Walkman line of digital portable music players did not support the MP3 de facto standard natively, although the software SonicStage provided with them would convert MP3 files into the ATRAC or ATRAC3 formats.

- Sony is currently touting its Blu-ray optical digital versatile disk format, which is likely to compete with Toshiba's HD-DVD. As of quarter one of 2006, Blu-Ray has the backing of every major motion picture studio except Universal.

- The PSP (PlayStation Portable) handheld gaming system uses the proprietary *Universal Media Disc* (UMD) format to distribute games, movies, and other media. The Memory Stick format is used for game saves and other multimedia features.

- Sony and Philips jointly developed the Sony-Philips digital interface format (S/PDIF).

- Sony and Philips introduced the high-fidelity audio system SACD in 1999, but it has since been entrenched in a format war with DVD-Audio. At present, neither has gained a major foothold with the general public. CDs are preferred by consumers because of their ubiquitous presence in consumer devices.

- OpenMG, a digital rights management system.

- ARccOS, a copy control system for DVDs.

Criticism

Fictitious movie reviewer

In July 2000, a marketing executive working for Sony Corporation created a fictitious film critic, David Manning, who give consistently good reviews for releases from Sony subsidiary Columbia Pictures, which generally received poor reviews amongst real critics.

Digital rights management

In August 2000 Sony Pictures Entertainment US senior VP Steve Heckler foreshadowed events of late 2005. Heckler told attendees at the Americas Conference on Information Systems "The industry will take whatever steps it needs to protect itself and protect its revenue streams...It will not lose that revenue stream, no matter what...Sony is going to take aggressive steps to stop this. We will develop technology that transcends the individual user. We will firewall Napster at source - we will block it at your cable company, we will block it at your phone company, we will block it at your [ISP]. We will firewall it at your PC...These strategies are being aggressively pursued because there is simply too much at stake."

Advertisements

To commemorate the tenth anniversary of the PlayStation (PS) gaming console in Italy, Sony released an ad depicting a man smiling towards the camera and wearing on his head a crown made of button symbols (Triangle, O, X, Square). At the bottom, the copy read as "Ten Years of Passion". This outraged the Vatican as well as many local Catholic believers, prompting comments such as "Sony went too far" and "Vatican excommunicates Sony". After the incident, the campaign was quickly discontinued.

Sony also admitted in late 2005 to hiring graffiti artists to spraypaint advertisements for their Playstation Portable game system in seven major US cities including New York, New York, Philadelphia, Pennsylvania, and San Francisco, California. The mayor of Philadelphia has filed a cease and desist order and may file a criminal complaint. As of early January 2006, Sony has not commented on the advertisements or on plans to keep or withdraw them.

Recent Trends

Sony Computer Entertainment boss Ken Kutaragi has lashed out at Sony's failure to compete in key sectors such as the MP3 player market in the past, in an unusually direct statement where he claimed that the firm is "growing up". Company's reluctance to compete with products such as Apple's iPod music players, mainly due to resistance from the firm's music and movie divisions. Until recently, Sony has insisted on sticking doggedly to proprietary formats such as the ATRAC music format, instead of using popular open formats such as MP3 which have been embraced by competitors.

According to Kutaragi, this approach - recently addressed by products such as PlayStation Portable, which supports open standards such as MP3 for music and MP4 for video - was driven by concerns over piracy from the media divisions. In a rare admission of mistakes and an unusually direct criticism of the company's management, Kutaragi said that Sony's innovation had been "diluted", but promised that these problems had now been identified. "It's just starting," he told reporters at the club; "we're growing up." Kutaragi is pushing the PlayStation Portable as a combined platform for games, music and movies, and the forthcoming PlayStation 3 home console is also expected to offer significant media functionality as well as a powerful videogames platform.

(Source: Adapted from **http://en.wikipedia.org/wiki/Sony** and http://www.gamesindustry.biz/articles/father-of-playstation-slams-sonys-strategic-failur)

Questions

1. Discuss the Sony's strategies with regard to brand change.
2. Why does Sony's failure to compete in key sectors such as the MP3 player market?
3. How does management style of Sony contribute for its limited success in competing with its rivals.

✦ ✦ ✦

(G) CASE STUDY 5

XEROX CORPORATION

The Xerox Corporation was incorporated ion April 18, 1906. The corporation is highly multinational oriented and is divided into four major segments; Document processing, insurance, third party financing, and finally investment banking services. Xerox corporation operates in the Western hemisphere, while its subsidiaries, Rank Xerox Ltd., operates in Europe, and Fuji Xerox which is responsible for the corporation's operations in Pacific nations.

Before the 1970's Xerox pretty much dominated the market for document processing. However, by 1970, the Japanese started to penetrate the world market with low-cost products. The public perception in the USA, and Xerox's board believed that low quality was directly linked to low-cost products. In 1974, Japanese Canon, Ricoh penetrated the market with cheap and efficient plain paper copiers. Xerox did not respond to this new idea and continued to sell copiers that required coated paper. As a result, by 1978, the Japanese companies controlled 25% of the world market.

In addition, the Japanese products started to gain a reputable reputation of being good quality copiers for a good price. Xerox realized that the company had to continue to improve products and services continuously in order to gain the lost market share, or even being able to retain the current share. In 1982, David Kearns became the President and the CEO, and he introduced a total quality strategy, which "gave Xerox employees the tools they needed to compete in the global market."

SWOT Analysis

The internal strengths of the Xerox Corporation relative to the competition in the industry include the following strengths. Xerox has a favourable brand name image. The company was one of the pioneers in the document processing business, and the name stands for quality, state-of-the-art technology, and good service. Many Japanese brands may not have such a favourable image. This image was enhanced by the introduction of the "Total satisfaction guarantee" where instead of monetary refunds, the products are replaced. Secondly, I believe that Xerox corporation has an excellent quality management team. This fact has enabled the corporation to increase its market share. Also, Xerox places a heavy emphasis on employee participation in operational decisions. Also, the people in the Xerox organization are of a proactive nature, rather than a reactive. This will make it possible for the company to set industry standards, rather than respond to the actions of competitors. Also, employee participation programs makes it possible for Xerox to gain valuable information from the "bottom up" and the company should be well prepared to meet new customer demands.

The weaknesses of the Xerox Corporation relative to the competition include all of the following; high overhead costs as a result of Total Quality management implementation, and a fairly weak financial position. First, keeping-up a close to perfect quality index costs a lot of money. It is possible the trade-offs associated with the "100% quality concept" may be too large, thus creating a negative competitive position for Xerox. How much are customers prepared to pay for exceptional quality and service?

In addition, the financial position of Xerox is not very good. It is true that the fixed asset turnover has increased in recent years, but the total asset turnover ratio has decreased. A possible explanation to that fact is that the company has increased its inventory requirements by its product replacement concept. Profitability ratios are decreasing steadily (returns on sales, return on equity, return on investment and du pont). In addition, leverage ratios are increasing.

The external opportunity that the Xerox Corporation can utilize includes all of the following; Diversification into more products lines, and finally, seeks expansion into more potential foreign markets. First, by diversifying into more product lines, Xerox will be able to utilize its good reputation and favourable image in new related products and services. By offering more diverse products and services, the company may be able to more effectively respond to international needs in the "office machine" market. Therefore, it may be less difficult to diversify into new potential markets, such as Europe and South East Asia. However, some international markets may not be able to pay the price for quality (such as less industrialized nations).

The external threats that Xerox faces are the following; Increased competition from low-cost-high-quality products from domestic and foreign manufacturers, economic recession, and finally, deregulation's of trade barriers by the implementation of the World Trade Organization on January 1st, 1995. First, in recent years, foreign competitors and domestic competitors have cannibalised a large market share of the copier market from Xerox. These competitors will most probably be able to improve quality and maintain low prices. Many companies may not be prepared to pay a high price for image and reputation. In addition, the copier market is highly sensitive to economic trends. As a result of economic depression, businesses are less willing to invest in assets and may chose to "sail through" the recession utilizing what the company already has.

Investments are therefore discouraged. This fact could certainly affect Xerox's market place. Also, unfavourable government intervention such as the lowering of import barriers of goods and services to the United States in accordance to the new GATT agreement may impose a major threat to Xerox's largest market, which is currently the USA. This will make imported copiers less expensive to buy in the domestic market, since importing foreign companies will face lower ad-valorem trade barriers.

Steps aimed to implement a quality strategy

The very first step that the Xerox had to take was to enhance and change the corporate culture, which usually is very difficult and time consuming, since the process involves changing the perceptions of the people in the organization. David Kearns decided that this "corporate culture turnaround strategy" was to be achieved by extensive training. A company motto was established, "the better the quality, the lower the overall costs." In 1983, Xerox implemented a "Quality through Leadership" program, which had three main objectives. First to improve profits as reflected in higher returns on assets. Second, to improve customer satisfaction, and third, to improve market share. David Kearns first believed that these three objectives were of equal importance. However, soon it was recognized that the objectives were in conflicting nature, and they could only be achieved on the expense of one other. Therefore, one particular objective was ranked as most important to improve customer satisfaction.

The cost of the implemented program was enormous, $125 million, and over 4 million hours of man-hours of work. However, the results of the program were positive. Customer satisfaction increased by 40% and customer complaints decreased by 60%. Promotions were based on criteria not related to quality. By 1989, 75% of Xerox workers participate in the drive for perfect quality, and over 7,000 quality improvement teams were formed. Company expenditure designated for training was increased to 2.5%-3.0% of the annual revenues. In the total quality control (TQC) concept, employees are empowered to take responsibility for quality.

In addition, Xerox closely examined companies such as American Express, American Hospital Supply and L.L. Beam in the purpose to learn how to increase efficiency. This process is known as competitive bench marking which is the "continuous process of measuring products, services, and practices against the company's toughest competitors or those companies renowned as industry leaders." This kind of strategy forces the corporation to examine and effectively respond to changes in the competitive environment.

Furthermore, since it is difficult to control the quality standards of several suppliers (Xerox had 5000), Mr. Kearns decided to cut down the number of suppliers to 300. This action made it possible for the corporation to gain more control over the quality of inputs and to reduce costs.

Did Xerox satisfy the ten elements from implementing a TQM program?

Total Quality Management (TQM) is viewed as a new organizational culture and way of thinking. There are ten essential elements of implementing total quality management. First, the organization has to define "quality". Company personnel should have a clear definition of what quality means in the job, department, and throughout the company. I believe that Xerox did satisfy this element. Xerox was able to "empowering employees to take responsibility for quality." Effective reward systems, and extensive training made this possible.

The second element in TQM is to develop a customer orientation, which emphasizes that quality is what the customer says it is. Xerox did fulfil this element. Employees were directly involved in the sales process, and became directly responsible for keeping customers satisfied. In the Xerox organization, "Employees are closest to the customer".

Third, TQM requires focus on the company's business processes. Processes in all functional areas of an organization should be closely examined, and the organization should look for ways to improve them. Again, Xerox did closely examine its functional areas, such as manufacturing processes. By better utilizing assets, including the employees, Xerox was able to increase its return on assets. Defect free products rose to 99.95 percent. The fourth element, which is to develop customer and supplier partnerships. This view suggests suppliers are partners in meeting customer needs, and customers are partners by providing input so the company and suppliers can meet customer product expectations.

Fifth, an organization must take a preventive approach. The management should be rewarded for being prevention oriented and seeking to eliminate non value-added work. The organization must be proactive. Sixth, the organization has to adopt an error-free attitude. Instil an attitude that "good enough" is not good enough anymore. Xerox clearly fulfilled this requirement, since it reached a nearly perfect quality index, and that David Kearns still emphasized a 100 percent fault free products.

Seventh, a company that is in the process of implementing a TQM program should "get the facts first."

TQM companies should make decisions based on facts, not on opinions. Xerox fulfilled this requirement, since the company was turned into an information company, as opposed to a copier company. Xerox was one of the first companies to conclude that the "Industrial age" is over and the "Information Age" has begun. Furthermore, research and development staff was reorganized and trained.

Eight, a TQM company should encourage every manager and employee to participate. Xerox was able to fulfil this element.

Employees were included in more management decisions. Line workers and other personnel was involved and were given the opportunity to provide input in finding ways of improving production and service through quality improvement teams. The ninth element is to create an atmosphere of total involvement. TQM cannot be achieved unless all areas of the organization apply quality concepts simultaneously. Xerox fulfilled this requirement as well. All functional departments in the organization were involved, and Finally, TQM companies should strive for continuous improvement. Quality is not only a one-time program of competitive response, for it creates a new standard to measure up to. Improving quality is not only good for the profitability of the business, but it is a necessity for long-term survival of the corporation. Xerox is clearly planning on preserving its TQM approach, and it is a vital part of the company's long-term strategy.

Problems in the 1970's

Xerox dominated the document processing industry before the middle of the 1970's. The company anticipated that no one single competitor would be able to penetrate the industry. Xerox believed that the barriers to entry were high, and that most Xerox customers would continue to be loyal towards the company. The company did simply not take the competition seriously. They underestimated the power of the competition, especially high potential Japanese manufacturers.

In addition, Xerox was not worried that the Japanese started to penetrate the international copier market in the early 1970's with their low-cost copiers, since Xerox believed that "low cost mean low quality." They believed that their products were untouchable since they were superior in quality and technology. They believed that "the Japanese products posed no threat, because their products were seen as cheap, unreliable, and of laughable quality."

What Xerox did not anticipate was the Japanese were able to catch up in the international market place, and that they were able to keep costs low, but the products were of good quality. In addition, Xerox did not respond to the plain paper copiers which the Japanese introduced in 1974. Furthermore, the Japanese were able to produce their products more effectively than Xerox, and the parts used in production were less complex, mass produced, more reliable, and easier to fix than Xerox products. In addition, the Japanese were able to sell their products instead of leasing them, which released tied-up capital. Xerox suddenly had to realize that the company was being out produced and under priced.

Xerox's Key Success Factors

The key success factors to Xerox successful strategy turnaround are very much employee related. First, increased involvement of employees has directly increased customer satisfaction. Employees are now directly responsible for keeping customers happy and satisfied. Also, since "employees are the closest to the customer", so they know the best how to please the customer. Furthermore, employees are involved in more management decisions. A large emphasis is placed on employee participation. In addition, plenty of money was spent on employee training. I believe that the funds spent on training paid off good returns. A large emphasis was based on changing the corporate attitude regarding the concept of quality; the training programs accomplished this massive cultural change. A new slogan was developed, "the better the quality the lower the overall costs."

In addition, the new customer supplier relationship, which was created, aided in the process of improving the quality standards of component products. It is logical that it is impossible to produce a superior quality product, when components do not meet required quality standards of the company. Also, by better utilizing assets, including the employees, Xerox was able to increase returns on assets (fixed assets) by almost 300 percent.

Furthermore, by reorganising the organization (particularly in the research and development staff and the marketing force), with the objective of viewing new product lines as systems in the organization. Also, Xerox was one of the first major corporations that recognized the need to move from a purely product-line oriented company (copier company) to an information company. Computer information networks such as Ethernet and other office communications networks made it easier for divisions and people in the organization to communicate with each other. One of the major problems that corporations face today are problems and interference in communication channels.

Examples of strategic and operational controls

There are numerous examples of Strategic controls in the Xerox case.

First, employees are Operational control systems guide, monitor, and evaluate progress in meeting annual objectives. Usually, in order to be effective, operational control systems involves setting four essential objectives; Set standard of performance, measure the actual performance, identify deviations from standards set, and finally initiate corrective action. There are several examples of operational controls in the Xerox case. Xerox has focused on "key success factors", such as improved productivity, high employee morale, improved product-service quality, and growth in market share.

Characteristics of the management style

The management style is decentralized. Employee input from all employee hierarchies in the corporate structure is crucial in maintaining Xerox's total quality concepts. Employees are considered to be very valuable, and ideas are taken seriously. Idea generation and basic change is originating from the "bottom" of the hierarchy level. Excellent information systems facilitate the need for the free flow of information between departments, employees, and subsidiaries. That is a necessity, since communication between the over 7000 quality teams is crucial for their effectiveness.

Management by Objectives (MBO) is a crucial component of Xerox's management style. MBO emphasizes employee participation in the decision-making processes. Employees meet together with the management, and together, they find possible and reasonable solutions to problems and opportunities. The Management by Objectives system creates effective bench marking (which is set bilaterally by employees and management), which it is possible to measure success factors effectively in individual quality improvement teams and in individual departments throughout the organization.

The leadership approach at Xeorx is a two-way system, and not an authoritarian style of management. Upper management at Xerox delegates much authority and decision making to line supervisors and employees. Furthermore, input from employees is taken seriously, and corporate leaders are open to opinions and changes, which requires a high degree of flexibility. Employees at Xerox are feeling that they are involved in the company.

In addition, I believe that the strategic control is centralized to the top management. Strategy decision-making, such as the implementation of new product lines and future expansions into foreign markets are made at a top-management level. The top management at Xeorx is keeping goals in sight, but is flexible enough to adopt to environmental changes both from within and outside the company.

Financial analysis

Overall, the Xerox Corporation is not financially doing as well as it did in earlier years. While examining a corporation it is important to analyse the internal financial capabilities and policies of an organization. By the use of a trend analysis, the economic health of the company can be determined and educated forecasts can be made concerning the financial future of the company. This trend analysis of the Xerox Corporation Company is for the years 1980 through 1989. The following financial ratios will be used; profitability, liquidity, leverage and finally activity ratios.

The activity ratios indicate how effectively a firm is using its resources. The Asset turnover ratio of Xerox has decreased in the last four years, while the fixed asset turnover has increased. That indicates that the turnover on plant and equipment is increasing, but the management is not able to efficiently manage Xerox's total assets. A possible explanation why the total asset turnover ratio is lower than the fixed asset turnover is that Xerox is forced to carry large amounts of inventory, in the purpose of being able to quickly satisfy customer demands and backup the corporation's product replacement program. Profitability ratios indicate how effectively the total firm is being managed. Returns on sales, return on investment, return on equity and the net profit margin are all decreasing. The total profitability of Xerox is therefore decreasing. A Du Pont analysis confirms this negative trend. These numbers may scare future stockholders away from the company. Therefore it may be difficult for Xerox to find future potential investors.

Leverage ratios identify the source of a firm's capital. Xerox's leverage ratios are increasing. The total debt to total assets ratio measures the percentage of total funds provided by debt. In 1990, Xerox's debt to total assets ratio was 0.86, way above the national average of approximately 0.50. In addition, creditors provide the long-term debt to equity ratio, which measures how much of Xerox's long term financing. This ratio has also increased in recent years.

Liquidity ratios are used as indicators of a firm's ability to meet its short-term obligations, such as current liabilities. Xerox's current ratio has decreased in recent years. In 1990, Xerox's current ratio was 1.51, which I believe is a bit too low. Most financial analysts believe that a current ratio of two to three is favourable to companies.

To summarize, I believe that the financial position of the Xerox Corporation is fairly weak. The company should carefully consider future expansions, which require major investments. Leverage ratios should be decreased, and Profitability, Liquidity and Activity ratios should be increased. It is important to improve profitability ratios, as low ratios may discourage future investments in the company. Xerox cannot only focus on excellent quality, but the company must also consider the profitability of the company. There is usually a trade-off between profitability and quality. The "QTL" program cost an estimated $125 million and over 4 million of man-hours, but to what extent did the program contribute to the profitability of the company? Xerox has to find the proper balance between the two.

(Source: Adapted from: http://www.geocities.com/TimesSquare/1848/xerox.html)

Questions

1. Discuss and identify strengths, weaknesses, opportunities and threats of Xerox.
2. To what Xerox could not implement TQM program successfully?
3. What are the key success factors of Xerox?
4. How could management style and organisation culture of Xerox helped it in achieving strategies?

◆ ◆ ◆

Subject Index

-A-

Acquisition Strategy, 203
Advantage Potentials, 243
Attitude Positive, 360
Attack Competitor's Strengths, 240
Attacking Competitor's Weaknesses, 241
Attacks Simultaneously, 241

-B-

Backward Integration, 206
BCG Matrix, 305
Board Committees, 493
Board of Directors, 492
Business Definition, 50, 69
– Broad/Narrow, 69
Criteria, 69
– Meaning, 69
Business Ethics, 477
– and Law, 480
– Meaning, 478
– Need for, 477
– Principles, 480
– Scope, 480
Business Unit Level Strategies, 226

-C-

Capabilities, 133, 146
Captive Company Strategy, 212
Cash Cows, 307
Career Development, 367
Collaborative Strategies, 187
Combination Strategy, 222
Company Situation Analysis, 158
Competencies, 134
Competency Mapping, 275
Competitors, 115
Competitor Analysis, 117
Competitive Advantage, 132
Competitive Advantage Potentials, 243
Competitive Profile Matrix, 302
Competitive Strength Assessment, 145
Concentration Strategies, 198
Conglomerate Diversification, 205
Controlling, 149, 429
Core Competencies, 134
Corporate Capability Factors, 146, 157
– Diagnosis, 157
Corporate Culture, 370
Corporate Governance, 490
– Meaning, 490
– Need for, 490
– and Strategic Management, 491
– Parties to, 492
– Principles of Good, 495
Corporate Level Strategies, 178
Corporate Profile, 193
Cost Advantage, 231
Customers, 226

-D-

Decision-Making, 39
Decision Stage, 321
Demographic factors, 114
Defensive Strategies, 183
– and Competitive Advantage 244
Differentiation Strategies, 233-237
Differentiation-cum-Low Cost, 237
Directing, 149
Directional Policy Matrix, 314
Distinctive Core Competencies, 142
Divestment Strategy, 214
Dogs, 309
Dot.Coms, 505

-E-

Economic factors, 171
Electronic business, 9
End-Run Offensives, 242
Enron Scandal, 502
Experience curve and Efficiency, 287
External Environment, 19, 85
– Analysis, 85

– Economic Environment, 96
– Industry Environment, 114
– Legal Environment, 111
– Natural Environment, 113
– Political Environment, 107
– Social and Cultural, 89
– Strategic Management, 85
– Technological, 94
External Factor Evaluation, 300
Environmental Scanning, 123
– Techniques of, 124
– Threats and Opportunities, 126

-F-

Financial Management, 153,170
Financial Policies, 410
First-Mover Advantages, 244
First-Mover Disadvantages, 245
Focus Strategy, 237
Focused Cost Leadership, 240
Forward Integration, 206
Functional Strategies, 262
– Financial, 268
– Human Resource, 271
– Information, 283
– Integrated, 285
– Marketing, 265
– Operations, 262
– Production, 262
– Research and Development, 282

-G-

Generic Strategies, 228
GE Nine-Cell Matrix, 311
Global economic trends, 7
Goal, 50
Geographic Environment, 115
Global Strategic Management, 164
– Peculiarities, 165
Global Strategic Management Process, 167
Grand Strategy Matrix, 317
Growth strategy, 197
– Internal Growth, 198
Guerrilla Offensives, 242

-H-

Harvesting Strategies, 255
Hofer's Nine-Cell Matrix, 315
Horizontal Integration, 204
Human Resource Development, 414
Human Resource Management, 156,170
Human Resource Matrix, 280
Human Resource Policies, 411

-I-

Information Strategies, 283
Industry Attractiveness, 319
Industry Biundaries, 122
Industry Environment, 114
– Competitors, 115
– Geographic, 116
– Market, 114
Input Stage, 300
Internal-External Matrix, 315
International Environment, 89, 130,170
– Resources and Capabilities, 130
International Product Portfolio, 183
International SWOT Analysis, 173
Inter-personal Roles, 32
Internal Environment, 22
Integrated Functional Strategies, 285
Intuitive-Emotional Approach, 40

-J-

Joint Venture, 179, 207—210

-K-

Knowledge Management, 277

-L-

Learning Effects and Efficiency, 286
Leadership, 361
Licensing, 179
Liquidation Strategy, 215
Low Cost Leadership, 182, 230
Low Cost Plus Conveniences, 231

-M-

Manager, 32
– Roles, 32
– Tasks, 32
Management Information System, 414
Mark-to-Market Accounting, 502
Marketing Management, 152,169
Marketing Policies, 398
Merger Strategy, 200
Mindset, 360
Mission, 18, 50, 54, 184
– Broad Statements, 65
– Characteristics, 59
– Contents, 64
– Evaluation, 68
– Functions, 64
– Inputs, 65
– Key Elements, 58
– Meaning, 55
– Redefining, 68

-N-

Non-Profit Organisations, 455
– Categories of Non-Profit, 455
– Strategic Management in, 457
– Types, 455

-O-

Objectives, 50,71
– Areas, 72
– Characteristics, 74
– Guidelines, 75
– Importance, 76
– Nature of, 78
Offensive Strategies, 182
– And Competitive Advantage, 239
Operations Management, 154
Operations Policies, 391-398
Opportunities, 142
Organisational Analysis, 131,168
– Resource-Based, 131
Organisational Change, 381
Organisational Development, 383
Organising, 148
Outsourcing, 141

-P-

Policy, 164
Political-Behavioural Approach, 41
Political Factors, 171
Power, 378
Pre-emptive Strategies, 242
Problem Children, 308
Production Management, 154,170
Portfolio Restructuring, 222
Profit Strategy, 196

-Q-

Question Marks, 308

-R-

Rational-Analytical Approach, 41
Research and Development, 156
Resource and Competitive Advantage, 132
Retrenchment Strategies, 211

-S-

Satisfying Approach, 41
Satyam Computer Services, 505
Seven "S" Framework, 374
Shared Values, 374
Situational Analysis, 192
Social Factors, 172
Social Responsibilities, 467-478
– Modern View, 467
– Traditional View, 467
Special Purpose Accounts, 503
Specialisation Strategy, 237
Stability Strategies, 195
Staffing, 149
Stars, 308
Status-Quo, 196
Strategic Alliances, 216
Strategic Change, 329
– Managing, 330

– Radical Change, 330
– Routine Change, 329
Strategy 2, 50,164
– Alliances, 216
– Criteria for effective, 5
– Concentration Strategies, 198
– Conglomerate Diversification, 205
– Corporate Level Strategies, 178
– Defensive Strategies, 183
– Divestment Strategy, 214
– Focus Strategy, 237
– Functional Strategies, 262
– Generic Strategies, 228
– Harvesting Strategies, 255
– Horizontal Integration, 204
– Integrated Functional Strategies, 285
– Joint Venture, 179, 207—210
– Licensing, 179
– Liquidation Strategy, 215
– Merger Strategy, 200
– Pre-emptive Strategies, 242
– Definition, 3-5
– Forms of, 6
– Kinds of, 6
– Need for, 2,7
– Meaning of,
– More complex, 7
– Profit, 196
– Retrenchment, 211
– Specialisation, 237
– Stability, 195
Strategic Choices, 166
Strategy Formulation, 192
– and Board of Directors, 324
– Guidelines for, 323
– and Politics, 324
Strategy Implementation, 331
– Organisational Structural, 331
– Procedural, 332
– Project, 331
Strategic Management, 9, 13,164
– Benefits of 15,
– Board of Directors, 35
– Shareholders, 36
– CEO, 36
– Entrepreneurs, 37
– Family operated firm, 37
– SBU Strategist, 37
– Historical Development, 14
– Meaning, 14
– Need for, 15
Strategic Advantage Profile, 158
Strategic Alternatives, 195
Strategic Audit, 435-451
Strategic Control, 430
– Process, 430
Strategic Decisin-Making, 39
Strategic Fit, 24
Strategic Cost Analysis, 145
Strategic Evaluation, 296
Strategic Failures, 503
Strategic Intent, 24
Strategic Issues, 146
Strategic Management Process, 17
– Challenges of, 26
Strategies for Industry Leaders, 253
Strategy for Runner-up Firms, 254
Strategies for Weak Firms, 255
Structural Implementation, 332
– Assessment, 351
– Entrepreneurial, 333
– Vertical Structure, 334
– Tall Structure, 334
– Horizontal Structure, 335
– Flat Structure, 335
– Functional Structure, 338
– Product Strcture, 341
– Geographical Structure, 341
– Decentralized Structure, 343
– Strategic Business Unit, 344
– Matrix Structure, 346
– Team Structure, 348
– Virtual Structure, 348
Strategic Management in Non-Profit, 455
– Categories of Non-Profit, 455
– Types, 455
Strategic Piggybacking, 461
Structure-Strategy Thesis, 338
SWOT Analysis, 23,192
Strategist, 34

Strategy-Situation Match, 245
Strengths, 142
Structural Implementation, 332
Superior Customer Service, 291
Superior Efficiency, 285
– and Customisation, 288
– and Information System, 289
– and Marketing, 289
– and Human Resources, 288
Superior Guarantee, 292
Superior Quality, 290

-T-

Tactics, 51
Take-Over Strtaegy, 203
Technological Factors, 171
Threats, 142
Total Quality Management, 291
TOWS Matrix, 303
Transformation Strategy, 214
Turnaround Strategy, 211
Turn Key Operations, 182

-V-

Values, 375
Value-based Management, 483
Value Chain Analysis, 137
Value Creation, 166,230
Vertical Integration, 205
Virtual Structure, 348
Vision, 18, 50, 52,164
– Characteristics, 52
– Meaning, 52

-W-

Weaknesses, 142